1001 PAINTINGS
YOU MUST SEE BEFORE YOU DIE

1001 PAINTINGS
YOU MUST SEE BEFORE YOU DIE

GENERAL EDITOR **STEPHEN FARTHING**

FOREWORD BY **GEOFF DYER**

 **CASSELL** ILLUSTRATED

A Quintessence Book

First published in Great Britain in 2006 by Cassell Illustrated
a division of Octopus Publishing Group Limited
Carmelite House, 50 Victoria Embankment
London, EC4Y 0DZ
www.octopusbooks.co.uk

An Hachette UK Company
www.hachette.co.uk

ISBN-13: 978-1-84403-920-3
QSS.KPIC4

A CIP catalogue record for this book is available from the British Library.

This book was designed and produced by
Quintessence Editions Ltd.
The Old Brewery, 6 Blundell Street
London N7 9BH
www.1001beforeyoudie.com

First edition published 2006
This edition first published 2016

Senior Editors	Jenny Doubt, Jodie Gaudet
Assistant Editor	Tobias Selin
Picture Researcher	Jo Walton
Editors	Mary Cooch, Carol King, Carla Masson, Karen Morden
Art & Design Director	Tristan de Lancey
Update Editor	Juliet Lecouffe
Update Designer	Dean Martin
Production Manager	Anna Pauletti
Editorial Director	Ruth Patrick
Publisher	Philip Cooper

Colour reproduction by Colourscan Co Pte Ltd, Singapore
Printed in China by Printplus Ltd.

Contents

Foreword | Geoff Dyer

They're so irritating, those lists of the best ten paintings, the best five novels . . . It's ludicrous: if you're ever in a position where your options are so reduced, then the chances are you won't have any choice. Okay, you might be torn between which books to take on a long flight or for a weekend in the country but, asked to choose in some definitive way between Tolstoy or Dostoevsky the only reasonable response is "both." Likewise, if you're forced to choose just ten great paintings, then what is at stake is probably not your personal preference but the fate of art and civilization itself.

When the catchment area is raised to 1001, however, the idea seems quite reasonable. (The extra *one* is crucial. A thousand is a logical cut-off point. Allowing in one more suggests that there is always room for one exception. So, implicit in the idea of a thousand and one is a thousand and two, and if there's room for a thousand and two, then . . .) It is generous—an inclusive kind of exclusivity. And, in all likelihood, in the course of seeing these 1001, you will accidentally catch ten thousand more.

One thousand and one is benign in the opposite way too. It is not off-putting. Some of the paintings in this book are in private collections and therefore often only on display when they are on tour. In the course of a normal lifetime, you could get to see many of the rest. There are, broadly speaking, three ways in which you might do so.

The first is when the work in question hangs permanently in your hometown or when an exhibition of works by that artist comes to a museum near you. What could be easier? You take a bus, buy your ticket, and get in line to see the masterpiece in question.

The second is when you happen to be visiting a city where the work is housed or where a temporary exhibition featuring it is in progress. This is quite convenient, but it is not always as simple as it seems. For years I had wanted, in the vague, passive way of these things, to see Gauguin's *Where Do We Come From? What Are We? Where Are We Going?* And then one day I found myself in Boston with some free time. I went to the Museum of Fine Art and deliberately refrained from asking where the picture was hung. I wanted to stumble upon it, as if by accident. Eventually, after traipsing through the entire building, I discovered that it had been removed for restoration or was out on loan (I forget which). Murphy's law.

This raises the third possibility: going to a place specifically to see a work or exhibition. Naturally, this does not mean that the only thing you do in Urbino is see the Piero della Francescas, but that was the reason my then girlfriend and I went there. It was a kind of pilgrimage and, as such, the act of getting there (involving trains, buses, wine, dinners, sex, heated arguments) became part of the experience of seeing the paintings.

Now, I could—to go back a paragraph—fly to Boston to see the missing Gauguin but, (a) I am not that desperate to see it and, (b) it is not a bad idea to have things up one's sleeve for the future, things to look forward to. I'm confident that I will at some point find myself in Boston again and see this painting that has so far eluded me. Not having done so yet gives my life purpose. As for whether it will live up to the interminable build-up, well, people say it is great but, as far I am concerned, I'll be the final judge of that. This is one of the reasons I want to see it—to see how it compares with its formidable reputation.

Whether seeing this or any other particular work will transform or even enhance one's life is open to question. It depends—on the painting and the person looking at it. Will looking at a good portion of the paintings in this book make you a better person (more polite, kinder, nicer to dogs, less grumpy)? Maybe not. So why bother? The best answer, I think, is a negative one that keeps the stakes as low as possible: because not to do so is a waste of one's eyes.

Personally, I would consider my life a waste if I'd not seen Death Valley, Angkor Wat, Varanasi, or Dead Vlei in Namibia. How do paintings compare with real places? Given the choice, would you rather see a painting or . . . ? The mere fact that you're reading this book means that you enjoy a degree of freedom from the realm of necessity. You can see places and you can see paintings of places. Chances are you won't be able to see everything or go everywhere but you'll be able to make a start. This book shows you how—and where.

London, UK

Introduction | Stephen Farthing

When you picked this book up for the very first time, you probably flipped through its pages to get a quick glimpse of what was inside. If you went for a second run-through, you probably paused at some point to wonder why a painting you did not much like the look of was included. During your reflections on that painting, you probably began to wonder how the selection was made. Then, you may have started checking to see if any of your top ten paintings were included.

Once readers have spent a little time with this book, they tend to make the very reasonable assumption that a book carrying this title might also be a catalog of good paintings. If that is true, which I hope it is, then they will eventually begin to wonder whether there is a common thread, running through time and around the globe, that connects good paintings.

Accepting that not every picture can match up to the absolute magic of the very best of the premier league—Velázquez's *Las Meninas*, van Gogh's *Wheat Field with Crows*, or any late Vermeer—what I hope we have ended up with is a rich and adventurous overview of quality painting, not simply an overextended Oscar nominations list or a romp through stuff I like.

Each painting that made it into the final cut did so because it was important or interesting, or both. Interesting because of its subject matter or the way it was painted; important because of its relationship with other paintings.

Within my personal sense of "great" and "good," I'm still not certain, for example, where Andrew Wyeth's painting *Christina's World* sits. It is without doubt a very memorable and popular image, but more important than that for me is the fact that it is one of the most popular paintings in the Museum of Modern Art, New York, and as such a necessary part of this book.

When I was an art student in London in the early seventies, my tutor struggled to explain to me the difference between good and bad painting. He started by telling me that drawing was at the heart of it all and that no amount of brightly colored paint could distract the eye from bad drawing.

He then told me that painting was all about producing memorable images and rattled off his inventory of successes: the *Mona Lisa*, van Gogh's sunflowers, Monet's waterlilies, Cézanne's bathers, Matisse's dancers. I got his point, but kept thinking how difficult it was for me to remember anything more than a series of disjointed fragments from Picasso's *Guernica* and how I could only remember Jackson Pollock's drip paintings as a concept, not as clear images. I also remember thinking that there has got to be more to van Gogh's sunflowers than the fact that they are simply memorable.

Toward the end of the tutorial, he moved on from "memorable images" to Mondrian, Abstraction, and Modernism and settled on more lyrical and abstract concerns. By the end, he had relegated subject matter to the second division and positioned the lyrical arrangement of line, form, and color as the essence.

This landed us in a "technical area" where we started thinking about the relationship between how something is made and what it is trying to say, the relationship between form (the shape of the thing) and content (not simply the subject matter, but what the artist is saying with the paint and the subject matter). We concluded by agreeing it was the degree of perfection in balancing those two components that governed the quality of any painting.

Although it is clearly not the whole story, much of what we talked about that day still rings true.

In the light of my subsequent experience making and looking at paintings, I would like to add a fourth element to the checklist, relating to meaning—the type of meaning that we generate as individuals, for ourselves while looking, as opposed to the meanings that art history, museum catalogs, and auction houses assign to paintings. I believe a good painting enables an interaction between itself and the viewer that encourages us to explore its meaning independent of fashion taste and art history, leaving only the bad ones and paradigm shifts of complete genius to leave us wondering. Unfortunately, to get to know a picture well enough to begin to engage with what I have just been talking about takes time.

The last time you saw a film, you will have spent two hours watching it unfold out of the darkness; the last time you read a novel, you probably lived with it for at least a week, absorbing then reflecting on the words. Now, try to remember the longest time you ever spent looking at a great painting.

Good and great paintings are like people: you can get some idea of what they are like from a photograph, but to find out what they are really like, you need to spend time getting to know them. With paintings this is clearly not an easy feat, especially since the average time a gallery visitor spends in front of a painting is no more than two or three seconds.

It remains a fact, however, that the only way to understand just how good a painting is, is not to take another's word for it, but to go and see it in the flesh and spend time with it. So this book sets out to be a visitor's handbook and traveling companion, not an armchair travel guide.

With these thoughts in the back of my mind, I began to build the list that became this book.

As my list grew, I realized its quality was less reliant on connoisseurship than on a decision made right at the start, which was to gather the 1001 paintings from the broadest geographical boundaries and longest timeline possible. (On this note, I should point out that I have elected not to include ancient cave paintings, such as those found at Lascaux in France, as they were not "painted" in the traditional sense, but drawn.)

I always kept the title of the book in mind, often taking it quite literally. When deciding whether a work was in or out, I would ask myself whether it was indeed worth the trip to go and see it. The object was, after all, to bring together the 1001 paintings we really should try to see before we die.

This list actually started in a minor way quite a few years ago when after dinner, or in a bar sitting with other artists, someone would pose the question: "If you could own five paintings, which would you hang in your home?" We would then go around the table naming our fantasy collection. I think the last time I played that party game, I came up with a classic Mondrian, that beautiful Titian in the Frick of a man with a fur collar, the Vermeer of a woman in a red hat, a massive Pollock drip painting that would replace the TV, and a Canaletto of the Grand Canal. Can you imagine living with those? Brilliant.

This time, with so many pictures to find, I started work on the back of an envelope making a list of the paintings I knew I couldn't work without: Rembrandt's *Night Watch*, Uccello's *Battle of San Romano*, and the ones I had chosen in the most recent party game.

At the beginning I thought I would test myself and tried to think of a really famous painting that I could leave out. I tried to remember my biggest disappointment, a painting that I had built up in my mind that when I saw it in the flesh just did not cut the mustard. I came up with probably the best-known painting in the world: Leonardo da Vinci's *Mona Lisa*.

The last time I saw it, it was a very long walk from the front door of the Louvre, surrounded by hordes of tourists, hung far too high on the wall, and locked away behind plated glass. I thought there was absolutely no point making others share my disappointment, but then I realized it was worth bothering, if only to ask the question you can never satisfactorily answer while looking at a reproduction in a book: "What is all the fuss about?"

By contrast, when I applied the same test to probably the largest painting in the book, the Sistine Chapel ceiling, there was no doubt left in my mind that it was worth the effort. Like the *Mona Lisa*, it is both a long walk from the front door, and positioned high above the crowds of tourists swarming to see it, but unlike the *Mona Lisa* the viewpoint and experience is more or less as the artist intended. Seeing that painting in person, on the ceiling above the *Last Judgment*, is an awe-inspiring experience.

Around two edges of the envelope I wrote the words "face painting," "murals," "hand painting/henna," "ceramic decoration," "masks," "illuminated manuscripts," and "destructive camouflage"—though given the specific remit of this title, I have ultimately chosen to concentrate just on watercolors, frescoes, and oils. Screen and woodblock prints have been excluded, as these are to a great extent reproducible, hence the absence of masters such as Hokusai and many famous pieces by Andy Warhol—I made it a criterion that all works of art should be painted by hand. (As an aside: wherever a frame plays an integral part in the painting—e.g. in the work of artists such as Howard Hodgkin, or in a triptych—it is also included as part of the reproduction in this book.) In the top left corner of the envelope, I noted the names of some countries and centuries that I would dig into more deeply as the project progressed. When I got to about nine hundred I stopped, knowing the rest would arrive as a result of bright ideas, forgotten names, and the inevitable gap-filling exercises.

As the list grew, a number of categories developed. There were the painters who created so many good works that I couldn't immediately select just one: Titian, Vermeer, Rembrandt, Monet, Turner, Picasso, and Pollock, for instance. Then there were painters who hadn't produced one outstanding painting in particular. Clearly, all paintings included should also be accessible to the public (some of those featured here belong to a private collection, true, but they are loaned out for exhibitions).

Once the works were assembled, it became time for the words. The point of the text was to illuminate both the pictures and the people who painted them. Artist biographies and the stories that sit behind the paintings can be interesting, but they are neither the point of painting nor the only key to the door. Van Gogh's career as a painter lasted just ten years, but in that time he completed almost 900 paintings, an average of one every four days.

Among the artists behind our list of paintings are murderers, drunks, frustrated bankers, and debt collectors. Among them, too, are dozens of decent people whose labor and vision produced some of the defining images of world civilization. Enjoy.

Title Index

PRE 1400S

Garden with Pool | Unknown

1420–1375 BCE | wallpainting (detail) | 25 x 30 in / 64 x 76 cm | British Museum, London, UK

Garden with Pool is a wallpainting detail from the tomb of Nebamun who was a powerful statesman in eighteenth-dynasty Egypt. His tomb is located on the western shore of Thebes. This wall fragment depicts a rectangular pool full of tilapia fish, wading birds, and lotus flowers with papyrus growing around the edge. The pool is surrounded by palms, sycamore fig trees, mandrakes, and other bushes. Viewed from above, as if through the eyes of the gods, the trees in the lowest register of the painting are rooted in the "wrong" direction, in an attempt to create a sense of depth. In the top right corner, the tree-goddess Hathor collects the pleasures of the garden—life-giving water in jugs and fruit in baskets—and offers the grace of her protection in the afterlife. It is thought likely that Nebamun and his wife Hatshepsut were originally depicted to the right of this scene. Hathor was also known as the Lady of the Southern Sycamore—the sycamore fig tree was sacred to her and was a common symbol of life. Hathor is an ancient goddess, often depicted as a young, attractive woman with cow's ears and cowlike eyes. Her garden is an otherworldly paradise symbolizing new life, while her talapia fish symbolize regeneration. In cool, indigo-blues and rich yellow-browns, the *Garden with Pool* portrays, in an orderly style, the delights of the plentiful afterlife awaiting Nebamun. It also provides the viewer with a fascinating glimpse of ancient Egyptian life and beliefs some four thousand years ago. **SWW**

Goldsmiths at Work | Unknown

1411–1375 BCE | wallpainting (detail) | Tomb 181, Valley of the Nobles, Sheikh Abd el-Qurna, Egypt

Goldsmiths at Work is a fragment of a wallpainting from the tomb of Ipuki and Nebamun who were craftsmen and sculptors who worked in the royal necropolis at Thebes during the reign of Amenhotep II. The eighteenth dynasty of ancient Egypt—often combined with the nineteenth and twentieth dynasties under the group title "New Kingdom"—was a time of great artistic flowering in ancient Egypt. Ipuki and Nebamun were involved in the royal building projects of the New Kingdom. Despite Nebamun's modest title of "scribe and counter of grain," he artfully prepared his own burial tomb to be shared by Ipuki, combining their skills to make a tomb as equally well crafted as any of the nobles' tombs surrounding it. At least one wall of these tomb chambers was reserved for celebrating the work of the deceased. *Goldsmiths at Work* portrays eleven craft workers engaged in various activities from the initial weighing of gold to the creation of gold objects. Gold was used to decorate temples dedicated by the pharaoh, and was placed alongside the kings in their tombs for use in the afterlife. *Goldsmiths at Work* is an elegant portrayal of work, with many hands animated in diverse actions. It also provides important historical information about ancient Egyptian workshops, and the high degree of skill required by goldsmiths. Nebamun and Ipuki, who were possibly brothers, or related through marriage, are two artists who cannot resist providing an intimate portrait of their vocation, and of the artistic process at large. **SWW**

Sailing Barge of Amenhotep Huy | Unknown

*c.*1330 BCE | wallpainting (detail) | Tomb of Huy, Qurnet Murai, Thebes, Egypt

Amenhotep Huy was Viceroy of Nubia, modern-day Ethiopia, during the reign of Tutankhamun (1336 to 1327 BCE). Although Tutankhamun's reign was very short, it marked a return to the old religion and the cult of Amun, which had been overturned by his predecessor Akhenaten. Thebes and its Valley of the Kings again became an important location for royal burials. From artifacts in Tutankhamun's tomb, it is known that Egypt mounted military campaigns in Nubia and the region of modern-day Palestine and Syria. In the tomb of Amenhotep Huy, wall paintings tell the story of the annexation of Nubia. Some paintings depict subservient Nubian princes paying tribute to the pharaoh. Another painting shows Huy's installation as viceroy. Huy is also shown worshipping the deities Anubis and Osiris. On another wall, Nubian chiefs, almost all dressed in the Egyptian fashion, bring precious stones, gold, and other valuable objects including a chariot to Egypt. *Sailing Barge of Amenhotep Huy* is one painting of several showing rows of ships bringing treasures from Nubia to Egypt. Although highly stylized, the viewer is given a vivid account of the barge sailing up the Nile, its massive oars pulled through the water by slaves below deck, its billowing sails picking up wind. The golden color of the painting puts the conquest of Nubia in context. Nubia's gold was coveted by Egypt. Amenhotep Huy wanted his tomb to reflect what he had done during his governorship of the region, and how faithfully he served the pharaoh. **MC**

Sethos I Before Horus | Unknown

*c.*1280 BCE | wallpainting (detail) | Temple of Sethos I, Abydos, Egypt

Sethos I (reigned *c.*1291–1278 BCE) was the son of Ramesses I, the founder of the nineteenth dynasty, and the father of Ramesses II, one of the greatest of all the pharaohs. Ramesses I had relatively humble origins, and his son Sethos came to the throne at a time of internal strife, warring neighbors, and a society recovering from the upheavals and subsequent decline of the eighteenth dynasty. Sethos I was preoccupied with consolidating the nineteenth dynasty and stabilizing the kingdom. Sethos built the temple at Abydos to honor the god Osiris, his wife Isis, and their falcon-headed son Horus. In Egyptian mythology, Osiris, king of Egypt, was murdered by his jealous brother Set who cut Osiris's body into several pieces and spread them all over Egypt. Distraught,

Isis traveled the country to find every piece of her husband. When she had gathered every fragment, she prayed to the gods to give him life again, just long enough to conceive an heir. They were given one night together and Horus was conceived. Horus spent much of his life in the body of a falcon searching for Set to avenge his father's death. Some scholars believe that Sethos, whose name may have meant "Man of Set," built the Abydos temple to propitiate Horus. In *Sethos I Before Horus,* Sethos is receiving his pharaonic regalia from Horus, including a headdress, which is blue to emphasize his military success, and a royal scepter. In his left hand, Horus holds the *ankh,* the ancient Egyptian symbol of life. The image is painted onto carved, polished limestone relief. **LH**

Etruscan Erotic Scene | Unknown

c.550 BCE | wallpainting (detail) | Tomb of the Bulls, Monterozzi Necropolis,Tarquinia, Italy

Discovered in 1892, the Tomb of the Bulls is one of the few remaining Etruscan antiquities. There is very little known about the Etruscans who left no written records. Information about them comes mainly from Greek and Roman writers, including Plato. The Romans and Greeks considered Etruscan culture to have been degenerate—sharing wives was said to be an established Etruscan custom, public nudity and sexual acts were apparently commonplace. The Tomb of the Bulls confirms the view that Etruscan culture was explicitly sexual—its wallpaintings depict both heterosexual and homosexual acts, rampant bulls, and symbols of fertility. The tomb has two arched entrances with a large, pillarlike centerpiece. Above each entranceway is an erotic scene involving bulls.

Etruscan Erotic Scene is one of them. The two figures on the right are believed to be male and female—the male is painted darker than the female according to the Greek tradition. The charging, rampant bull is an ancient symbol of fertility. Along the bottom of the painting, red circular objects with crosses form a decorative border. These are believed to be depictions of *omphalos*—a Greek word meaning "naval," which represented a source of divine energy. Their use shows that the Etruscans were influenced by ancient Greek culture, but it is unclear what they represented to the Etruscans. Nor is it known why a necropolis—a repository for the dead—was decorated with erotic paintings. It would seem that for the Etruscans, the sexual act connected life, death, and the afterlife. **MC**

Painting from the Tomb of the Diver | Unknown

c.480 BCE | fresco | Museo Archeologico Nazionale di Napoli, Naples, Italy

The practice of painting tombs in Etruria appears to have begun around the seventh century BCE. The earliest examples of Etruscan tomb painting are those discovered at Veii and Cerveteri (also known as Caere). The practice then spread to other cities, including Paestum, Chiusi, and Tarquinia. *Painting from the Tomb of the Diver* was painted at the end of the period known as Archaic (c.575–480 BCE). This period is characterized by a strong Grecian influence and this can be glimpsed in the figure of the diver himself, echoing figures seen on Greek vases. The Etruscans placed great importance on competitive sports, and many of the tombs at Tarquinia commemorate sportsmen and women. These include *The Tomb of Hunting and Fishing*, which depicts a man aiming at birds with a slingshot and a young boy fishing; *The Tomb of the Augurs*, showing wrestlers competing; and *The Tomb of the Jugglers*, a painting of a female acrobat, a male juggler, and a pipe-playing musician. Etruscan death rituals were lavish and several large cities of the dead have been discovered. Rich families tended to have large communal tombs, whereas tombs owned by the wealthy middle classes tended to be smaller, made either for married couples or a lone individual. No evidence of Etruscan literature has been found, so our knowledge of this ancient culture comes from their art, from the archaeology, and from contemporary writers from other cultures. By c.100 BCE, the Etruscan culture and people had been absorbed by the Romans. **LH**

Scene of Initiation into the Cult of Demeter | Unknown

60–50 BCE | fresco (detail) | Villa dei Misteri, North Wall, Pompeii, Italy

This panel is part of a larger mural that was discovered in the Villa dei Misteri, near Pompeii in Italy. Like much of the art from this period, it was constructed using the fresco technique. The eruption of Vesuvius in 79 CE destroyed many works of art in this region, but some were protected by lava or by their location in tombs and houses. Located in a large chamber, known as the *triclineum* or dining room, at the front of the villa, this fresco cycle comprises twenty-nine figures and runs continuously around the chamber. The composition of the frieze is typical of the Second Style (80–20 BCE), which is marked by its representational style and creates the illusion of receding space. The startled woman on the far right is an initiate engaged in a dance step with her purple veil. The type of ritual

has been hotly debated, but most agree that it depicts the initiation of a woman into rites associated with pleasure, probably sex or marriage, also called bacchanalia. Some people speculate that the scene depicts one of the mystery cults that was concerned exclusively with the lives and experiences of women. What has startled the woman is uncertain, but it is thought likely to be linked to the apprehension of hearing Silenus (center, playing the lyre) divining her future. The seated woman (far left) is a priestess and appears to be preparing to cleanse her hands. The rich color scheme includes blues and greens. These would have been very costly pigments for a fresco of this size, which suggests that the proprietor of the villa spared no expense. **PS**

Europa on a Bull | Unknown

*c.*20 BCE–45 CE | fresco (detail) | Museo Archeologico Nazionale di Napoli, Naples, Italy

This fresco from Pompeii is painted in the Third Style or ornamental style of ancient Roman wall paintings, but is now housed in a Naples museum rather than being located *in situ* in Pompeii. The painting, which was part of a larger collection, was probably copied from a Greek original. According to the myth, Zeus became enamored by the lovely Europa, a Phoenician princess. Zeus disguised himself as a bull and infiltrated her father's herd. While looking after the herd with her friends, Europa innocently caresses the bull and sits on him only to be carried off over the sea to Crete. Europa gives birth to three sons, becomes the first Queen of Crete, and Zeus puts the image of a bull in the heavens for her—we know it as the constellation Taurus. She also gave her name to the continent of Europe. In the Pompeii fresco, the artist depicts Europa soon after she has unknowingly straddled the bull, which is the focal point of the scene. Sexual innuendo is confined to the exposure of Europa's breasts as she has raised her cloak with her right hand. Surprisingly, there is little motion represented in the image, nor any feeling of violence or fear among Europa and her onlookers. Europa's three friends seem quite calm, one girl even pets the bull. It perhaps marks the moment of calm just before Zeus bolts away with his prize. This painting and the myth of the abduction of Europa have inspired artists throughout history—Veronese, Gustave Moreau, Titian, Rembrandt, and Matisse—to paint their own renditions of the tale. **SW**

Pan and Hermaphrodite | Unknown

*c.*50 CE | fresco (detail) | Museo Archeologico Nazionale di Napoli, Naples, Italy

When the Roman city of Pompeii, which is thought to have been inhabited by 10,000 people, was destroyed during a catastrophic eruption of the volcano Mount Vesuvius in 79 CE, many of the paintings on the walls of the building of the city were left intact. The volcano buried the city under many feet of ash and it was lost for 1,600 years before its accidental rediscovery in 1748. Four distinct styles of Roman mural have been identified. This mural is painted in the "architectural style"—space extends beyond the room with various perspective changes being employed. Roman artists came close to developing a true linear perspective. The artists used wet and dry plaster infused with powdered marble and alabaster to create a luster. The intent of the artist was a near photorealism although the murals found in Pompeii are often quite abstract. In *Pan and Hermaphrodite,* the notoriously lustful Pan is fleeing the advances of Hermaphroditus having seen his male genitalia. Hermaphroditus, the son of the messenger god Hermes and Aphrodite, the goddess of love, was pursued by a nymph who, having had her advances spurned, fused her body to Hermaphroditus thus causing him to become endowed with the physical traits of both sexes. Pan's intriguing features are well shown here. He was the deity who watched over shepherds and had the hindquarters, legs, and horns of a goat. This is a beautiful fresco, exquisitely executed, which captures the aching solitude of Hermaphroditus as well as the bestiality of the satyrlike Pan. **OR**

Sacrifice of Conon | Unknown

*c.*50 CE | wallpainting (detail) | National Museum, Damascus, Syria

The city of Doura Europos, in modern day Syria, was founded in *c.*300 BCE by Macedonian Greeks. By the first century BCE, it had been absorbed into the Parthian empire. The Parthians were a nomadic people of Iranian origin who rose to power under Mithradates the Great (171–138 BCE). By the first century CE, Doura Europos had become a melting pot of races and religious beliefs. In addition to the Temple of the Palmyrene Gods, a Jewish synagogue, a Christian baptistry, and temples to Mithras and Zeus have been discovered. All the wallpaintings in these buildings show a distinctly "Parthian" form of decorative art. There is a synthesis of the linear, two-dimensional forms and stiff poses of the ancient Near East, with the artistic traditions of ancient Greece.

"Parthian frontality" demanded that all figures, human or divine, face forward with eyes fixed on the viewer. In Near Eastern art from previous periods, figures were almost always shown in profile. *Sacrifice of Conon from the Temple of the Palmyrene Gods* is organized in three registers. In the top register, arches and walls create a three-dimensional space. In the second register, Conon and other dignitaries offer sacrifice to Bel, the god of the sky, using an ornamental brazier and ritual vessels. Perspective is suggested by the feet of the figures which seem to stand on a receding floor. In the lower register, small figures—Conon's family—stand just outside the painted stone frame. Parthian art was an innovative form of figurative painting that lasted until Doura Europos was destroyed in *c.*300 CE. **MC**

Theseus Freeing Children from the Minotaur | Unknown

50–79 CE | fresco | Museo Archeologico Nazionale di Napoli, Naples, Italy

Theseus Freeing Children from the Minotaur is a well-known example of a Pompeiian wall painting dating from the first century CE. Typically, the Romans painted directly on the walls of their rooms to enliven their otherwise dark and windowless living quarters. The depiction of Theseus freeing children from the Minotaur, from the House of Gavius Rufus, recalls the myth of the Athenian hero, Theseus, in the moment just after he has successfully killed the Minotaur. According to the legend, Athenians were obliged to send annual offerings of children and virgins to be sacrificed to the half-man half-bull monster because of an earlier obligation to Minos. In this painting, the children are gathered around Theseus expressing gratitude and relief for their narrow escape from

becoming the Minotaur's dinner. The artist ensures that Theseus is the main focus of the work by employing various painting techniques. His naked body is clearly highlighted while plentiful space separates him from the other figures in the work, and he is notably positioned in front of a lighter background. In addition, the doorway on the left of the painting is balanced by the group of onlookers on the right, which further emphasizes the centrality of the hero. This piece encapsulates elements typical of the Fourth Style, an intricate style of wall painting that emerged after the earthquake of 62 CE, after which architecture became more realistic. It is made from colored pigments that were applied to the wall of Gavius Rufus's home when it was still damp. **SW**

Portrait of a Woman | Unknown

3rd century | encaustic paint on wood | 21 ⅝ x 13 ⅜ in / 55 x 34 cm | Louvre, Paris, France

This sarcophagus portrait is from the Fayum region and was painted in the Greco-Roman period. The word "Fayum" refers to a very fertile region southwest of Cairo. It was centered around an artificial lake, Lake Qaroun, an ambitious engineering project dating from the twelfth dynasty, built in a natural valley. The people of the Fayum Valley came from Egypt, Greece, Syria, Libya, and other areas of the Roman Empire. They grew crops, including wheat and barley; the fish from the lake was considered a great delicacy throughout Egypt; and, under the rule of Amenemhet III (twelfth dynasty), the area became famed for lush gardens and abundant fruit trees. Today, the region is known for the number of papyrus documents unearthed during the nineteenth and twentieth centuries, as well as for the many "Fayum portraits" uncovered by archeologists. These life-size portraits were apparently used to decorate homes, as well as being employed for funerary purposes. The encaustic technique involved melting wax and mixing it with pigmentation and perhaps linseed oil or egg, then applying it like paint onto wood or linen. This painted portrait looks surprisingly modern. The woman's clear eyes and prominent nose and the artist's careful depiction of the jewelry suggest that this was painted to be a recognizable portrait. Art historians often credit the Fayum region with the birth of realistic portraiture and the many portraits uncovered in this region represent a time of groundbreaking artistic experimentation. **LH**

The Good Shepherd | Unknown

3rd century | fresco (detail) | Catacombs of Priscilla, Cubiculum of the Good Shepherd, Rome, Italy

The catacombs were dug between 150 CE and the early fourth century out of the soft volcanic rock that covers parts of Rome. They were originally excavated to provide burial grounds for Roman citizens in the late classical period, but were later used by Jews and Christians. Until 313 CE, Christians were persecuted in Rome, so Christian artists often used images already common in secular society to express their faith. The first Christian art used neutral images such as the Orant—a figure with hands uplifted in prayer; the dove—a symbol of peace; and the good shepherd which stood for humanitarian concern. In Christianity, an Orant symbolized the deceased in heaven, the dove was the Holy Spirit, the shepherd and his sheep represented Christ and his followers. These images appear on frescoes in each burial chamber or cubiculum painted in a style now known as "paleo-Christian." In the cubiculum of the Good Shepherd of the Arenas, the fresco *The Good Shepherd* bears a striking similarity to the "ram bearer"—a classical image of the Roman god Mercury, messenger to the gods and guardian of shepherds. In *The Good Shepherd,* Christ wears a short tunic and strikes a classical pose, framed by trees and birds. Like Mercury, he carries a ram on his shoulders, wears a pouch, and carries a staff. The shepherd is also clean-shaven, as are all early images of Christ. It would have been difficult to distinguish this Christ figure from late Roman representations of Mercury, but an early Christian would have recognized him immediately. **MC**

Hercules in the Garden of the Hesperides | Unknown

4th century | fresco | 33 ½ x 33 ½ in / 85 x 85 cm | Catacomb of the Via Latina, Rome, Italy

Hercules in the Garden of the Hesperides depicts one of the last labors of Hercules—the great hero of Greek mythology, known to the Greeks as Heracles. Hercules was ordered to steal the golden apples that Gaia, Earth goddess and mother of Zeus, had given to Hera as a wedding gift. The apples were guarded by a dragon named Ladon, by Atlas the titan who held the earth upon his shoulders, and by Atlas's daughters, the Hesperides, who were nymphs of the night and lived in a garden located at an extremity of the world. Journeying through northern Africa and Asia, Hercules fought with the son of the god of war Ares, the sea-god Poseidon, and Prometheus who finally revealed this coveted garden's location. Hercules obtained the apples by slaying the

dragon, represented in *Hercules in the Garden of the Hesperides* as a single-headed serpent. The fresco is one of many in Rome's catacombs that were painted in very early Christian Rome in a style known as "paleo-Christian." In paleo-Christian art, both classical and Christian stories are depicted and there is a synthesis of classical poses with a rather simplistic style of painting. Here, Hercules's stance and naked body with a cloth draped over his arm belong to classical art, but the serpent prefigures Christian art, entwined around a tree as the serpent is in the story of Adam and Eve. The story of Hercules and the Hesperides is one that painters throughout the ages have revisited many times to tell the compelling story of a hero triumphing over adversity. **SWW**

Bodhisattva Padmapani | Unknown

5th–6th century | mural (detail) | Ajanta Cave 1, Lenapur village, near Aurangabad, India

The Ajanta mural painting *Bodhisattva Padmapani*, located in Maharashtra state, western India, reflects the beauty and classical sophistication of the arts of the Indian Gupta dynasty. The Ajanta caves were carved out of rock over six centuries and functioned as a monastic retreat, and a place to worship. They were designed to spread the Buddhist doctrine via the pilgrims, monks, craftsmen, and merchants who traveled in the region. The caves were decorated and carved between 200 BCE and 650 CE, and most of the artworks were inspired by the life of the historical Buddha. The *Bodhisattva Padmapani* mural is one of the later murals, and is now regarded as an example of the indigenous style of that era *par excellence*. It shows an unprecedented attempt at realism, which was uncharacteristic of Indian painting at that time. The artist understood the use of light and shade in order to stress the importance of the protagonist. The natural pigments of green, black, and red were painted onto an added surface of lime plaster. The thin, black outlines of the figure as well as the delicate treatment of the face result in a deep, emotional, overall effect. The meditational quality of Padmapani is emphasized by the fullness of his lips, the slender waist and nose, the sinuous elongated eyebrow, and the lotus-shaped eyes. Although the divinity is extremely idealized, the realistic approach is conspicuous. One can infer that the crown and jewels are of secular inspiration. This mural is the perfect embodiment of the classical Guptan genre. **SZ**

Mayan Procession Scene | Unknown

790 CE | fresco (detail) | Temple of Frescoes, Bonampak, Mexico

The Maya are generally considered to have been the most advanced of all the pre-Columbian civilizations. The culture's beginnings have been traced back to 2000 BCE, and the civilization's classic period is placed between 300 and 900 CE. The *Mayan Procession Scene* fresco is at Bonampak, a classic period satellite center subordinate to the one at Yaxchilan, in Chiapas, modern-day Mexico. The work is in a three-room building called The Temple of Frescoes (also wrongly known as The Temple of Murals) which was discovered in 1946 by Giles Healy, an American film-maker. The frescoes were painted by using a dry fresco technique, which means that they were painted on dry plaster. The fresco shown here comes from the first room and depicts masked men and musicians accompanying a grand procession. The purpose of the festivities was the presentation of the heir of the ruler of Bonampak, Chaan Muan. There is a baroque quality to this work that is also evident in other Mayan works of art—brilliantly colored murals, polychrome ceramics, and intricately detailed stonework. This is a vibrant and graphically rendered painting—the empty top zone emphasizes the frenzied activity below. Little is known about the Maya and their beliefs, but the paintings at Bonampak establish them as superb masters of artistic techniques that, in some instances, rival those of the European Renaissance. A full-scale reproduction of the Bonampak temple can be found at the National Museum of Anthropology and History in Mexico City. **OR**

Kichijōten
Unknown

8th century | pigment on cloth | 21 x 12 ⅝ in /
53 x 32 cm | Yakushi-ji Temple, Nara, Japan

Mansions in the Mountains
Tung Yuan

10th century | ink and color on silk | 72 ⅛ x 47 ⅝ in /
183 x 121 cm | National Palace Museum, Taiwan

Kichijōten is the oldest extant color painting of a single figure in Japan and is a superb example of Nara period arts, which incorporated elements of the arts of the Chinese Tang dynasty (618–907). The Buddhist deity Kichijōten derives from Lakshmi, the Hindu goddess of prosperity. Buddhism was introduced to Japan from China and Korea in the sixth century and heavily influenced Japanese art. Yet, Buddhism's encounter with Shinto, the indigenous religion of Japan, distinguished Japanese Buddhism from other Asian traditions, and distinctive Japanese styles evolved. Painted in polychrome, *Kichijōten* depicts an idealized Asian beauty with full cheeks and crescent-shaped eyebrows dressed in the robes of the Tang court. Her right hand forms a mudra, a hand gesture symbolizing the special feature of a Buddhist deity and on her left hand lies a *hōju*, a sacred gem. **FN**

Tung Yuan (*b.*10th century) was active in the province of Jiangsu (modern Nanjing) within the Southern Tang court during the Ten Kingdoms Period. While northern China was ravaged by war, the south enjoyed peace, prosperity, and cultural growth. Tung Yuan was a founder of the southern school of landscape painting, and was seen as one of the best of four working artists in China. His elegant style became the standard for brush painting in China for the next nine centuries. His scenery was innovative in its use of techniques such as crosshatching. *Mansions in the Mountains* portrays a vast gorge that is penetrated by a mountain stream; the mountains lead down to the mansion covered by mist. With a complex harmony that recalls divine perfection as witnessed in nature, paradise is viewed from a high, heavenly perspective. Tung Yuan renders an atmosphere of peace, wisdom, and power. **SWW**

Boson de Rochechouart
Unknown

12th century | fresco (detail)
Les Salles Lavauguyon, Haute Vienne, France

The Church of Les Salles Lavauguyon was built in the late eleventh century. In 1986, plaster in the nave was removed to reveal twelfth-century frescoes—some indecipherable, but many in good condition. Boson de Rochechouart was prior superior of the adjacent priory in the eleventh century. He is depicted above one of the arches in the nave. Painted in typical Romanesque fashion, he is framed in a style reminiscent of Roman frescoes. The figure is Byzantine—the head is a little too small for the body, and the white robes are graphically rather than realistically drawn. There is little sense of perspective, and the arms, which are bent in a typically Byzantine-style gesture, are too long for the body. The hands are quite crudely rendered, especially the right hand in which the prior holds a book. These frescoes fuse ancient celtic and classical styles with Byzantine iconography. **MC**

Archangel Gabriel
Unknown

12th century | tempera on wood | 20 ½ x 17 in
State Russian Museum, St. Petersburg, Russia

Archangel Gabriel, also known as *Angel with the Golden Hair*, is one of the most famous Russian icon paintings. It is attributed to the Novgorod School of *c*.1130–90. During the tenth and eleventh centuries, Christianity spread northward from Constantinople, bringing Byzantine arts to the Slavic region of Russia. The revival of iconography in this era ushered in new thinking about icons as aids to meditation. Icons take earthly materials and create something that enables the viewer to approach the divine. From this perspective, the painting of icons is a form of prayer. The jewel in the angel's hair indicates that this is an archangel. It is thought to be Gabriel, God's messenger, although this is disputed. Painted with large, stylized eyes, the archangel looks away from the viewer toward the mysterious and ineffable. Detached but compassionate, he inspires the contemplation of beauty and purity. **MC**

Eldrad Leaving for Santiago de Compostela | Unknown

c.12th century | fresco (detail) | Chapel of St. Eldrad and St. Nicholas, Abbey of Novalesa, Piedmont, Italy

The Benedictine Abbey of Novalesa was founded in 726, built high above the Susa Valley. It is situated on a section of the Via Francigena, one of several routes taken by medieval pilgrims traveling between Rome and the three great centers of Christian pilgrimage—Jerusalem, Canterbury, and Santiago de Compostela. The abbey has a number of chapels including the Chapel of St. Eldrad and St. Nicholas. St. Eldrad was abbot of Novalesa in the ninth century. The entire chapel is frescoed with scenes from the lives of St. Eldrad, St. Nicholas, and biblical figures. The frescoes are dated to around 1100, and are typical of the Romanesque style that was prevalent in Europe at the time. They owe much to Byzantine art in their flat, stylized, exaggerated poses, which lack perspective,

but are full of color and life. The abbey probably spent a considerable amount on the intense greens, reds, and golds since paint was an expensive luxury. In *Eldrad Leaving for Santiago de Compostela*, St. Eldrad, dressed in a tunic and leggings, is stooping to receive a pilgrim's staff and priest's begging bag. The word *sacerdos* beside the other figure means "priest," which tells the viewer that St. Eldrad is being blessed before setting off on his pilgrimage. The figures are framed by an arch with classical Roman pillars topped by a church—the words *eclasci petri* reveal that it is St. Peter's in Rome. The borders, decorated with fruit and flowers in typical Romanesque fashion, add depth. This is a wonderful scene from a beautiful set of frescoes that are a stunning artistic achievement. **MC**

Maiestas Domini, San Clemente de Tahull | Unknown

12th century | fresco (detail) | Museu d'Art de Catalunya, Barcelona, Spain

The small basilica of San Clemente de Tahull is located in the Bohí valley of Catalonia, Spain, an area renowned for its superb Romanesque frescoes. The semi-dome of San Clemente de Tahull's central apse was adorned with this traditional *Maiestas Domini*, in which Christ appears in majesty surrounded by the four evangelists. The damaged fresco was acquired by the Museu d'Art de Catalunya in Barcelona in 1923. In this stunning composition, the formidable figure of Christ is seated, his right hand is raised in a gesture of benediction and his left holds open a book inscribed with the words *ego sum lux m(un)di* ("I am the light of the world"). His feet rest upon a hemisphere decorated with acanthus leaves, an allusion to both the earthly world and the rainbow from the Book of Revelation.

The four evangelists (not shown) are represented as winged angels—Matthew holds his Gospel and John cradles an eagle. Mark and Luke are depicted as half-length figures and are accompanied by their respective animal symbols: the lion and bull. An apocalyptic seraph (the highest class of angel) stands sentinel at either end of the composition, all six wings covered with a multitude of eyes. Represented in the damaged lower register are the Virgin Mary and the Apostles Thomas, Bartholomew, John, James, and Philip. This fresco was created by an unknown artist of possible Aragonese origin. The dramatic quality of the subject matter, in addition to the billowing draperies and dynamic composition, suggests that the painter was familiar with contemporary French frescoes. **NSF**

Rucellai Madonna | Duccio di Buoninsegna

1285 | tempera and gold on wood | 177 x 114 in / 450 x 290 cm | Uffizi, Florence, Italy

Duccio di Buoninsegna (c.1255–1319) was one of the most important painters to emerge during Siena's heyday in the thirteenth century. Duccio painted in the traditional Byzantine style, but he introduced innovations that began the transition to the genre now known as International Gothic. The *Rucellai Madonna* altarpiece was commissioned by a Dominican lay confraternity devoted to the Virgin. It was installed in the church of Santa Maria Novella in Florence. Originally placed above the altar, the *Rucellai Madonna* was later moved to the Ruccellai chapel within Santa Maria Novella, from where it acquired its name. Duccio's interpretation of the Madonna and Child theme reveals an emphasis on form that is not seen in earlier Madonnas by other artists. The bodies of the Madonna and the infant Christ are given realistic treatment, and Duccio makes good use of *chiaroscuro* (light and dark shading) to create the illusion of three-dimensionality. The Christ child sits convincingly in the Madonna's lap and gestures toward his mother—both innovative developments in paintings of this kind during this era. However, the Byzantine style is apparent in the surrounding angels, which seem to float in space, and in the typically Byzantine medallions, featuring figures from the bible, on the gilded frame. Another Madonna and Child, painted in 1300 by Duccio, was bought by the Metropolitan Museum of Art in New York for $45 million in 2004—a testament to the importance of this early Renaissance painter. **MC**

Crucifix | Cimabue

1287–88 | oil on panel | 176 x 153 ½ in / 448 x 390 cm | Basilica di Santa Croce, Florence, Italy

Originally known as Bencivieni di Pepo, Cimabue (c.1240–1302), as he is commonly known, was both a painter and a mosaicist. Cimabue is generally regarded as the last great painter working in the Byzantine style, which was characterized by relatively static images embellished in rich decorative gilt detail almost exclusively of Christian theme. He is also credited with discovering Giotto. Together, they were among the very first in the history of painting to depict people in lifelike proportion with individualistic features, earmarking a major shift toward naturalism in painting. Very little is known of his life outside of the handful of artworks that are securely attributed to his name. Cimabue was commissioned to paint two major frescoes for the Basilica of St. Francis in Assisi.

Unfortunately, the works of art on the walls of St. Francis have suffered throughout history from fire and earthquakes. His seminal painted *Crucifix* has influenced painters throughout the ages from Michelangelo to Francis Bacon. Sadly it too has suffered the ravages of time. When the Arno river burst in 1966, Santa Croce was flooded and Cimabue's *Crucifix* was badly damaged, with much of its painted surface washed away. Cimabue's lithe body of Christ turns in a sinuous contortion of death. It contrasts with the flatly colored panels that constitute the cross—the starkly naked body emerges from flat background, as does the semicircular halo which, with the use of shadow, projects at a slight angle into the viewer's space. **SP**

The Last Judgment | Pietro Cavallini

1293 | fresco (detail) | 126 x 551 in / 320 x 1,400 cm (full size) | Church of Santa Cecilia, Rome, Italy

Pietro Cavallini (c.1270–1330) was a painter and mosaic designer who worked mostly in Rome. Cavallini's work marks a significant development in early Renaissance art, and signals a transition from the heavy stylization of Byzantine art toward a more naturalistic and three-dimensional interpretation of figures. This detail comes from *The Last Judgment*, which was part of a fresco cycle in the Church of Santa Cecilia in Trastevere, Rome, and is considered to be one of his most important surviving works. The fresco in its entirety demonstrates the artist's grasp of three-dimensional figures, which are conceived in a monumental, almost sculptural manner, while retaining something of the Byzantine past in their arrangement. Significantly, Cavallini worked with the sculptor Arnolfo di Cambio on this fresco, which in part accounts for the sculptural quality of his figures and the convincing folds of drapery. This detail depicting angels demonstrates the particularly soft and colorful palette that the artist used in the cycle, especially through his treatment of their wings. He approached the angels' wings in an innovative manner, building up layers of dense color from dark to light to create an overall sparkling and ethereal effect. They appear fully three-dimensional, a fact that is further emphasized by the flat orbs of the angels' halos. *The Last Judgment* had a profound effect on Giotto, the Florentine master. His *Last Judgment* cycle in the Arena Chapel, Padua, from c.1305, was clearly influenced by Cavallini's fresco. **TP**

St. Francis Receiving the Stigmata | Giotto

1297–99 | fresco | 106 ¼ x 90 ½ in / 270 x 230 cm | Basilica di San Francesco, Assisi, Italy

Giotto di Bondone (c.1270–1337) worked in Tuscany, Naples, northern Italy, and possibly in France. A friend of kings and popes, and Grand Master of Florence, his name was renowned. This is one of twenty-eight frescoes depicting the *Legend of Saint Francis* in the Upper Church in San Francesco, twenty-five of which were by Giotto. Initially an apprentice of Cimabue, Giotto later took over the painting of the frescoes, which are his earliest known work in the medium. Each fresco depicts an event in the saint's life. *St. Francis Receiving the Stigmata* shows the saint having an apparition of an angel with six wings, and a crucified figure. After the vision, his hands and feet received the stigmata—the marks of Christ's crucifixion. In Giotto's rendition of the scene, rays from the vision fall onto St. Francis's hands and feet. The rocky landscape glows with the light of revelation. Without a technical knowledge of perspective or anatomy, Giotto indicates space and, in the seated monk particularly, weight. In his later frescoes he fully explores the transmission of human emotions beyond the rhetoric of gesture, which inspired other Renaissance artists. Giotto left behind the rigid stylization of medieval art and broke new ground in terms of realism. In his fresco painting we can see an impetus, which developed during the Renaissance into a tradition that existed until twentieth-century Cubism. In his *Decameron*, written twenty-two years after Giotto's death, Boccaccio recognized that the artist had resurrected the art of painting. **WO**

Legend of the Three Dead and the Three Living | Unknown

14th century | fresco (detail) | St. Benedict Sacro Speco, Subiaco, Italy

Legend of the Three Dead and the Three Living is in the Sacro Speco, Subiaco—a cave where sixth-century holy man St. Benedict, the father of Western monasticism, is said to have lived for three years. Subiaco is now a Christian center of pilgrimage. The legend of the three dead and the three living was a popular story between 1300 and 1600. In the earliest version of the legend, three nobles are riding through a wood when they are stopped by three animated skeletons who say: "Such as I was you are, and such as I am you will be. Wealth, honor, and power are of no value at the hour of your death." By the fourteenth century, this story had several variations. In one, the nobles are met by a hermit who shows them three bodies in differing states of decay. In the Sacro Speco fresco, only a noblewoman is depicted. The hermit shows her three corpses in coffins in various stages of putrefaction, representing her dead body and its decay. Attributed to the Sienese School, this is a simplistic painting, rather crudely rendered. The hands of the first corpse cross left over right, whereas the hands of the other two corpses cross right over left, suggesting a rather hurried execution. Yet the story is vividly told leading the viewer from the skeleton around to the hermit and the noblewoman and back again. There is a sense of perspective with the wood, the church, and foliage providing a backdrop to this cautionary tale. Seen in the context of the fourteenth century when the Black Death raged through Europe, this is a luridly effective painting. **MC**

Presentation of the Virgin at the Temple | Giotto

1304–06 | fresco | 78 ¾ x 72 ¾ in / 200 x 185 cm | Capella degli Scrovegni (Arena Chapel), Padua, Italy

Giotto di Bondone's (c.1270–1337) reputation as an artist was well established by the time he began working on this fresco around 1304. *Presentation of the Virgin at the Temple* forms one part of a much larger fresco cycle in the Capella degli Scrovegni, sometimes called the Arena Chapel because of its location on the site of a Roman amphitheater in Padua. At the time of the chapel's completion, Enrico Scrovegni was one of Padua's wealthiest citizens. Like his father, Enrico had acquired his riches by lending money at usurious rates. The fresco cycle within the chapel relates the lives of both the Virgin Mary and Jesus Christ. Each lateral wall comprises three rows of frescoes that function as an unfolding narrative and are read from left to right. *The Presentation of the Virgin* centers

upon the story of the Virgin when she was brought to the temple. When she was three years old, and to the amazement of everyone, she was able to climb the fifteen steps of the temple unassisted. Giotto's treatment of this scene here demonstrates what sets him apart from his predecessors. By abandoning the stilted treatment of the figure synonymous with an artist such as his teacher Cimabue, Giotto imbues Mary, her mother and the high priest with a psychological depth and verisimilitude that, up until that point, had been absent from the western pictorial tradition. Such qualities are slight, but their presence is enough to transform the figures into people or personages with discernable motivations and feelings that are resoundingly human. **CS**

The Meeting at the Golden Gate | Giotto

1304–06 | fresco | 78 ¾ x 72 ¾ in / 200 x 185 cm | Capella degli Scrovegni (Arena Chapel), Padua, Italy

Many of the episodes depicted within the Capella degli Scrovegni (Arena Chapel) fresco cycle hinge upon a moment of heightened emotional tension, either given in the context of some form of a departure, as in the case of *The Expulsion of Joachim from the Temple*, also by Giotto di Bondone (*c*.1270–1337), or entailing some form of encounter or meeting. *The Meeting at the Golden Gate*, which forms the last episode in the top register on the south wall is an example of the latter and what Giotto manages to achieve, in an exemplary manner, is to imbue the scene with a sense of truthfulness and intimacy. Immediately prior to this moving meeting between Joachim and his wife Anna, Joachim, while sleeping, receives a vision from an angel who had

told him that his wife had conceived a daughter, Mary. That particular episode, *The Vision of Joachim*, is depicted immediately prior to *The Meeting*. Joachim is then told to go and meet his wife at the Golden Gate of Jerusalem. Giotto captures a powerful and captivating sense of intimacy as Joachim confides in his wife the miraculous news he has recently been told. The two figures form a single, symmetrical pyramid as they embrace. As well as conveying a sense of stability, this also sets Joachim and Anna, to a certain extent, apart from the group of onlookers immediately to their left. What is particularly impressive is Giotto's ability to depict a powerful emotional scene while also foreshadowing the magnitude of events that are yet to come. **CS**

Noli Me Tangere | Giotto

1304–06 | fresco | 78 ¾ x 72 ¾ in / 200 x 185 cm | Capella degli Scrovegni (Arena Chapel), Padua, Italy

In this interpretation of Christ's resurrection, Giotto (c.1270–1337) conflates two separate events—Christ's resurrection and his subsequent meeting with Mary Magdalene. To the left of the picture an angel sits on a tomb and assumes the role of witness to the resurrection. On the right, Christ and Mary Magdalene can be seen enacting the scene known as *noli me tangere*. The phrase, from Latin meaning "touch me not," refers to the first miraculous appearance of Christ, before Mary Magdalene, after his apparent death. Mary, having found the tomb empty, mistakes Jesus for a gardener and implores him to reveal the location of Christ's dead body. Christ, in the instant he reveals himself to Mary, proclaims, "Touch me not, for I am not yet ascended to my father." This sense of

Christ inhabiting two realms is conveyed through the pose he adopts. Placed on the right, while the body of Christ motions away from Mary, he casts a glance over one shoulder. Giotto manages to imbue the scene with an unprecedented level of naturalism. However, it should be understood that "naturalism" here is not, strictly speaking, an entirely novel form of empiricism. Nor is it a sophisticated treatment of a figure's anatomy, although Giotto somehow wrests his treatment of the human form from the medieval conception of the body. Naturalism in Giotto's case entails giving the figures psychological depth, which ensures emotional resonance. Giotto's achievement is remarkable because he sustained this emotional pitch in the whole of the chapel's fresco cycle. **CS**

The Betrayal of Christ | Giotto

1304–06 | fresco | 78 ¾ x 72 ¾ in / 200 x 185 cm | Capella degli Scrovegni (Arena Chapel), Padua, Italy

The fresco cycle by Giotto di Bondone (c.1270–1337) in the Cappella degli Scrovegni is one of the most important masterpieces of Western art. While the upper register depicts the story of Joachim and Anna, the parents of the Virgin Mary, the lower two registers of the chapel narrate the life and Passion of Christ. Giotto's *Betrayal of Christ* is on the south wall. What perhaps distinguishes *The Betrayal of Christ* is Giotto's singular emphasis upon the confrontation between Christ and Judas. Directly to the left of the two protagonists, Giotto places the figures of Peter and the soldier Malchus. According to scripture, Peter cut off Malchus's ear in an uncharacteristic moment of rage. Christ, having miraculously healed the soldier, warned that those who live by the sword will ultimately perish by it. However, this scene assumes a secondary role in relation to the meeting between Christ and his traitor. As with the artist's treatment of other episodes in Christ's life, the emotional gravitas of this scene appears to hinge upon a psychologically charged moment between two people. According to the Gospels, Judas identified Christ to the soldiers by means of a kiss. The two figures are shown in profile; while Judas looks directly up into the eyes of Christ, Christ reciprocates Judas's stare with an unflinching look that shows neither indifference nor revulsion but humility—even compassion—for his betrayer. By depicting Christ this way, Giotto ensures that he remains a steadfast symbol of moral certitude amid the clamor of accusation, deceit, and betrayal. **CS**

The Marriage Feast at Cana | Duccio di Buoninsegna

1308 | 17 ⅛ x 18 ¼ in / 43.5 x 46.5 cm | tempera on poplar | Museo dell'Opera del Duomo, Siena, Italy

The life and times of Duccio di Buoninsegna (c.1255–1319) are hotly debated because of the paucity of his known works. Legal documents provide our only means of tracing Duccio's activities. His indisputable masterpiece was *Maestà* designed for Siena Cathedral's high altar. In 1302, according to state archive documents, Duccio received payment for another, earlier *Maestà*, commissioned for Cappella dei Nove in Siena's Palazzo Pubblico. Today, its whereabouts are unknown. Duccio later painted the reverse side of the *Maestà* of 1308 with thirty-eight *storie* or histories commemorating Christ's ministries from his Passion to his latter days. *The Marriage Feast at Cana* is one of these. The altarpiece was the most elaborate and expensive in the world, but it was sliced into separate panels in 1771. The majority are now in Siena Cathedral's museum. The others are held in public collections throughout the world. *The Marriage Feast at Cana* is a charming scene that tells the story of Jesus's first miracle. He is seated at the end of the table with the Virgin Mary on his right. At this time in his ministry, Christ had only five Apostles who are pictured sitting to his left. The servants, dressed in fourteenth-century clothing, are serving water that Jesus has miraculously changed into wine from earthenware jars. The Byzantine style is apparent in the rather stiff poses, extravagant halos, and lack of perspective, yet Duccio has given the scene his detailed, narrative treatment with a decorated tablecloth, tiled floor, wooden ceiling, and pointed arches. **SP**

Miracles of St. Nicholas of Bari | Ambrogio Lorenzetti

1332 | tempera on wood | 38 x 20 in / 96 x 52.5 cm | Uffizi, Florence, Italy

Ambrogio Lorenzetti (1290–1348) and his elder brother Pietro (c.1280–1348) belonged to the fourteenth-century Sienese School of painting dominated by the stylized Byzantine tradition developed by Duccio di Buoninsegna (c.1255–1319) and Simone Martini (c.1284–1344). While Pietro was more traditional than his sibling, and showed a propensity for harmony, refinement, and dramatic emotion, Ambrogio proved more realistic, inventive, and influential. The *Miracles of St. Nicholas of Bari* altarpiece was executed for the Church of St. Procolo in Florence. Painted during the artist's second visit to the city between 1327 and 1332, it presents all the components of Ambrogio's creativity—the influence of Byzantine art and the plasticity of duecento Sienese relief. Conceived as the

upper section of a side panel of a now dismembered triptych that would originally have had the Madonna and Child at the center, the vignette shows St. Nicholas reviving a child from his deathbed while other children are being carried away by black angels of death. The saint's behest is shown by the lines that project from his mouth and hands. The scene has great narrative power and affords the viewer a glimpse of contemporary interiors, down to details such as the bed covers and tablecloths. The composition of the panel foreshadows the art of the Renaissance. It is as remarkable for its vivid depiction of life, custom, and fourteenth-century Sienese architecture as for its extraordinary command of structure and the control of three-dimensionality and spatial arrangements. **AA**

The Scourging of Christ before Pontius Pilate | Ferrer Bassa

c.1333 | fresco | Monasterio de Pedralbes, Barcelona, Spain

Scenes from the life of Christ depicted by Ferrer Bassa (c.1290–1348) adorn the walls of the Chapel of St. Michael, which was used by nuns of the Order of St. Clare at the Monasterio de Pedralbes. Heavily influenced by fourteenth-century Italian art, Bassa modeled his painting on the work of Giotto. *The Scourging of Christ before Pontius Pilate* is a re-creation of a scene disturbing to all Christians, the torturing of Christ before the Roman Prefect of Judaea and the Jewish high priests. Both in its composition and reticent use of color, the scene resembles the work of Giotto. At the left of the painting, a seated Pilate converses with two Jewish high priests, seemingly oblivious to the scourging of the bound Christ by the Jewish scribes. A disciple—possibly Peter—watches helplessly from outside the gallery. However, some scholars have suggested that the fresco might depict Matthew's account of Jesus being brought before the High Priest Caiaphas, rather than Pontius Pilate, with Caiaphas being shown in discussion with two priests bearing witness against Christ. The piece is likely to provoke anger in the Christian viewer who must watch the son of God being brutally beaten at the hands of Jewish scribes, while neither those in authority nor Peter, who would deny Christ three times, make any attempt to intervene. In his painting Bassa implores the viewer to defend the Church against the Jews who have insisted upon his death. In 1391 anti-Semitism erupted in a pogrom during which hundreds of Barcelonese jews were killed. **WM**

The Annunciation with Two Saints | Simone Martini

1333 | tempera on wood | 104 x 120 in / 265 x 305 cm | Uffizi, Florence, Italy

Simone Martini (c.1284–1344), pupil of Duccio di Buoninsegna and one of the most original and influential artists of the Sienese School, built on techniques developed by his teacher to show three-dimensionality but elevated them in his own work by adding a more refined contour of line, grace of expression and serenity of mood as his signature. *The Annunciation with Two Saints* was created as an altarpiece for the Saint Ansano Chapel inside Siena Cathedral. It was executed by the artist and Lippo Memmi, his brother-in-law, to whom are attributed the lateral figures—St. Ansano, patron of Siena, and St. Giulitta. In the central panel, the Archangel Gabriel and the Virgin enhance the triptych's Gothic nature. Narrative details are implicit in the various symbols—

the pot of lilies symbolize Mary's purity; the olive branch, God's peaceful message; and, between the two figures, a rosette of cherubs surrounding a dove indicates the presence of the Holy Spirit. The gold-relief inscription emanating from the angel's mouth contains the words *"Ave gratia plena dominus tecum"* (Greetings, most favored one! The Lord is with thee). In a break from conventional religious iconography, Mary is visibly shrinking in fear. *The Annunciation* is perhaps the most splendid example of craftsmanship ever produced in Siena. Elaborately tooled in burnished and matte gold, it is a remarkable achievement in the use of outline for the sake of linear rhythm, two-dimensional pattern, and sophisticated enamel color harmonies. **AA**

The Effects of Good Government in the City | Ambrogio Lorenzetti

*c.*1338–40 | fresco | 116 ½ x 550 ⅜ in / 296 x 1,398 cm | Palazzo Pubblico, Siena, Italy

Ambrogio Lorenzetti (*c.*1290–1348) was a Sienese painter known for the sensitive, warm tones of his paintings and the inventiveness of his compositions. *The Effects of Good Government in the City*, by far one of his most important works, is part of a cycle of paintings generally known as the allegories of good and bad government, which were commissioned to adorn the walls of the Sala della Pace in the Palazzo Pubblico of Siena. In this painting (which adjoins *The Effects of Good Government in the Country*), Lorenzetti creates a picture of the harmonious Republic of Siena using a freely inventive approach that does not appear to follow any known prototype. Although at first glance the image appears to be a picture of an idealized "day in the life" of Siena, it has been proposed

that individual groups of figures represent different aspects of happy city life, for example the seven mechanical arts described by the philosopher Hugh of St. Victor. The group of dancers may, perhaps, relate to the mechanical art of music (dancing in the streets was, in fact, illegal in medieval Siena). The program of the entire cycle of paintings is still being debated, and it is possible that the picture was meant to be open to many interpretations. Medieval images such as these, in which a wealth of details are portrayed and in which the viewer's point of view is constantly changing, were constructed so as to invite the viewer to return over and over again to the picture and to contemplate its details, a process that Lorenzetti facilitates marvelously. **SS**

Christ on the Cross | Simone Martini

c.1340 | tempera and gold on panel | 9 x 5 in / 24 x 13 cm | Fogg Art Museum, Cambridge, MA, USA

Siena experienced its golden age in the early trecento under the artistic genius of Duccio di Buoninsegna (c.1260–1319) and his pupil, Simone Martini (c.1284–1344). Both artists developed a rich, courtly style dependent on a gracefulness of line and delicacy of interpretation rather than the monumentality and the sobriety of work by Florentine painters such as Giotto. This new method of painting developed an International Gothic style among the superb artists of the Sienese School. This crucifixion, conceived as the central panel of an altarpiece, captures beautifully the silent dignity and suffering of Christ. Suspended from the cross, the limp, ashen-colored body is stark against the gilded, Byzantine-style background. The agony of Christ's Passion is evoked through the frailty of his

mortal shell—the elongated and emaciated arms and legs, the delicate and exquisitely painted face inclined to one side, the almost transparent veil of the loincloth, and the waxlike flesh which accentuates the copious amounts of red blood streaming from wounds on his hands and feet. Up until Duccio and Martini, religious characters in Byzantine contemplative art wore rigid expressions devoid of human emotion. The illusion of space was seldom explored and flatness was used to emphasize the other-worldliness of its subjects. While retaining many Byzantine conventions, Martini moved away from the rigidity of Byzantine icons toward a new naturalism and a more direct appeal to human emotion that was revolutionary in Western art. **AA**

Beata Umiltà Altarpiece | Pietro Lorenzetti

*c.*1341 | tempera on wood | 70 ½ x 55 ½ in / 179 x 141 cm | Uffizi, Florence, Italy

Brothers Pietro (*c.*1280–1348) and Ambrogio (1290–1348) Lorenzetti—both said to have perished in the Black Death—were fourteenth-century Sienese painters who played a vital part in transforming early Italian Renaissance painting. Like Ambrogio, Pietro developed a style that moved away from the elegant Byzantine tradition toward the naturalism of the great Florentine painter Giotto. The work shown here is an altarpiece that was originally housed in the women's convent of San Giovanni Evangelista, in the northern Italian town of Faenza. The altarpiece tells the story of the life and miracles of Santa Beata Umiltà (St. Humility), an Italian abbess who founded two convents of the Vallumbrosan order during the thirteenth century. One panel (middle row, second from right) depicts Santa Umiltà's arrival in Florence to build the second of these convents, and shows her being guided toward the task by St. John the Evangelist. The figures in the various panels have the new kind of solidity for which the Lorenzetti brothers are famed, with a naturalistic, strongly sculptural quality. The scenes have been carefully constructed, with Pietro displaying convincing spatial illusion, architectural features that are attractively rendered, and an astute awareness of three-dimensional perspective. Pietro was a master of color, and the whole altarpiece is subtly harmonized and imbued with a gentle serenity—he is known for the emotional quality of his work. The sculptural, naturalistic, and emotional qualities show Pietro to be a talented and influential painter. **AK**

Scenes from the Life of Magdalene | Giovanni da Milano

1365 | fresco (detail) | Rinuccini Chapel, Santa Croce, Florence, Italy

The Italian Gothic era painter Giovanni da Milano (active 1350–69) was commissioned by Lapo di Lizio Guidalotti to execute a modest fresco cycle in the Rinuccini Chapel. The Lombard artist painted a series of five scenes on each of the side walls taken from the lives of the Virgin and Mary Magdalene. These scenes are regarded as variants of the cycles by Taddeo Gaddi in the Baroncelli Chapel and those by Giotto's circle in the Magdalene Chapel in the Lower Church of San Francesco in Assisi. This fresco depicts a little-known legend from the life of Mary Magdalene; she is set adrift in a ship toward Marseilles. There her preachings convert the local heathen prince and his wife to Christianity and her prayers grant the couple a son. On the way to Jerusalem to visit St. Peter, the princess dies giving birth. The prince leaves her body on an island with the infant beside it. On his homebound journey two years later, he alights where he had left his dead wife and child and is surprised to find the infant alive. His dead wife rises as he approaches and stretches her arms out to him. The family return to Marseilles to be baptized as Christians. Although it has been suggested that a more stylized manner dominated Florentine painting after the Black Death of 1348, the bulkiness and simplicity of Giovanni's figures and drapery modeling methods are more typically associated with Giotto's Florentine School and his crisp linearity with Simone Martini. His work is notably lacking in decorative detail, especially *sgraffito*, and the coloring is particularly subtle. **AA**

Annunciation | Giusto de' Menabuoi

1376–78 | fresco (detail) | Baptistery, Padua, Italy

Giusto de'Menabuoi (*c*.1320–91), was originally from Florence, but worked mainly in Padua, northern Italy. He possibly trained under Bernardo Daddi or Maso di Banco, and he was an imitator of Giotto. Working at the time of the Black Death in the 1370s, and under a decentralized Catholic papacy, Giusto de'Menabuoi, usually known as Giusto, was an innovator who expanded the pictorial and expressive possibilities of Christian art. *Annunciation* depicts the angel Gabriel informing Mary of her immaculate conception of Jesus. This is just one scene from an enormous series of frescoes in the Baptistery in Padua. Viewed *in situ*, this image is the first in the story of Jesus's conception and birth. Scenes in the lower register depict stories from the life of Christ. In this scene, the Annunciation

is quite conventionally drawn—the angel Gabriel and the Virgin are separated by a pillar to symbolize the division of the mundane and the divine. Mary receives the blessing of the Holy Spirit, represented by the dove. The lilies held by the angel Gabriel represent purity. The geometrically stylized background and clever use of perspective is part of a trompe l'oeil effect, which deceives the eye into thinking that the scene is recessed when it is not. Giusto was instrumental in establishing Padua as a major artistic center, and is credited with furthering and expanding the legacy of Giotto, while widening the stylistic gulf between the artists of northern Italy and the Florentine School. The frescoes at Padua are an astonishing, monumental artistic achievement. **MC**

Descent into Hell | Jaime Serra

1381–82 | tempera on panel (detail) | Museo Provincial de Bellas Artes, Zaragoza, Spain

An artistic disciple of the emerging Sienese style introduced to Spain by Ferrer Bassa, Jaime Serra (active 1370–95)—probably assisted by his brother and sister—painted an altarpiece for the convent of The Holy Sepulchre east of his native Barcelona, outside Zaragoza. The term "descent into hell" is from various New Testament references, particularly Peter's First Epistle. Jesus appears in the foreground on the left side of the painting about to step into the underworld through the wide-open "gates." In Italian and Byzantine works, the entrance to hell is a cave in rocks. In Serra's *Descent into Hell* it is a zoomorphic mouth of a water monster. Adam, the oldest human resident of hell, probably offers his hand to Jesus, desperate for his one-way ticket to heaven. The always-crowned King

David is notably absent—according to most accounts, he and Isaiah hold the gates open for Jesus. Above the royally clothed Jesus, the angels fondly watch over him framed by a formation of white clouds, in contrast to the horned demons in black who scamper about the monster. A descent into the underworld is a theme in other religions. Among others, Osiris of Egypt, the Hindu deity Krisha, the Aztec's Quexalcoatl, Prometheus, and Odysseus all descended into the underworld. The image is likely to have invoked intense feelings of fear at the gruesome image of the dark and slippery fish. However, Jesus willingly descended into hell to complete the divine cycle and bring righteous men to heaven, so this image also holds out the promise of salvation. **WM**

Dormition of the Virgin | Theophanes the Greek

*c.*1392 | tempera on wood | 34 x 27 in / 86 x 68 cm | Tretyakov Gallery, Moscow, Russia

A native of the Byzantine Empire—hence his nickname "the Greek"—Theophanes (*c.*1370–1404) established himself in Muscovite Russia around 1390. Byzantium and Russia both adhered to the Orthodox branch of Christianity and its tradition of icon painting. The dormition, or assumption into heaven, of the Virgin Mary was a recurring theme in Orthodox iconography. It was believed that the Virgin had been buried in the presence of all Christ's apostles, but her tomb was later found to be empty. The traditional iconic representation of the event, which Theophanes follows, shows the lifeless Virgin surrounded by the apostles exhibiting various signs of grief. Behind them two Fathers of the Church wear Orthodox white liturgical robes with crosses. The scene is dominated by the powerful figure of Christ. He holds the Virgin's soul, escaped from her body, in the form of a swaddled baby. The concept of the individual artist and his style is difficult to apply to icon painting, but Theophanes was recognized as unusual in his approach. According to a contemporary account: "When he was drawing or painting … nobody saw him looking at existing examples." Instead he is described as "considering inwardly what was lofty and wise and seeing the inner goodness with the eyes of his inner feelings." The attribution of this icon panel to Theophanes is sometimes debated, but the colors, dramatic force, coherence of the composition, and a relative freedom of brushstroke mark it as distinctive. This icon is an object of intense spiritual power. **RG**

Humay at the Gate of Humayun's Castle | Junayd Baghdadi

1396 | watercolor on paper | British Library, London, UK

Humay at the Gate of Humayun's Castle is one of several miniatures illustrating the poem *Humay and Humayun*, a love story from the fourteenth-century manuscript *Three Poems* by Khwaju Kirmani (*d*.1352). It was completed in 1396 by Junayd Baghdadi whose name implies that he came from Baghdad, but otherwise little is known about him. His style is typical of the synthesis of Chinese art—which arrived with the thirteenth-century Mongol invasion of Persia—and traditional Mesopotamian art. By the late fourteenth century, these two styles had been fully integrated and reached a pinnacle in the "romantic" style of painting known as the Shiraz School. In *Humay at the Gate of Humayun's Castle*, Humay, the suitor, woos Humayun who looks down from her gorgeously

decorated tower. It was typical of miniature painting of the time that the scene was viewed from a high point—sometimes called the "eye of God." Baghdadi pays little attention to perspective or realism, instead he focuses on composition. He does this by including all the elements of the story within a circular shape. The protagonists seem small and rather wooden as they play out their romantic drama. The influence of Chinese art can still be seen in the inclination of Humayun's head, and in Humay's hat and stylized horse. The fairy tale atmosphere is enhanced by the brilliantly colored landscape with its lush garden, fruiting trees, flowering plants and birds wheeling through the sky in the upper register. This is a charming love scene, stylishly executed. **MC**

The Wilton Diptych | Unknown

*c.*1399 | egg tempera on oak | 22 ½ x 11 ½ in / 57 x 29 cm (each panel) | National Gallery, London, UK

Richard II Presented to the Virgin and Child by his Patron Saint John the Baptist and Saints Edward and Edmund is commonly known as *The Wilton Diptych,* which takes its name from Wilton House, the seat of the Earl of Pembroke, where the painting was once housed. Consisting of two hinged panels, a diptych was a portable altarpiece, which its owner would carry on journeys and unfold as an aid to private prayer. This example was created for the ill-fated English monarch Richard II (reigned 1377–99). The unknown artist has represented the somewhat effeminate king kneeling, in the left-hand panel. The figures behind him are recognizable by their emblems. John the Baptist, Richard's patron saint, carries a lamb, while Edmund the Martyr holds one of the Danish arrows that killed

him, and Edward the Confessor has a ring. These holy men are presenting the king to the Virgin Mary, the infant Jesus, and the angels. The painting is scattered with the king's personal emblem—the white stag—worn by the angels as well as by the king himself. An angel holds what may be the banner of St. George, and in the silver globe atop the staff floats a tiny image of Britain. The diptych emphasized the sanctity bestowed on the monarch by God, but also provided a salutary warning against the vanity of kings. It is one of the finest examples of the graceful International Gothic style, prevalent in Europe at that time, and is a superb relic of a unique period in European art. It is also a very rare survivor of England's lost Catholic heritage. **RG**

1400S

The Old Testament Trinity | Andrei Rublev

c.1410 | tempera on wood | 56 x 44 ¾ in / 142 x 114 cm | Tretyakov Gallery, Moscow, Russia

Andrei Rublev (c.1360–1430) grew up in a period of revival in the Eastern Orthodox Church and came to be regarded as one of the greatest Russian iconographers. He received his training under Prokhor of Gorodets and collaborated with Theophanes the Greek in the decoration of the Annunciation Cathedral in Moscow. His unique style broke away from the severity of form, color, and expression of traditional Russian Byzantine icon painting and was infused with a gentleness of spirit that he cultivated in his ascetic life as a monk at the Holy Trinity-St. Sergius Lavra. *The Old Testament Trinity* was immediately considered important and its format was quickly copied and disseminated. The Church Council of Moscow even wrote *The Old Testament Trinity* into the official canon

as the ideal representation of the Holy Trinity. *The Old Testament Trinity* is also known as *The Hospitality of Abraham* because of its reference to Genesis 18, where three angels appear to Abraham at Mamre. Rublev chose not to depict narrative elements of this story in order to convey complex ideas about the trinity—much debated by theologians—through one symbolic image. This icon can be interpreted as the New Testament trinity, consisting of God the Father, Jesus Christ the Son, and the Holy Spirit. In this case the chalice corresponds to the Eucharist. The figures all hold staffs, signifying their divinity. In his peaceful, calm, and contemplative paintings, Rublev innovatively applied his craft in service of his passionate religious convictions. **SWW**

Entombment Triptych | Robert Campin

c.1410 | paint, gold leaf on panel | 25 x 21 in (center), 25 x 10 in (wings) | Courtauld Institute, London, UK

The *Entombment Triptych* is believed to be the earliest surviving work of Robert Campin (c.1375–1444), also known as the Master of Flémalle. With Jan van Eyck (c.1385–1441), Campin is considered to be one of the first great masters of the early Netherlandish School, which represented a radical break with the International Gothic style. The central panel of this work shows the entombment of the dead Christ as his mother Mary, Joseph of Arimathea, Nicodemus, and another Mary are about to wrap Christ's body in his shroud. The other figures in the scene remind viewers of different stages of Christ's suffering. Mary leans on St. John, alluding to the lamentation; Mary Magdalene rubs oil into Christ's feet, symbolizing the anointment; St. Veronica holds up a piece of fabric referring to

Calvary, and angels carrying various elements of the Passion represent the crucifixion. On the left wing is the patron of the work kneeling before the hill of Golgotha. The landscape is quite shallow, and the central cross between the two thieves has a ladder leaning against it, to remind us of Christ's descent from the cross. The right wing shows the resurrection with Jesus emerging from his tomb. All three panels are decorated with gold vines and grapes, symbolizing Christ, the true vine. The *Entombment Triptych* is an example of the transition toward the realistic observation of Netherlandish art, but it retains a traditional medieval decorative gold background. The influence of Claus Sluter (c.1350–1405) is evident in the sculptural quality of the figures. **SH**

Christine de Pizan | Unknown

1410–11 | ink on parchment | 5 ¾ x 7 in / 14.6 x 17.9 cm | British Library, London, UK

Christine de Pizan (1364–1430) was Europe's first professional woman writer. Born in Venice and raised in France, she was widowed at twenty-five and began writing to support herself and her three children. A prolific author and publisher, she produced poetry, prose, political commentary, and literary criticism. She is best known for her historical *Book of the City of Ladies*, and for her response to the misogyny in Jean de Muen's *Romance of the Rose,* which jump-started the *querelle des femmes*, the long debate on the status of women in society. This picture is taken from a beautifully decorated manuscript of Christine's collected works. The collection was planned, copied, and decorated under the supervision of Christine, before being presented to Isabeau of Bavaria, Queen of France, in 1414. In this picture, Pizan presents her book to Isabeau, surrounded by the ladies of the court. The artist, a master of the Cité des Dames workshop, allows the viewer a glimpse into what appears to be the private and colorfully decorated space of the queen's bedroom. Isabeau (*c.*1370–1435) was the wife of Charles VI, and took a prominent role in political affairs due to her husband's frequent bouts of insanity. She was an unpopular queen in difficult times, but she was a good patron of the arts and supported Christine. The decorated walls in the complicated background feature a combination of the French fleurs-de-lis and Isabeau's House of Wittelsbach arms. Centuries later, de Pizan's work continues to inform feminist thought. **KM**

Quaratesi Polyptych | Gentile da Fabriano

1422–25 | tempera on wood (detail) | 12 ½ x 24 ½ in / 32 x 62 cm | Vatican Pinacoteca, Vatican City, Italy

Gentile da Fabriano (1370–1427) was commissioned to paint the panels of the high altar polyptych for the church of St. Niccolò Oltrarno in Florence. The polyptych shows various episodes from the life of St. Nicholas of Bari, patron saint of seamen and travelers: his birth; his gift of a dowry to three penniless maidens; his resurrection of three youths; and his rescuing of a ship at sea. Brimming with naturalistic detail, this panel shows the saint in bishop's robes positioned over the troubled vessel within a radiant halo of light. His miraculous intervention—the act of driving back the menacing clouds and scaring away the mermaids threatening the vessel's safety—is in direct response to the supplication of the passenger seen clasping both hands in prayer while the rest of the crew are casting their cargo overboard. The scene unfolds as if in suspension or in a bubble with no obvious points of reference, such as a coastline or landmarks, pinning down its perspective. Da Fabriano was one of the founding fathers of the fifteenth-century courtly decorative style known as International Gothic. The Quaratesi Polyptych, one of only a handful of surviving works in this style, remained intact until 1830, when it was dismantled and sold as separate panels to galleries worldwide. Da Fabriano (who was praised by Michelangelo for his refined draftmanship) was a pioneer painter who mastered sophisticated techniques, such as the use of color and gold, to transform works of art into what looked like pages from an illuminated manuscript. **AA**

St. Anthony Beaten by Devils | Sassetta

1423–26 | oil on panel | 9 ¹/₂ x 15 ³/₈ in / 24 x 39 cm | Pinacoteca Nazionale, Siena, Italy

Stefano di Giovanni di Consolo (c.1400–50), known as Sassetta, may be the most innovative painter of the Sienese quattrocento. Alongside Florence, Siena was a leading cultural center in Tuscany. Sienese painting was characterized by decorative, mystical works, emphasizing the miraculous and divine. Sassetta emerged within this flourishing tradition, but began to incorporate innovations from the more naturalistic Florentine School. The *Altarpiece of the Eucharist* is his earliest known work, commissioned in 1423 for the Church of the Carmelite Order. It is a triptych depicting scenes from the lives of St. Anthony and Thomas Aquinas, the central panel of which was lost when the altarpiece was disassembled in 1777. *St. Anthony Beaten by Devils* is one of the surviving panels. The hermit St. Anthony is being bludgeoned with clubs by three devils intent on breaking his faith. This terrible scene has an emotional resonance typical of later Renaissance works, as the old man lies helpless beside his abandoned walking stick. The muted gray light pervading the sparse, rocky landscape of St. Anthony's isolation offsets the vivid glow of his halo and the fiery reds punctuating the devils. Sassetta's fusion of Sienese art with Florentine innovation was instrumental in bringing Sienese painting from the International Gothic into the Renaissance style. Although Siena's artistic progression would later be tempered by the city's economic and political decline, Sassetta's influence was widespread in Siena and beyond. **SLF**

Tribute Money | Masaccio

c.1426 | fresco | 100 x 235 in / 255 x 598 cm | Brancacci Chapel, Santa Maria del Carmine, Florence, Italy

Originally commissioned by Felice Brancacci, a wealthy silk merchant, *Tribute Money* forms part of a larger cycle of frescoes depicting the original sin of Adam and Eve and the life of the apostle Peter. In this particular scene from the cycle, Tommaso di Giovanni Masaccio (1401–28) conflates three separate moments from the story of the tax collector who asked Jesus whether he had paid his temple tax, as recounted in St. Matthew's Gospel. The episode begins at the center of the picture where the tax collector is seen with his back to us, making his request. From there the scene continues on the far left of the painting (where both Peter and Jesus are pointing). We see Peter collecting "a piece of money" from the mouth of a fish at the water's edge. Finally, on the far right, Peter presents the tax collector with his original request. That the viewer willingly accepts the artist's depiction of three discrete moments condensed into one whole painting is due, in no small part, to Masaccio's bold, naturalistic, and entirely convincing treatment of the figures. Their sculpturelike appearance conveys an almost palpable sense of volume. Moreover, the inherent dynamism of the scene and the psychologically charged atmosphere in the center is conveyed through the glances that are cast by both Jesus and his Apostles. It is a compelling painting, partly because of the very human set of emotions that the artist is able to imbue the characters with, and partly because he successfully fuses technical innovation with an underlying classicism. **CS**

Temptation of Adam and Eve
Masolino da Panicale

c.1426 | fresco | 82 x 34 ⅝ in / 208 x 98 cm | Brancacci
Chapel, Santa Maria del Carmine, Florence, Italy

Masolino da Panicale (Tommaso di Cristofano, c.1383–
1440) began to collaborate with Masaccio in 1424,
and by 1425 they were both working in the Brancacci
Chapel. Masolino's *Temptation* faces Masaccio's *Expulsion*,
and could hardly be more different in style, mood, or
composition. Time has stopped at this key moment in
Christian teaching, as Eve seduces Adam into eating
from the tree of knowledge. Woman and serpent are
one, as tail and arm thread sinuously around the tree
together. Adam and Eve hover in an undefined space
under the tree's canopy and the dark background
pushes forward the illuminated figures. The space
between them is filled with an arm that curls and an
arm that reaches out. Masolino is concerned with intent
rather than with instinctive reactions, as in Masaccio's
painting. Yet, for all its Gothic beauty it is clear that
Masolino was aware of anatomical form. **WO**

Virgin and Child
Masaccio

1426 | egg tempera on wood | 53 ⅛ x 29 in /
135 x 73.5 cm | National Gallery, London, UK

Of all the artists associated with quattrocento Italy, it is
perhaps Tommaso di Giovanni Masaccio (1401–28)
whom we look toward in order to appreciate most
fully the innovations that painting was subject to at
the time. Masaccio was able to work with conventional
subject matter in a highly innovative and technically
sophisticated manner. The *Virgin and Child* originally
formed the central panel of an altarpiece that had
been commissioned by the notary Ser Giuliano degli
Scarsi for his family chapel in Santa Maria del Carmine
in Pisa. Perhaps the most evident way the artist
imbues the scene with an unprecedented degree of
naturalism is through his use of light. A light source at
the far left invests the panel with a palpable sense of
volume, both through the surfaces that are directly
illuminated and through the coterminous areas of
shadow that are interspersed across the scene. **CS**

The Trinity
Masaccio

1428 | fresco | 262 ½ x 124 ⅞ in / 667 x 317 cm
Santa Maria Novella, Florence, Italy

Had Masaccio (1401–28) not died at the age of twenty-seven, he might have produced an oeuvre comparable with that of his Tuscan counterpart, Piero della Francesca. As it is, his legacy only affords glimpses into how deeply he could have contributed to the development of a style of painting we first see in Giotto. Masaccio's *Trinity* is compelling partly because of the way it plays off the devotional against the secular. Although on one level a depiction of the Trinity, the tripartite union of God the Father, Jesus the Son, and the Holy Spirit, the fresco also acted as a donor portrait. Domenico Lenzi and his wife, who are shown as pious onlookers on the outer edges of the fresco, commissioned it as a mural for the family chapel. What is most notable about this work is the way it employs one-point perspective. Yet it is Christ's face at the composition's center that remains omnipresent. **CS**

Dome of the Zodiac
Pesello

c.1430 | fresco | Old Sacristy,
Basilica of St. Lawrence, Florence, Italy

Giuliano d'Arrigo (c.1367–1446), known as Pesello, was greatly respected as an architect and was consulted over the construction of Florence Cathedral's dome. He built a model of the dome in 1419—which has since been lost—and in 1420 was elected as a standby architect to the cathedral's chief architect, Brunelleschi. Pesello was particularly skilled at depicting animals, as can be seen in the *Dome of the Zodiac*, which is in the Old Sacristy of Florence's oldest church, the Basilica of St. Lawrence. The dome is beautifully crafted with exotic, deep blue coloring and gold details creating a sumptuous vision of the sky. It shows the constellations of the heavens with some accuracy for the month of July in the period of its execution. The *Dome of the Zodiac* is a superb example of the artist's technical skill and draftsmanship, and reflects the growing interest in astronomy in Florence at that time. **TP**

Queen Trishala on Her Bed | Unknown

c.1432 | watercolor on paper | 13 x 5 in / 33 x 13 cm | Philadelphia Museum of Art, Philadelphia, PA, USA

The Jain Western Indian style developed originally at major trade centers such as Gujarat, Rajasthan, and Malwa after the tenth century. It is now considered to be a genre that had a great impact on subsequent Indian painting. Jain arts were mostly patronized by Jain merchants. The artists followed rigid conventions and did not attempt to create realistic effects. The palette was composed of rich natural pigments such as red, yellow, gold, ultramarine blue, and green. The flatness of the colors and the black angular outlines render the figures in static poses. According to Jain sacred texts, Kshatriyani Trishala gave birth to Mahavira, the twenty-fourth Jina. This event is recounted in the famous narrative Kalpasutra, which relates the life of Mahavira. This painting is on a page of a manuscript of the Kalpasutra, and exemplifies the major characteristics of the Western Indian School such as flat colors, angular outlines, static poses, and exaggerated proportions of the body and face. The stylistic paradigms are broad shoulders, narrow waists, and a three-quarter profile of the face. The protruding eyes of the figure is a distinctive feature of the Jain style. Although the composition is compartmentalized, a sense of balance is noticeable. The middle register shows Queen Trishala lying on her bed in an elegant posture. The upper section shows the introduction of temple architecture and fauna within the Jain style. The Western Indian style became a model for subsequent Indian paintings such as those of the Chaurapanchasika tradition. **SZ**

Ghent Altarpiece | Jan van Eyck

1432 | oil on wood | 138 x 181 ½ in / 350 x 461 cm (open) | Saint Bavo Cathedral, Ghent, Belgium

This great masterpiece of Netherlandish art has been admired by visitors to the Saint Bavo Cathedral in Ghent from the moment it was installed there on May 6, 1432. An inscription on the work provides this date and tells us that Jan van Eyck's (c.1385–1441) older brother Hubert began the work. It was finished by Jan at the request of Jodocus Vijd, deputy burgomaster of Ghent and warden of the Church of St. John, and his wife, Elisabeth Borluut. The exact involvement of Hubert in the execution of the work remains unknown. When closed, the altarpiece presents a unified setting on two registers. In the lower tier, the two donors kneel before John the Baptist and John the Evangelist, both represented as stone sculptures. Above them, in a low-ceilinged room stretching across the four panels, is the Annunciation. The shadows in this scene correspond precisely to the direction of the light as it entered the Vijd chapel for which the altarpiece was designed. The interior panels appear as two sets of almost unrelated scenes. In the top half, the central corpus shows God the Father with Mary and John the Baptist. On the inner pair of wings, angels are singing and playing musical instruments, and at each end stand the nude figures of Adam and Eve. Across the panels in the lower register, groups of gloriously arrayed figures— from left to right, the Warriors of Christ, Just Judges, apostles, angels, prophets, patriarchs, female saints, confessors, martyrs, holy hermits, and pilgrims—have gathered in paradise to worship the Lamb of God. **EG**

Man in a Red Turban | Jan van Eyck

1433 | oil on wood | 10 x 7 ⅜ in / 26 x 19 cm | National Gallery, London, UK

In 1550, Giorgio Vasari named Jan van Eyck (c.1385–1441) as the inventor of oil painting, a legend perpetuated until recent times. While Vasari's claim is now discounted, Van Eyck was undoubtedly instrumental in the explosion of oil painting on panel that occurred in the Netherlands in the fifteenth century. Van Eyck's meticulous technique using thin layers of transparent pigment, his extraordinary facility to create the illusion of reality and his erudite use of detail earned him his fame and his place—along with Rogier van der Weyden—as one of the founders of Western European oil painting. *Man in a Red Turban* has long been believed to be a self-portrait. The exotic red headgear appears in the reflections of objects in other works by Van Eyck, such as *The Arnolfini Portrait*.

An inscription, composed of letters made to look as if they are carved, has been painted onto the original, marbleized frame. The top line reads *Als ich kan*, which is thought to be a pun on Van Eyck's surname ("As I/ Eyck can"). The name of the painter and the date ("Jan van Eyck made me on October 21, 1433") appear on the bottom of the frame. Whether or not this is a self-portrait, the painting is extraordinarily powerful. Set against a plain, dark background, the sitter's features are picked out in a clear light that falls from the left. Tiny dots of light from the studio windows appear in his irises. The figure looks directly at the viewer. Nothing detracts from the concentration on this distinctive face, from the laugh lines around the eyes to the slight stubble of a beard. **EG**

The Annunciation | Fra Angelico

1432–34 | tempera on panel | 67 x 71 in / 175 x 180 cm | Museo Diocesano, Cortona, Italy

Fra Angelico's (Guido di Piero, c.1395–1455) earliest work stems from commissions related to the Dominican order of which he was a member. Starting as a manuscript illuminator, he became a renowned artist with a series of major commissions from the Vatican, and ran the largest and most important Florentine workshop of the day. Vasari wrote that he was, "humble and modest in all his works." Fra Angelico took a fresh, naturalistic approach, and created imagery that challenged the boundaries of fifteenth-century altarpiece painting. In *The Annunciation*, a beloved theme of the artist, both the angelic messenger Gabriel and the penitent Virgin are larger than appropriate for the scale of the architecture—if the angel were to stand erect he would be as tall as the column that supports the portico's roof. The congregation was often seated far from the altarpiece image, and by exaggerating the size of these two central characters, Fra Angelico heightens the drama of this holy visitation. The ornate furniture and dress imbue the scenery with luxurious Renaissance detail, bringing the story into a contemporary setting of the painting's making. As the colonnade recedes back into the upper left corner, an early use of linear perspective, the artist inserts a miniature depiction of the expulsion of Adam and Eve. Fra Angelico influenced Leonardo da Vinci (1452–1519), also a Tuscan, and today he rests in the canon with his student Fra Filippo Lippi, and with his peers Paolo Uccello and Andrea del Castagno. **SP**

The Decapitation of St. George | Bernardo Martorell

*c.*1432–34 | tempera on panel | 42 x 20 in / 107 x 53 cm | Louvre, Paris, France

Bernardo Martorell (*c.*1400–52) worked in Barcelona and was probably taught by Luis Borrassá (*d.*1424/5), the most prolific Catalan painter of the time. Only one surviving work is definitely attributed to Martorell—the *Altarpiece of St. Peter of Pubol* (1437), which is in the Museum of Gerona, Italy. However, the *Altarpiece of St. George* is so distinctively in Martorell's style that most experts believe that he was the artist. The altarpiece was created for the St. George chapel in the Palace of Barcelona. It is made up of a central panel showing St. George killing the dragon, which is now housed in the Art Institute of Chicago, and four side panels, which are in the Louvre in France. This side panel forms the final part of the narrative, and depicts St. George's martyrdom. The legend of St. George seems to originate in writings by Eusebius of Caesarea, dated to the fourth century CE. He was reputed to have been a Roman soldier of noble birth who was put to death in 303 CE for protesting against the persecution of Christians. He was canonized in the tenth century, and became the patron saint of soldiers. The legend of St. George was widespread throughout Europe in the Middle Ages, and although the story of the saint killing a dragon seems more mythological than miraculous, it is retold in many medieval paintings. In this last scene from the legend, as St. George is decapitated, lightning falls from a fiery red and gold sky. The style may be International Gothic, but the horrified faces, rearing horses, tumbling bodies, and expert handling of light belongs to Martorell. **MC**

Portrait of Giovanni Arnolfini and His Wife | Jan van Eyck

1434 | oil on wood | 32 x 23 in / 82 x 59.5 cm | National Gallery, London, UK

This enigmatic double portrait, commonly known as *The Arnolfini Portrait*, is set in the bedchamber of a Flemish house and is unique to Netherlandish art. The couple are usually identified as Giovanni di Nicolao Arnolfini, a wealthy merchant from Lucca living in Bruges, and his wife, Giovanna Cenami, although this is questioned by some scholars. As he did on other occasions, for example in *Man in a Red Turban*, Jan van Eyck (c.1385–1441) inscribed this picture in an original and witty way. The ornate Latin signature, which looks like graffiti on the wall between the chandelier and the mirror, translates as "Jan van Eyck was here 1434." The poses and unusually detailed setting have led to various interpretations of the couple's circumstances. It has been suggested that the picture depicted the couple's civil wedding. Giovanna is not pregnant, but holds up the full skirt that was highly fashionable in her day. More recently, it has been proposed that this is a posthumous portrait, painted after Giovanna's untimely death. The objects dotted around the room seem to point to the couple's relationship, such as the dusting brush hanging from the bedstead, which referred to a woman's domestic duties, and the carved figure on the bedstead that is probably St. Margaret, the patron saint of childbirth. This painting shows Van Eyck's extraordinary capacity to render detail and light. The elaborate mirror, each lobe decorated with a scene from the Passion, reflects the rear view of the couple and two figures standing in the doorway. One may be the painter himself, wearing a red turban. **EG**

Virgin and Child Enthroned with Four Saints | Fra Angelico

c.1433–36 | tempera on panel | 86 x 94 ½ in / 218 x 240 cm (overall) | Museo Diocesano, Cortona, Italy

Born at the dawn of the quattrocento, Fra Angelico (Guido di Piero, c.1395–1455) began life in obscurity, but rose to unprecedented heights in art-making, setting the scene for two hundred years of Italian dominance. Only after his death was he given the name "Angelico." Both he and his brother were trained in book arts. His brother Benedetto, who died in 1448, was a scribe, and young Guido was an illustrator. This early phase of his life proved useful in honing the skills required to become a masterful altarpiece painter. Guido entered the friary of St. Dominic, from which he assumed the name Fra Giovanni, and by 1425 he was experienced enough to be named for the authorship of a Medici-commissioned altarpiece. *Virgin and Child Enthroned with Four Saints* shows the mature artist successfully rising to a daunting challenge. Not only did Fra Angelico and his workshop have to create a seamless narrative flow of images but they had to frame them within a coherent order. The result is a gilt panoply of images and meaning layered over three major sequences. The image of Christ on the cross, on the central finial, presides over the focal image of the Virgin and Child below. Flanking both sides of the image are the saints poised with the attributions that mark their contribution to biblical history—Mark and John, authors of the Gospels, are shown bearing quills. The predella panel below shows Pope Innocent III meeting Saints Dominic and Francis. Here, Christian iconography is generously endowed with the pomp and power of the Italian Renaissance. **SP**

The Annunciation | Robert Campin

1430–40 | oil on panel | 30 x 27 ½ in / 76 x 70 cm | Museo del Prado, Madrid, Spain

The great movement of Flemish painting during the early Renaissance was initiated by two painters Robert Campin (c.1375–1444), known as the Master of Flémalle, and Jan van Eyck (c.1385–1441). The annunciation was a theme that Campin painted several times. In c.1425, he painted the famous *Mérode Altarpiece*, a triptych, the central panel of which also depicted the Angel Gabriel announcing to Mary her role as the mother of Christ. One of the most striking features of his painting is his detailed representation of contemporary interiors. This painting of *The Annunciation* takes place within a Gothic temple. The Virgin, seated in the porch, is dressed in the clothes of the fifteenth-century bourgeoisie. The Angel Gabriel kneels on the stairs, about to speak. It is produced in

Campin's usual taut style, and his customary symbols explain the event. An empty vessel stands before the carefully rendered folds of Mary's dress and an open cupboard, half revealing hidden objects, serves to remind us of the mysteries to follow in this young woman's life. An unexplained light—symbolizing the Holy Spirit—illuminates the Virgin, as yet undisturbed by her visitor. By depicting Mary reading, Campin implies that she is wise—an allusion to the throne of wisdom. But she sits at a lower level than the Angel Gabriel, so she is also the Virgin of humility. The painting is divided vertically by a pillar. The left-hand side with the Angel Gabriel is the divine half, while the right-hand side portrays the human aspect of Mary before her life changes irrevocably. **SH**

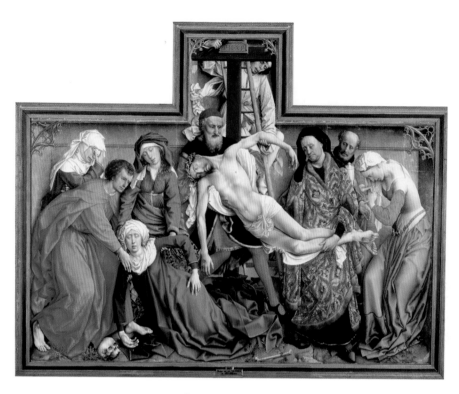

Deposition | Rogier van der Weyden

1435–40 | oil on oak panel | 86 ½ x 103 ⅛ in / 220 x 262 cm | Museo del Prado, Madrid, Spain

Rogier van der Weyden's (*c*.1399–1464) *Deposition* is a supreme example of the early Netherlandish tradition. Encompassing painters such as Jan van Eyck, the tradition was characterized by an acute attention to detail that was afforded by the use of oil paint. Although oil as a medium had been used as far back as the eighth century, it took artists such as Van Eyck and Van der Weyden to realize its full potential. Van der Weyden's painting was originally commissioned by the Guild of Archers in Louvain, Belgium. In the painting, the deposition—the moment when the dead body of Christ is taken down from the cross—takes place within what appears to be an enclosed, boxlike space. Although the Netherlandish tradition was notable for its use of domestic interiors, here the artist's use of space lends the overall scene a sense of intimacy. The body of Christ is gently lowered by Joseph of Arimathaea on the left and Nicodemus on the right. The Virgin Mary, shown traditionally in blue, swoons at the feet of St. John, who reaches out to the grieving mother. Visually, the diagonal that is formed by the Virgin's limp body echoes the lifeless body of Christ above it. This poignant mirroring is also evident in the positioning of Mary's left hand in relation to Christ's right hand. Van der Weyden raises the emotional register of the scene to an unprecedented level. The downcast eyes of the nine witnesses to Christ's death collectively speak of an inconsolable grief, the artist is able to portray a grief that is unrelenting in its sorrow and emotional pathos. **CS**

The Annunciation with Two Kneeling Donors | Fra Filippo Lippi

c.1440s | oil on panel | 61 x 56 ¾ in / 155 x 144 cm | Galleria Nazionale d'Arte Antica, Rome, Italy

The date of this painting has been disputed for some time. Early scholars insisted that it could have been painted no earlier than 1452, but more recent research suggests that it was painted during the 1440s, when Fra Filippo Lippi (c.1406–69) first began following the style of Fra Angelico. It has also been suggested that one of Lippi's assistants on this version of *The Annunciation* was Andrea del Castagno. The detail in this painting is exquisite, with the background painted as intricately as the foreground. Note the entwined statues in the alcove to the right of the Virgin Mary and the detailed painted trees behind her, as well as the delicate patterning of the stonework. The painting is rich with symbols associated with the Virgin Mary, such as the lily the angel Gabriel is giving to her, and

the dove, surrounded by a halo, flying toward her. Lippi is renowned for giving the characters in his paintings realistic facial expressions. Here, the angel Gabriel has such a young face—one would almost expect him to be a cherub, not an angel of great wisdom and renown—but this only adds gravity to the seriousness and sorrow implicit in Mary's face, as if she already knows the pain waiting in store for her with the crucifixion of her son. The two donors look stiff and somber, obviously painted on as an adjunct, their awkward presence in the holy bedchamber is forced. One feels that Lippi objected to including them in his painting. They stare straight ahead, unable to look directly upon the great religious figures of Mary and Gabriel. **LH**

The Battle of San Romano | Paolo Uccello

Begun c.1440 | tempera on panel | 71 x 126 in (each panel) | National Gallery, UK; Uffizi, Italy; Louvre, France

Paolo Uccello (c.1397–1475), also known as Paolo di Dono, was one of the great early masters of Renaissance perspective. Born in Florence, Italy, he trained in the workshop of the master Lorenzo Ghiberti. Being the son of a lowly barber surgeon, Uccello was first admitted to the Guild of Doctors and Apothecaries. In 1425, he moved to Venice, where he was employed to lay mosaic in the Basilica of San Marco. The Battle of San Romano comprises a series of three large panels probably painted for the Medici family, the most powerful of Florence's patrons. The paintings depict a minor battle in 1432 between Florence and Siena. The London panel (above) shows the Florentine commander Niccoló da Tolentino, backed by only twenty soldiers, surprising the Sienese during an attack at San Romano. This panel is a *tour de force* of war imagery, and demonstrates Uccello's fascination with perspective—a matrix of splintered spears, strewn bodies, and colorful heraldic armor leads the viewer through an exhilarating display of violence and bloodthirsty chaos. The panel housed at the Uffizi (above right) features da Tolentino unseating Bernadino della Ciarda. The Uffizi panel was once the center of the trio, and is the only one signed by the artist. The last panel, from the Louvre (below right), depicts the counterattack of Michelotto da Cotignola. Uccello introduced a new subject to fifteenth century art—the battle. He also used the panels as an unparalleled experiment in perspective, and set a new course in the art of painting. **SP**

Noli Me Tangere
Fra Angelico

1440–41 | fresco | 70 ⅞ x 57 ½ in / 180 x 146 cm
Museo di San Marco dell'Angelico, Florence, Italy

Fra Angelico (Guido di Piero c.1395–1455) is best known for the frescoes he painted in the monks' cells at San Marco, Florence. While there are traces of the International Gothic style in his work, it is clear that he was aware of the innovations taking place in Florentine art. There is nothing of Masaccio's blunt realism here, but there is the same interest in capturing the psychological moment. "Noli me tangere" (Touch me not) were the words that Christ spoke to Mary Magdalene (John 20:17) when, seeing him alive after the crucifixion, she tried to embrace him. The position of the trees in the background mirrors the distance between Christ's hand and that of Mary; the placing of the central tree also divides the composition into before and after, or mortality and spirituality. Mary's earthbound posture also contrasts with that of Christ, who seems to hover above the carpet of flowers. **WO**

Portrait of Leonello d'Este
Pisanello

1441 | tempera on panel | 11 x 7 in / 28 x 18 cm
Galleria Accademia Carrara, Bergamo, Italy

Due to the scarcity of his paintings, Antonio Pisano, known as Pisanello (c.1394–1455), is better known for his portrait medallions. These were reproducible sculptural reliefs that mimicked the coinage of ancient Rome. There is little information on his early career, though his name is thought to indicate that he came from Pisa. According to a poet, Pisanello completed the *Portrait of Leonello d'Este* in 1441 in direct competition with Jacopo Bellini. It is thought to be a companion to Pisanello's *Portrait of Ginevra d'Este*, which today hangs in the Louvre in Paris. Leonello d'Este (1407–50) was born illegitimately into the aristocratic ruling family of Ferrara, a city-state in northern Italy. He was legitimized by the Pope in 1435, and became Marquess of Ferrara in 1441. This portrait celebrates Este's rule—the roses, ornate clothing, and flawlessly coiffed hair reveal a man of culture and standing. **SP**

Adoration of Christ
Stefan Lochner

1445 | oil on panel | 14 ¾ x 9 ¼ in / 37.5 x 23.6 cm
Alte Pinakothek, Munich, Germany

Edward Grimston
Petrus Christus

1446 | oil on oak | 12 ¾ x 9 ½ in / 32.5 x 24 cm
National Gallery, London, UK

The skill of *Adoration of Christ* is that it evokes a delicate charm without being cloyingly sentimental. This makes it typical of the work of German painter Stefan Lochner (c.1415–51). This scene is a simple portrayal of the Nativity. Mary kneels before Christ in a stable. An angel announces the birth to shepherds on the left, whose flocks of sheep are in the distance. Lochner often gave his compositions a strong Gothic-style structure. Here it is provided by the Virgin kneeling in adoration of Christ. Her central position and triangular shape, formed from flowing robes spreading out across the picture, balance the whole image. The robes are painted with a softness typical of Lochner, but they also have a sculptural quality lending Mary a suitable monumentality. Lochner combines gemlike colors and flowing lines, common to Gothic art, with a Netherlandish eye for naturalistic detail. **AK**

Petrus Christus (c.1410–72/73) studied under Jan van Eyck in Bruges. He was a contemporary of Rogier van der Weyden, whose influence is evident in his paintings, and he advanced the Eyckian style by incorporating rooms and recognizable interiors into his work. The concept of portrait painting was relatively new in the fifteenth century, but Christus made the form his own. Edward Grimston was a diplomat in Henry VI's court, which he references with his chain of S-shapes symbolizing the Lancastrian house of the king. The painting is the earliest surviving portrait of an English commoner. Grimston is lit by an undefined source of light, but his face is clearly drawn from life with its mottled skin and dour countenance. His eyes are mismatched, which adds to the portrait's realism, and their expression of cunning and secrecy no doubt fueled the rumors that Grimston was a spy. **MC**

The Flood | Paolo Uccello

1447–48 | fresco | 84 ⅝ x 200 ¾ in / 215 x 510 cm | Chiostro Verde, Santa Maria Novella, Florence, Italy

Sadly, the masterful fresco *The Flood* by Paolo Uccello (Paolo di Dono, *c.*1397–1475) has faded badly inside Florence's impressive Santa Maria Novella basilica. The work illustrates the Old Testament tale of Noah and his ark surviving a great flood sent by God as punishment for the sins of humankind. The fresco depicts Noah's monumental ark twice, showing it enduring the initial deluge, and settling on land with the recession of the waters. The compression of these two parts of the Genesis story into a single visual narrative testifies to Uccello's willingness and skill in reinterpreting familiar images of the Church. It also displays Uccello's dexterity as a master storyteller. To the left of the image is a warrior atop his steed brandishing a saber against a club-wielding nude figure who is wearing what must be one of the great geometrical accessories of the Renaissance, the complex necklace known as the *mazzocchio*. The architect Alberti would be proud of the brilliantly engineered space, and at this time Uccello and Donatello (Donato di Niccolò di Betto Bardi, *c.*1386–1466) were working neck and neck in creating such masterful compositions. Other characters in the fresco are either dead or are shown struggling to survive—one comically floats at rest inside a barrel—the wrath of the heaven-sent cataclysm. The scene is full of horror and gore. In a nearly imperceptible section toward the rear of the image, painter and biographer Giorgio Vasari noticed a "dead body . . . whose eyes are being pecked out by a crow." **SP**

St. John in the Desert | Domenico Veneziano

1445–50 | tempera on panel | 11 ¼ x 12 ½ in / 28.5 x 32 cm | National Gallery of Art, Washington, DC, USA

St. John in the Desert is part of an altarpiece painted for the Church of Santa Lucia dei Magnoli, in Florence. This is the masterwork of one of the leading artists of the early Italian Renaissance, Domenico Veneziano (c.1400–61). Here is art at a crossroads, mixing medieval and emerging Renaissance styles with a new appreciation of light, color, and space. "Veneziano" suggests that Domenico came from Venice, but he spent most of his days in Florence and was one of the founders of the fifteenth-century school of Florentine painting. John is seen exchanging his normal clothes for a rough camel-hair coat—exchanging a worldly life for an ascetic one. Veneziano departed from the medieval norm of depicting John as an older, bearded hermit and instead displays a young man cast, literally,

in the mold of ancient sculpture. Classical art became a major influence on the Renaissance, and this is one of the first examples. The landscape's powerful, nonrealistic shapes symbolize the harsh surroundings in which John has chosen to pursue his pious path and recall scenes from Gothic medieval art; in fact, the artist trained initially in the Gothic style and very probably studied the northern European artists. What is also remarkable about this painting is its clear, open delicacy and its attention to atmospheric light effects. The space has been carefully organized but Veneziano in large part uses his revolutionary light, fresh colors (achieved in part by adding extra oil to his tempera) to indicate perspective, rather than the lines of the composition, and in this he was a pioneer. **AK**

Boccaccio | Andrea del Castagno

*c.*1450 | detached fresco | 98 ³⁄₈ x 60 ⁵⁄₈ in / 250 x 154 cm | Uffizi, Florence, Italy

A member of the Florentine School, Andrea del Castagno (Andrea di Bartolo di Bargilla, *c.*1418–57) was commissioned to paint the *Cycle of Famous Men and Women* at the Villa Carducci in Legnaia no later than June 1449, when Filippo Carducci, owner of the villa, died. The *Cycle* consists of nine portraits placed inside individual niches painted like monumental marble recesses and separated by pilasters. It features three Florentine military commanders (Farinata degli Uberti, Pippo Spano, and Niccolò Acciaiuoli), three famous women (the Cumaean Sibyl, Queen Esther, and Queen Tomyris), and three Tuscan poets (Dante Alighieri, Francesco Petrarch, and Giovanni Boccaccio). The elaborate architectural decoration of the ceiling and the walls emphasizes the monumentality of the figures. These austere figures, based on models by Masaccio and Giotto, give the viewer an exalted representation of the desirable qualities of Renaissance man: physical strength, moral virtue, and a keen intellect. All nine figures appear to be looking and gesturing toward each other. Boccaccio (1313–75), the Italian poet and scholar best remembered as the author of the *Decameron*, is the final figure and appears as a colored and draped lifelike statue set along the wall for the viewer to observe. He is shown holding a leather-bound volume and looking at Petrarch, emphasizing the fact that both men helped elevate vernacular literature to the level of the classics of antiquity, and served as iconic Renaissance models worthy of emulation. **AA**

Triumph of Death | Unknown

c.1450 | fresco | Galleria Regionale, Palazzo Abbatellis, Palermo, Italy

By the mid-fifteenth century, Sicily was enjoying a period of continuous rule under the house of Aragon, and forged close links with Spanish culture. The Catalan Gothic style became popular in contrast to Renaissance Gothic, which prevailed on the Italian mainland. The *Triumph of Death,* a suitably Gothic image, covers an entire wall and was painted for the chapel of a hospital. It is sometimes attributed to Pisanello (c.1394–1455) because of the similarity in style to Pisanello's *Vision of St. Eustace,* which is housed in the National Gallery, London. The detailed studies of animals in each painting are similar—Pisanello was famous for his portrayals of animals and birds—but it is unlikely that a definite attribution will ever be made. The theme of "triumph" was a common one

in the Middle Ages that was borrowed from classical Rome and adapted for Christianity. Triumphs of the Cross, of love, of patience, and of various saints, were popular throughout Europe. The *Triumph of Death* is a chillingly gory painting. Like one of the horsemen of the Apocalypse, Death rides a hideous, skeletal horse trampling the rich and the clergy while sparing the poor. On the right-hand side and above right, the lovers of pleasure and riches are only dimly aware of Death's approach, but it is too late for them to mend their ways. This Apocalyptic vision has an extraordinarily modern feel with the horse and dog almost graphically styled. An aid to medieval meditation, it retains its power to move the viewer to contemplate life and death. **MC**

The Melun Madonna
Jean Fouquet

c.1451–52 | oil on panel | 35 7/8 x 31 7/8 in / 91 x 81 cm | Koninklijk Museum, Antwerp, Belgium

As the original master of the French Renaissance, Jean Fouquet (c.1420–81) trained in the Italian tradition. He studied in Florence and Rome but returned to France where he excelled at naturalistic portraiture—his subjects included his patron Étienne Chevalier and Charles VII of France. Chevalier commissioned Fouquet to paint *The Melun Diptych* for the church at his home in Melun. The left-hand panel depicts Chevalier with St. Stephen and is now housed at the Staatliche Museum, Berlin. The right-hand panel, *The Melun Madonna*, is said to be modeled after Agnès Sorel, mistress of Charles VII who was also loved by Chevalier. The Madonna is an arresting figure, with one breast bare, in front of a throne surrounded by blue and red angels representing night and day. She has the bulging, shaved forehead fashionable at this period. The blanche-white skin, crown of stars, and pearls decorating the throne show Mary in her role as Queen of Heaven. The bare breast is abnormally placed and the waspish waist exaggerated, which separates the Virgin's image from more naturalized portrayals of nudity. This, along with the vivid coloring and her extreme beauty, gives the picture a strangely modern feel. Despite Fouquet's importance as the reconciler of the southern and northern Renaissance traditions, his legacy was neglected after the last of his pupils died in the sixteenth century. It was not until his work was assembled for a retrospective exhibition at the beginning of the twentieth century that his reputation was reassessed. **MC**

Scenes from the Life of St. John the Baptist: Herod's Feast
Fra Filippo Lippi

c.1457 | fresco | Santo Stefano Cathedral, Prato, Italy

Fra Filippo Lippi (c.1406–69) had been ordained into the Church as a teenager. He had always lived in a religious community, having been abandoned by his parents as a baby and brought up in a Carmelite friary. As an artist, he was acclaimed during his lifetime and counted the Medici family and Pope Eugenius IV among his patrons. In 1442, the Pope granted Lippi a steady income. Despite his ordination, Lippi scandalized the religious community by having an affair with a nun named Lucretia Buti—an affair that could no longer be concealed when she became pregnant. His powerful friends ensured they were able to leave their religious orders and marry—although history is divided about whether the couple ever did. Some contemporary sources claim that Lippi wanted to remain "free" so the couple lived together without marrying. After his death it was rumored he had been poisoned by the family of a woman with whom he was having an affair. This painting is from a series of frescoes, one depicting the life of St. Stephen and the other of John the Baptist. The figure of Salome at Herod's feast is believed to be a portrait of Lucretia Buti. Note the look of shock on the face of the female guest who is being shown the head of John the Baptist on its platter. It was Salome's mother Herodias, who instructed the girl that when Herod offered her anything she wanted she was to ask for the prophet's head. Most often Salome is portrayed as a scheming temptress, yet Lippi shows a compassionate Salome and suggests she is mourning for the dead man. **LH**

The Virgin Appears to Pope Callistus III | Sano di Pietro

1455–58 | oil on panel | 62 ¼ x 45 ¼ in / 158 x 115 cm | Pinacoteca Nazionale, Siena, Italy

In the fifteenth century, the city of Siena was an important religious and cultural center. Sienese artist Sano di Pietro (c.1405–81), and his workshop made altarpieces for most of the churches in the region. Siena saw some troubled times, and this painting deals with one such incident. The story told here concerns a terrible famine that struck Siena in 1455, when Pope Calixtus III (or Callistus III) sent help to relieve the city's starving inhabitants. It seems that the Virgin Mary had inspired him to take this action, and the painting shows her appearing to him in a vision. The two scrolls feature Mary's appeal to the pope and his reply to her, both in verse. At the foot of the picture a caravan of mules toils toward the city walls bearing sacks of grain (the picture was actually commissioned by the trade organization that controlled corn supplies in Siena). This picture has the lovely coloring common to the Sienese School, great charm, and a skillful blending of fact and fiction. The mismatched scale of the figures, buildings, and mules immediately conjures up the feeling of a dream. Everything is, however, painted with an eye for detail that brings the picture alive and reminds us that it deals with an actual event—especially little touches such as the mule shown halfway through the city gates. Sano di Pietro has created an elegant, beautifully colored, and slightly mystical work. It shows Florentine influence but also has the courtliness and realistic detail of the International Gothic style. Sano di Pietro was influenced by the master painter Sassetta. **AK**

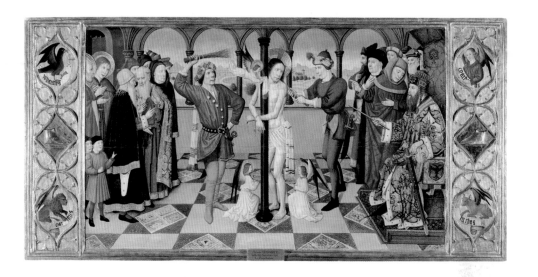

The Flagellation of Christ | Jaume Huguet

1450–60 | oil on panel | 36 ¼ x 61 ⅜ in / 92 x 156 cm | Louvre, Paris, France

The lands of Catalonia, centered on the city of Barcelona, saw a great golden age of art in the 1400s, and at the forefront of this revival was Jaume Huguet (c.1415–92). Huguet is famed for stunning altarpieces such as this, which typify the beautifully decorative religious art produced by the Catalan School at this time. At the center of this picture, Christ is being beaten prior to receiving a sentence of death by crucifixion. The man who delivered the sentence—Roman governor of Judaea, Pontius Pilate, is seated on a grand throne to the right of the painting. Huguet's image is filled with jewellike colors and bursting with fine detail—from the floor tiles to Pilate's throne and clothing. There is a well-constructed symmetry in the composition—Christ's central position, flanked by two men delivering the beating and two small angels at his feet, the receding floor tiles, the row of arches behind Christ, and the distant view of a landscape with evenly sized peaks. The whole effect is highly decorative, almost like a piece of tapestry. This piece was commissioned by the guild of shoemakers for the Saint-Marc chapel of Barcelona Cathedral, which is why shoes appear in the decorative border. The borders also feature images of an eagle, a lion, an angel, and an ox—symbols of the Evangelists St. John, St. Mark, St. Matthew, and St. Luke respectively. Huguet's work is broadly in the mold of fifteenth-century Catalan masters such as Bernardo Martorell, and his personal style helped to define the Catalan style. **AK**

The Flagellation of Christ | Piero della Francesca

c.1460 | oil and tempera on panel | 23 x 32 in / 58 x 82 cm | Galleria Nazionale delle Marche, Urbino, Italy

Ignored at the time of its creation (its very existence went unrecorded for three hundred years), it was only in the last century that the unique qualities of this small painting began to be appreciated. It is now generally acknowledged as one of the most enigmatic and formally sophisticated paintings ever made. Its creator Piero della Francesca (c.1415–92) was also a mathematician and geometer. As a painter he worked throughout central and northern Italy, including the Ducal Palace at Urbino where this painting still hangs. The painting's subject matter was a common theme in the art of the time but Piero's treatment is strikingly unconventional. Christ's flaying is displaced to the left background, and takes place in a tiled gallery which is depicted with a complete mastery of perspective and

foreshortening. The right foreground is dominated by three apparently detached characters whose identity and connection to the events behind them is the source of much of the painting's enduring mystery. Are they the Duke of Urbino and the counselors who allegedly conspired to assassinate him? Is the bearded figure Judas, could he be a medieval astrologer, or does he symbolize the Turks who had captured Constantinople in 1453 and who were threatening to sweep across Europe? Is the painting an allegory of the Church in peril, or is its meaning more personal and illusive? Whatever its "true" meaning may have been, the painting's mathematically precise composition and resistance to easy interpretation continues to appeal to modern viewers. **RB**

Journey of the Magi to Bethlehem | Benozzo Gozzoli

c.1460 | fresco (detail) | Chapel of the Palazzo Medici-Riccardi, Florence, Italy

In Italy during the fifteenth century there was a tremendous flourishing of the arts and literature combined with a great sense of national pride. Florence and Venice were wealthy and powerful cities at this time, and it was to Florence that Benozzo Gozzoli (c.1420–97) was summoned in c.1459 to commence work on the magnificent cycle of frescoes, *Journey of the Magi to Bethlehem*, in the Medici Chapel. Gozzoli's style is generally categorized as International Gothic, based on the elaborate detailing, pageantry and tapestrylike effect of his compositions, and this can be seen to good effect in this fresco cycle. *Journey of the Magi* covers three walls of the chapel and is rich in detail, sumptuous color, and superbly fictitious architectural structures. The

cycle, which was finished in 1461, was unusually lavish for Gozzoli, being markedly more ornate than the rest of his work. This reflected the expensive tastes of the powerful Medici family, whose portraits appear in the procession, alongside a portrait of the artist. Spatially, the composition appears rather unresolved and the perspective unconvincing, although aesthetically the coloring and vivacious figures are compelling and create a patternlike effect through the cycle. Gozzoli had a long and prolific career and, although his work did not have a particular influence on other artists, he was widely appreciated during his time. Interest in the artist was renewed in the nineteenth century and today his vividly colored, captivating works remain highly appealing. **TP**

Adoration of the Child with St. Bernard | Fra Filippo Lippi

*c.*1463 | tempera on panel (detail) | 55 ⅛ x 51 ⅛ in / 140 x 130 cm | Uffizi, Florence, Italy

Despite the religious themes of Fra Filippo Lippi's (*c.*1406–69) paintings—in part because he was an ordained priest, and in part because this was the primary style of art in fifteenth-century Florence—Lippi's paintings are always full of human interest. He imbues each character with a personality normally absent from strictly religious scenes. Painted toward the end of Lippi's life, *Adoration of the Child with St. Bernard* is a scene of great religious symbolism. St. Bernard lived in the twelfth century and remains one of the most important religious figures of his time. St. Bernard is often described as having begun "the cult of the Virgin," and he was largely responsible for the Virgin Mary's prominent position in the church. Lippi painted him on more than one occasion, most

famously in his *Saint Bernard's Vision of the Virgin* (*c.*1447). Lippi had been a keen follower of the painter Tomaso di Giovanni, known as Masaccio (*c.*1401–28). Masaccio died mysteriously at a young age—he left Florence for Rome and was never heard of again—but his work continued to inspire other Florentine artists after his death. Lippi's own style changed direction after 1440, becoming uniquely linear and using an increasing amount of decorative motifs. Lippi was also among the first artists to paint in the form of tondo—a circular canvas often depicting the Virgin and Child. Lippi and the nun Lucretia Buti's son, the painter Filippino Lippi (*c.*1457–1504), learned his craft alongside the young Botticelli, and it is likely that it was Lippi who taught them both. **LH**

The Resurrection of Christ | Piero della Francesca

c.1463 | fresco | 88 ⅝ x 78 ¾ in / 225 x 200 cm | Pinacoteca Civica, Sansepolcro, Italy

Piero della Francesca's (c.1415–92) life as an artist and theorist—he published several treatises on painting, including *De prospectiva pingendi*, continuing the debate on the new science of perspective—was, to a certain extent, peripatetic. His affiliations were toward no particular region; rather, his activities as a painter led him to make work in various locations across the Italian peninsula. *The Resurrection* currently resides in Piero's hometown, Borgo San Sepolcro (now called Sansepolcro). The fresco's provenance was originally the Residenza, an official government chamber, where it had been commissioned for the Sala dei Conservatori. The fresco centers around the risen figure of Christ, and the frontality of the pose Christ adopts denotes the certitude and solemnity of the Christian spirit. Organized around a dominant vertical line that splices the painting in two, Piero places winter on the left-hand side of the line, and summer on the right. Reading this painting from left to right the viewer understands that the change of the seasons is an elaboration on the "rebirth" of Christ himself. As well as reading the painting from left to right, one can read it from the bottom of the composition, where the soldiers lay asleep, to the standing, upright pose of Christ himself, his left foot placed on the ledge as if about to step upward and quite literally out of the scene itself. Such a change from passivity to action, from slumber to movement, conveys the painting's ultimate meaning—the indomitability of Christ himself. **CS**

Portraits of Federico da Montefeltro and Battista Sforza
Piero della Francesca

1465–66 | tempera on panel | 18 ½ x 13 in / 47 x 33 cm | Uffizi, Florence, Italy

Gazing toward each other across the centuries in front of a luminous landscape (the earliest landscape background in Italian Renaissance portaiture) are Federico da Montefeltro, powerful ruler of the city-state of Urbino, and his young wife Battista Sforza. The paintings were probably intended to be hinged together to form a diptych. On the back of the panels Piero della Francesca (c.1415–92) painted the couple set in allegorical landscapes, sitting on triumphal chariots. In Piero's only known portraits he depicts the sitters in absolute profile—painted versions of a Renaissance medal, as was the fashion at the time. Both realistic and idealized, each profile is held within a perfectly drawn outline. Dressed in bright red court clothes and hat of state, Federico is shown warts and

all, with skin blemishes and a hook nose damaged in a tournament. The same incident badly disfigured the right side of his face, which Piero has diplomatically hidden from view. Despite the realism of her exquisite coiffure, brocaded dress, and glinting string of pearls, Battista's face itself has an unearthly quality. It may be that Piero took her likeness from her death mask, for Battista died young. She married Federico when she was fourteen, and after producing eight daughters in eleven years, she offered her life to God in exchange for a son. In 1472 the longed-for son was born: six months later Battista died of pneumonia. Although scholars still debate the dating of this double portrait, it is likely that it is one of the works that Federico commissioned as a memorial to his wife. **JW**

Last Supper Altarpiece
Dierec Bouts

1464–67 | oil on wood | 72 ⅞ x 111 ⅞ in / 185 x 284 cm | Church of Saint Peter, Leuven, Belgium

Dierec Bouts (c.1415–75), originally from Haarlem, settled in Leuven around 1444. In 1464, four members of the Brotherhood of the Holy Sacrament of Saint Peter's Church in Leuven commissioned an altarpiece from Bouts. The contract, which has survived, stipulates that two theologians act as advisers on the subject matter. The Last Supper is a rare theme for Netherlandish panel painting. Bouts set the scene in the central panel—the moment when Christ announces that the host, or bread, is his body—in a Flemish interior. The twelve apostles sit stiffly around a square table that dominates the room. The Christ figure is at the exact center of the composition. The angle of vision is high, allowing us to look down on the spacious hall. The windows afford glimpses of the city outside, two cooks looking in from the kitchen, and a garden. Bouts was a master of spatial recession, which is particularly evident in the side panels. These wings each depict two relatively obscure scenes from the Old Testament that relate to the Eucharist. Their subjects are the Meeting of Abraham and Melchizedek (Genesis 14)—the first offering of bread and wine by a priest; the Gathering of Manna (Exodus 6), in which bread was sent from heaven to the starving Israelites; Elias in the Desert (I Kings 19), to whom an angel brought bread and wine; and the Feast of Passover (Exodus 12), the Jewish equivalent of the sacrament. In these scenes, Bouts employed an innovative way of placing figures along diagonal axes that lead the viewer's eye into the distance. **EG**

The Hunt in the Forest | Paolo Uccello

*c.*1470 | oil on canvas | 29 ⅛ x 69 ⅝ in / 74 x 177 cm | Ashmolean Museum, Oxford, UK

Paolo Uccello's (Paolo di Dono, *c.*1397–1475) elegant hunt—one of the great treasures of Oxford University—has been enjoyed by generations of bleary-eyed students tired of reading their classics. In this late work the great pioneer of matrix-making pictures brings his themes to bear upon the dark heart of night. Some theories link the image to Lorenzo de' Medici hunting outside Pisa, but there is no way to prove this; others think that the picture is an illustration of an unknown *novella*. Renowned art historian and leading authority on Uccello, John Wyndham Pope-Hennessy, regarded this painting as "one of the most unaffectedly romantic paintings" of its time. There certainly is no shortage of competitors, yet *The Hunt in the Forest* is as mysterious in origin as it is beguiling in formal inventiveness. As the eye adjusts to the darkness of the scene, one sees the characters light up in their regal costumes, soft caps, and assorted scarlet regalia. Never before in the history of painting had red been used for such a dappled orchestration of color. Rather than the broken bodies in the battle scenes for which he was famous, here Uccello adopts the same visual language of orthogonal lines in fallen wood. The verdant mesh of the forest floor give life to the flora that sprout and the fauna that spring into action. The four foregrounded trees, which expertly slice the scene into three equidistant spaces, balance the scene and draw the eye in from both directions toward an undefined vanishing point. **SP**

St. George and the Dragon | Paolo Uccello

c.1470 | oil on canvas | 21 ⅞ x 29 ¼ in / 55.5 x 74 cm | National Gallery, London, UK

There are two versions of *St. George and the Dragon* attributed to Uccello (Paolo di Dono, c.1397–1475). The earlier and notably less dramatic version is located in the collection of the Musée Jacquemart-André, Paris. Both paintings derive from the very popular thirteenth-century *Legenda Aureahe* (*The Golden Legend*), written by Jacobus de Voragine, which describes the lives of the saints. The London version of the painting is considered to be among Uccello's late works—the style of the figures and the location in perfect space are unmistakably that of this militaristic master of blood and violence. Uccello painted the lance at such an acute angle that, as early commentators agreed, we feel the violence of the image. Two stories are depicted in this startling canvas. The first is St. George's triumphal delivery of the death blow to the menacing dragon, which, while out on its rampage, was thought to be spreading the plague. Second, in dispatching the supernatural beast St. George rescues the fair princess, but it is significant that in this chivalric act he is aided by the gentle seduction of the dragon by the maiden, who, with only her belt as a leash, leads the dragon to its death. A remarkable feature of the composition is the eye of the brooding storm perched above the trees in the painting's top-right corner. While highlighting the sheer courage and superhuman strength required of St. George, Uccello leaves the viewer to wonder whether it is divine intervention, symbolized by the gray tempest, that will determine the outcome. **SP**

St. George and the Dragon
Sano di Pietro

---

*c.*1440–70 | tempera on panel
Museo Diocesano, Siena, Italy

Sano di Pietro (*c.*1405–81) was a successful artist in fifteenth-century Siena. *St. George and the Dragon* is typical of his approach—it has a simplicity, clarity, and decorative quality that he turned into a winning formula. Here England's patron saint is shown as a medieval knight slaying a dragon to save a king's daughter in return for a promise that the king's subjects would be baptized. This picture makes little attempt at showing realistic three-dimensional space, and harks back to a simple, medieval style of art. The composition is well-balanced, with each element well-placed in an overall design that creates an attractive pattern rather than a convincing scene. The work has a flat, decorative quality—the dragon, wound artfully around the legs of the horse, almost disappears because it is painted as a decorative element and not a frightening, naturalistic beast. **AK**

Portrait of an Old Woman
Hans Memling

---

*c.*1470 | oil on panel | 10 ⅜ x 7 in / 26.5 x 18 cm
Museum of Fine Arts, Houston, TX, USA

In the 1460s Hans Memling (*c.*1430–94) established himself in the Flemish city of Bruges, where his talent was rewarded with a stream of commissions. Many of these were for portraits, a genre in which the painter excelled. At a time when Italian portraitists were still producing profiles, Memling poses the sitter for a three-quarter view. Typically, the sitter's eyes do not engage with the viewer, looking down and to the side with an implication of piety. Memling habitually set his subjects in front of a landscape, whereas here the background is plain greenish-blue. This portrait exemplifies Memling's technical brilliance, especially in the highlights that model the strong nose and the folds of cloth. The composure that characterizes Memling's art presumably suited his subjects' view of themselves. There is a firm self-satisfaction in these features, as at the confident awareness of virtue. **RG**

Winter Landscape
Sesshū

c.1470 | ink on paper scroll | 18 x 11 ½ in /
46.5 x 29.5 cm | Tokyo National Museum, Japan

The Holy Family
Martin Schongauer

c.1470 | oil on wood | 10 x 6 in / 26 x 17 cm
Alte Pinakothek, Munich, Germany

Many consider the Zen Buddhist priest Sesshū (c.1420–1506) as the greatest master of Japanese ink painting. Traveling around the country as an itinerate priest, Sesshū devoted his life to art. As a youth, he entered Shukoku-ji Temple in Kyoto, where he received training in Zen and painting under the guidance of Shūbun. *Winter Landscape* was created in his personal version of the Xia Gui style, marked by its use of *hatsuboku* (splattered ink). The poetic legacy of his Japanese teachers is also recalled here. Sesshū depicted mountains, cliffs, and rocks in a technique known as *shumpu*, which combines bold outlines with more delicate lines to create a feeling of three-dimensionality. Long before the early modern period, he had already established his reputation as an artistic genius—the sheer number of disciples he had in his lifetime testifies to his influence and popularity. **FN**

Martin Schongauer (c.1440–91) came from the Alsatian city of Colmar. He became a leading artist of his time, specializing in engraving and painting. It is likely that he learned engraving from his father, and was later greatly influenced by Netherlandish art, in particular the work of Rogier van der Weyden. Schongauer often depicted religious subjects, such as this exquisitely painted Holy Family. The detail and fine linear quality show his superb draftsmanship. The balance of the composition is emphasized by his use of color, and is based on a harmony between vertical and horizontal planes. The rich red of Mary's robe is continued in Joseph's scarf and forms the base for the deep brown of the cow in the background, creating a strong vertical line and focusing the eye on the primary subject. This is countered by the pale blue used in the imaginary landscape, the lake, and the mountains. **TP**

Brera Madonna | Piero della Francesca

1472–74 | oil on panel | 99 x 67 in / 251 x 172 cm | Pinacoteca di Brera, Milan, Italy

Along with the artist's fascination with the effects of light, Piero della Francesca (*c*.1415–92) was deeply interested in architecture and geometry. Nowhere are these fascinations more keenly realized than in Piero's *Brera Madonna* altarpiece, also known as the *Montefeltro Altarpiece*. Piero sets the devotional scene below a cassetted, vaultlike space at the back of which is an inlaid scallop-shell design. Suspended from the tip of the scallop is an ostrich egg—most likely a symbol of resurrection. Overall the composition of the painting hinges on the contorted figure of the infant Christ, portrayed in the midst of sleep, which prefigures the Passion. The *Brera Madonna* is believed to have been commissioned by the then Duke of Urbino, Federico da Montefeltro, for his recently deceased wife Battista Sforza, who had died after giving birth to their son Guidobaldo. The features of the Virgin Mary are purportedly Battista's, while the infant Christ resembles the newborn baby. Although there has been some debate as to the credibility of this interpretation, the presence of the kneeling, pious figure of Federico would appear to suggest that this is a votive work, functioning as a means by which he can be presented to his intercessors. As one of the last paintings executed by the artist, the meditative nature of the onlookers, the cool, entirely rational treatment of light and space, and the overall sense of harmony, proportion, and compositional balance are representative of Piero's singular contribution to quattrocento painting. **CS**

The Annunciation | Leonardo da Vinci

1472–75 | oil on panel | 38 ⅝ x 85 ⅜ in / 98 x 217 cm | Uffizi, Florence, Italy

The year 1472 offers the first record that we have of Leonardo "the artist" when he enrols in Florence's illustrious confraternity of painters, joining the ranks of artists such as Botticelli, Ghirlandaio, Pollaiuolo, and Perugino. There is no doubt that Leonardo da Vinci's (1452–1519) apprenticeship under Verrocchio, a member as well, would have provided an entrée into the society. At some point during this period, Leonardo would have had to produce a veritable masterpiece in his own right. His ambitious first attempt is *The Annunciation*. Given the disparate ambitions of this image—from the meditative landscape to the dense drapery studies—one cannot fault the precocious artist's efforts. In 1867 the painting was moved to the Uffizi from the monastery of San Bartolomeo a Monte Oliveto in the Tuscan countryside. This somber panel by the young Leonardo certainly places him, at least in the subject's traditional layout, in direct lineage with his Florentine painterly tradition. The dainty fingers of the Virgin have irritated some critics who malign the feature for having come directly from Verrocchio's circle. Others complain about the lack of emotional intensity characteristic of the mature Leonardo. The right hand of the Virgin secures her place in the scriptures as the angel interrupts her. We might even see this inventive gesture as a first foreshadowing of Leonardo's use of hand placement—consider his depiction of the Apostles' reaction to the announcement of betrayal in his epic version of *The Last Supper*. **SP**

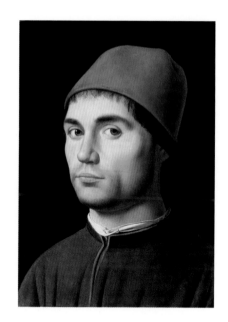

Virgin and Child Enthroned
Cosimo Tura

c.1475 | oil and egg tempera on poplar | 94 x 40 in / 239 x 101.5 cm | National Gallery, London, UK

Cosimo Tura (c.1430–95) trained alongside Andrea Mantegna (c.1431–1506), and the latter's influence can be seen in the work of Tura. However, Tura brought an idiosyncratic imagination to his work, which often resulted in a slightly surreal effect. This painting is part of the Roverella Polyptych and widely considered to be among his best work. It was commissioned by the Bishop of Ferrara, Lorenzo Roverella, and shows members of the Roverella family kneeling with saints. *Virgin and Child Enthroned* is believed to be the middle piece of the polyptych and shows a family member knocking for admission to the central vaulted space, while angels play music and the Virgin gazes down. There is an unemotional quality to the painting heightened by the impassive figures. Tura's style influenced several of his pupils, including Francesco del Cossa (c.1435–77), a leading figure of the Ferrara School of painting. **TP**

Portrait of a Man
Antonello da Messina

c.1475 | oil on poplar | 14 x 10 in / 36 x 25.5 cm
National Gallery, London, UK

This painting of an unknown male reflects two major developments in fifteenth-century Italian painting: the influence of the Classical era and the increasing interest in art from northern Europe. Although Antonello da Messina (c.1430–79) worked with paint, this work recalls Roman portrait busts in its composition and the incised vertical folds of the garment. Despite these characteristics, the portrait remains that of a quattrocento Italian rather than an ancient Roman. Most importantly, it shows an explicit awareness of northern European art and shares similarities with portraits of the Flemish school, and those by Jan van Eyck (c.1390–1441) in particular. Like this artist, Antonello depicts his sitter in a three-quarter pose, allowing for a greater connection between viewer and subject. Additionally, *Portrait of a Man* is set against a dark background and shows great attention to detail in the rendering of the hair and the folds of the collar. **WD**

Condottiero
Antonello da Messina

1475 | oil on wood | 14 x 12 in / 36 x 30.5 cm
Louvre, Paris, France

Martyrdom of St. Sebastian
Antonio and Piero del Pollaiuolo

1475 | oil on poplar | 114 ¾ x 79 ¾ in / 291.5 x 202.5 cm
National Gallery, London, UK

In what has become one of Antonello da Messina's (c.1430–79) most famous paintings, the artist depicts a military leader of Italy, known as a condottiere. Until the nineteenth century, Italy was composed of a set of independent city states, and condottieri were in high demand to fight in battles between conflicting states. Antonello takes an interest in displaying the rank of his sitter: he is seated before a black background in basic clothing and headwear with good posture, thus elevating his status above that of a simple warrior. Indeed, Antonello's subject most probably had the wealth to afford a title closer to that of a gentleman, and he would have commissioned this portrait to emphasize his social standing. However, Antonello reminds the viewer that this man is a ruthless fighter. A closer inspection of *Condottiero* reveals details such as the war wound on the sitter's upper lip. **WD**

Antonio del Pollaiuolo (c.1432–98) was one of the great masters of the Italian Renaissance. He lived and worked in Florence, often alongside his brother Piero (c.1441–96), who was also an artist. The two brothers collaborated on several works, including *Martyrdom of St. Sebastian*. Antonio was a superb draftsman and his understanding of anatomy and the human form was ahead of his time. In this painting, the figures in the foreground are massive and muscular, and demonstrate the artist's knowledge of classical pose and sculptural form. There is an innate rhythm across the picture plane created by the composition of figures in the foreground that are based on three poses seen from slightly different angles. This retains a sense of continuance through the composition, while the scenery in the background shows a new and heightened naturalistic observation of landscape details. **TP**

Portinari Altarpiece | Hugo van der Goes

c.1474–76 | oil on wood | 99 ⅝ x 230 ¾ in / 253 x 586 cm | Uffizi, Florence, Italy

Tomasso Portinari—a wealthy Italian businessman and representative of the Medici family in Bruges—commissioned this spectacular altarpiece for his family chapel in Florence. Evidently wanting to impress at home and to commemorate his success in Flanders, Portinari selected the Ghent painter Hugo van der Goes (c.1440–82) for the job. Van der Goes produced a masterpiece that was not only a suitably grand tribute to Portinari, but a highly personal interpretation of the Nativity. The large altarpiece represents the adoration of the holy family and the shepherds according to the account given by Luke (2:10–19). The central scene celebrates the joy at the birth of Christ, but at the same time emphasizes the humility of the family and the peasants. The artist reintroduced an archaic hierarchy of scale—the holy family appears largest and the donors and angels smaller in comparison. The figures are arranged in diagonal axes around Mary, whose hands are the center of the composition. This unusual composition produces a slightly unbalanced, dynamic movement. The angle of the floor in the central panel might reflect the practice of contemporary religious theater. The stage floor has been tilted up for a better view and the figures are clothed in costumes worthy of a mystery play. The donors kneel on the side wings and are flanked by their patron saints. In this extraordinary work, Van der Goes managed to fuse Van Eyck's astonishing illusionism with Rogier van der Weyden's monumentality as well as the naturalism of Dierec Bouts's landscapes. **EG**

St. Francis in Ecstasy | Giovanni Bellini

c.1480 | oil and tempera on poplar panel | 49 x 56 in / 125 x 142 cm | Frick Collection, New York, NY, USA

Standing in front of this large panel it is easy to lose oneself in the many and charming details of this landscape. However, the subject of this painting is St. Francis of Assisi. Dressed in his monk's habit, St. Francis is standing barefoot at the very foreground of the image. With his arms spread wide and his head and body arched backward, his mouth opens in awe as his face and eyes turn up toward the rays of golden light that pierce the blue sky in the top left corner. St. Francis was born into a wealthy family of merchants but renounced his wealth in favor of a simple life, eventually founding the Franciscan Order in 1209. This painting by Giovanni Bellini (c.1430–1516) evokes the moment St. Francis received the stigmata in 1224. The stigmata marks the wounds inflicted on Christ

at the crucifixion, which are believed to have miraculously appeared on the body of the saint during a retreat on Mount Alverna. Although faint wounds are visible on the open palms and foot of St. Francis, it is the landscape that dominates the composition. The dramatic rocks on the right create the home of the saint—his reading desk and sandals are visible beneath his grapevine trellis. A low stone wall in which juniper has been planted follows the curve of the rock, and provides home to a rabbit, which can be spotted beneath the saint's sleeve. A donkey and gray heron stand still in the middle ground, while a shepherd and his flock are seen in the distance. Soft, warm light unites this picture in which man and nature appear in harmony. **AB**

The Sultan Mehmet II | Gentile Bellini

1480 | oil on canvas | 27 ½ x 20 ½ in / 70 x 52 cm | National Gallery, London, UK

In 1453, the young Mehmet II shocked the Western world when he seized the city of Constantinople, the eastern capital of the Christian empire. In doing so, Mehmet II redefined Constantinople as a Muslim city, causing panic in the Christian church. Mehmet II's action also had a profound effect on Venice, a city that had benefited from political and trading links with Constantinople until the cities became locked in conflict. However, settlement terms were drawn up in an attempt to assuage these issues. As part of his terms, Mehmet II requested a Venetian artist to be sent to his court, and the government of Venice chose the established Gentile Bellini (1429–1507). Arriving in Constantinople in 1479, the purpose of Bellini's visit was to help restore the relationship between the two cities, and to execute a number of portraits, from which this work is believed to originate. Set beneath a classical, rounded arch, Bellini has depicted a reserved and regal leader. It is interesting that Mehmet II does not look out toward the viewer or adopt a frontal pose, two ways in which the sitter's authority can be affirmed. Instead, he is twisted away from the viewer, a format that recalls contemporary developments in Italian Renaissance portraiture. Although this work is signed by Bellini, its authenticity is often questioned, largely because it was almost entirely repainted in the nineteenth century. However, even if this work is a copy, it is not surprising to read contemporary documents stating that Mehmet II was very pleased with such an ornately detailed work of art. **WD**

St. Job Altarpiece | Giovanni Bellini

1480 | tempera and oil on panel | 186 x 102 in / 471 x 258 cm | Galleria dell'Accademia, Venice, Italy

This large altarpiece was painted by Giovanni Bellini (c.1430–1516) for the church of San Giobbe—St. Job—in Venice and the artist won immediate acclaim because of it. Born into the most important family of Venetian painters of the late fifteenth century, Bellini trained in the workshop of his father Jacopo Bellini (c.1400–70). He is best remembered for incorporating the subtle and detailed oil techniques of the northern Renaissance into the monumental tradition of early fifteenth-century Italian painting. Oil painting, which allowed artists much greater freedom, was thought to have been introduced to Venice by Antonello da Messina during his visit to the city in 1475. Oil paints could be used in dense strokes of vivid color or in thin, transparent glazes, allowing for much more gradual and subtle shading, enriched colors, and suffused lighting. In the *St. Job Altarpiece*, Bellini uses this new technique to subtly portray the drapery worn by the three musical angels. Seated on steps below an enthroned Madonna and Child, the angels' knees, instruments, and toes are sharply foreshortened and appear to come toward us. The darkening shadows and subtlety of lighting convince the viewer that the figures are seated in a real space. Playing a lute and a rebec—an early violin—the angels to the left raise their eyes toward figures beside the throne. Meanwhile, the angel on the right is focused on plucking the strings of his lute, echoing the visual concentration demanded by this contemplative and devotional painting. **AB**

The Donne Triptych | Hans Memling

1480 | oil on oak | 28 x 28 in (central panel) 28 x 11 ¾ in (shutters) | National Gallery, London, UK

The Donne Triptych, also known as *The Virgin and Child with Saints and Donors*, is among the finest examples of Flemish art of the fifteenth century. It was commissioned by a Welshman, Sir John Donne of Kidwelly, on a visit to Bruges, where Hans Memling (c.1430–94) worked. Donne is shown kneeling on the Virgin Mary's right. The kneeling figures on the other side of the central panel are his English wife, Elizabeth Hastings, and one of their daughters. Although their demeanor implies humble piety, their clothing exhibits wealth and style, and both husband and wife wear the white lion—the badge of English king Edward IV. On the outer panels are Donne's name-saints, John the Baptist (with lamb) and John the Evangelist. In the central panel, St. Catherine presents

Donne to the Virgin and Child, while St. Barbara presents his wife. The Virgin is flanked by angels playing music for the infant Christ. The man observing the scene from behind John the Baptist is probably the artist himself. Memling plays wittily with the convention that saints must be shown with their traditional attributes—St. Catherine's wheel becomes the waterwheel of a mill in the background. The Christ-child makes an ambiguous gesture with his right hand—he may be reaching for a fruit offered by an angel, or he may be blessing the donor. The landscape is charming—a miller unloads a sack from his donkey, a man rides a horse. The minute realism of the depiction of surfaces is integrated into a serene, symmetrical whole. **RG**

La Primavera | Sandro Botticelli

*c.*1477–82 | tempera on poplar | 80 x 123 ½ in / 203 x 314 cm | Uffizi, Florence, Italy

After training as a goldsmith, Sandro Botticelli (Alessandro di Mariano Filipepi, 1445–1510) was apprenticed to Fra Filippo Lippi (*c.*1406–69). Lippi had developed a style of portraying expressive interactions between figures, and employing highly decorative detailing inherited from the late Gothic period. Botticelli was also influenced by Antonio Pollaiuolo (*c.*1432–98), whose muscular modeling announced a new approach to figurative work accounting for human anatomy and proportion. Botticelli painted on many scales, and his delicate evocations of landscape and figuration ensure his place as one of the most beloved painters of all time. *La Primavera* (Spring) commemorated the Florentine Renaissance—a cultural, political, and economic rebirth of the Republic. The painting originally hung in the summerhouse of the Medici family as a companion piece to *The Birth of Venus*. In *La Primavera*, Botticelli has created a lively scene that includes, from left to right, the mythological figures Mercury; the Three Graces; Venus, goddess of love; the nymph Chloris; Flora, goddess of fecundity; and the west wind Zephyr. Above them, Cupid, the god of erotic love, aims his dart at the Three Graces. Some scholars have argued that the painting is an example of Botticelli's interest in Neoplatonism—a blending of pagan and Christian identities. However, it is probable that he painted this mythological scene because he was commissioned to do so by the Medicis, whose interest in classical history and art influenced many painters of this time. **SP**

Christ Giving the Keys to St. Peter | Pietro Perugino

1481–82 | fresco | 132 x 216 ½ in / 335 x 550 cm | Sistine Chapel, Vatican City, Italy

Pietro Perugino (Pietro Vannucci, c.1450–1523) must have established an impressive reputation early on to have been asked to paint this work—part of a major fresco cycle by various leading artists—for the Sistine Chapel. To have produced, at this stage, a work considered to be his finest masterpiece is an even greater achievement. The fresco is dominated by the powerful central image of a kneeling Saint Peter, Christ's first vicar on Earth, receiving the keys of the kingdom of heaven. Around them are the other apostles (Judas is the fifth person to the left of Christ) and contemporary figures—the fifth person from the right-hand edge may be Perugino. There is beautiful detail in the faces, hair, and clothing of this group, and a serene refinement suited to the subject. The middle ground depicts two stories from Christ's life—the tribute money (left) and the stoning of Christ (right). Back further still is the Temple of Jerusalem, given an Italian Renaissance style of architecture. Flanking it are triumphal arches modeled on Rome's Arch of Constantine and revealing the Renaissance interest in ancient art. In the farthest distance is a fine landscape, with the pearly blue light and delicate trees that countless future artists would also use as a way of depicting infinite space. Overall, the space in this fresco does not work in a logical three-dimensional way, but the simple, symmetrical composition tells the story clearly and effectively. This spatial clarity is one of the major aspects of Perugino's work that would become a feature of later Renaissance art. **AK**

Altarpiece of the Church Fathers | Michael Pacher

c.1483 | oil on wood | 85 x 148 in / 216 x 396 cm | Alte Pinakothek, Munich, Germany

Michael Pacher (c.1434–98) was born in Bruneck where he spent most of his career, primarily working for local churches. Little is known about him except that he was an accomplished sculptor as well as painter. His sculpture is late Gothic in spirit, but his painting is strongly reflective of Italian art, in particular that of Mantegna (1431–1506). This altarpiece was made for the Neustift Monastery near Brixen, and demonstrates the artist's striking synthesis of painterly and sculptural qualities. The four saints, from left to right, Jerome, Augustine, Pope Gregory the Great, and Archbishop Ambrose, are seated within a dramatically virtuoso architectural setting that appears to protrude from the picture plane into the viewer's space. However, the three-dimensional effect is in contrast to the figures themselves, which are relatively flatly modeled. There is also a disparity between the perspective implied by the foreshortened floor tiles and architecture, and the placement of the figures, which makes the figures themselves less convincing than the framework. The inclusion of the figure right at the forefront of the picture plane is reminiscent of Mantegna's work, and represents the Emperor Trajan being delivered from purgatory by Pope Gregory. The combination of Gothic and Renaissance is particularly evident in the beautiful detailing and patternlike quality with strong sculptural forms and areas of broad flat coloring. Pacher's work represents one of the first interpretations of Italian Renaissance ideals within the traditions of German art. **TP**

Adoration of the Child | Filippino Lippi

1483 | tempera on wood | 37 ¾ x 28 in / 96 x 71 cm | Uffizi, Florence, Italy

Filippino Lippi (1457–1504) was trained by his father Fra Filippo Lippi and, after his father's death in 1469, by Sandro Botticelli. This is an early painting and still shows the influence of his father as well as that of his master. The subject is the adoration of the child by the Virgin, a representation demonstrating the humanizing of holy figures, which happened during the Renaissance. The tenderness between mother and child is moving; she is no longer depicted as a remote and inaccessible figure, and her face is reminiscent of the face of Lippi's own mother, Lucretia Buti, who appears in many of Fra Filippo's paintings. Although *Adoration* is likely to have been painted before Hugo van der Goes's *Portinari Altarpiece* (1475–78) arrived in Florence, creating enormous artistic interest, there are significant references to Flemish painting, in particular the sparkling "carpet" of flowers, and the background landscape. Both may have been inspired by Leonardo's adoption of such northern features. His *Annunciation* (1472–75) for example also depicts a harbor in the background. Mary is known as "Star of the Sea" and is consequently associated with water. The harbor also symbolizes eternal life. The parapet wall—also a feature of both paintings—suggests an enclosed garden, a reference to Mary's virginity. At this stage Lippi had not adopted Leonardo's technique of *sfumato*, but had reduced his dependence on Botticelli's linearity. Shortly after this painting, Lippi was commissioned to complete the Brancacci Chapel frescoes begun by Masaccio and Masolino. **WO**

Birth of Venus | Sandro Botticelli

1482–86 | tempera on canvas | 68 x 109 ½ in / 172.5 x 278.5 cm | Uffizi, Florence, Italy

Birth of Venus is one of the most famous paintings in the world. It was painted by Alessandro di Mariano Filipepi (1445–1510), known as Sandro Botticelli, who was an Italian painter of the Florentine School. He served an apprenticeship under Fra Filippo Lippi, the best Florentine painter of that time. Botticelli made his name with his painting *Allegory of Fortitude* (1470), and he was subsequently commissioned to paint *Birth of Venus* for Lorenzo the Magnificent of the Medici family. In mythology, Venus was conceived when the Titan Cronus castrated his father, the god Uranus, whose severed genitals fertilized the sea. *Birth of Venus* depicts the moment when, having emerged from the sea in a shell, Venus lands at Paphos in Cyprus. She is attended by two winds who blow her toward the shore, while a nymph is poised to wrap a cloak, decorated with spring flowers, around Venus to cover her nudity. The stance of Venus is believed to be based on classical statuary, which was highly prized in Florence at that time. Despite the strange proportions of her body—the elongated neck and her overlong left arm—Venus is an arrestingly beautiful figure with her delicate skin and soft-flowing curls fresh from the sea. She is born to the world as the goddess of beauty, and the viewer is witness to this act of creation. She steps off a gilded scallop shell, the winds shower her with roses—each with a golden heart—and the orange blossom on the tree behind her is also tipped with gold. Historically, this is the most important depicted nude since classical antiquity. **MC**

The Annunciation, with St. Emidius
Carlo Crivelli

1486 | egg tempera and oil on canvas | 81 x 57 ⅝ in / 207 x 146.5 cm | National Gallery, London, UK

Carlo Crivelli (c.1435–95) painted this sumptuous altarpiece for a church in Ascoli, the town in the Italian Marches where he spent most of his working life. It was made to celebrate an important local event—the grant of a decree of self-government to the town by its ruler, Pope Sixtus IV, which occurred on the feast of the Annunciation in 1482. Crivelli depicts the Virgin kneeling in her room. Outside in the street the winged Archangel Gabriel, who has come to tell Mary that she is to give birth to the son of God, also kneels. St. Emidius, the patron saint of Ascoli, attempts to distract Gabriel at what might be thought an ill-chosen moment by showing him a model of the town, with its many towers. A shaft of golden light brings Mary the Holy Spirit. The ornate architecture constitutes a dazzling exercise in perspective, with lines converging vertiginously upon a vanishing point in the left third of the picture. Crivelli fills his strict geometrical structure with a rich proliferation of detail—the small child spying in on the scene from the top of a stairway on the left, the man reading a letter on a bridge in the background, the precisely detailed contents of Mary's room, the pot plant in her window. Much of this is significant—the peacock, for example, while offering the painter a splendid opportunity to demonstrate his skill, also symbolizes immortality and refers, in a bold flash-forward, to the assumption of Mary into heaven. But the viewer need not explore such arcane elements of the painting, for the visual thrills are overwhelming even to an ignorant eye. **RG**

Francesco Sassetti and His Son Teodoro
Domenico Ghirlandaio

c.1487 | tempera on wood | 33 x 25 in / 84 x 63 cm | Metropolitan Museum of Art, New York, NY, USA

Domenico di Tommaso Curradi di Doffo Bigordi, known as Domenico Ghirlandaio (c.1449–94), hailed from a long and proud tradition of successful craftsmen, merchants, and artists. An apocryphal story propagated by Vasari credits the origin of the name Ghirlandaio (from the word for "garland") to his father, who may have created a series of hair ornaments. Vasari also tells us that Ghirlandaio worked in the service of the Sassetti family. Employed in the Medici banks based in Avignon, Geneva, and Lyon, the wealthy patron Francesco Sassetti (1421–90) worked for both Piero de' Medici and Lorenzo Il Magnifico. This double portrait of father and son is complicated by the fact that Sassetti had two sons, both of whom were called Teodoro. The younger son was born the year

that the older one died. It is thought that the younger son is depicted here, which dates the painting to 1487, although this remains uncertain. The stern paternal image of the banker is only softened by the innocence of the son who gazes directly into the eyes of his father. Intended to be a formal portrait, the rigidity of the composition and the static, wide-shouldered man are offset by the floral patterning on the youth's clothing and his soft hands. The face and body of Sassetti are heavily repainted, which might explain the central figure's general blandness. In the background, Ghirlandaio has painted an oratory built by Sassetti in Geneva. The same building is included in Ghirlandaio's frescoes, which he painted for Sassetti in Florence—a painter's compliment to his patron. **SP**

The Vision of the Blessed Gabriele | Carlo Crivelli

c.1489 | oil and egg tempera on poplar | 55 ½ x 34 in / 141 x 87 cm | National Gallery, London, UK

Old Man with a Young Boy
Domenico Ghirlandaio

c.1490 | oil on panel | 24 x 18 in / 62 x 46 cm
Louvre, Paris, France

Gabriele Ferretti was a Franciscan friar who died in 1456 and was posthumously beatified in 1489 by the Pope in recognition of his miracles and visions. To celebrate this honor, the Ferretti family reconstructed Gabriele's tomb in San Francesco ad Alto church. Carlo Crivelli (c.1435–95) was probably commissioned to make this picture as part of the tomb reconstruction. The painting illustrates an event from Gabriele's life—the vision of the Virgin and Child accorded him outside the convent church, the building shown on the right of the picture. Gabriele kneels in religious ecstasy, wearing the gray robes of his order, as the Virgin and infant Jesus float above him enclosed in a flame-rimmed mandorla. The central point of the composition is Gabriele's hands joined in prayer. Fruit festoons the top of the picture in a witty appeal to the quattrocento taste for trompe l'oeil illusionism. **RG**

Domenico Ghirlandaio (c.1449–94) was a Florentine artist renowned for his frescoes and portraits. *Old Man with a Young Boy* is his most widely recognized image. A drawing in the National Museum in Stockholm provides evidence that Ghirlandaio made studies of the old man, including the skin defect on his nose. The man is believed to have suffered from the disfiguring condition rhinophyma as a result of acne rosacea. But the realism of the portrait is unusual for its time. Ghirlandaio's inclusion of this defect is thought to have influenced later artists, such as Leonardo, to paint their subjects "warts and all." The viewer is certainly touched by this scene. The old man's aging face contrasts with the soft, young skin of the child. As the child's hand reaches up to the old man, their eyes meet in an open display of affection. The warm reds emphasize this loving bond. **MC**

Battle of Mailberg
Hans Part

1489–92 | oil on wood (detail)
Klosterneuburg Monastery, Austria

The extraordinary beauty and detail in Hans Part's work makes it surprising that the artist has remained so obscure—even his birth and death dates are unknown. He produced an exquisite triptych known as the *Family Tree of the House of Babenberg*. The Babenbergs ruled Austria from 976 to 1248, when they were ousted by the Hapsburgs. This detail from the triptych depicts Leopold II of Babenberg (*c*.1055–1102), also known as Leopold "the Handsome," at the Battle of Mailberg in 1082. The battle was part of the Investiture Dispute—the most significant struggle for power between state and church in the Middle Ages. In this painting, the elegant Abbey of Melk, which was founded in 1089 when Leopold donated one of his castles to the monks, can be seen shimmering in the distance, while to the right of the picture is Leopold's home, the castle Thunau. **TP**

St. Augustine in the Cell
Sandro Botticelli

1490–94 | tempera on panel | 16 x 10 ½ in /
41 x 27 cm | Uffizi, Florence, Italy

Outside his work as a court painter to memorialize Lorenzo the Magnificent's victories, the deeply religious Sandro Botticelli (1445–1510) was fascinated by both Christian and pagan epics. This pious image was perhaps created for the Priory of Santo Spirito, the only convent for Augustinian hermits in Florence. Although Augustine was never a monk, here he wears a cope of a bishop over the robe of their fraternal order. The subject's peaceful affection for monastic life is clearly evoked in the calm demeanor in which the saint looks patiently upon his writing table. The small scale of the image and the drawn curtain emphasize the enclosed, devotional air of the penitent monk at work. At the foot of the panel, wispy scraps of paper lie scattered. This is a humbling reminder that even Augustine, one of the great authors in Christendom, had to revise several times in order to write meaningfully. **SP**

Calumny of Apelles | Sandro Botticelli

1494–95 | tempera on wood panel | 24 ¼ x 35 ¾ in / 62 x 91 cm | Uffizi, Florence, Italy

Sandro Botticelli (Alessandro Filipepi, 1445–1510) was born in Florence and eventually became an apprentice to the Florentine master Fra Filippo Lippi. Botticelli later befriended Cosimo de' Medici's famous grandson Lorenzo, known as "Il Magnifico." Botticelli was among the most important artists to be commissioned by Lorenzo and began an era that the artists' biographer Giorgio Vasari later called the Golden Age. It is known that Botticelli painted this picture for his own keeping. It is his last surviving image that depicts a secular history. The theme was a description by a classical Greek writer, Lucian, of a painting by a classical Greek painter, Apelles. Apelles's painting was a response to an accusation by another painter, Antiphilos, that Apelles was involved in a plot against the king. Antiphilos repeated this to the geographer and astronomer Ptolemy who believed the calumny. When a key witness testified to Apelles's innocence, Ptolemy awarded Apelles damages, which included Antiphilos as his personal slave and recompense of one hundred talents. Yet the painter "revenged himself with an allegorical picture." Botticelli's *Calumny of Apelles* was painted following Lucian's detailed description. Unlike other works by Botticelli, such as *La Primavera* and *Birth of Venus*, the intimate scale of this work belies its rich, finely wrought detail. To the right is a man with ass ears welcoming the beautiful Calumny as she enters from the left. The two women at his side appear to be Ignorance and Suspicion. **SP**

Pietà | Pietro Perugino

1494–95 | tempera on wood | 66 ⅛ x 69 ¼ in / 168 x 176 cm | Uffizi, Florence, Italy

This mature work, painted for the church of San Giusto near Florence, dates from the years that show Pietro Perugino (Pietro Vannucci, c.1450–1523) at his most productive peak—roughly 1490 to 1500. It is one of his greatest paintings and, content-wise, sits squarely within the tradition of Christian Pietà images. These images depict Christ after his death, his body supported by his mother, the Virgin Mary, and often surrounded, as here, by other figures, such as Mary Magdalene, who sits at his feet. Perugino's Pietà appears simple but it is ingeniously constructed to produce a moving tribute and a pious, reflective mood. The artist organizes his space with extreme precision. In the foreground is a carefully arranged group, with each member striking a graceful pose.

The group is set against a backdrop of impressive but simple Renaissance buildings that bring grandeur to the painting and frame the central event. In the far distance, a faintly glowing landscape hints at infinity, emphasizing the spiritual dimension. The foreground, mid-ground, and far distance are harmonized, partly through the rich overall coloration and balanced lighting that characterizes Perugino's work. The idealized figures have a statuesque solidity that, appropriately for the theme, lends them great presence. Perugino's harmonious compositions and sculptural figures had a great impact on Raphael, who worked in Perugino's studio as a young man and would take what he had learned from his master forward into the High Renaissance. **AK**

Dream of St. Ursula | Vittore Carpaccio

1495 | tempera on canvas | 108 x 105 in / 274 x 267 cm | Gallerie dell'Accademia, Venice, Italy

The arts were actively encouraged by the Venetian state and by the church during the fifteenth century, and accordingly they flourished with some of the greatest of fifteenth-century painters working in Venice. Vittore Carpaccio (c.1460–1526) was just such an early Venetian master, who is perhaps best known for his cycle of nine paintings depicting the *Legend of St. Ursula*, to which this picture belongs. He studied under Gentile Bellini (1429–1507) and Lazzaro Bastiani (1449–1512), and lived and worked in Venice, primarily painting commissioned works for the Venetian scuole, or confraternities. *Dream of St. Ursula* is one of the most beautiful of his works with its diffuse and soft golden light that drenches the scene, and is characteristic of his work. Carpaccio was, in effect, the

first Italian painter of genre, and his particular adherence to light and detail would influence the Dutch masters Johannes Vermeer (1632–75) and Pieter de Hooch (1629–84). The detail in Carpaccio's work provides an accurate account of the life of the times. Here a young girl has fallen asleep and is visited by an angel who tells her of her impending martyrdom. Though spiritual in content, the painting is also a reflection of simple human life, documenting the minutiae of everyday living from the girl's open book to the little dog at the foot of the bed. Carpaccio's depiction of light, which is seen in virtually all his work, and his attention to detail also seems to have influenced Canaletto (1697–1768), the Venetian master of the eighteenth century. **TP**

The Last Supper | Leonardo da Vinci

1495–98 | fresco | 180 x 346 in / 460 x 879 cm | Convent of Santa Maria delle Grazie, Milan, Italy

For centuries this spectacular mural has been seen as one of the world's finest paintings and perhaps the greatest expression of its creator, Leonardo da Vinci (1452–1519), who played a leading role at the forefront of the Italian Renaissance—the flourishing of learning that peaked in the sixteenth century. His genius lay in an inventive curiosity that embraced both the arts and sciences. *The Last Supper* is the perfect synthesis of Leonardo's talent. Cleverly situated and conceived, it looks down from its lofty position on the north wall of the Convent of Santa Maria's refectory. As the diners sat down to eat, Christ and his twelve disciples cast their inspiring spiritual presence over the pious individuals beneath. Leonardo subtly highlights Christ's status in the group by painting his figure slightly larger and framed against the light of the window. He introduces human drama to the mural by choosing to illustrate the point when the disciples ask Christ who would betray him. Each disciple is shown reacting in a way that reveals much about them without resorting to the symbolism favored by his contemporaries. Da Vinci painted this mural on dry plaster, which allowed him to work it as a whole, rather than having to finish one section at a time as was the norm with traditional wet-plaster frescoes. Sadly, decay set in early because the medium was less durable. This bold experimentation, along with his pioneering grasp of composition, light, and perspective, are among the reasons da Vinci achieved an eminence that has lasted across the centuries. **AK**

Self-Portrait with Gloves | Albrecht Dürer

1498 | oil on panel | 20 x 16 in / 52 x 41 cm | Museo del Prado, Madrid, Spain

Albrecht Dürer (1471–1528) was born in Nuremberg, the son of a Hungarian goldsmith. His achievements as an artist cannot be overestimated. He is known as the greatest printmaker of all time, his drawing and painting are unrivaled to this day, and he was an author of books on mathematics and geometry. In 1494 he went to Italy for a year where his work was influenced by Renaissance painting. Although Dürer's work had always been innovative, until then his work broadly belonged to the late Gothic style prevalent in northern Europe. In 1498, he produced *The Apocalypse*, a suite of fifteen woodcut prints illustrating scenes from the Book of Revelations. He also painted *Self-Portrait with Gloves* in which the Renaissance style is evident. He paints himself in the fashion of an Italian aristocrat, in a three-quarter pose that is typical of contemporary Italian portraiture. The background is reminiscent of Venetian and Florentine painting with its subdued neutral colors and an open window showing a landscape stretching to distant, snow-capped peaks. The face and hair are painted realistically—another Italian influence—while the gloved hands are typical of Dürer since he painted hands with especial skill. Dürer painted several self-portraits, which was an unusual subject at the time. *Self-Portrait,* painted in 1500, now housed at the Alte Pinakothek Museum, Munich, Germany is particularly famous. But it is *Self-Portrait with Gloves* that shows why Dürer is often thought of as the bridge between Gothic and Renaissance styles. **MC**

The Judgment of Cambyses | Gerard David

1498 | oil on panel | 71 ¾ x 125 ⅜ in / 182.5 x 318.5 cm | Groeninge Museum, Bruges, Belgium

Gerard David (c.1460–1523) rose to become the leading painter in Bruges at a time when the city was a thriving artistic and commercial center. *The Judgment of Cambyses* is an impressive painting—one of a two-part altarpiece that was commissioned by the city of Bruges, and is perhaps his most famous work. It is one of several major altarpieces that have sealed his reputation. The painting relates an ancient Persian tale from the time of King Cambyses, which deals with a corrupt judge named Sisamnes. This picture shows Cambyses arresting the judge as he sits on his throne of office. In the background, two figures in a doorway show the judge being bribed. The work was designed to be a powerful warning against dishonesty. Typical of David's mature works, it has a

stately, monumental composition that shows Italian influence and perfectly underlines its authoritarian message, as well as clever organization of space. Realistic, carefully arranged figures show the influence of his direct master, Hans Memling (c.1430–94). There are also the beautifully rich colors for which David is famed, and subtly observed light effects. Above the judge, *putti* (cherublike children) are seen holding out a garland. Putti and garlands were common to Italian Renaissance art but seldom seen in Flemish pictures at this time. *The Judgment of Cambyses* pays homage to earlier Netherlandish masters such as Jan van Eyck (c.1385–1441), but is too accomplished to be just a slavish imitation. His late works influenced later artists such as Adrien Ysenbrandt (c.1490–1551). **AK**

The Miracle of the True Cross near San Lorenzo Bridge
Gentile Bellini

1500 | tempera and oil on canvas | 127 x 169 ¼ in / 323 x 430 cm | Gallerie dell'Accademia, Venice, Italy

Although it is his brother Giovanni who is best remembered, Gentile Bellini (c.1429–1507) was the most celebrated Venetian artist of his day. This painting was commissioned by the Scuola Grande di San Giovanni Evangelista to decorate the great hall of their headquarters. Scuole were confraternities formed for religious purposes or to assist trade guilds; they played an important civic role. This large painting depicts an annual confraternity procession in which its highly prized property, a relic of the True Cross, was carried from the Scuola to the Church of San Lorenzo. According to legend, the reliquary fell into a canal. While a number of the confraternity jumped into the water to its rescue, it floated over the canal and did not allow itself to be saved until approached by the Scuola's Grand Guardian, Andrea Vendramin. Here he is seen in the water, dressed in his white robes and clutching the gold-and-crystal cross-shaped reliquary at the very foreground of the image. Although the scene is tightly packed with onlooking crowds, the overall effect and mood of the painting is that of ordered reverence. The canvas offers a panoramic view of Venice painted with documentary loyalty and charming details, such as the gondolier raising his hat in amazement. At the front, kneeling on a wooden platform, can be seen Caterina Corano, Queen of Cyprus on the left, and to the right a group of men who have been identified as the artist, his father, brother, and brother-in-law, all of whom were also renowned artists. **AB**

Ecce Homo
Andrea Mantegna

c.1500 | tempera on canvas | 21 ¼ x 16 ½ in / 54 x 42 cm | Musée Jacquemart-André, Paris, France

The work of Andrea Mantegna (c.1431–1506) has been criticized for being clinical, but some of his images of the Virgin and Child are deeply moving, as is this picture of Christ. It was painted toward the end of his life, by which time this major Renaissance figure had acquired a formidable reputation. A child prodigy brought up in the stimulating artistic and intellectual ferment of Padua, Mantegna went on to use his formative influences as official painter to the Mantuan court. In this crucifixion image, he was working within the *Ecce Homo* tradition of contemporary Christian art (Latin for "Behold the man"—believed to be what Pontius Pilate said to Jews asking for Christ's crucifixion). Such paintings usually focused on Christ's head or upper body, showing him wearing a crown of thorns, and often with a rope around his neck, tied wrists, and scourge marks. Typically he looks toward his accusers with compassion. All of this is here, but Mantegna characteristically makes it his own, using clear colors, well-defined forms, and a superior grasp of spatial organization. The vicious faces around Christ squeeze into the picture and we see just the fingers of their pawing hands. By triangulating the accusers behind Christ, Mantegna makes them seem more evil and Christ more triumphantly untouchable. Christ's sad expression is in stark contrast to the piercing eyes of those around him. Mantegna had a profound effect on the Renaissance, particularly on the art of his brother-in-law, Giovanni Bellini, and the German master Albrecht Dürer. **AK**

Hare | Albrecht Dürer

1502 | watercolor on paper | 9 ⅞ x 9 ⅛ in / 25 x 23 cm | Graphische Sammlung Albertina, Vienna, Austria

Albrecht Dürer (1471–1578) visited Italy in 1494 and 1505 but although he was influenced by the Italian Renaissance, non-Italian influences are always present in his work. His training with Michael Wolgemut, who was a highly respected painter and illustrator, and his subsequent travels during which he met masters such as Matthias Grünewald, must account for this. To the theories of Italian Renaissance humanism he added wit, humor, and a gritty expression achieved through line. He is known principally as a printmaker, but his woodcuts and engravings, paintings, drawings, and watercolors are as important. *Hare* carries the famous AD monogram, showing that this was not a preparatory study but a finished work in its own right. The image is so compelling that it is difficult to tear one's eyes away, and it is equally difficult to say why this is the case. The meticulous scientific detail is impressive, but it is not simply a scientific drawing. The magical quality comes from the golden light striking the hare from the left and casting a strange shadow. This light picks out the tip of each individual hair, brushes the folded ear, and gives life to the eye. The extraordinary result is that this creature appears to be contemplating the viewer. Dürer kept diaries and notes for most of his life. After his death, four books on mathematics and proportion were published. His theoretical writings and his diaries tell us about the context of his art as well as about the man himself. The variety and quality of Dürer's existing work demonstrates his importance in the history of art. **WO**

Mona Lisa | Leonardo da Vinci

1503 | oil on wood panel | 30 ³/₈ x 20 ⁷/₈ in / 77 x 53 cm | Louvre, Paris, France

Leonardo da Vinci (1452–1519) began life as the illegitimate son of a Tuscan notary, and arguably became the world's most discussed painter. Endless fascination on the part of scholars and the public alike ensued virtually from the day he began writing and painting, yet he was also a man with flaws and limitations. He was born in the Tuscan hillside town of Anchiano near Vinci, and moved to Florence at an early age to train as an apprentice to Andrea del Verrocchio, a famous sculptor of the day. From those early lessons, Leonardo gained a profound appreciation of three-dimensional space, a concept that served him well throughout his career—whether he was painting or drawing the intricacies of plants or parts of the human body, war machines or public water works, mathematical geometry or local geology. The title of the painting, which was not used until the nineteenth century, was derived from an early account by Vasari, which also provides the only identification of the sitter. Mona Lisa, also known as Lisa Gherardini, was painted in her mid-twenties after she married a silk merchant named Francesco del Giocondo, the man who may have commissioned the portrait. To this day, the Italians know her as *La Gioconda* and the French as *La Joconde*, which literally translates as the jocund or playful one. In more recent history, the painting's fame may also derive in part from the fact that it was stolen from the Louvre in Paris in a sensational heist in 1911 by an Italian nationalist but was thankfully returned two years later. **SP**

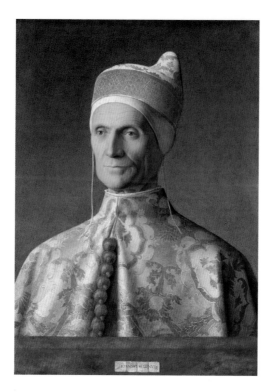

The Doge Leonardo Loredan | Giovanni Bellini

1501–04 | oil on poplar | 24 ³/₈ x 17 ³/₄ in / 62 x 45 cm | National Gallery, London, UK

This famous portrait is of Doge Leonardo Loredan, who ruled Venice from 1501 to 1521. He can be identified as a doge—an elected ruler of the Venetian Republic—as he is wearing his official hat and robes of state. His garment is made of luxurious, gold-threaded damask and is decorated with ornate buttons, while his hat, called a "corno," is worn over a linen cap. Painted by Giovanni Bellini (c.1430–1516) at the beginning of Loredan's rule, this is an official and formal portrait; nonetheless, the sitter's personality and individuality are felt. While his clothing is painted using thick touches of paint, his face is painted using thin transparent layers, or glazes, which allow for the subtle details of his face to be visible. The sitter's face is turned slightly toward the light on the left, so that

his facial wrinkles and slight stubble become apparent. Although he is standing perfectly still, with immobile features and with only his head and torso visible, one has the feeling that at any moment his mouth will break into a smile and his eyes will move to look toward the viewer. It is easy to focus on the richly decorated clothing and carefully observed facial features, as the rest of the painting is filled with a deep blue monochrome background. The high degree of realism and exquisite finish of this image may fool us into believing we might reach in and touch it. However, the parapet at the very bottom of the painting, on which a small piece of paper with the artist's signature is attached, reminds us of the division between the real world and the painted world. **AB**

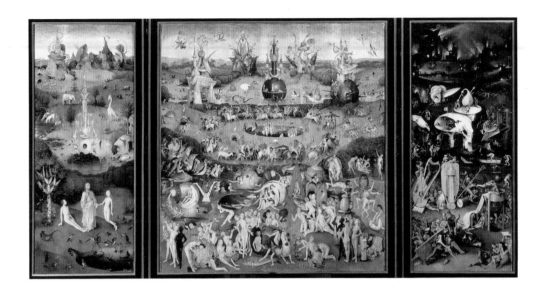

Garden of Earthly Delights | Hieronymus Bosch

c.1504 | oil on wood | 86 ⅝ x 76 ¾ in (panel) 86 ⅝ x 38 ⅛ in (shutters) | Museo del Prado, Madrid, Spain

Hieronymus Bosch (c.1450–1516) remains one of the most idiosyncratic artists of his time; his work was full of strange fantastical beasts, surreal landscapes, and the depiction of the evils of man. He was born into a family of artists in the Dutch town of 's-Hertogenbosch, from where he takes his name, and spent most of his life there. In 1481, he married a lady twenty-five years his senior; it was a propitious move on the artist's behalf for, by the time of his death, he was among the richest and most respected of 's-Hertogenbosch's residents. A sign of the artist's elevated social position was his membership in the conservative religious group The Brotherhood of Our Lady, who were also responsible for his early commissioned work. The extraordinary *Garden of Earthly Delights* is a large triptych that depicts

Bosch's account of the world, with the garden of Eden on the left, hell on the right, and the human world of fickle love moving toward depravity in the center. The perspective and landscape of the left and central panel match, suggestive of a progression toward sin from one to the other, while the right-hand panel of hell is structured separately and abounds with depictions of man's most despicable acts. Bosch's vision was highly fantastical with a strong moral message that made his work very popular during his time. His style was widely imitated, and his influence on Pieter Bruegel the Elder was particularly apparent. The imaginative quality of his work was to have a significant effect on the development of Surrealism in the twentieth century. **TP**

The Last Judgment | Luca Signorelli

1504 | fresco | Duomo, Orvieto, Italy

Luca Signorelli (*c.*1440–1523) was one of the most important and influential painters of the Italian Renaissance, although his reputation is greatly overshadowed by the generation of High Renaissance artists who followed him. Among modern scholars, he is most famous for his *End of the World* cycle of frescoes (1499–1504) in the chapel of San Brizio in the Orvieto Cathedral, which includes his painting of *The Last Judgment,* shown here. In the frescoes, Signorelli imagines the end of the world as a dark, chaotic sequence of events, and achieves a dramatic pitch that seemed very original to contemporaries. Medieval depictions of the Last Judgment often pictured hell diagrammatically by indicating the location and the nature of the punishment that each sinner would be allotted. Signorelli's vision, however, dispenses with this convention and brings the moment vividly to life. The inventive way in which he painted his demons exemplifies this: he has rendered their bodies with the skill of a great anatomist, but has exaggerated their skin coloring, an invention that made his figures seem both real and horrific. Michelangelo was known to have been influenced by Signorelli's conception, although in comparison to Michelangelo's painting of the same subject, Signorelli's figures appear stiff. Indeed, they are characteristic of the art of the Early Renaissance, in which artists had a firm grasp on the principles of anatomy but had difficulty articulating this knowledge so that it appeared natural. **SS**

Marriage of the Virgin | Raphael

1504 | oil on panel | 66 ⁷⁄₈ x 46 ½ in / 170 x 118 cm | Pinacoteca di Brera, Milan, Italy

The panel known as the *Sposalizio* (*Marriage*—or Betrothal—*of the Virgin*) was commissioned by the Albizzini family for a church in the Città del Castello. Early sixteenth-century viewers would immediately have recognized the politics of the image. Directly in the center of the foreground is the elegant ring, which the Virgin at left nonchalantly receives from Joseph. This is no ordinary gentleman down on bended knee. He carries the flowering staff, which marks him as the chosen one and differentiates him from those of his rival suitors, one of whom breaks his staff in consternation. The Virgin Mary's ring was the city of Perugia's sacred relic. It had been stolen and then retrieved in the years prior to the painting of this work. The picture celebrates the controversial

stance of the Virgin's centrality in the church, a position that was defended by the Franciscans of the day, and for whom Raphael (Raffaello Sanzio, 1483–1520) painted the picture. Perugino, Raphael's elder master, painted an earlier picture of the same theme and his influence is visible; nevertheless, the formal structure of Raphael's composition here is deserving of its fame. Who could replicate such a remarkably clear perspectival landscape with architecture so artfully conceived? The vanishing point penetrates the front door of the temple, and by doing so cleverly draws the eye of the viewer through the picture from the primary action of the foreground to the social context of the middle, and on to the azure sky of the horizon. **SP**

The Forest Fire | Piero di Cosimo

c.1505 | oil on panel | 28 x 79 ½ in / 71 x 202 cm | Ashmolean Museum, Oxford, UK

Piero di Cosimo (c.1462–1521) was a Florentine painter of unusual temperament, about whom contemporary stories abound—such as his refusal to eat anything except boiled eggs, his tendency to require hermitlike solitude, and tales of his fantastic, and probably highly dangerous, inventions conjured up for carnival time. Most well known for his religious paintings, he was also inspired by classical myths and painted portraits that verged on caricature. In *The Forest Fire*, smoke indicates that the animals' habitat is threatened; the more fortunate birds fly from their branches, while in the background a herdsman attempts to escape with all his charges. The animals in the foreground—those with which the viewer can identify most strongly—are those that are doomed.

The fact that many of the animals pictured would never coexist in the wild seems irrelevant to Piero's boundless imagination. His works also include *Perseus and Andromeda*, a fantastic and yet oddly bawdy scene inspired by mythology, and the spectacular *Visitation with St. Nicholas and St. Anthony Abbot*, in which Mary, pregnant with Jesus, meets Elizabeth, pregnant with John the Baptist. On first sight it is a traditional, peaceful religious scene yet in the background are images of a quiet Nativity alongside a hellish scene of children being massacred. It is a hallmark of Piero di Cosimo's paintings that they teem with life and unexpected incident; every time one looks at his paintings afresh there is always something new that escaped notice before. **LH**

Vision of St. Augustine | Vittore Carpaccio

1502–08 | oil on canvas | 55 x 82 in / 141 x 210 cm | Scuola di San Giorgio degli Schiavoni, Venice, Italy

There is little surviving documentation on Vittore Carpaccio's (*c*.1460–1526) life in Venice, but his paintings have provided an extraordinary account of Venetian life during his time. His works include, and relish, the observations of human life, and even his religious paintings have their foundations based on the trivia of the world at large. At this time in Venice there was a great tradition of pageants and processions and many of Carpaccio's paintings depict these flamboyant public occasions with intricate, decorative detail and luminous, clear light. Though he often included fictional buildings in these works, for the most part they reflect a sense of what Venice was like during the early sixteenth century. Carpaccio is most famous for two cycles of paintings, *Legend of St.*

Ursula, and *Scenes from the Life of St. George and St. Jerome*. This painting is the first of seven pictures from the *St. George* cycle, and depicts a quiet interior scene. In the middle of writing a letter, St. Augustine has been startled by the voice of St. Jerome telling him of his imminent martyrdom. Although this is a painting of a saint, the figure of Augustine appears as a humble man in his study, a room full of the accoutrements of a Humanist and academic. Carpaccio's attention to detail is all encompassing, as is his treatment of light. The study is bathed in light streaming through windows on the right, causing deep and sharp shadows to fall across the floor. Carpaccio's detailed treatment of his subjects would seem to pave the way for the work of Canaletto and Guardi. **TP**

Scene of Pork Butcher's Shop | Unknown

*c.*1510 | fresco (detail) | Castle Issogne, Aosta Valley, Italy

This scene of a sixteenth-century butcher's shop adorns the walls of Castle Issogne in northern Italy, alongside frescoes of other everyday scenes including tailor's, chemist's, and baker's shops, a guard, and a vegetable market. Such frescoes recall earlier Flemish market scenes, and viewers today might wonder why a wealthy Italian family would choose to adorn a wall of their vacation home's great hall with such a subject. In fact, it represents a form of elitist propaganda. The viewer's eyes are drawn to a crucifix shape formed by the suspended carcass of a darkly colored animal and the wooden shelf from which it hangs alongside sausages and various utensils. Similarly, the workmen's table appears as an ungodly altar in front of it. Sixteenth-century naturalists believed that the social

hierarchy mirrored a hierarchy of foods: the most delicate foods, suitable for noble, delicate natures, were deemed to be light-colored fish and flying fowl, while sausages stuffed with the dark ground meat of ground-dwelling animals were fit only for the stomachs of peasants. For the wealthy, the food in the peasants' kitchen justified the dehumanization of the poor: the problem of Christian poverty disappeared after seeing the sacrilegious kitchen of a peasant, where a dark animal replaces Christ on the cross. Thus Jesus's teaching about the spiritual worth of poverty could be ignored, and the nobles could enjoy their fish dinner—it was theirs by nature. Thankfully such distorted logic was unable to withstand the social mobility of the late sixteenth century. **WM**

Virgin and Child with St. Anne | Leonardo da Vinci

*c.*1510 | oil on poplar | 66 x 51 in / 168 x 130 cm | Louvre, Paris, France

Leonardo da Vinci (1452–1519) was apprenticed under the master sculptor Andrea del Verrocchio, after which he worked for some of the wealthiest patrons in France and Italy including the Sforza family of Milan, the king of France, and the Vatican in Rome. Had Verrocchio not switched to painting to compete with his rivals at the time when Leonardo was in his workshop, some scholars believe that it is conceivable that Leonardo would not necessarily have ever lifted a brush. Although his life and work are immensely important to the history of art, today there are roughly twenty securely attributed paintings in his oeuvre. The Virgin, her mother Anne, and the Child, the subject of this painting, comprise one of Leonardo's most popular themes, as evidenced

by several drawings and paintings. These include a lost cartoon of 1501, and *The Virgin and Child with St. Anne and St. John the Baptist* (*c.*1508, known as the Burlington House Cartoon); it may be assumed that the cartoon was intended for development into a large, fully painted work, but there is no evidence that such a painting was ever attempted. Here, however, the Virgin Mary rests on the lap of St. Anne, while the Christ child playfully fondles a young sacrificial lamb, a foreshadowed embodiment of the infant's fate. A small-scale pen and ink drawing for *Virgin and Child with St. Anne* exists in the collection of the Accademia, Venice. The informal posturing and the tender psychological engagement between the sitters constitute an all-time high in religious painting. **SP**

The Tempest | Giorgione

1505–10 | oil on canvas | 32 x 28 in / 90 x 73 cm | Gallerie dell'Accademia, Venice, Italy

Mystery continues to shroud the legacy of Giorgione (c.1477–1510), a painter whose dark visions continue to entice viewers. Dating and attributing paintings to this Venetian master have long presented varied challenges, both to his earliest commentators and to modern connoisseurs who fought to own a piece of his work. Restoration work revealed that Giorgione, contrary to a long-held opinion, made several under drawings rather than painting directly onto the canvas. The first known description of *The Tempest* in 1530 states, "the landscape on canvas with the storm, the gypsy and the soldier, made by the hand of Giorgio Barbarelli da Castelfranco [Giorgione's full name]." What is notable about this painting is that the landscape, in the form of the town stretched along the hill and the lightning in the center, is almost as important an element in the narrative as the figures in the foreground. It has even been said that this painting is the seed from which the tradition of seventeenth-century landscape painting grew. On the right of the image, the half-naked mother clad in an innocent white blanket is suckling her child, separated from the soldier on the left who is looking back at her. The impending storm adds to the tension of the scene, and the vertical axis that serves to emphasize the distance between the two adults. Yet this is not a blackened sky, the green and blue shades add a sense of natural beauty—there is a mood of expectation but not of foreboding. Giorgione uses the symmetry of the painting to draw the viewer into the landscape. **SP**

Adoration of the Shepherds | Giorgione

1505–10 | oil on panel | 35 ¾ x 43 in / 91 x 111 cm | National Gallery of Art, Washington, DC, USA

Giorgio Barbarelli da Castelfranco (c.1477–1510, known as Giorgione) commanded enormous respect and influence given his productive period lasted only fifteen years. Very little is known about him although it is believed that he was familiar with Leonardo's art. He began his training in the workshop of Giovanni Bellini in Venice, and would later claim both Sebastiano del Piombo and Titian as his pupils. Vasari wrote that Titian was the best imitator of the Giorgionesque style, a connection that made their styles difficult to differentiate. Giorgione perished from the plague in his early thirties, and his posthumous fame was immediate—Isabella d'Este of Mantua was unable to acquire a single painting by the late master. *Adoration of the Shepherds*, otherwise known as the *Allendale Nativity* from the name of its nineteenth-century English owners, is among the finest renderings of High Renaissance Nativities. It is also widely regarded as one of the most solidly attributed Giorgiones in the world. There is discussion, however, that the angels' heads have been painted over by an unknown hand. The Venetian blond tonality of the sky and the large and enveloping bucolic atmosphere differentiate this Nativity. The holy family receive the shepherds at the mouth of a dark cave; they are seen in the light because the Christ child has brought light into the world. Christ's mother Mary is clad in resplendent blue-and-red drapery in keeping with tradition: blue to signify the divine, and red signifying her own humanity. **SP**

The Fortune Teller | Lucas van Leyden

*c.*1508–10 | oil on panel | 9 x 12 in / 24 x 30.5 cm | Louvre, Paris, France

Lucas van Leyden's (1494–1533) principal fame rests on his extraordinary skills as an engraver, but he was also an accomplished painter credited with being one of the first to introduce Netherlandish genre painting. Born in Leiden, where he spent most of his life, he is thought to have trained with his father and later with Cornelis Engebrechtsz (1468–1533). He traveled to Antwerp in 1521, where he met Dürer, who recorded this event in his diary. Dürer's work appears to have had the most influence on him, although Van Leyden approached his subjects with a greater animation, concentrating more on the character of individual figures. *The Fortune Teller*, which is an allusion to the vanity of love and games, was painted early in Van Leyden's career, but already shows his draftsmanship

and skill as a colorist. It is a study of character, with each individual portrayed with a lively sensibility. The dark-bearded man in the background is especially captivating, with his piercing stare and sinister countenance that contrasts with the pale figure of the fortune teller. The picture surface is richly patterned, and the different textures, from fur and silk to glass and flesh, are superbly rendered. Pushing the composition to the front of the picture plane has the effect of placing the viewer in among the other figures. Van Leyden was famous during his lifetime, and though he had no direct pupils, his influence was profound on the development of Netherlandish art, paving the way for the Dutch tradition of genre painting. His work is also thought to have had an effect on Rembrandt. **TP**

School of Athens | Raphael

1510–11 | fresco | 303 ⅛ in / 770 cm (width at base) | Vatican Museums and Galleries, Vatican City, Italy

For Pope Julius II's private apartment, Raphael (Raffaello Sanzio, 1483–1520) painted a sort of school reunion for the intellectual powerhouses of antiquity, otherwise known as the *School of Athens*. The room (the Stanza della Segnatura) originally housed the church tribunal, and was intended by Pope Julius II to be filled with the portraits of the great thinkers of both Christian and pagan antiquity. On the wall opposite this masterpiece is the *Disputa*, which was completed first. This wall fresco, among the most important frescoed works in existence, reaches far beyond the reverent. Like Leonardo's *The Last Supper*, the architectural setting—thought to be inspired by Bramante's vision for the early Christian basilica of St. Peter's—is imposing, yet light enough to create

an incredible view as visitors look toward the ceiling of the Stanza della Segnatura from below. At the center of *School of Athens* are the dynamic duo of Artistotle, who props up a copy of his *Ethics*, and a balding Plato, who points skyward and holds a copy of *Timeus*. Pythagoras sits below and is sketching geometry, Diogenes reclines, and the arch pessimist Heraclitus—thought to be a portrait of Michelangelo, who was then at work on the Sistine ceiling—is passively writing on a bench of marble. Ptolemy is prominently featured with his celestial spheres. Euclid is patiently teaching the next generation of students. The overall theme of the painting, and the whole room, is the synthesis and celebration of worldly (Greek) and spiritual (Christian) thinking. **SP**

The Sistine Chapel Ceiling | Michelangelo

1508–12 | fresco | Sistine Chapel, Vatican City, Italy

Italian genius Michelangelo Buonarroti (1475–1564) was a sculptor, painter, architect, draftsman, and poet who dominated Florentine art during the Renaissance and his influence is still felt today. Born the son of a nobleman, he was apprenticed to the painter Domenico Ghirlandaio in 1488 but a year later moved to work under the sculptor Bertoldo Giovanni. He worked between Florence, Bologna, and Rome. The ceiling fresco of the Sistine Chapel was commissioned by Pope Julius II in 1508 as part of the rebuilding of St. Peter's in Rome. Initially, Michelangelo was reluctant to take on the project, since he saw himself primarily as a sculptor. But it came to dominate his life and he spent the next four years singlehandedly painting it, during which time his style evolved.

Michelangelo's knowledge of anatomy and sculptural skill is evident in many of the poses of the figures, which pay tribute to classical Roman and Greek sculpture. He made some three hundred preliminary drawings, which were enlarged into "cartoon" designs that were transferred to the ceiling. His sculptural thinking led him to abandon scenic detail to focus on the gesture and movement of the figures. The main panels represent scenes from the book of Genesis, from Creation to the drunkenness of Noah. Ten medallions portray scenes from the Old Testament and complement the scenes on the main panels. Prophets and sibyls are at the sides of the ceiling, while *ignudi*—naked male youths—are positioned at each corner of the central panels. **CK**

The Death of Adonis | Sebastiano del Piombo

1511–12 | oil on canvas | 74 ³/₈ x 112 ¹/₄ in / 189 x 285 cm | Uffizi, Florence, Italy

The Death of Adonis was painted by Sebastiano del Piombo (*c.*1485–1547) in the early part of his career, when he was still working within the school of Venetian art. He was influenced by his teacher Giorgione (Giorgio da Castelfranco, *c.*1477–1510), the master of Venetian Renaissance painting. This painting deals with the classical myth of Adonis, a beautiful youth who captures the heart of Venus (center of painting) before dying (left), but is later resurrected. As Venus is told of his death, handmaidens entreat Pan (the bearded figure on the extreme right) to stop playing his pipes at this sad moment. The composition—idealized nudes in the foreground against a serene landscape—echoes Giorgione's work, as does the typically Venetian feeling for rich color and light. Del Piombo's palette is beautifully harmonized but already there is a hint of the more subdued colors that he would later adopt. In this painting, there is a lovely, gentle interplay of light—from the sheen on human skin, to the soft reflections in the lake. However, there is more to this painting than Giorgione's influence. Del Piombo's off-center figure grouping, turning heads, and pointing fingers give much more movement than in earlier Renaissance works. His technical skills are such that each nude forms a marvelous life study. These nudes have a statuesque monumentality that del Piombo developed from the Renaissance interest in sculpture. He took this much further in the second half of his career, when he had settled in Rome. **AK**

Portrait of a Man | Titian

*c.*1512 | oil on canvas | 32 x 26 ⅛ in / 81.2 x 66.3 cm | National Gallery, London, UK

Titian's (Tiziano Vecellio, *c.*1485–1576) *Portrait of a Man*, otherwise known as *A Man with a Quilted Sleeve*, was painted shortly after the artist had painted three frescoes in the Scuola del Santo, his first major commission depicting the life of St. Antony of Padua. Although the picture is believed to be a portrait of the poet Ludovico Aristo, some have identified it as an early self-portrait. This would be an appropriate claim to make when one considers the number of Renaissance artists who used the genre of self-portraiture, including bystander self-portraits, as a means by which their status and reputation could potentially be elevated. Whoever the painting is actually of, the sitter addresses our gaze directly and this sense of confidence is given through a pose that

is relaxed, yet resolute. Although Titian's application of brushmark still harks back to the soft *sfumato* style of his master, Giorgione, his willful subversion of artistic convention appears wholly modern. While still adhering to Venetian convention by employing the parapet as a means by which the fictive space of the viewer can be distinguished from the actual space the viewer inhabits, Titian compromises the logic of this pictorial mode by subtly letting the sitter's sleeve spill over the parapet's edge. *Portrait of a Man's* flamboyant inventiveness, beyond producing a highly novel example of its genre, is characteristic of an artistic temperament that from this point on would persistently set out to confound and reinvent artistic precedent. **CS**

The Mass of Bolsena | Raphael

1512–14 | fresco | 259 ⅞ in / 660 cm (width at base) | Vatican Museums and Galleries, Vatican City, Italy

Raphael (Raffaello Sanzio, 1483–1520) was born in the central Italian town of Urbino where he worked under the auspices of great Renaissance courts including the Montefeltro family, the Gonzaga family, and a succession of Rome's popes. His father was a minor painter and poet who occasionally worked under the patronage of the Duke of Mantua, and this may have played a role in landing the young Raphael a position in the workshop of the master Pietro Perugino. Although he died in his late thirties, Raphael's prodigious years of painting produced several masterpieces. The frescoed door portal from the Stanza dell'Eliodor, known as *The Mass of Bolsena*, is one of four main stories from the biblical Apocrypha. Divine intervention by the Church is the theme of the subjects shown in the room—the large compositions are integrated into a complex, architectural space. *The Mass of Bolsena* envisions a miracle of the thirteenth century at Bolsena in central Italy, when it was reported that the blood of Christ seeped from a communion wafer. The depicted priest, who on his way to Rome was consumed with doubt about transubstantiation, or the idea that the bread and wine of communion are in reality the flesh and blood of Christ, is shown administering the sacraments. The insertion of Pope Julius I, kneeling directly to the right of the altar, commemorates the pontiff's visit to the relic in 1506. In doing so, Raphael's complex image amalgamates the history of the Church with the presence of the contemporary Papal lineage. **SP**

Sistine Madonna | Raphael

1513–14 | oil on canvas | 104 ³/₈ x 77 ⅛ in / 265 x 196 cm | Gemäldegalerie, Dresden, Germany

Raphael's (Raffaello Sanzio, 1483–1520) dramatic masterpiece known as the *Sistine Madonna* has a fascinating history that combines church rhetoric and the skills of practiced illusionism. It was originally commissioned to decorate the sepulchre of Pope Julius II. The image of Pope Sixtus I, seen at left, was chosen primarily because he was the patron saint of Julius's clan, the Della Rovere family. St. Barbara, painted on the right of the Virgin, inspects the scene with her downward glance toward the two winged putti, who gaze intently at the heavenly proceedings above them. Perhaps the most admired feature of the picture today, the putti are thought to symbolize the funeral procession. Reproductions of their passive embodiment of childlike curiosity have graced the T-shirts, mugs, and notepads of late-capitalist museum culture. This, however, should not distract the viewer by undervaluing the brilliance of Raphael's other characters. As the curtains part to reveal the ordered and triangular arrangement of the Virgin hoisting the Christ child, clouds billow out as stage smoke might engulf the modern audience. St. Sixtus, positioned in humble repose with his papal tiara teetering on the edge of the painting, points outward to the faithful, confirming his role in this tradition of enduring devotion. The canvas was first installed in the convent of St. Sixtus in Piacenza. It was later donated to Augustus III, King of Saxony. After World War II, it was taken from war-torn Germany to Moscow for safekeeping, only to return to Dresden in later years. **SP**

Isenheim Altarpiece | Matthias Grünewald

c.1512–15 | oil on panel | 198 x 312 in / 500 x 800 cm | Musée d'Unterlinden, Colmar, France

Little is known of Matthias Grünewald's (c.1475–1528) life, but he is famous for his undisputed masterpiece, the large folding altar painted for the Anthonite monastery hospital chapel at Isenheim in Alsace. The *Isenheim Altarpiece*'s physical structure is complex, comprising two sets of folding wings. By folding and unfolding these wings, the altarpiece offers three distinct views. This view shows the patron saint of the plague, St. Sebastian, on the left wing; the patron saint of the hospital's religious order, St. Anthony, on the right wing; and Christ being laid in his tomb on the lowest wing. In the middle panel is Grünewald's dark and harrowing depiction of the Crucifixion. The horribly wounded, etiolated, crucified figure of Christ, dead or close to death, is flanked by the pointing St. John the Baptist, the desperately praying Mary Magdalene, and the traumatized Virgin Mary who is held by St. John the Evangelist. The Isenheim hospital cared for victims of the plague and St. Anthony's fire—an intensely painful burning sensation in the limbs caused by eating cereals contaminated by ergot. Grünewald's Christ, who has clearly experienced a great deal of pain and is covered in sores like a plague victim, was intended to offer solace to the hospital's patients by suggesting that Christ understood and shared in their afflictions. Grünewald's astonishing and powerful work combines Gothic religious imagery with Renaissance technical advances, but its attempt to generate a passionate and transcendental state in the viewer is a product of earlier, less rational times. **PB**

Portrait of Lucina Brembati | Lorenzo Lotto

c.1518 | oil on canvas | 20 ⅛ x 16 ½ in / 51 x 42 cm | Accademia Carrara di Belle Arti, Bergamo, Italy

This frank yet enigmatic portrait is a fine example of the original and exuberant art of Venetian painter Lorenzo Lotto (c.1480–1556). Lucina Brembati was a noblewoman from the northern Italian city of Bergamo. Lotto represents her at night, with the moon faintly illuminating clouds in the dark background. At one level this is an admirably direct portrait of a woman, in no sense idealized or mythologized. Men were often portrayed in this way during the Renaissance, but women almost never. Her clothing is lavishly expensive and stylish—a damask dress, translucent shirtwaist tied with ribbons and embroidered with shells, large headdress, and a profusion of pearls. Her rather plain features are presented without apology; she meets our gaze with a direct look that is neither flirtatious nor modest. But is there a hidden side to the portrait, to be read by the initiated? Some critics have thought so. Lotto certainly knew how to appeal to a Renaissance taste for witty puzzles and allusions, for the sitter's name is encoded in a ring on her finger, which has the letters "CI" inside a moon (luna in Italian). It has been suggested that the moon motif also refers to the fact that Lucina is pregnant, indicated by the hand she lays on her midriff. But much that could seem significant is also open to practical explanation. The weasel or marten whose dead head startles the viewer could be a symbol of ill omen, or just a fashionable fur clothing accessory. The strange gold object hung around her neck has been identified simply as a toothpick. **RG**

Joseph with Jacob in Egypt | Pontormo

1518 | oil on wood | 38 x 43 ⅛ in / 96.5 x 109.5 cm | National Gallery, London, UK

Jacopo Pontormo (1494–1557) emerged as a painter at the pinnacle of the Florentine High Renaissance, having studied under Andrea del Sarto and Leonardo da Vinci. He is considered by many to be the first Mannerist painter. *Joseph with Jacob in Egypt* was commissioned for the nuptial bedchamber of Pierfrancesco Borgherini in 1515. In the work, four distinct episodes of Joseph's story are condensed into a single composition. In the left foreground, Joseph introduces his father Jacob to the Pharaoh of Egypt. On the right, Joseph leans down to receive a petition, while a later Joseph climbs the staircase with one of his sons to visit the dying Jacob. Finally, in the top right corner, the dying Jacob blesses Joseph's sons. Pontormo's Mannerism is evident in this panel,

with compositional design taking precedence over naturalism. He does not follow the rules of perspective slavishly and, where most high Renaissance painters sought compositional harmony, Pontormo places the precarious staircase as a strong diagonal across his painting. Infrared images have shown that the deathbed scene was originally drawn in the top left of the panel, but was altered for compositional effect. As he matured, Pontormo was influenced by Michelangelo and Dürer and, despite his distinctive portrait style, became almost exclusively a religious painter. He remains one of the greatest proponents of Florentine draftsmanship, and his Mannerist influence is visible in the works of his pupil Bronzino, Parmigianino, and even El Greco. **SLF**

Assumption of the Virgin
Titian

1516–18 | oil on wood | 272 x 142 in
Santa Maria Gloriosa dei Frari, Venice, Italy

Tiziano Vecellio, (c.1485–1576) known as Titian, worked under Giovanni Bellini, who was at that time Venice's leading painter. He worked closely with Giorgione, whose influence is apparent in Titian's paintings—a tonal approach to the use of color and an atmospheric landscape style. *Assumption of the Virgin* is his largest painting, and hangs over the high altar in the church of the Frari, Venice. It is an incredible piece of colorist execution on a colossal scale. The painting is designed to be seen from afar, attracting the viewer toward the altar from the other end of the church. The lower register represents the earthly plane where the apostles witness the assumption. In the second register, the Virgin Mary, flanked by angels, soars up toward the third register where God awaits her. The strong colors, golden light, and gesticulating figures caused a sensation when the painting was unveiled in 1518. **MC**

Charity
Andrea del Sarto

1518–19 | oil on wood transposed onto canvas
72 x 54 in / 185 x 137 cm | Louvre, Paris, France

In 1518 Francis I of France summoned the Florentine painter Andrea del Sarto (c.1486–1530) to his French court, where the Italian artist lived for a year. *Charity* is the only surviving painting from his French stay and was painted for the Château d'Amboise. The work is typical of the paintings favored by the French royalty at this time. It depicts the figure of Charity surrounded by children whom she nurtures and protects. It was an allegorical representation of the French royal family, and celebrated the birth of the Dauphin who is symbolized by the baby suckling, while the figure of Charity bears some similarity to the queen. The pyramidal structure of the composition is typical of the traditional form for this type of painting, and is also a reflection of the influence of Leonardo da Vinci on Andrea del Sarto. In particular the artist admired Leonardo's *The Virgin and Child with St. Anne.* **TP**

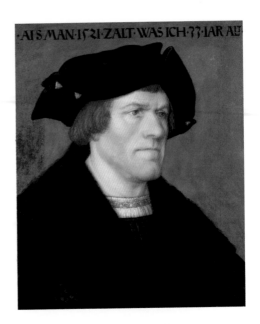

Portrait of Emperor Maximilian I
Bernhard Strigel

1510–20 | oil on panel | 21 5/8 x 15 in /
55 x 38 cm | Private collection

This is a stately but human portrait of a powerful man, Maximilian I (1459–1519), Holy Roman Emperor and a member of the Hapsburg family. The Hapsburgs ruled vast lands over many centuries. German painter Bernhard Strigel (1460–1528) here creates a picture that shows the status of its subject in a subtle way and bridges the traditions of Gothic and Renaissance painting. Strigel's portrait has a tight composition in which, fittingly for such a prominent ruler, the half-length figure of Maximilian dominates. The profile view shows the protruding lower lip that was a strong hereditary feature of the Hapsburgs. There is plenty of character in this face, it is not overidealized. True to the traditions of contemporary northern European art is Strigel's attention to details, such as the folds of Maximilian's clothes and the decorative panel behind him, but again he exercises stately restraint. **AK**

Portrait of a Beardless Man
Hans Maler

1521 | oil on lindenwood | 14 5/8 x 12 3/8 in / 37 x 31.3 cm
Kunsthistorisches Museum, Vienna, Austria

Hans Maler (c. 1485–1529) belongs to the most glorious period of German painting, generally considered to be 1500 to 1530. While overshadowed by Dürer, Grünewald, and Holbein, Maler was well known for his portraiture of the Hapsburg court. *Portrait of a Beardless Man* identifies the year it was painted and the age of the gentleman portrayed through Maler's German rhyme written at the top of the painting: "If one counts from 1521 he was thirty-three years old." The man's dress indicates his wealth: the two-piece split brim hat was common apparel for the wealthy men of the period, and the piece of fur around his neck as well as the gold chain hanging over a clean frock indicate that this is a man of considerable wealth, although not royalty. Typical of Maler, the man is looking at a forty-five degree angle toward the painter and is set against a blue-green background. **WM**

Bacchus and Ariadne | Titian

1520–23 | oil on canvas | 69 ½ x 75 ¼ in / 176.5 x 191 cm | National Gallery, London, UK

Painted while Titian (Tiziano Vecellio, c.1485–1576) was still in his thirties, *Bacchus and Ariadne* was commissioned by Alfonso d'Este as one of a series of canvases destined for his castle in Ferrara. Alfonso's original intention was to emulate an ancient picture gallery as described by Philostratus's *Imagines*. He initially commissioned Fra Bartolommeo and Raphael but they both died before the work could be realized and the commissions went to Titian. The subject matter of the painting is a conflation from two literary sources: from Catullus, Titian drew on the description of the abandoned heroine and Bacchus's endeavor to find her, and from Ovid he took the description of the actual meeting. This fateful meeting between the two figures and the very separate worlds they represent is shown through Titian's use of color. He uses a strong diagonal that traverses the entire scene, beginning with the bronze vessel on the bottom left-hand corner, and threads its way upward through the ensuing scene to the two quite literally divided realms. The upper left-hand side features heavenly blues and whites, whereas the bottom right consists of earthy rustic hues, reflecting the pleasures that a Bacchanalian frenzy would entail. (The drunken Silenus, slumped over his ass, is testimony to such indulgence.) Through his fusion of movement, energy, and imagination, Titian imbues the moment the two lovers meet with an almost hallucinatory vividness, creating a scene that is both compelling in its magical realism and emphatic in its use of color. **CS**

Landscape with St. Jerome | Joachim Patinir

1515–24 | oil on panel | 29 x 35 ¾ in / 74 x 91 cm | Museo del Prado, Madrid, Spain

Joachim Patinir (c.1480–1524) was born in southern Belgium, probably Bouvignes. In 1515, he is recorded as joining the Antwerp Painters' Guild. He lived in Antwerp for the rest of his short life and became close friends with Albrecht Dürer. In 1521, Dürer was a guest at Patinir's second wedding and drew his picture the same year, giving us a clear image of his appearance. Dürer described him as a "good painter of landscape", which is one of the most striking aspects of Patinir's work. He was the first Flemish artist to give equal importance to landscape in his paintings as to the figures. His figures are often small in comparison to the breadth of the scenery, which is a combination of realist detail and lyrical idealism. *Landscape with St. Jerome* tells the story of the saint's

taming of a lion by healing his wounded paw. The viewer looks down on the scene, which is cleverly composed so that the eye is led first to St. Jerome before wandering through the landscape as it unfolds in the background. It has a strange dreamlike quality, also evident in his work *Charon Crossing the Styx*, which is emphasized by the use of a glowing, translucent light. There are only five paintings signed by Patinir, but various other works can be reasonably attributed to him stylistically. He also collaborated with other artists, painting their landscapes for them, and worked with his artist friend Quentin Massys on the *Temptation of St. Anthony*. Patinir's depiction of landscape and his surreal, imaginative works greatly influenced the development of the landscape in painting. **TP**

Gian Galeazzo Sanvitale
Parmigianino

1524 | oil on panel | 42 ⁷⁄₈ x 31 ⁷⁄₈ in / 109 x 81 cm
Museo di Capodimonte, Naples, Italy

The School of Love
Correggio

c.1525 | oil on canvas | 61 ¼ x 36 in / 155.6 x 91.4 cm
National Gallery, London, UK

Admired for his landscapes and Mannerist religious paintings, Parmigianino (Girolamo Mazzola, 1503–40) was also one of the great Italian Renaissance portraitists. The viewer is immediately struck here by the vitality and physical presence of Sanvitale, count of Fontanellato. He sits in a fine chair wearing elaborate clothing, and stares directly and unflinchingly. He wears a sword, while an impressive pile of military equipment is heaped behind him. In his gloved right hand he holds a medal displaying what may be alchemical symbols. From the background, foliage crowds in on the sitter. In its way, this is a flattering portrait of a Renaissance nobleman. Yet it is hard to avoid the impression that the artist has created an unfriendly, critical portrait. The sitter's haughty expression seems close to petulance. But whether or not we warm to the count, the painting remains a masterpiece of representational art. **RG**

Antonio Allegri da Correggio (c.1494–1534) is perhaps one of the least-known masters of the Italian Renaissance. *The School of Love* was painted for Federigo II Gonzaga, Lord of Mantua, and was one of six erotic works based on mythological themes. The figures are softly modeled in rosy tones of pure clear color, while his details of the foliage, for example, and the figures' shining hair are exquisite. The painting itself does not represent a specific mythological event, but rather alludes to the themes of love and schooling. Venus and Mercury are seen with Cupid, instructing him in the ways of love, but also appear as a tight family unit. The sensuous Venus combines the exotic and the demure, carefully looking away from the viewer. Correggio's work foresaw the delicate romantic appeal of eighteenth-century Rococo art, and was greatly admired by artists touring Italy during the nineteenth century. **TP**

Portrait of Andrea Doria
Sebastiano del Piombo

c.1526 | oil on panel | 60 x 42 in / 153 x 107 cm
Doria Pamphilj Gallery, Rome, Italy

The Judgment of Paris
Lucas Cranach the Elder

c.1528 | oil on wood | 39 ¾ x 28 in / 102 x 71 cm
Metropolitan Museum of Art, New York, NY, USA

Sebastiano del Piombo (c.1485–1547) spent most of his life in Rome. He worked with Michelangelo, under whose influence he developed a unique, rather grand style. *Portrait of Andrea Doria* is a famous example of his Roman style and shows him at the peak of his powers. Andrea Doria was a much-revered figure in his native Genoa. A heroic naval commander, he had rescued Genoa from years of French domination and was made a prince for his pains. The solid, dark blocks of Doria's voluminous clothing and hat, the stark simplicity of the composition, and the somber, very limited color scheme all create the majestic quality that befits the subject. Sebastiano was inspired by Roman art, with its emphasis on clear-cut, heavy sculptural forms. This portrait is an extreme example of Sebastiano's later love of grays, but the dark colors here still have a richness. **AK**

Here one can see the influence the Italian Renaissance exerted on the German artist Lucas Cranach the Elder (1472–1553). *The Judgment of Paris* was a favorite theme of Cranach's and the Greek myth allowed him to show the female nude from three different perspectives. His rendering of anatomy was often inexact, as can be seen here, especially in the left arm and elbow of the goddess with her back toward the viewer. Cranach is portraying a German version of the myth in which Mercury presents the goddesses Juno, Venus, and Minerva to Paris in a dream and asks him to judge who is the most beautiful of the three. Each goddess disrobed in front of him and promised him a great reward if he chose her. Paris chose Venus and presented her with a golden apple (depicted here as a glass orb). Venus's victory is signified by the artist placing Cupid, her son, in the upper left of the painting. **LH**

A Lady with a Squirrel and a Starling
Hans Holbein the Younger

c.1526–28 | oil on wood | 22 x 15 ¼ in / 56 x 38.8 cm | National Gallery, London, UK

Hans Holbein the Younger (c.1497–1543) probably painted *A Lady with a Squirrel and a Starling* on his first trip to England while working under the patronage of the lawyer, author, and statesman Sir Thomas More. More was a friend and admirer of Holbein's previous patron in Basel, the Humanist scholar Erasmus. This portrait might originally have been one of a pair showing husband and wife. The sitter is thought to be Anne Lovell, as the starling and the squirrel may signify her name—squirrels, often kept as pets in England during this period, featured on the Lovell family's coat of arms. Yet the sitter is unlikely to have posed with either the squirrel or the starling. Holbein probably drew the animals separately and added them to the painting later. He frequently included pets, such as monkeys and marmosets, in portraits of women and children, whereas his portraits of men sometimes featured falcons, used by aristocrats for hunting. In this masterwork of representation and iconographic allusion, the sitter's severity and stillness is contrasted with the squirrel's hectic nut-chewing. Holbein's skillful, meticulous brushwork delineates many different finishes and surfaces: the flat blue background, with its decorative pattern of branches and leaves, sets off the woman's sharply drawn features and the various textures of her clothing, while the sumptuous white fur cap chimes with the rufous coat of her tethered companion. Holbein's superb character portraits later influenced British artists such as William Hogarth and Thomas Gainsborough. **PB**

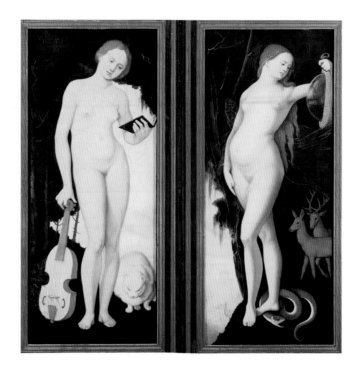

Allegories of Music and Prudence
Hans Baldung Grien

1529 | paint on pine panels | 32 x 14 in / 83 x 36 cm | Alte Pinakothek, Munich, Germany

Hans Baldung (1485–1545) adopted the nickname Grien, from the color green ("grün") while working in Albrecht Dürer's workshop in Nuremberg. A celebrated German Northern Renaissance painter and printmaker, Baldung uses complex composition to portray human comportment in a style that would later be known as Mannerism, a break from the pictorial and psychological content of High Renaissance paintings. While Baldung produced a series of altar pieces, religious subjects, and private portraits, in the latter part of his career he painted secular scenes from ancient legends, mythology, and history, even scenes of sorcery and witchcraft. Consisting of two separate panels, *Allegories of Music and Prudence* portrays the key pillars of high civilization through distorted female nudes. With the precision of a commercial draftsman, but with the charged strangeness of a progressive artist, Baldung depicts the human form in a manner that verges on grotesque. The rounds of flesh are disproportionate but elegant, disjointed but harmonious. The deep blacks contrast with the pale yellow flesh and the glowing greens. While the form and posture of Music is obviously feminine, her manner is intellectual and her face, arms, and hands possess a masculine animation. Prudence has a tortured, saint-like expression as she steps on the snake of temptation, while her protruding belly suggests pregnancy. Placed somewhere between paganism and Christianity, Baldung depicts human psychology and civil values in a wildly fantastic mixture. **SWW**

The Battle of Issus
Albrecht Altdorfer

1529 | oil on panel | 62 ³/₈ x 47 ³/₈ in / 158.4 x 120.3 cm
Alte Pinakothek, Munich, Germany

Albrecht Altdorfer (c.1480–1538) depicted biblical and historical stories set in stirringly evoked Alpine and Danube landscapes. In *The Battle of Issus* Altdorfer conjures up a vivid bird's-eye view of the scene—almost reminiscent of the spectacular, computer-generated battle scenes from war movies of today. The large panel hanging in the swirling clouds describes the scene: the Persian emperor Darius, to the center left of the painting, is fleeing on a chariot pulled by three white horses, having been defeated by Alexander the Great. The ranks of soldiers are almost incidental yet the painting shows an architect's eye for spatial perspective, and the setting looks distinctly like the Rhineland. It is the dramatic and moody clouds with the sun overshadowing the moon that gives a fantasylike element to an otherwise realistically depicted battle. **JH**

Portrait of Becuccio Bicchieraio
Andrea del Sarto

c.1528–30 | oil on panel | 33 x 26 in / 86 x 67 cm
National Museums of Scotland, UK

Andrea del Sarto (c.1486–1530) was working in Florence at a time when the style of the Italian High Renaissance was starting to develop into Mannerism, and his art can be seen to fall between the two. His work is characterized by a subtle use of color, which was beyond his Florentine contemporaries, combined with a convincing handling of line that makes his figures realistically three-dimensional. This work was for a long time thought to be a self-portrait, but has now been identified as a painting of the artist's friend, Becuccio Bicchieraio, who was a glassmaker. In the foreground, del Sarto has included a glass bowl that alludes to his friend's profession, and also serves to demonstrate his skill at depicting texture. This is also seen in the sleeve, which is a study of light and dark, and the dark material of the cloak set off against the brilliant white of his collar. **TP**

Adam and Eve
Lucas Cranach the Elder

c.1530 | oil on wood
Private collection

Jupiter and Io
Correggio

c.1530 | oil on canvas | 64 ⅜ x 29 ⅛ in / 163.5 x 74 cm
Kunsthistorisches Museum, Vienna, Austria

Lucas Cranach (1472–1553) was born Lucas Sünder, but changed his surname in honor of his German birthplace, Kronach. He later moved to Wittenberg, Germany, when he was appointed court painter to Frederick III of Saxony. Cranach gained renown for his skilled workshop of assistants; however, he was forced to move to Innsbruck, and later Weimar, when the new Elector of Saxony, John Frederick, was sent into exile. Cranach is often referred to as a member of the Danube School, a reference to a similarity of style among artists of the region. His paintings of religious subjects were intended to provoke strong emotional reactions in the viewer. In this version of the story of Adam and Eve, Cranach depicts Eve sympathetically as a sorrowful figure—as though she is aware of what she is doing by giving Adam the forbidden fruit to eat, but is powerless to resist the serpent's temptation. **LH**

Antonio Allegri da Correggio (c.1494–1534) was one of the leading artists of the Parma school of Italian Renaissance painting. Little is known about his training, but stylistically it would seem that he came under the influence of Leonardo da Vinci and Mantegna, especially in his grasp of perspective and foreshortening. *Jupiter and Io* was one of a series of paintings of mythological themes commissioned by Federico II of Gonzaga, Marquis of Mantua, and probably originally destined to hang in the Palazzo del Te. It is a study of rapturous emotion. The picture depicts the shy nymph Io captured in an amorous embrace by Jupiter, whose hand and face are just visible shimmering through the clouds. Correggio caught the erotic nature of the scene and the nymph's ecstatic state with the most delicate touch, creating an image of unrivaled beauty. **TP**

St. Donatian of Rheims | Jan Gossaert

1510–32 | oil on panel | 17 x 13 in / 43.1 x 34.4 cm | Musée des Beaux-Arts, Tournai, Belgium

In 1508, Flemish painter Jan Gossaert (c.1478–1532) accompanied Philip of Burgundy, the admiral of Zeeland, on a trip to Italy. This event was to prove significant in the subsequent development of art in the Netherlands, since Gossaert returned home with new ideas based on the Italian works he had seen, revolutionizing Flemish art at that time. The trip also initiated a fashion for Flemish artists to travel and study in Italy, which further emphasized the growing synthesis of traditional Flemish art with Italian themes and forms. Gossaert painted many mythological and religious subjects, but his portraits are considered to be among his best work. St. Donatian of Rheims depicts the saint against a dark background from which he seems to emerge, a technique the artist used often in his portraits before 1525. The painter's rendering of the saint's face is realistic yet sympathetic. The soft tones, smudged shadowing, and folds of skin are immediately convincing, although the stiff painting of the saint's hand is less so. The treatment of the saint in juxtaposition to his hand and the wheel demonstrate Gossaert's illusionary technique, as the latter two items appear to protrude from the picture frame. Gossaert did not achieve great fame until after his death, at which point his work became popular in Italy and later in the southern Netherlands. His highly personal and innovative style had little influence on his direct contemporaries, but it was significant on the development of subsequent artists working in the Netherlands. **TP**

The Ambassadors | Hans Holbein the Younger

1533 | oil on oak panel | 81 ½ x 82 ½ in / 207 x 209.5 cm | National Gallery, London, UK

One of the most staggeringly impressive portraits in Renaissance art, this famous painting by Hans Holbein the Younger (c.1497–1543) is full of hidden meanings and fascinating contradictions. The meticulous realism of Holbein's immaculate technique is breathtaking in itself, but virtually every object has a symbolic meaning too. The painting celebrates human achievement, but at the same time Holbein is reminding us that worldly success is ultimately meaningless—no matter what we achieve, we all must die. The full-length double portrait shows two French courtiers: Jean de Dinteville (on the left), ambassador to the court of Henry VIII, and his friend Georges de Selve, the young Bishop of Lavaur, whose visit to London in April 1533 the painting commemorates. The objects laid out between them include navigational, astrological, and musical instruments, a sundial (showing the date of April 11, 1533), and a hymn book. These objects reflect the two cultured men's interests and achievements, but the broken lute string, for example, is a traditional symbol of death, and may also refer to the Protestant split from the Church of Rome, something that the ambassadors were trying to prevent. Many portraits at this time contained an image of a skull as a *memento mori*, but none is more unusual than the one seen—or not seen—here. Holbein has distorted the perspective so that when the painting is viewed from a certain angle on the right-hand side, the strange shape in the foreground re-forms itself into a skull—the age-old reminder of death. **JW**

KVNIGIN · LEONORA · IST · GEBORN · DEN · ANDE
RN · TAG · NOVEMBRI · IM · M · D · XXX · iiii IAR

Portrait of Archduchess Eleonora of Mantua | Jakob Seisenegger

*c.*1536 | oil on wood | 13 ³⁄₈ x 10 ⁵⁄₈ in / 34 x 27 cm | Private collection

Jakob Seisenegger (*c.*1504–67) was an Austrian painter appointed to the Hapsburg court at Augsburg in 1531 by Emperor Ferdinand I. He was immediately sent by Ferdinand to Bologna, Italy, to paint Ferdinand's brother, the recently crowned Holy Roman Emperor Charles V. Seisenegger gained immediate notoriety and a place in art history for his novel use of full-length portraiture at a time when half-length representations were customary; his portraits created prototypes that were frequently imitated by artists such as Titian. Created a few years after his more famously recognized *Emperor Charles V with Hound* (1532), *Portrait of Archduchess Eleonora of Mantua* does not continue Seisenegger's trend-setting use of the full-length portrait, but returns to a more conservative representation as a diplomatic gesture to the newly appointed Mantuan nobility. The first duke of Mantua was Federico II of Gonzaga, who acquired the title from Emperor Charles V in 1530; the Archduchess Eleonora of Mantua was most likely Federico II's daughter and the portrait a gift as a sign of Charles's royal patronage. Seisenegger tended not to paint a true likeness in his portraits, preferring to opt for a few recognizable characteristic features. The Archduchess has an unusually focused expression for a small child, expressing the noble duty ascribed to her father. She is adorned with the accoutrements of civic standing, her necklace echoes her stoney eyes and her head jewel offsets her Roman forehead. **SWW**

Portrait of Henry VIII | Hans Holbein the Younger

c.1536 | oil on wood | 11 x 7 ¾ in / 28 x 19 cm | Thyssen-Bornemisza Collection, Madrid, Spain

The penetrating characterization and highly detailed style of Hans Holbein the Younger's (c.1497–1543) portraits create such a strong presence that his sitters appear as the living, breathing representatives of sixteenth-century Europe and have come to embody the look and feel of the Reformation in the public imagination. Entering royal service in England around 1533, one of his chief works for his benefactor, Henry VIII, was a dynastic group portrait of 1537 showing Henry with his third wife, Jane Seymour, and his parents, Henry VII and Elizabeth of York. It was probably commissioned to mark the birth of Henry's son Edward, later Edward VI. *Portrait of Henry VIII* was a preparatory painting for a full-length portrait, which was later destroyed in the Whitehall Palace fire

of 1698, and celebrated the strength and triumphs of the Tudor dynasty. Holbein's practice of painting from drawings instead of life emerged from the demands placed on him by his strenuous workload as court portraitist. As a consequence, many of his later images, like *Portrait of Henry VIII*, display a strongly linear, graphic style. Holbein completed the portrait around the time of Anne Boleyn's execution and the dissolution of the monasteries. It is a good example of Holbein's finely poised balance between individualized description and ideal appearance. Henry's flat face and small, wary eyes realistically depict his unique character, while his magnificent apparel, embroidered with delicate gold thread, elaborates on his regal authority. **PB**

Triumph of Titus and Vespasia | Giulio Romano

*c.*1537 | oil on panel | 47 x 67 in / 120 x 170 cm | Louvre, Paris, France

Born Giulio Pippi (*c.*1499–1546), the artist later became known as Romano after the city of his birth. At a young age, he went to study with Raphael, subsequently becoming his chief assistant, and on Raphael's death completed a number of the artist's works. Romano's vibrant palette and bold figurative style was in contrast to the subtlety of his teacher, but in terms of sheer imagination and dramatic illusionary effect achieved through the manipulation of perspective, Romano was a leader in his field. Apart from his painterly accomplishments, the artist was also an architect, he is responsible for designing the Palazzo del Te in Mantua, and an engineer. In *c.*1524, Romano was employed by Frederico Gonzaga, ruler of Mantua, and embarked on a massive project designing and rebuilding some of the town's buildings, as well as a number of decorative schemes. *Triumph of Titus and Vespasia* was commissioned by Gonzaga for the Room of the Caesars in the Palazzo Ducale. It depicts the Emperor Titus parading through Rome after a victory over the Jews. The composition is based on a scene on the inside of the ancient Arch of Titus in Rome, and retains much of the sculptural quality of the original, particularly in Romano's strident chariot horses. The brilliant colors and classical theme rendered in the Mannerist hand of the artist made this work very popular in its time. Romano's treatment of the landscape—which is beautifully detailed and bathed in a shimmering translucent light—is of particular note. **TP**

Venus of Urbino | Titian

1538 | oil on canvas | 46 ⅞ x 65 in / 119 x 165 cm | Uffizi, Florence, Italy

Inspired by Italian masters of the High Renaissance, such as Michelangelo, Titian (Tiziano Vecellio, c.1485–1576) was considered a master within the accomplished artistic circles of sixteenth-century Venice. He has also been cited as the first Venetian painter to earn international standing. He painted anonymous "courtesan" portraits, as well as altarpieces and mythological paintings. As a prolific portraitist, he produced flattering yet recognizably human likenesses of such prominent figures as the Pope, the Emperor, the Doge, and the Marquis of Mantua, yet despite the range of his prestigious commissions, Venus of Urbino is arguably his masterpiece. In his 1880 travel diary, A Tramp Abroad, American author Mark Twain described the painting as "the foulest, the vilest, the most obscene picture the world possesses." Allegorical touches, such as the clothed female figures in the background and the puppy asleep at Venus's feet, have led to thorough iconographic readings of the painting but perhaps Twain's atavistic, and prudish, reaction was closer to Titian's real intentions. The unselfconscious desire in the model's direct, lascivious expression might have offended Twain but her lovely, lustful gaze has also seduced countless viewers. Titian's breathtaking talent and his bold depiction of female sexuality is why this painting is often cited as the grandmother of many of Western art's most controversial images—including Manet's Olympia—and considered a model of empowered female sexuality, as well as a precursor to the pinup. **AH**

Sorcery, or the Allegory of Hercules | Dosso Dossi

1535–40 | oil on canvas | 56 ¼ x 56 ¾ in / 143 x 144 cm | Uffizi, Florence, Italy

Dosso Dossi (c.1490–1542) was a somewhat eccentric proponent of the High Renaissance style known as Mannerism, noted less for its naturalism than its complex, fantastical subjects and cryptic symbolism, often impenetrable to the modern mind. In 1514, heavily influenced by Giorgione and Titian, he became court artist for Duke Alfonso d'Este in Ferrara. A Renaissance center for culture and refinement, the court employed Bellini and Titian. Within this rich environment, Dosso painted complex mythological and literary works to appeal to the courtly scholars. *Sorcery, or the Allegory of Hercules* is a curious example of this dense symbolism; its meaning is much debated. Some view the work as an allegory to Alfonso's son Ercole, via his namesake Hercules. It may also warn against the seductions of courtly life, a touch of humor that the Este court would have embraced. An elderly Hercules focuses morosely on two stone spheres, ignoring his teasing companions. A smiling young man presents a distaff, symbolizing Hercules's feminine subjugation to Queen Omphale, while the light falls on a bare-chested woman bearing fruit. A tambourine and mask on the table hint at earthly love and frivolous pastimes. A buoyant colorist, Dosso skillfully rendered flesh and musculature. While the male faces fall just short of caricature, the females are purely classical. With frequent visits to Rome and Venice, Dosso learned to emulate Michelangelo, Raphael, and Correggio, yet produced some of the most original, if mysterious, works of his era. **SLF**

The Last Judgment | Michelangelo

1535–41 | fresco | 540 x 480 in / 1,370 x 1,220 cm | Sistine Chapel, Vatican City, Italy

The Last Judgment is generally regarded as one of Michelangelo Buonarroti's (1475–1564) greatest masterpieces. Inspired by Dante's *Divine Comedy*, the fresco was commissioned by Pope Paul III, begun in 1535, and finally revealed on October 31, 1541. Its creation required the destruction of Perugino's frescoes, which had previously adorned the altar wall of the Sistine Chapel. This work has become so iconic that it is difficult to remember that in its own time it was controversial. Not least of all the concerns regarding the image was its pervasive nudity, much of which was later covered up by Michelangelo's pupil, Daniele da Volterra, and finally uncovered again by restorers. Certainly Michelangelo was preoccupied with the glory of the human body—as is evident throughout his oeuvre—but the nudity of figures in *The Last Judgment*, combined with the emotional fury of their gestures, emphasizes their vulnerability in the midst of the chaos around them. Michelangelo groups figures to create some sense of a compositional structure, but he still fully investigates the emotional personality of each individual. This inventiveness is perhaps best exemplified by a character in the lower mid-right of the fresco, a damned soul descending to hell, who, amid the figures struggling around him, appears too horrified to resist his fate: he covers one eye with his hand and has an expression of pure terror on his face. The true genius of Michelangelo was that he could explore the psychological reaction of so many characters with equal conviction. **SS**

Nativity of the Virgin | Domenico Beccafumi

c.1543 | oil on wood | 91 x 57 in / 233 x 145 cm | Pinacoteca Nazionale, Siena, Italy

The Tuscan town of Siena had considerable power in Italy through the Middle Ages, and was rival to Florence in terms of artistic, social, and cultural wealth. However, by the fifteenth century the town's prestige was waning and war and disease had taken their toll. The artist Domenico Beccafumi (c.1485–1551) can be considered the last of the great painters of the Sienese School, and though he traveled beyond Siena to Rome, his style remained essentially true to his roots. His paintings show an unusual approach to his subjects and composition, and often included strange, almost fantastical, details. In *Nativity of the Virgin*, for example, he paid great attention to the elongated fingers and smooth pale hands of the figure to the right, who is captured in a strong plane of light. Behind this elegant figure of classical countenance hovers the face of another, whose ghostly form emerges from the drapery directing a level gaze at the viewer. The hand of the woman who is cradling the Virgin has again been carefully modeled with precise attention to detail. There is a strange atmosphere here, which is heightened by the planes of light and deep shadow. This was not unusual in his paintings, and indeed his great talent lay in the very unique concept of his works. When Beccafumi was in Rome he saw Michelangelo's ceiling in the Sistine Chapel and the work of Raphael, and the influence of both artists is tangible. Here Beccafumi has combined Mannerist and classical influences within his own framework. **TP**

An Allegory with Venus and Cupid | Agnolo Bronzino

1540–50 | oil on wood | 57 ⅝ x 46 in / 146.5 x 116.8 cm | National Gallery, London, UK

Agnolo Bronzino (Agnolo di Cosimo, 1503–72) was the adopted son and pupil of the master painter Pontormo and was to become a member of the illustrious sixteenth-century Florentine tradition of painting. The first work he carried out for Duke Cosimo I de' Medici—the great patron of the Renaissance—was in 1539, when he was involved in the decorations for the duke's wedding to Eleonora of Toledo. He soon became the official court painter and remained so for most of his career—responsible for a vast collection of images of the duke's family and courtiers. He was also a poet and produced portraits of other literary figures. Bronzino's style was almost identical to Pontormo's, but he was far more successful at portraits than religious paintings. His portraits were characterized by elegant posturing and his admiration of Michelangelo and Raphael is evident in his work. An Allegory with Venus and Cupid is Bronzino's paramount achievement. Commissioned by the duke, it is also known as Venus, Cupid, Folly, and Time. Here the eroticism of the central image of Venus and the fondling Cupid as well as the obscure imagery are characteristic of the Mannerist period. The winged elderly man pictured in the upper right supports an hourglass, which marks him as the personification of Time. The identity of the other figures is not as clear: the distraught figure at left has been interpreted as Despair or Jealousy, the boy scattering roses as Folly or Pleasure, and the top left figure as Oblivion. The overall meaning of the picture continues to tease, and appeal to, its audience. **SP**

The Story of Papirius | Domenico Beccafumi

1540–50 | oil on wood | 29 x 54 in / 74 x 137.8 cm | National Gallery, London, UK

Beccafumi was born Domenico di Pace (c.1485–1551), but took the name Beccafumi after his patron Lorenzo Beccafumi. The wealthy Sienese encouraged the boy to study art, first in his hometown of Siena and then in Rome between 1509 and 1511. During this period, the artist saw the work of Michelangelo and Raphael, and certain aspects of their style, and Roman classicism, influenced him. He returned to Siena and spent most of his working life there—much of his best works remain in his hometown. Beccafumi's style was unique, and was further advanced by his relatively isolated artistic environment. *The Story of Papirius* depicts an unusual story that has only recently been identified. A young boy, Papirius, accompanied his father to the Senate, where he was sworn to secrecy concerning the debate. The picture relates two scenes from the story. To the left is Papirius who, on being questioned by his mother, tells her that the debate concerned whether a man should have two wives or a woman two husbands. His mother returned the following day with her friends to petition for women to be allowed two husbands, to the chagrin and confusion of the senators. In the center of the picture, Papirius is explaining his mother's actions to the bemused officials. There is a surreal quality to this painting—the figures, some strangely elongated, float across the foreground, while in the background, Roman structures sit haphazardly in an artfully constructed setting. It is precisely this quirky approach that makes Beccafumi's work so intriguing. **SH**

Adam and Eve | Tintoretto

*c.*1550 | oil on canvas | 59 x 86 ½ in / 150 x 220 cm | Gallerie dell'Accademia, Venice, Italy

The masterful Venetian painter Jacopo Robusti, known as Tintoretto (*c.*1518–94), is considered the last of the major Italian Renaissance artists. He helped set a dramatic stage for a new period of Italian cultural progress known today as the Baroque. The seething energy of his canvases later gave rise to his nickname *Il Furioso*. In his lifetime, Tintoretto's characteristically brusque touch earned him much praise, although there were also those who lambasted him for the lack of painterly finish that resulted from this rushed, abbreviated style. Tintoretto painted many Old Testament themes. In *Adam and Eve*, he positions Eve so that the viewer is also presented with the fruit of knowledge. The leaning, healthy torsos of the two figures, their spines diagonally parallel to each other,

frame the seductive nature of the image, enhanced by the painting's warm, muted tones. The verdant vista of paradise, stretching on beyond the horizon, creates a wildness appropriate to the innocence of the scene. In the distance to the left of Adam is the darkest passage of paint—a carefully calculated foreshadowing of the imminent fall of man. Tintoretto spent virtually his entire career in the Venetian Republic, leaving only once in 1580 to work on a commission for the Gonzagas of Mantua. Although he painted the portraits of several prominent Venetians, he struggled to be accepted by the city's social elite. However, his reputation reached new heights after 1564, when he was given a major project in Venice's Doge's Palace and another in the Scuola Grande di San Rocco. **SP**

The Chess Game | Sofonisba Anguissola

1555 | oil on canvas | 28 ⅜ x 38 ⅛ in / 72 x 97 cm | Muzeum Narodowe, Poznań, Poland

Sofonisba Anguissola (c.1535–1625) was a fortunate young Italian woman in that her enlightened father endeavored to educate all seven of his children—including the girls—in the best humanist tradition. Although several of her sisters also painted, it quickly became clear that Sofonisba was a prodigy. She trained with the eminent masters Bernardino Campi and Bernardino Gatti, and—quite unusual for a woman—gained an international reputation. This is probably her most famous painting and signals a departure in portraiture. She dispenses with stiff formal poses and instead depicts three of her sisters—Lucia left, Europa middle, and Minerva on the right with someone generally considered to be a servant—in a relaxed, informal game of chess. The servant might appear as a chaperone to suggest the virtue of the girls, however, she also presents a contrast in both class and age to the three girls of noble birth. Chess was considered a masculine game requiring logic and strategic skills, rarely the attributes ascribed to females. In spite of the good humor of the painting, it is clear from Europa's impish delight in Lucia's imminent victory that the sisters took the game seriously. Access to nude models was denied to women artists at the time, so this restricted the available subject matter. Anguissola focused on bringing life to the genre of portraiture. Her achievement was recognized by Vasari who rated her above other female artists, writing that she showed application and grace in drawing and that she, "by herself," created beautiful paintings. **WO**

Self-Portrait at the Easel | Sofonisba Anguissola

1556 | oil on canvas | 26 x 22 in / 66 x 57 cm | Muzeum Zamek, Łańcut, Poland

Sofonisba Anguissola (c.1535–1625) produced several self-portraits during her life. This one is thought to be one of the first showing a woman artist at the easel. It is important because it demonstrates her profession and it is also notable that she depicts herself painting a devotional picture because it lends the work gravity. Although we now know that there were many women artists practicing in the Renaissance, it was more difficult for noblewomen to become artists. Women artists were restricted by the conventions of their time and had to be very careful to maintain standards of propriety. The colors of the painting and of her palette provide a vibrant contrast to the artist in her severe brown dress and dark room. The same light that infuses the painting seems to rest on Anguissola's face and hands, which connects her as intimately to her subject as does the brush poised above the canvas. The artist was only in her mid-twenties at the time of this painting, but stares out confidently at the viewer. She had good reason to: she had already been to Rome where she met Michelangelo, who expressed his admiration and requested work from her. The influence of Anguissola's teacher Bernardino Campi is evident in this work. A great portraitist, he even produced a self-portrait of himself at the easel painting a portrait of Anguissola. In 1559, she became court painter and lady-in-waiting to Elizabeth of Valois, Queen of Spain and the King arranged her first marriage. In 1569, she returned to Italy and continued to paint until the onset of blindness in old age. **WO**

St. George and the Dragon | Tintoretto

c.1558 | oil on canvas | 62 x 39 ½ in / 157.5 x 100.3 cm | National Gallery, London, UK

It is said that Jacopo Robusti (c.1518–94) began painting on the walls of his father's house from an early age. His father was a *tintore* ("dyer"), a profession that endowed Jacopo with the name Tintoretto ("little dyer"). He was apprenticed to the studio of the middle-aged Titian in 1533. Tintoretto's biographer, Carlo Ridolfi (1594–1698), wrote that Tintoretto drew such accomplished figures there that the jealous Titian dismissed him. Ridolfi also relates how Tintoretto inscribed the motto "The drawing of Michelangelo and the coloring of Titian" on his studio wall. Although influenced by their work, his own is distinctive for the exaggerated gestures of its figures, its dynamic composition, and dramatic use of light as in *St. George and the Dragon*. Here the concentric rings of divine light surrounding God at the top of the picture illuminate the scene and cap Tintoretto's depiction of the epic battle. According to legend, St. George was a knight from Cappadocia—now Turkey—who rescued a princess from a dragon at Silene, in Libya. This was a deed of Christian courage, which caused many to be converted. As the princess flees, St. George is shown ready to deliver the final blow to the dragon. The tension is heightened by Tintoretto's compositional choice to paint her running toward the viewer. Directly above her is a corpse laid out like the crucified Christ, which the beast was about to devour. Using a palette of pinks, reds, and blues, the artist leads the eye toward the background landscape, castle, horizon, clouds, and God. **SP**

Landscape with the Fall of Icarus | Pieter Bruegel the Elder

*c.*1558 | oil on wood | 29 x 44 in / 74 x 112 cm | Musées Royaux des Beaux-Arts, Brussels, Belgium

Early in his career, Pieter Bruegel the Elder (*c.*1525–69) worked for a successful publisher and print-seller with whom he produced many designs for engravings of popular proverbs. There was a huge demand for these, prompting the artist to reproduce some of the subjects as full-sized paintings. Here, Bruegel tackles the famous Greek legend about Daedalus and his son Icarus, who were imprisoned on the island of Crete. In a bid to escape, Daedalus made two sets of wings, using feathers and wax. He warned Icarus not to fly too close to the sun, but the foolish youth took no heed. The wax melted and Icarus plummeted into the sea and drowned. This myth was often included in proverb anthologies of the time, as an illustration of the folly of pride and ambition. Bruegel conveyed this

moral in an ingenious manner. The flight of Icarus has been miraculous. However, it causes barely a ripple in the tide of human affairs: the plowman and the shepherd go about their daily business, while the ship passes by, without noticing the drowning boy. Similarly, a casual spectator, unaware of the painting's title, might easily fail to spot the legs of Icarus, in the lower right-hand corner of the picture. Bruegel underlined the moral with other details. The shepherd, as careless as Icarus, is daydreaming, while his sheep wander off into the sea. On the ground, a wallet and sword refer to a popular proverb: "A sword and money need careful hands." In addition, there is a corpse in the thicket on the left, illustrating the saying: "No plough stops because a man dies." **IZ**

The Last Supper | Juan de Juanes

*c.*1560 | oil on panel | 45 ⅝ x 75 ¼ in / 116 x 191 cm | Museo del Prado, Madrid, Spain

This is one of the best-known paintings of a major event in Christ's life, painted by a Spaniard who came from a family of artists based in Valencia. Vicente Juan Maçip (*c.*1510–79), known as Juan de Juanes, was the son of noted artist Vicente Maçip and rose to become the leading painter in Valencia during the second half of the sixteenth century. *The Last Supper* shows the same kind of Italian influences seen in his father's work, but adds a distinctive Netherlandish twist. The picture shows Jesus and his disciples gathered for a last meal together, when Jesus offers his companions bread and wine as symbols of his body and blood. Bread and wine are clearly visible, as are the wafer and chalice used in the sacrament of the Eucharist that commemorates this event. There is a stylized drama to

the scene, with its *chiaroscuro* lighting and yearning, leaning figures, that makes it slightly Mannerist. Here too are the rather idealized figures, balanced composition, and graceful grandeur of the high Renaissance master, Raphael. Italian art—especially that of Raphael—was a great influence on Spanish art at this time, and Juan may well have studied in Italy at some point. He has even been called "the Spanish Raphael." There is plenty of adept technical skill in the depiction of the folded drapes of clothing, curling hair, and highlights glancing off dishes and vessels. Juan's style became very popular and was much copied. His appeal did much to establish a Spanish school of religious art known for being harmonious, affecting, and well designed. **AK**

The Rape of Europa | Titian

1559–62 | oil on canvas | 72 ⅞ x 112 in / 185 x 285 cm | Isabella Stewart Gardner Museum, Boston, MA, USA

The oeuvre of Titian (Tiziano Vecellio, c.1485–1576) was subject to a number of shifts in import and sensibility over the course of his career. Whereas the bacchanals, painted for the Duke of Alfonso d'Este's studio in Ferrara, were for the most part joyous and inflected with a certain youthful fervor, during the 1550s Titian worked under the patronage of King Philip II. From 1553 he produced seven mythological paintings, all of which were rather more complex in their treatment of the fallibility of the human condition. Titian defined these paintings as poesie or "painted poems". These took as their subjects themes from ancient mythology. In *The Rape of Europa*, the story (derived from Ovid's *Metamorphoses*) concerns the lovesick god Jupiter, who disguises himself as a white bull in order to kidnap the Phoenecian princess Europa. In what would prove to be the last of the poesies, Titian organizes the composition around a strong diagonal and depicts the tumultuous moment of Europa's abduction. Sharply contrasting in subject matter to his bacchanals, Titian's poesies also differ substantially in their execution. While a painting such as *Bacchus and Ariadne* is underpinned by a certain crispness in execution, the poesies can be identified through the employment of a considerably looser configuration of brushstrokes. *The Rape of Europa* represents a major development in Titian's work, extending not only the emotional breadth of Venetian painting, but the actual techniques by which such emotion could be conveyed. **CS**

Hunters in the Snow | Pieter Bruegel the Elder

1565 | oil on panel | 46 ⅛ x 63 ¾ in / 117 x 162 cm | Kunsthistorisches Museum, Vienna, Austria

Pieter Bruegel the Elder (c.1525–69) did much to establish the tradition of landscape painting in the Low Countries. This splendid winter scene, painted when the artist was at the peak of his powers, is his finest achievement in the field. In Northern Europe, landscape painting did not emerge as a separate genre, but as an offshoot of the calendar scenes that appeared in Books of Hours. This painting, for example, was not originally known as *Hunters in the Snow*, but was part of a series, *Months*, commissioned by Niclaes Jonghelinck, a wealthy banker from Antwerp. It probably represents the month of January. This can be deduced from the scene on the left, in which a group of villagers are singeing a pig, in order to remove its bristles. In purely compositional terms, *Hunters* also

seems to have the ideal structure for the initial item in a frieze of pictures. The trees on the left act as a framing device, while the huntsmen and their dogs lead the eye to the right, toward the remainder of the series. Public attitudes to landscape painting were very different at this time. While Bruegel paid great attention to minute details—the depiction of the tiny figures skating, tobogganing, and curling on the ice are a particular joy—he was not expected to produce an accurate view of a specific place. Instead, this is a composite scene. The mountains in the distance were based on sketches that Bruegel made from 1552 to 1553, when he traveled through the Alps on his way to Italy, while the rest of the panorama was inspired by the flat terrain of his native Belgium. **IZ**

The Jurist | Giuseppe Arcimboldo

1566 | oil on canvas | 25 x 20 in / 64 x 51 cm | Nationalmuseum, Stockholm, Sweden

The Italian Mannerist painter Giuseppe Arcimboldo (c.1527–93) was born in Milan to a family of painters. By 1549 the young artist had been commissioned, along with his father, to design stained-glass windows for Milan Cathedral. He also designed a series of tapestries for Como Cathedral. This early foundation in design formed the basis of the artist's subsequent astonishingly innovative style that was conceived in a thoroughly precise and linear manner. In 1562, Arcimboldo was employed by Emperor Ferdinand I, and left Milan for Vienna, and later Prague, to fill his position of painter to the Hapsburg court. On Ferdinand's death in 1564, he was taken on by his successor, Emperor Maximilian II, and later by Emperor Rudolph II, for whom he worked until 1587. It was during the first years of his courtly service that the artist's style emerged, seen in an early version of his *Four Seasons* series. By the time *The Jurist* was painted in 1566, Arcimboldo had established himself as one of the leading innovative painters of his time. He treated his subjects with an ironic wit that was greatly appreciated. The artist's feelings about his jurist are clear—the countenance is composed of plucked chicken carcasses and dead fish, and his mouth is pulled down in a sneer. These clever and humorous compositions, and Arcimboldo's particular ability to create recognizable personas from composite elements, was unsurpassed. Arcimboldo's work is considered a precursor to Surrealism, and the visual pun is a device used in advertising today. **TP**

The Peasant Wedding | Pieter Bruegel the Elder

1568 | oil on panel | 45 x 64 in / 114 x 163 cm | Kunsthistorisches Museum, Vienna, Austria

For centuries, Pieter Bruegel the Elder (c.1525–69) was known primarily as a painter of comic peasant scenes; in fact, he used his peasant subjects as vehicles for lighthearted moral allegories. According to an early account, Bruegel liked to visit country weddings, disguised as a peasant, so that he could observe the festivities first hand. Whether or not this is true, the artist's depiction of boisterous carousing is utterly convincing. There is, however, one minor mystery: where is the groom? The bride is easily identified, sitting in the place of honor, but the location of her husband is far less certain. One possible candidate is the man in the foreground, turning around to call for more drink. He has been suggested because of a theory that the woman is marrying a townsman, an

hypothesis that would also explain the presence of a few well-heeled, urban guests. The venue is furnished like a parody of a great man's hall, with a blanket serving as a makeshift tapestry and an old door as a banqueting tray. Ironically, the most distinguished-looking guest, the man on the far right, is seated on an upturned tub. For all the humor of the scene, Bruegel could not resist a little moralizing and some critics have interpreted this picture as a sermon against gluttony. In the foreground, for example, the child in the enormous hat is shown sucking its finger, a pose that was traditionally employed as an emblem of hunger. This reference would have seemed particularly pointed in Bruegel's day, as there had recently been a famine in the Netherlands. **IZ**

The Tailor | Giovanni Battista Moroni

1565–70 | oil on canvas | 39 ¼ x 30 ¼ in / 99.5 x 77 cm | National Gallery, London, UK

Giovanni Battista Moroni (1520–78) was one of the most talented portrait painters of his century and this picture is his best-known work. Although Moroni painted a host of distinguished people, he depicted them with the same honest, penetrating humanity that is so striking in his portrait of a working tailor. Moroni made every attempt to show the essence of the real person, no matter their status. As with most of the artist's portraits, his tailor instantly engages the viewer by looking directly out of the canvas. In this case, the stare is almost mesmerizing. The tailor's face, handsome but full of individual character, forms the main focus. It is subtly lit from above, giving highlights that mold the face and also glance off the eyes, connecting viewers with his gaze. His expression has

an intriguingly reserved shrewdness. In his cream and red clothing, the tailor stands out against the subtly muted background of soft gray that the artist often used. Typical for Moroni, the clothing is shown convincingly but not overly detailed, and the tunic is painted with the more economic strokes found in his later works. While the head dominates this picture, Moroni balances the work by use of sparkling highlights on the belt, cuffs, and scissor blades. Here is a picture of a man at work and yet the simple, natural grace of his pose and his absorbing face give him considerable presence. This same restrained serenity and elevation of the ordinary would, in the next century, distinguish the work of the great Dutch genre painters Vermeer and De Hooch. **AK**

The Vision of St. Helena | Paolo Veronese

c.1570 | oil on canvas | 77 ¾ x 45 ½ in / 197.5 x 115.6 cm | National Gallery, London, UK

Italian high Renaissance painter Paolo Caliari (c.1528–88) adopted the name Veronese from his native city of Verona. Initially he trained as a sculptor before being apprenticed to learn painting from Antonio Badile (c.1518–60), his eventual father-in-law. He is thought to have been influenced by the works of Giulio Romano (c.1499–1546), Parmigianino (1503–40), and Titian (c.1485–1576). He moved to Venice in 1553 and became one of the leading painters of the time, with a large studio where he employed his brother and sons, who continued to run it after his death. Veronese received many commissions for both paintings and frescoes, largely on religious, historical, and mythological themes, although he also painted portraits. The Vision of St. Helena depicts St. Helena of Constantinople, who is believed to have had a vision of the cross on which Christ was crucified while she was sleeping. As the mother of the Christian convert, Emperor Constantine I, she is said to have received divine powers to assist her search for the burial location of the True Cross. Veronese's The Vision of St. Helena adds an element of humanity to the saintly reverie by painting her in a relaxed pose within a domestic space. Yet the lush colors, sumptuous folds of clothing, and marbled interior are typical of the richly decorative nature of Veronese's work. This feeling of decorativeness is enhanced by the playful presence of two winged putti seen through a wide window floating in a delicately colored sky while carrying a heavy wooden cross. **CK**

Summer | Giuseppe Arcimboldo

1573 | oil on canvas | 30 x 25 in / 76 x 63.5 cm | Louvre, Paris, France

Giuseppe Arcimboldo (c.1527–93) was highly successful during his lifetime, but after his death his work quickly went out of fashion, and interest in it was not revived until the end of the nineteenth century. Stylistically, his fantastical and imaginative paintings fit into the popular world of Mannerist art. The courts all across Europe during the sixteenth century particularly favored this type of witty and clever illusionary painting, and testament to this was Arcimboldo's lengthy assignment as painter to the Hapsburg court between 1562 and 1587. *Summer* forms part of the series *Four Seasons* that the artist painted for Emperor Maximilian II (reigned 1564–76) in 1573. This was a subject that Arcimboldo painted several times during his career, and was one that became extremely popular. He first painted a series of *Four Seasons* in 1562, and his imaginative concept of creating a head from a collection of fruit and vegetables was received with great enthusiasm. The artist went on to develop this theme of painting, which in many respects was centuries ahead of its time. Arcimboldo's courtly duties for Maximilian were not confined to painting—the artist was also called upon as a stage designer, an architect, and an engineer. Later, while working for Emperor Rudolph II (reigned 1576–1611), he was also charged with finding antiques and rare objets d'art for the Emperor's collection. Arcimboldo's paintings create a thoroughly surreal effect, and they are certainly among the most imaginative and cleverly contrived of his time. **TP**

Feast in the House of Levi | Paolo Veronese

1573 | oil on canvas | 218 ½ x 503 ⅞ in / 555 x 1,280 cm | Gallerie dell'Accademia, Venice, Italy

Paolo Caliari (c.1528–88), known as Veronese after his birthplace, was one of the great Venetian painters. *Feast in the House of Levi* is typical of his work with its lush colors, dynamic moving figures, and decorative classical architecture. The dramatic and sumptuous feel of his painting with its bold perspective reflects the pomp and grandeur of the age. The vast canvas of *Feast in the House of Levi* was originally commissioned as a depiction of the Last Supper with Jesus and his disciples for the monastery of Santi Giovanni e Paolo. The patterned tiled floor and sweeping staircases lead the eye to the central figure of Jesus under the middle arch. But the ornate tone and style of this banquet, with its dogs and drunken servants, got Veronese into trouble with

the religious authorities of the time in the form of the Inquisition—it was perceived as a rowdy scene rather than a religious painting of a sacred event, and Veronese was charged with heresy. He was asked why he had crowded his painting with what were deemed to be unnecessary and sacrilegious figures such as a jester with a parrot, dwarves, a servant with a bleeding nose, and German mercenaries. Veronese defended his artistic interpretation saying: "I received the commission to decorate the picture as I saw fit. It is large and, it seemed to me, it could hold many figures." He was told to make changes but refused to overpaint any parts of the work that were thought to be objectionable. Rather, he solved the problem by changing its title to *Feast in the House of Levi*. **CK**

The Repentant Magdalene | El Greco

c.1577 | oil on canvas | 42 ½ x 39 ⅞ in / 107.9 x 101. 4 cm | Worcester Art Museum, Worcester, MA, USA

The Greek painter Domenikos Theotocopoulos (1541–1614), known as El Greco, referred to himself as a painter-philosopher, an allusion to his fervent religious beliefs at the height of the Spanish Counter-Reformation. After spending his youth training as an icon painter in Crete, he set sail for mainland Italy where he studied in Venice under Titian, short changing the Byzantine for his unique style. He then moved to Rome in 1570 where he met Michelangelo. El Greco's *The Repentant Magdalene* was painted just after his arrival in Spain, where he would stay for the rest of his life. There are five versions of the painting, and this one is arguably the clearest and most expressive. There is a similarity between El Greco's interpretation of the scene and Titian's

version of 1561. The penitent St. Mary Magdalene is shown living as a hermit against the backdrop of a bleak wilderness. To one side is an open landscape and the other a rock covered by ivy symbolizing the everlasting life possible after repentance. She looks to heaven and contemplates an eternal life after death. Heavy drapery ensconces the Magdalene, with her distended neck and sensuous flowing blonde curls. She was frequently depicted with long hair, which she used to wipe her tears from Jesus's feet. This biblical scene is again alluded to by the small flask on her right, representing the vase of ointment she used to anoint his feet. Also on her right is a still life of an ominously yellowed skull, to remind the viewer of their own mortality and need to repent. **SP**

The Witch Ankarut | Unknown

c.1577 | watercolor and ink on paper | 27 x 21 in / 68 x 53 cm | Victoria & Albert Museum, London, UK

This painting is from an illustrated manuscript of the *Hamzanama* commissioned by the Mughal emperor Akbar, who reigned from 1556 to 1605 and was a lover of tales of magic and adventure. It took fifteen years to complete the whole series, which may have begun as early as 1562. The *Hamzanama* tells the epic story of Hamza, the uncle of the Prophet Muhammad, and his ambition to Islamicize the world. Akbar had his own ambitions: to spread Mughal power throughout the Indian subcontinent. *The Witch Ankarut* is extraordinary for its comparatively large scale and for its Persian influence juxtaposed with Mughal themes. The main subjects of the story are represented in two separate trees: on the left is the witch Ankarut,

and on the right is Hamza's enemy Iraj. The witch is offering to free Iraj—whom she has captured and lashed to a tree—if he agrees to become her lover. The faces of the protagonists are smudged, perhaps consciously because of religious conflict and differences. There is a genuine attempt at naturalism—although the trunks of the trees are rendered less realistically than the leaves of the vegetation—and the building in the background reflects contemporary Mughal architecture. The depiction of the rocks points to Persian artistic influences on the work. The unknown artist applied his wide palette of colors densely and left no empty space in a composition that ultimately is well balanced and unified. **SZ**

Chinese Lions | Kanō Eitoku

1580–85 | ink and gold on screen | 88 x 178 ⅜ in / 223.4 x 453.2 cm | Imperial Collections, Tokyo, Japan

Splendorous images and the abundant use of gold leaf characterize the art of the Momoyama period. A union of architecture and painting in the building and decorating of castles and mansions of feudal lords and nobles resulted in an elaborate style of interior paintings of folding screens, sliding panels, and walls. Kanō Eitoku (1543–90) was the master painter of this style, establishing the aesthetic canons of the Kanō School, founded by Kanō Masanobu, Eitoku's grandfather. Eitoku excelled in brush techniques from an early age under the guidance of his grandfather, and he worked in a variety of styles and mediums. The *Chinese Lions* folding screen is one of the rare extant large-scale works by Eitoku. Commissioned by feudal lord Toyotomi Hideyoshi, it depicts two guardian lions

with their manes and tails in stylized flame patterns. These lions, believed to have mythic protective powers, traditionally stood in front of palaces, temples, tombs, and homes of the wealthy. Eitoku invented a new style of painting on gold-leaf backgrounds to achieve dramatic effects suitable for shoguns' displays of power. He might have taken the idea from newly arrived Spanish and Portuguese religious paintings. The Kanō School's influence was widespread and dominated Japanese painting from the fifteenth through the mid-nineteenth century. Kanō artists combined the Chinese Zhe School style of ink painting with decorative elements derived from the Japanese indigenous *yamato-e* style. They were also renowned for their monochrome ink landscapes. **FN**

The Burial of Count Orgaz | El Greco

c.1586 | oil on canvas | 189 x 141 in / 480 x 358 cm | Church of Santo Tomé, Toledo, Spain

Born Domenikos Theotocopoulos (1541–1614), this Greek painter, who was born on Crete and died in his beloved city of Toledo outside of Madrid, was known to the Spanish as El Greco ("The Greek"). He was active in Rome and Venice, where he inevitably encountered the prevailing painterly styles of the period dominated by Titian and Tintoretto. His use of Venetian coloring and the distortions of his elongated figures are considered to prefigure Expressionism. El Greco moved to Toledo in 1577, which was the religious capital of Spain at that time. The magisterial *The Burial of Count Orgaz* commemorates the death of the patron of the Santo Tomé church, the devout Count of Orgaz, Gonzalo Ruiz de Toledo, who had died 250 years earlier. According to legend, when he was laid to rest, two saints appeared to place his body in the tomb. The picture is divided into two parts, with heaven above and earth below. As the pallid corpse in a suit of armor is lowered into the ground, his soul is seen flying toward the lap of Christ at the precipice of heaven. The sour tones of mustard yellow, cherry red, and inky blue create a stark contrast to the black background that engulfs the scene in darkness. A face in the back row of the crowd, staring out of the painting, is thought to be a self-portrait of El Greco. The child standing to the lower left, carrying a torch, is thought to be based on the artist's son. Written on the handkerchief protruding from the boy's pocket is the artist's cleverly placed signature. **SP**

A Youth Among Roses | Nicholas Hilliard

c.1588 | watercolor on vellum | 5 ³/₈ x 2 ⁷/₈ in / 13.5 x 7.3 cm | Victoria & Albert Museum, London, UK

This exquisite painting is one of the most famous works of the leading limner, or painter of miniatures, at the court of England's Queen Elizabeth I. Miniatures were produced as part of the game of courtly love, to be exchanged as tokens of fidelity or coded messages. The young gentleman pictured in Nicholas Hilliard's (1547–1619) miniature, shown pining with hand on heart amid a bower of roses, has been identified by some scholars as the young Robert Devereux, Earl of Essex, a favorite of Elizabeth I. His stormy relationship with the queen was to end on the executioner's block in 1601. This identification remains uncertain, however, while the identity of the artist, on the other hand, is unmistakable. The miniature displays Hilliard's habitual fine use of line and his aversion to shadows.

The proportions of the figure are studiedly distorted, the legs and torso elongated and the head small, as if being seen from below. It would have suited the Elizabethans to give the elements of the painting an allegorical reading. The pose with hand on heart suggests love and devotion, a message reinforced by the tree trunk, a symbol of constancy. The young man's melancholy air hints at love's vicissitudes, a message reinforced by the roses—the flowers symbols of love's delights, the thorns signifying love's pains. This theme is spelled out in Latin on the painting's frame: *Dat poenas laudate fides*—My praised loyalty brings me suffering. To a modern eye, this originally private image has become a public object to be enjoyed for its refined and jewellike beauty. **RG**

Venus with a Satyr and Cupids | Annibale Carracci

*c.*1588 | oil on canvas | 44 x 56 in / 112 x 142 cm | Uffizi, Florence, Italy

Annibale Carracci (1560–1609), his brother Agostino (1557–1602) and their cousin Ludovico (1555–1619) formed one of the most important artistic family groups of the sixteenth century. The three artists, who opened their own academy in the 1580s, placed great importance on basic draftsmanship as fundamental to painting, and worked in a manner that combined the sensuous palette of the Venetian School with the linear quality of the Florentines. The sumptuous goddess of love in *Venus with a Satyr and Cupids* demonstrates Carracci's exquisite detailing and the particular skill the artist had for life drawing. It is his grasp of the actual figure and his understanding of the folds of flesh and structure of bone that make this composition, and indeed his painting as a whole, so

convincing. His use of rich colors and his attention to the different textural qualities, seen in the sheen of Venus's tightly coiled hair, the velvet of the cushion, the smooth folds of the silken cloth, and the warm blush of her skin, make this painting instantly captivating. It is a work that pervades the senses, and it is simultaneously coy and provocative. The work of Carracci in particular was of great importance to successive artists, and he can be credited with starting a number of different artistic trends. He is, for example, thought to have been one of the first artists to have used caricature, which can be seen in his early genre paintings, and his monumental and heroic figures in fresco were widely copied, becoming something of a standard for this type of character depiction. **TP**

Landscape with Fishing Scene | Annibale Carracci

*c.*1588 | oil on canvas | 53 x 100 in / 136 x 255 cm | Louvre, Paris, France

Annibale Carracci (1560–1609) was born in the Bologna area, and along with his brother and cousin, came to be recognized as one of the leading painters of the Bolognese School. He was a particularly skilled draftsman and placed great emphasis on correct drawing, often depicting scenes from life, and placing them within an imaginary or idealized landscape. The themes of hunting and fishing were popular for villa decoration in Bologna at this time. *Landscape with Fishing Scene* was painted as a companion piece to another work by Carracci, *Hunting*, and based on their dimensions both were probably designed to hang over doorways in a domestic villa. The two works were painted early in Carracci's career, and prior to his move to Rome in 1584, but already show the artist's highly accomplished style. In this work he has combined a number of different scenes within one painting, and cleverly devised his composition so that the eye is led from the foreground to each group of people and into the background, without missing any detail. The figures were probably based on studies direct from nature, and were then combined with the landscape. This painting is intriguing because it shows Carracci developing his use of gesture, seen in the pointing figure on the right. The use of convincing and articulate gesture was one of Carracci's particular skills, which influenced later painters of the Baroque period. Also evident is Carracci's compelling use of landscape, which is beautifully composed in a clear translucent light. **TP**

The Raven Addressing the Assembled Animals | Miskin

1590 | opaque watercolor on paper | 10 ½ x 7 ½ in / 27 x 19.4 cm | British Museum, London, UK

Miskin was one of the best painters in the imperial atelier of Akbar (1542–1605). Works that were executed under Akbar's atelier were known to be the collaborative efforts of several artists who specialized in one specific task in the painting—the designer, the colorist, and the illuminator. Miskin was first known as a colorist and then developed his skills and became an extraordinary designer. His skills as a draftsman were well appreciated by Akbar, who commissioned several manuscript illustrations from him. The *Anwar-i Suhaili*, (*Lights of Canopus*) is the second dated manuscript from the Akbari period. It shows the interest of Akbar for Sanskrit Indian tales—this manuscript had been translated for him into Persian. The moralistic fable is illustrated here with a blend of Mughal and foreign styles, which testifies to the contacts of the empire with Iran and China. The mixture of mythical beasts and realistic animals oriented toward a central vertical axis is typical of the complex structural composition of Miskin in his maturity. While the crocodile shows some central Asian influences, the pink color as well as the fashion of the rocks is reminiscent of Iranian miniature painting. The crane, dragon, and phoenix indicate Chinese inspiration. On the other hand, the elephant and the horses, which are represented on the lower right-hand corner of the composition, demonstrate the Mughal Indian style, characterized by a leaning toward realism. A remarkable sinuousness flows through the painting as a whole. **SZ**

Queen Elizabeth I | Marcus Gheeraerts the Younger

1592 | oil on canvas | 95 x 60 in / 241.3 x 152.4 cm | National Portrait Gallery, London, UK

Marcus Gheeraerts the Younger (1562–1636), son of the Flemish painter and engraver Marcus Gheeraerts the Elder, escaped from Bruges with his father to London to avoid religious persecution. Aged seven, Gheeraerts the Younger started a new life with his artist father, but little is known about him. We know that his father probably taught him to paint, and that his earliest paintings were created from the 1590s, but not much more. What is certain, however, is that this Flemish child in exile grew up to become the artist responsible for defining the public image of Shakespearean England's key players. While Gheeraerts the Younger clearly painted this portrait—also known as the "Ditchley" portrait—the architect of the concept was most probably the queen's champion, Sir Henry

Lee. Between them they engineered a magnificent full-length portrait whose main purpose was to flatter the monarch and regain her favor after Lee had annoyed her. It also gives a visual presence to Elizabeth's power and status. Elizabeth I is pictured, like a secular angel dripping with jewels and pearls, standing majestically on a map of the world with England (and Ditchley, Lee's Oxfordshire home) having risen to the top of the globe beneath her delicate feet. To her left there is a bolt of lightning, darkness, and a sonnet to the sun; to her right are light blue skies. Floating around her in three parts is a Latin inscription: "She gives and does not expect"; "She can but does not take revenge"; and "In giving back she increases [her power]." **SF**

Boy with a Basket of Fruit | Caravaggio

c.1593 | oil on canvas | 27 ½ x 26 ⅜ in / 70 x 67 cm | Galleria Borghese, Rome, Italy

At the time of this painting, Michelangelo Merisi da Caravaggio (1571–1610) lived in great poverty and was moving from studio to studio to find work. He eventually set up on his own in 1595 and found a patron, Cardinal Francesco del Monte, who not only gave him board and lodging, but opened the door to many commissions. This is a portrait of Caravaggio's friend, the Sicilian painter Mario Minniti, as a young man. The overt eroticism of the image is accentuated by the steep light, which picks out Minniti's bare shoulder, face, and hand. The sultry, provocative gaze may be an invitation to eat the fruit, but other interpretations are more convincing in the light of Caravaggio's treatment of similar subjects and his known sexual interests. The basket of fruit appears in many of Caravaggio's paintings, and on its own in *Basket of Fruit* (1597). He painted fruit with all its imperfections—bruised, rotten, and blighted. In this painting, however, the fruit is almost perfect. Fruit has many symbolic meanings, but the abundance here suggests that the artist painted them for their voluptuousness. Caravaggio led a disreputable life culminating in murder. He fled to Naples and then to Sicily, where Minniti sheltered him. Although he continued to paint, Caravaggio's last years were spent in flight from various authorities. A pardon arrived three days after his death. His work influenced Orazio and Artemisia Gentileschi in Italy, Georges de la Tour in France, Rembrandt van Rijn in Holland, and Diego Velázquez in Spain, to name only a few. **WO**

Captain Thomas Lee | Marcus Gheeraerts the Younger

1594 | oil on canvas | 90 ½ x 59 in / 230 x 150 cm | Tate Gallery, London, UK

This exotic portrait is of Captain Thomas Lee—a relative of Sir Henry Lee—an influential member of Elizabeth I's court who undertook a role somewhat similar to a modern-day PR consultant. It was painted by a leading society portraitist, Marcus Gheeraerts the Younger (1562–1636), but almost certainly to a plan designed by Sir Henry as part of an attempt to reconstruct the subject's damaged reputation. It appears that while he was a soldier in the English Colonial Army in Ireland, Thomas Lee's loyalty fell under suspicion to such an extent that, in the year this picture was painted, he felt obliged to travel to London to plead his innocence. This exercise clearly only delayed the inevitable, as he was executed for his part in the Earl of Essex's rebellion just seven years later. Looking more like an actor than a warrior, Captain Lee is unexpectedly pictured as a bare-legged foot soldier. Lee fought in Ireland in England's conquest of the island and Gheeraerts depicts him here rather like a semi-naked Irishman, against a pastoral background. Laden with flashy armor and sporting a limp wrist while his hand dangles over the wrong end of his pistol, this aristocratic, shoeless soldier appears as if he is going absolutely nowhere. Gheeraerts also produced the famous Ditchley portrait of Queen Elizabeth I and this example of his work exudes a similar romanticism. As a painting, the portrait *Captain Thomas Lee* is skillfully constructed, hauntingly beautiful, and one of the great oddities of English portraiture. **SF**

Akbar Rejoicing at the Birth of His Second Son | Unknown

1590–95 | watercolor, gold on paper | 13 x 7 ½ in / 33 x 19 cm | Victoria & Albert Museum, London, UK

This painting is an illustration from a page in the *Akbarnama*, or History of Akbar, a huge work in three volumes. It was commissioned by the third Mughal emperor, Akbar the Great, to provide an illustrated chronicle of the Mughal empire, and it took many years to complete. Akbar (1556–1605) expanded and centralized the empire, and the second volume of the *Akbarnama* records his achievements. In Akbar's atelier, Persian and Indian artists shared their knowledge, and even incorporated Western ideas about depth and perspective into their work. *Akbar's Household Rejoicing at the Birth of His Second Son, Murad* is a fine example of this artistic flowering. It celebrates the birth of Akbar's son some twenty years before the painting was created. The vivid colors are typical of Indian painting, while the Persian influence can be seen in the high horizon, which piles up the scenes of the narrative one on top of the other. The story begins in the top right-hand corner, where Akbar's wife has delivered their son and her female attendants cook for her in an inner courtyard. The eye is then drawn down to the open door, where another female attendant beckons the guests who queue to bring gifts in celebration of the birth. Beside them, in a cross-section of a room, court astrologers draw up the new baby's horoscope. The differing costumes of the figures emphasize the tolerance of Akbar's court, and the viewer can almost hear the din of the music rising from street level. The painting is a wonderful example of a creative fusion of artistic traditions. **MC**

Narcissus | Caravaggio

*c.*1595 | oil on canvas | 43 ¼ x 36 ¼ in / 110 x 92 cm | Palazzo Barberini, Rome, Italy

Michelangelo Merisi da Caravaggio's (1571–1610) enduring fame stems partly from his extraordinary life and partly from his even more remarkable art. In life he earned a reputation as a swaggering brawler, became a fugitive after killing a man over a bet, and died prematurely at the age of thirty-eight. Yet Caravaggio also produced paintings of breathtaking originality, becoming the most influential Italian artist of his generation. *Narcissus* belongs to the early part of Caravaggio's career, and comparatively little is known about his work at this stage—indeed, some critics have even questioned whether this painting is actually by Caravaggio. Nevertheless, some of the artist's trademarks are already apparent. From the outset, he favored the dramatic device of placing large, boldly lit figures in dark settings, like actors caught in a spotlight. He also had a tendency to use sensual young men as his models. More importantly, the composition is simple but eye-catching. Narcissus and his reflection form a loop, revolving around the boy's illuminated knee. A similar effect can be found in Caravaggio's *Conversion on the Way to Damascus*, which focuses on a horse's hoof. The subject is drawn from Ovid. Narcissus was a handsome youth who fell in love with his own reflection and gradually pined away. At his death, he was transformed into the flower that now bears his name. Here, the doleful expression of the reflection already hints at this fate. Mythological subjects are quite rare in Caravaggio's work, and the circumstances of any commission are unknown. **IZ**

The Deposition from the Cross | Unknown

c.1598 | watercolor, gold, and ink on paper | 7 ½ x 4 ½ in | Victoria & Albert Museum, London, UK

This painting reveals the interest of the Mughal emperor Akbar, who reigned from 1556 to 1605, in other cultures and testifies to his tolerance toward other religions. It also demonstrates the European presence in the Indian continent and the cultural exchanges that resulted from it. Indeed, the Portuguese established themselves in Goa in 1510 and Akbar often invited European delegations to his court. It is known that gifts were exchanged between Akbar and his visitors. Jesuit missionaries who attempted to preach their doctrine offered the Bible to him. The Portuguese embassy brought the Royal Polyglot Bible, which was written in Antwerp between 1568 and 1573 by Christopher Plantin. Biblical engravings then became a source of inspiration for local artists, who adopted the subject matter with some Mughal idioms. The floral scrolls in the border of the painting are typically Mughal. The strong European influence is clear in the division of space, the colors, and the middle-ground architecture of this painting. The artist must have been aware of European techniques and the biblical illustrations. The cross is used as a bracket idiom and divides the composition into left and right sections. The theatrical poses of the figures recall the European depictions of Christian scenes. The strong blue, green, and red colors, as well as the exaggerated folds of the draperies of the figures, are reminiscent of European practices. The small cherubs and angels flying across the clouds are also evident European imports. **SZ**

The Head of Medusa | Caravaggio

c.1598 | oil on canvas mounted on wood | 23 ½ x 21 ½ in / 60 x 55 cm | Uffizi, Florence, Italy

Commissioned as a ceremonial shield by Cardinal Francesco Maria Del Monte, the Medici family's agent in Rome, The Head of Medusa was presented to Ferdinand I de' Medici, the Grand Duke of Tuscany, in 1601. For its subject matter, Michelangelo Merisi da Caravaggio (1571–1610) drew on the Greek myth of Medusa, a woman with snakes for hair who turned people to stone by looking at them. According to the story, she was killed by Perseus, who avoided direct eye contact by using a mirrored shield. After Medusa's death, her decapitated head continued to petrify those that looked at it. Caravaggio plays with this concept by modeling himself for Medusa's face—making him the only one who is safe from Medusa's deadly gaze—and having to look at his reflection to paint the shield

in the same way that Medusa caught her own image moments before being killed. Although Caravaggio depicts Medusa's severed head, she remains conscious. He heightens this combination of life and death through Medusa's intense expression. Her wide-open mouth exudes a silent but dramatic scream and her shocked eyes and furrowed brow all suggest a sense of disbelief, as if she thought herself to be invincible until that moment. But Caravaggio's Medusa does not have the full effect of scaring the viewer, since she does not look at us, thereby transferring the power of the gaze to the viewer and emphasizing her demise. Caravaggio displays huge technical achievements in this work by making a convex surface look concave and Medusa's head appear to project outward. **WD**

Orpheus in the Underworld | Jan Brueghel the Elder

1594–1600 | oil on copper | 10 x 14 in / 26 x 35 cm | Palazzo Pitti, Galeria Palatina, Florence, Italy

Jan Brueghel the Elder (1568–1625) was born in Brussels and was initially taught painting by his grandmother, a specialist in miniature works. He was the son of Pieter Bruegel the Elder and was commonly nicknamed either "Velvet" Brueghel on account of the lush velvet quality to his paintings or "Flower" Brueghel with respect to his still-life paintings. He was one of the leading still-life masters of his time, but also painted landscapes and allegories. His work is characteristically brilliantly colored, as seen here, and populated with exquisite details. The artist traveled to Italy and Cologne early in his career, but by 1597 had settled in Antwerp. He enjoyed great success, and was appointed court painter to Archduke Albert and the Infanta Isabella, making many trips to the court in

Brussels. He was also friendly with Rubens, and the two artists often collaborated, with Rubens painting the figures and Brueghel concentrating on the landscapes. *Orpheus in the Underworld* shows the artist at his most exuberant. The painting has a searing, jeweled effect with magnificent, opulent coloring combined with a richly detailed and animated surface. The scene shows Orpheus who has traveled to the underworld to rescue his wife and plays the harp to calm the fantastical beasts of hell. Looming from the shadows lie creatures of all description, while the overall effect of the underworld's depths is heightened by the greenish hue. Brueghel's style was widely copied, and his influence can particularly be seen in the work of two of his sons, Jan II and Ambrosius. **TP**

St. Paul on Malta | Adam Elsheimer

c.1600 | oil on copper | 6 ¾ x 8 ½ in / 17.3 x 21.5 cm | National Gallery, London, UK

Adam Elsheimer (c.1578–1610), born in Frankfurt, Germany, painted beautifully crafted scenes on miniature copper panels. Equally adept at figurative and landscape painting, Elsheimer influenced the development of European landscape art and inspired such painters as his friend Rubens and Rembrandt. Moving to Venice, Italy, at the end of the sixteenth century, he was exposed to the work of leading Italian painters such as Caravaggio (1571–1610). He studied various types of light, methodically reproducing the effect of the sun, moon, torchlight, and firelight in his paintings. His nightscapes, in particular, were highly acclaimed and sought after by European collectors. By 1600, he had settled in Rome, where he painted several important works, including St. Paul on Malta.

Drawing on the New Testament's Acts of the Apostles, it shows St. Paul and his followers shipwrecked on the island of Malta. As lightning flashes in the night sky and a storm beacon beckons from a cliff top, huge waves crash against the rocks, tossing the remains of a boat around in the turbulent sea. In the foreground, some travelers cluster around a fire, while others try to dry their wet clothes, helped by natives from the island. St. Paul stands near the spitting fire, a deadly viper fastened to his wrist, although he seems entirely unaffected by it. Elsheimer suffered from melancholia, rendering him unable to work at times. He fell into debt and was sent to prison just before his death. Elsheimer left behind fewer than forty paintings, some unfinished. **AV**

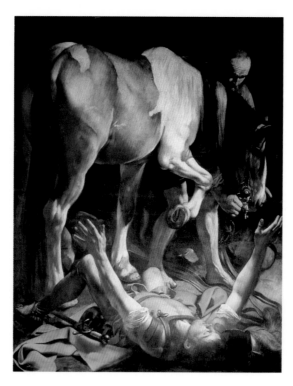

The Conversion on the Way to Damascus | Caravaggio

1601 | oil on canvas | 90 ½ x 69 in / 230 x 175 cm | Cerasi Chapel, Santa Maria del Popolo, Rome, Italy

Caravaggio (1571–1610) transformed the religious art of his time, using bold compositions and an uncompromising sense of realism to give his pictures a genuine feeling of immediacy. This is one of his best-known paintings, produced when he was at the height of his powers. The biblical story of Saul's conversion was a popular subject for artists. A Roman citizen (he is dressed as a Roman soldier in this picture), he was actively persecuting Christians when, on the road to Damascus, he was thrown from his horse and blinded by a heavenly light. Following his conversion he changed his name to Paul. Characteristically, the artist played down the supernatural element, reducing the blinding, celestial rays to a modest glimmer in the upper right-hand corner of the picture. The

process of the saint's conversion is internalized—the unkempt groom is unaware of the drama, and seems more concerned with calming the frightened horse. Caravaggio's critics accused him of undermining the sanctity of his religious themes by focusing on squalid details. Here, for example, they were unhappy with the veins on the groom's leg, and at the dominant role of the horse's behind in the composition. Nevertheless, Caravaggio's talent was recognized at the highest level. *The Conversion* was commissioned by Tiberio Cerasi, the Treasurer-General of Pope Clement VII, to hang in his chapel in the church of Santa Maria del Popolo. The picture was viewed from the side, which accounts for the exaggerated perspective and foreshortening. **IZ**

Still Life with Game Fowl | Juan Sánchez Cotán

*c.*1602 | oil on canvas | 26 ¼ x 34 in / 67.8 x 88.7 cm | Art Institute of Chicago, Chicago, IL, USA

Juan Sánchez Cotán (*c.*1560–1627), born at Orgaz in the province of La Mancha, is perhaps most closely associated with a conception of still life inherited from classical antiquity. According to Pliny the Elder, the rival painters Zeuxis and Parrhasius tried to outdo one another through displays of technical virtuosity. To this end, Zeuxis painted a still life of grapes so convincing in their verisimilitude that some birds swooped down and tried to peck at the apparent fruit. Parrhasius then asked his rival to draw back a pair of curtains so that Zeuxis might see Parrhasius's own painting. When Zeuxis attempted this, he realized that Parrhasius had painted a pair of curtains so lifelike that they were able to deceive the eyes of an artist. While Cotán's still lifes perhaps fell somewhat short of such

an ambition, the artist, who often went to meticulous lengths to arrange a few objects in a sparing and highly selective manner, was concerned with getting his paintings as close to reality as possible. Only recently discovered, *Still Life with Game Fowl* places a number of objects within a shallow, boxlike space. Either suspended or resting upon an apparent ledge, each object carries its own integrity, while collectively working in harmony to instill an over-arching design or arrangement. In a display of artistic virtuosity, Cotán suspends the duck in front of the actual frame and toward the space occupied by the viewer. As well as instilling the palpable nature of the objects, Cotán's approach is more widely indicative of the artist's wholly singular approach to the genre of still life. **CS**

Poem Scroll with Deer | Tawaraya Sōtatsu and Hon'ami Kōetsu

1603 | ink and gold on paper (detail) | 13 x 363 in / 34 x 939 cm | Seattle Art Museum, Seattle, WA, USA

The calligrapher Hon'ami Kōetsu (1558–1637) and the painter Tawaraya Sōtatsu (1576–1643) collaborated to produce a series of fine handscrolls. Born into a distinguished family of sword connoisseurs, Kōetsu was a versatile artist most renowned for his calligraphy, but who also excelled at lacquerware, ceramics, poetry, and the arts of tea. Little is known about Sōtatsu's life—he began his career as a painter at the Tawaraya fan shop, and later revived *yamato-e* (Japanese style painting) themes and produced large-scale paintings. Originally twenty meters (sixty-five feet) long, this fragment is the longest continuous portion of a scroll fragmented in 1935. The text presents twenty-eight poems from the poetry anthology *Shin kokin wakashū*. Deer was a popular theme, for its poetic connotations of autumn and loneliness as well as its religious associations in Shinto and Buddhism. Underpaintings on paper for calligraphy are attributed to a tradition of decorative paper popularized in the Heian period. Kōetsu and Sōtatsu formed a style at the artisan community Takagamine in Kyoto, which later came to be called Rinpa. The Rinpa style is known for its lavish use of bright colors, gold, and silver, and its adaptation of native classical literature, reinventing the elegant Heian period aesthetics through modern techniques. The Rinpa artists favored simple natural subjects. The format of the handscroll served to express the transience of nature well, because a view from the continuing scene was exposed as the handscroll was unrolled. **FN**

The Entombment | Caravaggio

1602–04 | oil on canvas | 118 x 80 in / 300 x 203 cm | Pinacoteca Vaticana, Vatican City, Italy

Michelangelo Merisi da Caravaggio's (1571–1610) *The Entombment,* as well as being one of his most admired works (several artists, including Sir Peter Paul Rubens, Jean-Honoré Fragonard, and Paul Cézanne made copies or adaptations of it), represents a point at which he began to depict mainly religious themes. The most striking aspects of the painting—the emphatic naturalism, the stark almost cinematic use of light (Caravaggio, in effect, radicalized the technique of *chiaroscuro*), and the depiction of figures frozen in a moment of heightened emotional tension—are all representative of his mature style. Compositionally, the painting is organized around a strong diagonal that begins at the point of the Virgin Mary's sister Mary Cleophas's raised left hand, continues down through

Mary Magdalene's slumped shoulder and the elbow of Nicodemus, to finally rest upon the corner of the shroud within which Christ's dead body is about to be wrapped. The four figures who surround Christ's body are remarkable for their unconventional treatment; the Virgin Mary appears as a nun and the arched figure of Nicodemus, historically a man of means, is dressed modestly as a symbol of his humility. Caravaggio makes the viewer occupy a position directly below ground level—essentially, the same space where the dead body of Christ is soon to be interred. This, along with Nicodemus's imploring gaze, demonstrates the artist's unflinching desire to evoke a degree of empathy within the viewer that is entirely at one with the emotive force of the scene itself. **CS**

Landscape with Salmacis and Hermaphroditus | Carlo Saraceni

*c.*1608 | oil on panel | 16 ⅛ x 20 ⅞ in / 41 x 53 cm | Museo di Capodimonte, Naples, Italy

Baroque painter Carlo Saraceni (1579–1620) dressed in French clothes, spoke French fluently, and had French followers, but he never visited France. Born and trained in Venice, he settled in Rome in 1598. Saraceni's painting style was mostly influenced by the poetic landscape settings of the German artist Adam Elsheimer (1578–1610) and the dramatic storytelling of the Italian Caravaggio. Saraceni painted small-scale biblical and mythological subjects in an expressive Baroque style that was suggestive of the more elegant and elaborate Rococo style of art to come. *Landscape with Salmacis and Hermaphroditus* interprets the mythical tale of dual gender. Hermaphroditus was the illicit son of Hermes and Aphrodite, who was later entrusted to the nymphs of Mount Ida and grew up as a wild creature of the woods. Salmacis was an atypical water nymph, who rejected the ways of the virginal hunting goddess Diana in favor of vanity and idleness. She loved, and according to some accounts raped, Hermaphroditus and was allowed to be with him on the condition that the gods place them in one body. Fresh and layered, *Landscape with Salmacis and Hermaphroditus* portrays the two naked bodies struggling and merging in a dark, wooden cove next to a spring. With their colorful clothing lying by the wayside, the engrossing curves of the trees and boulders mimic the curves of the coupling bodies. *Landscape with Salmacis and Hermaphroditus* portrays in an emotive, Baroque style the ancient tale of gender, dominance, and dual sexuality. **SW**

Flight into Egypt | Adam Elsheimer

1609 | oil on copper | 12 ¼ x 16 ⅛ in / 30.6 x 41.5 cm | Alte Pinakothek, Munich, Germany

Adam Elsheimer (c.1578–1610) lived to the age of thirty-two and produced only a small body of work. He is little known outside specialist circles today, but was one of the most influential painters of the early seventeenth century. Born in Germany but active in Rome, he worked on a small scale, producing exquisite paintings on copper that are astonishingly rich in detail and invention. This extraordinarily poetic landscape dominates the actual subject of the painting, the Holy Family's flight into Egypt. Despite the darkness of the night, this landscape exudes a sense of peace and calm. The scene is illuminated by three symbolic sources of light, which also clarify the composition. Joseph carries only a small torch that barely illuminates the face of the child and symbolizes Christ's humility. The full moon in the distance, which reflects in the calm water below, and the countless stars in the sky testify to the presence of God. In the left foreground, shepherds tend to a campfire sending sparks up into the air. This group probably refers to the shepherds in the field who received the nocturnal annunciation of the birth of Jesus. This is the first moonlit nocturnal scene in the history of European painting, and the first representation of the Milky Way. Elsheimer must have been in contact with scholars who were making rapid advances in the knowledge of the stars. Elsheimer's representation of the heavens was so accurate that we can recognize constellations and see the surface of the moon. This is remarkable given the early date of the painting. **EG**

St. George Killing the Dragon | Domenichino

c.1610 | oil on wood | 20 ¾ x 24 ¼ in / 53 x 62 cm | National Gallery, London, UK

The Bolognese artist Domenichino (Domenico Zampieri, 1581–1641) achieved great acclaim during his lifetime, mainly because of his decorative frescoes. However, he was also an important landscape painter and this picture is an excellent example of his approach. It is a retelling of the legend about St. George, patron saint of England, who was said to have saved a princess, and a city, by slaying the dragon who threatened to destroy both. The simple tale is told clearly, but it is the tranquil landscape that dominates. The picture shows a beautifully harmonized, muted palette. Lighting adds to the restrained effect; the carefully blended greens and blues, receding to a pale, hazy distance, plus the softer forms of the city buildings, and the highlights glancing off George's armor, reveal an understanding of natural light. Beautifully rendered details on the armor and the clothing of the fleeing princess show Domenichino's superior draftsmanship and his compositional skills. This balanced composition has been diligently worked out, with trees framing the image and other elements designed to lead the eye back through the entire painting. A potentially highly dramatic scene is being played out in the foreground and yet it is seamlessly absorbed into the serene whole. All of these elements proclaim that this is the direct forerunner of groundbreaking work by Claude Lorraine and Nicolas Poussin. In helping to lay the foundations of the poetic landscape, Domenichino made a major contribution to the landscape tradition. **AK**

Descent from the Cross | Peter Paul Rubens

1611–14 | oil on wood | 165 ¾ x 242 ⅞ in / 421 x 617 cm | Cathedral of our Lady, Antwerp, Belgium

In 1611, Antwerp's Guild of the Arquebusiers ("Musketeers"), commissioned Peter Paul Rubens (1577–1640) to paint this triptych for their altar in the cathedral. The guild's dean was Burgomaster Nicolaas Rockox, a close friend of Rubens, whose portrait appears in the altarpiece's right wing. Rubens began the work after his return from a prolonged visit to Italy, and the resulting altarpiece is rife with lessons he learned there, from the rich Venetian colors to the dramatic lighting of Caravaggio and the muscular perfection of Classical sculpture. In the central panel, an extraordinary group of interlocking figures is arranged around the slumped form of the dead Christ. The diagonal composition is astonishingly dynamic, following the movement of Christ's pale yet muscular body as he slides off the cross—from the figure of Nicodemus, who clenches the shroud in his teeth at the upper right, to the three Marys, whose outstretched arms form a triangle at the lower left. Each figure participates not only in this activity, but in the grief and emotion of this moment. The scenes on the wings do not form a continuum with the composition of the Descent, but have an iconographic link. The patron saint of the Arquebusiers was St. Christopher, whose Greek name means the "Christ bearer," and who appears on one of the altarpiece's outer panels. All three scenes on the interior—the Descent (center), the Visitation (left), and the Presentation in the Temple (right) depict incidents in which Christ is physically carried or supported. **PB**

Jahangir Preferring a Sufi Shaikh to Kings | Bichitr

*c.*1615–18 | watercolor on paper | 10 x 7 ⅛ in / 25.5 x 18 cm | Freer Gallery of Art, Washington, DC, USA

The artist Bichitr (active 1615–1650) flourished under the great Mughal emperor Jahangir and this painting marks a unique development in Mughal portraiture. One of the striking innovations in this work is Bichitr's self-portrait in the lower left-hand corner—the first time a Mughal artist had dared to include his representation among an important delegation and, furthermore, standing in front of the emperor. Jahangir is seated on an hourglass, perhaps exposing his concern with being mortal and his impossible desire to control time. Yet Jahangir also used the painting to reinforce his social, political, and spiritual supremacy. The four men represented to the left of Jahangir were probably ordered according to the emperor's idea of hierarchical importance. The

man offering him the sacred book is a Sufi Shaikh, proving that spirituality mattered more to Jahangir than politics. The second man is the Ottoman sultan, the third is James I of England, and the last is Bichitr. Judging by the different style of clothes worn by each of the men, one assumes that the artist was aware of other styles of arts. The four cherubs show some clear Western influence. On the other hand the gigantic halo decorated with a sun motif is archetypal of the haloes that were painted under Jahangir's reign. The Persian and Mughal features may also be distinguished by the elaborate floral scroll and scriptural borders. Bichitr surpasses stylistic cultural boundaries by blending Mughal, Persian, and Western styles in a single harmonious canvas. **SZ**

Portrait of Shah Jahan as a Prince | Abu'l Hasan

c.1616–17 | watercolor and gold on paper | 8 x 5 in / 21 x 12 cm | Victoria & Albert Museum, London, UK

Abu'l Hasan (b.1588; active c.1600–30) was the son of Aqa Riza, an Iranian artist who worked in the imperial workshop of Jahangir. Abu'l Hasan continued his father's style and also flourished in the atelier of Jahangir. His expertise is attested to by the number of portraits that Jahangir commissioned from him, calling Abu'l Hasan "Nadir al-Zaman," the "Wonder of the Age." His technique juxtaposed European realism and chiaroscuro with Persian Safavid types of decorations and landscapes. Prince Khurram, the future Shah Jahan, was twenty-five years old in this miniature portrait, which is signed by the artist. As the portrait testifies, the prince was fascinated by jewelry. His orange costume contrasts greatly with the spinach-green background of the painting. The details of the textiles, the jewelry, and the facial features are extremely realistic. The painting reveals the personality of the subject but also that of the painter, who consciously chose to represent the green background as a flat color so that it would emphasize the accurate representation of the prince. The prince's halo refers to the divinity of the royal family, who often used the visual arts to legitimize their political authority. Besides its subject matter, the courtly patronage of the painting may be observed by the richness of the pigments and the illuminations. A Persian influence is seen in the incorporation of calligraphies in the painting and in the floral borders. This way of representing the ruler became a model for the Rajput states of India, such as Bikaner and Jaipur. **TP**

Return of the Prodigal Son | Guercino

*c.*1619 | oil on canvas | 42 x 56 in / 107 x 143.5 cm | Kunsthistorisches Museum, Vienna, Austria

Return of the Prodigal Son is one of the best examples of the early style of Giovanni Francesco Barbieri, nicknamed Guercino (1591–1666). His nickname (meaning "Squinter") was given to him because of his cross-eyes resulting from a childhood accident. Although born in a small town between Bologna and Ferrara and having virtually no formal artistic training, Guercino came to be one of the leading artists of the Bolognese School of painting. His contrasting of lights and darks is reminiscent of Caravaggio (1571–1610), but it is debatable whether Guercino would have seen Caravaggio's paintings at this early date. He was certainly influenced by Ludovico Carracci (1555–1619) who had founded a painting academy in Bologna in 1585. Guercino took the cool, clear tones and accomplished coloring of the older artist and gave it new life through his use of dramatic gesture and shadowing. This painting depicts the prodigal son, who has returned contrite to his father, who has forgiven him and is providing him with new clothes. It is a scene of forgiveness but devoid of joy, and was commissioned by Jacopo Serra the papal legate in Ferrara. Typical of Guercino's early style, the action occurs at the front of the picture, drawing in the viewer. The asymmetrical composition of figures lit by irregular brilliant light was characteristic of the artist, yet after visiting Rome later in his career, his style became quieter and his compositions more balanced. Guercino is considered to be one of the leading painters of Italian Baroque art. **TP**

Raising of Lazarus | Guercino

c.1619 | oil on canvas | 78 ⅜ x 91 ¾ in / 199 x 233 cm | Louvre, Paris, France

Giovanni Francesco Barbieri (1591–1666), nicknamed Guercino, was born in poverty in the small town of Cento, between Ferrara and Bologna in Italy, and was largely self-taught as an artist. He became one of the leading painters of the Bolognese School, taking over Guido Reni's (1575–1642) busy studio upon his death (ironic, since accounts indicate that Guercino was regarded with ambivalence by Reni). Guercino's style changed quite dramatically during his lifetime, with works such as this one from early in his career showing a highly Baroque approach with dramatic use of contrasting lights and darks. Typical of Baroque paintings, the composition is complicated and full of dramatic gesture, energy, and feeling. The figures are crowded into the foreground, almost as though part of a frieze, while the middle and background are virtually indiscernible. This technique puts the viewer nearly in the same spatial plane as the figures in the painting, thus evoking a powerful emotional response. The event is that of the dead man Lazarus being raised by Jesus. Guercino imbues the scene with a rapt intensity and a spiritual fervor that would have been greatly admired during his period. A few years before this painting was executed, Guercino had met the artist Ludovico Carracci (1555–1619) and was inspired by Carracci's handling of color and emotion. Carracci's influence is discernible in the *Raising of Lazarus*, although this work is altogether more energetic in style. A prolific and sought-after artist, Guercino died a rich man. **TP**

Allegory of Sight | Jan Brueghel the Elder and Peter Paul Rubens

c.1619 | oil on wood | 25 ⅝ x 42 ⅞ in / 65 x 109 cm | Museo del Prado, Madrid, Spain

Collaborations between artists, even those as prominent as Peter Paul Rubens (1577–1640) and Jan Brueghel (1568–1625), were not uncommon in seventeenth-century Flanders. In this painting, Rubens contributed the figures. The other painter, Brueghel, was the second son of the famous artist Pieter Bruegel the Elder. Specializing in landscape and still life, Brueghel was one of the most successful and celebrated Flemish painters of his day. He was known as "Velvet Brueghel" for his subtle and detailed rendering of surfaces. This picture belongs to a series of five allegorical works painted by Rubens and Brueghel for the Spanish regents of the Netherlands, Archduke Albert and Archduchess Isabella. Known as *Allegory of the Senses* or *The Five Senses*, each image is

devoted to one of the senses. This painting, which represents sight, is set in an imaginary gallery, filled with paintings and precious objects—astronomical instruments, carpets, portrait busts, and porcelain. The large figure seated at the table is a personification of sight, particularly relevant to collectors. The painting of Madonna and Child ringed with flowers in the bottom right corner is in reality an actual work by Rubens and Brueghel. The double portrait behind the table depicts the two patrons. Pictures of (oftentimes imaginary) art collections became extremely popular in seventeenth-century Antwerp. Usually commissioned by a connoisseur, these paintings recorded a collection and frequently included a portrait of the owner. **EG**

Judith Beheading Holofernes | Artemisia Gentileschi

1620 | oil on canvas | 78 ³⁄₈ x 64 in / 199 x 162.5 cm | Museo di Capodimonte, Naples, Italy

Artemisia Gentileschi (1597–1651) was trained by her father and received tuition from Agostino Tassi, a painter of seascapes. This is her first version of the story in which, according to the Old Testament, Judith decapitated the drunken Assyrian general Holofernes, who was laying siege to her town, Bethulia. Later, she and her servant returned to Bethulia with his head. Gentileschi deals with this subject in an astonishingly new and explicit manner. Although influenced by Caravaggio, her interpretation is far removed from his anodyne depiction of the subject. Limbs radiate to and from the head making it the unavoidable focus in a semicircle of brilliantly lit action. In the story, Judith severed the head with two strokes, and there is no doubt that this muscular Judith is capable of such a

feat. The rich Baroque gowns and the rendering of linen and skin show her skills at their best. Recent literary and filmic accounts link this painting with Gentileschi's biography, seeing in it her desire for revenge after being raped by Tassi, and her subsequent torture during the trial. This tends to eclipse her real achievements as the first woman artist to be accepted into the Academy of Drawing in Florence and as one of the first to paint historical and religious subjects, then considered impossible for women to attempt. Highly respected by patrons and fellow artists in life, on her death some publications referred to her notoriety rather than to her talent. It is only in the recent past that she has been reinstated as one of the great painters of the Baroque period. **WO**

Zebra | Ustad Mansur

c.1621 | watercolor and ink on paper | 7 ¼ x 9 ½ in / 18.3 x 24 cm | Victoria & Albert Museum, London, UK

Ustad Mansur (*c*.1590–1630) has been attributed the title of "Ustad," meaning "master," for his extraordinary, naturalistic depictions of fauna and flora. No other artist could compete with his understanding of natural science and his skills at representing animals and vegetation with such great realism. He worked in the imperial atelier of Akbar, who reigned from 1556 to 1605, and then that of his son and successor, Jahangir. When Mansur was an apprentice under Akbar he was known as a colorist and then a designer. Under the reign of Jahangir, the themes of the paintings that were commissioned changed tremendously. The Akbari epic themes were substituted by natural history subjects. The style of Mansur matured with his animal studies. *Zebra*

echoes the Chinese contemporary academic animal studies that tended to focus on the animal study only. The floral scrolls on the frame and the script written within the main composition are reminiscent of Persian miniature paintings. He adopted Chinese and Persian stylistic elements and Mughalized these in order to fit the Mughal tastes of the emperors. However, the thin black outline of the zebra as well as the intense expression of the eyes evidences the perfectly controlled brushwork of the artist. He has depicted the animal in profile, to enable an ideal view of his study. The creamy background of the miniature contrasts with the colored skin of the zebra. Mansur's animal studies were highly esteemed and many Mughal artists at court attempted to copy him. **SZ**

Adoration of the Shepherds | Gerrit van Honthorst

1622 | oil on canvas | 64 x 74 in / 164 x 190 cm | Wallraf-Richartz Museum, Cologne, Germany

Gerrit van Honthorst (1592–1656) achieved great fame through his "night paintings" of which *Adoration of the Shepherds* is one. The artist had trained in Utrecht under Abraham Bloemaert, before traveling to Italy in 1610 where he achieved great success. Once there he was deeply affected by the hyper- naturalism and dramatic use of *chiaroscuro* in the work of Caravaggio. On his return, Honthorst brought the work of Caravaggio to the northern Netherlands through his own interpretation of the Italian artist, and in this respect his work was important for a number of artists, including Rembrandt and Georges de la Tour. Honthorst was made a member of the Guild of St. Luke in Utrecht in 1622, the same year in which he painted *Adoration of the Shepherds*. The

influence of Caravaggio is apparent in the painting, but the artist had also started to evolve a more personal approach through the use of a softer palette and treatment of his figures. The faces of the shepherds and Virgin Mary, for example, are flushed with the warm, delicate hues of human flesh, while dramatically contrasting against the brilliant white unearthliness of the Christ Child, thereby emphasizing the disparity between the spiritual and secular. Later, Honthorst moved away from the dramatic Caravaggesque night scenes with which he is most commonly linked. However, it was his role as joint leader of the Utrecht Followers of Caravaggio, along with Hendrik Terbrugghen, that was his most significant contribution to Dutch art. **TP**

The Laughing Cavalier | Frans Hals

1624 | oil on canvas | 32 x 26 in / 83 x 67.3 cm | Wallace Collection, London, UK

Frans Hals (1582–1666) was born in Antwerp but grew up in Haarlem to become the leading painter of the Dutch Golden Age. He was particularly famous for his large group portraits, but *The Laughing Cavalier* is his most iconic portrait of all. Catching our eye with a knowing gaze, the "cavalier" is neither laughing nor a cavalier. In fact, not much is known about the sitter except what the painting itself reveals. An inscription in the top right tells us he was twenty-six in 1624. He was wealthy and fashionable, as shown by the intricately embroidered doublet and extravagant lace collar and cuffs. On his sleeve, flaming torches, hearts and arrows, lover's knots, and bees can be seen; all symbols of love, suggesting that this was a betrothal portrait. Hals has captured the moment brilliantly. Is he a lover thinking of his fiancée or, as a five-year-old once observed, has he got a tasty sweet in his mouth? Is he just confident, swaggering, and glad to be alive, observing us with a twinkle in his eye? The turned body allows a good view of the finery of his clothes, depicted by Hals with amazing technique using bravura brushstrokes on the ruff, scribbles of black paint on the sash, the delicate rendering of lace on the cuffs, and bold highlights on the embroidered motifs. In financial difficulty most of his life, Hals rapidly faded into obscurity after his death. His reputation was not re-established until 1865, when the Marquis of Hertford outbid Baron Rothschild for *The Laughing Cavalier* at auction. This was a milestone in the revival of Hals's reputation, particularly among the Impressionists. **EB**

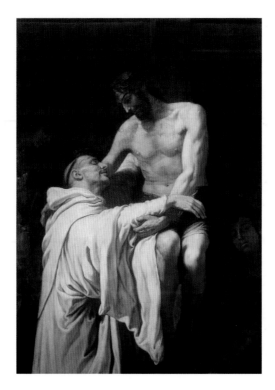

Christ Embracing St. Bernard | Francisco Ribalta

1625–27 | oil on canvas | 62 ¼ x 44 ½ in / 158 x 113 cm | Museo del Prado, Madrid, Spain

Spanish painter Francisco Ribalta (1565–1628) reached the pinnacle of his mature style with *Christ Embracing St. Bernard*—and transformed the Spanish Baroque in the process. A pioneer in discarding Mannerist conventions for a new type of naturalism, in doing so, Valencia's leading artist set a course for Spanish art that paved the way for masters such as Velázquez, Zurbarán, and Ribera. With its virile realism, *Christ Embracing St. Bernard* achieves a synthesis of naturalism and religiosity that defined the art of the seventeenth-century Counter Reformation. Playing off rapturous limpness against divine strength, and the human against the transcendent, the painting shows both a scene of devout piety and of distinctly human interaction. The corporality of Christ's body

(descended from the cross), as well as the careful attention to the draping of St. Bernard's habit (juxtaposed with the taut and suspended body of Christ), give a sense of intimacy and weighty presence to a mystical vision. In its introspective and expressive depiction of deep religious experience, the painting proposes a redemptive vision of mankind. The sculptural modeling and dramatic *chiaroscuro* that define the two figures—against a stark background in which two others are barely visible—recall Italian tenebrists such as Caravaggio. Although it is uncertain whether Ribalta ever visited Italy, the painting reflects many of the features of the Italian Baroque, and is most likely drawn from a replica of a Caravaggio altarpiece Ribalta is known to have copied. **JR**

Lomellini Portrait | Anthony van Dyck

1626–27 | oil on canvas | 106 x 100 in / 269 x 254 cm | National Gallery of Scotland, Edinburgh, UK

As a young artist, Sir Anthony van Dyck (1599–1641) spent six years in Italy. He traveled extensively, but returned mainly to Genoa, where he found a ready market among the local aristocracy for his sumptuous full-length portraits. This is the most grand and ambitious of Van Dyck's Italian works, and is also one of the most unusual. It depicts the family of Giacomo Lomellini, Doge of Genoa from 1625 to 1627. As a Genoese tradition forbade portraits of the Doge while in office, in order to prevent personal propaganda, he is absent here. The two young men at the left have been identified as Giacomo's sons born to his first wife, Nicolò. The elder one, in armor, holds a broken staff, probably referring to Giacomo's defense of the Republic against its bellicose neighbor, the Duchy of

Savoy. To their left are the Doge's second wife, Barbara Spinola, and their children Vittoria and Agostino. A classical statue of the Venus Pudica, the chaste protector of the family, underlines the theme. The picture can, therefore, be read as the defense both of the Republic and the home. Despite the grand setting, with its massive columns, rich carpet, and imposing drapery, this is hardly a stiff family grouping. Gestures and poses project a strong sense of character for each individual, from the proud, defensive stance of the oldest son to the tender, protective gesture of the mother. Van Dyck had a particular gift for portraying children, which is evident here. The youngest boy pouts with impatience, while his sister is obediently still in her sumptuous orange silk dress. **EG**

Two Old Men Disputing | Rembrandt van Rijn

1628 | oil on panel | 29 x 23 ½ in / 72 x 60 cm | National Gallery of Victoria, Melbourne, Australia

Narrative painting comes into its own with Rembrandt van Rijn (1606–69), who excels at conveying a moment in an ongoing sequence of events. This painting is also a gripping study of old age, a subject that Rembrandt returned to in his later self-portraits. It has been known by different titles over the years, but one more than plausible interpretation is that the subjects of the narrative are the apostles Peter and Paul who are disputing a point in the bible, which may have a specific theological significance in the context of Protestantism in the Netherlands at that time. The light strikes Paul's face as he points at a page in the bible, while the obdurate Peter is in darkness. Seated like a rock, as Jesus had described him ("Thou art Peter; and upon this rock I will build my church." Matthew 16:18) he listens attentively to Paul. But his fingers mark a page in the huge bible on his lap, suggesting that he has another point to make as soon as Paul stops speaking. In this way, Rembrandt suggests the continuation of time. The contrasting light in this painting reveals the Dutch master at his most Caravaggesque. Rembrandt uses it not only to delineate form, but also to suggest the character of each man. Paul, in the light of reason, is learned and rational. (Rembrandt identified with Paul so closely that, in 1661, he painted himself as the saint.) Peter in the shadow, bullish and headstrong, thinks intuitively. It is astonishing that at the tender age of twenty-two Rembrandt was able to paint these old men with such penetrating psychological insight. **WO**

The Arcadian Shepherds | Nicolas Poussin

1628–29 | oil on canvas | 39 ¾ x 32 ¼ in / 101 x 82 cm | Chatsworth House, Derbyshire, UK

During the seventeenth century certain artists sought to emulate classical precedent, specifically antique sculptures, in order to engender what might be considered a new form of classicism. Perhaps the artist most closely associated with this period in painting's history is Frenchman Nicolas Poussin (1594–1665). The esteem with which Poussin is held partly resides in his elevated intellectual status. As a "philosopher-painter," Poussin was keen to instill his painting with a classical ideal rooted as it was in Greek and Roman antiquity. *The Arcadian Shepherds*, painted around 1628–29 depicts three shepherds and possibly a shepherdess (although her style of dress may in fact denote a different status) gathered around a tomb. Etched into the stone are the words

Et in Arcadia Ego, which translates as "I too once lived in Arcadia." The concept of Arcadia originated in the Latin poetry of Virgil's fifth Eclogues and subsequently became a prevalent theme within both Renaissance and Baroque poetry. For Virgil and the poets who came after him, Arcadia was seen as an idyllic land, blissful and bucolic. The treatment of the figures is at one with the surrounding landscape; both are classical, restrained, idealized, and harmonious. By portraying the figures such that they take up the best part of the foreground, Poussin ensures our attention is fixed upon their discovery, namely that death is omnipresent. The skull resting on the top of the tomb further impresses upon the figures gathered around it the fate that will eventually befall everyone. **CS**

A Boy with a Violin | Frans Hals

1625–30 | oil on panel | 7 x 7 ½ in / 18.4 x 18.8 cm | Private collection

The Impressionists may have claimed to have invented the technique of painting unromanticized life in the 1870s, but with the exception of Degas's drawings and watercolors of life in the brothel where he lived, they never came near to capturing the seedy, grimy underbelly of life with the power and empathy of Frans Hals. Hals (1582–1666) was born in Antwerp before the Thirty Years' War. He learned to paint from Flemish master Karel van Mander, but his style bore little resemblance to Mander's. By 1616, he had become known in Haarlem through his life-size group portrait, *The Banquet of the Officers of the St. George Militia Company*. Early in his career he was known to drink heavily and surround himself with prostitutes, gamblers, thieves, and other people of "ill repute." Hals

reached his peak during the 1620s and 30s, the period when he painted *A Boy with a Violin*. The spontaneous, pathos-ridden expression of the boy, peering up from his violin with a mixture of both hope and fear, appears caught in motion. This is emphasized even more by the bold brushstrokes and daring diagonal angle of the figure in relation to the canvas. These qualities exemplify what made his portraits so dynamic and appealing to his contemporaries, and later to the Impressionists, who revived his reputation. Though he remained a successful, sought-after painter, art dealer, and restorer his entire life, and even rose to become chairman of the Painters Corporation at Haarlem, he was left destitute by 1664. He died in 1666 and was buried in the city's St. Bavo's Church. **AH**

Minerva Protects Pax from Mars | Peter Paul Rubens

1629–30 | oil on canvas | 80 ⅛ x 117 ⅜ in / 203.5 x 298 cm | National Gallery, London, UK

Artist Peter Paul Rubens (1577–1640) also enjoyed a considerable career as a diplomat. Between 1621 and 1630, the Spanish Hapsburg rulers entrusted Rubens with a number of diplomatic missions. Rubens almost certainly executed this work in London, where he attempted to negotiate peace between England and Spain. This painting (also known as *Peace and War*), full of Rubens's voluptuous nudes, rich colors, and lively movement, is actually a political allegory. At the center of the painting is Pax (Peace), who squeezes milk from her full breast to feed a child, usually identified as Plutus, the god of wealth. To the right of Pax is Minerva, the goddess of wisdom. She protects Pax from Mars, the god of war, and Alecto, the fury of war. In the right foreground, two young girls are led forward by a winged cupid and the goddess of marriage, Hymen. The children, the fruit of marriage, are offered a cornucopia, or horn of plenty. This is held up by a satyr, one of the entourage of Bacchus, the god of wine and fertility. From the left, two young women enter: one holds an armload of riches, while the other dances to the beat of a tambourine. A winged angel hovering in the air holds an olive wreath, the symbol of peace, and the caduceus of Mercury, messenger to the gods. This picture may be crowded with allegorical figures, but its meaning is obvious—peace brings prosperity, wealth, bountiful harvests, and a happy family life. Rubens presented the painting to Charles I of England, presumably in the hope that his vision of peace would be achieved. **EG**

A Game of Tric-Trac | Judith Leyster

c.1630 | oil on panel | 16 ⅛ x 12 ¼ in / 41 x 31 cm | Worcester Art Museum, Worcester, MA, USA

Judith Leyster (1609–60) was a master of Holland's Golden Age. Born the eighth child of a local brewer and clothmaker in Haarlem, she became the only woman painter from her era who is believed to have played an active role in the public art market when private collectors began replacing the Church as patrons of the arts. Her vivid paintings of candid, often slightly bawdy everyday activities, such as drinking and idle pursuits including games of backgammon (then known as tric-trac), were popular among private clients. By 1633, she was a member of the Haarlem Guild of St. Luke, whose only other female member was a house painter. Within two years of her entry into the guild, she had three male apprentices. Legal records show that she sued Dutch artist Frans Hals (c.1582–1666) for stealing a student from her workshop. In A Game of Tric-Trac, Leyster situates the viewer as if he or she were approaching the table with the intention of joining the players. The woman at the table, who may have been a courtesan, offers a clay smoking pipe and glass of red wine to the man seated in the foreground, who instead leers wantonly at the viewer. Leyster's masterful use of candlelight spotlights the various "vices" and heightens the painting's sense of enclosure, intimacy, and seduction. Her obvious ease in this environment puts her demonstrably on a par with her male contemporaries. Sadly, Leyster's artistic output dramatically diminished after her marriage to the lesser known Haarlem painter Jan Miense Molenaer. **AH**

Portrait of Archimedes
José de Ribera

1630 | oil on canvas | 49 ¼ x 31 ⅞ in / 125 x 81 cm
Museo del Prado, Madrid, Spain

This striking portrait by Spaniard José (Jusepe) de Ribera (1591–1652) shows the influence of Caravaggio on Ribera's early career. Archimedes emerges from rich, dark shadow, as dramatic spotlights—in the manner of Caravaggio—highlight certain areas. Ribera's toothless Archimedes has a wrinkled face and gaunt frame. The way he grasps papers in one hand and a compass in the other tells us he is a man of learning but also emphasizes his bony fingers with their dirty nails. The great man looks less like a revered scholar and more like an impoverished old man from a contemporary Spanish village. Ribera painted a series of eminent scholars in this way, in a bold move away from the accepted artistic traditions that favored painting important people in an idealized and heroic classical style. There is harsh detail in this picture, but this is a man with a personality, and not an aloof icon. **AK**

The Rejected Offer
Judith Leyster

1631 | oil on panel | 12 ¼ x 9 ½ in / 31 x 24 cm
Mauritshuis, The Hague, Netherlands

Judith Leyster (1609–60) is one of the few Dutch female artists of the period to have made a living from her art. Working in Haarlem, she specialized in genre scenes. In this painting, also known as *The Proposition*, a young woman is seated in a dark room, mending clothes by the light of an oil lamp. She sits by a table, warmed by the glowing coals of a footwarmer. A man wearing a fur cap touches her shoulder, trying to attract her attention. In one hand he holds a pile of coins, perhaps offering her money in return for her affection. The painting's theme is ambiguous; it has been interpreted as an improper proposition, a subject that was popular in seventeenth-century Dutch art. Yet the woman in the painting bears no resemblance to a prostitute and does not respond to the man's gesture. The psychological tension between the man and woman is heightened by the dramatic lighting. **EG**

Christ on the Cross
Diego Velázquez

c.1632 | oil on canvas | 98 ³/₈ x 66 ⁷/₈ in / 250 x 170 cm
Museo del Prado, Madrid, Spain

Diego Velázquez (1599–1660) produced few religious works, but this intensely powerful image is his finest. This is a convincingly real study of a man's body, but with hints of a more monumental sculptural quality that raises it to a higher plane, in keeping with the spiritual subject matter. The composition is starkly simple yet dramatic, with the contrast of the white body against a dark background echoing the work of Caravaggio, whom Velázquez had admired greatly as a young man. There is a realistic naturalism in the way that Christ's head falls on his chest, his matted hair partly obscuring his face and painted with the looseness that Velázquez admired in the Venetian masters, especially Titian. This work offers a religious subject dealt with in a highly original way: a real character shown in a natural pose, with a pared down composition that concentrates solely on the subject. **AK**

Khusraw Kills a Lion with His
Bare Hands | Riza-i Abbasi

1632 | ink, gold, and pigment on paper | 18 x 13 in / 44 x 34 cm | Victoria & Albert Museum, London, UK

Khusraw Kills a Lion with His Bare Hands was executed by, or under the direction of, Riza-i Abbasi (also known as Reza Abbasi; 1565–1635), the greatest Iranian painter and calligrapher of the Isfahan School, which flourished under Abbas I, Shah of Iran. This painting once illustrated a copy of the *Khamsa* (Five Poems), by the twelfth-century Persian poet Nizami, which included the narrative poem *Khusraw and Shirin*. The poem tells of the love between the sixth-century King of Persia Khusraw II and his Armenian princess, Shirin. Mounted with nineteenth-century borders, this miniature depicts one of the king's several adventures, in which Khusraw, dressed in his nightclothes and watched by two servants, strikes a lion prowling outside Shirin's tent to protect the princess. Riza-i Abbasi's skill can be seen in detailed facial expressions and the intricacy of the architectural design. **AS**

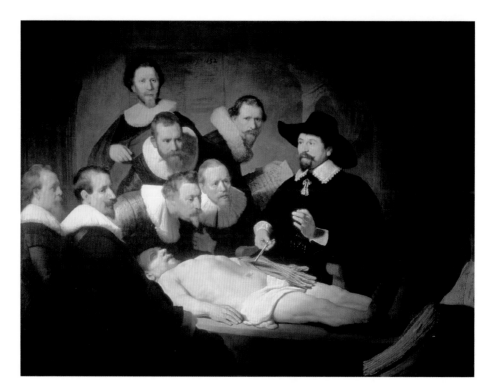

Anatomy Lesson of Dr. Nicolaes Tulp | Rembrandt van Rijn

1632 | oil on canvas | 66 ¾ x 85 ¼ in / 169.5 x 216.5 cm | Mauritshuis, The Hague, Netherlands

In January 1632 the Amsterdam anatomist and lecturer Dr. Nicolaes Tulp performed his second public autopsy in front of seven members of the Guild of Surgeons. Rembrandt van Rijn (1606–69) was still a young man when he received this important commission from the guild and it was his first group portrait. The subject of the dissection and center of focus is a common criminal. The arrangement of the six heads on the left form an arrow pointing to Tulp's right hand. The seventh man holds a list of the participants and links Tulp to the group compositionally. Rembrandt chose the moment when Dr. Tulp dissected the forearm of the corpse to illustrate the muscle structure. The painting is anatomically incorrect, but Rembrandt focuses instead on displaying psychological intensity. The eager inquisitiveness of the onlookers is striking, as is their proximity to the corpse given the stench that must have accompanied such dissections. Rembrandt's use of *chiaroscuro* is often compared to Caravaggio although it is unlikely that Rembrandt had seen a painting by him. He probably learned the technique through Dutch artists who had visited Italy and had been influenced by Caravaggio. The staged nature of this painting suggests public dissections were considered "performances." There is also a moral message connecting criminality and sin to dissection, and an implicit warning that death awaits everyone. In 1656 Rembrandt was commissioned to paint another dissection and firmly established this genre. **WO**

Still Life with Lemons, Oranges and a Rose | Francisco de Zurbarán

1633 | oil on canvas | 24 ½ x 43 ⅛ in / 62.2 x 109.5 cm | Norton Simon Museum, Pasadena, CA, USA

The Spanish artist Francisco de Zurbarán (1598–1664) is best known for his numerous paintings of saints; nonetheless, although this is his only signed and dated still-life painting, this simple image is now acknowledged as one of his masterpieces. The viewer is presented with a symmetrical arrangement of domestic wares: a silver plate with four lemons, a wicker basket filled with oranges, and a silver saucer on which rests a cup of water and a pink rose. Everything is aligned along a table's edge, which is at the foreground of the picture plane and tantalizingly close to the viewer's touch. This is an extraordinarily still and silent image; no air is felt rustling the leaves and petals of the blossom branch, no ripple is seen across the water's surface in the cup. With the exception of sound, all of our senses are awakened. Standing in front of this image it is easy to imagine the smell of the orange blossom and pink rose, the taste of the sour lemons and sweet oranges, and the feel of the cold hard surface of the metal dishes alongside the rough texture of the wicker basket. The soft yellows, oranges, pinks, and greens of the natural forms cannot help but entice, as does the strange, strict order of this geometrical arrangement. The stark austerity and humility of this image has led to the interpretation that it is a painting of religious symbols and especially of the Virgin Mary. The lemons are a fruit associated with Easter, orange blossom suggests chastity, the water-filled cup is a symbol of purity, and the rose is an allusion to the Virgin. **AB**

The Crossing of the Red Sea | Nicolas Poussin

c.1634 | oil on canvas | 60 ½ x 32 ¼ in / 154 x 210 cm | National Gallery of Victoria, Melbourne, Australia

While stylistically Nicolas Poussin's (1594–1665) early work is recognizable through the influence of Raphael and classical statuary, and was often based upon a literary theme, the latter canvases realized by the artist derive from biblical narratives. Originally *The Crossing of the Red Sea* was conceived along with *The Adoration of the Golden Calf* as constituting a complementary pair. (Both were first recorded as being in the collection of Amadeo dal Pozzo, the cousin of Cassiano dal Pozzo, who later became the artist's most important patron.) In this canvas, various figures are seen emerging from the water that, having parted, allows the "children of Israel" to cross the Red Sea. Compositionally, this is perhaps one of Poussin's most ambitious canvases and demonstrates his skill in organizing what is, in effect, a tumultuous scene. The energy and heightened sense of drama of the work is primarily carried through the expression of the various figures that occupy the foreground of the frame. Unlike Poussin's earlier compositions, which conveyed a sense of tranquillity, and often only depicted a lone figure almost dwarfed by the pastoral landscape they inhabited, *The Crossing of the Red Sea* relinquishes such luxury in favor of dramatic gravitas. Utilizing almost every square inch of canvas in order to convey the moment when the Red Sea parted, the strained almost contorted poses some of the figures adopt, along with the gesturing of Moses toward the heavens, forcefully conveys the magnitude and dramatic sweep of the event as it unfolds. **CS**

The Fortune Teller | Georges de la Tour

c.1632–35 | oil on canvas | 40 x 49 in / 102 x 123.5 cm | Metropolitan Museum of Art, New York, NY, USA

Georges de la Tour (1593–1652) appears to have traveled little, but he was from a wealthy middle-class family with good connections and his reputation spread. He managed to secure an important patron, the Duc de Lorraine and, in the late 1630s, he came to the notice of King Louis XIII. The king was so impressed that it was said he insisted a painting by La Tour be the only one to be hung in his bedchamber, reputedly having all previous paintings removed. In 1639, the painter was ordered to Paris, where the king paid him 1,000 francs and gave him the title of "Sir Georges de la Tour, painter to the King." Although many of La Tour's works have been lost, it seems that his religious works tend to contain fewer and more detailed figures (usually just one or two people), whereas his morality

pictures, such as *The Fortune Teller*, tend to be more crowded. In this painting, a fashionably dressed young man adopts an arrogant stance, paying so much attention to the fortune teller that he fails to notice his pockets being picked by her three assistants. The fortune teller is almost a caricature in her ugliness and her client has an expression of compelled revulsion on his face, leading him to be blind to the young thieves around him. He may also be distracted by the suggestion of eroticism in the eyes of the pretty young woman standing between him and the old woman, and may even think he is about to be rewarded in more ways than one. La Tour painted several similar cautionary tales of young men being cheated, often at cards. **AK**

The Surrender of Breda | Diego Velázquez

1634–35 | oil on canvas | 120 ⅞ x 144 ½ in / 307 x 367 cm | Museo del Prado, Madrid, Spain

As court painter to King Philip IV of Spain for most of his life, Diego Velázquez's (1599–1660) output focused predominantly on portraits. With *The Surrender of Breda*, however, his only surviving historical painting, he created a masterpiece considered to be one of the finest historical paintings of the Spanish Baroque. This picture depicts one of the major events of the Thirty Years' War, the Spanish capture of the strategically important Dutch city of Breda, in 1625. The Dutch commander is handing over the city key to the famed Spanish general, Ambrogio Spinola. Velázquez painted this after his return from Italy, a trip inspired partly by his friendship with the Flemish Baroque artist, Rubens. Painted to adorn the throne room of King Philip's Buen Retiro palace, as part of a series of images showing Spanish military triumphs, there is a directness and natural quality that is typical of Velázquez's work. Although the composition was diligently devised—and in fact resembles the work of Rubens—it gives a sense of being in the center of a very real, human drama. Soldiers look in various directions and the foreground horse is trotting away from the viewer. The artist abandons detail to create realism, showing the main protagonists with lifelike accuracy, while leaving nameless troops more sketchy. The natural lighting and broad brushwork were undoubtedly influenced by Italian masters. It is easy to see from this picture why Velázquez became a favorite of the Impressionists and this image retains its potency today. **AK**

Interior of the St. Bavo Church, Haarlem | Pieter Jansz Saenredam

1636 | oil on panel | 16 ⁷/₈ x 14 ⁵/₈ in / 43 x 37 cm | E. G. Bührle Collection, Zürich, Switzerland

The Thirty Years' War of 1618 to 1648 fought a cross Europe signaled the decline of the Holy Roman Empire and saw Catholic churches stripped of their ornament to reveal pale, austere interiors. Pieter Jansz Saenredam (1597–1665) traveled extensively through the Netherlands making precise and accurate drawings documenting the interiors of numerous churches. The church of St. Bavo, where Saenredam would eventually be buried, was one that he painted frequently. Saenredam was acquainted with the architect Jacob van Campen (1595–1657), and it is thought that the artist learned the techniques of architectural drawing from him. Saenredam would make drawings on site, which would then be worked into full-size, mathematically accurate construction drawings in the studio. Often the actual paintings were begun years after the initial drawings were made. Though his work was fundamentally true, he would on occasion, and especially in the latter part of his career, stretch his perspectives to exaggerate the height and magnitude of the interiors for pictorial effect. In *Interior of the St. Bavo Church, Haarlem,* the wide angle of the choir stalls and the towering height of the dome is greater than the eye can perceive from a single viewpoint. The whitewashed interior flooded with pale light is designed for reflection and contemplation, with human figures to emphasize the scale of the building. Saenredam's style was often copied but never truly emulated—his manipulation of space can be sensed in the Modern movement. **TP**

Lady Elizabeth Thimbleby and Dorothy, Viscountess Andover
Anthony van Dyck

1637 | oil on canvas | 52 x 59 in / 132 x 149 cm | National Gallery, London, UK

In England, Anthony van Dyck (1599–1641) fashioned a unique image of Charles I and his court. He transformed conventional English portraiture from highly formal presentations to extraordinarily relaxed and elegant images. In Van Dyck's hands, portraits became infinitely more lively, lighter in tone, and perfectly suited to the taste of the courtiers. They were to have an impact on many subsequent generations of painters, not only in the British Isles, but throughout Europe. This work was owned by the great British portraitist, Sir Peter Lely. Van Dyck was a master of the double portrait, and this is a particularly fine example. Lady Thimbleby and Viscountess Andover were the second and third daughters of Thomas, Viscount Savage. The painting might have been commissioned

to mark the wedding of the eldest daughter, Dorothy, in 1637. Dorothy appears here seated on the right, receiving roses from a cupid. The flowers are also an attribute of her namesake, Saint Dorothy. The poses of the sisters are both dignified and relaxed, and they are animated by the cupid, whose glowing red drapery provides a shimmering contrast to the sisters' elegant silks. The ladies' dress is highly fashionable—their pearls, hair, and the cut of their bodices are perfectly up-to-date. Yet there is a nonchalance about their costumes that lends them a classical appearance. Dorothy is not wearing a lace collar, exceptional for the time; her décolletage is unencumbered. It is for this reason that Van Dyck was known for introducing "timeless romance" to his sitters' attire. **EG**

The Bean King
Jacob Jordaens

c.1638 | oil on canvas | 63 x 84 in / 160 x 213 cm | State Hermitage Museum, St. Petersburg, Russia

Jacob Jordaens (1593–1678) was one of the most famous of the Flemish Baroque painters. He produced religious, mythological, and historical paintings, portraits and genre scenes, as well as monumental decorations. Unusually for a Flemish artist of his time, Jordaens did not visit Italy, but ran his own large, successful workshop in Antwerp, as well as working for Peter Paul Rubens and occasionally alongside Anthony van Dyck. In 1650 the artist adopted Calvinism, but continued to receive commissions from the Catholic Church. Jordaens's lively style was inspired by Rubens in its muscular figures and dynamic compositions and by Caravaggio in its strong contrasts of light and shade and affection for humble characters. This combination is particularly evident in Jordaens's genre paintings, which drew on subject matter from fables, proverbs, and folk tales. In *The Bean King* he presents an animated scene with humorous touches. The subject of the painting is one to which Jordaens returned many times. A raucous company celebrates the feast of Epiphany—January 6. According to Flemish tradition, friends and family gathered to eat, drink, sing, and make merry. A bean was hidden in a large cake and whoever found it became "the Bean King" and presided over the festivities. Other guests played supporting roles, including the queen (the only female part), the carver, the cupbearer, the jester, and so on. This painting portrays the moment when the king raises his glass and the whole company shouts, "The king drinks!" **EG**

Equestrian Portrait of Charles I
Anthony van Dyck

1637–38 | oil on canvas | 144 ½ x 115 in /
367 x 292.1 cm | National Gallery, London, UK

In 1632 the Flemish master Sir Anthony van Dyck (1599–1641) moved to London, where he became court painter to King Charles I. Van Dyck created an extraordinary group of portraits that has shaped our image of the Stuart court. Here Charles I sits astride a huge steed, dressed in a suit of Greenwich armor. On a chain, he wears a gold medallion with the likeness of St. George, which identifies Charles I as Garter Sovereign. An equerry stands behind him, holding his helmet topped with a magnificent set of plumes. This portrait probably dates to just before the outbreak of the Civil War, which led to the king's execution in 1649. Van Dyck has cast the king in the role of a supreme commander, in full control of his horse, his knights, and his country. More than just a grand portrait, this work functions as royal propaganda, proudly asserting Charles's belief in Divine Kingship. **EG**

St. Joseph the Carpenter
Georges de la Tour

1635–40 | oil on canvas | 54 x 40 in /
137 x 101 cm | Louvre, Paris, France

The story of the life and works of Georges de la Tour (1593–1652) is patchy. Although he enjoyed success in his own lifetime, La Tour was forgotten for several centuries—his work was rediscovered at the start of the twentieth century. A French painter, it is often claimed he was influenced by the paintings of Caravaggio. However, it may be that La Tour did not know Caravaggio's work, and that he independently explored the effects of shadow and light cast by a single candle. A devout Roman Catholic, La Tour often painted religious scenes. He returned several times to the theme of Mary Magdalene's repentance as well as painting this touching scene of Joseph teaching Jesus in the carpenter's shop. The style is realistic, detailed, and carefully planned—Jesus holds the candle because, in Christian belief, he is the light of the world illuminating the darkness of the world. **LH**

Hélène Fourment in a Fur Wrap
Peter Paul Rubens

1635–40 | oil on canvas | 69 x 33 in / 176 x 83 cm
Kunsthistorisches Museum, Vienna, Austria

This remarkable portrait captures Sir Peter Paul Rubens's (1577–1640) second wife, Hélène Fourment in what seems to be a private moment. She stands wearing nothing but a fur cloak and white chemise. Although this portrait has the spontaneity of a modern snapshot, it was in fact meant to cast Hélène in a mythological role as Venus. Rubens drew on a combination of classical sources for Venus's pose and setting. The fountain in the shape of a lion in the background refers to traditional images of Venus standing by a fountain or urn. The pose is derived from that of the Medici Venus, or Venus Pudica. Rubens also made a deliberate nod to Venetian painting. Rubens's erudite references did not hamper him from producing an intensely alive painting that communicates Hélène's sensuality and warmth. It also depicts a very real body, in all its glory. **EG**

Shah Jahan with Birds
of Paradise | Balchand

c.1640 | watercolor on paper | 9 ⅝ x 6 ⅜ in
Victoria & Albert Museum, London, UK

It was under the emperor Shah Jahan—famously responsible for building the Taj Mahal—that the refined Mughal style of painting truly came into its own. The emperor, who reigned 1628–58, was a great supporter of the arts. Paintings of this period were characterized by their ornate quality and lavish details, and formed a bridge between realism and lush idealism. They were brilliantly colored and highly patterned, and depicted a utopian paradise that implied this was the reality of Shah Jahan's empire. Balchand (c.1596–1640) was a popular miniature painter who had a long career. His work was based on realistic interpretations of what he saw, and as such the emperor is clearly recognizable here. This is an exquisite image typical of the artist's style, and shows his interest in tiny details, creating a flattering depiction of the elegant emperor. **TP**

Anne of Austria with Her Son Louis XIV | Unknown

c.1640 | oil on canvas | 47 x 38 in / 120 x 96.5 cm | Château de Versailles, Versailles, France

Louis XIV (1638–1715) was born when his parents, Louis XIII of France and Anne of Austria had been childless for twenty-three years. He acceded to the French throne in 1643, just before his fifth birthday, and ruled France for seventy-two years, the longest reign of any European monarch before or since. Dubbed "The Sun King," he was an absolute monarch who ruled from his palace at Versailles, and was a great patron of the arts and culture. The Baroque style, which reached its zenith under Louis XIV's patronage, dominated European painting in the seventeenth century. Baroque art is ornate, elaborate, decorative, and richly colored with a love of obvious symbolic detail. In *Anne of Austria with Her Son Louis XIV*, Louis is a very small child and has not yet acceded to the

throne. Anne has recently given birth to his brother Philippe d'Anjou (later Philippe I, Duc d'Orléans). The rich red and gold drapery and sumptuous furniture are typically Baroque, but the tone is subdued. Anne's pride in her son is palpable as she tenderly holds his hands to steady him. The dramatic emotion so typical of Baroque art has been put aside in favor of the simple bond between mother and child. Louis's lavish costume in "Spanish" style may refer to Anne's father Philip III of Spain. Around 1643 the artist Charles Beaubrun (1604–92) painted Louis and his brother with Louis in an identical costume. Beaubrun painted Anne of Austria several times, and the rendering of the hands and face is similar. The artist probably came from the same school of painting. **MC**

Self-Portrait at the Age of 34 | Rembrandt van Rijn

1640 | oil on canvas | 40 ⅛ x 31 ½ in / 102 x 80 cm | National Gallery, London, UK

Rembrandt van Rijn (1606–69) bought a large house in 1639, which precipitated later serious financial problems in spite of the fact that he was the most successful painter in Amsterdam. This portrait shows a man still young, at the height of his powers, consciously drawing a comparison between himself and Dürer in his self-portrait of 1498. It is a declaration of having arrived at prominence as well as a demonstration of Rembrandt's knowledge of Italian art. He had not visited Italy but knew and admired two portraits in particular, Raphael's *Portrait of Baldassare Castiglione* (1514–15), and Titian's *A Portrait of a Man* (1510). An etching of the previous year shows that he had been thinking of this type of composition for some time. His arm rests on a stone balustrade and he turns toward the viewer. Despite the fact that he wants to impress—with his references to other masters—it is an honest representation. He is plump and pasty-faced with a wispy mustache and unkempt beard. There is though, a dignified air of seriousness enhanced by the furrow between the brows, and the clothes, although expensive, have none of the flamboyance of the sitter's clothes in the Titian—that famous blue sleeve that falls over the sill into our space. Some of the many Rembrandt self-portraits in existence (estimates include fifty oil paintings, thirty or more etchings, and countless drawings) show him in costume, playing with identities, but here there is a hint of the brutal self-scrutiny that he would subject himself to in the later portraits. **WO**

A Dance to the Music of Time | Nicolas Poussin

1640 | oil on canvas | 33 ³/₈ x 42 ³/₈ in / 84.8 x 107.6 cm | Wallace Collection, London, UK

The reputation of Nicolas Poussin (1594–1665) rests, to a certain extent, upon his classicist credentials, that is, as an artist who was concerned with maintaining a certain fidelity to the artistic and intellectual precedents that were set during Greek and Roman antiquity. An exquisite example of Poussin's classicism is this relatively small painting that was originally commissioned by Cardinal Giulo Respiglio, who later became Pope Clement IX. Within an idyllic setting, Poussin places four allegorical figures who respectively represent wealth, poverty, industry, and pleasure. Together they dance to the music played by the winged figure to the right of the foreground who is assumed to be Old Father Time. His presence acts as a sobering reminder that death is ever-present, and even accompanies us in the midst of such revelry and abandon. The theme of time is further elaborated by the two putti who frame the overall composition. While the putto on the right fixes his gaze upon an hourglass, the bubble-blowing infant on the left refers to the concept of *homo bulla*, or "man the bubble," symbolizing the emphemerality of life. Above the putto on the left is a sculpture representing Janus, the two-faced Roman god who looked toward the past and the future simultaneously. Above Apollo's retinue toward the top of the painting, the sun god holds a circle, representing eternity. The symmetrical pyramidal composition lends the overall scene a sense of harmony, stability, and balance—all aspects that underpin Poussin's highly classical sensibility. **CS**

Venus at Vulcan's Forge | Le Nain Brothers

1641 | oil on canvas | 59 x 46 ⅛ in / 150 x 117 cm | Musée St. Denis, Reims, France

The Le Nain brothers, Antoine (c.1598–1648), Louis (c.1600–48), and Mathieu (c.1607–77) worked together in Paris in the 1630s and 40s. Art historians no longer try to identify which brother was responsible for any given painting and they are now treated as a single artist. The Le Nains are famous for their realistic genre paintings showing scenes from rural life in the French provinces, but they also painted religious and mythological subjects. This striking work depicts Vulcan, the Roman god of fire and metalworking, as a village blacksmith. The story of the relationship between Venus, goddess of love, and her aging husband Vulcan was a well-known myth. Besotted with his glamorous wife and humiliated by her infidelities, Vulcan was a figure of fun. In this version, Venus is a Renaissance goddess who has strayed into the genre context of a lowly blacksmith's shop. The seated Vulcan looks suitably disarmed by her beauty, his hammer idly grounded while his workmen get on with their jobs. One of the workers in the background, silhouetted against the blaze of the forge, looks at Venus with an amused expression, presumably a silent comment upon the boss's marital difficulties. The treatment of Venus and her son Cupid may seem uninspired, but Vulcan and his workers are rendered with a naturalism that reveals great powers of observation. The light effects are exquisitely judged and the background figures in particular have the feel of a momentary gesture captured, centuries before photography made this commonplace. **RG**

The Clubfoot | José de Ribera

1642 | oil on canvas | 64 ⅝ x 37 in / 164 x 94 cm | Louvre, Paris, France

Few people could fail to be intrigued by this genre picture of an obviously disabled beggar from Naples looking at them cheekily with a toothy grin. Spanish-born José (Jusepe) de Ribera (1591–1652) spent most of his career in Naples, which was then controlled by Spain, and became the city's leading artist. He probably intended simply to portray a Neapolitan beggar boy, as he had a great interest in ordinary people. However, the way he has blended realism with tradition heralded a new direction in art. The boy in this mature painting is probably a dwarf, with a clubfoot (a birth defect that made walking difficult) and possibly deformed hands, who exists by begging. Life has not smiled upon him but he is cheerily defiant. He carries his crutch jauntily over his shoulder and

casually, rather than desperately, holds out the paper that gives him permission to beg—compulsory in Naples at that time—it reads in Latin: "Give me alms for the love of God." Rather than being shown crouching in a dirty side street, he stands tall against a serene landscape that recalls historical, mythological, and religious works painted in the classical style. Ribera gives him an impressive stature, made greater by the low viewpoint, and a humane dignity. His beggar could almost be a little prince. The loose brushwork becomes softer on the landscape, making the boy stand out even more. Ribera's ability to convey a sense of people's individuality with realism and humanity had a great impact on art, and on the Spanish School in particular. **AK**

The Night Watch | Rembrandt van Rijn

1642 | oil on canvas | 143 x 172 in / 363 x 437 cm | Rijksmuseum, Amsterdam, Netherlands

The Night Watch, originally known as *The Company of Frans Banning Cocq and Willem van Ruytenburch* (the painting's famous title was erroneously given to it due to its thick, dark yellow varnish), is ostensibly a genre scene out of the seventeenth-century Dutch Baroque. Painted in 1642, at the height of Rembrandt van Rijn's (1606–69) career, the colossal painting is a commissioned group portrait of a militia company. Such portraits traditionally depicted their members in neat rows or at a banquet. Rembrandt's version, however, makes the prosaic subject into a dynamic work of art; with its masterful *chiaroscuro* and dramatic action, the conventions of traditional portraiture are overturned. *The Night Watch* depicts the captain of the guard as he leads his yellow-clad lieutenant in rounding up the uniformed ranks. Only eighteen of the thirty-four characters in the scene are portraits; the remaining figures are symbolic, such as the young girl in yellow as the allegorical emblem of the guard. The brilliant illusionism and the sense of theatricality and movement in the painting are enforced by the choreography of gestures, glances, muskets, and banners, and by the building up of pigment in the foreground that flattens as the perspective recedes. The painting was originally even larger, but was cut down in the eighteenth century. By mixing charged symbolism and reality, action and allegory, Rembrandt takes a subject steeped in tradition and creates a masterpiece transcending time and genre. **JR**

The Interior of the Buurkerk at Utrecht | Pieter Saenredam

1644 | oil on wood | 23 x 19 in / 60 x 50 cm | National Gallery, London, UK

Pieter Jansz Saenredam (1597–1665) is believed to have trained with the history and portrait painter Frans Pietersz de Grebber in Haarlem, before being accepted into the Guild of St. Luke in 1623. Several years later he was commissioned to make illustrations detailing Haarlem's history, and it was at this point that he made his first drawing of a church interior. His fame rests on his distinctive paintings of church interiors that are characteristically cool and muted in tone and composed around soaring perspectives. Saenredam was the first celebrated artist to base his perspective on the methods used by architectural surveyors. He made meticulous, accurate drawings from which he composed his paintings. *The Interior of the Buurkerk at Utrecht* is taken from the right half of a drawing he

dated "16 August 1636," which is now in the Kimbell Art Museum, Fort Worth, Texas. The blond tonality of the painting is typical of his works and reflects the austere interiors of the strict Dutch Reform Church. Saenredam has taken his view from the north door, looking into the nave, and has focused on the lofty Gothic architecture in comparison to the diminutive figures. In the foreground a child draws on the wall, depicting a popular medieval tale of chivalry. A second child teaches a dog tricks—a Dutch symbol of obedience and learning. There is an abstract quality to Saenredam's work—the picture plane is formalized into blocks of space and white-blond color that would later influence the work of such modern masters as Piet Mondrian (1872–1944). **TP**

Self-Portrait as a Philosopher | Salvator Rosa

c.1645 | oil on canvas | 45 x 37 in / 116.3 x 94 cm | National Gallery, London, UK

Neapolitan Salvator Rosa (1615–73), painter and subject of this brooding portrait, was probably the first artist to assert the principle of painting only if inspired to do so—when "carried away by the power of his raptures." Many myths that once accumulated around Rosa's life have been dispelled by modern scholarship. He was, for example, never a brigand or a revolutionary as had previously been suggested. But his pose as a rebellious outsider at odds with society marked an important step in the evolution of the Romantic image of the artist. This is one of a number of self-portraits Rosa painted during a stay in Florence in the 1640s. An actor as well as a painter, he chose to portray himself in a series of theatrical dramatizations. The simple brown gown and black bonnet here cast him in the role of an impoverished student of philosophy. His right hand supports a plaque with a Latin inscription that roughly translates as "Be quiet, unless your speech be better than silence." The artist exemplifies this stoic tag with a tight-lipped pose, his brow furrowed as if in weighty thought. Half of his face is cast menacingly in shadow. His hair is long and wild, although he is clean-shaven—other self-portraits show him with mustache and beard. The backdrop of stormy sky hints at emotional turbulence. This is a thoroughly romantic and idealized self-portrait. Rosa presents himself as an isolated outcast, a stern and serious critic of the frivolities of society. There may be more outer show than inner truth to the image, but it makes for a dramatic canvas. **RG**

The Archery Contest | David Teniers the Younger

c.1645 | oil on wood | 21 ¼ x 34 ½ in / 54 x 88 cm | Museo del Prado, Madrid, Spain

The prolific Flemish artist David Teniers the Younger (1610–90) was trained by his father, and was influenced early in his career by Adriaen Brouwer, Adam Elsheimer, and Sir Peter Paul Rubens. Teniers became a master in the Antwerp Painters' Guild in 1632, and from 1645 to 1646 was made a dean—he went on to become court painter and keeper of the pictures for Archduke Leopold William, governor of the Netherlands. The artist painted a wide variety of subjects, but it is his genre scenes for which he remains most famous. Many of these depict domestic interiors with peasants engaged in various activities. However, he also painted a number of outdoor scenes and it is these, including *The Archery Contest*, that show him at his most effective and demonstrate his

accomplished treatment of light in landscape settings. Here he has used broad areas of flat color that reflect a golden haze as sun streaks down through the thick cloud cover. The painting evokes the sensation of a sudden lull sensed either before or after a heavy rainfall, and is richly atmospheric. The figures are frozen in motion—with the archer on the point of releasing his bow—and appear suspended in animation. The architectural features of the scene form a natural "stage" on which the archery takes place, emphasizing the spectator nature of the event. Teniers was widely celebrated as an artist in his day, and was one of the founding forces behind the establishment of the Brussels Academy of Fine Arts in 1663 and the Academy of Fine Arts in Antwerp. **TP**

Cavalry Making a Sortie from a Fort on a Hill | Philips Wouwermans

1646 | oil on canvas | 54 x 75 in / 139 x 190.5 cm | National Gallery, London, UK

Philips Wouwermans's (1619–68) paintings of camps, hawking, traveling parties, and military skirmishes such as this one were extremely popular, and by the time of his death he was a wealthy and highly respected man. At the age of nineteen he married a Catholic girl and fled to Hamburg to avoid his family's disapproval, but two years later he was back in his hometown of Haarlem, and lived and worked there for the rest of his life. He is thought to have trained with Frans Hals, though the two artists share few similarities, and Pieter van Laer, who had traveled to Italy and absorbed the Italianate treatment of light. Wouwermans's paintings are universally bathed in a pure, golden, translucent light, which adds to their particular aesthetic beauty. *Cavalry Making a Sortie* *from a Fort on a Hill* is typical of his military paintings, and it is a purely fictitious scene. He favored paintings with equestrian themes and included horses in almost all of his works. His great skill in depicting the horse clearly revealed a thorough understanding of anatomy. He painted using short, quick, and light brushstrokes with a delicate touch that would seem to anticipate the Rococo style. This particular painting is darker in color than was normal for the artist, but, despite the billowing smoke and somber tonality, he demonstrates his affinity for effect through the glowing shell of the burning castle. Wouwermans's paintings were greatly sought after in France during the eighteenth century, and have long been collected by the English monarchy and aristocracy. **TP**

The Bull
Paulus Potter

1647 | oil on canvas | 92 ¾ x 113 ⅜ in / 235.5 x 339 cm | Mauritshuis, The Hague, Netherlands

Despite the fact that Paulus Potter (1625–54) died at the age of twenty-eight, his work was both original and influential. From very early in his career, he concentrated on the depiction of animals, and was one of the first artists ever to depict them as subjects in their own right. Considered by many to be a quintessentially Dutch picture, this work elevates the humble subject of a bull to a heroic status. Painted when Potter was only twenty-one, it shows what appears to be an ordinary animal in a meadow, but on a monumental scale. The bull is accompanied by a cow, three sheep, and a farmer leaning on a willow tree. In spite of the large size of this work, Potter lavished attention on small details, such as a frog in the foreground, the carefully delineated plants, and the flies buzzing around the animals. In the far background is the spire of the church in Rijswijk, a town near The Hague. Although the painting was long assumed to depict an actual animal, Potter actually fabricated it from various studies of bulls of different ages. In general, it looks like a yearling, but has adult teeth, horns of a two-year-old, and a mature chest and dewlap below the neck. On closer examination, the bull's body is somewhat unbalanced, with slight, undeveloped hindquarters grafted onto a powerfully muscular neck, chest, and shoulders. Potter evidently selected the best of several studies in order to create a beast that literally improved on reality. Who commissioned this extraordinary work or where it was meant to hang remains a mystery. **EG**

Landscape with the Marriage of Isaac and Rebecca
Claude Lorraine

1648 | oil on canvas | 60 x 79 in / 152.3 x 200.6 cm | National Gallery, London, UK

A modern viewer, seeing this painting for the first time, might assume that the artist was simply continuing a long tradition of landscape painting. In fact, Claude Lorraine (known as Claude, 1600–82) was treading new ground in work such as this, becoming the father of the idealized landscape and of a whole new tradition of landscape painting. Nominally a biblical tale, but showing few signs of the Old Testament story, this picture's real star is the scenery, shown relatively realistically in a way that owes everything to Claude's endless sketching of his beloved Italian campagna—he lived in Rome for most of his life. Few painters had set their paintings in the Italian countryside unless it was to highlight classical ruins. Claude's breakthrough was in creating a special mood that exuded love of the landscape, with acutely observed outdoor color and light. The painting also contains very convincing portraits of clouds, of the way light plays across a landscape, and also of the way light rises up from the horizon toward the viewer, harmonizing the whole scene—which no artist had really shown before. The view is anchored and framed by trees that serve, along with strategically placed people, boats, buildings, and spurs of land, to lead the eye to the horizon. Claude's innovation lies in exploring mood, light, and color for their own sake, a major trend that continued through the Impressionists. His work also made him a founding force in the influential picturesque movement of the late eighteenth and early nineteenth centuries. **AK**

The Ashes of Phocion Collected by His Widow | Nicolas Poussin

1648 | oil on canvas | 45 ¾ x 70 ¼ in / 116.5 x 178.5 cm | Walker Art Gallery, Liverpool, UK

Nicolas Poussin (1594–1665) holds a canonical position within the tradition of seventeenth-century Western painting. His oeuvre is indebted to classical precedent. He was preoccupied with the legacy of Greek and Roman antiquity, and it was paramount for Poussin that his paintings embody a virtuous set of ideals discernable within certain characters and their exploits. It seems perfectly in keeping with Poussin's artistic sensibility that he should base two canvases on Phocion, the noble Athenian leader who was held in such high esteem by the stoic philosophers. *The Ashes of Phocion Collected by His Widow* is the second of the two Phocion landscapes and, as the title implies, depicts the widow of Phocion and a maidservant gathering the leader's ashes on the outskirts of Megara. Phocion, a statesman who lived during the fourth century BCE, was sentenced to death for what were seen to be political errors. Because a decree was passed banning the lighting of a funeral pyre preventing his cremation, his body was carried out of Athens to Megara where it was burned. Whereas the first of the two Phocion landscapes centers upon the very public grief of the slaves who bear Phocion's body out of Athens, the second is much more understated. In the foreground we see Phocion's widow discretely gathering the ashes, as if not wanting to draw attention to what she is doing. Overall, Poussin's treatment of the setting is remarkable for its pastoral splendor and treatment of nature as fecund, majesterial, and harmonious. **CS**

Gambling Scene at an Inn | David Teniers the Younger

*c.*1649 | oil on oak panel | 16 x 23 in / 40.2 x 57.9 cm | Wallace Collection, London, UK

David Teniers (1610–90) was born in Antwerp where he studied under his artist father. From a young age, he became more successful than his father and he soon attracted the patronage of prominent church officials and of the newly appointed governor of the southern Netherlands, Archduke Leopold Wilhelm, who made him court painter in Brussels and curator of his painting collection. After Wilhelm left, Teniers remained as court painter to the new governor, Don Juan of Austria, whom he taught to draw and paint. A genre painter from the start, Teniers painted local people enjoying life, especially the agricultural classes of Brabant and Holland. His villagers are natural and jolly. They drink, play cards, chat, and dance; but seldom quarrel or fight, and Teniers never seemed to tire of showing rustic merrymakings and joyous peasants. *Gambling Scene at an Inn* is sparkling with life and it demonstrates his mastery at grouping characters. Two men play cards at a table, watched by two other men and the innkeeper. In a recessed room in the background, four men are in deep discussion, while scattered around are objects and paraphernalia —a coat flung over a stool, a discarded shoe, and a stick. The work is fresh, bright, and technically precise, rendered in delicate brushwork. In his lifetime, Teniers produced more than nine hundred paintings. Few artists ever worked with greater ease and some of his smaller pictures have been termed "afternoons," because of the time he spent in producing them. His work was imitated by many followers. **SH**

Wooded River Landscape | Salomon van Ruysdael

*c.*1640–50 | oil on canvas | Private collection

Originally Salomon van Ruysdael's (*c.*1602–70) last name was De Goyer, but he and his brother Isaack changed it, taking Ruysdael from the name of a castle near their father's birthplace, Blaricum. As with many artists of his time, Ruysdael traveled extensively around his native Holland and drew on material from his travels to produce his finished compositions. Although born near Amsterdam, he spent most of his life working in the town of Haarlem, which was enjoying an economic and cultural boom based on expanding industries such as linen, tulip bulbs, and beer bringing in revenue that in turn afforded the burgeoning population money to spend on luxury goods such as art. Paintings would still be commissioned, but artists also worked speculatively,

painting works that would be put up for sale through dealers or sold privately. The scene in this painting, with prominent trees and a slowly gliding ferryboat, was one that Ruysdael returned to several times. During the 1640s and 50s he often used a tree motif as a grounding compositional element, drawing the eye in and across the scene and creating drama through the opposing verticals and horizontals. He became interested in the effects of light, especially light on water. The cows in the boat are gently emphasized by the gleaming river behind them, which is drenched in the mysterious glow of an ominous sky. Ruysdael's riverscape paintings were influential on a number of Dutch landscape artists, including the early works of his nephew Jacob van Ruisdael. **TP**

Dordrecht from the North | Aelbert Cuyp

1650 | oil on canvas | 26 ⁷⁄₈ x 75 ⁷⁄₈ in / 68.3 x 192.8 cm | Anthony de Rothschild Collection, Ascott, UK

During the seventeenth century there was a tremendous feeling of civic pride in the town of Dordrecht, considered to be the first and oldest established town in the Netherlands. Built between the convergence of a number of major inland waterways, including the Rhine, Merwede, and Maas, the town was ideally situated for waterborne trade. The artist Aelbert Cuyp (1620–91) lived in Dordrecht throughout his life, and his paintings are imbued with an affection for a town that saw the artist prosper and thrive. This large canvas depicts the town from the northeast at a point where several of the waterways converge. Characteristic of Cuyp, the water is still and mirror-calm with boats and buildings reflected and shimmering across the luminous surface. This was

a high traffic area, yet he has depicted boats of all shapes and sizes serenely passing by. An interesting detail is the inclusion in the middle ground of wooden rafts that were used for floating timber from Bavaria to Dordrecht to supply the thriving ship-building industry. These rafts were rarely depicted in paintings and Adam Willaerts (1577–1644) seems to be the only other artist to have done so. Cuyp's work was relatively slow to appear on international markets, not becoming popular with collectors until the late eighteenth century. However, once realized, his work had a profound effect on the development of landscape painting, especially on the work of J.M.W. Turner (1775–1851), Augustus Wall Callcott (1779–1844), and Richard Wilson (1713–82). **TP**

Portrait of Pope Innocent X
Diego Velázquez

1650 | oil on canvas | 55 ½ x 46 ⅞ in / 141 x 119 cm
Galleria Doria-Pamphilj, Vatican City, Italy

Woman Bathing in a Stream
Rembrandt van Rijn

1654 | oil on oak panel | 24 ⅜ x 18 ½ in /
61.8 x 47 cm | National Gallery, London, UK

Diego Velázquez (1599–1660) was the leading painter in the court of King Philip IV, renowned for his portraits of the Spanish royal family. A Realist, Velázquez focused on depicting the world around him, instead of creating elaborate allegorical images. The paintings are remarkable for their attention to the models' often unromanticized appearance. Velázquez painted this portrait of Pope Innocent X when the Pope was seventy-five. A remarkably vigorous man for his age, he was also known as exceptionally ugly, hot-tempered, and a workaholic. The color red dominates the composition. The pope is seated, wearing his sumptuous papal robes, in a red armchair, which highlights his ruddy complexion and fleshy cheeks. While faithfully reproducing his sitter's physical unattractiveness, Velázquez also captures his powerful bearing in his stern expression and piercing gaze. **AH**

Rembrandt van Rijn (1606–69) soaked up influences from the Italian Baroque through Dutch followers of Caravaggio. He painted this small oak panel in the year that his housekeeper Hendrickje Stoffels became his mistress, seven years after the death of his wife Saskia. The warmth and intimacy suggests that Hendrickje was the model. She is totally absorbed in the sensation of cold water on her legs and feet. Rembrandt worked with a limited palette on a dark brown background so that the image seems to emerge from dark to light. The brushstrokes are rapid and free, particularly in the crumpled linen, which makes a strong contrast with the smoother texture of the skin. The lighting is typically theatrical, illuminating the figure from the top left and just picking up the red robe on the bank. Yet paradoxically the viewer is not emotionally distanced from the figure. **WO**

Parental Admonition
Gerard Terborch

1654–55 | oil on canvas | 27 ½ x 23 ⅝ in / 70 x 60 cm
Staatliche Museen zu Berlin, Germany

Dutch painter Gerard Terborch (1617–81) painted mainly portraits and genre scenes, treating his subjects with a cultivated elegance and paying infinite attention to details, especially the texture of fabrics. *Parental Admonition* is particularly beautiful in its delicate handling of the figures. Here a young girl is being quietly told off by her father, while her mother looks away. It has been suggested that the painting depicts an exchange at a brothel, although the calm, refined atmosphere of the piece makes this setting seem unlikely. There is something sensuous in the girl's pose; little can be seen of her except for a glimpse of silver-rose skin at the back of her neck. Terborch's work was imbued with an elegant grace, his careful scenes shot through with rich and warm coloring and his virtuoso depiction of fabrics and textiles was virtually unequaled. **TP**

Flowers
Xiang Shengmo

1656 | ink and watercolor on paper | 12 x 9 in /
31 x 23.2 cm | Victoria & Albert Museum, London, UK

Xiang Shengmo (1597–1658) was born late in the Ming dynasty (1368–1644) which was a period of great achievement in Chinese literature and art. Xiang was a grandson of the famous Ming art expert and collector Xiang Yuanbian. Though Xiang never met his grandfather, he inherited his artistic talents and became an accomplished painter and poet. He was taught by the painting theorist Dong Qichang who passed on the first law of painting, which was to express the spirit of an object through accurate representation. In his series of four paintings of flowers, Xiang focused on a spray of flowers and explored the details that interested him. Each flower and leaf is observed and executed in a tidy, dainty fashion. The brushstrokes are well controlled and precise. *Flowers* is typical of Xiang's acute observation of the natural world and is a work of great grace and beauty. **HC**

Las Meninas | Diego Velázquez

1656 | oil on canvas | 126 x 108 ⅝ in / 320 x 276 cm | Museo del Prado, Madrid, Spain

Originally known as "The Family of Philip IV," *Las Meninas* shows Velázquez (*c*.1599–1660) late in his career and at the height of his highly impressive powers. Few works have excited more debate than *Las Meninas*. The size and subject matter place it in the dignified tradition of portraiture familiar to Velázquez's contemporaries. However, what, or who, is the subject? Velázquez shows himself at the easel in his studio in Madrid's Alcázar Palace, with the five-year-old Infanta Margarita and her entourage in the foreground, other courtiers elsewhere in the picture, and the King and Queen reflected in the mirror on the back wall. Is Velázquez painting the royal couple as they pose beyond the easel, or is he painting Margarita, who has been surprised by her parents'

entry into the room? The seemingly "casual" scene has been very carefully constructed using extensive knowledge of perspective, geometry, and visual illusion, to create a very real space, but one with an aura of mystery, where the spectator's viewpoint is an integral part of the painting. The artist shows how paintings can create all kinds of illusions while also showcasing the unique fluid brushwork of his later years. Just a series of daubs when viewed close up, his strokes coalesce into a richly vivid scene as the spectator pulls back. Often called "a painting about painting," *Las Meninas* has fascinated many artists, including French Impressionist Manet, who was especially drawn to Velázquez's brushwork, figures, and interplay of light and shade. **AK**

View of Deventer Seen from the North-West | Salomon van Ruysdael

1657 | oil on wood | 20 x 30 in / 51.8 x 76.5 cm | National Gallery, London, UK

Salomon van Ruysdael (c.1602–70) was born in Naarden, outside Amsterdam, but spent his entire life in the cosmopolitan town of Haarlem, where he became one of Haarlem's leading landscape artists. Though his training is unknown, his work in particular shows the influence of Esaias van de Velde (c.1591–1630), Peter Molijn (1595–1661), and Jan van Goyen (1596–1656). He is perhaps most famous for his spectacular depictions of inland waterways. His work is infused with a delicate translucent light and stillness that evokes a seemingly infinite air of pastoral calm. This view of Deventer is not topographically correct, but is still recognizable. Fishermen and sailing boats populate the river, viewed against the vast backdrop of Dutch sky. It is an impressive landscape that implies

the elegant sailing boats are on the point of embarking out to sea, whereas Deventer was actually some way inland. The town is seen in the distance across the River Ijssel, and the low horizon is punctuated by the belfry of the Grote Kerk creating a marked vertical against the sweeping horizontals and diagonals of the scene. During the early part of his career, Ruysdael painted genre scenes of travelers outside inns as well as sandy dune landscapes, and toward the end of his life turned to still-life depictions. It is his landscapes of quiet waterways and simple compositional form bathed in soft light from the middle of his career that remain the most influential however, and hold their place at the top of Dutch seventeenth-century landscape painting. **TP**

The Courtyard of a House in Delft | Pieter de Hooch

1658 | oil on canvas | 28 ⁷/₈ x 23 ⁵/₈ in / 73.5 x 60 cm | National Gallery, London, UK

Pieter de Hooch (1629–84) lived for a relatively short time in the city of Delft, but his work from this period remains largely his most famous. De Hooch trained with the landscape painter Nicolaes Berchem (1620–83), probably in Berchem's hometown of Haarlem, and is not recorded as being in Delft until August 1652. At this time Delft was blossoming as an artistic center and was nurturing a new genre of architectural painting, based largely on the innovative work of Gerard Houckgeest (c.1600–61), Emanuel de Witte (c.1617–92), and Hendrick van Vliet (c.1611–75). Although influenced to an extent by the soaring perspective dynamics of architectural works, De Hooch developed his own unique style, a synthesis of domestic interiors, courtyards, and gardens within a sharply honed architectural framework. He frequently painted scenes that detail the minutiae of ordinary Dutch life with an earthy realism. This is one of two paintings the artist made using the same architectural composition, which would suggest that the arched courtyard was taken from life, and indeed the tablet seen above the arch has survived, and been traced to the Hieronymusdael Cloister in Delft. *Courtyard* was one of two paintings that were sold at the prestigious P. de Smeth van Alphen sale in Amsterdam in 1810. From this point on, De Hooch's work became increasingly popular and influential. His influence has been far reaching from Hendrick van der Burch (c.1627–99) and Jan August Hendrick Baron Leys (1815–69) to Millet (1814–75) and Bonnington (1802–28). **TP**

Captain Job Jansz Cuyter and His Family | Nicolaes Maes

1659 | oil on canvas | 43 ½ x 60 in / 110.5 x 152.4 cm | North Carolina Museum of Art, Raleigh, NC, USA

This rather theatrical portrayal of a wealthy shipping merchant and his family is a relatively early portrait by Nicolaes Maes (1634–93), and it tells a rich artistic story. Painted just before Maes turned from a mix of genre, history, and portrait subjects to concentrate solely on portraiture, it shows elements from the gifted works of the first part of his career. Mixed in are certain Dutch portrait traditions, a hint of his great teacher, Rembrandt, and stirrings of a dramatic change toward a more personal, brighter style. Maes was born in Dordrecht, and he painted many portraits of the elite of this prosperous Dutch port. In this painting, Cuyter, his wife, and children are standing on a quay in Dordrecht harbor. Rolling dark skies recall the *chiaroscuro* effects of Rembrandt, and there is also

something of the rich, deep, reddish quality seen in Maes's early, Rembrandt-influenced genre pictures. Expertly handled details, such as the baby's wooden cart, show a genre-like approach, as does the sentimentality of depicting three deceased Cuyter offspring as cherubs in the clouds. The buildings, broad skies, and open water suggest the expansive designs of history painting, albeit with a naturalistically genre-like air. Maes's subjects adopt quite stiff, conventional poses and restrained expressions—true to the school of contemporary Dordrecht portraiture. However, Maes starts to break away from the school's somber palette, using paler reds and white. In later years, Maes was influenced by Van Dyck, and became a central figure of his age. **AK**

River Landscape with Horsemen and Peasants | Aelbert Cuyp

1658–60 | oil on canvas | 48 x 94 in / 123 x 241 cm | National Gallery, London, UK

Aelbert Cuyp's (1620–91) hometown, Dordrecht, was affluent and conservative with a burgeoning patrician class, of which Cuyp was a part. During his lifetime he became a respected pillar of Dordrecht's community, serving as a deacon and elder of the Dutch Reform Church, a member of the tribunal of Zuid Holland, and active within social and charitable circles. In 1658 he married Cornelia Boschman, a wealthy widow, after which point his artistic output seems to have slowed. The majority of his patrons were fellow Dordrecht residents and, as such, by the time of his death his artistic reputation seems to have been little known outside his immediate area. The artist never traveled to Italy, but was greatly influenced by the Italian-inspired works of Jan Both (c.1618–52)

and Cornelis van Poelenburch (1594–1667). As this painting masterfully demonstrates, Cuyp took the Italian idiom of the classical Arcadian landscape and infused it with his very Dutch realism to create the perfect combination of Dutch and Italian expression. *River Landscape*, which is widely regarded as the culmination of Dutch seventeenth-century landscape painting, is transfused with a clear golden light that has rarely been surpassed. It is on first glance a scene of utter tranquillity, but the detail of a hunter crouched in the foreground, gun poised, lends the composition an edge, a hint at the disturbance about to happen. Cuyp's work became influential on the development of a number of landscape painters, including J.M.W. Turner, Augustus Wall Callcott, and Fitz Hugh Lane. **TP**

Rubens Painting the Allegory of Peace | Luca Giordano

c.1660 | oil on canvas | 132 x 163 in / 337 x 414 cm | Museo del Prado, Madrid, Spain

Luca Giordano (1634–1705) was perhaps the most prolific of the seventeenth-century great masters, and was nicknamed "Luca Fà-presto," meaning "Luke Fast Work," a name thought to have derived from his father urging the boy on with financial gain in mind. Giordano's prodigious talent was discovered at a young age and he was subsequently sent to study first with José de Ribera (1591–1652) in Naples and then with Pietro da Cortona (1596–1669) in Rome. His work shows the influence of both these teachers, and also that of Paolo Veronese (c.1528–88), but he also developed his own expression using bright colors, and is reputed to have said that people were more attracted by color than by design. Giordano's flamboyantly Baroque style can be seen to great

effect here in this painting depicting Peter Paul Rubens (1577–1640) at work. The allegorical subject matter was one that was particularly popular at this time, and Giordano's inclusion of the venerated Rubens would have been widely praised. He has used a complicated structural composition with figures and cherubs massed together on the right side crowded into a small picture plane, from which they seem to burst forth. The white dove in the foreground forms a focal point, radiating energy and action to direct attention to the figure of Rubens in the rear. In 1687 Giordano moved to Spain where he was employed by the royal court for ten years. A wealthy man on his return to Naples in 1702, he donated large sums of money to the town. **TP**

The Slippers
Samuel van Hoogstraten

1654–62 | oil on canvas | 39 x 28 in / 100 x 71 cm
Louvre, Paris, France

Samuel van Hoogstraten (1627–78) was a skillful painter of portraits and interiors who was concerned with the correct use of perspective. *The Slippers* exemplifies the artist's characteristic use of Dutch tiled floors to accentuate the depth of the picture. This is emphasized by the distinct receding picture planes, marked by the frame of the picture, the door casings, and finally the two pictures at the back of the painting. By showing part of the open door in the foreground, the artist places the onlooker in the doorway, which heightens the illusory effect of the painting. Hoogstraten's subject is alluded to by the subtle details. The discarded broom, house slippers, and closed book (reading has been interrupted) indicate an amorous liaison is occurring just beyond view. The gently moralizing tone of the painting was one that Hoogstraten returned to several times. **TP**

A View Down a Corridor
Samuel van Hoogstraten

1662 | oil on panel | 104 x 53 in / 264.2 x 136.7 cm
Dyrham Park, Gloucestershire, UK

Dutch tiled floors proved an invaluable tool for artists such as Samuel van Hoogstraten (1627–78), Pieter de Hooch, and Vermeer, who manipulated the strong geometric shapes to accentuate the dominant perspective lines of their interiors. *A View Down a Corridor* depicts a greater perspective field than the eye can see from one vantage point, a device that cleverly places the onlooker directly at the front of the canvas, almost below the birdcage. The sharply receding corridor creates the illusion of great depth, encouraging the eye to travel swiftly through the house to the rear, before coming back to assess the details. It is these subtle details that place Hoogstraten's paintings above those of simple illusory virtuosity. The shadowy figures of the man and woman indicate that domestic chores have been abandoned in favor of an amorous interlude. **TP**

Woman Holding a Balance
Jan Vermeer

c.1664 | oil on canvas | 15 ⅞ x 14 in / 40.3 x 35.5 cm
National Gallery of Art, Washington, DC, USA

Held lightly between a woman's slim fingers, a delicate balance forms the central focus of this painting. Behind the woman hangs a painting of Christ's Last Judgment. Here, Jan Vermeer (1632–75) uses symbolism to play on this so that he can tell a lofty story through an ordinary scene. This painting employs a carefully planned composition to express one of Vermeer's major preoccupations—finding life's underlying balance. The central vanishing point of the painting occurs at the woman's fingertips. On the table before her lie earthly treasures—pearls and a gold chain. Behind her, Christ passes judgment on humanity. There is a mirror on the wall, a common symbol of vanity or worldliness, while a soft light raking across the picture sounds a spiritual note. The serene, Madonnalike woman stands in the center, calmly weighing transitory worldly concerns against spiritual ones. **AK**

The Girl with the Red Hat
Jan Vermeer

c.1665–66 | oil on wood panel | 9 x 7 in / 22.8 x 18 cm
National Gallery of Art, Washington, DC, USA

This painting belongs to the period when Jan Vermeer (1632–75) produced the tranquil interior scenes for which he is famed. For such a small painting, this has great visual impact. Like Vermeer's *Girl with a Pearl Earring*, a girl with sensuously parted lips looks over her shoulder at the viewer while highlights glint off her face and earrings. Here, however, the girl looms larger, placed in the foreground of the picture, confronting us more directly. Her extravagant red hat and luxuriant blue wrap are flamboyant for Vermeer. In contrasting the vibrant colors with a muted, patterned backdrop he increases the girl's prominence and creates a forceful theatricality. Vermeer employed painstaking techniques—opaque layers, thin glazes, wet-in-wet blending, and points of color—that help to explain why his output was low and why both scholars and the public find him endlessly fascinating. **AK**

The Artist's Studio | Jan Vermeer

c.1665–66 | oil on canvas | 47 ¼ x 39 ⅜ in / 120 x 100 cm | Kunsthistorisches Museum, Vienna, Austria

Jan Vermeer's (1632–75) *Woman Holding a Balance* uses potent symbolism, but in this work he goes further and creates a full-blown allegory, commenting it seems on the painter's art and role in society. This allegorical approach, and the fact that it is one of his largest paintings, makes it an unusual piece for Vermeer. What is not unusual are the light effects and the detailed compositional planning. His passion for optical effects and aids may well have led him to use a camera obscura to plot the picture's main lines. Viewers look through a tantalizingly parted curtain to a brightly lit studio beyond. An artist sits at his easel with his back to us. Could this be Vermeer himself? The artist's model would have been readily recognizable to Vermeer's contemporaries as Clio, the muse of History, because she wears a laurel crown and carries a book and trumpet. On a table lie a sketch book, treatises on painting, and a mask (a symbol of imitation). A wall map shows the provinces of the Low Countries prior to 1581. This painting seems to say that history inspires the artist, provides art's most worthy subject matter, and confers status on artists who choose it as their subject. However, as Vermeer's work appears to go against that trend, others suggest that the painting refers to the ways in which artists use skillful illusion to turn fleeting effects into something eternal. This picture is often said to be Vermeer's finest and his family kept it, despite the fact that, when Vermeer died, his wife Catherina and their eleven children were left bankrupt. **AK**

Girl with a Pearl Earring | Jan Vermeer

1666 | oil on canvas | 17 ½ x 15 ³/₈ in / 44.5 x 39 cm | Mauritshuis, The Hague, Netherlands

It is easy to see why this irresistible image has become Johannes (Jan) Vermeer's (1632–75) best-loved work. Here he uses the simple, balanced composition, air of mystery, trademark blue and yellow palette, and delicately pearlized light effects unique to him and arguably unprecedented. *Girl with a Pearl Earring* shows Vermeer as being much more than simply a painter of charming small-scale "genre" scenes of everyday life. Vermeer draws the spectator into the painting by making his subject look lingeringly over her shoulder, directly at the viewer. Slightly parted lips add sensuality to the mystery—who is she? Her turban lends exoticism to this enticing mix, but is in fact simply explained. The picture is not a portrait but a study of a woman's head known in Vermeer's day as a tronie. Tronies represented certain emotions or types, with this one showing an exotic type. The colors of the painting are fresh, the brushwork smooth but just lively enough to capture every nuance of light, the unusual composition is powerful but harmonious, and the whole is unified by limpid light effects. The pearl, captured in just two main strokes, clearly reflects the model's white collar, her eyes sparkle, and tiny, dotted highlights play across her turban. Despite becoming head of the painters' guild in Delft, Vermeer acquired only a modest local reputation in his lifetime, and more widespread recognition had to wait until much later. His techniques, in particular his mastery of light, have inspired modern artists of all kinds, including Dalí. **AK**

Barbara Villiers, Duchess of Cleveland as St. Catherine of Alexandria | Sir Peter Lely

c.1665–67 | oil on canvas | 49 x 39 in / 125.7 x 100 cm | Private collection

Around 1641 Peter Lely (1618–80) moved from Haarlem to London, concentrating on landscapes and history painting before turning to a career as a portrait painter and art dealer in the English capital. It was a propitious time to do so because portraiture was highly fashionable during seventeenth century England, and Lely was able to step into the footsteps of Sir Anthony van Dyck. His early works showed the influence of Van Dyck and also of the Dutch Baroque, but through his career he developed a style that was uniquely his own. Lely received prestigious commissions from Charles I, then Oliver Cromwell, but it was during the reign of Charles II that he reached the height of his success. In 1660 he was appointed Principal Painter in Ordinary by Charles II, and enjoyed considerable fame and fortune. It was the same year that Barbara Villiers became the king's mistress, and Lely painted her many times. Her outstanding beauty became the model for Lely's depiction of women, and he recreated her languid sensuality with a soft and evocative hand. She was as promiscuous and bold as her characteristic heavy-lidded gaze suggests. It is Lely's luxuriant palette and attention to texture—the glistening of her pearls, sheen of her silken robes, and glow of her skin—that makes his work so aesthetically delightful. After Van Dyck's death Lely was considered the leading portrait painter in England, and thus was able to redefine court portraiture. His work became highly influential and was important in the course of portrait painting in both England and Haarlem. **TP**

Equestrian Portrait of Louis XIV
Charles Lebrun

c.1668 | oil on canvas | 129 ½ x 73 ½ in / 329 x 187 cm | Musée de la Chartreuse, Douai, France

When Charles Lebrun (1619–90) was appointed First Painter to France's King Louis XIV in 1662, it marked his ascension to a virtual dictatorship over French art. Lebrun's version of classicism was imposed as the rule of taste through the Academy, which he also headed, and he controlled the vast building projects of the Sun King's reign, including the royal palace at Versailles. Lebrun's talent, however, was in no way diminished by being devoted to the glorification of royal authority. This fine portrait shows the king as an energetic monarch in his early thirties, setting out to prove himself through leadership in the first of the many wars that would mark his reign. The shiny black armor reveals his martial intent, but it is the pose of the horse that contributes most to the dynamic effect.

The portrayal of a ruler on a rearing horse was not unprecedented; Louis's father-in-law Philip IV of Spain was painted in a similar pose by Rubens, but the French king is presented as surprisingly relaxed and confident on his steed. He is looking away to the side, rather than fixing the viewer with a haughty stare as might have been expected. Handsome and stylish, he shows his authority through the firmness with which he controls his lively mount. Light floods in from the left to illuminate the horse's exaggerated barrel chest and the rider's three-quarter profile. The backdrop of landscape, curtain, and pillars is little more than a formal setting for man and horse. This is a portrait devoid of pomposity, full of dash and boldness, showcasing a ruler in the springtime of his reign. **RG**

A Waterfall in a Rocky Landscape | Jacob van Ruisdael

c.1660–70 | oil on canvas | 38 x 33 in / 98.5 x 85 cm | National Gallery, London, UK

The son of Iszaack van Ruysdael, a frame maker and painter, and nephew to the landscape artist Salomon van Ruysdael, Jacob van Ruisdael (c.1630–81) made the distinction of spelling his name with an "i." Born and raised in Haarlem, he later moved to Amsterdam, where he spent the rest of his life. Sadly, there is little surviving documentation about him—not a single self-portrait, portrait, or contemporary account of his work exists. He was prolific during his career, with more than 800 known works, and was unusually diverse in his subject matter and techniques. Ruisdael was an avid recorder of the exact details of nature, and many specific trees and plants have been identified in his paintings. He paid the same attention to depicting the rushing torrent seen in *A Waterfall in a Rocky*

Landscape. Yet, despite the virtuosity of the natural appearance of this landscape, Ruisdael had never visited this Scandinavian scene. From the mid-1650s, he embarked on a series of monumental paintings of waterfalls surrounded by towering trees based on the work of fellow artist Allart van Everdingen, who had traveled through Norway and Sweden in 1644. Ruisdael painted 160 of these Nordic landscapes, which were considered among the most influential of their kind and set a precedent for the depiction of nature for a succession of landscape artists. Though the artist enjoyed only relative success during his life, by the eighteenth century his work was in demand and was greatly admired by Thomas Gainsborough, Joshua Reynolds, and John Constable. **TP**

Still Life of Fruit | David de Heem

c.1670 | oil on canvas | 11 x 9 in / 28 x 23 cm | Ashmolean Museum, Oxford, UK

On a stone sill before a niche lie grapes, apricots, cherries, blackberries, and a peach devoured by ants, with a cabbage-white butterfly and a bumblebee. This rich visual composition combines an elegant harmony of color with hyper-accurate renderings of objects, very much in keeping with the Dutch Masters, including the artist's most famous grandfather Jan Davidsz de Heem (1606–84)—one of the greatest painters of still life in the Netherlands. This painting is signed on the edge of the sill on the left: "D.De HEEM". The form of the signature recalls the large letters with which David de Heem's (c.1663–1701) father—Cornelis de Heem—signed his name. A letter "J" would be added on some paintings to give the impression that the painting was by Jan Davidsz.

This painting has been attributed to the grandfather, probably thanks to clerical confusion soon after the painting's completion. It is likely to have been begun by Jan Davidsz, but was almost certainly completed by his grandson, using his grandfather's style as a model and his barely-begun canvas as a foundation. The work must have been painted early in De Heem's career but it is difficult to date because it is not known when he died and he did not date any of his known paintings. But it is known that De Heem was born in Antwerp, Belgium, and that he moved later to Holland and was married in the Hague in 1690. His lineage is known but not the date of his death. Remarkably also, all known works by him are still life paintings of fruit and flowers. **JH**

Interior of the Burgomasters' Council Chamber
Pieter de Hooch

1661–70 | oil on canvas | 44 x 39 in / 112.5 x 99 cm | Thyssen-Bornemisza Collection, Madrid, Spain

Pieter de Hooch (1629–84) moved from Delft to Amsterdam around 1660, and remained there until his death (in an insane asylum). Amsterdam at this time was one of the main artistic centers in the Netherlands, and attracted artists in droves. By the mid to late 1660s De Hooch had received several notable commissions, yet how or why the artist ended his life in such tragic circumstances remains a mystery. The Amsterdam Town Hall was designed by Jacob van Campen and built between 1648 and 1665. The building was so spectacular that it was referred to as the "Eighth Wonder" of the world, and was considered a monument to the city's great artistic and cultural accomplishments. This painting, which is one of three the artist made, is accurately rendered from life except for the inclusion of De Hooch's characteristic light flooding into the room from the rear. By using such a device the artist has added depth and dimension to an otherwise relatively narrow visual field. Just visible behind the sumptuous red cloth is Ferdinand Bol's painting, *Gaius Lucinus Fabritius in the Camp of King Pyrrhus* and in the bottom right corner is De Hooch's signature, drawn in perspective on the tiled floor. De Hooch's paintings from Delft, courtyard scenes and domestic interiors, remain his most influential. However, the use of a richer, broader palette and greater imaginative detail with strong accents of light in the Amsterdam paintings may have had greater influence on artists such as Pieter Janssens Elinga and Michel van Musscher. **TP**

An Extensive Landscape with a Ruined Castle and a Village Church | Jacob van Ruisdael

1665–70 | oil on canvas | 43 x 57 in / 109 x 146 cm | National Gallery, London, UK

During the late 1660s Jacob van Ruisdael (1628–82) began painting a number of panoramic scenes with low horizons and big skies interrupted by spiky church steeples and the iconic Dutch windmill. Many of these views are of the area outside Haarlem, the town of his youth, though this painting's location cannot be succinctly identified. It is these paintings that have come to represent the epitome of the Dutch landscape, and are instantly recognizable. Here the artist has used bold horizontal planes, crossed with the strong diagonals created by the two church steeples and the ruined castle. The oppressive cloud cover merges from left and right, but the brilliance of the light-flooded field in the distance diverts any sense of melancholy. In the foreground there are two shepherds, painted by Adriaen van de Velde, which add a sense of scale and proportion to the mysterious scene. Ruisdael's extraordinary attention to detail, and the exact depiction of foliage lends the painting a hyperrealism. The painting has an interesting history and is thought to be one of the first Ruisdaels to be seen in the USA. It was exhibited in New York in 1830 by an English picture dealer, Richard Abrahams, who acquired the picture illegally. Abrahams and his accomplice were caught, and Abrahams imprisoned briefly before being allowed to exhibit the painting. Shortly afterward the picture was returned to London and sold at auction. During its brief stay in the USA it would seem the painting, now one of his most famous, received little recognition. **TP**

Negro with Parrots and Monkeys | David Klöcker Ehrenstrahl

1670 | oil on canvas | 56 x 47 in / 144 x 120 cm | Nationalmuseum, Stockholm, Sweden

The German painter David Klöcker (1628–98) was given the honorary title "Ehrenstrahl" in respect of his ennoblement by the Swedish royal court in 1674. It was a mark of the respect that the artist had won in Sweden, which was further heightened in 1690 when he was made a court steward. He initially studied in the Netherlands but by 1652 had already traveled to Sweden where he painted the equestrian portrait of Field Marshal Carl Gustaf Wrangel, and followed this trip with a stay in Italy and France. It was there that the artist truly developed his style, being influenced by the drama of Baroque art, and later combined this with his own startling realism. *Negro with Parrots and Monkeys* is an excellent example of this. It shows the artist's skill at painting animals and his use of dramatic effect. The painting is an exotic work, in subject and in execution. The dark yet rich palette is enlivened by the brilliant white-yellow of the parrot that appears to fly into the viewer's space. Compositionally, the painting is cleverly contrived with the forms based around a pyramidal structure picked out through the sharply contrasted lights and darks, with the parrot forming the peak, the man's sleeve and birdstand the sides, and the horizontal ledge the base. Ehrenstrahl worked primarily as a portrait painter but also produced lively allegorical paintings and was one of the first artists working in Sweden to paint genre scenes. His distinctive style and fluent depiction of landscape, nature, and people made him a leading figure in seventeenth-century Swedish art. **TP**

Interior of a Church | Emanuel de Witte

c.1680 | oil on canvas | 47 ¼ x 41 in / 120 x 104 cm | Hamburger Kunsthalle, Hamburg, Germany

During the seventeenth century there was a tradition of architectural painting that was particularly associated with the Dutch town of Delft, and it was there that the approach to this type of painting was revolutionized by the innovative works of Gerard Houckgeest. By 1641 Emanuel de Witte (c.1616–92) had moved to Delft, where the artist's style is considered to have fully evolved. At this time he focused on painting church interiors, both real and imaginary. Like Houckgeest, De Witte chose unusual views of his churches, depicting the interior from an angle with an expressive use of space and perspective. He moved to Amsterdam in 1652, but continued to paint the churches of Delft, and to create his own imaginary interiors. This interior shows his characteristic use of figures to create a busy scene. De Witte's lively interiors contrasted with the solemn scenes of most Dutch architectural painters. This work demonstrates the angled view that the artist favored and his use of strong lights and shadows. The planes of light in particular create a sense of pattern across the canvas, heightened by the use of broad distinct areas of flat, muted color. The figures here are dressed in the dark clothes of the churchgoer, and the inclusion of the dog is again typical of his painting. Although he led a troubled life, his work was of great importance to the development of architectural painting and, together with Gerard Houckgeest and Hendrik van Vliet, De Witte gave the church interior a new expression. **TP**

Angel with a Harquebus | Circle of the Master of Calamarca

*c.*1680 | oil on canvas | 63 x 43 ¼ in / 160 x 110 cm | Museo Nacional de Arte, La Paz, Bolivia

Among the most memorable reinterpretations of traditional European iconography in the new Spanish colonies is the angel or archangel as musketeer or "flame of God"—hence the firearm as a reference. This type of representation is particular to Bolivian mestizo and high Andean art, in some ways even typifying it. As the Latin inscription in the left-hand corner explains, this messenger has come to execute the mandate of God. The angel is portrayed in an extremely stylized way—an exaggerated, almost effeminate cut of dress, delicate cuffs and collar, enormous sleeves, silk stockings, colorful ribbons, and jaunty, plumed hat. This reminiscent of Flemish fashion and was a standard feature in paintings of this kind. As with all colonial art schools, heavy gilt brocade ornamentation has been applied over the folds of the drapery using stencils but not necessarily following the flow of the fabric in a naturalistic manner. This particular depiction of an angel cocking a harquebus, the fifteenth-century matchlock gun, in preparation to release the trigger, is slightly more unusual within this genre of painting. A more familiar pose for these winged defenders of the Christian faith would be fully facing the viewer with a weapon—whether musket, harquebus, or flaming sword—held up in one hand as a warning. Typically the subject wears high-heeled footwear and wide, flowing robes adorned with lace. The asexual appearance and beatific facial expression are in marked contrast to the aggressive tones set by the presence of the firearm. **AA**

Angel Holding a Firearm | Circle of the Master of Calamarca

c.1680 | oil on canvas | 63 x 43 ¼ in / 160 x 110 cm | Museo Nacional de Arte, La Paz, Bolivia

This example of an angel holding a rosary in one hand and brandishing a firearm in the other was painted in the seventeenth century in the Bolivian/Peruvian region surrounding Lake Titicaca. Such armed angels or archangels were a religious motif unique to the Andean New World. It would most probably have been found in the presbytery of a church. The composition is traditionally flat and lacking in perspective with a preference for a dark or neutral background. Flat, primary colors with few tonal variations are used with a touch of gold ornamentation on the garments. The iconography and opulent accessories of these warriors come chiefly from Antwerp. The angels symbolize the defense of the Christian faith in a brave new world.

There is a symbolic tension between the possibility of punishment as meted out by these heavenly guardians and their delicately embroidered attire and placid expressions. The polychromatic coloration of the wings—like tropical birds' feathers—is an artistic curiosity never before explored by European religious painters who had invariably always shown solid-color wings. This detail is remarkable given that criollo, indian, or mestizo apprentices would most probably have been working from black and white European engravings. Such imaginative reinventions of Old World images created a colonial framework that gave rise to new creative vocabularies that allowed the Andean artistic traditions of the schools of Cuzco and Lake Titicaca to flourish for nearly three hundred years. **AA**

Landscape with Ascanius Shooting the Stag of Sylvia
Claude Lorraine

1682 | oil on canvas | 47 x 59 in / 120 x 150 cm | Ashmolean Museum, Oxford, UK

This is Claude Lorraine's (c.1604–82) last picture, painted in the final year of his life, and it is a fitting epitaph to his work. It relates a tale from Virgil's *Aeneid*, as classical mythology was considered a suitably elevated subject for art in Claude's time. Claude has lent a uniquely poetic mood of an idealized Arcadia to the scene. Ascanius is on a hunting trip when an angry Juno directs Ascanius's arrow to kill the stag Sylvia, daughter of Tyrrheus, which sparks war. The trees bending in the wind signify the storm to come and the presence of Juno's helper, Allecto. The classical columns that help to frame the work are a reference to the emblem of the Colonna family for whom this was painted. This picture is typical of the landscapes of Claude's mature years, when he concentrated increasingly on the effects of light. A high viewpoint directs the eye over a breathtaking vista to the misty horizon. The artist has captured how certain light seems to lend solid forms a shimmering, ethereal quality—the gods here look like elongated ghosts. The episode depicted is not a peaceful one, yet Claude has chosen to show the calm before the storm, as Ascanius takes aim and the trees sway portentously, retaining his usual timeless serenity and at the same time adding poignancy to the story. Works such as this show Claude at the vanguard of artistic development, sharing his understanding of light with contemporaries, such as Vermeer and future masters such as Turner, who cited him as a major influence. **AK**

The Island in the Tiber
Gaspar van Wittel

1685 | oil on canvas | 19 ⅛ x 38 ¾ in / 48.5 x 98.5 cm | Kunsthistorisches Museum, Vienna, Austria

Gaspar van Wittel (1653–1736) was born in Amersfoort, Holland where he trained in the workshop of Matthias Withoos. With his family, he moved to Rome in about 1675 and it is there that he made his career depicting topographically accurate views of the city. At first, though, he worked as a draftsman on a scheme to regulate the Tiber. It may have been this that gave him the idea of making large, very accurate drawings that could eventually be worked up into painted views of the city. "*Vedute*" is a term that had been used before Van Wittel's arrival to describe pictures of Rome, but he is credited with developing this as an independent category of painting. Over time it has come to mean paintings of any city and their sites. Van Wittel's oeuvre includes views of Venice, Florence, Bologna, Naples, and other places in Italy. Over a thirty-year period, his technique influenced many other Italian artists, including Pannini in Rome and Canaletto in Venice. About half of Van Wittel's Roman *vedute* are views of the Tiber, painted from fifteen different locations. He usually chose a high vantage point from which to work in order to give a sweeping panorama and to include as many of the architectural features as he could. He portrayed the city as it was at the time rather than focusing on the remains of antiquity as so many had done before him. This *vedute* is a wonderful composition, with its large stretch of water and the cityscape in the distance. In this painting, Rome takes second place to the river that sustains it. **TS**

Queen Anne | Willem Wissing and Jan van der Vaardt

1685 | oil on canvas | 78 ½ x 50 ½ in / 199.4 x 128.3 cm | Scottish National Portrait Gallery, Edinburgh, UK

Born in Amsterdam, Willem Wissing (1656–87) trained in both The Hague and Paris. He became assistant to Sir Peter Lely on his arrival in London in 1676, and after Lely's death four years later, Wissing helped to finish Lely's uncompleted portraits. Subsequently he became a fashionable portrait painter. He painted many portraits of members of the Stuart court, including Princess, later Queen, Anne (1665–1714). In 1684, he was sent to Holland by King James II to paint the Prince of Orange and Princess Mary. Jan van der Vaardt (1647–1721) was born in Haarlem in the Netherlands, and moved to London in 1674 where he spent the rest of his life. He became Wissing's assistant, painting mainly the landscapes, still lifes, and draperies in his pictures. After Wissing's death

in 1687, Van der Vaardt established his own portrait practice, basing his style on Wissing, though his work is less polished. The portrait *Queen Anne* was painted before Anne ascended to the throne in 1702. Princess Anne was twenty in 1985, and the portrait was painted two years after Anne married Prince George of Denmark. There were probably several versions of this painting which would have been given as gifts to friends and family. The dog at her feet alludes to marital fidelity, the pillar represents spiritual strength, and the roses signify purity. During her marriage, Anne had many miscarriages, and gave birth to twelve children, none of whom survived. Queen Anne was the last of the Stuart dynasty to occupy the British throne. **SH**

Beauty Looking Back | Hishikawa Moronobu

1690 | ink and color on silk scroll | 24 ¾ x 12 ¼ in / 63 x 31 cm | Tokyo National Museum, Japan

Hishikawa Moronobu (1618–94) is often credited with the advancement of the *ukiyo-e*, a style of Japanese print and painting developed during the Edo period. *Ukiyo-e* was a popular pictorial expression of the world of the Kabuki theater, the Yoshiwara pleasure district, and other scenes of urban life, often peopled with actors and courtesans. The word *ukiyo* was originally used in the religious context of Buddhism, referring to the ephemeral nature of human life, but in the Edo period it acquired a new connotation as it became associated with the fleetingness of urban society. Born into a family of textile embroiderers near Tokyo, Moronobu's first artistic experience was making underdrawings on fabrics. After moving to Edo (present day Tokyo), he produced book illustrations using woodblock prints. By making sets of single-sheet illustrations independently from their accompanying text, he established a new *ukiyo-e* idiom. His prints were usually monochrome and often hand-painted. *Beauty Looking Back* is an example of a genre which portrayed beautiful women from the Kanbun period. Hand-painted *ukiyo-e* pictures were not the original pictures used for woodblock print reproductions, but singular pieces made to be viewed in their own right. By showing the back of a woman, Moronobu effectively displays the fashions of the day as seen in the hairstyle and kimono pattern. *Ukiyo-e* prints were a source of inspiration for Art Nouveau and many Impressionist painters, including van Gogh and Monet, in nineteenth-century Europe. **FN**

1700s

Irises | Ogata Kōrin

1702 | gilded folding screens | 59 x 133 ⅜ in / 150 x 338.8 cm | Nezu Institute of Fine Arts, Tokyo, Japan

Ogata Kōrin (1658–1716) was born into a rich merchant-class family, who owned a textile shop in Kyoto patronized by the ladies of feudal lords and nobles. Kōrin was influenced by the tradition that the artists Kōetsu and Sōtatsu had developed at the artistic community Takagamine, where his grandfather was a member. The Rinpa ("School of Rin") style established by his two predecessors in fact takes its name from Kōrin, who consolidated the style with his brother Kenzan. After losing the family fortune, Kōrin and Kenzan made their living by designing textiles, screens, lacquer, and ceramics. *Irises* is a symbolic representation of a scene from the *Eight Plank Bridge* of the *Tales of Ise*, a compilation of lyrical episodes written in the Heian period. By removing the hero and the bridge central to the tale from his depiction, Kōrin created a rhythmic composition based on repetition in an almost abstract manner. The flowers are painted in *mokkotsu*; the boneless brushwork style without ink outlines. Kōrin made a number of drawings of nature from life, but in his paintings objects are often reduced to the essence, presented in flat and simplified designs. Kōrin reworked the decorative style and the *yamato-e* (native Japanese painting) themes employed by Sōtatsu, whose paintings Kōrin copied to learn the techniques. The Rinpa school is known for its abundant use of colors, gold leaf, and silver. One hundred years later, Sakai Hōitsu revived the Rinpa tradition in Edo, present-day Tokyo, after studying Kōrin's works. **FN**

Flowers and Insects | Rachel Ruysch

1711 | oil on panel | 18 ¼ x 24 ¼ in / 46.2 x 61.6 cm | Uffizi, Florence, Italy

A moth sits beside a wicker basket containing a profusion of roses, tulips, primulas, and daisies. It is the work of a female artist, not in itself uncommon in eighteenth-century Holland, and the subject matter, a floral still life, was highly popular. The paintings, as here, often had insects such as caterpillars and butterflies included to enhance the naturalism of the image. Rachel Ruysch (1664–1750) was the most celebrated Dutch flower painter of her day. Born in Haarlem, Ruysch studied with the flower painter Willem van Aelst. She was one of several female flower painters inspired by Jan Davidsz de Heem's Baroque floral still lifes some fifty years before. Women were not allowed to attend life-drawing classes and were thought unable to paint portraits or historical scenes with figures, which were viewed as activities for men. Hence women focused on paintings of flowers, which were deemed a suitable domestic subject. Her choice of subject matter may also have been influenced by her upbringing, since her father Frederik Ruysch was a botanist. Given paintings such as these often included flowers that would rarely be in bloom at the same time and flowers quickly wilt, painters would use botanical illustrations as an aid when painting. The painting itself is a *vanitas*, with references to death and the emptiness of life—flowers fade fast. Such still-life paintings were admired and sought after at this time in Dutch society, as the emerging merchant class had the money to spend on objects that would reflect their own wealth. **JH**

The Pilgrimage to Cythera | Jean-Antoine Watteau

1717 | oil on canvas | 51 x 76 ½ in / 129.5 x 194.5 cm | Louvre, Paris, France

In 1717, Jean-Antoine Watteau (1684–1721) presented this picture to the French Academy as his diploma piece. It was acclaimed as his finest work, as well as a key influence on the emerging Rococo style. The subject started out as an illustration of a minor play. In Florence Dancourt's *Les Trois Cousines*, a girl dressed as a pilgrim steps out from the chorus line and invites the audience to join her on a voyage to Cythera—the island of love, where everyone will meet their ideal partner. Watteau's first version of the theme, dating from c.1709, was a very literal depiction, but here he has dispensed with the theatrical framework, and has turned the incident into a dreamy, romantic fantasy. Significantly, he has chosen to portray the end, rather than the beginning, of the journey. The lovers have

paired off, have garlanded the statue of Venus on the right with flowers, and are about to return home. By focusing on this moment, the artist was able to create the air of gentle melancholy that is so characteristic of his work. While most of the couples are making ready to leave, two lovers have remained by the goddess's shrine, spellbound by love and blind to everything else. One of the departing women turns and looks back at them sadly, aware that this part of love is the most fleeting. After Watteau's death, his art fell dramatically out of fashion. To many, his depictions of amorous escapades seemed too closely bound up with the old days of the monarchy. During the Revolutionary period, art students used his *Cythera* for target practice, hurling bread pellets at it. **IZ**

Examination of Country Magistrates | Unknown

1700–20 | watercolor on paper mounted on silk | Bibliothèque Nationale, Paris, France

The Qing Dynasty was established in 1644 when the Manchus, a semi-nomadic people from the north of China, conquered the decaying Ming state and took control of the whole of China. The § Emperors, realizing that the adoption of some Han Chinese culture would help tie their vast territory together, protected its art and literature. Three main groups of artists worked during the Qing Dynasty. The Traditionalists sought to revitalize painting through the imaginative reworking of past models. The Individualists practiced a deeply personal form of art that sometimes carried a message of political protest. A third group of courtiers, officials, and professional artists served at the Manchu court. This painting was probably produced under the rule of the Kangxi or Yongzheng emperor by an artist serving the court. The scene shows the examination of country magistrates under a pavilion—the Chinese characters tell us this is a "provincial examination." Successful candidates were awarded general government posts. As with all traditional Chinese art, this painting is two-dimensional. Realistic representation is put aside in favor of an attempt to capture the nature of the scene. The high horizon—a view above the action—allows a narrative to unfold, as in this painting in which the scholars enter in the lower register, sit the examination in the middle register, and hand their papers to the official in the top register. This is embellished with trees, vegetation, and a misty sky to express the spiritual values of this story. **OR/HC**

Gilles | Jean-Antoine Watteau

1718–20 | oil on canvas | 72 ½ x 59 in / 184.5 x 149.5 cm | Louvre, Paris, France

This is one of the last paintings Jean-Antoine Watteau (1684–1721) produced in his brief career. It shows a clown gazing out at his audience, with a wistful expression that may echo the melancholy mood of the artist. "Gilles" was a generic name for a clown in France, probably stemming from Gilles le Niais, a seventeenth-century acrobat and comedian. By Watteau's day, there was considerable overlap between this character and "Pierrot," the leading clown in the commedia dell'arte—an Italian theater tradition that was hugely popular in France. Both figures played the innocent fool who became the audience's favorite—a prototype for Charlie Chaplin and Buster Keaton. This picture was probably produced as a theatrical signboard designed to tempt passers-by into a show.

It may have been created for the premiere of *Danaë*, a comedy in which one of the characters was turned into an ass. Alternatively, it may have advertised the *parades*—the brief, farcical sketches before the main performance. In these, a donkey was often led across the stage to symbolize the sheer stupidity of Gilles. Watteau used a smaller version of this clown as the main figure in *The Italian Players*, a picture that he produced for his doctor in 1720. In both cases, the gloomy figure of Gilles was reminiscent of an *Ecce Homo* (Behold the Man) painting. This popular religious theme depicted an episode in the Passion of Christ, when Pontius Pilate presented Jesus before the people, hoping that they would call for his release. Instead, the mob called for his crucifixion. **IZ**

The White Stallion "Leal" en Levade | J.G. Hamilton

1721 | oil on canvas | 18 x 24 in / 47 x 82 cm | Lippizans Museum, Vienna, Austria

Originally based on training methods for horses required to work on the battlefield, classical riding had, by the eighteenth century, become a highly respected discipline, as well as a genteel pursuit. This painting was commissioned by Emperor Charles VI of Austria, who was a keen horseman. The famous Spanish Riding School was the pinnacle of equestrian perfection, and the trained Spanish Lipizzaner horses were highly sought after. J.G. Hamilton (1672–1737) is renowned for his enigmatic portraits of these equine gymnasts. Hamilton was the son of the Scottish still-life painter James Hamilton (c.1640–1720). He was born in Brussels but spent most of his working life in the courts of Europe. He was appointed Court Animal Painter to Emperor Charles VI, and recorded in

exquisite detail the Emperor's favorite mounts. This painting of the magnificent gray horse Leal combines an idealized Italianate landscape with a natural representation of the horse, painted with a delicate, soft Rococo palette. Hamilton painted the horse executing a complicated dressage movement known as "the levade." The picture is designed to flatter by illustrating the beauty, intelligence, and prowess of the horse, which would in turn be a reflection of the owner. Hamilton's work is uniformly beautiful with an appealing combination of the ideal and the real that makes it visually stunning. His particular skill lay in capturing the individual character of the horse—all his equine portraits display a unique expressiveness that was not matched by his contemporaries. **TP**

The Stonemason's Yard | Canaletto

1727–28 | oil on canvas | 48 ¾ x 64 ⅛ in / 124 x 163 cm | National Gallery, London, UK

This is not a typical scene by Canaletto (Giovanni Antonio Canal, 1697–1768), who was famous for painting landmark views of Venice, filled with carnivals, processions, and parades. Here, the viewer is offered an ordinary domestic urban picture filled with details of everyday life and activity. From a raised viewpoint, the viewer is given an unhampered view of an open square, which, framed on either side by tall buildings, creates the stage in which countless events are taking place. To the left a mother throws up her arms toward her little boy; a lady leans over a first-floor window to see the commotion, and a crowing rooster announces the morning. In the middle distance, gondoliers ferry passengers across the canal, and laundry is hung out to dry. In the center, stonemasons shape blocks of stone, while on the right a woman is spinning yarn at her window. This is not an imagined view, but a faithful record of the Campo San Vidal. In the middle distance is the Grand Canal and beyond is the church of Santa Maria della Carità. This painting is considered to be one of Canaletto's finest works, made with more care than later formulaic images that proved so lucrative on the tourist market. This square still looks much the same today, except for the addition of a wooden bridge over the canal and for the transformation of the church of Santa Maria della Carità; its bell tower collapsed in 1741, taking with it the two white houses adjacent to it. The building later became the Accademia di Belle Arti—Venice's principal art gallery. **AB**

St. Joseph and the Christ Child | Unknown

1670–1730 | oil on canvas | 43 x 32 in / 109 x 82 cm | Brooklyn Museum of Art, Brooklyn, NY, USA

Informal paintings of the Holy Family were popular in Spain and its colonies during the seventeenth and eighteenth centuries. Certain characteristics make this work typical of the Peruvian Cuzco School. The figures do not have blond hair, unlike conventional Spanish copies, and St. Joseph is portrayed as a youthful, handsome man. The combination of Baroque details and a balanced composition—another peculiarity of Peruvian and Alto Peruvian art—differentiate this type of painting not only from European Baroque but also from that of Mexico, Columbia, Brazil, and Ecuador. In iconographic fashion characteristic of the Cuzco School, the Christ Child carries a basket of carpenter's tools, and St. Joseph bears a triple-branched lily—a symbol of the Trinity and of the bearer's virtue and chastity. Roses and native lilies adorn part of the border of the painting; originally the entire border would have been decorated in this way but was removed, probably to allow the image to fit the current frame. The gilt brocade (brocadel sobredorado) decoration on the figures' garments, hems of their robes, and haloes, is extremely ornate, and has been superimposed by the artist on the folds in the drapery using stencils. Other hallmarks include the predominance of the color red, and the Incan style sandals worn by the child. These unique variations are the result of sincretismo, the process by which indigenous details were worked into the picture by local artists alongside Spanish elements imported from Europe. **AA**

The Young Schoolmistress | Jean-Siméon Chardin

1735–36 | oil on canvas | 24 x 26 in / 61.6 x 66.7 cm | National Gallery, London, UK

Jean-Siméon Chardin (1699–1779) is one of the finest painters of the eighteenth century whose treatment of his subjects, generally still lifes and genre scenes, is characterized by a lightness of touch and a delicacy of color. His compositions find their source in the Golden Age of Dutch painting. They have a unique clarity of vision and are generally of a modest scale and devoid of any superfluous content. *The Young Schoolmistress* shows a small child being taught by a rather stern-faced young girl. The scene takes place in a plain interior, redolent of the simple domesticity of French bourgeois life, and Chardin avoids any of the sentimentality that such a subject might generate in a lesser painter. Chardin repeated his design for *The Young Schoolmistress* on several occasions. The version

that is now on display in London's National Gallery was exhibited for the first time in 1740 at the Salon, the official art exhibition of the Académie des Beaux-Arts in Paris. It was reproduced in a contemporaneous print by the engraver François-Bernard Lépicié with the following inscription: "If this charming child takes on so well the serious air and imposing manner of a schoolmistress, may one not think that pretence and artfulness come to the fair sex no later than birth." Many of Chardin's paintings are marked by the timeless intensity of their visual description and this is certainly true of *The Young Schoolmistress*. The clock appears to have come to a standstill in Chardin's classroom and his little pupil is forever on the end of a life-improving lesson. **PB**

Christ at the Pool of Bethesda | William Hogarth

1736 | oil on canvas | 236 x 118 in / 600 x 300 cm | St. Bartholomew's Hospital, London, UK

Born in St. Bartholomew's Close, London, William Hogarth (1697–1764) was apprenticed as a silversmith and engraver. He had only been painting seven years when he offered his services free of charge to St. Bartholomew's Hospital. Hogarth adopted the "grand historical style" here to illustrate the biblical account (John 5: 2–11) of one of Christ's miracles. Christ tells the central figure, a man lame for thirty-eight years, to "rise, take up thy bed, and walk." The other thirteen figures are suffering from a variety of disorders, such as gout, blindness, anemia, rickets, jaundice, cancer, and cretinism (congenital thyroid hormone deficiency), and were probably based on patients in the hospital. The voluptuous woman on the right was a known courtesan, Nell Robinson,

who is depicted as suffering from arthritis due to either gonorrhea or syphilis. Bethesda, in Aramaic, means "house of mercy." The pool was discovered in Jerusalem in 1956, and the story went that, to obtain a cure, the sick person must be the first to enter the pool after the "troubling of the waters," which was attributed to a passing angel. Hogarth was committed to depicting life in the raw and making comment on the "ills of society," both medical and social. Here, he portrays charitable and uncharitable acts, the latter exemplified by the rich man who offers a bribe to facilitate early entry into the pool. Hogarth produced this work to advertise his skills as a painter with the hope of attracting other commissions for works on a similar scale; his aspiration was never fulfilled. **MF**

Reception of the French Ambassador in Venice | Canaletto

*c.*1740 | oil on canvas | 71 ¼ x 102 ⅛ in / 181 x 260 cm | State Hermitage Museum, St. Petersburg, Russia

Known as Canaletto, meaning "little canal," Giovanni Antonio Canal (1697–1768) is not just remembered as a painter from Venice but as a painter of Venice. He trained under his father, Bernardo Canal, a scenery painter for the theater, from which he learned to master the art of linear perspective. Canaletto furthered his ability to depict coherent and realistic urban spaces from topographical artists whose work he encountered in Rome. Throughout his career he produced a vast number of paintings of Venice: its civic pageantry and festivals, its well-known buildings and canals. These sunlit and picturesque views became the favorite purchases of eighteenth-century "Grand Tourists," sons of wealthy European aristocrats completing their education by traveling to the main European cultural centers. This vast view shows the colorful and stately arrival of Jacques-Vincent Languet, Comte de Gergy, on November 4, 1726. Having been appointed as French Ambassador to the Republic of Venice, his ceremonial welcome took place outside the Doge's Palace, the facade of which is seen in sharp perspective on the right. The panoramic view and its endless detail are perfectly visible throughout. The dramatic sky fills half of the painting and through the darkening clouds the sunlight casts shadows on the palace facade and highlights the richly decorated gondolas at the very front. The ambassador can just be marked out in the center of the crowd, followed by a row of senators and preceded by a line of men in uniform. **AB**

Girl with Shuttlecock | Jean-Siméon Chardin

1740 | oil on canvas | 32 ¼ x 26 in / 82 x 66 cm | Uffizi, Florence, Italy

Jean-Siméon Chardin (1699–1779), often called "The Good Chardin" in contemporary critical literature, was born in Paris, the son of a master cabinetmaker. A lifelong resident of his native Paris, he was at a disadvantage as a painter because, while other artists favored splashy history paintings and fashionable portraits of fashionable people, his talents lay in overlooked and undervalued subject matter such as still lifes and genre scenes. Chardin's technique—he uses paint as if it were pastels—and formal concerns (composition, color, texture) are at their most remarkable in *Girl with Shuttlecock*, in which a young girl absentmindedly toys with a badminton racket and a feathered shuttlecock. There is no overt drama in the painting; in fact she seems bored herself, as if waiting for her partner to get ready and play the game, yet the interplay of soft hues and surfaces is mesmerizing. The blush on her cheeks, the velvety fabric of her dress and billowy skirt are all in perfect harmony with, yet perfectly distinct from, the space surrounding her and the wood of her racket and chair. The more political and rigorous Neoclassical artists of the day dismissed Chardin as a fluffy sentimentalist, but instead of his humble interests hampering his talent, he elevated banal objects and everyday scenes to a height where latter-day intellectual greats, such as Proust and Matisse, were proud to admit they admired his art. Most viewers are still struck by the smoothness of his surfaces, and by his breathtaking, sensual rendering of mundane objects. **AH**

Entrance to the Grand Canal, Venice | Bernardo Bellotto

c.1741 | oil on canvas | 23 ¼ x 37 ¼ in / 59.3 x 94.9 cm | Fitzwilliam Museum, University of Cambridge, UK

The Venetian-born artist Bernardo Bellotto (1721–80) trained in the studio of his uncle, the great Canaletto, before traveling to Rome and Florence. These two artists collaborated on several works and, confusingly, Bellotto not infrequently signed his name Canaletto. However, although Canaletto had previously painted a version of the *Entrance to the Grand Canal, Venice*—and there are obvious parallels—Bellotto's interpretation is his own and his mature style became very different from Canaletto's. This magnificent view of the Grand Canal, characteristic of Bellotto's early style, is superbly accurate, with mathematically formulated perspective and intense attention to detail. He concentrated particularly on the exact quality of light in his locations, not for an atmospheric or emotive effect, but for a completely realistic rendering of the landscape. He developed this approach throughout his career and his later work became characterized by the use of strong light and shadow, and a painterly approach to skies similar in manner to his Dutch contemporaries. Here, however, his uncle's influence can still be seen in the inclusion of the busy figures working along the canal and the emphasis on the activities of daily life. Bellotto moved to Dresden in 1747 and later to Warsaw, devoting himself mainly to working for the various European courts. Among his greatest legacies are his detailed paintings of views of Dresden before it was flattened by bombing during World War II, and his views of Warsaw, which were used as a guide to rebuilding the city after it too was destroyed. **TP**

Shortly After the Marriage | William Hogarth

1743 | oil on canvas | 27 ½ x 35 ¾ in / 70 x 91 cm | National Gallery, London, UK

One of the most influential figures in English art, William Hogarth (1697–1764) was a highly skilled Realist portrait painter, engraver, satirist, critic, aesthetic philosopher, and editorial cartoonist. *Shortly After the Marriage*, also known as *The Tête-à-Tête*, is the second of a sequence of six scenes in Hogarth's *Marriage A-la-Mode* series. In this series, Hogarth illustrates the all-too-common story of a young aristocratic woman who contracts the pox from her arranged marriage. The series was commissioned by Mary Edwards, a wealthy art patron who had managed to escape from an arranged marriage herself. She hired Hogarth to educate society about the dangers of such marriages, where syphilis was only one among many possible horrid outcomes for young women forced to marry strangers to appease their parents' mercenary desires. Hogarth's original oil paintings were reproduced on copper plates, from which the series circulated in various publications. In this scene we see the couple engaged in an intimate morning in which their mutual disdain for each other and their separate social and sexual lives are very much in evidence. The drunken, bored lord still wears his hat and sword from the previous evening, while the wife stretches out before a table set for one. An exasperated steward leaves the scene after attempting to interest the couple in their flagging financial situation. While many of the iniquities of society Hogarth portrayed are still common today, the artist's sensibility, insight, and talent remains a historical rarity. **AH**

Sir James MacDonald and Sir Alexander MacDonald
William Mosman

1749 | oil on canvas | 69 ½ x 58 in / 176.5 x 147.5 cm | Scottish National Portrait Gallery, Edinburgh, UK

William Mosman's (c.1700–71) work is often described as part of the "Scottish Baroque" School of portraiture, alongside contemporary Scottish painters William Aikman (1682–1731), with whom Mosman studied briefly in the 1720s, and Allan Ramsay (1713–84), who became one of the leading British portraitists of his day. Ramsay and Mosman produced the same kind of fashionably styled portraits in the European manner—a refined approach with attention to fabrics and lighting. However, while Ramsay's work was cosmopolitan and sophisticated, this double portrait has Mosman's simpler charm and more down-to-earth quality. It shows the sons of great Highland chieftain Sir Alexander MacDonald, who owned estates on the Scottish Isle of Skye. The older boy,

James (1741–65), poses with his gun, which gives him a more senior and serious air than his younger brother Alexander (1744–1810), seen enjoying the more innocent pastime of playing golf (already a popular hobby in Scotland among the well-to-do). The landscape receding into a hazy distance hints at the estates of this important family and, along with the cleverly suffused, harmonizing lighting, echoes the poetic landscapes painted by Poussin and Claude. The boys' clothes feature three different tartans—family or clan tartans would not become common for another fifty years or so. Mosman ended his career in the northeast of Scotland, establishing a drawing academy in Aberdeen and leaving a pictorial record of some of the leading families of the region. **AK**

Mr. and Mrs. Andrews
Thomas Gainsborough

*c.*1750 | oil on canvas | 27 x 47 in / 70 x 119.5 cm | National Gallery, London, UK

This is Thomas Gainsborough's (1727–88) first masterpiece, painted early in his career. It shows his blossoming talent, not just as a portraitist but also as a landscape painter. The picture was probably commissioned as a marriage portrait. The sheaves of corn on the right were a standard symbol of fertility, often used in images of this kind. The couple were married in 1748 in the nearby town of Sudbury, faintly visible in the background, and are shown here on their private estate. The composition, with the figures pushed to one side, is unusual, although it does give the newly-weds a proprietorial air, as if they were proudly displaying their land to the outside world. There is another possibility, though: Gainsborough loved this part of the country, having been born in Sudbury, and he may have been more interested in painting the landscape than in his patrons. Gainsborough's inexperience is evident from the poses of the figures, which are a little stiff and doll-like. This may also account for the unflattering haughty expressions of the couple, which raises the question of their relationship with the artist: Gainsborough had known them both since childhood, though never as social equals. He had attended the same school as Robert Andrews, but while the latter had gone to Oxford University, he had become a lowly apprentice. Similarly, when Gainsborough's father had run into financial difficulties, Frances's family had come to his assistance. This social gulf may explain the disdainful way in which the couple are looking at the artist. **IZ**

Exhibition of a Rhinoceros at Venice | Pietro Longhi

*c.*1751 | oil on canvas | 23 ¾ x 18 ½ in / 60.5 x 47 cm | National Gallery, London, UK

In 1741, Dutch sea captain Douwe Moot van der Meer landed a female Indian rhinoceros in Rotterdam. It was only the fifth rhinoceros seen in Europe since the time of the Roman Empire. Exploiting the curiosity this naturally aroused, Van der Meer toured the animal around the continent for many years, exhibiting it to paying customers. When it was shown in Venice during the carnival of 1751, fashionable Venetian genre painter Pietro Longhi (1701–85) was twice commissioned by aristocratic clients to record the event. This version was painted for the nobleman Girolamo Mocenigo. The rhinoceros stands calmly in its arena munching straw. It appears docile and sad, with none of the fierce aggression typically associated with its kind. Its harmless appearance is emphasized by the absence of a horn. This had reportedly fallen off during a sojourn in Rome the previous June, after the animal rubbed its horn against the cage. The rhinoceros's handler brandishes the detached horn along with a whip, while pointing at the animal with his other hand. The masks traditionally worn in Venice during the carnival give a sinister touch to the audience. The woman in the back row wears a small black oval *moreta*, while three of the tricorne-hatted figures in the front row sport the white mask known as a *bauta*. A sense of jollity may be intended, but the effect of the scene is one of bizarre incongruity in the juxtaposition of the fashionable audience and the grotesque beast, deflated and resigned to the indignity of its fate. **RG**

Reclining Girl | François Boucher

1751 | oil on canvas | 23 ⅓ x 28 ¾ in / 59.5 x 73.5 cm | Wallraf-Richartz Museum, Cologne, Germany

François Boucher (1703–70) made two very similar pictures of this voluptuous nude, the second of which, painted in 1752, is one of his most famous. Produced at the peak of his powers, they underline his reputation as one of France's greatest Rococo artists. The Rococo style flourished at Louis XV's court before the French Revolution. It emphasized elegance and refinement, but it was also extremely lighthearted and exuded a playful sense of eroticism. Aristocratic patrons adorned their walls with the frolicking escapades of nymphs and goddesses. To meet this demand, Boucher became an expert at portraying the female form, producing thousands of sketches of different models that he used repeatedly in his larger compositions. *Reclining Girl* stands out from most of his other nudes

because of its directness. There is no attempt to place the model in a mythological or narrative context. It is, instead, a hymn to sensuality. The heady perfume of the rose, flung casually on the carpet, conjures up the sense of smell, while the tactile fabrics—the rumpled velvets and silks—evoke the sense of touch. The overall mood is one of pampered innocence. The girl is usually identified as Louise O'Murphy, the daughter of an Irish cobbler. She began modeling at the age of fourteen to escape her impoverished background and soon became renowned for her ravishing looks. For a time, she was one of Louis XV's mistresses. She also met Casanova, who described her in his memoirs as "white like a lily, possessing all the beauty that nature or the painter's art could possibly bestow." **IZ**

Portrait of Lu Tai Tai | Unknown

*c.*1755 | watercolor on silk | 72 x 44 in / 183.5 x 112 cm | Victoria & Albert Museum, London, UK

The Qing, or Manchu, Dynasty, was the last imperial dynasty of China, ruling from 1644 until 1911. At its height, the empire ruled much of central and eastern Asia under a strong, centralized government. This portrait of Lu Tai Tai, wife of General Lu Chian-Kuei, was painted under the leadership of Qianlong (1736–95), when China viewed its kingdom as the center of world power. However, as commercial and religious prowess came from Europe, so China regulated trade with the threatening foreigners. By 1800, China was more isolated than it had been in the fourteenth century, and faced population problems, rebellions, and political turmoil. The stately Lu Tai Tai in no way suggests the exotic concubine with bound feet, or the domesticated China doll of the clichéd Chinese woman. Many wives in Chinese history were described as being ugly, but on the other hand also extremely wise; the position of the wife was sacrosanct with authority and power as the commander of home and progeny, and as her husband's chief confident in his civic duties. Lu Tai Tai's black gown shapes a womanly curve, reminiscent of her past sexual power and reproductive fertility. Her hands and feet are hidden, but appear as aggressive claws that are rather part of the chair, suggesting her indirect but potent social control. Her red hat is the most significant symbol of all—Chinese brides wore red wedding gowns and walked on red carpets toward their grooms. Lu Tai Tai is crowned with the superiority of her position as wife of a general. **SWW**

Madame de Pompadour | François Boucher

1758 | oil on canvas | 28 x 22 in / 72 x 57 cm | Victoria & Albert Museum, London, UK

François Boucher (1703–70) had an unparalleled gift for portraying feminine charms, finding fame with his mythological scenes of nubile nymphs and shepherdesses. However, he was equally adept at depicting the less frivolous side of the female psyche. This is one of a series of portraits produced for his chief patron, the Marquise de Pompadour (1721–64). Born Jeanne-Antoinette Poisson, she gained her title after becoming the mistress of Louis XV in 1745. By the time of this portrait, she was no longer the king's lover, though the pair remained good friends and she was known as the *maîtresse en titre* (the king's official mistress). With true diplomacy, Boucher reflected this unusual situation in the portrait. The marquise is not depicted with regal pomp and majesty, nor as a great beauty. Instead, with the prominent display of books, he emphasized her intellectual and cultural gifts. This is hardly surprising, since her loyal patronage did much to ensure the success of his career. She commissioned numerous paintings from Boucher, along with decorations for her home, the Château de Bellevue. She also engaged him to produce many designs for the new porcelain factory at Sèvres. For all his versatility, though, Boucher was not a great portraitist. He only produced about a dozen portraits and, of these, seven were of Madame de Pompadour. She was well aware of his shortcomings in this area, remarking about one of the portraits that it was "very pretty, but not a good likeness." In spite of this, Boucher remained her favorite artist. **IZ**

The Guitar Player | Jean-Baptiste Greuze

1755–60 | oil on canvas | 27 ¾ x 22 in / 71 x 56 cm | Musée des Beaux-Arts, Nantes, France

This painting was executed when Jean-Baptiste Greuze (1725–1805) was at the peak of his career. His popularity with critics and the public had grown since he showed *Father Reading the Bible to his Children* at the 1755 Salon, an art exhibition held biannually in Paris. *The Guitar Player* is, however, different to many of Greuze's better known paintings in that it lacks the allegorical quality or social issues that can often be found in his work. Instead, Greuze depicts a man listening to the sound of a guitar, which he has probably just finished constructing, as implied by the various tools on his disorganized table. The picture reveals the artist's interest in seventeenth-century Flemish genre scenes, which influenced the rich and detailed style of the painting. One of the most striking

elements of the picture is its composition, which is loosely arranged around a cross. The subject holds the guitar at an awkward angle so that it is almost vertical, and the line this makes contrasts with the horizontal planes of the table and the wide stripes of his trousers. The guitar player is also dramatically lit from the right, creating a strong juxtaposition between his glowing, white clothing and his surroundings, which are painted in dark greens and browns. Together, these different aspects of Greuze's work reflect the player's intense mental focus. While we are stimulated visually, the guitar player, however, is wholly consumed by the sound of the instrument to the extent that, although he looks in the direction of the viewer, he fails to acknowledge the viewer's presence. **WD**

Venice Across the Basin of San Marco | Francesco Guardi

*c.*1760 | oil on canvas | 21 ½ x 34 in / 54.5 x 86.5 cm | Private collection

Francesco Guardi (1712–93) is most often associated with *vedute*—detailed "view" paintings—of his native Venice, such as this one pictured here. However, he actually painted a variety of different subjects, and is believed to have only turned to painting scenes of Venice in the second half of the 1750s. Guardi was born into a family of painters who ran a busy workshop. In 1735 he moved to the studio of Michele Marieschi, where he stayed until 1743. During this time he worked on several collaborations with his brothers. Guardi's early paintings of Venice show the influence of Canaletto, but his style quickly evolved into a far more emotive depiction of the city. His work was, however, less commercially successful than Canaletto's precisely drawn and accurate views.

Guardi often depicted his Venetian scenes with heavy cloud-filled skies, and this painting is no exception. Here the rapid brushstrokes of his painterly style are evident, as is his use of spots of bright pigment that throw the busy figures into focus. The contrast of lights and darks, along with the dots of color, lend the scene a shimmering quality which captures the effect of a watery atmosphere, with a clarity that foresaw the work of the Impressionists many years later. Similarly, the buildings along the canal are suggestions of the scene rather than topographically accurate representations, and are broadly painted in comparatively flat areas of color. Guardi's evocative paintings of Venice were indeed held in great esteem by the French Impressionists. **TP**

Young Woman with Macaw | Giovanni-Battista Tiepolo

*c.*1760 | oil on canvas | 27 ½ x 20 ½ in / 70 x 52 cm | Ashmolean Museum, Oxford, UK

Giovanni-Battista (Giambattista) Tiepolo (1696–1770) is best known for his frescoes in the palaces of Germany, Venice, and Madrid. Venetian-born Tiepolo traveled a great deal; his work was renowned throughout Europe where he was employed by a number of very wealthy and influential patrons. He was usually assisted in his work by his sons— Domenico (also known as Giandomenico) and Lorenzo. Tiepolo's portraiture is less well known, but was equally sought after. The identity of the model in *Young Woman with Macaw* is not recorded, but it is believed to be Tiepolo's daughter. The provenance of this painting is not certain, but it was probably produced for the Empress Elizabeth Petrovna of Russia. Paintings of women with parrots were popular during the eighteenth century, and symbolized the exotic world, along with lavish, decadent lifestyles, and hinted at sexual indiscretion. The themes for Tiepolo's large-scale works were based on classical mythology, ancient literature, biblical stories, or grand events in history—always high-blown and glorious, but also witty and hinting at irreverence. This portrait's detailed brushwork highlights the intense clarity for which his fresco and mural work was famed. This arresting work demonstrates Tiepolo's excellent draftsmanship, impressive understanding of anatomy, and use of brilliant colors. British author Philip Pullman has cited the painting as among the inspirations for the daemons in his *His Dark Materials* trilogy. **LH**

Still Life with Bottle of Olives | Jean-Siméon Chardin

1760 | oil on canvas | 28 x 38 ½ in / 71 x 98 cm | Louvre, Paris, France

Paris-born Jean-Siméon Chardin (1699–1779) resisted the wishes of his father, a cabinet maker, to follow in his footsteps, and instead became an apprentice in the studio of Pierre-Jacques Cazes and Noel-Nocholas Coypel in 1719. Throughout his life, Chardin remained a loyal member of the French Academy but, despite his success, he was prevented from becoming a professor because he was nominated as a painter "in the domain of animals and fruit." The early still lifes for which he is best known were completed in a short space of time demonstrating the speed at which he acquired his masterful technique. It has been estimated that a quarter of his total output was produced before 1732. His style is characterized by richly textured brushwork that owed a considerable debt to Dutch painting, in particular the influence of Rembrandt in the handling of paint. This separates his work from the more familiar style of eighteenth-century French painting. Chardin painted simple domestic scenes and familiar household items. However, more sustained attention reveals a deliberate composition and, importantly, the harmonization of disparate elements through his orchestration of a subtle range of related tones. Still Life with Bottle of Olives is typical of his restrained mood, mellow lighting, and uncanny realism giving everyday objects and scenes a magical aura. It is no surprise that his admirers dubbed him "the great magician." His talent lay in producing paintings of perfect completeness with unaffected, yet supreme technical skill. **RW**

Whistlejacket
George Stubbs

c.1762 | oil on canvas | 115 x 97 in / 292 x 246.4 cm
National Gallery, London, UK

George Stubbs (1724–1806) was arguably the greatest horse painter who has ever lived. Contemporaries thought that this picture had been planned as an equestrian portrait of King George III until the owner of Whistlejacket, the Marquess of Rockingham, who commissioned the painting, fell out of favor with the king and the painting was left unfinished. Instead it seems likely that Stubbs intended the horse to be seen as it is—in splendid isolation against a blank background. The artist's knowledge of the anatomy and physiology of the horse was second to none. But the greatness of the painting is not just in its technical skill or its striking physical presence, but in its powerful psychological intensity—we are confronted with the straining energy of the magnificent Whistlejacket as he rears dramatically and turns to flash his wild eyes. The effect is both moving and unforgettable. **JW**

De Español y Mestiza, Castiza
Miguel Cabrera

1763 | oil on canvas | 52 x 39 ¾ in / 132 x 101 cm
Museo de América, Madrid, Spain

Miguel Mateo Maldonado y Cabrera (1695–1768) was an indigenous Zapotec painter during the Viceroyalty of New Spain—now Mexico. Colonial society in what was known as the New World consisted of many groups of people from different areas of the globe. Those of Spanish or Portuguese descent born in Latin America, were called *criollos* or creoles. Cabrera was one of several artists to produce paintings depicting the different *castas* or castes. *De Español y Mestiza, Castiza* shows a family group surrounded by the tools and materials of the father's trade. They have been included in the painting to illustrate that belonging to a certain *casta* was linked primarily to skin color but also limited social status. The status of such individuals is also visible in their European style clothing. The fruit in the foreground is a symbol of the exotic and the natural resources that the New World had to offer. **HH**

The Brown Boy
Sir Joshua Reynolds

1764 | oil on canvas | 91 x 58 ⅛ in / 231 x 147.5 cm
Bradford Art Galleries and Museums, UK

The Honorable Colonel William
Gordon | Pompeo Batoni

1765–66 | oil on canvas | 101 ⅝ x 73 ¼ in / 258.2 x 186.1 cm
Fyvie Castle, Aberdeenshire, Scotland, UK

History has proven Sir Joshua Reynolds (1723–92) to be one of the most important influences on English painting—during his life he almost singlehandedly raised the status of artists in England. Much of this was because he made portraits of the famous and influential people of the day, and developed an approach that mixed lofty classical allusion with a desire to capture something personal about his sitters. This picture of twelve-year-old Thomas Lister shows what made Reynolds the foremost portraitist of his time. The artist has given the boy's face a flattering, slightly idealized look, but it still combines a child's sensitivity with the pensive air that says he is on the brink of growing up. Reynolds's technique brings out the plush fabric of the boy's costume; it blends harmoniously with the serene Arcadian backdrop, which is reminiscent of classical landscapes by Poussin or Claude. **AK**

Pompeo Batoni (1708–87) moved to Rome in 1727 where he studied painting and made copies of antique sculptures and the paintings of earlier Italian masters. These romanticized "Grand Tourist" portraits made him sought after among foreign, especially English, sitters who desired a souvenir of their travels. This painting portrays William Gordon of Fyvie, second son of William, Second Earl of Aberdeen. He is shown in the uniform of the Queen's Own Royal Highlanders wearing the Huntley tartan. Batoni has used the folds on his subject's plaid to suggest classical drapery. Sword in hand, the Scot strikes a dashing pose before a backdrop that features the ruins of the Colosseum. The painting epitomizes the sophisticated traveler who is interested in the grandeur of classical antiquity while maintaining his own national identity. Batoni's work influenced artists like Sir Joshua Reynolds. **AA**

David Hume | Allan Ramsay

1766 | oil on canvas | 30 x 25 in / 76.2 x 63.5 cm | Scottish National Portrait Gallery, Edinburgh, UK

Born in Edinburgh, Scotland, portraitist Allan Ramsay (1713–84) studied in London under the Swedish painter Hans Hysing, and at the St. Martin's Lane Academy. He spent three years in Italy, where he worked under Francesco Solimena and Francesco Imperiali. He attracted attention with his full-length portrait of the Duke of Argyll and numerous bust-portraits of Scottish gentlemen and their ladies, before he finally settled in London. His pleasant manner and skillful mastery in portraying grace and individuality earned him many commissions, and helped him achieve status as court painter to King George III. Ramsay's fellow Scot represented here is the philosopher, economist, and historian David Hume (1711–76), who is considered one of the most important figures of Western philosophy. Part of the Scottish Enlightenment, and heavily influenced by empiricists Locke and Berkeley, along with Isaac Newton, Hume's philosophy is based on skepticism, claiming that all human knowledge comes to us through our senses. Hume dealt with the problem of causation in his *Treatise on Human Nature* and *Enquiry Concerning Human Understanding*, by stating that although we perceive one event following another, we do not perceive any necessary connection between events. *David Hume* portrays a man of stature and sophistication who gazes ahead with exceptional directness. The features of Hume's face and the details of his dress display Ramsey's excellent draftsmanship and conservative use of light. **SWW**

The Swing | Jean-Honoré Fragonard

1767 | oil on canvas | 32 x 26 in / 83 x 66 cm | Wallace Collection, London, UK

This is Jean-Honoré Fragonard's (1732–1806) most celebrated painting, as well as one of the best-known images in eighteenth-century art. It illustrates the elegance and playfulness of the Rococo style, which dominated French art during this period. The risqué subject was chosen by the Baron de Saint-Julien, who wanted a portrait of himself with his young mistress. The baron is the lover concealed in the shrubbery and, in his original brief, he specified that the swing should be pushed by a bishop. This was meant as a harmless, private joke, as Saint-Julien held an important post in the Church, as Receiver General of the French clergy. Even so, the suggestion shocked the first artist that the baron approached. Fragonard was more accommodating, although he did insist on replacing the bishop with the more traditional figure of a cuckolded husband. Fragonard made the subject of the swing, a conventional symbol of inconstancy, his own by adding a host of witty details. In the foreground, a tiny lapdog—a symbol of fidelity—raises the alarm by yapping loudly, but the husband takes no notice. The statues, which seem half alive, share in the conspiracy. The putti—traditional attendants of Venus, the goddess of love—gaze up adoringly at the girl, while Cupid raises a finger to his lips. The girl is caught in a shaft of sunlight, while the frills and flounces of her dress echo the luxuriant foliage in the trees. Her two admirers, meanwhile, are bathed in shadows, and the outstretched arm of the baron has an obvious, phallic significance. **IZ**

John Campbell, 4th Duke of Argyll | Thomas Gainsborough

1767 | oil on canvas | 92 x 60 ¾ in / 235 x 154.3 cm | Scottish National Portrait Gallery, Edinburgh, UK

This portrait was commissioned and produced while Thomas Gainsborough (1727–88) was still based in Bath, prior to his move to London. He was nevertheless attracting an increasingly prestigious range of clients. For much of his career, Gainsborough maintained a fierce rivalry with Sir Joshua Reynolds (1723–92). The two artists had very different approaches. Reynolds, with his academic background, would have tackled a sitter of this kind by painting him in the grand manner. The pose would have echoed a classical statue or a painting by an Old Master, while the monument in the background would have featured carvings with some mythological or allegorical allusion. Gainsborough detested this sort of pomposity. His own training had included a stint with Hubert Gravelot (1699–1773), a popular illustrator and engraver, and this had influenced his own approach, which was lighter, more direct, and less artificial than any portrait by Reynolds. Here, Campbell's pose is entirely natural and the monument, while imposing enough to hint at a military background, was essentially nothing more than a prop. Gainsborough relied solely on the man's uniform and the symbols of his office to convey his exalted rank. The duke carries the ceremonial staff that signified his post as the Hereditary Master of the Royal Household. He also belonged to the Order of the Thistle, and is proudly displaying its badge across his chest. He had been a distinguished soldier and had served as Colonel of the North British Dragoons. **IZ**

Experiment with a Bird in an Air Pump | Joseph Wright of Derby

1768 | oil on canvas | 72 x 94 ½ in / 183 x 244 cm | National Gallery, London, UK

Industrial Revolution meets scientific experiment meets Caravaggio-style light and shade as a white cockatoo (or dove) flutters in panic while the air is sucked from the glass in which it has been placed. One girl recoils in horror, the other looks on forlornly as the bird suffocates. The imposing "scientist" may be about to flood back life-giving air but the outcome is uncertain. English genre and portait painter Joseph Wright of Derby's (1734–97) paintings, engraved later as prints, were highly popular in the 1760s, with their blend of scientific experiment and awe-struck onlookers: an absorbing mix combining the potential of danger inherent in experiments with the elation of success. But what really marked him was his play on candlelight, moonlight, and lantern-light and how this framed the details within his paintings, especially the faces on the individual onlookers. As with his other treatments of the time, Wright utilized a strong *chiaroscuro* effect emanating from a single light source. These are essentially contrived domestic scenes, painted for a wealthy market, and images of the scientific world. This was the age after all—especially in the Midlands—of the pioneers of science and industry, of James Watt, Matthew Boulton, Josiah Wedgwood (from whom Wright of Derby later took commissions), and Joseph Priestley—and Wright of Derby captured the zeitgeist perfectly. His nickname is derived from the fact that he spent his entire life in the British town (apart from brief stints in Bath, London, and Italy). **JH**

The Blue Boy | Thomas Gainsborough

1770 | oil on canvas | 70 x 48 in / 178 x 122 cm | Huntington Art Collections, San Marino, CA, USA

This dazzling portrait won great acclaim when it was first exhibited in 1770, cementing Thomas Gainsborough's (c.1727–88) reputation as one of the finest painters of his day. At the time, the artist was earning a good living in the fashionable city of Bath, but was anxious to make his name in London. He hoped to do this by showing *The Blue Boy* at a prestigious new venue, the Royal Academy, which had staged its first exhibition in 1769. The picture was probably not commissioned—it was painted on a used canvas, over another portrait. The sitter was Jonathan Buttall, the son of a London ironmonger, and a close friend of Gainsborough's—Buttall was one of the pallbearers at his funeral. The youth's fancy clothing is reminiscent of that found in the costume portraits of Anthony van Dyck (1599–1641), one of Gainsborough's chief influences Like van Dyck's pictures, Gainsborough's works are flamboyant, supremely elegant, and display a brilliant, virtuoso technique. Gainsborough liked to paint in subdued lighting conditions, particularly candlelight, which probably accounts for his flickering, feathery brushstrokes. He also rejected the contemporary taste for a smooth, detailed finish, insisting that his work should always be viewed from a distance. He commented dryly that paintings were "not made to be smelled" to a client who ignored this advice. Gainsborough also took particular care with his landscape backgrounds, ensuring that they complemented the mood of the picture. **IZ**

The Death of General Wolfe | Benjamin West

1770 | oil on canvas | 60 x 84 ½ in / 152.5 x 214.5 cm | National Gallery of Canada, Ottawa, Canada

The American artist Benjamin West (1738–1820) moved in 1763 to England, where he quickly gained a reputation as portraitist to King George III before painting his most famous and monumental work, *The Death of General Wolfe*. When it was first exhibited at London's Royal Academy in 1771, it was initially criticized for being overambitious. However, by the end of the century, opinion had changed. Three full-scale copies were commissioned from West, including one for the king, while smaller prints of the work became one of the best-selling reproductions of the period. This Neoclassical painting depicts the British Major-General, James Wolfe, dying at Quebec in 1759, during the war that established Canada as British colony. Wolfe won this fight, but lost his life, and West presents him as a modern, noble hero. Flanked by fellow officers and a Native American, each figure responds to Wolfe's death, focusing the viewer's attention on this central scene. West has distorted actual events to heighten the painting's drama. Here, the battle is in full swing right behind the dying general; in fact he died further afield as the battle was ending. Wolfe's body in the painting also alludes to Christ's descent from the cross, and the shape of the brooding clouds echoes his slumped figure. West also unconventionally depicts his figures in contemporary dress, rather than working within a classical or allegorical manner, thus emphasizing the work's veracity. **WD**

Portrait of a Child Holding a Rattle | Niels Rode

1771 | oil on canvas | 36 x 31½ in / 92 x 80 cm | Private collection

Portrait of a Child Holding a Rattle was painted by the Danish Rococo artist Niels Rode (1732–94). After flourishing in France for the first half of the eighteenth century, the Rococo style had almost come to an end in that country, but Rococo did not reach Denmark until the 1730s, and by the time of this painting it was still popular there. Rode was taught by Johann Georg Ziesenis, a recognized Danish Rococo painter who worked as a portraitist to the Danish, English, and German courts. It is likely that Ziesenis brought Rode to Holland around the late 1760s, where Rode would have been introduced to other Rococo artists in the Painters' Guild in The Hague, Netherlands. The subject of this painting is a small girl, probably about two years of age. She is holding onto her rattle quite firmly, just as a cord, tied to the chair, is holding onto her. She is dressed in the finest of clothes, suggesting she must be of noble family. Soft colors of pink, white, and beige surround the girl—even her head is covered by a pink cap with a fine border of white lace. She is looking straight at us, with kind eyes and a little smile, both of which are mannerisms often seen in the Rococo portrait. These new artistic traits somehow seem to open up the space between the viewer and the person being portrayed, creating a sense of intimacy. Rode's skills as a portrait painter remained true to the existing artistic styles that were practiced throughout Europe during the eighteenth century, livening up portraits and landscapes by the use of pastel colors and lighthearted subject matters. **SML**

Pencerrig | Thomas Jones

1772 | oil on canvas | 12 ½ x 8 ½ in / 32 x 22 cm | Tate Collection, London, UK

Pencerrig was the Welsh family estate of Thomas Jones (1742–1803), who was to have followed the typical path of a landowner's younger son and trained for the Church. However, the money for this was unavailable and he turned instead to landscape painting. The ability to sketch and paint was regarded at the time as an accomplished pastime for members of genteel families. Although Jones painted professionally, he still remained something of a "gentleman painter," recording views in Naples on his version of the Grand Tour undertaken by many contemporary young aristocrats. This painting of a view of his family's estate was produced on a holiday there in 1772. The scale of his painting is surprisingly small, yet the colors are rich and deep,

showing bright skies and solid banks of clouds whose forms echo the mountains and fields below. The vibrant colors and specific composition of the clouds indicate a work painted outside in the open air. This was unusual for oil paintings at the time; it was only because he was working on such a small, transportable scale that the artist was able to paint in this method outdoors, yet it enabled Jones to convey a timeless immediacy and freshness. At a time when landowners chose to have quasi-portraits of their estates painted by professionals, Jones created an innovative, intimate record of the landscape associated with his family, rather than of his house and garden. Jones eventually inherited the estate and died there in 1803. **SC**

Ariadne Abandoned by Theseus on Naxos | Angelica Kauffmann

1774 | oil on canvas | 25 ⅛ x 35 ⅜ in / 63.8 x 90 cm | Museum of Fine Arts, Houston, TX, USA

Angelica Kauffmann (1741–1807) with Mary Moser comprised the only two women of the thirty-six founding members of London's Royal Academy in 1768. It was in part due to her art training that Kauffmann was able to inhabit what was a predominantly male institution, and moreover, that she was able to work within history painting, a genre considered to be strictly the reserve of male creativity due to the technical and intellectual demands it placed on the artist. The plight of Ariadne was not the only mythological story Kauffmann tackled; the artist also depicted representations of Zeuxis (a superlative artist whose exploits were described in Pliny's *Natural History*), Cornelia, and Sappho. It is significant to remember that Kauffmann was painting her mythological scenes while the frescoes of Pompeii were being excavated; Pompeii itself was found during an excavation that began on March 23, 1748. Kauffmann takes up the story of the daughter of the Cretan King Minos recounted by Ovid at the point when, having slayed the minotaur with Theseus, she is abandoned on the island of Naxos. Here, Ariadne adopts a refined, yet heartfelt pose. Unlike Titian's depiction of Ariadne, wherein she appears caught in a moment of heightened emotional tension, Kauffmann's figure, while distressed, bears such an emotional response with a modicum of restraint and repose. The treatment of Ariadne is unprecedented in how the artist was able to retell the story in a manner entirely at one with her artistic sensibility. **CS**

Varaha | Mahesh of Chamba

1750–75 | opaque watercolor on paper | 8 x 11 in / 20.4 x 28 cm | Rietberg Museum, Zürich, Switzerland

Mahesh was active at the Chamba court between 1730 and 1770. Little is known about him, but it is believed that he worked as a carpenter-painter with prestigious artists such as Laharu. Mahesh is mostly known for his *Dashavatara* and *Bhairava*—illustrated texts of religious stories. The Pahari state of Chamba, in the Himachal Pradesh—a region in the foothills of the Himalayas—was ruled by the Rajput dynasty in the eighteenth century. At that time, Chamba was a refuge for many artists, and it became renowned for its miniature painting style. This style was a deliberate innovation that was intended to symbolize political resistance to the Mughalization of the Pahari states. The Rajput dynasty practiced Vaishnavism, a form of Hinduism that focuses on the worship of the god

Vishnu, and the ruler Umed Singh (reigned 1748–64) commissioned many works of art. *Dashavatara* tells the story of the tenth incarnation or avatar of Vishnu who is known as Varaha or the man-boar. In *Varaha*, Mahesh's hallmarks are apparent—the predominance of dark blue to represent water, the conceptual representation of the horizon, the architecture and the clouds. The horizontal format recalls traditional miniature paintings. Varaha is conventionally rendered in blue with a gemmed crown, a yellow lower garment, auspicious marks on his torso, and a garland of wild flowers. Holding the four attributes of Vishnu—the conch, the disk, the lotus, and the mace—in his four arms, he defeats a demon. Mahesh has told a traditional tale in his unique style. **SZ/MC**

Mr. and Mrs. Ralph Izard (Alice Delancey) | John Singleton Copley

1775 | oil on canvas | 68 ¾ x 88 in / 174.6 x 223.5 cm | Museum of Fine Arts, Boston, MA, USA

During the two decades that preceded the American Revolution, a portrait by John Singleton Copley (1738–1815) was the ultimate sign of status for affluent New Englanders and New Yorkers. While expressing the wealth and taste of his sitters, Copley nevertheless created psychologically penetrating portraits. *Mr. and Mrs. Ralph Izard (Alice Delancey)* depicts an intimate moment between a married couple. At the time of this portrait, Ralph Izard, a Southern-born gentleman, was living abroad in London, Paris, and Tuscany, which perhaps explains why Copley paints him and his wife in "Grand Tour portrait style"—the fashion for portraying sitters surrounded by the artifacts and art they had collected during their tourist travels. Yet in 1780, Izard would

pledge his large estate to finance warships to fight in the Revolutionary War and would later become the delegate and senator from South Carolina. Izard's ideological and political beliefs, as well as his interests as a collector, are symbolically expressed through the décor that surrounds him. In addition to representing an important transitional period in his sitters' lives, this painting is often seen as bridging the gap between Copley's earlier colonial style and his more extravagant later works. In 1774, Copley emigrated to London, became a member of the Royal Academy of Art, and began painting in the well-regarded historical genre. However, his most historically significant contributions remain his paintings of the reality and aspirations of prominent Colonial Americans. **AH**

The Bolt | Jean-Honoré Fragonard

c.1777 | oil on canvas | 28 ½ x 36 ½ in / 73 x 93 cm | Louvre, Paris, France

Jean-Honoré Fragonard (1732–1806) was one of the leading painters in the Rococo style. His pictures were frivolous but sensual, typifying the elegance of French court life, in the years leading up to the revolution of 1789. To his contemporaries, Fragonard was known above all as a master of *sujets légers* (light subjects). These themes were openly erotic, but were handled with a degree of taste and delicacy that made them acceptable, even in royal circles. Indeed, it speaks volumes about the fashions of the day that this picture appears to have been commissioned as a companion piece for a religious painting. According to an early source, the Marquis de Véri approached the artist seeking a picture to hang alongside one of Fragonard's rare devotional images—*The Adoration of the Shepherds*. To modern eyes, this may seem a strange juxtaposition, but Véri probably intended the combination to represent Sacred and Profane Love— an artistic theme that had been popular since the Renaissance. Usually, artists conveyed this idea in a single picture, but sometimes they paired a painting of Eve with a subject relating to the Virgin Mary (who was often viewed as the new Eve). Here, the apple, which is prominently displayed on the table, is a conventional reference to Eve's temptation in the Garden of Eden. *The Bolt* was painted when the Rococo style was beginning to go out of fashion; yet the dramatic lighting and the high degree of finish show that Fragonard was adapting to the Neoclassical style, which was coming into vogue. **IZ**

The Skater | Gilbert Stuart

1777 | oil on canvas | 96 ¼ x 58 in / 245.5 x 147.4 cm | National Gallery of Art, Washington, DC, USA

The perfectly poised and polished composition with its wash of vibrant surfaces tell of an artist totally at ease with his subject matter. Gilbert Stuart (1755–1828) was primarily a painter of head and shoulders so his full-length skater was something of a rarity. Painted in Edinburgh, this eye-catching picture by Stuart of his friend William Grant combines cool colors with flawless portraiture. As with many of his paintings, Stuart works up from a dark mass, in this case the ice providing a solid foundation for the skater. The figure rises above the ice with tilting hat, crossed arms, and an almost jaunty face, in dark clothes that provide a contrast to the background whites and grays. From the age of fourteen, Stuart was already painting on commission in colonial America.

In 1776 he sought refuge in London during the American War of Independence. There he studied with Benjamin West, the visual chronicler of early U.S. colonial history. It was West who aptly described Stuart's skill for "nailing a face to the canvas." For his ability to capture a sitter's essence, Stuart was regarded by his London peers as second only to Sir Joshua Reynolds; and he was head and shoulders above his American contemporaries—with the exception of Bostonian John Singleton Copley. But finances were not Stuart's forté and he was forced to flee to Ireland in 1787 to escape creditors. Returning to America in the 1790s, Stuart quickly established himself as the country's leading portraitist not least with his paintings of five U.S. presidents. **JH**

The Shepherd Girl | Sir George Romney

*c.*1778 | oil on canvas | 46 ½ x 35 ⅜ in / 118 x 90 cm | Philadelphia Museum of Art, Philadelphia, PA, USA

English artist George Romney (1734–1802) was born in Kendal in the Lake District. Almost self-taught as an artist, he moved to London in the 1760s and established himself as one of the most fashionable portrait painters of his day, alongside Reynolds and Gainsborough. Romney was often asked to paint the children of his clients, for this was the period when the modern idea of family life was gaining ascendancy. Here he has posed the child of a wealthy London family as an unlikely shepherd girl, a popular fantasy of the period as Marie Antoinette famously illustrated at Versailles. The unruliness of the girl's flock suggests she may be playing the role of the notoriously lax Little Bo-Peep, from the nursery rhyme. The charm of the fantasy image is irresistible, especially as it is carried off with such technical skill. The surfaces of skin and clothing, the delightful hat, and the wool of the sheep comprise a series of harmonious variations on white. Romney's celebration of country life here is pure artifice; it pretends to be nothing else. But the background is romantic and moody, reflecting a darker side to his work. The painting is saved from sentimentality by Romney's talent for capturing expressive details of posture and expression. The girl's face is alert and her gaze, shaded by the brim of the hat, is far from saccharine. There is a bold firmness to the upright figure and the unsmiling mouth. Romney's consummate skill and perceptive eye deliver an image that is unashamedly frivolous but enduringly impressive. **RG**

The Nightmare | Henry Fuseli

1781 | oil on canvas | 40 x 50 in / 101 x 128 cm | Detroit Institute of Arts, Detroit, MI, USA

This is Henry Fuseli's (Johann Heinrich Füssli, 1741–1825) most famous painting, as well as a landmark in the development of the Romantic movement. It has become an iconic image that is familiar in popular culture and much parodied. *The Nightmare* owes its enduring fame to two principal factors. It was one of the first paintings to successfully depict an intangible idea, rather than an event, a person, or a story. In addition, the precise intentions of the artist remain elusive. The likeliest of many theories about the source of Fuseli's inspiration is perhaps that this picture started out as a visual pun. The creature squatting on the woman is an incubus or *mara*. It is this demon who is causing the nightmare, rather than the horse (or "night-mare") that peers from behind the drapes. In contemporary folklore, horses were often linked with nocturnal visitations. They were ridden by night-hags and witches, and "hagridden" was used as a term for someone troubled by nightmares. The horror is heightened by the unsettling pose of the woman, which creates an air of sexual menace. There is a theory that the picture was designed as an act of sexual revenge. On the reverse of the canvas, there is an unfinished portrait of a girl, who may have been the object of Fuseli's unrequited affections. However, the pose may simply reflect contemporary scientific theories, which fascinated Fuseli, about the physical causes of nightmares, such as sleeping with the head lower than the feet. **IZ**

Self-Portrait in a Straw Hat | Élisabeth Vigée Le Brun

1782 | oil on canvas | 38 ½ x 27 ¾ in / 98 x 70.5 cm | National Gallery, London, UK

In this painting, a supremely confident, fashion conscious and beautiful young woman returns the viewer's gaze as she stands against a cloud-flecked blue sky. She has a gorgeous complexion, piercing eyes, a delicate nose, thin lips, pendant earrings, and natural wavy hair below a jaunty straw hat. Inspired by the Flemish master Sir Peter Paul Rubens, Élisabeth Vigée Le Brun (1755–1842) explores the play of outdoor light radiating on skin tones to charming effect. The palette and brush signify the sitter's profession, and the hat—adorned with a dashing ostrich feather and wreath of handpicked wild flowers—her desire to heighten her good looks and engage the viewer's attention. The viewer's eyes are drawn to her pale neck spreading down to her natural cleavage (not constrained by any corset as was the convention of the time) revealed by her low décolletage. Similarly, her hair is her own—not a wig—and is left unpowdered. It was this soft and flattering style that made Vigée Le Brun so sought after by Europe's ruling classes. She was the most famous female eighteenth-century portraitist, dispensing with standard aristocratic props to reveal her subjects as naturally as possible, effectively pioneering a new portraiture style for the period. Vigée Le Brun was not only talented but also highly prolific, painting, according to her lively memoirs, *Souvenirs* (published in 1835 and 1837), some 877 works, including 622 portraits and more than 200 landscapes. **JH**

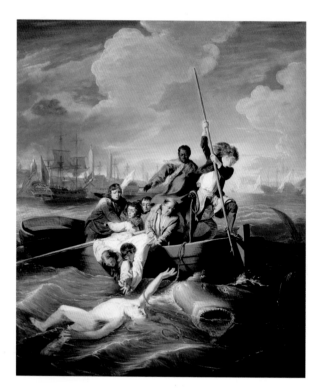

Watson and the Shark | John Singleton Copley

1782 | oil on canvas | 36 x 30 ½ in / 91.5 x 77.5 cm | Detroit Institute of Arts, Detroit, MI, USA

John Singleton Copley's (1738–1815) *Watson and the Shark* was inspired by a celebrated incident that took place in 1749 off the shore of Havana, Cuba. Fourteen-year-old Brook Watson, an orphan serving as a crew member on a trading ship, was attacked by a shark while swimming alone in the harbor. He suffered three attacks by the shark and his leg was bitten off before his shipmates managed to rescue him. in this dramatic, emotionally intense painting, Watson appears as an almost mythic creature. Here, he struggles in the water but his naked, white body appears to melt with the waves, as if he were already half part of the sea. Yet Watson survived the ordeal and went on to become a highly successful merchant and politician in London, where he served a term as

mayor from 1796 to 1797. Watson himself is believed to have commissioned the painting from Copley. Recent critical analysis has been devoted to the sociohistorical context for the black sailor standing in the center of the boat. Although Copley probably had little political interest in including this character, and it was not uncommon at this time for black free men to work on the seas, the figure is one of the earliest examples of an African American as a heroic figure in Western art. The themes of courage, teamwork, perseverance, and self-made success are typical ideals that the colonialist Copley became famous for expressing in his paintings. They also illustrate ideals that the revolutionaries hoped to realize in the new United States of America. **AH**

Soap Bubbles | Johann Melchior Wyrsch

1784 | oil on canvas | 19 x 18 in / 48 x 46 cm | Musée des Beaux-Arts, Besançon, France

Johann Melchior Wyrsch (1732–98) was born in Buochs, Switzerland. In 1753 he went to Rome to study with Gaetano Lapis and then at the Académie Française. He moved to Besançon in the Franche-Comté region of France where he was the founder and then director of the Academy of Painting and Drawing. He excelled in religious paintings and was also in demand from the aristocracy of the region for portrait painting. In 1784 Besançon proclaimed him a "citizen of honor" in gratitude for his work, and a street there still bears his name. He moved to Lucerne in Switzerland where he founded a school for painters, but his residence there was short lived as his eyesight failed due to untreated cataracts. He then retired to his native city of Buochs, where his fellow citizens named him "the blind painter." In this picture, a solemn young boy blows bubbles through a pipe. Soap bubbles were a conventional symbol of the transitory nature of life and the consequent vanity of worldly pursuits. Paintings of this genre, known as *vanitas* images, were to inspire the Pre-Raphaelist artist John Everett Millais (1829–96) to paint *Bubbles* in 1886, a painting subsequently made world-famous for its use over many decades in advertisements for Pears soap. Wyrsch's much earlier version is a fine example of the theme and showcases the artist's talent for portraiture. Tragically, Wyrsch was shot and killed in 1798 by Napoleon's troops who, in the process of attacking Buochs, also burned down his house and destroyed many of his paintings. **TS**

Oath of the Horatii | Jacques-Louis David

1785 | oil on canvas | 130 x 158 in / 330 x 401.5 cm | Louvre, Paris, France

Jacques-Louis David (1748–1825) is arguably history's most extraordinary political propaganda painter. Court-painter to Napoleon, much of what we know of the emperor's mythic persona and the iconography of the French Revolution comes from David's theatrical, allegorical paintings. David was the father of the Neoclassical art movement, which depicted classical myths and history as analogous to contemporary politics. Oath of the Horatii tells the story, recorded around 59 BCE by the Roman historian Titus-Livy, of sons from two families, the three Horatii brothers and the three Curiatii brothers, who fought in the wars between Rome and Alba around 669 BCE. The men are required to fight but one of the women from the Curiatii family is married to one of the Horatii brothers, and one Horatii sister is betrothed to a brother in the Curiatii family. Despite these ties, Horatii senior exhorts his sons to fight the Curiatii and they obey, despite the lamentations of their grief-stricken sisters. In depicting the moment when the men chose political ideals over personal motives, David asks viewers to regard these men as role models during their own politically tumultuous time. As concerned with realism in painting as he was with idealism in politics, David traveled to Rome in order to copy the architecture from life. The result was an enormous success when the painting was exhibited in the 1785 Salon in Paris. David's paintings still resonate powerfully with viewers because the strength of his skill was eminent enough to articulate his strong beliefs. **AH**

The Death of General Montgomery | John Trumbull

1786 | oil on canvas | Yale University Art Gallery, New Haven, CT, USA

John Trumbull (1756–1843), a graduate of Harvard, was greatly influenced by his fellow American, the artist Benjamin West, to create a series of paintings of the War of Independence that would encourage nationalism among Americans. The paintings, which utilized both the paintings of West and John Singleton Copley for creative inspiration, are highly constructed and moralized so as to uphold America and its causes as historically virtuous. A stylistic feature the contributes to this effect is the gesturing of the figures: even when dying, they assume graceful and elegant positions, exhibiting the Neoclassical style for which Trumbull's teacher, West, was known. The elegant Neoclassicism of Trumbull's *The Death of General Montgomery* greatly benefits from his carefully balanced composition. Placed roughly in the middle of the painting, the dying General Montgomery is at the center of a composition structured loosely around an "X" pattern. Our eye travels from the lower left-hand side of the canvas by following the sweeping diagonal line formed by the outstretched arms of the soldiers in front of the general, and then upward to the general himself who is framed by the dramatic line of the flags and the black sky beyond. In this work, Trumbull has successfully synthesized elements of the current academic style of painting to create a lively and interesting painting that effectively imagines a politically potent moment in American history. His painting is highly skilled propaganda. **SS**

Goethe in the Campagna | Johann Tischbein

1786–87 | oil on canvas | 64 ½ x 81 in / 164 x 206 cm | Städelschen Kunstinstitut, Frankfurt, Germany

Johann Heinrich Wilhelm Tischbein (1751–1829) came from a large family of painters from Hesse, and received his early training from his uncle Johann Heinrich Tischbein the Elder (1722–89) in Kassel. He later moved to Hamburg and studied with another uncle, Jacob Tischbein (1725–91). Much of his early work was in a late Baroque style popular in Germany at that time, and in 1777 he moved to Berlin and became a portraitist for the Prussian court. The defining moment of his career was when he made his first trip to Italy in 1779, where he studied in Rome with Alexander Trippel, a sculptor working in the Neoclassical style. Tischbein turned to the cool classicism seen in his later works, and eventually became one of the leading Neoclassical artists of his

day. *Goethe in the Campagna* is his most famous work, and was painted while the artist was in Rome for the second time. He met Johann Wolfgang von Goethe in 1786, and Tischbein accompanied Goethe to Naples in 1787. Based on their friendship and the success of this painting, Tischbein earned the nickname "Goethe-Tischbein." The elegant rendering of Goethe reclining among classical ruins and set against a distant view of the Roman Campagna was Tischbein at his best. Tischbein's work was of some importance in spreading the ideals of Neoclassicism, especially through his illustrations accompanying works by Homer. In 1799 he returned to Germany and from 1808 became painter to the court of Oldenburg in northern Germany. **TP**

Mrs. Richard Brinsley Sheridan | Thomas Gainsborough

1785–87 | oil on canvas | 86 ⅝ x 60 ⅝ in / 220 x 154 cm | National Gallery of Art, Washington, DC, USA

In this bewitching portrait, Thomas Gainsborough (1727–88) captured a compelling likeness of the sitter, while creating an air of melancholy. This emphasis on mood was rare in the portraiture of the day, but became an important concern for the Romantics in the following century. Gainsborough had known the sitter since she was a child and had painted her, together with her sister, when he was living in Bath (*The Linley Sisters*, 1772). He was a close friend of the family, largely because they shared his passion for music. Indeed, Elizabeth was a talented soprano and had performed as a soloist at the celebrated Three Choirs Festival. She had been obliged to abandon her singing career, however, after eloping with Richard Brinsley Sheridan (1751–1816)—then a penniless actor. Sheridan went on to achieve considerable success, both as a playwright and as a politician, but his private life suffered in the process. He ran up huge gambling debts and was repeatedly unfaithful to his wife. This undoubtedly accounts for Elizabeth's wistful and somewhat forlorn appearance in this picture. One of Gainsborough's greatest assets was his ability to orchestrate the various elements of a picture into a satisfying whole. In all too many portraits, the sitter resembles a cardboard cut-out, when placed against a landscape background. Here, the artist has paid as much attention to the sumptuous pastoral setting as to his glamorous model, and has ensured that the breeze, which is making the branches bend and sway, is also stirring the gauze drapery around Elizabeth's neck and blowing her hair into fetching disarray. **IZ**

Robert Burns
Alexander Nasmyth

1787 | oil on canvas | 15 x 12 ⁵⁄₈ in / 38 x 32 cm
Scottish National Portrait Gallery, Edinburgh, UK

Alexander Nasmyth (1758–1840) has been dubbed the "father of Scottish landscape painting," but no other work he painted is as well known as this portrait of Scotland's most famous poet. It was commissioned by Edinburgh publisher William Creech to adorn a new edition of Burns's poems in 1787, but Burns and Nasmyth were already good friends before the sittings. A half-length portrait framed in an oval, the picture shows Burns confident and well dressed, a trace of amusement around his eyes and lips. The landscape background, suggestive of Burns's native Ayrshire, supplies a note of melancholy. It is a Romantic portrait, identifying the poet with nature and self-will, but tempered by a flavor of Enlightenment rationalism. The picture has been left partially unfinished because Nasmyth stopped painting once he was satisfied with what he had achieved. **RG**

Self-Portrait
Angelica Kauffmann

1787 | oil on canvas | 93 ½ x 50 ½ in /
128 x 93.5 cm | Uffizi, Florence, Italy

Angelica Kauffmann (1741–1807) enjoyed greater status than was usual for eighteenth-century female artists. She was well versed in classical and Renaissance art and architecture having lived in Italy. Women artists were restricted to still life and portraiture but Kauffmann refused to be confined to these areas. She was interested in the women of myth and history such as Helen, Venus, and Cleopatra. Her history paintings were criticized at the time, and have been since, for their disregard for the heroism of Neoclassicism. Kauffmann produced many self-portraits to engage the attention of prospective patrons. In this portrait she looks away from the viewer, a green ribbon in her loose hair. The white robe suggests Roman dress, but in the Neoclassical style caught above the waist with a belt. Seated between pillars with open views to mountains, she holds the tools of her trade. **WO**

Marie Antoinette
Élisabeth Vigée Le Brun

1788 | oil on canvas | 106 ¾ x 76 ¾ in / 271 x 195 cm
Palace of Versailles, Versailles, France

This is one of many portraits that the Rococo artist (Marie-Louise) Élisabeth Vigée Le Brun (1755–1842) painted of French queen Marie Antoinette. In 1779, the artist was summoned to paint the queen, and the two women became good friends. Vigée Le Brun painted Antoinette in a variety of costumes and poses, many of which are displayed at the Palace of Versailles. In an extremely male-dominated art world, Vigée Le Brun's powerful patron gave her freedom to paint. While the clichéd props of marbled pillar and heavy drapes are in evidence, Marie Antoinette is shown in a very open and flattering pose—about as casual and relaxed as one could get for that strait-laced, corsetted time, when reputations were built and destroyed on the flimsiest of ridicules. In the wake of the Revolution, Vigée Le Brun fled France and became one of the most famed portrait artists of her time. **JH**

Mrs. Siddons as the Tragic Muse
Sir Joshua Reynolds

1789 | oil on canvas | 94 ⅜ x 58 ⅛ in / 239.5 x 147.5 cm
Dulwich Picture Gallery, London, UK

In this painting, Sir Joshua Reynolds (1723–92) combines a theatricality that instantly identifies its subject with an extreme example of his "Grand Manner." Reynolds casts Sarah Siddons as the mythical Greek "Tragic Muse" Melpomene. Behind her, allegorical figures Pity (left) and Terror (right) hold the dagger and cup that symbolize Melpomene. Her clothes reflect the stage costumes of the day, but showing a throne flanked by attendants echoes Michelangelo, while her pose is similar to a painting by Baroque artist Domenichino. Smooth brushwork on the actress's face recalls classical sculpture, and Reynolds places her pale face and upper body in a theatrical spotlight, making her the main player emerging from the rich browns and shadows. The unusual monochrome coloring brings a harmonized, monumental classicism to the whole. **AK**

Mozart at the Pianoforte | Joseph Lange

1789 | oil on canvas | 13 ½ x 11 ⅝ in / 34.3 x 29.5 cm | Mozart Museum, Salzburg, Austria

One of the most celebrated musical geniuses in the world, Wolfgang Amadeus Mozart has long fascinated audiences. Several leading artists have produced paintings of Mozart, but many works were executed after the musician's death when his importance was fully acknowledged. There are only about a dozen or so authentic pictures of Mozart, most commissioned by the musician's father and only three produced at Mozart's own instigation. Only four of these paintings exclusively depict Mozart, including the celebrated *Mozart at the Pianoforte*. This unfinished portrait by Wolfgang's brother-in-law, Joseph Lange (1751–1831), is a romantic representation of the musician. Lange created a sympathetic and naturalistic depiction of the young Mozart, just a couple of years

before his death in 1791. The Mozart of Lange's painting has an extraordinary depth of expression, and seems caught up in his own thoughts. Even though the painting is unfinished, the bottom part of the canvas left blank, it is still one of the most realistic portrayals of the musician sitting at the pianoforte. Here we imagine him at work playing or composing, whereas many portraits show him in elaborate costumes or posed stiffly with his family. Indeed, Mozart's wife, Constanze, is known to have said that Lange's portrait was the best likeness to her husband. Lange's own relationship with Mozart may have been complicated, however. The artist's wife, Aloysia, was Constanze's older sister, and had been involved with Mozart before her marriage. **AV**

Sketches of a Black and White Rabbit | Maruyama Ōkyo

*c.*1770–90 | ink and color on paper | 7 ⅝ x 10 ⅜ in / 19.4 x 26.5 cm | Private collection

Maruyama Ōkyo (1733–95) was a versatile artist, known as the precursor of contemporary Japanese art for his fusion of Western Realism with a traditional East Asian painting technique. Born into a family of farmers, Ōkyo moved to Kyoto and worked as an apprentice in a toy shop. Fascinated by perspectivism and realistic depiction of European *camera obscura* pictures, Ōkyo began to study Western painting techniques, and produced a series of *megane-e*, or "eyeglass pictures," showing scenes from Kyoto for a peepshow. He also studied the Kanō style and Chinese painting and excelled in traditional brush technique. The set of album leaves from which this image is taken is an example of his carefully observed sketches of flora and fauna in the manner of a European botanical study. A sketchbook of natural history by Watanabe Shikō (1638–1755) was a major influence to Ōkyo's realistic approach. However, Ōkyo's methods of sketching are marked by their synthesis of realistic elements with more decorative aspects of Kanō style. Despite his realistic depictions of nature, his images have a reflective feel and his motifs include imaginary creatures such as dragons and ghosts. He was possibly the first Japanese artist to draw nudes from life. Ōkyo took on many students, and with Matsumura Goshun (1752–1811) created styles that came to be known as the Maruyama-Shijō School or the Kyoto School. The tradition they established continued to exert its impact on Japanese painting of later periods. **FN**

Death of Marat | Jacques-Louis David

1793 | oil on canvas | 65 x 50 in / 165 x 127 cm | Musées Royaux des Beaux Arts, Brussels, Belgium

Jacques-Louis David (1748–1825) was devoted to the cause of the French Revolution. His painting *Oath of the Horatii* (1784), which hangs in the Louvre, has often been described as a call to arms for the French people, urging them to join the revolutionary cause. David had lost none of his political fervor by the time *Death of Marat* was produced. It commemorates the death of Jean-Paul Marat (1743–93), one of the Revolution's most controversial leaders. By 1793, the high ideals of the Revolution had descended into a general bloodbath, known as "the Terror." Although nicknamed "the friend of the people," Marat was one of the instigators of this phase and eventually the violence caught up with him. On July 13, 1793, he was murdered in his bath by Charlotte Corday, a supporter of a rival political faction. By this stage, David was deeply involved in the revolutionary government—he was an elected member of the National Convention, which voted for the death of the king—so it was natural that he should be chosen to record the event. He knew that Marat used his bathroom as an office, owing to a severe skin complaint, and that he wore a vinegar-soaked turban to ease the discomfort. He changed the appearance of Marat's bathroom, giving it a spartan look that was more fitting for a revolutionary leader. Marat's body strikes a pose highly reminiscent of the dead Christ. David is known as one of the greatest Neoclassical painters—his style deliberately distinguishing itself from the Rococo tastes of the despised French royal family. **IZ**

Pinkie | Sir Thomas Lawrence

1794 | oil on canvas | 58 x 40 in / 148 x 102 cm | Huntington Art Collections, San Marino, CA, USA

Hovering on the threshold of adulthood, this eleven-year-old girl also seems to hover above the landscape in which she is placed. Her filmy skirts and satin ribbons fly up in the brisk wind that sets the clouds racing in the vast sky behind her. This image seizes the imagination with its energy, brilliance, and romance. As such, it is typical of the work of its creator—a dashing, handsome, and largely self-taught prodigy who rose from humble beginnings to become the leading English portraitist of his day, president of the Royal Academy, and knight of the realm. Only in his mid-twenties when he painted this picture, Thomas Lawrence (1769–1830) was already painter to the king and a Royal Academician. Sarah, whose nickname was "Pinkie," came from a wealthy family in colonial Jamaica. When she was sent to school in London, aged nine, her godmother in Jamaica arranged a portrait of her because she missed her so much. The unusually low viewpoint makes Sarah part of the breezy sky, a child of nature echoing the Romantic ideas of French philosopher Jean-Jacques Rousseau, which were popular at the time. The brushwork is breathlessly adept: fluid strokes make Sarah's clothing dance weightlessly in the wind; hard-edged ones keep them from melting into nothing. This is one of the most popular images of all time, an enduring vision of youthfulness that appeared on Cadbury chocolate tins in the 1920s. It is poignant that Pinkie, the subject of such a life-affirming painting, died the year after the portrait was completed. **AK**

Titania Awakes, Surrounded by Attendant Fairies | Henry Fuseli

1794 | oil on canvas | 67 x 53 in / 170 x 134.5 cm | Kunsthaus, Zürich, Switzerland

One of the leading figures of the Romantic movement, Henry Fuseli (1741–1825) created pictures that explored the darker side of the human psyche. This image is in a similar vein to *The Nightmare* (1781), which blends horror and eroticism, though it also focuses on another of the Romantics' favorite themes: fairies. Fuseli drew much of his inspiration from literary sources, most notably Shakespeare, Milton, and Dante. Fortunately for him, there was a major revival of interest in the former at the time. In 1789, John Boydell (1719–1804), a future lord mayor of London, decided to promote the cause of British art by opening a purpose-built Shakespeare Gallery, devoted solely to paintings of scenes from the plays. Then, four years later, James Woodmason set up a similar gallery in Dublin. Fuseli contributed paintings to both these projects—nine to Boydell and five to Woodmason. *A Midsummer Night's Dream* provided material for two of Fuseli's chief interests: fairies and dreams. This picture comes from the Woodmason series and the fairies are considerably less sinister than those in the Boydell paintings. While Titania dotes on Bottom, Peaseblossom massages his ass's head. To the right, Cobweb has donned a suit of armor and is killing a bee, to steal its honey-sack for the queen's lover. In the foreground, other fairies dance and sing, among them one with an insect's head, who was borrowed from a figure in the commedia dell'arte. In the top right-hand corner, Puck surveys the scene, prior to releasing Titania from her enchantment. **IZ**

A Direct North General View of Sydney Cove | Thomas Watling

1794 | oil on canvas | 36 x 47 ½ in / 91 x 121 cm | Dixson Galleries, State Library of NSW, Sydney, Australia

Scotsman Thomas Watling (1762–1814) was the first professional artist to arrive in New South Wales, Australia, and this is the earliest known oil painting of Sydney. However, Watling was not a willing traveler—he was convicted of forging banknotes in his native town of Dumfries and sentenced to fourteen years in the recently established penal colony in Botany Bay. He arrived at Port Jackson in 1792 and became well known for his prolific sketches of birds, fish, mammals, plant life, and Aboriginal people; many of his sketches are now in the British Museum. His topographical studies, such as this detailed picture of Sydney Cove, depict the flora and fauna surrounding the fledgling colony, although the Italianate composition perhaps softens the reality of what was a rough, isolated prison settlement that housed some 2,000 convicts. The identity of the author of this work has been debated because the canvas is dated 1794 on the reverse and there is no record of any colonial artist using oils until 1812—over a decade after Watling received a full pardon and returned to Scotland. It is most likely that he did paint the scene, but perhaps at a later date, by referring to previous drawings. Considering his crime of forgery, it was ironic that Watling's plans for a book of his collected works from the colony were usurped by the Governor's Secretary, who published his own book using uncredited copies of Watling's illustrations. Therefore, only subsequent generations of Australians would be able to appreciate Watling's documentation of their country's foundations. **OW**

The Rev. Robert Walker Skating on Duddingston Loch
Sir Henry Raeburn

*c.*1795 | oil on canvas | 30 x 25 in / 76.2 x 63.5 cm | National Gallery of Scotland, Edinburgh, UK

Raeburn (1756–1823) was the leading Scottish portraitist of his day but, unlike many of his compatriots, he chose to remain in his native land, rather than work in England. This was fortunate, as his career coincided with the heyday of the Scottish Enlightenment and Raeburn was ideally placed to record this unique flowering of the nation's cultural and intellectual life. Based in Edinburgh, far away from the rivalries and competing influences that he would have experienced in London, he also developed a bold and highly distinctive style. Raeburn's originality is readily apparent in this, his most famous painting. Sometimes known as *The Skating Minister*, it depicts the clergyman Robert Walker (1755–1808), who was attached to Canongate Church in Edinburgh and later became chaplain to the Royal Company of Archers. A prolific author and a keen sportsman, Walker had been a member of the Edinburgh Skating Club since 1780. In Raeburn's picture, he is shown with his arms folded across his chest, which a contemporary treatise on skating described as the "proper attitude for genteel rolling." The portrait demonstrates Raeburn's fondness for ingenious lighting effects: the minister's face is shown in strict profile and the figure is virtually depicted as a silhouette, outlined against the pale, ominous sky and the indistinct landscape. These broad masses contrast sharply with a number of fine details, such as the ribbons on the skates and the delicate tracery of skate-marks on the ice, which hark back to Raeburn's early training as a goldsmith. **IZ**

George Washington
Gilbert Stuart

1796 | oil on canvas | 96 ¼ x 60 ¼ in / 244.5 x 153 cm | Brooklyn Museum of Art, Brooklyn, NY, USA

Once a gentlemanly planter, this portrait of America's first president shows a regal—even republican—countenance. The vibrant skin surface may be on an expressionless, even charmless, face but it oozes sturdiness, patience, and dependability. Little wonder this image became the icon still circulating on the country's dollar bills today. George Washington posed for the first time for his fellow countryman Gilbert Charles Stuart (1755–1828) in Philadelphia in November 1794. From that sitting and a number of follow-ups, Stuart went on to produce more than one hundred pictures of Washington. Along with an unfinished portrait (known as the "Athenaeum") this "Landsdowne" portrait is one of the most famous. Stuart would start his portrait paintings by blocking in the large masses and then working through the details. This allowed him to avoid initial line studies. His grasp of flesh tones, as seen here, was remarkable. He did not pay homage to any particular Old Master, instead he relied on what his own eyes, and human nature, showed him. Stuart produced flesh tones by using all the colors available, but did not mix them. Instead he liked to see each color shine through the subsequent layer, as in transparent skin. George Washington stands authoritatively, so much so that the artist can dispense with pomp and circumstance. Stuart painted the first five U.S. presidents, but he was much more than simply a celebrated portraitist of the Founding Fathers: he set the standard for much of the country's national art that was to follow. **JH**

Cornelia Adrienne Gräfin Bose | Johann Friedrich August Tischbein

1798 | oil on canvas | 83 x 54 in / 210 x 138 cm | Germanisches Nationalmuseum, Nuremberg, Germany

Johann Friedrich August Tischbein (1750–1812), also referred to as Friedrich Tischbein, was born in Maastricht into a large family of successful German painters. He first trained under his father and then his uncle, Johann Heinrich Tischbein the Elder (1722–89), a leading portraitist of his time. Friedrich followed in his footsteps and carved a career based on elegant depictions of the bourgeois and upper classes. In 1772, he moved to Paris, where his paintings adopted a delicately Rococo style, and then to Rome in 1777, where his style evolved along Neoclassical lines yet retained the soft and subtle palette of his earlier work. Here he came into contact with the works of Anton Raphael Mengs and Jacques-Louis David, which had a great effect on him. Tischbein was later influenced by

the English painters Thomas Gainsborough and George Romney, going on to develop his own eclectic approach to the portrait, which combined realism, Neoclassicism, and Romanticism. This portrait of the Countess Bose demonstrates his skillful synthesis of Neoclassical calm with warmer Romanticism. Tischbein became a master of pose with portraits that captured the essence of the sitter. Here he conveys the stately grace and social position of the Countess, while also alluding to her motherly skills. There is an air of melancholy in her wistful gaze, which adds to the nostalgic, romantic atmosphere of the painting. Establishing himself in Leipzig, Tischbein achieved great success as a portrait painter during his lifetime with his sensitive and insightful depiction of his subjects. **TP**

Berry Pomeroy Castle, Devon | Thomas Girtin

1798 | watercolor on paper | 10 7/8 x 15 3/8 in / 27.5 x 39 cm | Sotheby's, London, UK

J.M.W. Turner allegedly said that had "Tom Girtin lived I should have starved," and though perhaps an exaggeration, it indicates the extraordinary talent of Thomas Girtin (1775–1802). Girtin's artistic training began with drawing lessons and an apprenticeship with the topographical watercolorist Edward Dayes. As teenagers Girtin and Turner became friends, and the two frequented Dr. Thomas Monro's famous academy. Monro employed them to copy works by J.R. Cozens, the "father" of the English watercolor tradition, with Girtin supposedly making the drawings and Turner filling in the washes. Girtin's distinctive style of clearly defined lines, solid tonality, and broad areas of restricted color can be seen in *Berry Pomeroy Castle*. There is a precise and structural

quality to this work. By combining a pared-down vision of nature without extraneous detail with an accomplished understanding of the effects of light and atmosphere, Girtin created works that were immediately recognizable and appreciated for their aesthetic effect. He died tragically young, his cause of death being variously attributed to asthma or a heart condition. However, during his short life he was prolific, and his works have had a profound effect on the development of watercolor and landscape painting, particularly in England and the United States. Though Turner's success has overshadowed that of Girtin, it is perhaps Girtin who truly paved the way for subsequent watercolorists, and his bold style was frequently copied during the nineteenth century. **TP**

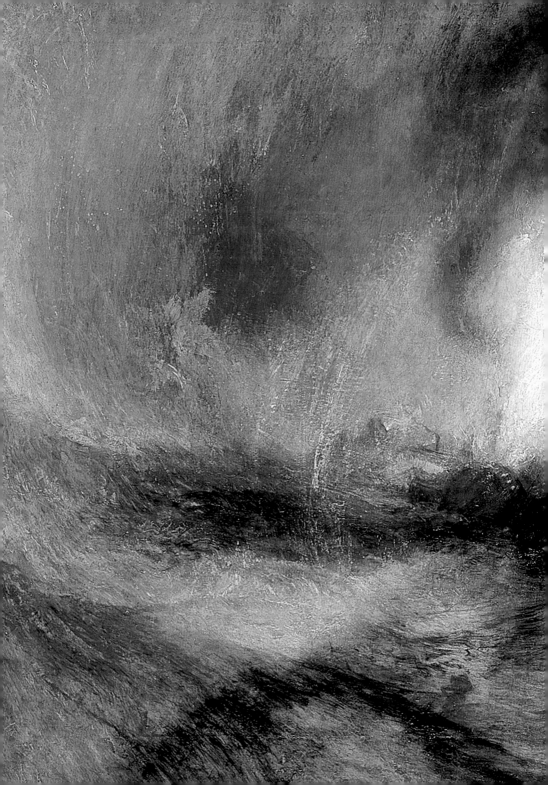

Vishnu Visvarupa, Preserver of the Universe, Represented as the Whole World | Unknown

1800–20 | watercolor on paper | 15 ¼ x 11 in / 38.7 x 28 cm | Victoria & Albert Museum, London, UK

Vishnu is one of the three principal deities in the Hindu godhead, along with Shiva the destroyer and Brahma the creator. Worshiped as the protector and preserver of the world and restorer of moral order, Vishnu is known by his various incarnations in animals and prophets, of which Krishna is the most well known. This cosmic manifestation of Vishnu is known as Visvarupa. Often depicted as a young and handsome man with a crown, Vishnu is studded with cult figures that tell stories from the holy text Bhagavad Gita. Most likely a painting of the Jaipur School in northwest India, made for the enjoyment of a local nobleman or ruler, such paintings are intended to inspire and instruct human practitioners. In *Vishnu Visvarupa, Preserver of the Universe, Represented as the*

Whole World, Vishnu appears in front of a nimbus cloud with four arms holding various items, an indication of his ability to perform several functions at the same time. The conch, also a musical instrument, represents Vishnu's vital role in the immensity of the primordial waters. The disk is a solar symbol, holding the power to destroy ignorance and darkness with the unifying, intellectual tendency of a human being. The lotus bud, one of the most ancient Hindu symbols of purity and spiritual power, when open represents the realization of human development in this process of illumination. The final item, the mace, represents individual existence. In a luminous but flat style of painting, Vishnu's body is a royal blue color, suggesting the infinite sky. **SWW**

Hambletonian, Rubbing Down
George Stubbs

1800 | oil on canvas | 82 ¼ x 144 ⅝ in / 209 x 367.5 cm | Mount Stewart House, County Down, UK

No artist has bettered George Stubbs (1724–1806) in depicting a likeness of the horse. Stubbs harnessed the materiality of paint in order to arrive at seamless, naturalistic images of horses, but what is often overlooked is his ability to render the human figure and capture the essence of landscape with a similar mastery. Stubbs's fascination for nature and its relationship with mankind are reflected in his obsessive attention to detail. His career as a painter of horses was rooted in his exhaustive knowledge of equine anatomy. In his early thirties, Stubbs spent eighteen months dissecting and drawing the bodies of horses at an isolated farmhouse in Lincolnshire. Out of this gory, Enlightenment-driven industry came his treatise *The Anatomy of the Horse* and a steadfast commitment to the pursuit of reality. Painted when Stubbs was seventy-five years old, the almost life-size *Hambletonian, Rubbing Down* signifies the climax of the artist's concern for reality and his late-flowering interest in comparative anatomy. Stubbs has chosen to picture the moment when the racehorse is being cleaned off following his exertions on the racecourse. The trainer and groom are attempting to pacify the exhausted thoroughbred, but Hambletonian's heaving flanks and anxious demeanor overshadow the landscape and everything in it, relegating all further incident to the margins of the picture. Even if Stubbs had never produced another painting, *Hambletonian, Rubbing Down* would have assured him a prominent position in Western art. **PB**

Nightmare | Nicolai Abraham Abildgaard

1800 | oil on canvas | 16 ⅛ x 13 ¾ in / 41 x 35 cm | Private collection

In 1781, the Swiss artist Henry Fuseli painted an image that would terrify and inspire audiences for centuries. In Fuseli's oil painting, a voluptuous, supine young woman in a white, sweat-drenched, clinging tunic is being crushed by the weight of an incubus crouched on her chest. An incubus was a term used synonymously for "nightmare," but it also referred specifically to a mythological creature believed to descend on women and have sexual intercourse with them while they slept. The painting is thought to illustrate the all-consuming pain of lost love. Fuseli's social circle included the Danish painter Nicolai Abildgaard (1743–1809), who created his own version of Fuseli's chilling image. Abildgaard had studied under former pupils of the baroque painter Boucher, and Neoclassicists Claude Lorrain and Nicolas Poussin. He moved to Rome in 1772 where he met Fuseli, whose influence led him to produce work with Romantic elements. He was known throughout his life as one of the foremost Dutch history painters and a leading figure in the Romantic movement. In Abildgaard's version of *Nightmare*, the leering incubus is perched on the beautiful woman's splayed, dormant body while she lies naked next to her sleeping lover. The addition of the second body, with its back turned to the victim and her demonic rapist, renders the image more blatantly erotic and perhaps more nightmarish. It is no longer the portrayal of a psychological state but an image of pure physical terror. **AH**

Portrait of Madame Récamier | Jacques-Louis David

1800 | oil on canvas | 68 ⅞ x 96 ⅛ in / 175 x 244 cm | Louvre, Paris, France

This is widely acknowledged as Jacques-Louis David's (1748–1825) finest portrait. With its grace, simplicity, and economy it is also regarded as one of the most successful examples of Neoclassical art. David's model, Juliette Récamier, was the darling of Parisian society. She was the wife of a wealthy banker from Lyons, though she received the attentions of a host of other men, all of whom were modestly rebuffed. David drew inspiration from Récamier's virtuous reputation. With her bare feet, white dress, and antique accessories, she resembles a latter-day vestal virgin. This is reinforced by the pose. The woman's gaze is candid and direct, but her body is turned away, unapproachable. The portrait sittings did not run smoothly: the painter was irked by Juliette's persistent unpunctuality, while she objected to some of the artistic liberties taken. In particular, she resented the fact that David lightened the shade of her hair, because it did not suit his color scheme. As a result, she commissioned another portrait from one of the artist's pupils. When he learned of this, David refused to continue. "Madame," he declared, "ladies have their caprices; so do painters. Allow me to satisfy mine. I shall keep your portrait in its present state." This decision may have been beneficial, for the stark severity of the picture gives it much of its impact. The lamp and some of the other details are said to have been painted by David's student, Ingres. The latter was certainly impressed by the picture, for he borrowed Récamier's pose for one of his most celebrated works, *La Grande Odalisque*. **IZ**

Naked Maja | Goya

1800 | oil on canvas | 38 ¼ x 74 ¾ in / 97 x 190 cm | Museo del Prado, Madrid, Spain

It is likely that Francisco Goya y Lucientes (1746–1828) painted the famously controversial *Maja desnuda* (*Naked Maja*), for Manuel Godoy, nobleman and prime minister of Spain. Godoy owned a number of paintings of the female nude, and hung them in a private cabinet dedicated to this theme. The *Naked Maja* would have seemed daring and pornographic displayed alongside works such as Velázquez's *Venus and Cupid* (otherwise known as the *Rokeby Venus*, *c*.1650). The model's pubic hair is visible—considered obscene at the time—and the lower-class status of the maja, along with her blatant pose, with breasts and arms facing outward, suggests the subject is more sexually accessible than the traditional goddesses of Western art. However, she is more than merely an object of male desire. Here, Goya may be portraying the new *marcialidad* ("forthrightousness") of Spanish women of the day, and is exploring the forbidden subject of female sexuality. The maja's pose is complicated by her confronting gaze and cool flesh tones, which signify her autonomy. As art critic Robert Hughes wrote, she "is defiantly herself, alluring certainly, but decidedly on her own terms. She is not a sweet little thing, a passive and receptive appeal to male fantasy. . . . Even without her clothes (or perhaps especially so), she is the real maja, tough, sharp, and not to be pushed around." Goya paid for his taboo-breaking act in 1815, when the Inquisition interrogated him about this painting and he was subsequently stripped of his role as court painter. **KM/SP**

Family of Carlos IV | Goya

1800–01 | oil on canvas | 110 ¼ x 132 ¼ in / 280 x 336 cm | Museo del Prado, Madrid, Spain

In 1799 Francisco Goya y Lucientes (1746–1828) was made First Court Painter to Carlos (Charles) IV of Spain. The king requested a family portrait, and in the summer of 1800 the artist prepared a series of oil sketches for the formal arrangement of the various sitters. The final result has been described as Goya's greatest portrait. In this painting, the family members wear sparkling, sumptuous garments, and sashes of various royal orders. Yet despite the pomp and splendor, the artist has employed a naturalistic style, capturing the individual characters so that each, as one critic put it, "is strong enough to disrupt the unity expected of a group portrait." Nevertheless, the most dominant figure is Queen María Louisa in the center. She, rather than the king, took charge of political matters, and her illicit relationship with royal favorite (and patron of Goya) Manuel Godoy was well known. Yet a tender side is evident in her tactile engagement with her son and daughter. Though some critics have interpreted the sometimes unflattering naturalism as a satire, Goya is unlikely to have endangered his position in this way. The royals approved of the painting and saw it as a confirmation of the strength of the monarchy in politically tumultuous times. Goya also pays homage to his predecessor Velázquez here with the insertion of a self-portrait similar to *Las Meninas* (1656). However, while Velázquez painted himself as artist in a dominant position, Goya is more conservative, emerging from the shadows of two canvases on the far left. **KM/SP**

Portrait of Mademoiselle Charlotte du Val d'Ognes
Constance Marie Charpentier

c.1801 | oil on canvas | 64 x 51 in / 162.5 x 129.5 cm | Metropolitan Museum of Art, New York, NY, USA

In 1917, the Metropolitan Museum of Art acquired the unsigned *Portrait of Mademoiselle Charlotte du Val d'Ognes*, believing that it was painted by Jacques-Louis David. The sitter's classical white tunic, Grecian curls, and Spartan setting all reinforced this attribution, but in 1951 Charles Sterling, then director of the museum, concluded that it had actually been painted by one of David's students, a woman named Constance Marie Charpentier (1767–1849). Since then, whether the painting, one of the Met's most popular, is the work of Charpentier or another woman painter of the era, Marie-Denise Villers (1774–1821), has been actively debated among art historians and critics. This magnificent, luminous image of the subject at her drawing board can be read as a moving portrait of mutual respect between two female artists. Sterling's reattribution caused this intimate portrait to be recognized as one of the most accomplished and well-regarded works by a female artist in Western history. Yet once the painting was attributed to a woman and not to David, its monetary value plummeted. At the same time, critics began to ascribe "feminine attributes" to the image. French composer Francis Poulenc called the painting a "mysterious masterpiece," and it was termed "an eighteenth-century Mona Lisa." In his assessment, Sterling wrote: "Its poetry, literary rather than plastic, its very evident charms, and cleverly concealed weakness, its ensemble made up from thousands of subtle attitudes, all seem to reveal the feminine spirit." **AH**

Napoleon Crossing the Alps
Jacques-Louis David

1801 | oil on canvas | 107 x 91 in / 272 x 230 cm | Louvre, Paris, France

Jacques-Louis David (1748–1825) was the ultimate political artist. He was a fervent advocate of the French Revolution (1789–99), almost losing his life on the guillotine. Then, in the next wave of political events, he became an equally enthusiastic supporter of Napoleon Bonaparte, using his talent to glorify the new emperor. This painting commemorates Napoleon's journey across the Alps in 1800, leading his army on the invasion of northern Italy. The scene was chosen by Bonaparte himself, and instructed the artist to show him "calm, mounted on a fiery steed." The emperor's features are idealized, largely because he refused to attend any sittings. As a result, David had to ask his son to sit at the top of a ladder in order to capture the pose. The costume was more accurate,

however, as the artist was able to borrow the uniform that Napoleon had worn at the Battle of Marengo (1800). First and foremost, David's painting serves as an icon of imperial majesty. The horse's mane and the emperor's cloak, billowing wildly in a howling gale, lend a sense of grandeur to the composition while, carved on the rocks below, are the names of Hannibal and Charlemagne (Karolus Magnus)—two other victorious generals who had led their armies across the Alps. As with all the best propaganda, the truth was rather more prosaic. Napoleon had in actuality made the journey in fine weather conditions. Similarly, although David based the rearing horse on an equestrian statue of Peter the Great, in reality, Napoleon had ridden across the Alps on a mule. **IZ**

Melancholy
Constance Marie Charpentier

1801 | oil on canvas | 51 ⅛ x 64 ⅞ in / 130 x 165 cm | Musée de Picardie, Amiens, France

The twentieth-century writer and cultural theorist Susan Sontag defined depression as "melancholy minus its charms." Those charms are self-evident in Constance Marie Charpentier's (1767–1849) image of melancholy embodied in a beautiful, introspective young woman. Little is known of Charpentier's life, besides the facts that she was a pupil of Neoclassicist François Gérard and of the great political painter Jacques-Louis David. She was awarded a gold medal from the Paris Salon, where she exhibited from 1795 until 1819. Whether she suffered from melancholia is unrecorded, but her image still resonates with viewers as a representation of her era's views on the illness. The woman's dress and profile are recognizably Roman, reflecting both Charpentier's training in Neoclassicism and the notion that melancholy was a noble, artistic, philosophical emotion. Despite this romanticized idea about melancholy, the model's hunched shoulders, flaccid hand, and glazed expression are vividly recognizable as physical signs of depression. Her contemporary critics, and many today, have been eager to define her principally by gender, as her choices in genre have often been traditionally feminine subjects such as sentimental rural scenes and portraits of women and children. But pigeonholing Charpentier's oeuvre by gender alone displays a limited awareness of her work. Regardless of gender, she produced highly original and impressive works of portraiture, such as those of revolutionary Georges Danton's scarred, piglike visage. **AH**

Battle Between Russians and Kościuszko Forces in 1801
Aleksander Orłowski

1801 | watercolor on paper | 13 x 21 in / 33.5 x 53 cm | Muzeum Narodowe, Warsaw, Poland

Aleksander Orłowski (1777–1832) was born in Warsaw, the son of aristocratic but poor hotelier in Russian-occupied Poland. As a teenager his artistic talent was noticed by the visiting Princess Isabella, who arranged for him to be taken on as a pupil at the studio run by her family's court painters, one of whom was Jan Piotr Norblin. Yet despite aristocratic patronage, Orłowski always remained a rebel. He was a fervent supporter of the Polish nationalist cause in its struggle for freedom from Russia. The subject of *Battle Between Russians and Kościuszko Forces in 1801* was one Orłowski knew well: it records a battle led by the rebel leader Tadeusz Kościuszko, who spearheaded the fight for Polish liberation; Orłowski was a volunteer in Kościuszko's army. The battle was unsuccessful and the bid for

liberation failed. The lighting effects employed in the painting add great emotional depth; the center of the scene is the most brightly lit, immediately drawing one's eye to the figures of fighting men. At the forefront of the picture, swathed in shadow, are the dead and broken bodies of men, horses, and the paraphernalia of war. For some time after Kościuszko's defeat, Orłowski traveled around Poland, Lithuania, and Russia, at one point joining a group of itinerant actors. Many of his portraits are of working people and record the struggles of their domestic daily life. He worked in a variety of media, including charcoal, chalks, pen and ink, oils, watercolors, and pastels, and became one of the earliest pioneers of the art of lithography. **LH**

Chirk Aqueduct | John Sell Cotman

c.1804 | watercolor | 12 ½ x 9 ⅛ in / 31.6 x 23.2 cm | Victoria & Albert Museum, London, UK

During his lifetime the prolific artist John Sell Cotman (1782–1842) received little public recognition. He was largely self-taught, though he had spent a little time in the famous London academy of Dr. Munro, whose pupils also included J.M.W. Turner and Thomas Girtin. Cotman spent most of his life working from just outside his birthtown of Norwich, England, an area that attracted artists and artisans. One of the leading members of the Norwich School of Painting, he taught drawing, allowing students to copy his works. His influence in this respect was profound on a generation of emerging watercolor artists, most notably his two sons, Miles Edmund and John Joseph Cotman, and the artist John Thirtle. In 1834 he was appointed Drawing Master at King's College, London.

The haunting and evocative watercolor *Chirk Aqueduct* is possibly one of his best in this medium. For many years it was believed to depict the Welsh aqueduct of the same name, but the drawing of the structure is not accurate and the background appears imaginary. The aqueduct reflects a sense of ancient Roman architecture with the soaring height and simple majesty reminiscent of a temple portico. It is a brilliant synthesis of real and imaginary, the ancient conceived and portrayed in a bold, modern way. Cotman's grasp of spatial organization and his use of solid blocks of color and strong forms, as well as his sense of design, would seem to predict the emergence of the modern movement, although his works always retained a vestige of the romantic style of his early career. **TP**

Self-Portrait | Sir David Wilkie

1804 | oil on canvas | 30 x 25 in / 76 x 63 cm | National Gallery of Scotland, Edinburgh, UK

Painted when Sir David Wilkie (1785–1841) was just twenty, this portrait represents a defining moment in the artist's life: Wilkie was about to leave his native Scotland for England. Having studied in Edinburgh, Wilkie left Scotland to attend the Royal Academy School in London. The portrait shows a fashionably dressed young man looking unerringly out of the canvas, but with the gaze directed beyond the viewer, as if the subject is looking toward his own future. The colors employed in this painting are cleverly chosen, with the wall. hair, and jacket complementing one another. The brilliant gold hue of his waistcoat suggests a more flamboyant side to the sitter's personality than the more somber tones used elsewhere. One might have expected the self-portrait of an artist to include the tools of his trade, such as brushes, paints, or charcoal, but interestingly the artist has chosen to portray himself holding a pen. After just five years of artistic training, Wilkie was already becoming known for his landscapes and the realism of expression in the figures who inhabited his scenes. He would go on to enjoy great success during his lifetime, being made a full member of the Royal Academy in 1811. In 1830, he was named Painter to the King and he received a knighthood in 1836. His early works were influenced by painters of the Flemish schools and exhibited a tendency toward dark colors and slightly oppressive tones. In the 1850s, Wilkie traveled around the Mediterranean, after which his works began to reveal a strong Spanish influence. **LH**

Clothed Maja | Goya

*c.*1805 | oil on canvas | 37 ³/₈ x 74 ³/₄ in / 95 x 190 cm | Museo del Prado, Madrid, Spain

Several years after painting the *Naked Maja* for his patron Manuel Godoy, Francisco Goya y Lucientes (1746–1828) painted a clothed version of his subject. He appears to have used the same model, in the same reclining pose, in the same surroundings. There is much debate as to the identity of the model, and it is possible that Goya used several different sitters for the paintings. Majos and majas were what might be described as bohemians or aesthetes. Part of the Madrid art scene of the early nineteenth century, they were not wealthy but placed great importance on style and took pride in their flamboyant clothes and considered use of language. The maja in this picture, also referred to as a gypsy, is painted in the artist's later, looser style. When compared with the *Naked Maja* the *Clothed Maja* may seem less pornographic or more "real," as her dress gives the subject more of an identity. The *Clothed Maja* is also more colorful and warmer in tone than the *Naked Maja*. The clothed maja wears rouge and her face is much softer and conventionally pretty, further emphasizing the stark power of her naked counterpart. This unusual work may have acted as a smart "cover" for the nude picture which had caused such outrage in Spanish society, or perhaps was intended to enhance the erotic nature of the *Nude Maja* by encouraging the viewer to imagine the figure undressing. Goya's thought-provoking painting influenced many artists, notably Manet and Picasso, and his work continues to fascinate today. **KM**

Seashore with Boats | John Sell Cotman

c.1806 | oil on board | 11 ⅛ x 16 ⅛ in / 28.3 x 41 cm | Tate Collection, London, UK

John Sell Cotman (1782–1842) was born the son of a shopkeeper in the bustling market town of Norwich. He traveled to London in 1798 to further his artistic training, and was swiftly immersed in the active art circles of the time. Although he never received much in the way of formal training, he quickly became one of the leading watercolorists working in the city. He returned to the Norwich area around 1804 and immediately became integral to the Norwich School of painting, which was less a school and more of a provincial movement of art formed by a group of largely self-taught artists. Characteristically the artists of the Norwich School focused on the landscape and seascape of their local area, although they also drew inspiration from other areas of natural beauty.

Seashore with Boats is one of Cotman's relatively few works in oil, and is thought to be of Cromer Beach north of Norwich. In 1809, shortly after this work was completed, the artist married Anne Miles who lived close to Cromer beach. Over the following year he exhibited four subjects inspired by this area. The work is particularly distinctive by its broad areas of flat color with bold forms that create a pattern effect across the surface. It was a piece typical of his style that was startlingly modern in concept for its time, and would seem to anticipate the works of Paul Nash. Though Cotman was relatively little known during his time, he enjoyed a huge revival during the twentieth century that saw his work equal—if not surpass—that of J.M.W. Turner in popularity. **TP**

The Hülsenbeck Children
Philipp Otto Runge

c.1806 | oil on canvas | 51¾ x 56⅜ in / 131.5 x 143.5 cm | Hamburger Kunsthalle, Hamburg, Germany

Philipp Otto Runge (1777–1810) is among the leading figures in German Romantic painting. His theoretical approach, however—aiming to express notions of a superior harmony in his works through the symbolism of color, motifs, and numbers—was not easily accessible to his contemporaries. Yet he was well known for portraits such as *The Hülsenbeck Children*. This painting shows the three children of a Hamburgian trader's family playing. What makes this painting unique is that before the nineteenth century children had been depicted as small adults, here the children are shown life size and instead of looking down at them the viewer is placed on the same level. The central child actively confronts the viewer while the smallest child, in the cart, holds on to the sunflower plant that frames the scene. From left to right, the three represent in ascending order the different states of awareness, turning from unconscious grasp to vital activity to considerate caregiving and communication. This autonomous world of their own is carefully fenced in and sheltered from the adult world—or is it the latter that is excluded? A sharply defined garden fence aligns with the eldest child's toe and then suddenly trails off toward the family home. Behind it opens up an extended view of the city of Hamburg in the distance, representing cultivated nature, buildings, and labor. It is a different world still far away in the children's future, barred from their reality and, for now, out of their sight. **SaP**

Sun Rising Through Vapour: Fishermen Cleaning and Selling Fish
J.M.W. Turner

c.1807 | oil on canvas | 52 ¾ x 70 ⅝ in / 134 x 179.5 cm | National Gallery, London, UK

In many ways, this relatively early work by Joseph Mallord William Turner (1775–1851) is a traditional portrait of a pleasant, generalized scene. Established influences at work here include seventeenth-century Dutch marine artist Willem Van der Velde the Younger, and earlier Italianate landscapes by Claude Lorraine and Richard Wilson. These artists had a love of creating mood in a landscape, while Van der Velde and Claude developed a mastery of the effects of luminosity, atmosphere, light, and color—all central to Turner's work. In this painting, Turner seems to take these influences and begins to move into a realm of his own. This work is filled with early versions of the perfectly captured atmospheric effects for which Turner is famed, with bright sun bursting through cloud to light up the water and glance off the boats and the fishermen at work on the shoreline. It seems that this painting does not depict a specific place, but it is painted with great affection and knowledge. Turner spent all his life living near water, be it rivers or the sea, and had a deep love of watery places and subjects. He also spent some of his childhood with relatives of his mother who were fishmongers. In his will, Turner requested that this painting, along with his *Dido Building Carthage* (1815), should be hung in London's National Gallery alongside his two favorite Claude paintings. Many art critics have said that, although Turner forged a startlingly new style, he never totally strayed from traditional roots, and perhaps his bequest is proof of just that. **AK**

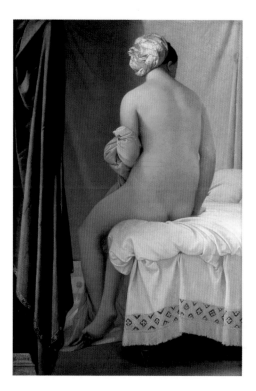

Bather of Valpinçon | Jean Auguste-Dominique Ingres

1808 | oil on canvas | 57 ½ x 38 ¼ in / 146 x 97 cm | Louvre, Paris, France

In 1801, after studying under the artist, Jacques-Louis David, the French artist Jean-Auguste-Dominique Ingres (1780–1867) won the prestigious Prix de Rome. This was a prize awarded by France's Academie Royale, who paid for their best artists to visit Rome for four years and study the Italian masters of the past. Unfortunately, the state could not afford to send artists to Italy at this time because of France's failing economy. Ingres eventually went to Rome in 1808. *Bather of Valpinçon* was one of Ingres's first paintings to be executed in Italy and, although the artist was surrounded by centuries of important Renaissance art, it breaks with tradition. Rather than reveal his subject's identity, Ingres has featured his almost monumental subject facing away from the viewer with her torso twisted slightly to open her back. This allows the viewer to admire and even objectify the bather without her challenging us—she remains anonymous, undetermined, her character undecipherable. Ingres's later works of female nudes often adopted more frontal poses and looked toward the viewer. It is interesting to note that Ingres's limited palette of greens, creams, and browns changes from the dark tones of the curtain on the left to the light tones of the backdrop and bed cover on the right. This gradation of tone can be seen to echo the symbolic nature of bathing, an act that cleanses and purifies one's soul: as the sitter moves away from the bath she become whiter, and therefore more pure. **WD**

Two Leopards Playing | Jacques-Laurent Agasse

1808 | oil on canvas | Private collection

For popular amusement in the early nineteenth century, an array of wild beasts—from tigers to boa constrictors—was exhibited at Exeter Change in London. The animals were kept in small cages and displayed to the curious public for educational purposes. The menagerie also became a creative haunt for artists such as Swiss-born Jacques-Laurent Agasse (1767–1849) and poets such as Wordsworth and Byron. Exeter Change presented a unique and invaluable opportunity for Agasse, who had trained in dissection and veterinary science, to intimately observe animals in motion. *Two Leopards Playing* depicts the beasts' languid movement, but also sympathetically represents the discomfort of their living conditions. The painting demonstrates Agasse's evocative skill and wonder at nature. The two leopards appear as if captured in the middle of intimate play. The lying female leopard's left leg arched suggestively against the dominant male's belly, tells us that she is not dead or even defeated—she is still in charge of the game. The contrast between the animals' feral flirtation and the indignity of captivity gives the painting its potent emotional charge. Agasse illustrates these tensions with characteristic physical accuracy and emotive sensitivity. Agasse's empathy for animals and ability to represent their physical and psychological states made him renowned in Victorian England as the creator of some of the nineteenth century's most exquisite animal studies. **SWW**

Adoration of the Kings | Friedrich Overbeck

1813 | oil on panel | 19 x 26 in / 49.7 x 66 cm | Hamburger Kunsthalle, Hamburg, Germany

The German painter Friedrich Overbeck (1789–1869) is chiefly remembered as one of the founding members of the Nazarene movement, a group of young, idealistic German artists. Nazarenes believed that art should have a religious or moral content, and looked to the Middle Ages and to early Italian art for their inspiration. Overbeck was born into a religious Protestant family. He moved to Rome in 1810, remaining there for the rest of his life, living in the old Franciscan monastery of San Isidoro. He was joined by a succession of like-minded artists, who lived and worked together. They earned the derogatory label "Nazarene" in reference to their biblical clothing and hair styles. In *Adoration of the Kings,* the sharply defined color lends the work an enamel quality, while the perspective generated through the tiled ground appears unresolved. The painting is typical of Overbeck's precisely drawn style, as is his use of clear, brilliant color. In 1813 Overbeck joined the Roman Catholic church, and in so doing believed his work to be further imbued with Christian spirit. In the 1820s the Nazarenes dispersed, but Overbeck's studio remained a meeting place for people of similar aspirations. The moralizing spirit of Overbeck's work earned him many supporters, among them Jean-Auguste-Dominique Ingres (1780–1867), Ford Maddox Brown (1821–93), and William Dyce (1806–64). Overbeck's influence in particular can be found in aspects of the work of the Pre-Raphaelites. **TP**

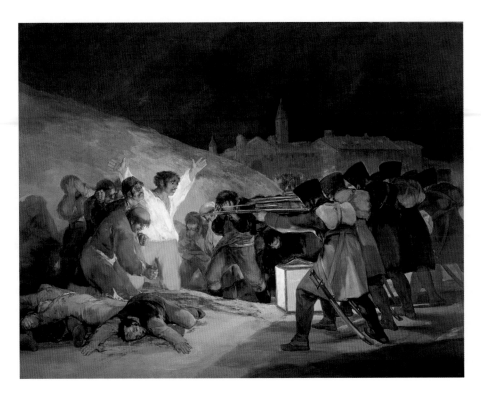

The Third of May 1808 | Goya

1814 | oil on canvas | 104 ¾ x 136 in / 266 x 345 cm | Museo del Prado, Madrid, Spain

On March 17, 1808, the Mutiny of Aranjuez ended the reign of Carlos IV and María Luisa, the royal patrons of Francisco Goya y Lucientes (1746–1828). Carlos's son, Ferdinand was made king. Taking advantage of the factionism of the Spanish royal family and government, Napoleon moved in and eventually gained power. *The Third of May 1808* portrays the execution of the Spanish insurgents by French troops near Príncipe Pío Hill. Napoleon's brother, Joseph Bonaparte, took the crown, and the French occupation of Spain lasted until 1813. It is unclear what Goya's political leanings were but he spent most of the occupation recording the atrocities of war. His acclaimed print series *The Disasters of War* included perhaps the most poignant and

unadulterated images of war that Europe had ever seen. The prints were etched from red chalk drawings and the artist's innovative use of captioning recorded a blunt commentary of the brutality of war. *The Third of May 1808* is Goya's most unapologetic piece of propaganda. Painted once Ferdinand had been restored to the throne, it champions the patriotism of the Spaniards. The central figure is a martyr: he assumes a Christlike pose revealing stigmata on his palms. The Spaniards are shown as human, colorful and individual; the French inhuman, faceless, and uniform. The image remains one of the most iconic visions of militaristic violence in art, together with Édouard Manet's *The Execution of Maximilian* (1867–68) and Picasso's *Guernica* (1937). **KM/SP**

The Temple of Isis and Osiris | Karl Friedrich Schinkel

c.1816 | painted opera set design | Staatliche Museen, Berlin, Germany

Karl Friedrich Schinkel (1781–1841) was a Prussian Neoclassical architect and painter who designed some of Berlin's grandest architecture. Born in Brandenburg and a student of Friedrich Gilly in Berlin, Schinkel decided at the 1810 Berlin art exhibition that he would never reach a mastership in painting and turned his talents to architecture, creating in his lifetime the Neue Wache, the Schauspielhaus at the Gendarmenmarkt, and the Altes Museum. A noted proponent of Classical revival, he defined a distinct Teutonic style based on the vocabulary of ancient Greek mythology and architecture. *The Temple of Isis and Osiris where Sarastro was High Priest* is the background set design for the final scene of Wolfgang Amadeus Mozart's *The Magic Flute* in which Sarastro, the wise priest of Isis and Osiris King of the Underworld, releases Pamina and others from the influence of the Queen of the Night. Schikaneder, who wrote the original libretto, Mozart and Schinkel himself were all freemasons. The opera's ideas are masonic in content and echo Enlightenment motifs: Sarastro's symbolizes the sovereign who rules with reason, wisdom and enlightened insight, overcoming the irrational darkness. The beasts in the columns as protectors of the underworld, are an innovative variation on the Greek temples commonly used in Schinkel's real-life architecture. In this, the last scene, the electric sky is dominated by architecture representing the justice and order of the enlightened Greek spirit. **SWW**

Wanderer Above the Sea of Fog | Caspar David Friedrich

*c.*1818 | oil on canvas | 38 ¾ x 29 ½ in / 98.5 x 75 cm | Hamburger Kunsthalle, Hamburg, Germany

The sublime power of nature was a dominant theme in Caspar David Friedrich's (1774–1840) paintings. The landscape of his native Germany was a source of inspiration, but his personal history might also explain the ominous tension between beauty and terror in his representation of nature. When he was a child, he was skating with his brother on the frozen Baltic sea when the ice cracked. Caspar slipped, and his brother died saving him. Friedrich's adult depression led to a suicide attempt in Dresden. After he tried to slit his own throat, he always wore a beard to hide the scar. The relationship between trauma and inspiration is evident in Friedrich's statement: "The painter should paint not only what he has in front of him, but also what he sees inside himself. If he sees nothing within,

then he should stop painting what is in front of him." A frightening, raging sea crashes in front of the lone, elegant figure in *Wanderer Above the Sea of Fog*. This utterly arresting painting, which Friedrich produced the year he married, could express his own personal struggle to tame his surging emotions for the sake of his young bride. Friedrich, who only began painting in oils after the age of thirty, demonstrates a profound understanding of the medium in the depths of dark color he employs to execute his emotionally wrenching imagery. Events corrupted Friedrich's legacy when Adolf Hitler chose to appropriate one of his paintings for use as Nazi propaganda. Despite that anachronistic connection, the mystical, melancholic beauty of his landscapes has endured. **AH**

The Bay of Naples, Seen from Chiaja | Joseph Rebell

1813–19 | oil on canvas | 25 ½ x 38 ½ in / 65 x 98 cm | Musée Conde, Chantilly, France

Joseph Rebell (1787–1828) was born in Vienna, Austria, and educated at the Akademie der Bildende Künste. In later years, he would return to the Akademie as a teacher. In 1810 he traveled to Switzerland and then to Milan and Naples before spending almost a decade in Rome, where he associated with a number of international artists. He was influenced by the work of Joseph Anton Koch, Claude Lorraine, Joseph Vernet, and the English Realists. He returned to Austria in 1824 where Emperor Franz I made him Director of the Belvedere Art Gallery in Vienna. The emperor admired Rebell's own artistic skills greatly—he had first discovered the young man's work while in Rome, where he purchased four of his pictures. He also employed Rebell to paint a number of the imperial residences around Austria. Although best known for his paintings, Rebell was also a talented etcher and printmaker. *The Bay of Naples, Seen from Chiaja* magnificently depicts the working Italian port at the base of the smoking volcano Vesuvius and showcases Rebell's talent for architectural painting, figures, and landscapes. Rebell's initial interest had been in architectural painting, which he had studied at the Viennese Akademie, but his time in Italy seems to have persuaded him to change direction, in favor of landscape works. Rebell died just a couple of weeks before his forty-second birthday, but the work he left behind has earned him a reputation as one of the most important Austrian landscape artists. **LH**

Raft of the Medusa | Théodore Géricault

1819 | oil on canvas | 193 ¼ x 281 ⅞ in / 491 x 716 cm | Louvre, Paris, France

Few people could look at this painting and not be overwhelmed by its passion and power. Painted by the flamboyant prime mover of French Romanticism, Théodore Géricault (1791–1824), it is now seen as the defining statement of that movement. The Romantics broke away from classical eighteenth-century art to stress realism and emotion. This painting is especially interesting because it so clearly bridges Classicism and Romanticism. When *Raft of the Medusa* appeared at the 1819 Salon exhibition, it caused a major scandal, horrifying the establishment. The scene tells the true tale of the shipwrecked French government frigate, *La Méduse*, whose incompetent captain and officers took the only lifeboats for themselves and left all but fifteen out of a 150 crew and passengers

to perish on a makeshift raft, sinking into despair, savagery, and cannibalism. Géricault dared to show a sordid, disturbing episode from contemporary history (the wreck occurred in 1816) that reflected badly on all involved, in a way that resembled the huge heroic history paintings much loved by traditionalists. On the one hand, there is a macabre level of realism here (Géricault studied corpses to get the details right), with extraordinarily energetic brushwork heightening the swirling movement and emotion. On the other hand, the bodies and pyramid-shaped composition are classical in style. Despite the outrage, the picture won artistic approval for Géricault, and had an enormous influence on other artists, most notably Delacroix. **AK**

Norwegian Mountain Landscape | Johan Christian Dahl

1819 | oil on canvas | 29 x 41⅜ in / 74 x 105 cm | Nationalmuseum, Stockholm, Sweden

This painting dates from the last years that Johan Christian Dahl (1788–1857) spent in his native Norway. He left to travel in Italy and improve his artistic education before moving finally to Germany, where he would live for the rest of his life. In 1823 he was offered the opportunity to teach art at the Dresden Academy. Despite having relocated to Germany, Dahl loved his native country and made regular trips back to Norway, delighting in the inspiration its scenery gave him. Dahl specialized in landscapes and this dramatic painting is an exciting example of his work. It manages to combine Realism and fantasy and was championed by the philosopher, author, and painter Johann Wolfgang von Goethe (1749–1832). The rocks undulate invitingly and at first sight appear to be mossy, gentle, and welcoming—one is tempted to reach out and touch them—yet they are also commanding and undoubtably threatening. Dahl takes what could be a simple scene and fills it with dramatic intent and rich light effects. The lowering clouds threaten in the distance to the right, amassing to potentially mar the scene and block the penetrating light. Small details enhance the majesty of the scene, such as the lowly tree haloed by the sunlight and the speckled, sun-daubed stones. Toward the end of his life, Dahl helped to found an art gallery in his former city of Christiana (now the city of Oslo). In his will, he bequeathed his art collection to the gallery. **LH**

Anatomical Pieces | Théodore Géricault

1818–20 | oil on canvas | 20 ½ x 25 ¼ in / 52 x 64 cm | Musée Fabre, Montpellier, France

In this painting, Théodore Géricault (1791–1824)—a French artist and the pioneer of the Romantic movement—presents the viewer with a depressing view of humanity. As the title suggests, it depicts a selection of dismembered human limbs, executed in such a way that celebrates neither life nor death. Instead, the body parts are represented as pieces of meat with no sense of pathos. They also appear to encourage cannibalism, for this painting is more of a brutal and raw still life than a figurative image. Géricault does not offer the viewer any respite from this gruesome subject matter. It is tightly cropped, leaving little pictorial space around the limbs, forcing the viewer to acknowledge the disturbing content. The parts are dramatically lit in comparison to the dark background, helping to emphasize their effect. Géricault exhibits his technical ability by foreshortening one piece that projects toward the viewer to bare its raw flesh. This study is one of many by Géricault that depict human limbs, and is often seen in relation to the artist's most prolific work, *Raft of the Medusa*. However, unlike other studies, *Anatomical Pieces* does not feature fleshy and muscled bodies that recall the idealized forms of ancient Greek and Roman sculpture to help to subdue the shocking effect of his subject matter. Here, the artist has stripped the limbs of any distracting or pleasing elements to create a more extreme painting that reflects the pessimism in post-Revolution France as the hope of the people subsided. **WD**

Allegory of the Four Continents—America | José Teófilo de Jesus

c.1820 | oil on canvas | 25 ⅝ x 32 ¼ in / 65 x 82 cm | Museu de Arte da Bahia, Salvador, Brazil

The artist depicting this idealized scene of a native man unassaulted in the landscape was José Teófilo de Jesus (c.1763–1847), a principal figure in the Bahian School of painting. Jesus worked under religious orders to produce delicately colored murals on church ceilings in the Bahian capital. He was also commissioned to paint a portrait of the Emperor Pedro I. Painted after approximately four hundred years of oppression, resistance, and social disintegration, *Allegory of the Four Continents— America* is an unusually peaceful representation of an indigenous Indian in Brazil. The "naked savages" of Bahia in eastern and southern Brazil were originally the Gé people, then the Tupinambá who encountered the first Europeans in 1500. The objectives of the colonial era were control, revenue, and religious conversion under royal policy and papal interests. As a landscape, *Allegory of the Four Continents— America* is uncommon in Bahian painting. Jesus's engagement with this genre reveals his intellectual roots in a European painting tradition. His use of paint suggests movement, harmony, and a wealth of lush, natural details. The muted but luminous coloring and unusual gray greens create an idyllic, pristine sense of abundance, though it is unclear if the box at the native's feet is an offering or a gift. Closely linked to the interests of the church and the government of the later half of the nineteenth century, Jesus represents a historical scene from Bahia's past as if it were merely a tame, tropical illusion. **SWW**

The Hay Wain | John Constable

1821 | oil on canvas | 51⅜ x 73 in / 130.5 x 185.5 cm | National Gallery, London, UK

The son of a prosperous miller, John Constable (1776–1837) was born in rural Suffolk, England, an area of idyllic scenery to which he referred throughout most of his artistic career. Even after his move to London in 1799 to begin his formal training at the Royal Academy, he still returned to the landscape of his youth on sketching trips. The artist used sketches to document the transitory effects of light and natural phenomena as they occurred. It was not unusual for him to return to his sketches, sometimes years later, and create finished works that evoke all the immediacy of a passing moment. The tangible presence of a warm summer's afternoon is strikingly apparent in this, probably Constable's most famous work. The imposing six-foot canvas was painted in 1821 in his London studio and based on a series of oil sketches made the summer before. Constable developed the unusual technique of producing a full-size oil sketch of his large works that enabled him to fully resolve the composition, and which offer a fascinating insight into the artist's working practices. *The Hay Wain*, which was exhibited in 1821 but failed to receive much recognition, depicts a still millstream near Flatford Mill in Suffolk. It was bought in 1824 by the French art dealer John Arrowsmith and exhibited at the Paris Salon where it won a gold medal. It was greatly admired by Delacroix and Géricault, among others, and was to prove influential on the development of landscape painting, especially in France, and in particular on the Barbizon School. **TP**

Portrait of a Kleptomaniac | Théodore Géricault

1819–23 | oil on canvas | 24 x 19 ¾ in / 61 x 50 cm | Museum of Fine Arts, Ghent, Belgium

As with his *Raft of the Medusa*, this picture shows Théodore Géricault (1791–1824) embracing Realism and up-to-the-minute contemporary events with typical fervor. One of the artist's friends was a young psychiatrist named Etienne-Jean Georget. Dr. Georget was an influential "alienist," believing that psychiatric patients should be treated with dignity. He also subscribed to the new concept of "monomania," where a patient suffered from one specific type of delusion, compulsion, or obsession. Géricault made a series of ten portraits of monomaniacs in Dr. Georget's care. Of the five that survive today, the kleptomaniac is perhaps the most arresting. In this portrait, Géricault treads the fine line that combines an almost scientifically detached, ultra-realistic portrayal of a "distasteful" subject with a more subjective Romantic sympathy. We can see at once that this is a disturbed person, as the artist's considerable technical skills convincingly depict staring eyes, a slightly twisted face, unkempt hair, and sadly drooping shoulders. We feel rather unsettled as we look at what appears to be a very real person. What we can also see is plenty of movement in the vigorous, fluid brushwork, which lends a certain sketchy quality to the picture and helps to stir up an emotional connection with the picture and sympathy for its subject. The other surviving monomaniac portraits show a compulsive gambler, an obsessively envious person, a child molester, and someone suffering from delusions of being a military commander. **AK**

Saturn | Goya

1821–23 | mural transferred to canvas | 57 ½ x 32 ½ in / 146 x 83 cm | Museo del Prado, Madrid, Spain

In 1819, Francisco Goya y Lucientes (1746–1828) bought a house west of Madrid called the Quinta del sordo ("Villa of the deaf man"). A previous owner of the house was deaf, and the name remained apt as Goya himself had lost his hearing in his mid-forties. The artist painted directly on to the plaster walls of the Quinta the series of psychologically brooding images popularly known as the "black" paintings (1819–23). They were not intended to be shown to the public, and only later were the pictures lifted from the walls, transferred to canvas, and deposited in the Prado. The haunting *Saturn* illustrates the myth of the Roman god Saturn, who, fearing that his children would overthrow him, ate them. Taking the myth as a starting point, the painting may be about God's wrath, the conflict between old age and youth, or Saturn as Time devouring all things. Goya, by then in his seventies and having survived two life-threatening illnesses, is likely to have been anxious about his own mortality. The artist may have been inspired by Rubens's Baroque portrayal of the myth, *Saturn Devouring His Son* (1636). Goya's version, with its restricted palette and looser style, is much darker in all senses. The god's wide-eyed stare suggests madness and paranoia, and disturbingly he seems unselfconscious in carrying out his horrific act. There is also evidence to show that in the original image Saturn had a partially erect phallus. In 1823 Goya moved to Bordeaux. After a brief return to Spain, he went back to France, where he died in 1828. **KM/SP**

Sir Walter Scott | Sir Henry Raeburn

1823 | oil on canvas | 30 x 25 in / 76 x 63.5 cm | Scottish National Portrait Gallery, Edinburgh, UK

Largely self-taught, Scottish painter Sir Henry Raeburn (1756–1823) was initially apprenticed to a goldsmith; his marriage to a wealthy widow in 1780 allowed him to pursue his career as an artist. By the late 1780s, he was considered the foremost portrait painter of the country, and was responsible for painting some of the most influential Scottish figures of the period. In 1819, Raeburn was commissioned to paint the writer and national hero Sir Walter Scott. Scott initially showed some reluctance. He had sat for the artist in 1808 and, despite widespread critical acclaim for this early painting and its impact on the course of Romantic portraiture, Scott had reportedly been unhappy with the deeply serious appearance he had been given. Raeburn started work on the new portrait of Scott in the early 1820s. Working in dark contrasting colors and with his distinctive bold brushstrokes, Raeburn depicted a man at the very peak of his career and influence. A few days after the completion of the painting, Raeburn was dead. His portrait of Scott was to be one of his last, as well as one of his greatest, works. By choosing to remain in his homeland, Raeburn sacrificed some of the opportunity available to many London portraitists. Yet his decision enabled him to develop a more individual style and to spearhead the blossoming Scottish School of the period. Elected president of the Edinburgh Society of Artists in 1814, his significant influence was further recognized in a knighthood, bestowed by George IV a year before the artist's death. **JB**

Brighton Beach with Colliers | John Constable

1824 | oil on paper | 5 ⅞ x 9 ¾ in / 14.9 x 24.8 cm | Victoria & Albert Museum, London, UK

The death of John Constable's (1776–1837) father in 1816 left the struggling artist financially secure, and finally able to marry Maria Birknell whose family had opposed the union for some years. By 1824 Maria had fallen seriously ill, and Constable moved her and their children out of London and down to Brighton for an extended visit. The fashionable seaside town was a popular health resort, but on his trips to visit his family from his London studio the artist found it stifling and disliked the frivolous atmosphere. He referred to the town as "Piccadilly . . . by the seaside" and found the bustle of the bourgeoisie at leisure irritating. He made many sketches on his visits, turning his back to the town and capturing in oil the expanse of blue-gray sea punctuated by colored sails and the honest labor of fishermen. One of the artist's most famous Brighton sketches, this piece shows the dark collier boats delivering coal to the expanding town. Just visible behind the boats is the end of the Chain Pier, built in 1823, and the subject of paintings by both him and his contemporary J.M.W. Turner. Constable was greatly concerned with the depiction of changing light and atmosphere. With a muted palette and short, sensitive brushstrokes he suggests a single moment on a warm summer evening—one of "very white and golden light," as he refers to it in an inscription on the back of the small sketch. It is this immediacy and shimmering luminous quality of his work that was so influential on the painters of the Barbizon School, and in turn on the development of Impressionism. **TP**

Lion: A Newfoundland Dog | Edwin Landseer

1824 | oil on canvas | 59 x 77 in / 149.8 x 195.6 cm | Victoria & Albert Museum, London, UK

Dogs had been frequently included in family portraits, but it was only in the eighteenth century that they began to take center stage in pictures of their own. Animal painting remained a minor, specialized genre until the following century, when artists such as Sir Edwin Henry Landseer (1802–73) brought it to the fore. Landseer attracted clients at the highest level, most notably Queen Victoria, while his sentimental pictures made him a favorite with the public at large. He was something of a child prodigy, exhibiting at the Royal Academy by the age of sixteen. These prestigious shows brought him a string of lucrative commissions, including this particular picture, which was ordered by the dog's owner, W.H. de Merle. The animal is not shown in its domestic setting, but outdoors in the Scottish Highlands, where Landseer was a frequent visitor. The artist gained even greater celebrity from his sentimental paintings, which underlined the devotion and loyalty of man's best friend. The most famous example, perhaps, is *The Old Shepherd's Chief Mourner*, where the dog is shown alone in a cottage, resting his head on his master's coffin, long after the shepherd's human friends have gone home. This painting of a Newfoundlander illustrates a breed that originated in Canada. They were working dogs, mainly used for hauling in fishing nets and known for rescuing swimmers in distress. Landseer painted these dogs on many occasions, and in honor of his services to the canine world, a breed of dog was named after him: a black and white variety of the Newfoundland. **IZ**

Ruins of the Holyrood Chapel by Moonlight | Louis Daguerre

1824 | oil on canvas | 83 ⅛ x 100 ¾ in / 211 x 256 cm | Walker Art Gallery, Liverpool, UK

The captivating photorealism of this painting becomes less surprising when one considers who the painter was. Louis Daguerre (1787–1851)—stage designer, painter, and inventor—created the diorama (an early version of cinema) and a groundbreaking method of early photography that bears his name: the daguerrotype. Although best known today for photography, Daguerre began his career as a draftsman and painter. With his partner, Charles-Marie Bouton, Daguerre worked on very large paintings, akin to theatrical backdrops, which were part of the interactive experience that came to be known as a diorama. Their life-size paintings of buildings were executed on transparent linen and then hung onto a skeleton shell, which was rotated so that spectators

could marvel at the way the clever use of lighting suggested the passing of time, as though they were watching an entire day, from morning to evening. Daguerre first exhibited a solo painting—*Interior of a Chapel of the Church of the Feuillants*—at the Paris Salon in 1814. His similar painting, *Ruins of the Holyrood Chapel by Moonlight*, was exhibited to acclaim at the Paris Salon of 1824, earning him a Legion d'honneur. There is no record of Daguerre ever having visited Edinburgh in Scotland, but he painted this scene more than once. Daguerre and Bouton opened their first diorama in Paris in 1822 although it was destroyed in a fire in 1839. In 1823 they opened another in London, but it was the daguerrotype in 1837 that made Daguerre's name widely known. **LH**

Autumn Grasses | Sakai Hōitsu

1800–25 | ink, color, and gold on silk | 56 x 34 in / 143.5 x 87 cm | Seattle Art Museum, Seattle, WA, USA

Sakai Hōitsu (1761–1828) revived the Rinpa school tradition of Ogata Kōrin, Kōetsu and Sōtatsu in Edo, present-day Tokyo, a century after Kōrin's time. His style came to be known as the Edo Rinpa School. Hōitsu was an admirer of Kōrin's works, and studied them systematically. Hōitsu was the second son of the lord of prosperous Himeji Castle, who owned a fine collection of Kōrin's works. Hōitsu grew up in a scholarly and artistic environment, which enabled him to study haiku poetry, *kyōka* comic verse, calligraphy, and painting. As a youth, Hōitsu studied various painting styles including *ukiyo-e*, the Kanō School as well as Chinese academic painting. However, after entering Buddhist priesthood at the age of thirty-seven—possibly because he wished to distance himself from his family's feudal holdings and devote himself to art after his brother's death—he worked exclusively in the Rinpa style. His paintings of autumn plants and grasses mark the most sophisticated expression of nature in the Rinpa tradition. The distinctive beauty of autumn has long been a popular subject in Japan. Autumn grasses allude to the melancholy sentiments of the fleeting season. Hōitsu produced a large number of paintings such as *Autumn Grasses,* and other motifs from nature, combining certain elements of the Rinpa School with techniques and themes from other contemporary schools, and created a more delicate and elegant style. He preferred the use of silver ground rather than gold common in the Rinpa tradition. **FN**

Landscape with Repose of the Holy Family | Samuel Palmer

1825 | oil and tempera on panel | 12 ¼ x 15 ⅜ in / 31 x 39 cm | Ashmolean Museum, Oxford, UK

Samuel Palmer (1805–81) belonged to a group of Romantic artists known as the Ancients, who aimed to breathe new life into the religious art of the day. This painting dates from the start of their association in the mid-1820s. The subject is a variant of *The Flight into Egypt*, which had long been a popular theme in Western art. After learning of the birth of Christ, Herod took brutal measures to find and kill the Holy Child. Joseph took his family into Egypt to escape the slaughter. In some accounts (the pseudo-Gospels in the Apocrypha), they broke their journey to rest under a palm tree. There, angels brought them food or, in alternative versions, Christ caused the tree to bend its branches, so that they could reach its fruit. Palmer specialized in painting idyllic landscapes, suffused with poetic mysticism, so the subject held an obvious appeal for him. With the exception of the palm tree, however, there was no attempt to conjure up a Middle-Eastern scene. Instead, the landscape depicts the countryside near Shoreham, the Kent village where the artist settled in 1826. The picture appears to have been painted for Palmer's cousin, John Giles. He was a stockbroker, rather than an artist, though he was also a member of the Ancients, providing invaluable financial support for the group. In artistic terms, the Ancients took their lead from William Blake (1757–1827). They admired the visionary quality of his pictures and strove to translate this into their own work. They also mimicked his use of archaic media— hence Palmer's use of tempera in this scene. **IZ**

River Scene, with Steamboat | J.M.W. Turner

*c.*1826 | watercolor on paper | 5 ½ x 7 ⅜ in / 14.1 x 18.7 cm | Tate Collection, London, UK

Although linked in most people's minds with oils, James Mallord William Turner (1775–1851) is regarded by many as the father of watercolor landscape painting. Watercolor afforded the artist a way to perfect his craft throughout his life, and studies painted in this medium would often form the basis of large oil works. Watercolor helped Turner to understand how to portray the landscapes that he loved so much, and to advance stylistically, because it allows such a free exploration of the effects of color and light. The work belongs to a period, from about 1814 to 1830, during which Turner traveled around Britain and Europe, sketching landscapes as he went. He made his first visit to Italy a few years before painting *River Scene, with Steamboat* and experiencing

the light abroad made his colors purer and his lighting more natural. It is not surprising, therefore, that Turner inspired Monet and Pissarro, and that the French regard him as the greatest of English painters. In this work, minimal brushwork captures the scene perfectly. A few light strokes indicate the steamboat's watery reflections, while opaque gouache deftly picks out foreground figures and distant rocky outcrops; the whole is infused with a convincing outdoor light. The technique is spare and, typical of Turner, some areas are more detailed than others, yet the scene has a real sense of perspective, space, and distance. Turner also liked to mix the old and the new, and here a steamboat from the age of industry and engineering chugs through a gentle pastoral scene. **AK**

The American Wild Turkey Cock | John James Audubon

1826 | oil on canvas | 60 x 48 in / 155 x 123 cm | University of Liverpool Art Gallery, UK

Raised in France, John James Audubon (1785–1851) relocated to a farm near Philadelphia at the age of eighteen. He was fascinated by birds, and sought to record every bird of North America, a mission that saw him traveling extensively across the country. In order to draw a bird, he shot it, and then wired it into position, posing it in its normal habitat. This process allowed him to imbue his work with great naturalness, making his birds universally graceful and convincing. Unable to find a publisher for his portfolio, Audubon set sail for England, arriving in Liverpool in 1826. *Birds of America* was eventually published in 1838. Audubon painted *The American Wild Turkey Cock* shortly after his arrival in Liverpool, and is one of two canvases of the same subject.

The first painting, which was allegedly painted in just twenty-three hours, was presented by the artist to the Liverpool Royal Institution to thank them for the generous welcome and support they had given him. The second version of *The American Wild Turkey Cock* was given to Richard Rathbone, a wealthy businessman who had introduced the artist to the founder of the Royal Institution. Audubon returned to America in 1829, where he continued his studies of birds and began work on his second great volume of drawings. His bird drawings in particular are exquisitely colored and detailed, often with a strong sense of pattern, and in this capacity they have been influential on the development of textile designs, particularly in England. **TP**

Portrait of a Young Woman | Franz Seraph Stirnbrand

1827 | oil on canvas | 24 ⅝ x 20 ⅝ in / 62.5 x 52.5 cm | Private collection

Franz Seraph Stirnbrand (1788–1882) was born in what is now Croatia and, at the age of seventeen, was apprenticed to a painter. Wishing to escape from military service, he crossed the border into Germany and began to market himself as a portrait painter. In Frankfurt he was commissioned by a tobacco company to paint portraits of famous people, such as Napoleon and his wife, Marie Louise, on their tobacco tins. Eventually he graduated to painting genuine portraits, such as this one of an unnamed young woman. While in Rome he painted a portrait of the Pope, Leon XII. Other important figures who feature in portraits by Stirnbrand include Queen Charlotte Mathilde von Wurttemberg, Baron Johann Wilhelm von Muller, Prince Friedrich von Hohenlohe, Tsar

Alexander II of Russia, and Kaiser Wilhelm I. It is uncertain whether all these great figures actually sat for Stirnbrand; it is more likely that he simply painted their portraits from other popular representations of them. *Portrait of a Young Woman* is a flattering, and no doubt idealized, image painted in a Romantic style. The even, creamy tones of the young woman's skin and the glossy sheen of her hair suggest Stirnbrand's portraiture was intended to flatter rather than reflect a realistic portrayal. The rose and rosebud attached to her waist ribbon are suggestive of romance, first love, and the blossoming of an adolescent into a woman. Her face appears slightly apprehensive and shy. Stirnbrand paints her looking to the side, as if she were too demure to look directly at the viewer. **LH**

The Death of Sardanapalus | Eugène Delacroix

1827 | oil on canvas | 154 ³/₈ x 195 ¼ in / 392 x 496 cm | Louvre, Paris, France

Often said to be the greatest of the French Romantics, Eugène Delacroix (1798–1863) was truly a painter of his times. Like his friend Géricault, Delacroix retained certain classical elements from his early training but showed a daring energy, a rich, individualistic use of color, and a love of the exotic that made him a trailblazer. The massive canvas *The Death of Sardanapalus* explodes onto the senses with wild movement and sumptuous color, an orgy of indulgent exoticism. Sardanapalus was an Assyrian ruler of ancient legend with a taste for extreme decadence. In response to the shame of a major military defeat, Sardanapalus made a huge pyre on which he burned himself to death along with all his palace treasures, mistresses, and slaves. Delacroix reveled in such Byronic drama. He appears to have abandoned any attempt at realistic perspective or compositional coherence. Distorted bodies and objects swirl around in a nightmare world choked with intense color and hot, encroaching shadow. The detailed painting of glittering jewels and rich fabrics clearly conveys the extravagant world being depicted, while the cool detachment with which Sardanapalus surveys the mayhem around him strikes a sinister mood. Delacroix experiments with gray and blue tones on human skin to give shape to his unconventional modeling of bodies. It is easy to see how the uninhibited exploration of violence, along with the frantic energy and bold coloring techniques, spoke volumes to later artists. **AK**

Apotheosis of Homer | Jean-Auguste-Dominique Ingres

1827 | oil on canvas | 152 x 201½ in / 386 x 512 cm | Louvre, Paris, France

By the time this was painted, Ingres (1780-1867) was a self-proclaimed leader of traditional, classical painting, pitting himself against the headstrong art of French Romantics such as Delacroix. This particular painting could hardly be a better example of Ingres' academic approach, and in fact he intended it as a hymn of praise to classicism. Although he did have a more sensual side (for example, his famous *Bather of Valpinçon*, 1808), it has been totally suppressed here. Also known as Homer Deified, this work shows Ancient Greece's famous poet as a god, being crowned with laurels by the mythological figure, Victory. Two women at his feet represent Homer's great epic works, *The Iliad* and *The Odyssey*. Around him cluster an adoring crowd of artistic giants from ancient and modern times, including fellow Greeks: the dramatist Aeschylus offers up a parchment left of Homer, while the Athenian sculptor Phidias holds out a hammer on the right. The more modern figures are dominated by artists from France's 17th-century classical period, such as playwright Molière and painter Nicolas Poussin. The triangular, symmetrical composition exudes classical idealism, with Homer placed centrally against an antique temple bearing his name. Sadly this painting was poorly received at the time. Ingres withdrew to Rome for a few years, but returned in the 1840s to be re-acclaimed as a leading classicist. It became fashionable to damn Ingres' traditionalism, but he is now seen as a highly influential artist of considerable technical skill. **AK**

Portrait of Nino Eristavi | Unknown

1829 | oil on canvas | 54 x 35 in / 139 x 90 cm | Georgian State Picture Gallery, Tbilisi, Georgia

Early nineteenth century Persia was marked by political conflict; a series of disruptive wars reorganized land principalities and established regional dominance. Between 1805 and 1834 Iran lost control over areas of the Caucasus to Imperial Russia; the year 1829, also the year of the painting of *Portrait of Nino Eristavi*, saw the end of the first and second Russian-Persian war. Despite such turmoil, under the Fath Ali Shah Qajar court, classical Iranian poetry and portraiture experienced a revival. While the trend in Iranian painting later moved toward small lacquer and enamel portraits, the Qajar court's large portraits remain some of the most dramatic Iranian representations. Georgia was irrevocably intertwined with Iran in language and culture, and

Portrait of Nino Eristavi a vivid, diplomatic portrait. Persia was changing from tribal to centralized rule; the tumultuous mountains with an insidious black, silver lake at its foot are brought into bold relief by an intricately adorned woman, in bright, regal dress. The young woman's sheer veil is decorated with jewels and pearls, she holds a flower as an offering of peace. The plant design on her chest suggests the regeneration of civilizations. Her hands and feet are staid, as she appears to be floating out of perspective from the land behind her. Nino Eristavi's face is warrior-like, deeply Persian, and deeply unsettled. As Russia increasingly dominated the vast lands behind her, she offers peace not as a supplicant, but as a proud, cultural representative. **SWW**

Miss Cazenove on a Grey Hunter | Jacques-Laurent Agasse

1820–30 | oil on canvas | 12 x 10 in / 30.5 x 25.5 cm | Private collection

Born into an influential, wealthy Huguenot family in Geneva, Jacques-Laurent Agasse (1767–1849) spent his childhood observing nature at his family's estate. He first devoted himself to dissection and veterinary science in Paris before studying painting under Jacques-Louis David and Horace Vernet. In 1800, after he was commissioned to paint the portrait of an Englishman's beloved deceased dog, the patron invited Agasse to move with him to England. There he quickly became one of the era's most celebrated painters as a master of that most British genre: the racehorse portrait. The true subject of *Miss Cazenove on a Grey Hunter* is not the rider or the ride, but the intimate relationship between horse and equestrian. With his exquisite understanding of animal anatomy

and his poetic use of color, Agasse conveys the beauty of an equestrian in command of her horse. Within the muted, misty surroundings, Miss Cazenove's dress, gaze, and posture convey the complex power pull between horse, rider, and dog—all equal characters rendered with equal importance by Agasse. To illustrate their harmony, the woman's white front neckpiece draws attention to the elegant neck of the horse, while the dark slip of her dress falls behind the horse's legs, thereby visually linking her to the dog. Passionate about representing the perfection of the animal form, Agasse first directs our eyes to the horse, yet it is the dog whose gaze engages the viewer directly. The woman is left as essentially a conduit between dog and horse. **SWW**

Liberty Leading the People | Eugène Delacroix

1830 | oil on canvas | 102 ³/₈ x 128 in / 260 x 325 cm | Louvre, Paris, France

This work belongs to the period between 1827 and 1832 during which Eugène Delacroix (1798–1863) produced one masterpiece after another. This is no exception. Painted to commemorate the revolution of July 1830 that brought Louis-Philippe to power, the image has come to symbolize the spirit of revolution. It caused a sensation at the Paris Salon of 1831, and, although Louis-Philippe bought the work to mark his accession, he kept it away from public view because it was considered to be potentially inflammatory. The picture cleverly combines gritty contemporary reportage with allegory in a monumental way. Place and time are clear: Notre Dame is visible in the distance and people are dressed according to their class, with the scruffy boy on the right symbolizing the power of ordinary people. The allegorical figure of Liberty that bestrides the scene, tricolor raised above her, caused outrage because rather than personifying idealized beauty, the vibrant brushwork shows a very real woman—half-naked, dirty, and stepping over corpses in a way that might suggest how liberty could bring some oppression of its own. This picture also shows Delacroix turning toward the more subdued approach of his later work, in which he made increasingly subtle forays into the ways in which colors worked next to each other in order to convey a sense of reality or express truths. Such use of color would be enormously influential among the Impressionists and Modernists to come, from Renoir and Seurat to Picasso. **AK**

Old Elms in Prater | Ferdinand Georg Waldmüller

1831 | oil on panel | 13 x 10 in / 31.7 x 25.9 cm | Hamburger Kunsthalle, Hamburg, Germany

Ferdinand Georg Waldmüller (1793–1865) made a living as a portraitist before branching out into landscapes and genre paintings, becoming the leading master of the Viennese *Biedermeier* period. After Napoleon's defeat in 1815, Vienna entered a period of government oppression and censorship, prompting artists to move away from high concepts and focus on domestic, non-political subjects. Fuelled further by the growth of a new middle class, the city was suddenly brimming with family portraits, genre paintings, and landscapes that rediscovered the native beauty of Austria. This painting of 1831 demonstrates Waldmüller's mature technical mastery, enhanced by years spent copying from Old Masters. Having reached a peak in his portrait painting he

began to see the study of the actual world around him as the only aim of painting. With an almost photographic clarity, he depicts a peasant couple wandering peacefully among the trees of the Prater. His attention to detail is second to none as his delicate colors create the illusion of natural daylight. Although he precedes the Realist movement by many years, Waldmüller declared himself an enemy of both academic art and Romanticism, and a firm advocate of realism. Despite this, his genre works often idealize a peasant existence that was, in reality, full of hardship. His compositions and exact rendering had a seminal influence on the development of landscape painting, evident in the work of later painters such as Von Guérard. **SLF**

Landscape with Shepherds and Cows | Joseph Anton Koch

1832–34 | oil on canvas | 29 ⁷/₈ x 40 ⁷/₈ in / 76 x 103.7 cm | Hamburger Kunsthalle, Hamburg, Germany

Joseph Anton Koch (1768–1839) was one of the leading Romantic painters of the early nineteenth century, but unlike his more famous counterpart, Caspar David Friedrich, his work was not solely a response to the landscapes of his native Germany. Koch established a tradition of Germano-Roman painting that combined the intense and emotional atmosphere of the rugged Alps with the idealized vistas of Italian landscapes and the classical outlook of French painters such as Claude and Poussin. Koch was born in Tyrol, Austria, but lived most of his life in Rome where he raised a family. As an expatriate living in Italy, he became unofficial tutor and mentor to a colony of young German and Austrian artists in Rome including the Nazarenes, a group that wanted to revive religious iconography and medievalism in art. *Landscape with Shepherds and Cows at the Spring* reveals how the time Koch spent on his parents' farm and on excursions into the Swiss Alps would later inform his paintings of "heroic landscapes" as he called them. Although the painting presents the viewer with a rural idyll full of nostalgia for simpler days spent tending animals and living off the abundant land, it is actually a carefully crafted composition of space that resembles an amphitheater or stage set. The viewer is seated in a slightly raised position from which to watch the action below. This raised vantage point also allows us to gaze out over the horizon to the distant hilltops and the eternal, timeless blue of the sky—another symbol of God's creation of nature. **OW**

The Stages of Life | Caspar David Friedrich

1834 | oil on canvas | 28 ³/₈ x 37 in / 72 x 94 cm | Museum der Bildenden Künste, Leipzig, Germany

Caspar David Friedrich (1774–1840), the leading artist of the German Romantic movement, translated his melancholy temperament into some of history's most masterful landscapes. Friedrich painted *The Stages of Life* when he was sixty-one, six years before his death. Though it was a pastiche of sketches he had made during different travels in his youth, *The Stages of Life* was an anomaly in his oeuvre because it was a painting of an imaginary location. The recognizable geographical references in the work are all highly personal and the landscape serves almost as an autobiography for the deeply introspective artist. The main body of the painting appears loosely based on the harbor of Greifswald where he was born. Five ships are depicted at various distances in the water.

They symbolically represent the passing of life. On the shore, an old man stands in the foreground facing toward the water and it is assumed that he is Friedrich at the time of this painting. Nearby stands a young man in a top hat, modeled after his nephew, who in this context represents maturity. Playing beyond them both is a graceful young girl, modeled after his eldest daughter, who represents youth, and portraits of his two youngest children playing with a Swedish flag, who represent childhood. The mast of the central ship forms a crucifix, a sign of Friedrich's deep faith, yet the tranquil, luminous, poetic painting is not filled with redemptive hope, or the yearning for heaven after death, but with the bittersweet awareness that mortal life is precious and passes quickly. **AH**

Flowers | Johan Laurents Jensen

1835 | oil on canvas | 7 x 6 in / 19 x 17 cm | Hamburger Kunsthalle, Hamburg, Germany

Flowers was painted in 1835 during the Danish Golden Age, a time characterized by much ambiguity. Politically and economically Denmark was struggling due to the great fires in Copenhagen at the end of the eighteenth century, the British bombardment of 1807, and later the state's bankruptcy. However, amid this chaos, Danish culture still managed to grow rich in spirit and in thought. The same year that Johan Laurents Jensen (1800–56) painted these flowers he was appointed professor at the Royal Academy of Art in Copenhagen. He began his education at the Academy when he was fourteen, taught by Claus Detlev Fritzsch (1765–1841), a specialist in floral painting. After his training Jensen soon became a prominent artist within the genre of still-life paintings,

predominantly depicting flowers. In this painting Jensen presents us with a flower vine with leaves, buds, and a big open dog rose in the center. The vine stretches from the bottom right-hand corner and into the center of the painting. The red, white, and green colors stand out from the neutral, light-beige backdrop. Jensen played with optical illusions; true to nature the flowers seem to grow naturally on the canvas. Jensen was very well received in his time and at the Academy many students followed his style. Ladies of the middle class attended his courses or lessons, as did the wife of King Christian IX, Queen Louise. His attention to detail, precision, and color revived the genre of still-life flower painting, thus making it possible to bring the glory of nature indoors. **SML**

A View of the Artist's House and Garden in Mills Plains, Van Diemen's Land | John Glover

1835 | oil on canvas | 30 ⅛ x 45 in / 76.4 x 114.4 cm | Art Gallery of South Australia, Adelaide, Australia

Established English landscape artist John Glover (1767–1849) was in his sixties when, in 1831, he arrived in Tasmania. His romantic, Claudean landscapes had received much acclaim in Britain, yet he chose to turn his back on the English scenes that had brought him success and embrace the challenge of a new and strange environment. Glover's new setting, combined with his ability to accurately record his subject, allowed the artist to work with new and excited eyes and freed him from his former precise approach. The sheer scale of the terrain (which dwarfed the tight vistas of his native country), the grayish greens of the landscape, and the bright Australian sunlight entered Glover's paintings as he skillfully recorded "the remarkable peculiarity of the

trees" and the sublime beauty of the horizon. The effect of *A View of the Artist's House and Garden in Mills Plains, Van Diemen's Land* verges on the surreal. The artist contrasts a pastoral scene of a home and newly planted garden, populated with neat rows of English flowers, against the open, unknown landscape beyond. The subject reflects the artist's experience of using his English sensibilities to carve out a home and create a personal Eden in the context of a foreign and seemingly uncharted setting. Not only did Glover find a new personal aesthetic, he created a visual language for describing his new environment. Known for creating some of the most significant paintings to come out of the Australian terrain, he is considered "the father of Australian landscape painting." **JB**

The Burning of the Houses of Lords and Commons, October 16, 1834 | J.M.W. Turner

1835 | oil on canvas | 36 ¼ x 48 ½ in / 92 x 123.2 cm | Philadelphia Museum of Art, Philadelphia, PA, USA

Joseph Mallord William Turner (1775–1851) is known as the great English Romantic painter and as one of the major fathers of modernist painting. His depiction of London's Houses of Parliament in flames, inspired by real events, brings the viewer to the border between abstraction and reality. Turner had witnessed the fire firsthand from a boat on the River Thames. He had made some rough sketches but some months elapsed before he made a large-scale painting of the subject. The right side of the painting is dominated by the bridge, which leads across the Thames to the smoldering ruins on the other side. The twin towers of Westminster Abbey are visible in the background with the Thames and its reflections in the foreground. From a distance, however, it is difficult to recognize a realistic three-dimensional scene. The painting seems a powerful but undefined mélange of colors ranging from the bright gold and oranges at the left to the deep greens and purples to the right. The boats on the river fade into vague brown streaks. The final result is an embodiment of the Romantic sublime: the terror of fire and the radiant beauty of its light combine, putting the viewer into contact with the infinite forces of nature. When Turner exhibited the painting at the British Institution in 1835, he knew that it would cause a stir. The painting flaunts the Western tradition of realistic visual depiction in order to reach for a deeper emotional response, and foretells the birth of abstract art. This makes the painting as dynamic to viewers today as it was nearly two hundred years ago. **DK**

King Gustav I Vasa of Sweden Addressing Men
from Dalarna in Mora | Johan Gustaf Sandberg

1836 | fresco | Uppsala domkyrka, Sweden

Gustav Vasa, venerated as the founder of modern Sweden, is a legendary figure in Swedish history. Indeed, many myths and legends have grown up around him, but the subject depicted in this painting is not one of them. Around 1520, the Swedes were skirmishing with the Danes who had invaded the southern part of the country. Gustav Vasa went to the province of Dalarna, in the north, to round up a small army. After a few years of fierce fighting he had successfully pushed the Danes back, united the various provinces as one country, and had been elected king. Here we see the future monarch depicted three hundred years later on the wall of the Chapel of Our Lady in Uppsala domkyrka, the cathedral that houses his tomb. Johan Gustaf Sandberg (1782–1854) shows Gustav Vasa as a man of the people, in the same puritanical outfit as his compatriots, though slightly less frilly. He is encouraging the townsfolk to take up arms and fight for their country. The focal point of the composition is the young hero and soon-to-be-king high on the left but the eye is drawn along the diagonal to the man in black set apart from the crowd, seemingly hesitant to join the cause. The work is part of a group of scenes from Gustav Vasa's life painted in the 1830s by Sandberg, who was a professor at the Royal Academy of Fine Arts in Stockholm and had built a reputation as a portrait painter and a master of lighting. The commission was a chance for him to indulge his interests in peasant life and history. **RA**

The Course of Empire: Destruction
Thomas Cole

1836 | oil on canvas | 39 ¼ x 63 ½ in / 100 x 161.2 cm | New-York Historical Society, New York, NY, USA

Thomas Cole (1801–48) was an American Romantic landscape painter who added moral meanings to his work, leading to monumental historical allegories like the epic five-painting series *The Course of Empire*. *Destruction* comes second to last in the series, which charts the rise and decline of an imaginary empire. The cyclical nature of civilizations and the tension between the timeless natural world and fleeting man-made "progress" preoccupied many thinkers in Cole's day— the French and American Revolutions were recent memories and the Industrial Revolution in full swing. Cole himself migrated as a youth from the new industrial center of Lancashire, England, to the open spaces of America. In *Destruction*, the forward-leaning stance of the conqueror's huge statue in the foreground—presiding, ironically, over the city's destruction—leads us into the picture, to see doom at every turn. The sky thunders, waters swell, magnificent buildings burn, and warring soldiers bring a bridge crashing down—the overwhelming destruction wrought both by war and by nature. The buildings, in ancient Roman style, remind us of that empire's fall, and Cole seems to see the same potentially fatal arrogance and decadence in modern America. The dark skies and billowing smoke, expertly portrayed, show the influence of Turner's paintings (Cole visited England again as an adult). This series was the peak of Cole's successful career and his passion for an art dealing with universal truths helped to elevate and give an identity to American landscape painting. **AK**

Danish Artists at the Osteria la Gensola, Rome
Ditlev Conrad Blunck

1837 | oil on canvas | 29 x 40 in / 74.5 x 99.4 cm | Thorvaldsen's Museum, Copenhagen, Denmark

This entertaining painting was created in 1837, supposedly commissioned by the famous Danish sculptor Bertel Thorvaldsen. Ditlev Conrad Blunck (1798–1854) has illustrated the everyday life at an Italian inn in Rome, where both the local residents as well as a group of Danish artists are gathered. During the first half of the nineteenth century many Danish artists traveled to Rome, where they explored another way of life to that of the North. The depiction of Danish artists, positioned to the right in the painting, are all seated together around a table where they are being served Italian delicacies. Thorvaldsen sits by the end of the table; behind the waiter is the Danish artist, Albert Küchler, who is busy with his sketchbook portraying the Italian family to the left. Blunck has also included a self-portrait; he is sitting next to Jørgen Sonne, the artist with the gray top hat. The union of the artists and the local people make up a vibrant yet somewhat idealized setting. This subject matter, of prosperous, happy life in Rome around the first half of the nineteenth century, was hardly applicable to all Italian life at the time, yet this portrayal proved very popular when recounting the lifestyle of Southern Europe to people back home. Blunck returned to Denmark in 1838. Two years later he was commissioned by King Christian VIII to paint four paintings dealing with the allegory of human age. Today, as then, the painting *Danish Artists at the Osteria la Gensola, Rome* stands out as one of Blunck's most lively and joyful paintings. **SML**

The Fighting Temeraire Tugged to Her Last Berth to Be Broken Up
J.M.W. Turner

1839 | oil on canvas | 35 ¾ x 48 in / 90.7 x 121.6 cm | National Gallery, London, UK

J.M.W. Turner (1775–1851) loved this work and wrote: "No considerations of money or favour can induce me to loan my Darling again." His scene is a poignant memorial to the graceful, tall-masted warships of the Royal Navy and a mourning for the great days of British naval power. It shows the *Fighting Temeraire*—famed for her heroic role in the Battle of Trafalgar in 1805—being towed up the River Thames to a shipyard to be broken up. As the modern steam-powered tug pulls the ethereal sailing ship to her fate, Turner testifies to the massive technological changes ushered in during his lifetime. The techniques and colors are typical of the later works that were to make him arguably the most revolutionary of landscape painters. This painting demonstrates Turner's fascination with elemental subjects: water, air, and fire. The sun sets in flaming colors in homage to the ship's former glories, but also shows Turner's virtuoso skills. This was painted when the artist was in his sixties, and when he was just about to move into his more abstract final phase. It is filled with the contrasts he loved: loose brushwork and thick paint on the sky versus detailed work on the sailing ship; the painting's left side is cool in color, the right boldly hot; the comments on the old world versus the new. Works like this show clearly how Turner began the breakdown of recognizable forms, the emphasis on light and color, and the emotional brushwork that would mark the work of the Impressionists and of countless abstract painters. **AK**

View of the Grande Galerie of the Louvre | Patrick Allan-Fraser

1841 | oil on canvas | 43 ¼ x 36 ⅝ in / 110 x 93 cm | Louvre, Paris, France

The son of a successful weaver merchant, Patrick Allan-Fraser (1813–90) rejected the opportunity to follow his father into a commercial career in favor of pursuing his artistic leanings. Studies took Allan-Fraser to Edinburgh, Rome, London, and finally Paris, where he encountered the magnificent Grande Galerie within the Louvre. When painting *View of the Grande Galerie of the Louvre* the artist took his inspiration from a group of Victorian artists known as The Clique, whom he had encountered in London. The Clique dismissed academic high art in favor of genre painting. The seemingly infinite Grande Galerie, stretching for a quarter of a mile, was a place where artists and craftsmen often congregated, yet here we encounter a serene atmosphere of appreciation

and reflection. In later years Allan-Fraser would immerse himself in the restoration and construction of fine buildings and his admiration for the Grande Galerie was paramount when undertaking this. The sporadic rays of light not only allow the viewer to gaze at the activity within, but also reveal the magnitude and elegance of the hall. Allan-Fraser was elected to the Royal Scottish Academy in 1874 and he commissioned the portraits of members of The Clique, in deference to those who had inspired him. The paintings reside at the home of the Hospitalfield Trust in Arbroath, the registered charity Allan-Fraser set up before his death to provide a place where young artists could practice and nurture their talents; something they still do to this day. **SG**

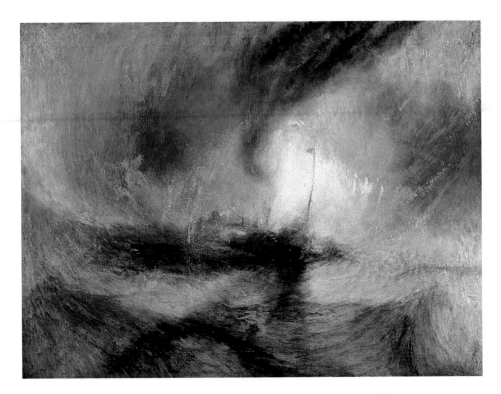

Snow Storm—Steamboat off a Harbour's Mouth | J.M.W. Turner

c.1842 | oil on canvas | 36 x 48 in / 91.5 x 122 cm | Tate Collection, London, UK

Joseph Mallord William Turner's (1775–1851) increasingly experimental work drew heavy criticism during the 1840s, and this painting was damned by some critics as "soapsuds and whitewash." Influential contemporary art critic John Ruskin, however, who was Turner's great champion, loved it. The famous tale attached to this painting is that Turner had himself lashed to the mast of the steamboat *Ariel* that appears in the picture while it crashed about in a sea storm. This story seems unlikely, but shows the artist's passion for getting inside the heart of the natural world. Viewers of this painting are sucked rapidly into the vortex-shaped composition that was much-used by Turner, and the careering compositional lines induce giddy disorientation and chaos, true to the subject matter. This is an unusually subjective picture for Turner's day, and the fairly limited color palette and crazily merging swaths of water and light evoke a dreamlike state. Despite this, Turner is in control of every well-observed element—only he, with his knowledge of color and light, would recall that the fires burning below deck need to be shown in that lemon-yellow shade created by looking through a curtain of snow. At the vortex's epicenter, a steamboat is tossed about perilously, used symbolically as in the *Fighting Temeraire*, but here specifically reflecting Turner's belief that man is helpless at the mercy of nature's vast forces. Turner apparently said of this work: "I did not paint it to be understood, but I wished to show what such a scene was like." **AK**

Odalisque and Slave | Jean-Auguste-Dominique Ingres

1842 | oil on canvas | 29 ½ x 41 ½ in / 75 x 105.4 cm | Walters Art Gallery, Baltimore, MD, USA

Ingres (1780–1867) began his training in the arts at a young age, starting under his father before studying in Toulouse and then Paris. He enjoyed a long career, executing *Odalisque and Slave* near the end of it, a work that is characteristic of his style because of its flat, linear quality and focus on contour. *Odalisque and Slave* is a product of both Ingres's and a more general interest in the Near East. Contemporary travelers were writing accounts on the culture of this area, with many focusing on harems. Ingres picks up on this subject through his reclining figure of an odalisque, a young virgin slave who acted as chambermaid for the rest of the harem. An odalisque would not usually have contact with the sultan, yet Ingres presents an erotic and sensual depiction of an idealized and nubile young woman. Her sexuality is heightened by the numerous phallic details including the lute that follows the line of her body, a column, and the hookah in the bottom right. By portraying his main figure so explicitly, Ingres has either misunderstood an odalisque's role, or is suggesting that she will soon be promoted to the position of a concubine. Although this painting's depiction of the Near Eastern setting is highly detailed, Ingres never traveled to this area. This explains why the odalisque recalls the Western tradition of the reclining Venus, as well as the stereotypical viewpoint: Ingres makes a blatant contrast between the white skin of his nude and the black eunuch who guards her, and he would continue to make such crude observations in similar work. **WD**

American Lake Scene | Thomas Cole

1844 | oil on canvas | 18 x 24 in / 46 x 62 cm | Detroit Institute of Arts, Detroit, MI, USA

Despite his English birth, Thomas Cole (1801–48) became one of the greatest American landscape painters of the nineteenth century. Having emigrated to America in 1818, the young Cole found himself enamored with the beauty of the Ohio countryside. Determined to become a painter, he learned rudimentary skills from a traveling portraitist named Stein before dedicating himself to landscape. In 1825, Cole executed a series of paintings along New York's Hudson River that were to make his fortune, attracting the attention of the city's most important patrons. *American Lake Scene* is a mature work of 1844, just four years before Cole's premature death. Having spent several years in Europe studying the work of the Old Masters, Cole greatly admired the landscapes of Claude Lorrain, and the weighty concepts of Italian history paintings had encouraged him to introduce a morality into his own works. In this painting, a lone Native American under a luminous sky contemplates the silent lake, evoking the tranquillity of the early settlement years. A true Romantic, Cole had campaigned against America's railroad fever, believing that nature reinforces man's morality and must be preserved. His skillful rendering of color, naturalism, and atmosphere is second to none at this time, causing one contemporary critic to proclaim that the work "looks like the earth before God breathed on it." Cole is now seen as the founder of the Hudson River School, a Romantic movement in which artists produced realistic landscapes with moral narratives. **SLF**

The Balcony Room | Adolf von Menzel

1845 | oil on cardboard | 23 x 19 in / 58 x 47 cm | Staatliche Museen, Berlin, Germany

At first glance, this painting resembles those of the French Impressionists. In fact, it was produced by a German painter and engraver popular during his lifetime for historical works glorifying Prussian power. From around 1840, Adolph Friedrich Erdmann von Menzel (1815–1905) began to produce low-key interiors and landscapes that used his talent as a Realist in a progressive way. In *The Balcony Room*, a flimsy curtain blows over the open door of a balcony, as a shaft of sunlight cuts dramatically across the floor. A chair is positioned just inside the balcony doors, caught in the light to reveal its delicate elegance. Highlights glance off another chair and off a large mirror, itself reflecting part of the room we cannot see. Fluid brushstrokes evoke the effect of strong sunlight outside the room and the way delicate material lifts in a breeze. It seems a simple picture: the corner of an unremarkable room with haphazardly placed objects, but it is filled with mood and mystery. The viewer is curious about the rest of the room and the world outside. Has someone just been sitting in the chair by the doors? What did they see outside? Menzel's genre paintings have unorthodox viewpoints. The off-center composition here, chopped off at each side as a casual snapshot of everyday life, anticipates French Impressionism, as does the free brushwork, natural light effects, and use of reflections. Curiously, Menzel kept paintings like this hidden and disparaged Impressionism when it came along. Only after his death did such works gain the admiration they deserve. **AK**

Fur Traders Descending the Missouri | George Bingham

1845 | oil on canvas | 29 x 36 ½ in / 73.5 x 92.5 cm | Metropolitan Museum of Art, New York, NY, USA

George Caleb Bingham's (1811–79) paintings immortalize the vanished world of the North American frontier. Bingham's solemn reverence for the landscape is characteristic of many mid-nineteenth-century Realists, yet he represents its beauty with a unique sensitivity to color and light. After completing only a few months of formal training at the Pennsylvania Academy of Fine Arts, Bingham traveled through Europe and North America before settling in Missouri. There he dedicated himself to producing landscape scenes and representing the fishermen and trappers who had recently occupied the area. In 1856, Bingham traveled to Düsseldorf, Germany, to study, mastering the academic style of painting he then taught as the Professor of Art at the University of Missouri. In addition to his art, he also served as a local politician. His later work is often criticized for its dry formalism and pedantic political undertones. But this earlier painting—showing two trappers in the early morning, eyeing the viewer from their canoe, in which lie a dead duck and a tethered cat or bear cub—particularly appealed to urban viewers, who were fascinated by its glamorization of the violence necessary for daily survival on the American frontier. Originally titled *French-Trader—Half Breed Son*, it was renamed when bought by the American Art Union. Bingham elegantly employs deft brushwork, a striking, geometric composition and clear, pure use of light to expose the hard-scrabble life of settlers and river men involved in the risky adventure of creating a new world. **SWW**

Comtesse d'Haussonville | Jean-Auguste-Dominique Ingres

1845 | oil on canvas | 51 ⁷⁄₈ x 36 ¼ in / 132 x 92 cm | Frick Collection, New York, NY, USA

Jean-Auguste-Dominique Ingres (1780–1867) was trained by his father as a painter, sculptor, and violinist. As a child, his musical talent dominated but later he focused on painting and studied under Jacques-Louis David. In 1801, he won the Grand Prix for *Ambassadors of Agamemnon in the Tent of Achilles*, which now hangs in the École Nationale Supérieure des Beaux-Arts, Paris. Ingres became the leading exponent of Neoclassicism at a time when Romanticism, as practiced by artists such as Delacoix and Géricault, was in fashion. Ingres lived in Italy for many years, and returned to Paris in 1834. It was then that he became popular as a portrait painter. Ingres's great skill was in employing his flat, linear style to represent his sitters' personalities while depicting them as beautifully as possible. He captured the most attractive qualities of even his most unattractive patrons without sacrificing their characters or making them unrecognizable. Expressing his sitter's beauty was no challenge though when painting Comtesse d'Haussonville who, despite her demure appearance, was an outspoken liberal, author and well-regarded intellectual. The sumptuous rendering of textures, such as the folds in her silk dress and the sheen of her hair ribbon, are characteristic of Ingres's painting. A master of technique, Ingres is sometimes critcized for being "bourgeois," and to this day his work is often satirized by cartoonists. He was a man of many contradictions, but this elegant portrait remains one of the most iconic images in art. **AH**

Crossing the Sands | David Cox

1848 | oil on panel | 10 ½ x 15 in / 26.5 x 38 cm | Birmingham Museums and Art Gallery, UK

David Cox (1783–1859) was one of the leading English watercolor landscape painters of the nineteenth century. In his later years, however, he turned to oil painting, producing highly atmospheric and evocative works such as *Crossing the Sands*. He began his artistic career painting miniature portraits, before working as a scene painter for the theater in Birmingham and again in London after his move in 1804. He supplemented his income through teaching, and took up watercolor painting around 1805, making the first of many sketching trips to Wales. Throughout his life he traveled widely through England, recording the landscape with his distinctive appreciation for a natural composition. After initially struggling, Cox went on to become a successful painter within his own lifetime, and was highly regarded as both a teacher of art and as an artist. In 1840 he moved back to Harborne, near Birmingham, and took up oil painting. He took lessons from the Bristol artist William James Müller (1812–45), who was proficient in both watercolor and oil painting. *Crossing the Sands* is typical of Cox's style, and shows the artist exhibiting every bit as much skill in oils as he had through his watercolors. The painting depicts a theme that he addressed several times: that of travelers crossing open flat landscapes in windy or stormy weather. There is a great sense of hope here, as the travelers, who appear weary, leave the dark skies behind them and head toward the light, a feeling that is further symbolized by the flock of birds soaring ahead. **TP**

Frederiksborg Castle | Ferdinand Richardt

1848 | oil on canvas | Private collection

Joachim Ferdinand Richardt (1819–95) established himself as an artist excelling in the depiction of Danish architecture, predominantly manor houses, churches, and castles. After a brief period as a carpenter's apprentice in 1835, Richardt studied at the Royal Academy of Arts in Copenhagen and was taught by some of Denmark's most important artists from the Danish Golden Age (c.1800–1850). By 1848 Richardt had sold twenty-six paintings to the Danish King Christian VIII, having been given a five year stipend by the Crown in 1847. In this painting Richardt has positioned Frederiksborg Castle—located twenty-two miles (thirty-five km) north of Copenhagen—in the center of the canvas, retaining a portion of the surrounding lake as well as two bridges, which guide our eyes in from the sides. The red castle stands out in sharp contrast to the pale blue sky and water. It rises from the lake as a crown worthy of King Frederik II who had the place built in 1560 and whose son, later King Christian IV, built the main buildings between 1600 and 1620. Richardt is known to have stayed at the castle for a period of two years, studying it from all angles and in all sorts of weather, resulting in a publication in 1852 purely focusing on Frederiksborg. This painting clearly demonstrates Richardt's skills by depicting architecture and nature with great accuracy, something he developed further after traveling to America in 1855, and in 1873, when he settled there. His work was hugely inspired by the vast American landscape, particularly the majesty of Niagara Falls. **SML**

Isabella | John Everett Millais

1848–49 | oil on canvas | 40 ½ x 56 ¼ in / 103 x 143 cm | Walker Art Gallery, Liverpool, UK

Originally titled *Lorenzo and Isabella*, this is the first painting that John Everett Millais (1829–96) exhibited as a member of the Pre-Raphaelite Brotherhood. The initials of the group appear after his signature and as a carved decoration on Isabella's seat. The subject is taken from a poem by John Keats, based on a story by the fourteenth-century writer Boccaccio. Isabella falls in love with Lorenzo, a workman employed by her brothers. They are incensed, having planned a far more lucrative match for her. The brothers murder Lorenzo and hide his body in the woods, but the suitor's ghost returns, advising Isabella of the crime. When she finds his remains, she takes his head and keeps it by her, buried in a pot of basil. In typical Pre-Raphaelite fashion, Millais used a host of tiny details to hint at the tragic outcome of the tale. Lorenzo hands Isabella a blood orange, while the plate in front of her depicts a biblical scene of decapitation. The cruel brothers are accompanied by a bird of prey, and one of them kicks their sister's dog. Finally, in the background is the ominous sight of the flower pot that will shortly contain Lorenzo's head. Millais used friends and family to model for the scene. His sister-in-law posed for Isabella, his father for the man with the napkin, while fellow Pre-Raphaelite Dante Gabriel Rossetti was the drinker at the back. The picture was generally well received by critics, who recognized the artist's intention of mimicking early Italian art with his angular poses and archaic sense of perspective. The painting was sold to a tailor for £150 and a suit of clothes. **IZ**

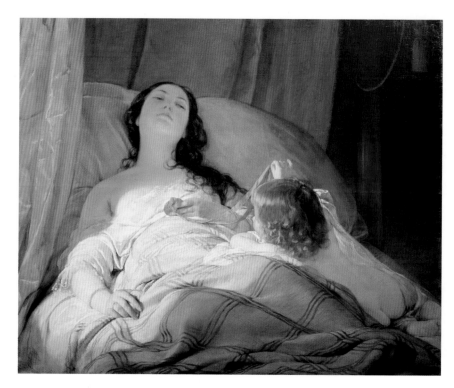

The Drowsy One | Friedrich von Amerling

1830–50 | oil on canvas | 20 x 14 ½ in / 51.4 x 37.4 cm | Uffizi, Florence, Italy

One of the most distinguished exponents of Austrian portrait painting, Friedrich von Amerling (1803–77) was also a major artist of historic and genre pictures. Emperor Franz Josef I commissioned works, as did members of Vienna's elite whom Amerling captured in elegant settings with vivid colors. *The Drowsy One* presents a typified likeness of feminine charm with a young woman in a state of apparent languor. The circumscribed close-up, a stylistic device frequently employed by Amerling, emphasizes the intimacy of the scene. One of Amerling's favorite compositional devices was to position the sitter turned away from the beholder as he does here with the child. The luminosity of the woman's exposed skin harmonizes with the white of the nightgown, which has slipped from her shoulder, and the patterned bedspread. The recumbent position of abandonment is offset by the restlessness of the child intent on distracting the woman with a yellow satin ribbon. The finely painted features and suffused rosy cheeks contrast with the energetic brushstrokes of the dark unruly locks, the corkscrew curls on the child's head and the wrinkles on the bedspread. This work is a successful blend of portrait and genre, which played a dominant role in the Biedermeier period (1815–48). *The Drowsy One* showcases nineteenth-century ideals of femininity—the soft gleam on the young woman's face and the child's curls, the head inclined sideways, the sentimental gaze, and the gently sloping line of the neck and shoulders all suggest sensitivity, gentleness, and vulnerability. **AA**

The Buffalo Hunt | Paul Kane

*c.*1850 | oil on canvas

In 1845, the Irish-Canadian artist and explorer Paul Kane (1810–71) left Toronto to document the customs of the indigenous people of Canada before they largely vanished as a result of Western influence. Guided by traders for the Hudson's Bay Company, he arrived at Fort William in May 1846 and then traveled to Fort Garry, where he sketched the last great buffalo hunt to take place there. This image, for which there is also a watercolor sketch now held in the collection of the Stark Foundation, Texas, depicts the Métis buffalo hunt. The hunt was accomplished by carefully herding buffalo toward a cliff over which they would fall to their deaths, or would be killed shortly thereafter. For various reasons the prairie bison became extinct around 1880, and as such *The Buffalo*

Hunt is particularly poignant as Kane, a Westerner—and hence member of that group of people who were leading native culture to "extinction"—here portrays natives in the process of rendering the buffalo extinct. As in many of the oil paintings that Kane reworked in his Toronto studio following his journeys across Canada, Kane has altered details to make the image more palatable to European audiences. One small example of this is the dramatic, cloudy sky, a hallmark of European Romanticism, which replaces the clear sky in his original sketch. Kane's art continues to fascinate today, for the historic details of Canadian Aboriginal culture, which seep into his works, and also for the way in which it articulates the desires of the audience for whom they were made. **SS**

The Bookworm
Carl Spitzweg

c.1850 | oil on canvas | 19 x 10 ⅝ in / 49.5 x 27 cm
Museum Georg Schäfer, Schweinfurt, Germany

Carl Spitzweg (1808–85) is sometimes referred to as a "German Hogarth." His small-scale genre paintings portray German middle-class life with a gentle humor and technical mastery learned from copying the Dutch Masters as a young man. Spitzweg began painting during the Biedermeier period, an artistic era following Napoleon's defeat in 1815 that valued comfort, stability, and domesticity over high political concepts. *The Bookworm* has become a much-reproduced emblem of bookish eccentricity: an elderly scholar totters on a ladder, thoroughly absorbed amid towering bookshelves and bathed in Spitzweg's favorite golden light. Although commercially successful, Spitzweg also craved academic recognition. In 1868 he was made an honorary member of the Munich Art Academy, and in later life his style became much looser under the influence of the Impressionists. **SLF**

The Gypsy Boy and Girl
José Agustín Arrieta

c.1850 | oil on canvas | 44 ⅞ x 35 in / 114 x 89 cm
Private collection

In the mid-nineteenth century there was a dramatic increase in the number of locally trained or self-taught Mexican artists and a rise in art schools throughout the country, especially the Puebla School of which José Agustín Arrieta (1803–74) was its most representative artist. Mexican painters no longer copied continental styles but sought to produce works that captured their country's indigenous or primitive traditions. Although famous for his still lifes, Arrieta was also a frequent painter of *chinas poblanas* (native women). His painting of a gypsy couple eating their lunch displays a provincial approach that lacks traditional modeling and a use of space that shuns traditional perspective. The young woman's gaze lures the viewer into the scene. Local dress, custom, and foods are given center stage. During this era, women's apparel remained in the indigenous style, while men adopted newer, imported styles. **AA**

The Sower
Jean-François Millet

1850 | oil on canvas | 40 x 32 in / 101.6 x 82.6 cm
Museum of Fine Arts, Boston, MA, USA

The Sower was one of Jean-François Millet's (1814–75) most influential pictures, produced at a time when the Realist style was causing ripples in the art world. Images of peasant life had been popular for centuries, usually small and picturesque, presenting the town-dweller with an unthreatening view of the countryside. But Millet's peasants were unidealized and shocked the critics with their heroic scale, normally reserved for classical deities or historical celebrities. The Revolution had swept away the old order, leaving the future uncertain and, as a result, any large-scale canvases of peasants were bound to seem inflammatory. The revolutionary intentions of such works by Gustave Courbet, leader of the Realists, were undoubtedly intentional, though Millet's own politics are far less clear. Nonetheless, *The Sower* was greeted enthusiastically by republican critics, but negatively by conservatives. **IZ**

Side Portal of Como Cathedral
Rudolph von Alt

1850 | oil on cardboard | 10 ½ x 8 in / 25 x 21.5 cm
Hamburger Kunsthalle, Hamburg, Germany

Rudolph von Alt (1812–1905) began painting in the Biedermeier era, a movement that focused on everyday scenes and objects. On trips around Austria and Italy, he produced landscapes, cityscapes, and interiors noted for their realism and attention to detail. Although watercolor was becoming his preferred medium by the time of this mature study, its golden depiction of late afternoon shade demonstrates the masterful rendering of light and atmosphere that still characterized his oil works. The rich, earthy palette differs from the cool crispness of his Alpine watercolors. In 1861, he helped establish the Kunstlerhaus, a conservative art society; but his own style continued to evolve, later works demonstrating a freedom akin to Impressionism. In 1897, he left the Kunstlerhaus and joined the Viennese Secession, embracing the avant-garde alongside Gustav Klimt, foreshadowing Austrian Expressionism. **SLF**

A Converted British Family Sheltering a Christian Priest from the Persecution of the Druids | William Holman Hunt

1850 | oil on canvas | 43 ¾ x 55 ½ in / 111 x 141 cm | Ashmolean Museum, Oxford, UK

William Holman Hunt (1827–1910) was a founding member of the Pre-Raphaelite Brotherhood, and remained truest to its original aims. This picture dates from the early days of the group, when its work was still attracting fierce criticism in the press. Hunt produced paintings with a strong moral purpose, executed in a scrupulously detailed manner. This particular subject began as an entry for a competition at the Royal Academy on the theme of "An Act of Mercy." The Academy's size restrictions proved too limiting, and the picture was eventually acquired by Thomas Combe, one of the Pre-Raphaelites' chief patrons. Combe was a keen supporter of the High Church revival that was taking place at the time, spearheaded by the Tractarians. Among other things,

these revivalists were keen to stress the historical continuity of the Church of England along with the importance of the sacraments and clerical vestments. Hunt's picture contains many symbolic references to Tractarian ideas. The missionary's pose is reminiscent of Christ's descent from the cross, while the girls who tend to him carry a thorn branch and sponge—two of the instruments of the Passion. On the left, the bowl of water symbolizes the rite of baptism while, behind it, two children squeeze grapes into a cup, a reference to the eucharist. At the back of the hut, a painted cross and hanging lamp form a makeshift altar while the hanging nets allude to the Church's role as "fishers of men." Hunt expanded the theme still further, with a series of biblical quotations on the picture frame. **IZ**

Washington Crossing the Delaware
Emanuel Gottlieb Leutze

1851 | oil on canvas | 149 x 255 in / 378.5 x 647.7 cm | Metropolitan Museum of Art, New York, NY, USA

Any visitor to the American Wing in New York's Metropolitan Museum of Art will not forget seeing Emanuel Leutze's (1816–68) *Washington Crossing the Delaware*. More than twelve feet tall and twenty-one wide, this iconic picture is truly larger than life. The painting depicts Washington and his army dramatically crossing the icy river for a surprise dawn attack on the British at Trenton, New Jersey, on December 25, 1776. Leutze uses every imaginable device to heighten the drama and elicit an emotive response in the viewer; jagged chunks of ice, whinnying horses, wounded soldiers, and a morning star speak of danger, courage, and hope. The heroic Washington stands noble and erect at the center of the scene. His demeanor suggests fortitude and moral

purpose. He brings with him an army of Americans ready to face any hardship and battle any foe in the name of freedom and truth. Strangely enough, this symbol of America was actually painted in Germany. The German-American Leutze insisted on using American art students at the famous Düsseldorf Academy as his models. At the time, the United States had recently expanded its boundaries to the Pacific Ocean through its victory in the Mexican War. Leutze, while painting the Delaware, imagined the spirit of Washington crossing western rivers, bringing the stars and stripes and thousands of American settlers with it. The original version of the painting was destroyed in the bombing of Bremen, Germany, in 1942. This surviving version was completed in 1851. **DK**

Monarch of the Glen | Edwin Landseer

1851 | oil on canvas | 64 ½ x 66 ½ in / 163.8 x 169 cm | John Dewar and Sons Ltd., London, UK

Sir Edwin Henry Landseer (1802–73) was the greatest animal painter of his age, often endowing his subjects with human qualities. His pictures of dogs were frequently humorous or sentimental, but his paintings of stags were more romantic, displaying an epic sense of grandeur that was in keeping with their wild surroundings. He produced a powerful series of deer paintings in the 1840s, culminating in this imposing depiction of a royal stag at Glenorchy. The popularity of this type of theme was linked to the changing image of the Scottish Highlands, which had been made fashionable by the novels of Sir Walter Scott and the patronage of Queen Victoria at Balmoral. He visited the area frequently. Landseer was always well aware of his paradoxical attitude to stags. On one hand, he found them the finest and noblest of animals, yet he also enjoyed the spectacle of seeing them hunted and killed. He wrote: "There is something in the toil and trouble, the wild weather and scenery that makes butchers of us all. Who does not glory in the death of a fine stag." *Monarch of the Glen* was originally commissioned for the refreshment room at the House of Lords, but after being deemed too expensive by the Commons, it was sold off privately. Its subsequent fame is due mainly to its use in advertising, a field that expanded rapidly after the abolition of advertising duty in 1853: the Pears soap company, the whisky industry, and an insurance firm have all been associated with it. The image has also appeared on American banknotes. **IZ**

Ophelia | John Everett Millais

1851–52 | oil on canvas | 30 x 44 in / 76 x 112 cm | Tate Collection, London, UK

This is one of the most popular Pre-Raphaelite paintings, produced when the youthful enthusiasm of the group was at its peak. Its painstaking attention to detail and love of poetic symbolism were characteristic traits of their style. Shakespeare was a favorite source of inspiration for all the Pre-Raphaelites. Here, John Everett Millais (1829–96) depicts a scene from *Hamlet*, where Ophelia throws herself in the river and drowns after her father has been killed by her lover. Shakespeare had emphasized the plight of his deranged heroine by describing how she garlanded herself with a variety of flowers, each of which had appropriate, symbolic associations. Millais followed this lead, portraying the blooms with botanical accuracy and adding examples from the Victorian language of flowers. Among others, he included pansies (love in vain), violets (fidelity), nettles (pain), daisies (innocence), pheasant's eyes (sorrow), forget-me-nots and poppies (death). This final association is also suggested by the outline of a skull, formed by the foliage on the right. It refers not only to Ophelia's death, but also to the famous graveyard scene which followed it, featuring Hamlet with Yorick's skull. Millais's obsession with accuracy was not limited to the flowers. He spent four months working on the background, at a spot near the Hogsmill River in Surrey, England. The model, too, was obliged to suffer for his art. She was Lizzie Siddall, Dante Rossetti's future wife. For weeks on end, she posed in a bath full of water, heated from below by a number of lamps. **IZ**

The Awakening Conscience | William Holman Hunt

1853 | oil on canvas | 30 x 22 in / 76 x 56 cm | Tate Collection, London, UK

As a member of the Pre-Raphaelite Brotherhood, William Holman Hunt (1827–1910) painted one of the defining images of Victorian Christianity, *The Light of the World* (1851–53), which became a popular print. *The Awakening Conscience* is a direct response to that painting. The young woman looks up and starts forward suddenly—her posture indicates that she has done so in response to something she has seen or heard from outside. At first glance this is a scene of domesticity in comfortable surroundings. Such intimacy between man and woman is rare in Victorian painting, yet among all her rings her wedding finger is bare. She is a "kept woman," a mistress. All around her are symbols of her entrapment—the clock under its glass, the bird trapped by the cat—and of her wasted life—the unfinished tapestry, the music for "Tears, Idle Tears" on the floor. She turns to a world outside the house she is imprisoned in, a happier world, seen in the shaft of sunlight falling on the bottom right corner of the painting, and which is reflected in the mirror behind. She has "seen the light." This painting is a direct expression of mid-Victorian religious revivalism that swept across all sections of the Church of England, yet the very same religiosity took offence at the subject. Contemporary sensibilities even frowned on paintings of men and women talking together freely in railway carriages. The circumstances in which Hunt's young lady finds herself may not now be immediately obvious, yet this is still a powerful portrayal of spiritual emotion. **SC**

A Country Home | Frederic Edwin Church

1854 | oil on canvas | 32 x 51 in / 81.5 x 130 cm | Seattle Art Museum, Seattle, WA, USA

A pinnacle of his formative painting years, and a poetic evocation of the rural American countryside as God and Nature intended, *A Country Home* by Frederic Edwin Church (1826–1900) portrays a pioneer homestead in a scene of wild, primeval beauty. America was coming to terms with urban and industrial shifts in its landscape—Henry David Thoreau had just published *Walden*, his famous celebration of the simple life, and Church captured this longing for the backwoods with poignancy and drama. Church was a member of the Hudson River School founded by another key American painter, Thomas Cole (1801–48). Its artists followed in the tradition of Romantic Classicism and saw themselves as "God's stenographers," painting America as the

"final frontier." Panoramas were *de rigueur*. Cole taught Church for the last two years of his life and Church repaid the tutelage by mirroring Cole's love of nature even more resplendently. *A Country Home* is Church's ultimate homage to Cole. It turned out to be Church's last painting idealizing the New England landscape. In 1853 he made his first sketching trip to South America in search of exploding volcanoes and lush impenetrable forests. When he returned to painting American scenery, it was of a land fighting for ecological survival. Church was forced to abandon painting in 1877 because of arthritis in his hands. Today, thousands of people visit his Victorian castle museum "Olana" with its spectacular views—the same views he captured in several of his paintings. **JH**

Bonjour Monsieur Courbet | Gustave Courbet

1854 | oil on canvas | 50 ¾ x 58 ⅝ in / 129 x 149 cm | Musée Fabre, Montpellier, France

In the 1850s, Gustave Courbet (1819–77) was the most controversial artist in France. Outspoken rebel against bourgeois society and acknowledged leader of the Realist School, he was subject to a torrent of ridicule for the alleged vulgarity and ugliness of his paintings. He had the luck to find a wealthy patron, Alfred Bruyas, who solved his acute financial problems. In May 1854, Courbet traveled to Montpellier in southern France to stay with Bruyas. It was during this sojourn that *The Meeting*—popularly known as *Bonjour Monsieur Courbet*—was painted. *The Meeting* takes place under a light-filled, sunny sky. The effect of the figures looming above the nondescript landscape is monumental and strangely dreamlike. The redheaded Bruyas makes a sweeping gesture

of welcome with his doffed hat; he is standing erect but with eyes modestly cast down. Behind him, his servant Calas bows respectfully. Only Bruyas's dog Breton seems unawed by the artist's presence. With his staff and his backpack crammed with painting materials, Courbet's pose was based on a woodcut of the Wandering Jew, a symbolic representative of suffering humanity. He stands in full sunlight, casting a defined shadow, while Bruyas and the servant are muted by shade. With the arrogant tilt of his head and his protruding beard, the artist accepts the deference shown him as his right. Although classified as a Realist, Courbet here produced a definitive statement of the Romantic view of the artist as prophet and rebel, deserving of humanity's homage. **RG**

The Horse Fair | Rosa Bonheur

1853–55 | oil on canvas | 96 x 200 in / 245 x 507 cm | Metropolitan Museum of Art, New York, NY, USA

The unconventional artist Rosa Bonheur (1822–99) was born in Bordeaux and learned the fundamentals of art from her father, the artist Raymond Bonheur (*d.*1849). Her style changed little throughout her career, and remained grounded in Realism. Working at the same time as the Realists Gustave Courbet (1819–77) and Jean-François Millet (1814–75), her work was based on accurate observation from nature combined with excellent technical skills. She had a great affection for animals, in particular horses, and her understanding of animals, their nature, and their anatomy is obvious in her paintings. Her enormous canvas *The Horse Fair* is considered the artist's greatest work, but is also unusual within her style. Although the foundation of the painting is Realist, she

approached her subject with a combination of the color and emotion of the Romantics, and in particular was influenced at this point by the work of Théodore Géricault (1791–1824), himself a great admirer of the horse. She based the scene on sketches made while visiting the horse market in Paris near the asylum of La Salpêtrière. Bonheur made sketching trips twice a week for a year and a half before starting the painting, and on her trips dressed as a man to avoid attention from passersby. Bonheur enjoyed financial success during her lifetime, yet was never properly appreciated by the critics and the art world; it may be that her feminist views and unconventional lifestyle led to her lack of popularity within the male-dominated academic art circles. **TP**

The Scapegoat | William Holman Hunt

1854–55 | oil on canvas | 13 ¼ x 18 in / 34 x 46 cm | Manchester Art Gallery, UK

William Holman Hunt (1827–1910) is most renowned for his links with the Pre-Raphaelites but, in his own time, he gained even greater fame as a leading religious painter. *The Scapegoat* is one of his earliest and most unusual ventures in this field. In 1854, Hunt embarked upon a two-year stay in the Middle East. His aim was to endow his religious scenes with an authentic flavor, by producing them in genuine biblical locations. This picture, for example, was painted by the Dead Sea, close to the original site of Sodom. The subject is taken from the Jewish rites relating to the Day of Atonement. Two goats were chosen as sacrificial animals, in a symbolic act of expiation for the sins of the faithful. One of the goats was sacrificed in the temple, while the other was cast out into the wilderness, bearing away the people's sins. The ritual was also seen as an echo of Christ's sacrifice. To stress this further, a red ribbon was placed around the goat's horns, as a symbolic reference to the crown of thorns. On the left-hand side of the picture, a reflection of the moon encircles a pair of goat's horns like a halo, emphasizing the sanctity of the event. Hunt went to considerable trouble to make the scene as realistic as possible. He took great pains to find a rare white goat—the color was vital, to indicate that the animal was free from sin. Then, when his model died on the return journey to Jerusalem, Hunt had to find a second animal. This time, he painted it while it was standing in a tray of salt and mud, taken from the shores of the Dead Sea. **IZ**

The Last of England | Ford Madox Brown

1855 | oil on panel | 32 x 29 in / 82.5 x 75 cm | Birmingham Museum and Art Gallery, UK

This poignant scene is Ford Madox Brown's (1821–93) masterpiece. It deals with the issue of emigration, which was topical at the time and had some personal significance for the artist. Brown began work on the picture in 1852, when emigration was reaching a peak in the UK, with almost 370,000 Britons leaving their homeland. The immediate inspiration came from the departure of Thomas Woolner (1825–92), a Pre-Raphaelite sculptor, who was emigrating to Australia. The artist, too, was thinking of leaving. He painted this scene when he was "very hard up and a little mad," and was contemplating a move to India. For this reason, perhaps, Brown based the two main figures on himself and his wife. The grim-faced couple are sailing away from their native land, without even a backward glance at the white cliffs of Dover. The name of their vessel is "Eldorado," but there is nothing in the picture to suggest that their future will be rosy. In the cramped conditions of a cheap passage, they huddle together for warmth. Their baby is wrapped up in the woman's shawl and only its tiny hand can be seen. In a customary, Pre-Raphaelite quest for accuracy, Brown was determined to ensure that his working conditions matched the inclement setting of his picture. He painted most days in the garden, rejoicing when the weather was poor: "Today fortune seemed to favor me. It has been intensely cold, no sun, no rain—high wind, but this seemed the sweetest weather possible, for it . . . made my hand look blue with the cold, as I require it in the work." **IZ**

Habitants Sleighing
Cornelius Krieghoff

1855 | oil on canvas | 12 ⅛ x 18 in / 30.8 x 45.7 cm | Art Gallery of Ontario, Toronto, Canada

Although Cornelius Krieghoff (1815–72) was born in Amsterdam, and died in Chicago, he is known as one of the fathers of Canadian painting. *Habitants Sleighing*, a sentimental depiction of French Canadian peasants, was created during the artist's greatest period of productivity, when he was living in Quebec City. Paintings such as this appealed to the aristocracy there as it represented the French peasants and Canadian Aboriginals—two greatly marginalized groups of people during this period—as simple, harmless, and diverting. Many images such as *Habitants Sleighing* were bought by European military men stationed in Quebec, who then brought them home as a souvenir of Canada. The politics of Krieghoff's images are still an issue of sensitivity to this day, but his unique achievement was that he brought Canadian subjects into the field of painting, in much the same way that seventeenth-century Dutch genre painters brought the everyday life of the Dutch middle class into the popular imagination. Krieghoff could never be called a masterful painter, but here he has artfully composed his subject along the lines of conventional European genre painting of the time. He has very closely observed the Quebec landscape, with its sugary snow and crystal-like sky, which serves as a backdrop for his depiction of the habitants. The idealistic nature of the Quebec landscape very strongly supports the notion that his paintings were highly constructed fantasies of how people wanted to remember the country and its people. **SS**

Portrait of Emperor Pedro II
Luiz de Miranda Pereira Visconde de Menezes

1855 | oil on canvas | Museu Historico Nacional, Rio de Janeiro, Brazil

Despite his European ancestry, Dom Pedro II was born in Rio de Janeiro, making him Brazil's only native-born monarch. He came to the throne at the age of fourteen, and during his forty-nine-year rule he laid the foundations for modern Brazil. When he was painted by Luiz de Miranda Pereira Visconde de Menezes (1820–78), at age thirty-one, Dom Pedro II was already a well-loved liberal, progressive emperor who encouraged industrialization, the abolition of slavery, and the modernization of Brazil. *Portrait of Emperor Pedro II* is a classic Baroque portrait honoring a great and popular ruler. Little is known about Menezes; however, the complex expression on the emperor's face reveals an exceptional talent. Menezes captures discernment, sense of duty, and playful curiosity in the emperor's handsome face. He also employs the remnants of classical European portrait style to illustrate the vast earthiness of tropical Brazil. Characterized by a highly decorative appearance, the painting possesses a remarkably harmonious balance of gilding and earth tones. Dom Pedro II is seen as representing his own mixed heritage, as well as embodying his hopes for Brazil's developing hybridized and industrialized society. With modernization, the monarchy became an increasing obstacle to Brazil's economic powers and to the integration of large-scale immigration from Europe. Although still popular among the people, Dom Pedro II was removed from power and exiled in 1889. He died in 1891 in Paris, France; his remains, along with those of his wife, were reburied in Brazil in 1922. **AH/SWW**

The Studio of the Painter, a Real Allegory | Gustave Courbet

1855 | oil on canvas | 142 ¼ x 235 ½ in / 362 x 598 cm | Musée d'Orsay, Paris, France

Gustave Courbet (1819–77) was the founder and leader of Realism, the influential nineteenth-century literary and artistic movement that focused on ordinary people, everyday themes, and visual verisimilitude. Courbet was particularly interested in France's peasantry and he painted many of his most important pictures in his hometown of Ornans. *The Studio of the Painter, a Real Allegory* differs significantly in tone and topic from Courbet's depictions of rural domestic dramas and radiant landscapes, yet his most visually elaborate and densely narrative painting is still considered one of his greatest masterpieces. The painting's title is a clever pun, since it is both a genuine allegory and Courbet's allegory of the philosophy behind Realism. At the center of the composition

Courbet sits painting one of his more typical canvases, which symbolically represents his ethos of "truth" in painting. The nude model watching him paint acts as the embodiment of unidealized beauty. All around are sights of an artist's studio such as a skull, a model contorted into a complex pose, and another wearing a traditional Chinese costume and waiting to be called to the platform. Included in the crowd are also portraits of Courbet's friends, collectors, and patrons. Yet Courbet directs his attention to a little peasant boy, whose opinion seems to matter more to the artist than those of the affluently dressed scholars and collectors observing him, demonstrating the importance for artists to observe and represent the beauty of their contemporary reality. **AH**

Autumn Leaves | John Everett Millais

1855–56 | oil on canvas | 41 x 29 in / 104 x 74 cm | Manchester City Art Galleries, UK

This is one of John Everett Millais's (1829–96) most poetic scenes. It was painted after the initial furor over the Pre-Raphaelites had died down, and the artist was replacing the complex symbolism of early works, such as *Isabella*, with subjects that were more ambiguous and evocative. As the 1850s progressed, Millais was increasingly drawn to themes that revolved around a paradox. In *The Blind Girl*, a sightless woman is juxtaposed with the visual splendor of a rainbow; in *The Vale of Rest*, a nun is engaged in back-breaking labor. In a similar way, *Autumn Leaves* depicts a group of young girls—the epitome of youth and innocence—in a setting that is redolent of decay and death. The smoke, the dead leaves, and the setting sun are all images of transience, and the

gloomy expressions of the girls confirm this. Millais began work on this picture in October 1855. It was set in the garden of his home at Annat Lodge in Perth, Scotland—the outline of the local church can just be seen in the misty background. He is quoted to have "intended the picture to awaken by its solemnity the deepest religious reflection." The elegiac mood was equally influenced by Lord Tennyson, whose work he was illustrating at the time, and by his own melancholy fondness for the season of fall. "Is there any sensation more delicious," he once remarked, "than that awakened by the odor of burning leaves? To me, nothing brings back sweeter memories of the days that are gone; it is the incense offered by departing summer to the sky...." **IZ**

Madame Moitessier | Jean-Auguste-Dominique Ingres

1856 | oil on canvas | 47 ¼ x 36 ¼ in / 120 x 92 cm | National Gallery, London, UK

Jean-Auguste-Dominique Ingres (1780–1867), a pupil of Jacques-Louis David, painted some of the world's most memorable and admired portraits, yet as an academician he considered the genre inferior to history painting. He wrote that expression in painting demands a great science in drawing, and believed that the best way to achieve this skill was to copy from classical sources and continue in the tradition of Raphael. This set him against the artists such as Delacroix, who believed in expression through color. For Ingres there should be no visible brushstroke; the paint should be "as smooth as an onion skin." This portrait of Marie-Clotilde-Inès Moitessier, the wife of a banker, was begun in 1844. It did not leave his studio until many years later, during which time her clothing changed several times. The pose is taken from a Roman wall painting in Herculaneum. The huge mirror is a statement of wealth, along with the vase, the furniture, and the sitter's jewelry and sumptuous dress. It is also a technical device to create depth, and to recreate Madame Moitessier in profile. Ingres frequently framed women with mirrors, displaying them as beautiful, decorative objects. This doubling also enabled him to demonstrate his skills by painting the reflected image. Many nineteenth-century painters such as Whistler and Manet adopted this device for different reasons. Ingres's successor was Degas, who admired and emulated his skills of draftsmanship. Matisse and Picasso took his legacy into the twentieth century. **WO**

The Stonebreaker | Henry Wallis

1857 | oil on canvas | 25 ⅝ x 31 ⅛ in / 65 x 79 cm | Birmingham City Museum and Art Gallery, UK

Most famous for his painting *The Death of Chatterton* (1856, Tate Britain, London), which Ruskin called "faultless" and "wonderful," Henry Wallis's (1830–1916) *The Stonebreaker* is more Realistic in tone than the Romantic *Chatterton*, showing a manual laborer who, at first glance, may appear to be asleep but who has actually been worked to death. Whereas *Chatterton* is rich with jewel-like colors—purple trousers and vivid copper-colored hair—*The Stonebreaker* displays a much more muted tonal structure. The autumnal colors emphasize that the man has died too early. Wallis is believed to have painted the picture as a comment on the effects of the Poor Law of 1834 which forced the destitute into workhouses. To stay out of the workhouse, some laborers worked themselves to death. On the picture's frame is written a line from a poem by Tennyson: "Now is thy long day's work done." *The Stonebreaker* was exhibited at the Royal Academy, London, in 1858 to great acclaim. Initially, many viewers believed it represented a working man asleep—it was only when reviews appeared that people realized the true resonance of the picture. *The Stonebreaker* marks Wallis's move away from the principles of Pre-Raphaelitism toward Social Realism. In 1859, Wallis came into an inheritance which meant he no longer needed to earn money from painting, He continued to paint, but his later work lacked the fire of his early works. Wallis was also an art historian and collector—he bequeathed his ceramics collection to London's Victoria & Albert Museum. **LH**

View of the Großglockner Mountain | Marcus Pernhart

1857 | oil on canvas | Karnter Landesgalerie, Vienna, Austria

In the nineteenth century, Marcus Pernhart (1824–71) was one of the most famous painters in Austria. His stunning romantic landscapes focused on the beauty of lakes and mountains, particularly in the hard-to-reach passes and peaks that only a true mountaineer could explore. As a young boy, Pernhart's artistic talent was appreciated by the Archbishop of Gorica, who arranged for him to attend school in Klagenfurt. The young artist quickly made a name for himself and over the next twenty years came to dominate Austria's landscape market under the name "Pernhart" (the German version of his true name Pernat). Pernhart particularly enjoyed mountain climbing and constantly tried to capture the stunning panoramas available from some of the world's highest peaks.

The oil painting *View of the Großglockner Mountain* is one of several paintings made from sketches he took on the mountainside. The distinctive vista showered with sparkling snow underscores the magnificence of Großglockner, the highest mountain in Austria. Continually fascinated by its untouched majesty, he climbed it eight times between 1857 and 1859. As well as the natural world, Pernhart was commissioned to capture the details of Austrian castles and monuments before they fell into disrepair. By 1855 he had created a series of 197 detailed drawings, and when he died he left around 1,200 oil paintings and more than seventy books of sketches. His legacy is to have captured Austria's natural and manmade beauty in a way that has not been reproduced since. **JM**

The Morning Hour | Moritz Ludwig von Schwind

1858 | oil on canvas | 13 ³/₈ x 15 ³/₄ in / 34 x 40 cm | Schack Galerie, Munich, Germany

Viennese-born Moritz Ludwig von Schwind (1804–71) studied at the famous Akademie der Bildende Kunst. *The Morning Hour* is not typical of his work; he became best known for frescoes and for depictions of fairytales and medieval history. Greatly inspired by literature, he absorbed the works of the brothers Grimm, Achim von Arnim, and others. Von Schwind traveled throughout Austria, Germany, and Italy, where his work was always in great demand. A highly strung, temperamental man, his moods veered wildly. He would lose himself in a commission and then suddenly decide that he was being stifled; as a result, his style was changeable and unpredictable. His frescoes are often peopled with such a hectic number of figures that they can be bewildering, yet they hold the viewer's interest as the artist's attention to minute detail is superb. Von Schwind also illustrated the music of his friend the composer Franz Schubert. *The Morning Hour* was painted when the artist was focusing on personal works, paintings he did not intend for the public. It is one of several intimate domestic paintings and seems startlingly modern; it would not be surprising if one were to learn that it had in fact been painted in the 1950s. Most notably unusual for a nineteenth-century work is the length of the woman's skirt, high above the ankle. Her dressing gown lies discarded on a chair, but Von Schwind has captured her at a moment before she is ready to be seen, a dreamy time when she is captivated by the beauty of the view outside. **LH**

L'Angélus | Jean-François Millet

1857–59 | oil on canvas | 21⅝ x 26 in / 55 x 66 cm | Musée d'Orsay, Paris, France

This celebrated painting was one of the most widely reproduced images in the nineteenth century. Prints of it were displayed in thousands of Christian households, though it was equally popular with cartoonists, who loved to lampoon its sentimental approach. The Angelus is a prayer that was traditionally recited three times a day in Catholic countries, in the morning, at noon and, as here, at sunset. The name comes from the opening words of a passage relating to the Annunciation—*Angelus Domini nuntiavit Mariae* or "The Angel of the Lord announced to Mary." Jean-François Millet (1814–75) was not prompted to paint the scene out of religious fervor. He was not a churchgoer, and his private life would certainly have been frowned upon by the authorities (he lived with a common-law wife with whom he had several children). Rather, he was inspired by nostalgia. He came from peasant stock himself, and remembered the Angelus from his childhood. At the sound of the church bell, his grandmother had always instructed the family to stop working, to remember "those poor dead people." He also recalled how peasant women seemed much more devout than their menfolk—it is no accident that, in this picture, the woman's head is bowed and her hands are clasped in a formal attitude of prayer, while her husband simply holds his hat. *L'Angélus* escaped the controversy that surrounded some of Millet's other paintings and rapidly became his most famous work. It sold in the 1890s for a huge sum, and its fate was national news in France. **IZ**

En Gondol | Johan Julius Exner

1859 | oil on canvas | 13 ¾ x 13 ⅜ in / 35 x 34 cm | Statens Museum for Kunst, Copenhagen, Denmark

As one of Denmark's finest Romantic painters, Johan Julius Exner's (1825–1910) patriotic feelings for Denmark after the Napoleonic Wars compelled him to focus predominantly on Danish rural and folk themes. Originally aspiring to be a history painter, Exner instead directed his traditionally trained talent to genre painting and portraiture. For many years he painted local scenes in Amager, an island south of Copenhagen, where Dutch farmers had settled in 1521 but were still relatively unknown to their fellow Danes. The few grand tableaux he completed represented scenes from classical Danish folklore and myth, considered treasures of the Danish tradition. Set in Italy, *En Gondol* (In a Gondola) was a lovely anomaly in the Copenhagen-based artist's prolific and illustrious

career. Here Exner applied his refined sense of local intimacy to a foreign scene. Painted during a two-year journey around central Europe, *En Gondol* offers the perspective of a painter on holiday from his ardent dedication to Danish folklore and rural island cultures. The painting depicts a young woman looking out from the plush interior of a covered gondola. Resting across from her is a fan with a small rose attached. A gondolier on the right-hand side of the central archway, bathed in light, leans in toward the center of the painting in a gesture that creates movement and very subtly decentralizes the focus of the painting. Beyond is a glimpse of the waterway and other boats. The effect is dreamy and sensual, as if Exner were experiencing the scene as a memory already in the past. **SWW**

The Kiss | Francesco Hayez

1859 | oil on canvas | 44 x 34 ½ in / 112 x 88 cm | Pinacoteca di Brera, Milan, Italy

Francesco Hayez (1791–1882) was one of the leading artists of Italian Romanticism, although much of his career is difficult to assess since he often neither signed nor dated his works. Born in Venice into a relatively poor family of French and Italian parentage, he was apprenticed to an art restorer and later the artists Antonio Canova, Teodoro Matteini, and Francisco Magiotto. He received a Neoclassical training that he applied to a variety of historical paintings, political allegories, and finely rendered portraits realized throughout the course of his career. He was also the key figure in the transition from Neoclassicism to Romanticism in Italy, although his form of Romanticism is more apparent in his subject matter than in his technique. Remarkable in its intense clarity of light, it depicts a genteel young couple engaged in a charged, passionate encounter. The man and woman embrace as if they are stealing a forbidden kiss in a forbidden place; the woman's hand is electrified with passion, the man's hand soft on her face. The lyrical shadow to their right draws our eyes to the length of her sensuous, draping skirt. Eroticism and emotion are carried in the dimension and interplay of highlights within this intricately rendered silk. A famous symbol of Italian Romanticism, *The Kiss* is shadowed with an air of hazy nostalgia and tender melancholy. It demonstrates Hayez's ordered, Neoclassical composition and refined, narrative style, but it is his luscious use of light that makes it a truly intimate pleasure. **SWW**

Self-Portrait | Anselm Feuerbach

c.1860 | oil on canvas | 36 ¼ x 28 ¾ in / 92 x 73 cm | State Hermitage Museum, St. Petersburg, Russia

Anselm Feuerbach (1829–80) was allied with a group of German artists called the "German-Romans" who believed that Germany and Italy had a special affinity and aimed to create a noble, idealized art out of the purest ideals of Germanic Classicism and Italian Renaissance art, with a preference for the grander branch of Venetian painting. Feuerbach absorbed his lofty ideas from his background—his father lectured in classical archaeology and his uncle Ludwig was a philosopher. When he painted this self-portrait, he was in Italy, where he lived from 1855 to 1873, producing much of his best work. The picture shows his love of ancient Greek and Roman art, a fashion that drove much of the Renaissance. He is dressed in nineteenth-century clothes, yet the garment thrown over his

shoulder recalls a classical-style toga. The alabaster sheen of his skin is reminiscent of a classical sculpture, while the profile view, much used in his portraits, was common in Renaissance portraiture. The rich, vigorous brushwork, however, particularly in the background, comes from a Romantic impulse that he often suppressed. It echoes the style of the Flemish master Rubens, whom Feuerbach greatly admired. In fact, the Rubens self-portrait that now hangs in Vienna's Kunsthistorisches Museum has the same dark, loosely painted background, somber palette, and profile view. Feuerbach also painted history scenes and landscapes, but his portraits are widely considered his best work. His ideas foreshadowed the Symbolism movement that emerged a few years later, just after his death. **AK**

Lovers
Unknown

1860 | Sangram Singh Collection, City Palace, Jaipur, India

Jaipur, the Western Indian capital of Rajasthan, has a folkloric history of chivalry and romance—a spirit that is missing in the ungainly image of *Lovers*. Maharaja Jai Singh II founded Jaipur in 1727, offering patronage to court artists fleeing Dehli and the declining Mughal empire. It was the later Maharaja Pratap Singh, however, who led the golden age of painting in Jaipur. Artists refined the opulent Mughal style of the oval-faced females with fishlike eyes, by incorporating more elaborate techniques and traditional Indian themes into technicolor miniatures that define the Jaipur School of painting. Hardly suggestive of the sweet love escapades of Krishna or the mystical practice of tantric sex, *Lovers* portrays a complex image of sexual power. While the almond-shaped limbs of the lovers are entwined in sexual intercourse, the objects about them are rather more suggestive: the tall, phallic column; the woman's pink couch reminiscent of female genitals; the translucent white veil coming from her spine suggestive of sexual fluids. The open, flowered curtain compartmentalizes the picture and suggests the potential transience of the man—his entrance and exit assured. Jaipur rulers, in addition to being patrons of art, were proud kingdom builders, shrewd politicians, and daring army commanders; ambition clearly found in the man's eyes, in his clarity of purpose, and in his direct, physical control of the woman. The woman looks away, resigned yet present in ways that are entirely inaccessible to the man. **SWW**

Still Life of Papaya, Watermelon and Cashew
Agostinho José da Mota

1860 | oil on canvas | 21 x 25 ½ in / 53.5 x 65 cm | Museu Nacional Belas Artes, Rio de Janeiro, Brazil

Agostinho José da Mota (1824–78) was born and died in Rio de Janiero, but he studied in Europe before returning to Brazil to teach art. Mota's *Still Life of Papaya, Watermelon and Cashew* is a dramatic play between bright and somber hues, reminiscent of the detailed textures and realistic light effects of still-life paintings from the Dutch Golden Age. When he painted this elegant image, Mota was already one of Brazil's most notable landscape artists. His work in Rome with the Italian Carlo Magini, a well-regarded still-life painter, and a commission from the Brazilian Empress to paint a still life, encouraged Mota to master the still-life genre. While landscapes represent the main body of his work, Mota's still-life paintings highlight the most compelling qualities of his technique, demonstrate his skill for composition and atmosphere, and reflect his nuanced observation of nature. Created during the later Baroque period of Brazilian art, the combination of European and local influences in *Still Life of Papaya, Watermelon and Cashew* is characteristic of its time, and of Mota's sensual aesthetic. Mota creates an overall sense of pictorial harmony by highlighting the deep oranges, lively pinks, and soft yellows of the fruit against a muted, earthy background. Similarly, he juxtaposes the fruits' forms, so that the individual geometry of the precisely cut papaya and roughly split watermelon complement one another. Mota influenced Brazil's painting tradition during a period of upheaval as Brazil became an industrialized society. **AH/SWW**

Frederiksborg Castle, the Departure of the Royal Falcon Hunt
Heinrich Hansen

1861 | oil on canvas | 15 ¾ x 19 ⅝ in / 40.5 x 50 cm | Private collection

A Danish artist who focused on architecturally detailed scenes, Heinrich Hansen (1821–90) spent four years (1842–46) studying decorative painting at the Academy in Copenhagen. Works such as *The Room of the Four Doors, Palazzo Ducale, Venice* (1883) show his minute attention to detail and his great talent for recreating perspective and dimension. They also illustrate his figure painting, with the delicate draperies and rich colors of the cloth evoking a bygone era. This is also demonstrated in *Frederiksborg Castle, the Departure of the Royal Falcon Hunt*, in which the viewer can appreciate his aptitude for painting animals. The various elements of this painting—humans, animals, flowing water, static buildings, and a changeable sky—are a showcase for the artist's

versatility. A well-respected figure in his native Denmark, Hansen taught at the Academy, where he specialized in perspective and design and was at the forefront of several Danish artistic movements. This is one of many studies Hansen made of the castle. His use of color is superb, especially in the tones of the brickwork, delicately changing with the effects of the passing sunlight and shadow; in areas mellow, in other areas rich in hue, yet never losing the sense of continuity. The amazing attention to architectural detail that characterized Hansen's work proved historically invaluable when Frederiksborg Castle was damaged by fire in 1859. Hansen's detailed paintings enabled the architects to complete the reconstruction accurately. **LH**

The First Landing of Christopher Columbus in America
Dióscoro Teófilo de la Puebla Tolin

1862 | oil on canvas | Ayuntamiento de La Coruña, La Coruña, Spain

Until the nineteenth century, the genre of historical tableaux was considered the most esteemed and serious of artistic genres. It enabled artists to combine historical fact with myth and allegory and provided them with an opportunity to flaunt their compositional skills. Dióscoro Teófilo de la Puebla Tolin (1831–1901), who studied in Madrid and Rome, worked in the tradition of Historicism, a subgenre of history painting, which focused on the interplay of religious pride, patriotism, and notions of glory. Tolin's technical style is referred to as Eclecticism for its wide-ranging, and often superficial, borrowing from European techniques and visual trends. Paintings in this genre were often funded by official organizations and art academies, which treated them as opportunities for propagandistic interpretations of history. *The First Landing of Christopher Columbus in America* provides no shortage of drama. In this pro-colonialist image, naked savages retreat in ignorant fear of the explorers, who arrive bearing symbols of religious and national pride. In a single grand gesture, the figure of Christopher Columbus looks heavenward while authoritatively striking his sword on the ground. This painting implies that the settlers have a divine right to claim the natives' land. With this grand image, Tolin seeks to justify what we now understand to be a brutal, selfish, and arrogant episode in history. Today, his depiction of Columbus's landing is seen for what it is—the glorification of a shameful conquest of indigenous peoples. **AH/SWW**

The Railway Station
William Powell Frith

1862 | oil on canvas | 46 x 101 in / 117 x 256 cm | Royal Holloway College, Egham, UK

At the height of the Victorian era, there was a tremendous interest in crowded panoramas depicting a broad cross-section of modern society. William Powell Frith (1819–1909) built his reputation on scenes of this kind, winning particular acclaim for three large canvases—*Life at the Seaside* (1854), *Derby Day* (1858), and this picture. The phenomenal success of *Derby Day* enabled Frith to market his work in a highly lucrative manner. *The Railway Station* was commissioned by an art dealer, Louis Flatow (shown in the background, talking to the engine driver). He paid a record sum for the picture, but made a fortune from exhibiting it privately (more than 21,000 people paid to see it when it was shown in London) and selling engravings of the work. It took Frith two years to complete the painting, which was surrounded by a blaze of publicity, long before it was unveiled. As in his previous works, he used a combination of photographs and specialist assistance to create the setting. In this case, the architectural artist, William Scott Morton, helped with the background details of Paddington Station, while the train was based on a photograph of the "Sultan" engine. Frith included portraits of himself and his family in the center of the composition. The main talking point of the picture, however, was provided by the detail on the right, where the police are arresting a fugitive. For these figures, Frith employed two genuine detectives, who were celebrities at the time, after taking part in a number of high-profile cases. **IZ**

North-east View from the Northern Top of Mount Kosciuszko
Eugène von Guérard

1863 | oil on canvas | 26 ½ x 46 ⅝ in / 66.5 x 116.8 cm | National Gallery of Australia, Canberra

Australian landscape painting surged in the 1850s, as the gold rush attracted European artists to Australia. Austrian-born painter Eugène von Guérard (1811–1901) arrived in Australia in 1852, shortly after the death of British-born John Glover (1767–1849), widely considered the father of Australian landscape painting. Like Glover, Von Guérard had been greatly impressed by the works of Claude (1600–82) and Poussin (1594–1665), but had become a devotee of high German Romanticism, exemplified by Caspar David Friedrich (1774–1840). By 1863, Von Guérard had become the foremost landscape painter in the colonies. Typically Romantic, he depicts the mountain view as an untouched wilderness, a theme commonly favored by painters wishing to rebel against nineteenth-century urbanization. A cluster of figures in the foreground appears small and insignificant against the awesome backdrop, while careful contrasts of light and shade emphasize the sublime drama of nature. They also hint at Von Guérard's earlier association with a group of German artists called the Nazarenes, keen proponents of medieval draftsmanship who believed that nature could bring man closer to God. From 1870, Von Guérard spent eleven years teaching at the School of Painting in the National Gallery of Victoria before migrating to England. Von Guérard's art and writings have a special historical significance today, documenting the way in which gold mining and urbanization transformed the Australian landscape. **SLF**

Le Déjeuner sur l'Herbe | Édouard Manet

1863 | oil on canvas | 82 x 104 in / 208 x 264 cm | Musée d'Orsay, Paris, France

Long before his association with the Impressionists, Édouard Manet (1832–83) was a controversial figure in the French art world. This was the first of his pictures to create a scandal, when it was exhibited in 1863. A year earlier, Manet's taste for experiment had received an unexpected boost. His father had died, providing him with a sizable inheritance, which meant that his art did not need to be commercially viable. Neither did he have to be concerned about upsetting his family, since Manet knew that Le Déjeuner sur l'Herbe would cause a stir. Most critics acknowledged that Manet was a talented painter but they were baffled by the subject. They were aware that it was loosely based on the Pastoral Concert, a famous sixteenth-century painting in the Louvre. However, while the original was clearly a fantasy, set in an imaginary past, the clothing in Manet's picture was both real and modern. This raised questions of morality. Why were two gentlemen sitting beside a naked woman? Manet's picture was also puzzling in other ways. The pose of the right-hand figure, for example, was copied from an engraving by Marcantonio Raimondi (c.1480–1534). In its original context, the man's gesture made perfect sense, but in Le Déjeuner sur l'Herbe it served no obvious purpose. The figure in the background was equally disconcerting. She was obviously too large, particularly when compared to the nearby boat. Manet, it seemed, was deliberately flouting the laws of perspective, as well as the conventions of composition. **IZ**

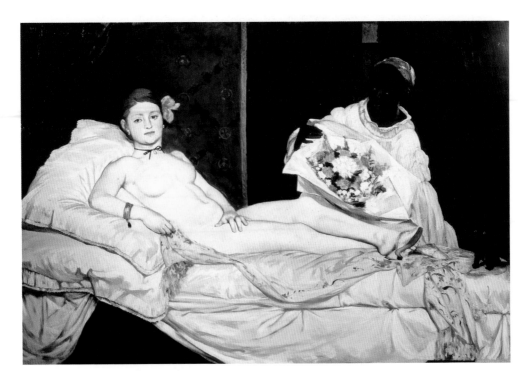

Olympia | Édouard Manet

1863 | oil on canvas | 51 x 74 in / 130 x 190 cm | Musée d'Orsay, Paris, France

During the 1860s, Édouard Manet (1832–83) was France's most notorious artist. Two years after the furor that surrounded his *Le Déjeuner sur l'Herbe*, he scandalized the public once again by exhibiting the provocative *Olympia*. In both pictures, Manet was reinventing an Old Master painting, translating it into a modern idiom. In doing so, he was well aware that he was crossing the boundaries of contemporary taste. So, when *Olympia* was shown at the Salon of 1865, the model was derided as "a female gorilla" and "the Queen of Spades stepping out of the bath." The controversy stemmed from nineteenth-century attitudes to the nude. Here, the problem lay not in the nakedness of the model, but in its context. Manet's source, for example, was a famous Renaissance painting, the *Venus of Urbino* (1538) by Titian, which was deemed perfectly respectable. Similarly, many nineteenth-century artists were able to exhibit highly erotic pictures of Venus or Diana without censure. Provided that the subject was presented as a classical goddess or nymph, however thin the disguise, nudity was not an issue. Manet's picture was shocking, because the nude was modern. As a result, many critics interpreted her as a prostitute. Worse still, her direct gaze placed the spectator in the role of the prostitute's client. Manet did nothing to counter this interpretation. The woman is wearing a single slipper, which was a conventional symbol for loss of innocence, while the orchid in her hair was believed to have the qualities of an aphrodisiac. **IZ**

Stańczyk | Jan Matejko

1862 | oil on canvas | 34 ⅝ x 47 ¼ in / 88 x 120 cm | Muzeum Narodowe, Warsaw, Poland

Historical painting has always been a vital thread in Polish art and Jan Matejko (1838–93) chronicled Polish history with a verve and romance that earned him a central place in his homeland's artistic consciousness. Court jester to several Polish kings, Stańczyk (c.1480–1560) was said to be a man of extraordinary wisdom. Not afraid to wield his satirical wit to criticize those in power, he came to personify the fight for truth over hypocrisy and even Poland's struggle for independence. In this painting, Matejko has turned the jester into a symbol of his nation's conscience. While a ball at the court of Queen Bona is in full swing, Stańczyk sits slumped in depression, having just discovered—presumably indicated by papers on the table—that the Polish city of Smolensk has been lost during war with Moscow. Seating him apart from the rest of the court emphasizes that only he foresees that the war will be disastrous for Poland. This is like a scene from a play, with Matejko's characteristic theatricality and lighting. The principal player, in a fanciful costume that highlights his seriousness by its contrast, is placed centrally in a spotlight. In the wings, we glimpse the bit-players, while out of the window a comet falls portentously. The face is a self-portrait of Matejko himself and the artist's finely detailed style adds to the mood, picking out everything from the plushness of the drapes to the distant sparkle of a chandelier. For centuries Stańczyk featured in the work of an array of Polish artists and writers, but this striking image is the one that has endured. **AK**

Souvenir de Mortefontaine | Jean-Baptiste-Camille Corot

1864 | oil on canvas | 25 ½ x 35 in / 65.5 x 89 cm | Louvre, Paris, France

Jean-Baptiste-Camille Corot (1796–1875) began his career as a draper, before deciding to pursue artistic training. With the backing of his father he studied first with Achille Etna Michallon (1796–1822) and then with Jean-Victor Bertin (c.1767–1842), though Corot later denied that his training had affected his art. He traveled widely throughout his life, spending several years in Italy, exploring Switzerland and covering much of the French countryside. On his trips he made numerous oil sketches and *plein air* paintings capturing the immediacy of light and atmosphere, while also working on exhibition-style paintings within the studio. *Souvenir de Mortefontaine* is one of the best paintings from his late career, and is bathed in a soft, diffuse light. It is a work of utter tranquillity, the epitome of a lyrical

and poetic assimilation of the artist's world. The scene is not taken from nature, but combines key elements of the natural setting to create the perfect, harmonious image. The graceful tree in the foreground, the expanse of still water behind and quiet figures picked out in soft color were motifs used often by the artist to render a work of beautiful, quiet reflection. Working at first along the lines of the Realists, Corot's style developed to encompass a dreamy, Romantic perception. As such, his work can be considered something of a bridge between the Realists and the Impressionists, and indeed he is often referred to as the father of Impressionism. This painting in particular would seem to have influenced Monet's views of the Seine in early morning light painted during the 1890s. **TP**

The Suez Canal | Albert Rieger

1864 | oil on canvas | Museo Civico Revoltella, Trieste, Italy

In *The Suez Canal,* Albert Rieger (1834–1905), a painter known for his landscapes and lithographs often featuring water as their main theme, captures in oils a tremendous undertaking in history. Stretching its way across the canvas, the partially completed man-made canal leads the viewer's eye into the distance as it cuts its way through the uncultivated lands of Egypt. This scene documents the progress of a massive technological achievement. Planned by the French engineer Ferdinand de Lesseps and more than a hundred miles long, the Suez Canal intended to link the Orient and the Occident, the Mediterranean to the Red Sea. Soon trade routes would be shorter and less hazardous, new markets would emerge and before long the Suez Canal would become the center of the world. Rieger painted *The Suez Canal* five years before the project's completion. Like an old map, it captures the world as it was at the moment it was created and it shows the difference between Port Said then and now: a calm, uncultivated land versus the unstable, industrial state. Interestingly, this record of a moment showing the whole world on the brink of change ended up in the office of one of the men who helped to create that change: Baron Pasquale Revoltella, a wealthy Trieste entrepreneur who was one of the canal's major backers. The painting is located above his desk in Museo Civico Revoltella, a museum in the building where Revoltella spent his last years and that is now considered one of the most important modern-art galleries in Italy. **JM**

Orpheus | Gustave Moreau

1865 | oil on canvas | 60 ⅝ x 37 ⅜ in / 154 x 95 cm | Musée d'Orsay, Paris, France

Gustave Moreau (1826–98) was one of the pioneers of the Symbolist movement, which played a significant role in French art in the latter part of the nineteenth century. *Orpheus* was one of his early successes, winning him official recognition. During this period, the most prominent artistic rebels (the Realists, the Impressionists) reacted against academic art, with its clichéd depictions of classical myths and historical scenes. However, artists such as Moreau preferred to reinvent this approach rather than supplant it. Orpheus was a mythical Thracian poet famed for his musical ability, who could charm not only humans but animals, trees, and even rocks. He died when he spurned the Maenads, the wild female followers of the wine god Dionysus. Angered, they tore him limb from limb, and cast his remains into the River Hebron. But his head continued to sing plaintively as it floated away. Moreau reinvented this scene as a means of stimulating the viewer's imagination. In a dreamlike setting, the musician's head, recovered by a young woman, has become fused with his instrument. For some, this represented a timeless image of the martyred artist, undervalued when alive, but venerated after his death, though Moreau denied any such specific meaning. The provocative imagery he developed—severed heads, listless poets, androgynous men, and sinister femmes fatale—recur frequently in his works and appealed to both the Symbolists and the Surrealists. The latter with their enthusiasm for Freudian analysis, read into this imagery a fear of impotence or castration. **IZ**

First and Second Corps of the Army Ready for Attending Mass at Batei | Cándido López

1865 | oil on canvas | Museo Historico Nacional, Buenos Aires, Argentina

The Argentinian painter and soldier Cándido López (1840–1902) was hugely affected by the Triple Alliance War (1864–70), one of the bloodiest conflicts in the Americas. It was fought by the joint armies of Argentina, Uruguay, and the Brazilian empire against Paraguay. There were several causes of the war, one of which was the expansionist ambition of the Paraguayan dictator, Francisco Solano López, who declared war on Argentina. By the end of the conflict, vast numbers of the Paraguayan people had been killed and the country was utterly devastated. Cándido López enlisted when he was in his early twenties, a decision that nearly ended his artistic career. In 1866, at the Battle of Curupaity, he broke his right wrist irreparably and his arm was later amputated. He carried on painting and drawing with his left hand, his work continuing to focus on sympathetically evoking both the majesty and tragedy of war. The artist painted around fifty scenes from the Triple Alliance War, including *The Battle of Tuyuti* (1866). The blood-red color of the soldiers' uniforms in the latter painting contrasts sharply with the more somber tones employed here. This work, like López's *Landing of the Argentine Army in Front of the Trenches at Curuzu* (1891), is typical of López's style of depicting the war in miniature. Both these works are painted on an oblong canvas that enables the viewer to appreciate the artist's devoted attention to detail as well as the breadth of the war's devastation. López is regarded as one of Argentina's most important artists. **LH**

Work
Ford Madox Brown

1865 | oil on canvas | 54 x 77 ¾ in / 137 x 197.5 cm | Manchester City Art Galleries, UK

Ford Madox Brown (1821–93) provided inspiration for the young artists who founded the Pre-Raphaelite Brotherhood and, in turn, was influenced by their ideals. This, his most elaborate painting, demonstrates his close links with the movement. Initially at least, the Pre-Raphaelites wanted to paint scenes of modern life that were true to nature, as well as morally improving. Brown's picture accords well with these aims. On one level, it portrays workers installing the new sewerage system in Hampstead, north London; on another, it is a parable about the value of labor. Brown began the painting in 1852, but then laid it aside for several years, until he found a definite buyer. This patron, T.E. Plint, asked for a number of alterations, to bring the painting into line with his own evangelical beliefs

(among them, the addition of the woman on the left, handing out religious pamphlets). For modern commentators, the painting is remarkable for the freshness and originality of its composition, and as a detailed document of Victorian social life. Ironically, its reputation has been slightly undermined by the artist's exhaustive explanations about its symbolism. Brown intended to highlight the moral worth of labor. This was exemplified by the naval workers in the center, and the two "brainworkers" standing on the right—the writer and philosopher Thomas Carlyle and F.D. Maurice, the founder of a notable Working Men's College. In contrast, the chickweed seller on the left represents the poor, and the lady with the parasol and the couple riding behind her are the idle rich. **IZ**

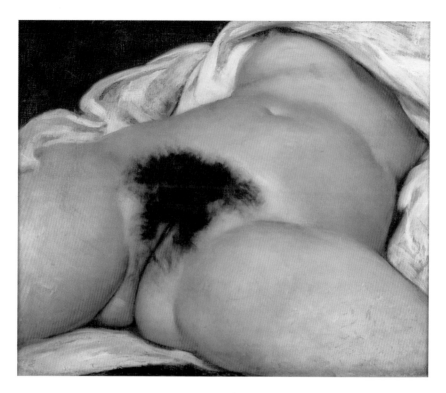

L'Origine du Monde | Gustave Courbet

1866 | oil on canvas | 18 ⅛ x 21 ⅝ in / 46 x 55 cm | Musée d' Orsay, Paris, France

At the commission of his wealthy Turkish patron, Khalil-Bey, who was a former diplomat and perhaps history's most known collector of erotic art, French Realist painter Gustave Courbet (1819–77) painted a series of erotic works, including *The Sleepers*, featuring a loving lesbian couple asleep in bed, and *L'Origine du Monde*, which depicts a woman's belly, spread legs, genitals, breast, erect nipple, and pubic hair, with her head covered by a sheet. The title of the painting pays homage to women's capacity to give birth, thereby propagating the species (the world) but also refers to Courbet's own obsession with sex and fascination with seeing female nudity. Pubic hair was never shown in art outside images of pornography, and Courbet's gorgeous rendering of the woman's soft hair is both an evidence of Khalil-Bey's intentions for the painting to be pornographic and a testament to the tenets of Realism, the philosophy Courbet pioneered that promoted strict adherence to reality in art. These paintings were on public display, which only increased their infamy and Courbet's notoriety, both as an artist and Lothario. In defiance of the conservatism of his times, Courbet established a "Federation of Artists" for the free and uncensored expansion of art. Figures such as Andre Gill, Honoré Daumier, and Manet were members. In the twentieth century, this painting caused outrage among feminist scholars, who perceive it as the ultimate example of female objectification but it has inspired many artists to appropriate or reference it. **AH**

The Bellelli Family | Edgar Degas

1858–67 | oil on canvas | 78 ¾ x 98 ½ in / 200 x 250 cm | Musée d'Orsay, Paris, France

Edgar Degas (1834–1917) started his career painting relatively traditional-looking portraits, but while *The Bellelli Family* seems such a work, it bears clear signs of his mature style and is extremely unusual and accomplished for a younger artist. Some of Degas's relatives lived in Italy and this picture shows his aunt Laure, her husband Baron Bellelli, and her two daughters, Giula and Giovanna. It was painted while Degas was in Italy for some years, studying the masters. There is an echo of Flemish portraiture such as those by Van Dyck in this work, but Degas has added his characteristic "freeze-frame" approach. Everyone looks in different directions, and only one of them out toward the viewer, while Bellelli turns in his seat but essentially has his back to us. One of the

girls has her leg crossed up under her and the little family dog disappears partly out of frame. This is on one hand a fleeting moment, but it is also a very truthful family portrait. Each family member remains stoically isolated in their own space. Laure is in mourning after the recent death of her father, whose portrait hangs on the back wall, while Bellelli, an Italian patriot living in exile in Florence, sits in profile. The pictures, mirrors, reflections, and doorway, plus the fairly restricted somber colors, heighten the claustrophobic mood. Already Degas has established the core of his approach, where certain things seem casual and others very carefully studied and constructed. He famously said of himself: "No art was ever less spontaneous than mine." **AK**

The Lyric (Il canto di uno stornello) | Silvestro Lega

1867 | oil on canvas | 62 x 38 ½ in / 158 x 98 cm | Palazzo Pitti, Florence, Italy

Silvestro Lega (1826–95) was an Italian Realist painter working during the Mazzini political movement that created modern Italy by subscribing to the move in Europe toward popular democracy in a Republican state. Lega's work depicts the sentiments and domestic pleasures that characterize the Italian *petite bourgeoisie* of this political era. After fighting in military campaigns for Italian independence, Lega began his series of large-scale paintings. *The Lyric* depicts three women singing before a piano, the large window behind them is open to the vast Italian countryside. Suggestive of the Three Graces in Greek mythology, these simple and understated figures portray a scene of peace, leisure, and intimacy. Lega studied at Luigi Mussini's school of painting, which emphasized the fifteenth-century Florentine principles of refined detail and orderly construction. Here the curves of the women's waists are elegantly mirrored in the full-bodied droop of the drawn curtain. The soft, dark browns and muted pastels convey a sense of nostalgia, and of fecundity governed by restraint. *The Lyric* is reminiscent of the 1950s paintings of the American Norman Rockwell, whose idealized representations of wholesome town and family life express conservative national values. Lega promoted the unified, modern Italian state by crafting morality into the content of his paintings. Images of family, civility, and simple pleasures encourage the values and behaviors that lead a nation into social stability, by constructing a common memory of social harmony. **SWW**

Niagara Falls | Frederic Edwin Church

1867 | oil on canvas | 102 x 91 in / 260 x 231 cm | National Gallery of Scotland, Edinburgh, UK

Here is nature powerful and untamed, spectacular scenery literally cascading through the gigantic canvas (over eight feet by seven feet). American landscape painter Frederic Edwin Church (1826–1900) reveled in painting on a huge scale. In this view of Niagara Falls from the American side, in New York State, his treatment of the rainbow, mist, and spume are all highly credible and his management of light and color shows great skill. It is a vivid record of pristine, virginal nature, and Church's worship of the wilderness strikes a chord with modern-day concerns about the environment. (Church was so concerned about Niagara Falls that he campaigned for the establishment of public parks on both sides to protect it.) Emerging from the Hudson River School tradition of charting the great river and its tributaries, Church painted Niagara Falls on more than one occasion, each time from a different vantage point. His wanderlust also took him much further afield—to South America, from the Amazon to the Andes—following in the footsteps of the great Victorian explorer Baron von Humboldt. Church was influenced by Humboldt's multi-volume *Kosmos* writings on the physical world and how artists should relate to it, and Church's paintings of jungle and mountain terrain and the flora found at different elevations show a planet still in formation. His powerful and evocative landscapes were highly popular in Victorian times, with painter and poet Edward Lear calling the him "the greatest landscape painter after Turner." **JH**

The Execution of Maximilian | Édouard Manet

1867–68 | oil on canvas | 99 x 120 in / 252 x 305 cm | Staatliche Kunsthalle, Baden-Baden, Germany

In January 1866, three years after having persuaded the Hapsburg Archduke Maximilian to accept the Mexican throne, Napoleon III decided to withdraw the French troops from Mexico, leaving Maximilian totally defenseless. The guerillas led by Benito Juárez captured and executed Maximilian soon after. Drawing inspiration from Goya's *The Third of May 1808* (1814) and contemporary pictorial reportage, Édouard Manet (1832–83) painted *The Execution of Maximilian* in 1867–68. It is the definitive canvas of five studies on the same theme that Manet produced. That same year the French writer Émile Zola published a biographic and critical study of Manet's work. Zola defended Manet's art, which had been rejected by the academics. Born in Paris to a judge and the goddaughter of the Swedish crown prince, Manet pursued art against the will of his father, who wanted him to have a career in law. Strongly influenced by the Realism of Gustave Courbet, and close to the Impressionists, such as Edgar Degas, Claude Monet, Paul Cézanne, and Pierre-Auguste Renoir, Manet is generally considered to have bridged the gap between Realism and Impressionism. Several qualities made Manet a modern artist, such as the typically rough painterly style, and the careful attention to the surface of the picture plane. This work was first shown to the public in 1879 in New York—Manet could not exhibit this painting in France because it was considered to be politically incorrect by the imperial regime of the time. **JJ**

Studio at Batignolles | Henri Fantin-Latour

1870 | oil on canvas | 80 x 108 in / 203 x 274.5 cm | Musée d'Orsay, Paris, France

As the nineteenth century drew to a close, the powerful elite of traditionalists who controlled the galleries and salons of Paris held the work of the artists depicted in this painting in contempt. Threatened by the accelerating shift toward Impressionism, the establishment rejected more and more of the new works. Every exhibition provoked alternative exhibitions featuring the work of the avant-garde, to the fury of the public and critics alike. Édouard Manet, who is seated at the center of the composition staring defiantly out at the viewer, was a figurehead for this new movement and bore the brunt of much reactionary criticism. For Henri Fantin-Latour (1836–1904), his friend and admirer, the decision to paint *Studio at Batignolles* constituted a personal

petition in favor of Manet's genius and the desire to capture a moment of revolution in the history of art. It has the feel of an early daguerreotype, thanks to the quality of light and the carefully posed stance of each subject. Although he was closely allied with the revolutionaries depicted here, including Auguste Renoir and Claude Monet, Fantin-Latour was in fact a far more traditional painter than any of them, and this work is therefore a brave statement of support. Toward the end of his life, Fantin-Latour became increasingly absorbed in music and developed a passion for Wagner. The composer inspired Fantin-Latour's more imaginative works that, both in subject and style, were to exert a significant influence on the Symbolist movement. **RW**

The Rescue | Honoré Daumier

1870 | oil on canvas | 11 x 13 ¾ in / 280 x 350 cm | Hamburger Kunsthalle, Hamburg, Germany

French caricaturist Honoré Daumier (1808–79) lampooned lawyers, politicians, and the pretensions of the bourgeoisie. In his cartoons of oafish, ugly, cruel-faced men and women, Daumier eloquently expressed the avarice, duplicity, and stupidity which Balzac described in his satire of the Louis-Philippe era. During his career, Daumier published more than 4,000 lithographs brilliantly depicting the psychology of this corrupt society. Born to a poor family in Marseille, Daumier was trained in Paris as an apprentice draftsman, but the proliferation of political journals after the 1830 revolution led him to cartooning. His impoverished early life and frequent imprisonment for his antimonarchical cartoons exposed him to the injustices of bureaucracy, but censorship and hardship only inspired his acid wit. Daumier was also thematically obsessed with the circus, other artists, and ancient myths. In the mythic painting *The Rescue*, a man and woman on a beach carry a naked child in their arms, whom they have apparently saved from drowning. Daumier's hazy brushwork creates the effect of an adrenalin drop—the view of a witness whose sight is obscured by exhaustion, making us feel as if perhaps we also had been swimming to save the child. Despite being known primarily as a satirist, Daumier's painting earned him the admiration of later artists including Picasso, Cézanne, and Francis Bacon. Charles Baudelaire aptly described Daumier as "one of the most important men I will say not only in caricature, but in the whole of modern art." **AH**

The Artist's Studio. Nine rue de la Condamine | Jean-Frédéric Bazille

1870 | oil on canvas | 38 ½ x 50 ½ in / 48 x 128.5 cm | Musée d'Orsay, Paris, France

A talented early Impressionist, Jean-Frédéric Bazille's (1841–70) work is little known due to his untimely death—he was killed in the Franco-Prussian War, at the age twenty-nine. His works exhibit a distinct, but often varied style, as Bazille sought to create his own artistic identity. His paintings show a freshness, great attention to detail, understanding of anatomy, and realistic facial expression. Had he lived for longer, it is likely his name would be as well known today as that of Monet and Renoir. Born in Montpellier, Bazille moved to Paris as a young man, where he studied at the studio of Swiss painter Charles Gleyre. His fellow pupils included Auguste Renoir, Claude Monet, and Alfred Sisley. Gleyre was an exponent of *plein-air* painting and Bazille embraced this concept of painting in the open, rather than a studio. Bazille was from a wealthy family and was studying to become a doctor. He gave a great deal of financial assistance to Monet. During the 1860s, he gave up his medical studies in favor of art. He shared studios with Monet and Renoir, and he exhibited at the Paris Salon from 1866 onward. Among his finest paintings are the sexually charged *Toilette* (1869–70), *After the Bath* (1870), and *The Improvised Field Hospital* (1865), actually a portrait of Monet recovering from a leg injury. Bazille's later works were strongly influenced by Édouard Manet. *The Artist's Studio* depicts Bazille's own studio. Among the figures in this scene are Manet, Monet, Renoir, and the writer Émile Zola. The tallest figure is Bazille himself, added in by Manet after Bazille's death. **LH**

La Vicaria | Mariano Fortuny y Carbó

1870 | oil on canvas | 23 ⅝ x 36 ⅝ in / 60 x 93.5 cm | Museum of Modern Art, Barcelona, Spain

Mariano Fortuny y Carbó (1838–74) was probably the most important Catalan painter of the nineteenth century, and enjoyed great international prestige in his lifetime. He was awarded a residency in Rome in 1857 and was subsequently sent to North Africa by the Barcelona Provincial Council to make sketches from life of the Hispano-Moroccan war. The impact of the light and vibrant colors of Morocco can be seen in many of his later works. By 1866, he had become interested in painting eighteenth-century interiors. Exceptionally skilled and an outstanding colorist, when Fortuny painted *La Vicaria* (*The Spanish Wedding*) it met with great acclaim from both critics and the public, helping his rise to fame and commercial success. Although he had painted this

subject before, *La Vicaria* became one of his masterpieces. It depicts the moment at which the witnesses of an eighteenth-century Spanish wedding sign the marriage certificate in the sacristy of a magnificent church, while the wedding guests are waiting. The style, composition, and color of the work point to the influence of Francisco de Goya on the Catalan artist. The painting highlights Fortuny's appreciation of the idiosyncracies of individual people. He fills the canvas with numerous quaint characters, including a bullfighter, a naval officer, a clergyman, an old woman, and a smattering of fashionable ladies. His love of detail was instinctive and this gave him every opportunity to display his artistic dexterity and luscious sense of color. **SH**

Max Schmitt in a Single Scull | Thomas Eakins

1871 | oil on canvas | 32 ¼ x 46 ¼ in / 82 x 117.5 cm | Metropolitan Museum of Art, New York, NY, USA

Thomas Eakins (1844–1916) was one of the greatest American artists of the nineteenth century, instilling a powerful and sometimes shocking sense of realism into his paintings. He spent most of his life in his native city of Philadelphia, though this picture dates from the start of his career, when he had just returned from four years studying in Europe (1866 to 1870), mostly in France and Spain. It was hardly surprising after such time away that he was anxious to turn his attention to the places and the activities that he had missed while abroad. Above all, he was drawn to the idea of rowing scenes, producing several paintings on this theme between 1870 and 1874. This is probably the most famous of them. It shows a boyhood friend, Max Schmitt (1843–1900), turning around to face the viewer. Although a lawyer by profession, Schmitt was a keen amateur oarsman and had recently won a prestigious single-scull race. In his usual, fastidious way, Eakins arranged the entire composition so that it included a number of references to this victory. The autumnal setting was chosen to tally with the date of the race (October 5, 1870); the late-afternoon sky indicated the time that it took place (5 p.m.); and Schmitt's scull was even located on the precise spot where the finishing line had been situated. As he was equally fond of rowing, Eakins decided to add his own portrait to the picture, in the guise of the rower in the middle distance. To make things doubly clear, he painted his signature and the picture's date on the side of the boat. **IZ**

Nocturne: Blue and Silver—Chelsea
James McNeill Whistler

1871 | oil on wood support | 19 ½ x 23 ⅞ in / 50 x 61 cm | Tate Collection, London, UK

Originally this painting was called *Harmony in Blue-green Moonlight*, but in 1872 Frederick R. Leyland, the shipping magnate and patron, suggested the name *Nocturnes* for James McNeill Whistler's (1834–1903) paintings of views of the River Thames. Whistler was immediately drawn to this alternative title because it suggested that painting could aspire to having the same effects as music—a nocturne is a piece of prayerful music for nighttime. Moreover, the title corresponded to Whistler's overarching concern that art should be necessarily autonomous—a dynamic force driven by its own internal logic and momentum. *Nocturne: Blue and Silver—Chelsea* is the earliest study from Whistler's *Nocturne* series and depicts a view across the Thames from Battersea looking toward Chelsea. When it was first exhibited at the Dudley Gallery in 1871 with its original title, it was not altogether well received. One of the main criticisms leveled at the painting was that it appeared to be unfinished. Whistler was not the only artist to be accused of this—the mature work of J.M.W. Turner and the late work of Cézanne were the subjects of similar criticism. Admittedly, Whistler does pare down the view to only a handful of basic elements, but the economy that underpins this "impression" belies a deftness of touch and a heightened sensitivity to capturing the prevailing quality of light through the simplest of means. Moreover, Whistler manages to convey a vision of London that is lyrical, wistful, fleeting, and entirely his own. **CS**

Arrangement in Grey and Black: The Artist's Mother
James McNeill Whistler

1871 | oil on canvas | 56 ⁶/₈ x 63 ⁷/₈ in / 144 x 162 cm | Musée d'Orsay, Paris, France

The singular vision that James McNeill Whistler (1834–1903) brought to bear on his *Nocturnes*, the series of paintings that largely consisted of views of the River Thames, he also applied to the genre of portraiture. Moreover, what connected the two series was an indubitable conviction that it was the task of the artist to reveal what resided underneath the surface appearance of observed, empirical reality. First exhibited at the Royal Academy in 1872, *Arrangement in Grey and Black: The Artist's Mother* was acquired by the French state in 1891. Whistler presents a pared-down, analytical study organized around a series of discrete and overlapping axes, both vertical and horizontal. Indeed, it is only the contour of Anna Whistler's body that provides any form of visual contrast with and visual respite from the painting's overarching angularity. Although the formal qualities of the painting provide some form of visual counterpoint, the actual appearance of Anna Whistler, seen in profile, remains consonant with the painting's overarching pictorial style—both are foregrounded by an austerity and economy of means, and both, in effect, are lacking any extraneous, unnecessary detail or embellishment. *Arrangement* is unprecedented and remarkable when one considers that the painting also functions as a portrait. If the artist's *Nocturne* series anticipated the experiments carried out under the rubric of lyrical abstraction, then *Arrangement* predates a related movement, Geo-abstraction, by at least half a century. **CS**

Snap the Whip | Winslow Homer

1872 | oil on canvas | 22 x 36 in / 56 x 91.5 cm | Butler Institute of American Art, Youngstown, OH, USA

When *Snap the Whip* appeared in 1872, Winslow Homer (1836–1910) was already a well-known and admired painter. However, this painting can be said to have ushered in a new period in Homer's career, a transition from his early years through to a more reflective, yet equally productive, middle period. The immense popularity of the work, probably his best loved, cemented his reputation and assured his place in American history. Homer made it his mission to chronicle the people who lived in a symbiotic relationship with the rugged American countryside around them. *Snap the Whip* shows a group of children playing the age-old game of the same name outside the "little red schoolhouse" in which they are taught. The white shirts of three of the boys are offset by the striking red of the schoolhouse. The figures, the building, and the landscape behind are set in perfect balance. In one sense, *Snap the Whip* is a lighthearted piece that celebrates youth and play. It calls to mind the "good bad boys" of nineteenth-century American art and literature—boys like Huckleberry Finn. However, in its form and content there are a number of subtle tensions: the stillness of the land and the movement of the children, the running of some boys and the falling of others, the interior mental life of the schoolhouse and the "fun" outdoor life of the field. Homer's last depiction of a large group of people, *Snap the Whip* has remained one of the finest examples of his brilliantly original, quintessentially American, naturalistic style. **OR**

Self-Portrait with Death Playing the Fiddle | Arnold Böcklin

1872 | oil on canvas | 30 x 24 in / 75 x 61 cm | Staatliche Museen, Alte Nationalgalerie, Berlin, Germany

Death was a recurring theme in the work of Swiss painter Arnold Böcklin (1827–1901) and so it is fitting that the most famous image of him should be this striking self-portrait. From the mid-1850s, Böcklin developed a highly personal, allegorical art peopled with figures out of myth, legend, and superstition. Fleeing Paris at the outbreak of the Franco-Prussian War, Böcklin and his family settled in Munich. Several of his children had died in infancy and a cholera epidemic loomed, so it is little surprise that his paintings from this period should be full of morbidity. Working in the Romantic tradition, this self-portrait epitomizes the conception of the artist as heroic individual, gazing haughtily at the viewer in bold *chiaroscuro*. The leering figure of Death seems to simultaneously undercut this idea and reinforce it. Böcklin may be listening intently to Death's tune, but is he acknowledging life's transience or defying Death and suggesting his art will secure him an immortality denied to most? In the coming years he produced the work for which he is most famous, paintings with dreamlike qualities that linked him with the Symbolist School and influenced the Surrealists. At the time of his death, Böcklin was regarded as the greatest painter in the Germanic world—indeed, the second movement of Mahler's *Symphony No. 4*, "Death Takes the Fiddle," which premiered that year, was inspired by this painting. In 2001, the Swiss issued a stamp reproducing this self-portrait to mark the centenary of the artist's death. Tellingly, Death himself is absent. **RB**

Three Boys in a Dory | Winslow Homer

1873 | oil on panel | 5 ⅞ x 10 in / 14.9 x 25.4 cm | Private collection

Winslow Homer's (1836–1910) *Three Boys in a Dory* embodies a particular blend of personal and historical nostalgia popular in nineteenth-century American art. Homer began his artistic career as a Civil War–time sketcher and drawer for *Harper's Weekly*, yet evolved to become a landscape artist and chronicler of American rural life. With his penchant for the New England coast (in this case, stormy Gloucester, Massachusetts), Homer expresses his equation of a calmer, pre–Civil War America, before urban blight and the Industrial Revolution, with the inevitable transition from childhood to adulthood. This was a theme shared with literature at the time. Writers such as Mark Twain and Louisa May Alcott were part of a generation who idealized and celebrated children's supposedly carefree nature, and for whom nature offered a last possible refuge from the corruption and responsibilities of adulthood. Despite being painted in oil, *Three Boys in a Dory* retains Homer's signature breezy, light, and spontaneous style. Homer is often compared with Thomas Eakins, whose work shared maritime settings and a preoccupation with light. Yet Homer's work differed from that of his fellow genre artists, in his rendering of the figure. His generic depiction of figures transcends portraiture to create universal images of man in nature. *Three Boys in a Dory*, a painting emblematic of Homer's style and sensibility, would have a profound influence on successive quintessential American painters such as Edward Hopper, Robert Henri, and Rockwell Kent. **SE**

Meeting with the Village Mayor | Józef Chełmoński

1873 | oil on canvas | 25 ³/₈ x 57 ⁵/₈ in / 64.5 x 147 cm | National Museum, Warsaw, Poland

While the Barbizon School of painters in France were propounding their theories on realism in art from around 1830 to 1870, there was a similar trend for realism in Poland. One of the leading figures in Polish Realist art was Józef Chełmoński (1849–1914) whose paintings are unerringly convincing. Although the artist traveled to Paris in 1875, where his work was received with enthusiasm, he never lost the distinctly Polish quality to his paintings. He trained in Warsaw under Wojciech Gerson (1831–1901), who taught many of the masters of nineteenth-century Polish art, and who influenced Chełmoński in his realism and also in his patriotic depictions of Poland. This imposing canvas is strongly horizontal in form and presents the scene almost as a frieze. The action, that of the mayor meeting his people, is thrust sharply toward the foreground, so the viewer becomes a part of the scene. Chełmoński has included three realistically painted horses, which were a favorite motif of the artist. His dark palette is restricted to the subdued tones of winter, which are contrasted against the brilliant and cold white snow of the background. The figure in red on the left stares diagonally toward a small splash of red in the distance that draws the eye through the composition. Chełmoński traveled comparatively widely through his life, but his best works are considered those that were done when he was living in Poland, the contact with his homeland inspiring a great depth and feeling that was reflected in his work. **TP**

Impression, Sunrise | Claude Monet

1873 | oil on canvas | 19 x 24 in / 48 x 63 cm | Musée Marmottan Monet, Paris, France

The artistic movement Impressionism owes its name to this influential work by Claude Monet (1840–1926). *Impression, Sunrise* was first shown in 1874 at an independent exhibition organized by a group of artists including Monet, Renoir, and Degas. The show served as an alternative to the traditional, state-run Salon, allowing artists to work in radically new ways. In a review of the exhibition, the critic Louis Leroy condemned *Impression, Sunrise*, arguing that it was nothing more than a sketch and, in a negative context, titled the show "The Exhibition of the Impressionists," a term that the group proudly adopted. Leroy's response is understandable: Monet's painting broke many artistic conventions. The artist's work does indeed have a sketchlike quality, due to his loose, broken brushwork that does not define what it represents. This technique is largely the result of the Impressionist desire to capture the fleeting moment *en plein air*. *Impression, Sunrise* was not executed in a studio but from a window overlooking the harbor of Le Havre from which Monet painted the modern city awakening at dawn, requiring quick brushstrokes before the view changed. Conversely, *Impression, Sunrise* is also a calculated work that shows an interest in color theory. While the sun appears to pierce the morning mist because of its intense orange color, in reality it has the same luminance as its surroundings. In a black-and-white photograph, the sun is almost indistinguishable, an effect that Monet did not achieve by accident. **WD**

Picnic in May | Pál Szinyei Merse

1873 | oil on canvas | 50 ³/₈ x 64 ³/₈ in / 128 x 163.5 cm | National Gallery, Budapest, Hungary

Pál Szinyei Merse (also known as Paul von Szinyei-Merse, 1845–1920) began his career as a portraitist and Realist but his style soon expanded to include *plein-air* painting and examinations of light and color. Szinyei Merse, a native of Hungary, was credited as being the artist who brought the concepts inherent in Impressionism to central Europe. He managed this before visiting Paris, which he did not do until 1908. Szinyei Merse studied in Munich, so his development of the revolutionary brushwork styles and concepts of Impressionism was simultaneous and distinct from the work of the French artists. Coloration based on the harmonious effect of complementary and contrasting colors and color values full of light is

fully developed in *Picnic in May*, considered to be his most influential work. The painting was rejected by the general public when it was first shown, but grew in acclaim years later. Both the use of light and shade and the subject matter are free and uninhibited. The group of figures is shaded by a tree that is not itself visible, but its pattern is markedly distinct in the shadow on the grass. The ladies' dresses, however, splayed in circular patterns on the grass, seem to glow with a light of their own. The couples are engaged in various stages of flirtatious conversation replete with enraptured glances and modest rebuffs. In addition to his artistic career, Szinyei Merse was a politician who fought for the modernization of arts education in Hungary. **RA**

The Dance Class | Edgar Degas

c.1874 | oil on canvas | 33 ½ x 29 ½ in / 85 x 75 cm | Musée d'Orsay, Paris, France

The first part of the 1870s saw Edgar Degas (1834–1917) defining his style, and the dance pictures he painted at this time—often "through-the-keyhole" glimpses of backstage life—were radical for the times. Sharing the Impressionists' passion for contemporary subject matter, Degas's depiction of the dramatic world of ballet and theater added a certain titillation. But he was also an outstanding draftsman with great admiration for the Old Masters and the work of Ingres. This helped to foster the fascination with human forms that is so clearly present here. This painting, one of two of the same scene, shows dancers waiting to be assessed by ballet master Jules Perrot. Degas prepared assiduously by making numerous drawings of dancers posing for him in his studio. His lively brushwork and light, bright colors were typical of the Impressionists. Their use of color was partly influenced by Japanese prints, which also made dramatic use of the "cut-off" composition—where the subject is chopped off at the frame—that Degas deploys so cleverly here and throughout his work. Degas was heavily influenced by photography and by overturning traditional compositional rules. This work looks like a snapshot but it is meticulously planned, with the eye drawn instantly to the arresting foreground group of two dancers before being taken into the picture by the receding floor planks. Degas admired the Dutch School and here shows the same ability to combine both traditional and modern approaches to give a new status to everyday life. **AK**

The Cotopaxi, Ecuador | Rafael Troya

1874 | oil on canvas | Museo Guillermo Perez Chiriboga del Banco Central, Quito, Ecuador

In this picture, the Ecuadorean artist Rafael Troya (1845–1920) depicts his country's Cotopaxi region—an area that was already famed for its own artwork in the form of ceramics. Troya was self-taught, and as a young man he was greatly influenced by the works of fellow Ecuadorean Rafael Salas (1824–1906), an artist and teacher who worked in Quito. While in his late twenties, Troya was hired by a group of German scientists to accompany them on their expedition as an illustrator. From 1870 until 1874, Troya toured Ecuador with them, making studies of the land, its flora, and geological formations. The expedition's geologist, Alfons Stübel, taught Troya how to make exact scientific paintings. This magnificent landscape, painted at the very end of the expedition, is a superb example of how the artist's image of his country was affected by the four years he spent with the group. Stübel's training in such detailed workmanship, combined with Troya's talent and love of the Romantics, resulted in a painting style that was accessible and collectible. In The Cotopaxi, Ecuador, the richness of the colors—especially the effects of the rising or setting sun—demonstrate Troya's ability and the reason why his work became so popular. Troya did not only paint scenes from nature; he was also commissioned on several occasions to produce religious paintings for Ecuador's many—and very influential—churches. In later years, Troya turned to portraiture, and found himself in great demand among the cream of Ecuadorean society. **LH**

Landscape with Lake Geneva | Gustave Courbet

c.1874 | oil on canvas | Musée des Beaux-Arts et d'Archeologie, Besançon, France

Through Gustave Courbet's (1819–77) undeniable talent and relentless self-promotion, he made his Realist style one of the most dominant prototypes in Western painting within his own lifetime. He was an outspoken opponent of the French government and, during the violent days of the Paris Commune (1871), took part in the destruction of the Vendôme Column, an official government monument. For this he was imprisoned and exiled from France, forced to spend the final years of his life in Switzerland where he painted several landscape scenes, including this one. He had always been fascinated with capturing the sea in his paintings; now, in land-locked Switzerland, he was forced to turn his attention to the country's Alpine lakes. The strong horizontals and the cool blues and greens create an atmosphere of peace and resolution. The sails of the small boat mirror the vertical branches of the tree protruding from the cliffs. A gentle breeze helps it on its way, furthering the feeling of cooperation between man and nature. Courbet, literally set apart from the tumultuous politics of Paris, seems to find comfort in his residing love of the natural world and solace for his forced exile in the beauty of the Swiss scenery. It captures one of the great paradoxes that make Courbet's art so interesting: dynamic, blunt, and bombastic in his social and political life, chauvinistic in his relationships with women, he nonetheless demonstrates a sensitivity to natural beauty and an uncanny ability to depict both the sublime power and the gentle moods of nature. **DK**

Nude on the Beach at Portici | Mariano Fortuny y Carbó

c.1874 | oil on canvas | 5 ⅛ x 7 ½ in / 13 x 19 cm | Museo del Prado, Madrid, Spain

After four years of artistic study in Barcelona, Catalan painter Mariano Fortuny y Carbó (1838–74) won the Prix de Rome scholarship in 1857, and spent the rest of his short life in Italy, except for a year in Paris in 1869 where he entered into business relations with the noted art dealer Goupil. The association brought Fortuny large sums for his work and an international reputation. He became one of the leading artists of his day, contributing to the revival and transformation of painting in Spain. Characteristically, he painted small genre paintings in meticulous detail. His innovative way of depicting light, particularly in his late works, and his exceptional skill in the handling of paint made him an inspiration to many others in nineteenth-century Spain and beyond. He was

outstandingly proficient at realistic drawing and painting, and had a stunning flair for color. *Nude on the Beach at Portici* is a consummate example of his late style. The brightly lit study of a naked child's body casts strong shadows around him. The viewpoint is from above and Fortuny mingles complementary colors to give a fresh feel to the subject. At the time this was painted, in France several young artists were experimenting with effects of light and color, making painting *en plein air* a new and exciting departure from studio work. Fortuny, while not embracing Impressionism, certainly explores similar themes. Sadly, he died a few months after completing *Nude on the Beach at Portici*, having contracted malaria while painting this work in southern Italy. **SH**

Paraná Landscape | Juan Manuel Blanes

*c.*1875 | oil on canvas | Private collection

Known for introverted and somber portraits of lone *gauchos*, or South American cattle herders, Juan Manuel Blanes (1830–1901) creates in *Paraná Landscape* a playful and dreamy scene that expresses deep individualism coupled with intimacy and hope. Blanes was born in Montevideo, at the time when Uruguay gained political independence and underwent a mass genocide of the original Charrúa Indian population. Moving frequently between Europe and Brazil, Blanes struggled as an artist, perpetually fraught by economic insecurities and personal loss. Self taught, he earned a government grant to travel to Florence in 1860 to work under the painter and commercial artist Antonio Ciseri. Yet the fresh and honest style of Blanes's paintings are free from the heavy influence of European academia, conveying a unique narrative of the people and history of his nation. Hardly a classic landscape but more an intimate portrait of a youth, *Paraná Landscape* is more suggestive than descriptive. A barefoot, young peasant woman reclines on a rock next to her fruit basket and reaches for an elusive yellow butterfly, a symbol of change and transformation. Blanes depicts a moment of leisure, magic, and spirit. While the woman reaches in tender fascination for what may be seen as an elusive future, she is set in earthy surroundings; her dirty feet are a sharp contrast to the bright butterfly. An allusion to the hope of youth, it is also an allusion to the hope of a developing nation. **AH/SWW**

Rural Scene | Jean-Baptiste-Camille Corot

1875 | oil on canvas | Musée Toulouse-Lautrec, Albi France

Jean-Baptiste-Camille Corot (1796–1875) is often associated with the painters of the Barbizon School, who produced works of a Realist nature, in part as a reaction against the more rigorous Romanticism of that period. However, while Corot painted with the eye of a Realist, he painted with the heart of a Romantic. Consequently his work forms a bridge between the two movements. Though he essentially worked from nature and reproduced natural scenes, his paintings were typically drenched in a sense of Arcadian harmony, and not infrequently recalled classical vestiges from his early artistic influences. This *Rural Scene*, painted in the last year of his life, is full of dreamy poetic lyricism. It incorporates large trees in the foreground, a compositional form that the artist favored, allowing a glimpse through the branches to a series of idealized buildings on the left, and a view across calm water ahead. The two figures were also characteristic of his work, and invariably he would include a single spot of bright color, such as a red cap or shawl, to direct the attention and focus the scene. Within his Parisian circle he became known as "Père Corot," due to his charitable nature and habit of helping out young and struggling artists. Today Corot is considered one of the leading landscape painters of his time, and was influential on the development of a number of artists, including Eugène Boudin (1824–1898), François-Louis Français (1814–1897), Alexandre DeFaux (1826–1900), and Stanislas Lépine (1836–1892). **TP**

Nocturne in Black and Gold: The Falling Rocket
James McNeill Whistler

*c.*1875 | oil on wood | 23 ¾ x 18 ⅜ in / 60.5 x 46.5 cm | Detroit Institute of Arts, Detroit, MI, USA

Having decided to move from Paris to London in 1859, the American-born James McNeill Whistler (1834–1903) became an instrumental figure within the English Aesthetic movement. In 1877, when *Nocturne in Black and Gold* was exhibited at the Grosvenor Gallery, John Ruskin accused it of being a "pot of paint [flung] in the face of the public," which led to a high-profile libel trial. Although Whistler successfully defended the painting, and by extension the set of aesthetic beliefs that *Nocturne* embodied—that art was necessarily autonomous and not therefore constrained by its responsibility to inscribe a "lifelike" effect—he was only awarded the token sum of a farthing in damages. *Nocturne* is one of six paintings loosely based on a site in London called the Cremorne Gardens. This

was a park wherein various forms of entertainment took place, including firework displays. It is relatively easy to appreciate why *Nocturne* would have proved such a provocative painting. Rather than organize the painting around some form of figure/ground relation, Whistler instead creates a rather indeterminate pictorial impression given through the incandescent glow of the fireworks themselves. Without any overt figurative reference, *Nocturne* instead appears almost entirely abstract. It is this unwillingness to yield to received opinion, represented in this case by the critic Ruskin, that gives the painting its vitality as an image and ensures its pre-eminence within discourses leading to the historical development of an abstract model of painting. **CS**

Woman at Her Toilette
Berthe Morisot

c.1875 | oil on canvas | 23 ¾ x 31 ⅝ in / 60.5 x 80.5 cm | Art Institute of Chicago, Chicago, IL, USA

Berthe Morisot (1841–95) is the only female painter who is consistently included in discussions about the Impressionists. The supposed grand-niece of the Rococo painter Jean-Honoré Fragonard, she was born into a wealthy family and grew up in an artistic home, but nonetheless shocked her family by choosing to become a professional artist. While in her teens she was sent to the École des Beaux-Arts in Paris, where she studied for three years. In 1860, she became a pupil of Jean Baptiste Camille Corot, whose work was her chief influence until she met Édouard Manet in 1868. Theirs was to prove a lasting friendship; she was accepted into his social group and went on to marry Manet's brother in 1874. Morisot's *The Cradle* (1873), showing an exhausted mother rocking her baby's crib, was included in the very first Impressionist exhibition, in 1874. The Impressionists' desire to perfect the ways in which light was portrayed is apparent in *Woman at her Toilette*: the manner in which the light changes when it falls upon the lady's skin, in contrast to the way it falls upon her dress, is masterful. Degas once wrote, "The fascinating thing is not to show the source of light, but the effect of light," and this seems to be the technique that Morisot used in this painting. Like Manet, Morisot was slightly more reserved in her method than the other Impressionists, preferring to work in a more accurate, less abstract style. Her paintings often concentrate on women, either as portraits or, like this one, as more general studies of women and their everyday domesticity. **LH**

L'Absinthe | Edgar Degas

1876 | oil on canvas | 36 ¼ x 26 ¾ in / 92 x 68 cm | Musée d'Orsay, Paris, France

Dancers, the theater, the circus, horse races, and here a bar—all the kinds of potentially seedy subjects that Edgar Degas (1834–1917) painted. This glimpse of real, modern life was a little too modern and real for many. Originally called *In a Café*, it acquired the title *L'Absinthe* (which refers both to a highly alcoholic beverage and those who drink it) when shown at the Grafton Gallery, London, in 1893, where it caused a massive stir. For some, this was a ghastly affront to Victorian morals. How could what was obviously an alcoholic prostitute (drinking absinthe) and her equally depraved sidekick (drinking a hangover cure) in a backstreet Paris bar possibly be a fit subject for a painting? Even more scandalous, the couple were well known—actress Ellen André and bohemian artist Marcellin Désboutin. Others thought it a radical masterpiece. What was Degas's motivation? Some see the slumped shoulders and glazed eyes of addiction here, others an off-guard moment of pensive companionship. It is unlikely that Degas was warning of the horrors of alcoholism, and more probable that he was capturing a truthful snapshot of modern life. The artist produces a powerful composition by placing his main subject off-center with a large area of "blank" space in the foreground—something he often did. The tones are somber but balanced harmoniously across the canvas, with dramatic use of shadow. Those who judged this to be a scrappy little image of street life failed to see it as the technically adept piece of portraiture and reportage that it undoubtedly is. **AK**

On Reconnaissance | Józef Brandt

1876 | oil on canvas | 18 ¾ x 44 ¾ in / 47.6 x 113.7 cm | Walters Art Museum, Baltimore, MD, USA

Józef Brandt (1841–1915) was born in Radom, Poland. He studied engineering first in Warsaw and then in Paris, where he was persuaded to abandon his scientific career for painting. He continued to study in Paris and then in Munich, where he settled, becoming known as one of the foremost artists of the Munich School. He painted and taught in Germany, opening his studio to expatriot Polish artists and only returning to the family estate in Radom in the summer. Brandt was a prolific artist, financially and professionally successful, and was known for large canvases depicting violent war scenes and their aftermath. His specialty was battle scenes of the seventeenth-century Cossack wars—fought between Ukraine and the Polish-Lithuanian commonwealth—as well as the Tartar and Swedish invasions of Poland. His works were nonrealistic, glamorized scenes, yet he attempted to portray with accuracy the armor, ammunition, cavalry mounts, and weaponry of the time, often filling his studio with props and models from which to work. Brandt was known for his consummate skill and anatomically astute images of war horses and their riders. Action, movement, and the frenzy of combat were among his specialties. *On Reconnaissance* anticipates this frenzy, as two riders gallop ahead, scouting for soldiers lying in ambush, followed behind on the hill by the amassing army. The feeling of imminent death and destruction permeates the painting. **RA**

The Red Roofs | Camille Pissarro

1877 | oil on canvas | 21 ½ x 25 ⅞ in / 54.5 x 65.5 cm | Musée d'Orsay, Paris, France

This scene shows farm buildings on a hillside called La Côte des Boeufs, near Pontoise. It was painted when Camille Pissarro (1830–1903), often considered the father of French Impressionism, was spending much of his time in this rural area, northwest of Paris. He painted many landscapes here, often in the company of Cézanne, and the two had a profound influence on each other. What may seem a charming country scene is far from straightforward from an artistic point of view. Pissarro chooses to show houses glimpsed through a screen of trees, a difficult task, but the screen makes the viewer's eye move quickly beyond it, into the heart of the painting to try and sort out the many layers of color. The artist has built the painting up from many short brushstrokes, sometimes in thick layers, in a wide range of colors. From a distance the colors harmonize, many of the individual brushstrokes disappear, and the scene comes fully alive. The center of the composition is strongly horizontal, thanks to the roofs and the shape of the hillside, while on the right the buildings are at an angle to the picture surface and the hill slopes down. This gives the picture movement, helping the eye to pick objects out of the pattern of strokes. Pissarro was reconsidering his style at the time of this painting. He experimented with many approaches through his career, but what is clear in this work is his devotion to making art that was an almost subconscious reaction to the scene before him, and to recording the pure effects of color and tone in nature, a theme central to Impressionism. **AK**

The Music Lesson | Lord Frederic Leighton

1877 | oil on canvas | 36 x 37 in / 92.8 x 95.3 cm | Guildhall Art Gallery, London, UK

Lord Frederic Leighton (1830–96) is probably best remembered today for his scenes of classical mythology, but his range of subjects was varied. His extensive travels in the Arab world, for example, led him to produce a number of Orientalist pictures. Orientalism was a popular theme in nineteenth-century European art. The trend arose after Napoleon's campaigns in Egypt (1798–1801), and was given further impetus by a series of important archaeological discoveries and the publication of early travelers' tales. Most artists based their pictures on these secondary sources, but Leighton was one of a select band who toured the area in person. He visited Algiers in 1857 and soon developed a passion for Arab art, amassing a large collection of tiles and ceramics. He even installed an Arab Hall in his London home. In spite of his thorough knowledge of the Middle East, Leighton did not attempt to make his Orientalist scenes authentic. Instead, he described them as "fatal, inevitable potboilers," which were designed to finance his travels, by appealing to Western tastes. In *The Music Lesson*, the enclosed setting and the girls' bare feet were meant to hint at a harem subject, which always sold well. The rich costumes were part of a collection that Leighton had purchased during a trip to Damascus in 1873. The models, however, were obviously European. The little girl was Connie Gilchrist (1865–1946), who also posed for Whistler and for the camera of Lewis Carroll. **IZ**

Apple Tree in Blossom | Carl Fredrik Hill

1877 | oil on canvas | 19 ⅝ x 24 in / 50 x 61 cm | Nationalmuseum, Stockholm, Sweden

Carl Fredrik Hill's (1849–1911) father was a professor of mathematics at Lund University in Sweden—he was deeply opposed to the idea of his son being an artist. Despite this setback, Hill moved to Stockholm where he studied at the Academy of Fine Arts and then moved to Paris. In France, he was inspired by Jean-Baptiste-Camille Corot, Jean-François Millet, and other landscape artists. While in Paris, his works, which had once been somber, began to exhibit more defined color and to demonstrate a much-improved understanding of tone, as can be seen here in *Apple Tree in Blossom*. Hill benefited from the tutelage of fellow artists such as Corot and his works took on a Realist style. Hill's works were continually rejected from academic circles;

only one was shown at the Paris Salon and another in the Exposition Universelle of 1878. This constant rejection led to depression and Hill struggled with mental illness, exacerbated by the deaths of his sister and father in Sweden. In the late 1870s, his mental illness became more marked and he began painting in bold, harshly vibrant colors, clashing hues, and mixing strange styles. Hill was eventually admitted to an asylum, where he was diagnosed with schizophrenia and treated for persecution mania. His doctor claimed that the bizarre paintings resulted from a series of hallucinations. Hill returned to his hometown of Lund for the latter years of his life, spending part of it in an asylum. His family cared for him until his death in 1911. **LH**

Interior of the Rosenborg Palace, Copenhagen | Heinrich Hansen

c.1870–80 | oil on panel | Private collection

Although painters from the nineteenth century Danish Golden Age had a different sensibility and technical virtuosity from that of the Impressionists, they were just as interested in the depiction of sunlight and the quality of light generally. The most prominent artists studied at Copenhagen's Royal Academy of Art, founded in 1754, and began introducing their local artistic communities to a rigorous set of visual and compositional values that exhibited a mastery of light effects and pictorial geometry. Heinrich Hansen's (1821–90) snapshot-like piece, *Interior of the Rosenborg Palace, Copenhagen*, with its acute observation of the gradations of late-afternoon light, crystalline clarity, and impeccably balanced composition, calls to mind the work of Vermeer. Hansen's optical Realism delineates shadows with precision and controls the colors with an exactitude that captures the strength and clarity of natural sunlight as it pours in through the windows and over the two figures, the marble floor, the stucco ceiling and the objects around the room. The careful plotting of detail achieves a verisimilitude of atmosphere that draws the viewer intimately into the scene. Denmark's desire for national identity is reflected in much of its nineteenth-century art: images of a bright and confident nation on the brink of change. Yet *Interior of the Rosenborg Palace* is also imbued with a feeling of nostalgia for a golden age, its Romanticism expressing a deeply felt nationalist sentiment for commemorating a glorious past. **AA**

Head of a Peasant Girl | Wilhelm Leibl

c.1880 | oil on wood | 12 x 11 in / 30 x 27.5 cm | Österreichische Galerie Belvedere, Vienna, Austria

Wilhelm Leibl (1844–1900) famed for his naturalistic genre paintings, became one of the most influential German Realists of the late nineteenth century. At his birth, Romanticism was still a leading artistic movement in Europe, emphasizing emotion, individuality, and sublime nature as the ultimate aesthetic ideals. Leibl was among a group of international painters who rejected the artificial sentimentality of Romanticism in favor of accurate depictions of everyday life. Leibl's early paintings were influenced by the Dutch Old Masters, treating everyday subjects with an obsessive focus on technique. His Realist leanings became even more pronounced when he visited Paris in 1869, in the company of Gustave Courbet. *Head of a Peasant Girl* is characteristic of Leibl's work during what is known as his "Holbein period." Living in rural Bavaria at this time, Leibl drew on local peasant life for his subject matter, seeing ordinary people as worthy subjects for art. Inspired by Dutch genre paintings and the strict naturalism of Holbein's portraits, his young subject is depicted dispassionately, with no attempt at sentimentality or flattery. The beauty of the painting lies primarily within Leibl's exquisitely detailed rendering of color and light, with fresh, florid skin tones set against crisp, tactile fabric. In later life, Leibl began to adopt more fluid brushstrokes, achieving an Impressionistic style, but his Realism was to leave a lasting legacy, attracting a circle of painters in Munich known as the "Leibl group." **SLF**

Paraguay: Image of Your Desolate Country | Juan Manuel Blanes

c.1880 | oil on canvas | 39 x 32 in / 100 x 80 cm | Museo Nacional de Artes Visuales, Montevideo, Uruguay

Uruguayan Juan Manual Blanes (1830–1901) is known for his canvases depicting great national historic events. This Realist nineteenth-century painting commemorates the almost apocalyptic aftermath following Paraguay's defeat in the Triple Alliance War (1864–70), its greatest military and humanitarian disaster. General Francisco Solano López, its president, dictator, and paranoid megalomaniac, declared war on Argentina, Brazil, and Uruguay, and later ordered the executions of his brothers, tortured his mother and sisters, and sent his bravest soldiers and generals to their deaths. After years of fighting, the country was in ruins and its two-million-strong population decimated by three-quarters, leaving mostly women and children. During the war, a generation of artists were lost on the battlefield or in the trenches. The lone and pensive woman looking down with her arms crossed is a *mestizo* (mixed-blood Guaraní and Spanish), hers the face of a devastated nation paralyzed by despair. Her blouse is torn at the shoulder as a grim reminder of the futile bloodshed. Around her waist is wrapped a sash bearing the colors of the Paraguayan flag and behind her stretches a silent battlefield littered with corpses and other debris. To this day, the debate continues in Paraguay as to whether Solano López was a fearless leader who led his troops to the bitter end, or whether he thought himself the "Napoleon of South America," willing to reduce his country to ruin and his countrymen to beggars in his quest for glory. **SWW**

Luncheon of the Boating Party | Pierre-Auguste Renoir

1880–81 | oil on canvas | 51 x 68 in / 129.5 x 172.5 cm | Phillips Collection, Washington, DC, USA

In the background of this painting is one of the many railway bridges that had recently been built by the French government and that were considered a symbol of modernity. These new lines allowed people such as those depicted here by Pierre-Auguste Renoir (1841–1919) to leave Paris and enjoy the countryside. Set on a balcony overlooking the River Seine in Chatou, France, a group of Renoir's friends stand in a complex composition, framed under a wide awning. The figures represent the diverse Parisian social structure, ranging from wealthy, well-dressed bourgeoisie to a young seamstress, Aline Charigot, in the foreground on the left, whom Renoir would marry in 1890. In *Luncheon of the Boating Party*, Renoir appears to create a typically Impressionistic scene, capturing a moment when his friends join him by the river on a sunny afternoon. In reality, Renoir—one of the founding members of the Impressionist movement—executed the portraits of each figure either separately or in smaller groups in his studio. In doing so, he was beginning to move away from his contemporaries. Indeed, shortly after finishing this painting, Renoir began to use more traditional methods of painting. The way in which *Luncheon of the Boating Party* is painted remains Impressionistic however. Working in bright and warm colors, Renoir captures the effects of the light diffused by the awning. He suggests movement in his figures through loose brushwork, while using a thicker handling of paint for the still-life on the table. **WD**

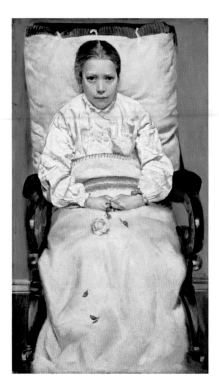

Sick Girl | Christian Krohg

1880–81 | oil on canvas | 47 x 41 ½ in / 120 x 105.5 cm | Nasjonalgalleriet, Oslo, Norway

Norwegian Christian Krohg (1852–1925) was a Realist painter and writer who portrayed the underbelly of society in both his painting and his writing, focusing on the problems of the poor or the unwell, as in *Sick Girl*. His social conscience led to some infamy, particularly after his 1886 novel *Albertine*, about a poor girl who becomes a prostitute, caused a scandal and was confiscated by the police. Yet his own fame was surpassed by that of his pupil Edvard Munch, who became Norway's greatest painter. From 1909 to 1925, Krohg was the director of Oslo's art academy. It was there he taught Munch, to whom he became a friend, mentor, and close supporter, especially when Munch's own work *The Sick Child* of 1885 was badly received by critics for its innovative psychological depiction of

Munch's feelings about the death of his sister Sophie. Krohg's *Sick Girl* shows a young girl swathed in a chaste white blouse and blanket. She is only a few years away from her swaddling clothes, but she is already almost a mummified corpse. The pure white material surrounding her heightens the deathly pallor of her face. The reddened rims of her eyes are accentuated by the red rose she holds like a rosary, its beautiful petals falling away like drops of blood on her blanket. She is well cared for, as she sits in a large chair whose shape reminds the viewer that this girl may never reach curvaceous womanhood. Yet despite the attention the girl is receiving, Krohg reminds the viewer that death and disease are society's great levelers, which pay no attention to wealth or class. **CK**

The Tepidarium | Sir Lawrence Alma-Tadema

1881 | oil on panel | 9 ½ x 13 in / 24 x 33 cm | Lady Lever Art Gallery, Wirral, UK

This exquisitely painted picture carries a strong erotic charge, rare for a Victorian painting of the nude. Sir Lawrence Alma-Tadema (1836–1912) was Dutch born but found fame in London for his fantasies of ancient Roman luxury. To wealthy Victorian businessmen, these pictures were an escape from the drabness of London life, with its gray, foggy weather, rigid social codes, and constricting dress. Alma-Tadema's work was informed by an extensive knowledge of Roman art and archaeology. He collected photographs of ancient sites and excavated objects, which he used as source material for his paintings. In this work, a woman reclines, in a pose of exhaustion, on a marble couch beside the *tepidarium*, the Roman lukewarm bath. Her face is flushed, perhaps because she has just emerged from the hot bath or *caldarium*. In one hand is a strategically placed ostrich feather fan, barely concealing her genitals. She holds the fan tantalizingly, as if it is about to drop from her grasp. In the other hand she toys with a *strigil*, a bronze implement used to scrape oil or sweat off the body. These were found in large numbers at the baths of Pompeii. The *strigil* combines archaeological authenticity with an explicitly phallic shape, and the general air of sensuality is enhanced by the contrast of the fur rug and the silken cushions with the naked body. Alma-Tadema's virtuoso technique, derived from seventeenth-century Dutch interior painters, enabled him to paint surfaces such as the sheen of marble with extraordinary illusionism. **JT**

Christ Before Pilate | Mihály Munkácsy

1881 | oil on canvas | 164 x 250 in / 417 x 636 cm | Déri Museum, Debrecen, Hungary

This dramatic depiction of Christ standing up to Pontius Pilate is one of a trilogy of works—inspired by Tintoretto's great Passion cycle—by Hungarian Realist artist Mihály Munkácsy (1844–1900), which he painted at the height of his career. The enormous scale of the work means that the defiant central figure is literally larger than life—it dominates the crux of tension between the baying crowd on the left and the pensive Roman Governor seated on the right. The later images show Jesus being presented as a criminal in *Ecce Homo* of 1896 and then crucified in *Golgotha* of 1884. Munkácsy's Christ trilogy was not exhibited in its entirety until over a century later, in 1995, when the three works were united for the first time, fittingly in Debrecen, Hungary. All three

had been bought by American millionaire John Wanamaker, who exhibited them in his department store in Philadelphia every Easter. Munkácsy studied in Vienna, Munich, and Düsseldorf, before art dealer Charles Sedelmeyer convinced him to paint bigger and bolder compositions in place of his genre images of Hungarian peasants. Munkácsy achieved acclaim at the Paris Salon of 1870 for a dark, haunting interior scene of a condemned convict facing his last day on earth. In spite of becoming Hungary's most famous artist and earning an international reputation for his large-scale biblical paintings, Munkácsy was incredibly sensitive to criticism and was troubled by a terrible depression that led to a spell in a mental institution, where he eventually died in 1900. **OW**

Phosphorus and Hesperus
Evelyn de Morgan

1882 | oil on canvas | 23 ⅝ x 17 ⅜ in / 60 x 44 cm
De Morgan Centre, London, UK

The Victorian artist George Frederick Watts described Evelyn de Morgan (1855–1919) as "the first woman artist of the day—if not of all time." She was certainly a pioneer, being one of the first women to enroll at London's then-new Slade School of Art. This is a dreamy evocation of the Greco-Roman myth of Phosphorus and Hesperus, the morning and evening stars respectively—hence the lit and spent torches. It shows off de Morgan's grasp of the human form and impressive drawing skills. Working during the later phase of the Pre-Raphaelites, she was influenced by artists such as Edward Burne-Jones. Her talent for tight, decisively planned composition comes into its own here with the close intertwining of her two centrally placed figures. De Morgan was a prolific artist who developed a very personal symbolic style and became a pivotal figure among artists who were moving away from traditional approaches. **AK**

The Water Sprite
Ernst Josephson

1882 | oil on canvas | 57 ½ x 45 in / 146.5 x 114 cm
Nationalmuseum, Stockholm, Sweden

In *The Water Sprite*, also known as *Näcken*, Ernst Josephson (1851–1906) combined Nordic folklore with Renaissance painting and the French Symbolism of the late nineteenth century. In ancient Nordic tales, Näcken was a destructive spirit who wandered through wild wetlands, playing music on his fiddle, and, sirenlike, lured people to their deaths. The sprite therefore symbolizes the hidden dangers in nature, but Näcken's story also functioned as a personal allegory for Josephson's own sense of isolation. The artist's skillful and sensual use of color is evident in this painting: the bright, wet green of the sprite's long hair and the reeds in which he kneels are balanced by patches of a complementary red, such as on the violin, rocks, and the spirit's lips. The loose, multidirectional brushstrokes bring to life the turbulent, rushing water, creating a melancholy yet angry and energetic mood. **KM**

Proserpine
Dante Gabriel Rossetti

1882 | oil on canvas | 30 ½ x 14 ¾ in / 77.5 x 37.5 cm
Birmingham Museum and Art Gallery, UK

In classical mythology, Proserpine was the daughter of Ceres, the goddess of agriculture. Pluto, the god of the underworld, fell in love with the maid and carried her off to his bleak domain. Enraged, Ceres threatened to prevent all crops from growing unless her daughter was returned. At length, a bargain was struck. Proserpine would be freed, provided she ate nothing during her captivity. Unfortunately, she had eaten four pomegranate seeds and was obliged to spend four months each year in the underworld, as Pluto's bride. Dante Gabriel Rossetti's (1828–82) picture shows Proserpine during her captivity. She looks doleful; a shaft of daylight has passed through a chink into the underworld, reminding her of her lost freedom. The subject had a personal resonance for Rossetti: he was in love with his model for *Proserpine*, Jane Morris, who was already married to fellow artist William Morris. **IZ**

The Damsel in Distress
James Ensor

1882 | oil on canvas | 39 ½ x 31 ⅜ in / 100.5 x 79.5 cm
Musée d'Orsay, Paris, France

In the early 1880s, Belgian artist James Ensor (1860–1949) worked on traditional subjects, such as portraits, still lifes, and seascapes. His work was described as "trash" by one critic. With constant rejection, his insecure personality became more inward-looking and he increasingly blended reality with dreams. His interior paintings of the period show this transition. They evoke unsettling moods through his use of light and subtle color. This work depicts a room in his parents' house. Heavy curtains screen the sunlight, excluding the outside world and the atmosphere is eerie and oppressive. A muted, almost imaginary light pervades the darkness, lending a sense of drama to the dismal atmosphere. The light alienates objects such as the fabric loops holding back the curtains, transforming them into strange birdlike figures that appear to watch over the silent young woman on the bed. **SH**

Roses in a Dish | Henri Fantin-Latour

1882 | oil on canvas | 14 ³/₈ x 12 ¹/₈ in / 36.5 x 46 cm | Musée d'Orsay, Paris, France

Henri Fantin-Latour (1836–1904) was a painter of romantic figure subjects, portrait groups, and still lifes. He received his earliest training from his father, a portrait painter, and in 1850 entered the studio of Lecoq de Boisbaudran. Later he studied under Gustave Courbet at the Ecole des Beaux-Arts. Fantin-Latour was known for his regular attendance at the Louvre, where he made countless studies of the works of the great masters. Here the artist depicts a simple subject—roses in a dish—and finds within it a delicacy and ephemeral beauty. He painted with an elegant restraint that greatly appealed to his growing number of supporters and collectors in England. Fantin-Latour was a man of contradictions, for while his own work was heavily indebted to the Old Masters

he socialized with the young and daring new artists of the time. Also, despite Fantin-Latour's desire to paint images of fantasy and reverie inspired by music, it was his flower paintings that became his signature subject matter. Greatly admired by his contemporaries, Jacques Emile Blanche wrote, "Fantin studied each flower, each petal, its grain, its tissue, as if it were a human face . . . " Eventually, however, Fantin-Latour began to feel frustrated and constrained by the focus on what he considered to be lesser facet of his artistic practice, and the flower paintings, which he was almost creating under duress, betrayed his boredom with the subject. Yet he was not able financially to give up the lucrative market for these works for many years. **RW**

Pears on a Chair | Paul Cézanne

c.1882 | oil on canvas | Barnes Foundation, Merion, PA, USA

The superlatives that Paul Cézanne's (1839–1906) work engenders are entirely appropriate. Not only did he reinvigorate a number of genres, such as the nude and the landscape, but Cézanne also radicalized both the representational basis of painting, and the means by which this conception of a representational idiom is created. His still-lifes are indicative of his original sensibility, and it is from them that the assertion of Cézanne as the father of Cubism, if not modern art, is primarily drawn. Painted during a period in the artist's career when he was attempting to make sense of Impressionism's implications for painting and its applicability for his own activities, *Pears on a Chair* is composed of Cézanne's distinctive manner, what the philosopher Maurice Merleau-Ponty described as his "patient hatchings." While the elliptical shape formed by the plate appears entirely in proportion, the surface of the chair appears to be organized around a different spatial plane. In effect, this type of visual disjunction was exactly what the Cubists, certainly in their analytical phase, were keen to explore. A robust black line delineates the fruit arrangement, and the chair seat is severely cropped, which contributes to the overall abstract sense of the painting. *Pears on a Chair* is not only remarkable for the way it is unrelenting in its pursuit of rendering reality—or the world of appearances—truthfully, it also anticipates the more experimental direction Cézanne took, a direction that nevertheless remained anchored within the sensate world. **CS**

A Bar at the Folies-Bergère
Édouard Manet

*c.*1882 | oil on canvas | 37 ¾ x 51 ⅛ in / 96 x 130 cm | Courtauld Institute of Art Gallery, London, UK

Édouard Manet (1832–83) painted this, his last great masterpiece, when he was terminally ill. In it, he returned to his favorite subject matter, the celebration of Parisian life. The Impressionists often showed people enjoying themselves, and many of their most familiar scenes were set in bars, cafés, and dance halls. The Folies-Bergère was the most famous of the café-concert halls, which provided entertainment as well as refreshment. A sample of this entertainment can be seen in the upper left-hand corner of the picture, where the legs of a trapeze artist are visible. Manet also gives some prominence to the electric lighting in the Folies-Bergère, which was still a novelty at this time. The girl was a barmaid, rather than a professional model. At first glance, the structure of the composition is confusing, as most of the picture is a reflection in a large mirror behind the barmaid. Manet employed artistic license here, shifting the girl's reflection to the right and tilting it slightly, to make the image more attractive. The man in the top hat shares the same viewpoint as the spectator. Manet was too ill to paint this picture in the Folies-Bergère itself. Instead, most of it was completed in the studio, where he had an imitation bar installed. As a result, the details in the foreground were painted with careful precision. Manet even added his signature to the wine bottle on the left. The background, by contrast, was less distinct. The artist had to work from memory, producing a shimmering, hazy reflection of the glamorous world that he was leaving behind. **IZ**

Jan Sobieski Vanquisher of the Turks at the Gates of Vienna
Jan Matejko

c.1883 | oil on canvas | 180 x 360 in / 460 x 920 cm | Sobieski Room, Vatican City, Italy

Krakow-born Jan Matejko (1838–93), the most popular creator of romantic visions of Polish history, declared that art is "a weapon . . . not to be separated from the love of one's homeland." Poland was partitioned and occupied by foreign powers at the time and his political aim was to encourage his compatriots to defend their country by depicting its great historical events. This action-packed painting of infantry and cavalry figures, military costumes, and paraphernalia commemorates the victory of Christian knight and Polish king Jan III Sobieski (1629–96) outside the gates of Vienna. At the Battle of Vienna on September 12, 1683, Sobieski's troops joined up with Austrians and Germans in a united front of about 81,000 men against the 130,000-strong Ottoman army under grand vizier

Kara Mustafa. This large-scale battle of the Hapsburg-Ottoman Wars was the turning point in the three hundred-year struggle between the Holy League and the Ottoman empire. Sobieski was dubbed the "Lion of Lechistan" by the Turks and the "Savior of Vienna and Western European civilization" by the Pope. A towering example of epic battle scene painting, it occupies the entire north wall of the Vatican's Sobieski Room. With this canvas, and his famous 1878 masterpiece, *The Battle of Grunwald* (the 1410 Polish-Lithuanian victory over the Knights of the Germanic Order of the Cross), Matejko took upon himself the task of rebuilding national identity through the immediacy of art. His grandiose painted histories had an impact on several twentieth-century Polish artists. **AA**

Bathers at Asnières | Georges Seurat

1884 | oil on canvas | 79 1/8 x 118 1/8 in / 201 x 300 cm | National Gallery, London, UK

Images of "lowly" working men were more typical of small-scale genre paintings, but in Georges Seurat's (1859–91) first large-scale painting these ordinary factory workers relaxing in the sunshine by the River Seine are given a subversive monumental grandeur. The picture was rejected by the Salon of 1884, and was shown instead at the Salon des Indépendants, set up by Seurat and other artists to rival the "establishment" showcase of French art. Seurat was the founder of Neo-Impressionism—a term coined by the art critic Félix Fénéon (who bought this painting) to describe the artistic movement that both evolved from Impressionism and reacted against it. Impressionist and Neo-Impressionist artists were alike in many ways—in their interest in light and color, and in painting modern life. But while painters such as Monet sought to capture the fleeting moment, Seurat worked painstakingly to present a moment transformed into timelessness. The painting's formal geometry and stillness recalls the paintings of the Renaissance master Piero della Francesca. Fascinated by color theories of the day, Seurat developed the technique called pointillism, in which small dots of pure color are carefully and systematically applied to the canvas, so that the colors mix and merge in the viewer's eye. He has used this technique in various areas of the canvas, including the foreground bather's red hat. The technique was adopted by the painters Signac and Pissarro, and had an influence on other artists, including Vincent van Gogh. **JW**

Madame X | John Singer Sargent

1884 | oil on canvas | 82 ½ x 43 ¼ in / 209.5 x 110 cm | Metropolitan Museum of Art, New York, NY, USA

John Singer Sargent (1856–1925), an American citizen largely brought up in Europe, painted this remarkable portrait near the start of his career, when he was living in Paris. He hoped that it would make his name and, indeed, it did, although not in the way he had envisaged. When it was exhibited, the picture caused a scandal, prompting the artist to leave France. He had approached Virginie Gautreau, a famous society beauty, and asked to paint her portrait. She was a fellow American and was the wife of a wealthy French banker. She readily agreed to his request, but progress on the painting was slow. Virginie was a restless model and Sargent found her beauty "unpaintable." He altered the composition several times before finally settling on a pose that accentuated her distinctive profile. The painting was finally displayed at the Paris Salon of 1884. The sitter was not formally identified, but Virginie was so famous that many people recognized her. The public were shocked by her low-cut dress, bemused by her deathly white makeup, repelled by the awkward, twisted pose of her right arm, and, above all, outraged by the fact that one of her dress-straps was hanging off her shoulder—a sure sign of sexual impropriety. Gautreau's family were appalled and begged the artist to withdraw the painting. He wanted to repaint the shoulder-strap, but was not allowed to do so until the exhibition was over. In the wake of the scandal, Sargent left Paris under a cloud, though he always maintained that the portrait was the finest thing he ever painted. **IZ**

After the Pose
Sven Richard Bergh

1884 | oil on canvas | 57 x 79 in / 145 x 200 cm | Malmö Museum, Malmö, Sweden

After the Pose by Sven Richard Bergh (1858–1919) looks forward to the coming innovations in Swedish art of the late nineteeth and early twentieth centuries. Painted when Bergh was in Paris to escape the rigorous academicism he experienced as a student at the Swedish Royal Academy, the image assimilates French nationalism and realism, while foreshadowing the emergence of, and emphasis on, a specifically Nordic art. As a scene of contemporary life, the painting depicts Carl Jaensson, a fellow Swedish expatriate artist, absorbedly playing the violin after a session of painting a nude model. Situated in the center foreground of a bare, monochromatic studio anchored by vertical and horizontal lines, the model slowly and distractedly dons one of her stockings among the scattered remnants of the artist's studio. Bergh's canvas also conveys attitudes towards the arts and integrates other artistic influences of the period, most notably the style of Japanese prints. The violin represents the ideal of music as the most indescribable of the arts and thus the purest. Significantly, beginning in the 1890s in Sweden, Bergh occupied a central role in the development of a more intrinsically Swedish art—a Swedish Romantic style that drew inspiration from the Swedish landscape and the unique quality of Nordic light. Bergh and others formed the Artist's Union, founded on principles of cooperative action and based on the ideas of William Morris and John Ruskin. In 1915, the Nationalmuseum in Stockholm appointed Bergh as its head. **AEH**

Bringing Home the Body of King Karl XII of Sweden
Gustaf Cederström

1884 | oil on canvas | 104 ¼ x 146 in / 265 x 371 cm | Nationalmuseum, Stockholm, Sweden

Coming from an aristocratic family, Gustaf Cederström (1845–1933), like many Swedish artists of his era, began his career as an army officer. After receiving artistic training in Düsseldorf under another Swede, Ferdinand Fagerlin, he moved to Paris—one of the first of his generation to do so. Although slightly older than the artists who introduced French Realism to Swedish painting in the 1880s, Cederström chose to specialize in history painting. His favorite subject was the Swedish King Karl XII and his illustrious military campaigns. This was also the theme of his initial great success—the first 1878 version of *Bringing Home the Body of King Karl XII*, which won him an award at the Exposition Universelle in Paris that same year. The 1884 version, however, is impressive in the way that it successfully infuses a distant historical subject with immediacy, gritty realism, and an evocative atmosphere. Cederström studied reality closely and developed a keen understanding of the workings of *plein air* compositions. This canvas was partly painted outdoors and the scene was set up with real models dressed in replicas of authentic early eighteenth-century uniforms. Even though Cederström made a notable contribution to nineteenth-century historic painting, he was not the most representative of this genre in Sweden. The Nationalmuseum, however, acquired this work at the end of the nineteenth century because it represents a veritable cornerstone in the glorification of Sweden's historical past and in the power of art to create national symbols. **AA**

Breakfast in the Garden | Giuseppe de Nittis

1884 | oil on canvas | 31 ⅞ x 46 ⅛ in / 81 x 117 cm | Pinacoteca Giuseppe de Nittis, Barletta, Italy

An artist who achieved international fame during his lifetime, Giuseppe de Nittis (1846–84) attained recognition early in his career. His excellent painting skills and choice of themes, portraying modern life, made his works accessible and collectible. He was born in Barletta to a wealthy family and traveled to Turin, Rome, Naples, and Paris for an education. In Naples, he showed paintings at a public exhibition for the first time in 1863, but was expelled from the city's Accademia di Belle Arti for bad behavior the same year. In Paris, he was befriended by Degas and met other Impressionists. He took part in the first Impressionist exhibition in 1874 and has become known as "The Italian Impressionist." *Breakfast in the Garden* poignantly depicts his small family, his wife and preferred model Léontine and son Jacques, in a tranquil domestic setting. It has an informal still life on the table of empty plates, glasses, and discarded napkins, their form suggested by his use of color in Impressionist style. He uses light and composition to show this is summer and that even at breakfast time the sun is hot, as the family are already sitting in the shade. De Nittis's promising career was cut short when he died of a stroke aged thirty-eight, the same year he completed this canvas. It is very much a representation of everyday intimate family life: his son playfully feeds the ducks, and the empty chair in the foreground had no doubt been inhabited by the artist, perhaps even while painting this, not knowing his chair would soon be permanently empty. **LH**

The Reception | James Tissot

1883–85 | oil on canvas | 56 x 40 in / 142.2 x 101.6 cm | Albright-Knox Art Gallery, Buffalo, NY, USA

James Tissot's (1836–1902) work is renowned for its accurate depictions of the fashions of his day and for its enigmatic qualities. Born in Nantes, France, Tissot moved to Paris at the age of twenty. The artists and writers he met there were to have an enormous influence on his career and his style of painting. He was particularly indebted to James McNeill Whistler, whose work Tissot strongly emulates. This painting is also known as *L'Ambitieuse*, "The Political Woman." The dual title provides a pleasing double entendre—is the woman's smile one of sincerity or diplomacy? Is she there as the central figure or as a beautiful accompaniment to the man on her arm? Can the viewer glimpse any clues in the chattering, perhaps conspiratorial, crowd? Tissot's interest in fashion

helped his works become highly collectible and they sold well, although the critics were less enamored with him than the public. In 1871, he fled the dangers of the Paris Commune (in which it was rumored he had played a part) for London. His works became as sought after in England as they had been in France, and he exhibited regularly at the Royal Academy. He remained in London until 1882, when the tragically early death of his lover and model, Kathleen, from tuberculosis, spurred him to return to Paris. In the late 1880s he underwent a religious conversion and began a new era in his career, painting only religious scenes. He traveled to the Middle East where he made many sketches, which he worked into illustrations for versions of the Bible. **LH**

Kaiser Franz Josef I of Austria in Uniform | Karl von Blaas

c.1885 | oil on canvas
Private collection

Louis Pasteur in His Laboratory
Albert Edelfelt

1885 | oil on canvas | 60 ⅝ x 49 ⅝ in / 154 x 126 cm
Musée d'Orsay, Paris, France

Karl von Blaas (1815–94) rose from humble peasant beginnings to become one of the most sought-after society portraitists in Europe. This painting is of Kaiser Franz Josef, the last ruler of the Austrian empire. Von Blaas also knew him as a friend of the arts: the great Kunsthistorisches Museum of Vienna was one of the kaiser's initiatives. Franz Josef is depicted in military regalia, as a vigorous and alert man of action. Bearing the red and white colors of Austria, he is the physical embodiment of his nation and its empire. Yet despite the military rigidity and cool Spartan atmosphere of the painting, a close look at the emperor's face suggests that he is deep in thought. His eyes do not engage with the viewer—he seems to have more pressing matters at hand than sitting for a portrait. Von Blaas allows us to sympathize with the man who stood at the center of an empire for nearly seventy years. **DK**

Finnish painter Albert Edelfelt (1854–1905) studied in Helsinki and Antwerp before being lured to Paris by the prospect of fame. Most of his paintings were portraits, and his bright, informal, and Impressionistic canvases show the influence of the contemporary vogue for Realism on his art. His portrait of the scientist Louis Pasteur in his laboratory is his most well-known work. Edelfelt was fascinated by Pasteur, and he spent several months studying his work before he began painting the portrait of the chemist. Here, the dapper scientist is seen dressed for an evening out yet still engrossed in an experiment. His elegance and dedication are rendered as desirable qualities. This portrait expertly demonstrates how an artist can balance the demands of representing his sitter while also creating an arresting image regardless of biographical context. **AH**

Lady at the Tea Table
Mary Stevenson Cassatt

1885 | oil on canvas | 29 x 24 in / 74 x 61 cm
Metropolitan Museum of Art, New York, NY, USA

The Umbrellas
Pierre-Auguste Renoir

c.1881–86 | oil on canvas | 71 x 45 ¼ in /
180.3 x 114.9 cm | National Gallery, London, UK

Mary Stevenson Cassatt (1845–1926) was the Jane Austen of painting. Like literature's "drawing room Shakespeare," the artist's deceptively calm and casual paintings, which depict women in everyday situations, contain underlying layers of dramatic tension, emotional depth, and psychological insight. Cassatt, who was born in Pennsylvania but settled in Paris in 1874, was the only North American woman artist invited to exhibit with the French Impressionists. Cassatt painted Mrs. Robert Moore Riddle, her mother's first cousin, for *Lady at the Tea Table*. This picture is remarkable for the subject's air of authority and the economical yet eloquent use of line and color. Mrs. Riddle's daughter was offended at Cassatt's realistic representation of her mother's nose, but the painter herself was so attached to the painting that she kept it until gifting it to the Metropolitan Museum of Art in 1923. **AH**

The Umbrellas is a visual record of an important development in Pierre-Auguste Renoir's (1841–1919) career. It is believed to have been painted at two different times, in between which Renoir moved away from Impressionism and began to work in a more formal manner. It is generally agreed that Renoir began by painting the group on the right in the late 1870s. The woman and girls are treated in a soft manner that makes them appear to be almost flat against the canvas. In contrast, the left side shows a greater interest in the more traditional notions of line and form rather than color. Figures such as the young woman in the foreground are still painted smoothly but in a way that suggests solidity through her well-defined contours, dating this section closer to 1885. Renoir's blues, greens, browns, and creams reflect the weather and the sober mood of this scene. **WD**

A Sunday on La Grande Jatte—1884 | Georges Seurat

1884–86 | oil on canvas | 81 ¾ x 121 ¼ in / 207.5 x 308 cm | Art Institute of Chicago, Chicago, IL, USA

In the 1880s the lower-middle classes flocked to the Grande Jatte in suburban Paris for a riverside stroll and a picnic on Sunday afternoons. This was the kind of subject matter that the Impressionists had made fashionable, but Georges Seurat (1859–91) was far from embracing that art movement's pursuit of the fleeting and spontaneous. He made more than seventy preliminary oil sketches and drawings for this formalized image, with its careful composition and stress on simplified geometric forms. During his two years working on *La Grande Jatte*, Seurat was also developing the *pointilliste* technique of applying color in dots that were intended to fuse when seen from a distance, and it coexists here with his more conventional earlier style. Some forty figures crowd

the canvas, mostly in profile or full face. They appear static and frozen in an uncommunicative proximity. Many figures have been identified as known Parisian stereotypes. For instance, the woman standing in the right foreground, with the striking bustle, is identified by her pet monkey—symbol of lasciviousness—as a woman of loose morals. The seated man with the top hat on the left is a fashionable stroller of boulevards. The shift from a shaded foreground to a bright background creates a strong sense of depth to which the recession of figures contributes, although there are some disorienting shifts in scale. Seurat said that his aim was to represent modern life in the style of a classical Greek frieze. The overall effect, intended or not, is dreamlike, haunting, and utterly unreal. **RG**

Summer Night | Kitty Lange Kielland

1886 | oil on canvas | 39 x 53 in / 100.5 x 135 cm | National Gallery, Oslo, Norway

Kitty (Christine) Lange Kielland (1843–1914) became a part of an important group of Norwegian Realist artists working in Munich when she moved there in 1875 and immersed herself in the artistic community. Although over the age of thirty at the time, she had only recently embarked on an artistic career, having been hindered by the chauvinistic attitudes of her time. She started her training in 1873, taking private lessons with Hans Gude (1825–1903), from whom she received a foundation in Realism that would perpetuate throughout her career. During her time in Munich she painted open landscapes of a windswept and somber nature, drawing inspiration from the scenery of her native Norway. She moved to Paris in 1879 along with several other Norwegian artists. There

she was influenced by the work of the landscape artist Léon Pelouse (1838–91) and her works became infused with a lighter and more romantic quality. *Summer Night* is one of her most evocative paintings from this period. It is a work of tranquillity and reflection, with the still waters peppered with lilies and glowing with the light of early evening. Appearing almost photographic in the clarity of form, *Summer Night* is clearly reminiscent of her early training, but it is infused with an atmosphere of nostalgia and gentle affection for Norway. Kielland's art was important in the development of Realism in Norway, and she paved the way for successive female artists, both through her paintings and her active participation in the fight for women's rights in the arts. **TP**

The Island of the Dead | Arnold Böcklin

1886 | oil on wood | 31½ x 59 in / 80 x 150 cm | Museum der Bildenden Künste, Leipzig, Germany

In the latter part of the nineteenth century, Symbolist painters reacted against the naturalistic aims of the Impressionists and their contemporaries. Instead of focusing on the everyday world, they preferred to dwell on themes of mystery and the imagination. The Swiss artist Arnold Böcklin (1827–1901) was one of the seminal figures of the movement. This particular image haunted him for several years. He created the original picture in 1880, at the request of Marie Berna, whose husband had recently passed away, but went on to produce no fewer than five versions of the subject. The title was suggested by the art dealer, Fritz Gurlitt. Böcklin disapproved of titles; over the years, he described it as *The Silent Island*, *The Island of the Graves*, *The Still Place*, and, perhaps most aptly of all, "a picture for dreaming over." He avoided depicting precise subjects wherever possible, encouraging spectators to find their own meanings in his paintings, but the starting points for his fantasies usually came from classical literature. Here, for example, the image of the hooded figure accompanying the coffin calls to mind Charon, the boatman who ferried the souls of the dead to Hades. Since Böcklin's time, *The Island of the Dead* has proved every bit as evocative as the artist might have hoped. It inspired a piece of music by Rachmaninoff, it fascinated Adolf Hitler, who owned one of the versions, it was used for the set of a horror film starring Boris Karloff, and it inspired a modern interpretation by another Swiss artist, H.R. Giger, best known as the designer of the movie *Alien*. **IZ**

Eight Bells | Winslow Homer

1886 | oil on canvas | 25 x 35 in / 63.5 x 89 cm | Addison Gallery of American Art, Andover, MA, USA

A one-time Civil War illustrator, Winslow Homer (1836–1910) would, particularly after an extended visit to England in the early 1880s, find his muse away from the land. He painted in Prout's Neck, Maine, in the summer and in Key West, Florida, or the Bahamas in the winter. His work is a meditation on life and the nearness of death. In the middle of the 1880s, the time at which *Eight Bells* was produced, Homer became a recluse, preferring in his later years to paint storms instead of sunny skies. One of Homer's best-known paintings and the last of the series of great sea pictures that had commenced with *The Life Line* three years earlier, it was completed in 1886 but not shown until 1888. The title refers to the regulation of the sailors' duty watches. Bells were sounded every half hour, with one bell after half an hour, two bells after an hour, and so on. Eight bells signified the end of a standard four-hour watch. Two sailors dominate the foreground, but the details of the ship and its riggings have been minimized. Homer became renowned as a watercolorist but he was equally adept with oil, and *Eight Bells* is emphatic proof of this. Homer would paint scenes of women working in coastal towns, living with the fear of seeing their husbands die at sea while at the same time, as in this picture, showing those same husbands out on their ships, dealing with the more tangible danger of the ocean. The waves are gathering around the boat and there are clouds in the sky. All are detailed in a strikingly direct hand, realistically, objectively, and in splendid color. **OR**

The Tub | Edgar Degas

1886 | pastel on card | 23 ⅝ x 32 ⅝ in / 60 x 83 cm | Musée d'Orsay, Paris, France

In the 1880s, Edgar Degas's (1834–1917) sight began to deteriorate, and he turned increasingly to working with pastels, a medium he enjoyed. Women had always been a favorite subject, and his later work included numerous studies of women in highly intimate moments, bathing and doing their toilette—as in this pastel piece. This work appeared at the eighth Impressionist exhibition, in 1886, and as before, certain people were shocked. This is not romantic, idealized womanhood, but a more truthful depiction of a woman's body, in a pose that some considered vulgar and voyeuristic. However, there is a delicacy and vulnerable beauty in the way this picture shares a very private moment. Far from being animallike as some critics said, the crouching position was based on the "crouching Aphrodite" pose of classical sculpture, and the body's lines echo the classicism of Degas's early training. True to form, Degas's picture seeks to freeze a truthful moment in modern life, with the unorthodox viewpoint, chopped-off composition, and strange perspective of Japanese prints. In his later years his work moved closer to the Impressionists in some ways—seen here in the purer coloration, sparkling natural lighting, and interesting textures. Here is a timeless classical nude and traditional still life so seamlessly blended with a modern approach that it stands as one of the artist's finest, bravest works. Little wonder that Pissarro counted him the "greatest artist of our epoch" and artists as diverse as Matisse and Picasso found themselves inspired by him. **AK**

The Garden of Pan | Edward Burne-Jones

1886–87 | oil on canvas | 60 x 73 ½ in / 153 x 187 cm | National Gallery of Victoria, Melbourne, Australia

Although the original Pre-Raphaelite Brotherhood was short-lived, bursting onto the art scene in 1848 and disbanding by 1853, its ideals were more enduring, influencing British art for the rest of the century. Sir Edward Burne-Jones (1833–98) belonged to the second wave of Pre-Raphaelites, making his mark in the 1870s. He studied for a time under Rossetti, sharing his passion for early Italian art, which is clearly evident in *The Garden of Pan*. Burne-Jones visited Italy in 1871 and returned full of new ideas for paintings. One of these was to be "a picture of the beginning of the world, with Pan and Echo and sylvan gods . . . and a wild background of woods, mountains and rivers." He soon realized this scheme was too ambitious and painted only the garden. The mood and style of this work is reminiscent of two early Italian masters, Piero di Cosimo (*c*.1461–1521) and Dosso Dossi (*c*.1490–1541). Burne-Jones may have seen their work on his travels, but it is more likely he was influenced by the examples owned by one of his patrons, William Graham. As was his custom, Burne-Jones put a new slant on the classical legends. Normally, Pan is shown with goatlike features, but Burne-Jones presents him as a callow youth (his own name for the picture was "The Youth of Pan"). The setting is Arcadia, a pastoral paradise that serves as a pagan equivalent of the Garden of Eden. Burne-Jones admitted that the composition was slightly absurd, declaring that it was "meant to be a little foolish and to delight in foolishness . . . a reaction from the dazzle of London wit and wisdom." **IZ**

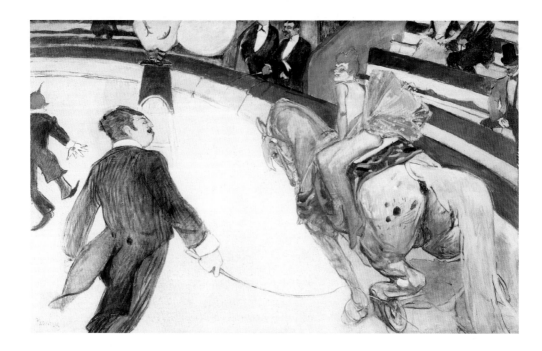

At the Cirque Fernando: The Ringmaster | Henri de Toulouse-Lautrec

1887–88 | oil on canvas | 40 x 63 in / 103 x 161 cm | Joseph Winterbottom Collection, Chicago, IL, USA

The circus, which was hugely popular in Paris at this time, had been a source of inspiration for many artists, including Degas and René Princeteau. The Cirque Fernando was at the height of its fame in the 1880s. Not far from Henri de Toulouse-Lautrec's (1864–1901) studio, it became the subject of a series of works he produced during the short period from 1886 to 1887. He later returned to the subject of the circus in 1899 when recuperating from mental illness, and produced a number of fine and evocative drawings. This large painting was probably produced for the exhibition of "Les XX," a Brussels exhibition society, in 1888, and has the appearance of being unfinished. There is in particular a striking disparity between the roundly modeled figure of the ringmaster, horse, and rider,

and the two-dimensional clowns who appear partially truncated by the edge of the picture. The picture edge to the right is undetermined, as if the artist had been undecided what to do, and even small drips of paint and smudges remain across the surface. It was painted quickly, and the speed with which the artist worked also reflects the speed with which the horse and rider race around the small circus ring. Despite this, Lautrec clearly considered the work complete and was happy to exhibit it as such. It was later hung above the bar at the Moulin Rouge. Lautrec's unique approach to his art and the expressiveness of his painting style played a valuable role in the development of art and, in particular, elevated the role of the poster to an art form. **TP**

The Vision After the Sermon | Paul Gauguin

1888 | oil on canvas | 28 ¾ x 36 ¼ in / 72.2 x 91 cm | National Gallery of Scotland, Edinburgh, UK

Paul Gauguin (1848–1903) worked closely with the younger artist Emile Bernard in Pont-Aven in Brittany between 1888 and 1891. Both artists were influenced by the Symbolist movement, both were interested in the "primitive," and both reached a similar form of representation at about the same time. Gauguin's, *The Vision After the Sermon*, also known as *Jacob Wrestling with the Angel*, was, by a few weeks, predated by Bernard's startlingly innovative but compositionally weak *Breton Women at a Pardon*, giving rise to accusations of plagiarism. Customarily, on particular saints' days, devout Bretons dressed in traditional costume to receive pardons. In Gauguin's painting, the composition is divided into two distinct halves separated by a tree. On the left, the women in their crisp, white bonnets are presented as patterns against the red of the field. The viewer is invited to see their vision, generated by the sermon, of Jacob wrestling with the angel, which is a story from Genesis. Conflated with the religious subject matter is the well-documented Breton custom of wrestling—a less devout occupation. Gauguin stated that, "the landscape and the wrestling . . . exist only in the imagination of the praying people as a result of the sermon." To denote this otherworldliness, he distorted scale and used vivid, arbitrary color. In a final and irrevocable break with Realism and Impressionism he flattened and simplified forms surrounding them with dark *cloisonnist* outlines. Unfortunately, the painting caused a rift between Gauguin and Bernard. **WO**

Christ's Triumphant Entry into Brussels in 1889 | James Ensor

1888 | oil on canvas | 99 ½ x 169 ½ in / 252 x 431 cm | J. Paul Getty Museum, Los Angeles, CA, USA

During James Ensor's (1860–1949) lifetime, his home town of Ostend in Belgium developed from a small fishing village to a seaside resort. Carnival time was celebrated by the locals by wearing masks and they became one of Ensor's recurring motifs and a metaphor for his loneliness. This is his largest painting, showing Christ caught up in a procession—half carnival, half political demonstration. The location is not Jerusalem but Brussels, the capital of Ensor's own country. Instead of palm branches, people are waving political slogans on banners. On the right-hand edge of the picture is the cry: "Long live Christ, King of Brussels." Ensor has made Jesus his contemporary. Citizens of Brussels are led by a military band. Someone in authority wearing a white sash stands on a green podium while a red banner proclaims: "Long live the social revolution." Following months of strikes and uprisings, two years before this painting's completion; the king of Belgium had declared that the working classes' lot needed improvement. Nine years before, a liberal government had banned religious education in schools, intending to weaken the power of the church. The controversy escalated into a war of religion. Pro-Catholic parties eventually regained the majority. By painting these crowds, Ensor emphasized such events. The masks and faces are hideously distorted yet the haloed Christ is not ugly, but resembles Ensor himself. A small figure, he has an important message for the Belgian people, but they do not seem to have noticed. **SH**

"Hip Hip Hurrah!" Artists' Party at Skagen | Peder Severin Krøyer

1888 | oil and acrylic on canvas | 53 x 65 ⅛ in / 134.5 x 165.5 cm | Göteborgs Konstmuseum, Sweden

Peder Severin Krøyer (1851–1909), born in Stavanger, Norway, was one of the leaders of a group of artists who gathered together at Skagen in Denmark and was the most famous of the Danish "painters of light." While training at the Academy of Copenhagen, he traveled widely as a student, especially to France, where he was influenced by the Impressionists and their attention to the qualities of light. He wanted to capture the complex effects of light in his work, especially daylight and lamplight. Like many Danish artists of the last half of the nineteenth century, he was attracted to the beautiful, dramatic surroundings of Skagen in Denmark's northernmost cape and began spending time there. He began *"Hip Hip Hurrah!" Artists' Party at Skagen* probably around 1884, inspired by a gathering at the Danish painter Michael Ancher's house. The painting depicts a happy group of Scandinavians at an outdoor party. The men stand at the far end of the table toasting each other, while the women are seated near the viewer, looking on at their menfolk, almost indulgently. A young girl in a white dress with a large pink bow leans drowsily against her mother. The open and mostly empty bottles and glasses on the table show that this has been a long, relaxed celebration. The scene, framed by lush, green countryside, is bathed in soft, gentle sunlight. The countryside was not typical of Skagen's harsh, sandy seascape. Krøyer's picture captured and came to symbolize the camaraderie and sense of community felt by the artists who gathered in Skagen. **AV**

The Bedroom at Arles | Vincent van Gogh

1888 | oil on canvas | 22 ½ x 29 in / 57.5 x 74 cm | Musée d'Orsay, Paris, France

Vincent van Gogh (1853–90) did the first version of this painting in the autumn of 1888, during one of the happiest interludes in his life. He believed that his move to Arles would mark a new chapter in his art. He asked his brother, Theo, to persuade Paul Gauguin to come and join him and rapidly painted a series of pictures to hang on the walls and create a welcoming atmosphere for his new guest. To a large extent, these paintings were designed simply as decorations for the house, but van Gogh also wanted to show that his own works could bear comparison with those of Gauguin's, whose talent he was in awe of. In *The Bedroom at Arles*, many of the items are shown in pairs—two chairs, two pillows, two pairs of pictures—signaling his expectation of companionship. Yet his friendship with

Gauguin turned sour just two months after his arrival and van Gogh had a mental breakdown. Recuperating in a lunatic asylum in St. Rémy, he painted this third version of the painting, for his mother. Although structurally very similar to the first two, certain details are significantly different. In the first version, van Gogh painted the floor a rosy pink; here it is a brownish-gray color, reflecting his more depressed mood. The two top right-hand paintings are different in each version as well. In the first two versions, the portraits are indistinct and cut off. In this version, though, they are very much discernible—the one on the left is van Gogh himself and the one on the right is of his sister, Wil. Ten months after he painted this picture, van Gogh committed suicide. **IZ**

Man Warping | Bruno Liljefors

1888 | oil on canvas | 47 ¼ x 58 ¼ in / 120 x 148 cm | Nationalmuseum, Stockholm, Sweden

Born in Uppsala, Sweden, Bruno Liljefors (1860–1939) was famous for his depictions of hunting life. Influenced by the evolutionist Charles Darwin, Liljefors became fascinated by anatomy and sought to paint realistic portrayals of his subjects. A frail child, Liljefors spent much of his childhood entertaining himself by drawing. As a teenager he was taken hunting, and developed a lifelong passion for the sport, and he later attributed this to his increased physical strength and improved health. After studying art at the Royal Academy in Stockholm, Liljefors moved to Germany, where he studied with the artist Carl Friedrich Deiker and began specializing in animal painting. He lived and worked in several European countries, and studied the art of the Impressionists and their depiction of light and color, which was so different from the darkness and somberness of German Realism. Liljefors eventually returned to Uppsala, where he struggled to survive as an artist for many years. In 1901, he received financial aid from a patron, however. Liljefors's 1906 exhibition established him as a reputable artist, particularly of wildlife subjects. *Man Warping* shows the influence of Impressionism on Liljefors's work. A soft, almost dreamy painting in pastel tones, *Man Warping* depicts a group of men gathered on a beach on a spring or summer's day. While some of the men are involved in a game, others crouch on the white sand or stand by silently watching. The scene is tranquil, relaxed, and peaceful; birds soar in the pinkish-blue sky and the sea gently laps at the sand. **AV**

Isabella Stewart Gardner
John Singer Sargent

1888 | oil on canvas | 74 ¾ x 31 ½ in / 190 x 80 cm
Isabella Stewart Gardner Museum, Boston, MA, USA

Sunflowers
Vincent van Gogh

1888 | oil on canvas | 36 ¼ x 28 ¾ in / 92 x 73 cm
National Gallery, London, UK

After the debacle surrounding the *Madame X* (1884) portrait, John Singer Sargent (1856–1925) revived his career in London. He also gained portrait commissions from fellow Americans, and the most important of these came from Isabella Stewart Gardner, the founder of the museum in Boston that bears her name. In comparison with *Madame X*, Isabella's portrait was a model of decorum, but her décolletage still created a stir when it was shown in Boston, and her husband asked her never to exhibit the picture publicly again. The model's pose is both frontal and symmetrical, an unusual combination in Sargent's work, although the picture's most striking feature is the background. This was based on a piece of fifteenth-century velvet brocade. Sargent enlarged the pattern considerably to create a halo effect around Isabella's head. As a result, the picture has the air of a religious icon. **IZ**

Vincent van Gogh (1853–90) painted a series of sunflower paintings to decorate the "Yellow House" in Arles, France, which he hoped to share with Paul Gauguin. This is the most famous of the series and one of the most famous pictures in the world. The flowers are set against a flat, butter-yellow background, separated from the darker ocher of the table top by a sketchily drawn blue line. The interplay between the color and lines of the table top, wall, and two-tone vase binds the surface of the painting together, and echos the design of Japanese prints. The angular yellow petals are thickly painted with an almost manic energy, while jabbing dabs of paint create the grainy texture of the deeper orange seedheads. Unlike the Impressionists, van Gogh was not trying to reproduce what he saw, but wanted to "use color more arbitrarily, so as to express myself with more force." **JW**

Self-Portrait with Bandaged Ear
Vincent van Gogh

1889 | oil on canvas | 23 ½ x 19 ½ in / 60 x 49 cm
Courtauld Institute of Art Gallery, London, UK

Few artists have recorded their own life as graphically as Vincent van Gogh (1853–90). In the last five years of his life, he produced more than forty self-portraits. This one, as the bandage confirms, was painted shortly after his breakdown. In 1888, Vincent moved to Arles, France, and invited Paul Gauguin to join him. Unfortunately, Gauguin's arrogance and van Gogh's fragile mental state proved a disastrous combination, and Gauguin fled. In despair, the Dutchman sliced off his left earlobe and sent it to a local prostitute. The artist painted two striking self-portraits, showing the extent of his injury. His main intention was to reassure his brother, and it is significant that van Gogh included a Japanese print of Mount Fuji in the background. He was passionately fond of these colorful images, which exerted a strong influence on his own style, and wanted to show that his optimism was returning. **IZ**

Georg Brandes at the University in
Copenhagen | Harald Slott-Møller

1889 | oil on canvas | 36 x 32 in / 92 x 81 cm
Detroit Institute of Arts, Detroit, MI, USA

This portrait is seen as the changing point in Harald Slott-Møller's (1864–1937) artistic career; leaving the completeness of Naturalism in favor of a visual language dominated by detail, symbols, and a new aesthetic. In *Georg Brandes at the University in Copenhagen*, the artist portrays his good friend within a very constructed and simple setting. The blackboard, the dark brown podium, and Brandes's black coat and hair stand out in a strong contrast to the beige wall, to his white shirt, and to the light coming from the two lamps above him. Slott-Møller has presented the viewer with an elemental construct, visually as well as theoretically: a lecturer within a bare room only consisting of contrasting colors. In the following years Slott-Møller turned toward a more symbolic world, affirming his association with the Symbolists and his interest in the Pre-Raphaelites. **SML**

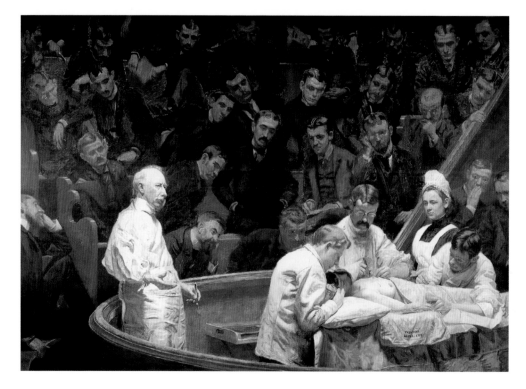

The Agnew Clinic | Thomas Eakins

1889 | oil on canvas | 84 x 118 ⅛ in / 213 x 300 cm | University of Pennsylvania, Philadelphia, PA, USA

Master of nineteenth-century American Realism Thomas Eakins (1844–1916) had spent time studying in Paris but, unlike many of his contemporaries, he chose to return to his homeland, intent on contributing to the establishment of a distinctly American School. Committed to a scientific approach to painting that drew upon his knowledge of anatomy and physics, he sought to both accurately record the truth of what he saw and convey the psychological meaning of his subjects. Instead of a more traditionally posed portrait, in *The Agnew Clinic* Eakins chose to depict Dr. David Agnew, Professor of Anatomy at the University of Pennsylvania, in the context of his lecture theater, mid-operation, surrounded by his assistants, and framed by his students. Agnew stands out, a beacon of knowledge and skill, illuminated against the dull and tangled mass of flatly painted students. The scalpel in his hand, a sign of his engagement with the operation to his left, shows that this is a man of practical achievement as well as academic learning. Like the many sportsmen Eakins also chose to paint, the doctor is depicted as a new type of American hero, one whose position is based on democratic public achievement rather than social status. Typical of the artist, the painting is informed by intense observation as well as research into anatomy, perspective, and motion. His approach to painting reinvigorated Realism and paved the way for the emergence of the early twentieth-century Ashcan School. **JB**

The Olive Pickers, Saint-Rémy, 1889 | Vincent van Gogh

1889 | oil on canvas | 28 ½ x 35 ⅜ in / 72.4 x 89.9 cm | Private collection

This painting dates from a pivotal point in Vincent van Gogh's (1853–90) brief life. Artistically, he had reached his peak, producing pictures that were radically different from those of his contemporaries. His fragile health, however, had started to fail him. Following a breakdown in December 1888, he was admitted to the asylum of Saint-Paul-de-Mausole in Saint Rémy. During his lengthy period of recuperation, van Gogh began painting olive trees. In all, he produced fourteen canvases on this subject between the summer of 1889 and the following spring, including this harvest-time scene. Van Gogh liked to express his emotions through natural forms and the olive trees proved an ideal vehicle for conveying his personal anguish. The gnarled, twisting branches of the trees reminded him of human arms, outstretched and yearning; the artist's agitated but controlled brushstrokes conveying a calm cry for help. In addition, there were the biblical associations. For van Gogh, who had been a lay preacher in his youth, they were inextricably linked with Christ's suffering in the Garden of Gethsemane, on the Mount of Olives. The biblical link was in the forefront of van Gogh's mind, because in 1889 Gauguin painted a version of Christ in the Garden of Olives in which he replaced Christ's features with his own. Van Gogh admired the concept, but was never comfortable with the idea of producing imaginary scenes himself. He preferred to give "an expression of anguish without aiming at the historic Garden of Gethsemane." **IZ**

The Conflagration | Albert Bierstadt

1860–90 | oil on paper | Worcester Art Museum, Worcester, MA, USA

Albert Bierstadt (1830–1902) was born in Solingen, Germany, then moved with his family to New Bedford, Massachusetts, at the age of two. In 1853, he returned to Germany to train with members of the Düsseldorf School. He taught drawing briefly before deciding to devote himself to painting. On his return to America, he began painting the landscape of New England and upstate New York. In 1859, he traveled westward in the company of a land surveyor to make sketches of the majestic mountain landscapes, which he later developed into paintings on enormous canvases, dwarfing those of his contemporaries and causing criticism and resentment in some cases. After renting a studio in New York, his reputation grew. People on the East Coast found his paintings thrilling, avidly buying them for large sums of money, but contemporary critics were unimpressed by the almost sentimental evocation of such wild landscapes, featuring mists and clouds with what they considered exaggerated light effects. This style later became known as Luminism. In *The Conflagration*, Bierstadt shows his skill in depicting clouds, in this instance contrasted with the oily blackness of the smoke issuing from the burning building. The result is atmospheric and dramatic. A member of the Hudson River School—two generations of American artists who were inspired by the romantic images of the American wilderness painted by Thomas Cole—Bierstadt's love of mountain landscapes led to Mount Bierstadt in Colorado being named in his honor. **TS**

Wheat Field with Crows | Vincent van Gogh

1890 | oil on canvas | 20 x 40 ½ in / 50.5 x 103 cm | Van Gogh Museum, Amsterdam, Netherlands

This is one of van Gogh's final pictures. It was painted in Auvers in July 1890, shortly before his suicide. According to some reports, it is actually the same field where the artist shot himself. In a brief note about the scene, van Gogh said: "Returning there, I set to work. The brush almost fell from my hands . . . I had no difficulty in expressing sadness and extreme solitude." Echoes of the artist's despair are plainly evident in the painting. Elements of the natural world, which he had so often celebrated joyously in his art, have now taken on a threatening tone. The overripe corn does not sway gently; it pulsates, almost like a raging fire. Above, the sky darkens and huge black crows, reduced to simple stabs of paint, advance toward the viewer, like portents of death. Even the structure of the picture is unsettling. Instead of converging toward the horizon, the composition is pulled toward the foreground by three rough paths. The two at the side disappear off the canvas, while the central one ends abruptly. The spectator, like the artist, feels hemmed in. During his final years, van Gogh worked at phenomenal speed, sometimes completing one or two pictures in a day. He worked right through the hottest part of the afternoon, and there is a theory that his illness was brought on by sunstroke. This frenetic activity is clearly visible in the finished works. Van Gogh applied his paint very thickly, making no attempt to smooth out the surface or blend his colors carefully. This is what gives his paintings such a sense of intense and vibrant energy. **IZ**

Poole Harbor | Philip Wilson Steer

1890 | oil on canvas | 18 x 24 in / 45.5 x 62 cm | Leeds City Art Gallery, UK

Philip Wilson Steer (1860–1942) was the son of an undistinguished English portrait painter Paul Wilson Steer (1810–71). He did not initially pursue a career in the arts but, after being unsuccessful in his entrance exams for the civil service, he studied first at the Gloucester School of Art and then at the South Kensington Drawing School. Between 1882 and 1884, he lived in Paris, where James McNeill Whistler (1834–1903), Édouard Manet (1832–83), and the French Impressionists were a profound influence on him. Upon his return to England, he developed his style of British Impressionism painting landscapes and beach scenes of incredible beauty, distinctive by their silver, translucent light. This painting of Poole Harbor was one of several scenes of harbors that

the artist painted and is an excellent example of the atmospheric effect that he was able to capture. It is an infinitely tranquil image of silver blue enlivened by the dark rowboats that form a pattern across the surface leading the eye from the foreground diagonally past the jutting harbor and beyond. Steer continually explored the depiction of light, and concentrated on breaking up his colors, somewhat in the manner of Claude Monet (1840–1926), to achieve the shimmering quality seen here and in so many of his works. Steer is generally considered the leader of British Impressionism, along with Walter Sickert (1860–1942), and was also the founder of the New English Art Club, which from 1886 offered an alternative to the Royal Academy. **TP**

Snow-covered Buildings by a River | Fritz Thaulow

1890 | oil on canvas | Private collection

Fritz (also known as Frits) Thaulow (1847–1906) is—after Edvard Munch (1863–1944), who was his pupil—probably the most celebrated of Norwegian artists. He originally intended to be a marine painter, but after studying in Karlsruhe, Germany, with Norwegian Hans Gude, Thaulow decided to become a landscape painter. He continued his studies in Pris between 1875 and 1879 and there was greatly influenced by the French Realists. He shared with Claude Monet (1840–1926) the preference for outdoor painting, and the two men spent a summer together working *en plein air*. Thaulow avoided repetition by constantly changing location. He spent time in various parts of France, Spain, Italy, Belgium, and the Netherlands—all of which provided contrasting subjects for his versatile brush. Although he admired the Impressionists (Gauguin was his brother-in-law), he did not regard his work as being of that school. Indeed, in Norway his progressive techniques were hailed as something completely original in that nation's art. Thaulow was particularly adept at capturing the play of light on water, and many of his paintings—including this one—feature rivers, lakes, and canals. This urban scene demonstrates the artist's versatility in capturing the subtle reflections in the dim light of a Norwegian midwinter, and the complex eddies on the slow-flowing river. Thaulow was also noted for his wintry scenes and reveled in depicting snow in all its manifestations, from pristine whiteness to sludgy thaw. **TS**

By Lamplight | Harriet Backer

1890 | oil on canvas | 21 x 26 in / 55 x 66.5 cm | Rasmus Meyers Samlinger, Bergen, Norway

In the latter part of the nineteenth century, art in Scandinavia was heavily influenced by the latest developments in Paris. Naturalism was the most pervasive style, while the work of the Impressionists led to a greater interest in the depiction of light. Harriet Backer (1845–1932), one of the leading artists in Norway, was deeply affected by these trends. She soon adopted the techniques associated with *plein air* painting although, rather than applying them to the more obvious field of landscape painting, she preferred to record the way that daylight falls as it enters a room. Backer herself described this as *"plein air* in the interior." By the 1890s she expanded this theme to include artificial sources of light. *By Lamplight* is arguably the greatest of these nighttime

scenes, and received generous acclaim when it was shown at the Autumn Exhibition in Kristiania (modern Oslo) in 1890. One critic compared it favorably with Edvard Munch (1863–1944). The nocturnal scenes added a new dimension to Backer's style: her daylight scenes were highly naturalistic but, in the night pictures, there is a much stronger emphasis on mood. Here, the light from the oil lamp and the fire in the stove are rendered with the artist's typical accuracy, but the looming shadows suggest an air of mystery. The darkness also accentuates the loneliness and isolation of the figure—a theme explored by other prominent Scandinavian artists, such as Munch and Vilhelm Hammershøi (1864–1916). **IZ**

Country Festival | Anders Zorn

1890 | oil on canvas | 17 ¾ x 14 ⅛ in / 45 x 36 cm | Pushkin Museum, Moscow, Russia

Anders Zorn (1860–1920) sprang from humble beginnings, but became one of Sweden's greatest artists. The Swedish painter and etcher traveled widely, spending time in England, Spain, and North Africa, and took international commissions, including portraits of three American presidents. His talent was first recognized in his wooden sculptures but he soon turned toward painting in watercolor, which was unusual at the time. This remained his primary media until he traveled to Cornwall in England in the late 1880s. This was a turning point in his career and saw him working in oils for the first time. An early oil painting, *A Fisherman in St. Ives*, was exhibited at the Paris Salon in 1888 and bought by the French state. One of the overriding aspects of Zorn's work, and in particular that of the 1890s, was his treatment of light. Here in *Country Festival*, his use of thick, white, dry paint scattered through the canvas creates a flickering effect of brilliant sunlight reflecting off moving forms. He has composed the painting so that the white shirts form a gentle diagonal that draws the eye in through the picture and along the line of dancers in a most effective way. The rapid brushstrokes and crumbly quality of the paint add to the sense of energy and movement in the painting. Zorn was a tremendously innovative painter and he strove to define new boundaries and develop new techniques in his work, most famously seen in his experiments with depicting water, one of his favorite motifs. **TP**

Lovemaking in the Evening | Fritz Syberg

1889–91 | oil on canvas | 40 x 60 in / 101.5 x 153 cm | Nationalmuseum, Stockholm, Sweden

Fritz Syberg (1862–1939), together with Peter Hansen and Johannes Larsen, created an association of artists in Copenhagen known as the Funen painters, who actively defined Danish Impressionism. In the late 1800s, Impressionism and Post-Impressionism experienced a delayed but forceful entry into Danish and Scandinavian art, as museums and collectors invested in French artists such as Paul Gauguin, also an influential friend to the Funen group. The Nordic artists adopted the emotional elements of Impressionism, molding an entirely new style of Nordic painting that adapted the Impressionist palette and *pointilliste* techniques to their own countryside and character. *Lovemaking in the Evening* portrays a courting couple exchanging a few words by the roadside after a day's work. Standing apart from the crowd, they hold their arms defensively yet express an empathic similitude. The tilt of the gentleman's hat is bold in line and color, rivaling only the arching road behind them for visual dominance, while the woman stands expectant but reserved. The road suggests the path of marriage, while the clouds signify the turmoil and moodiness of love. The small path at left is both the man's escape and his access—both his path home and the way he will return again for a similar exchange. After the death of his first wife, Syberg married the sister of his fellow painter Peter Hansen. *Lovemaking in the Evening* perhaps suggests Syberg's own courtship, one that would have taken place apart from the community, but also witnessed by it. **SWW**

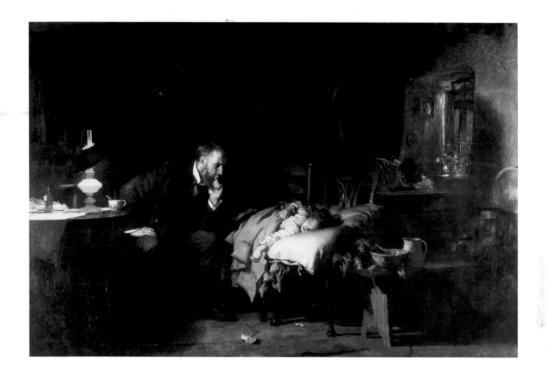

The Doctor | Sir Luke Fildes

1891 | oil on canvas | 65 ½ x 95 ¼ in / 166.5 x 242 cm | Tate Collection, London, UK

Sir Luke Fildes (1843–1927) was a painter and illustrator who made his name with a series of works dealing with contemporary social issues. *The Doctor* was probably the most famous of these. It became a star attraction at London's Tate Gallery when it opened in 1897. In the latter part of the nineteenth century, the growth of literacy brought an increasing range of illustrated magazines onto the market, which in turn offered greater opportunities for artists. One of the most significant new arrivals was *The Graphic*, which first appeared in 1869 and made a splash with its full-page engravings of everyday, working life. Fildes was a regular contributor and often turned his popular illustrations into full-size paintings. The somber realism of his work impressed the tycoon Sir Henry

Tate, who commissioned him to paint a subject of his own choosing. Fildes opted for *The Doctor*, a theme that was inspired by the death of his first child in 1877. He translated this memory into a working-class setting, creating an elaborate mock-up of a fisherman's cottage in his studio. In artistic terms, Fildes's main concern was with the dual light source, showing the contrast between the warm glow of the oil lamp and the bleak, first glimmerings of daylight. For the public, however, the picture's lasting achievement lay in its moving depiction of the doctor's devotion. The medical profession was well aware of this and instructed its students to "remember always to hold before you the ideal figure of Luke Fildes's picture, and be at once gentle men and gentle doctors." **IZ**

In the Souk | Moritz Stifter

1891 | oil on panel | 16 x 12 ½ in / 41 x 32 cm | Berko Fine Paintings, Knokke-Zoute, Belgium

Austrian artist Moritz Stifter (1857–1905) made a living painting Near Eastern subjects, a popular genre with Europeans throughout the nineteenth century. The taste for "oriental" exotica started with Napoleon's invasion of Egypt at the beginning of the century. It was fueled by literature, prints, and paintings by Western travelers to the Ottoman Empire, who included the novelist Gustave Flaubert, the anthropologist E.W. Lane, and the explorer Richard Burton, who famously translated the "unexpurgated" version of *One Thousand and One Nights*. By the late nineteenth century, mass tourism had arrived and was sufficiently common for the writer Mark Twain to write a spoof of a tour group traveling to the Holy Land. Thomas Cook's company was running tours to

Egypt, where grand hotels had been built along the banks of the Nile to cater for travelers seeking winter sun. *In the Souk* is a painting about tourism and fantasy. The elegantly dressed Western lady fingers a proffered tablecloth with a gloved hand. The gesture of the fez-wearing merchant suggests the exquisite quality of the piece under discussion. This scene, familiar to tourists even today, is almost photographic in its realism, yet it was almost certainly created in Stifter's studio in Haag in Lower Austria, using props such as the hookah and the coffee table, which he kept handy for his genre painting. Despite criticism from the late Edward Said, who argued that such falsified depictions of the Near East amounted to a form of racism, Orientalist works remain very popular at auction. **CR**

A Break Away! | Tom Roberts

1891 | oil on canvas | 54 x 66 ⅛ in / 137.5 x 168 cm | Art Gallery of South Australia, Adelaide, Australia

Born in Dorchester, England, Thomas William Roberts (1856–1931) emigrated with his widowed mother to Australia in 1869, where they settled in a suburb of Melbourne. He became a photographer's assistant, a job he kept for ten years, while studying art at night under Louis Buvelot. Roberts became the first major Australian painter to study at the Royal Academy of Arts, London, which he did for three years from 1881. He also studied Impressionism in Europe, returning to Australia in 1885 where he dedicated himself to painting the light and color of the bush. Roberts became foundation president of the Society of Artists in 1895 and was one of the first to paint outback subjects; *Shearing the Rams* and *A Break Away!* are among his best known works. Many of his contemporaries

considered the life of ordinary Australians an unfit subject for "fine" art, but his studies of life in the bush were to become his most enduring creations, loved by subsequent generations of Australians for their dignified and affectionate depiction of working people. *A Break Away!* certainly earns the exclamation mark of the title, showing a tumultuous chase, as a drover charges headlong down a steep slope after an escaped sheep. The rising dust, the panic-stricken animals, and the barking dog all give the impression of a bit of welcome action in an otherwise uneventful day. Whether it was sheepshearing, wood splitting, or droving, Roberts's paintings are heartfelt, exhilarating works that capture the spirit of nineteenth-century working Australians. **TS**

Haystack at Sunset, Frosty Weather | Claude Monet

1891 | oil on canvas | 25 ½ x 36 ¼ in / 65 x 92 cm | Private collection

Today the name Claude Monet (1840–1926) is virtually synonymous with the artistic movement known as Impressionism. Indeed, the name of the movement derives from a painting the artist himself executed in 1873, entitled *Impression, Sunrise*. If there is one salient aspect that sets Monet's oeuvre apart from his fellow Impressionists, it would perhaps be his meticulous exploration of the behavior of natural light at different times. Monet's *Haystack* (also known as "Grainstack") series was painted between 1890 and 1891, and reflected the artist's passion for rendering his everyday experiences. The stacks themselves stood directly behind his house in Giverny. The series as a whole tracks the effects light, both seasonal and during different times of the day, has upon the appearance

and the actual structure of the haystack. In *Haystack at Sunset, Frosty Weather*, the haystack occupies the left foreground of the painting wherein its apex abuts the line of the horizon. This subtly elevates the painting from being merely an instance of naturalistic description to something which is entirely more abstract. The stack is seen in shadow and forms a silhouette that, although it is set apart from its immediate surroundings, provides continuity through Monet's palette, which is comprised of a significant amount of white. What Monet brings to such an apparently mundane subject is a sense of wonder and awe, and renders concrete the idea that nature, far from being static and fixed, is in fact dynamic and even revelatory. **CS**

Haystack in the Morning, Snow Effect | Claude Monet

1891 | oil on canvas | 25 ¾ x 36 ⅜ in / 65.5 x 92.5 cm | Museum of Fine Arts, Boston, MA, USA

In October 1890, Claude Monet (1840–1926) wrote in a letter to his future biographer Gustave Geffroy: "I am hard at it, grinding away at a series of different effects, but at this time of the year the sun sets so quickly I cannot keep up with it. . . ." He was describing his *Haystack* ("Grainstack") series of paintings, and went on to say that what he was after was what he called "instantaneity"—the "enveloppe" of light that unifies a scene for an instant, before changing to create a new momentary effect. Though the paintings were begun out of doors, they were "harmonized" in the studio, and Monet intended them to be viewed together. Compare this image to *Haystack at Sunset, Frosty Weather* (opposite). The powerful compositions are very similar, with an almost abstract simplicity. But in

Frosty Weather the stack and the entire scene glow hot in the fiery sunset, while in this painting the dark shape of the haystack is enveloped in the chilly light of a late winter afternoon, and set against the ice blue of the snow-covered field and the cool blue of the landscape "band" behind it. The winter sun is low in the sky, and lights the stack from behind, casting a long elliptical shadow across the canvas. When fifteen Haystack paintings were exhibited together in 1891, the show was a triumph. Critics not only saw Monet's unique rendering of light effects, but also responded to the French rural subject matter. The artist may also have been concerned with the haystacks themselves as symbols of the fertility and prosperity of the French agricultural landscape. **JW**

The Flowered Dress | Édouard Vuillard

1891 | oil on canvas | 20 x 32 ½ in / 51 x 83 cm | Museu de Arte de São Paulo, Brazil

Édouard Vuillard (1868–1940) lived with his mother for sixty years as she ran her corsetière in a succession of apartments around Paris. After her husband died in 1878, Vuillard's mother set up a dressmaking business. It was in such private observations that the stay-at-home child sharpened his eye for detail through the colors, materials, patterns, and shapes of the dresses. Many of this French painter's most touching works, including *The Flowered Dress*, record with exquisite intimacy his mother and sister sewing and sorting fabrics with other women in the workroom. Influenced by Gauguin and Japanese woodcuts, Vuillard shared a studio with Pierre Bonnard and together they developed the Intimist style of painting. Then with other artists they formed the Post-Impressionist *Nabis* (Hebrew for "prophet"). This group sought to go beyond Gauguin's pure color approach to render beautiful, symbolic harmonies. Certainly Vuillard captured these harmonies gloriously in his small-scale, "snug" scenes, heightened by his flat patterns taken from the textiles themselves. The part reflection (in this case of the emphatically patterned dress) in the mantelpiece mirror was a technique Vuillard used recurringly. What is extraordinary is how he could project this intimate vision onto large murals (he painted murals and designs in many public buildings) without losing his sure touch and detailed observation. Sadly, his later paintings are often written off as merely competent compared to his earlier nineteenth-century work. **JH**

Tiger in a Tropical Storm | Henri Rousseau

1891 | oil on canvas | 51 1/8 x 63 3/4 in / 130 x 162 cm | National Gallery, London, UK

The naive and primitive style of Henri Rousseau's (1844–1910) work is instantly recognizable, yet in his time and for some years after his death, the artist was repeatedly ridiculed and his work deemed "childish." He was born in Laval in the Loire Valley and raised within fairly impoverished circumstances. He spent four years in the army before moving to Paris in 1868 and working as a clerk in a law office. Rousseau did not turn to art until late in his life: his first known work, *Landscape with a Watermill* is dated 1879, and he did not launch his public artistic career until 1885. *Tiger in a Tropical Storm* (or *Surprised!*) is the first of the series of jungle scenes that Rousseau painted, and was exhibited at the Salon des Indépendants in 1891. The artist claimed that he had encountered such exotic jungle scenes while serving as a regimental bandsman in Mexico in 1860, but in fact, he had never left France. It is more likely that his inspiration came from the botanical gardens in Paris including the Jardin des Plantes. Rousseau worked from the background to the foreground layering his paint meticulously, and using an enormous range of greens to express the verdant lushness of the jungle. To achieve the slashing rain he devised a method of trailing thin silver strands of paint diagonally across the canvas, adding to the unusual three-dimensional effect of the work. Though derided by critics of the period, Rousseau's work was much admired by some of his fellow artists, including Matisse, Picasso, Toulouse-Lautrec, and Robert Delaunay. **TP**

The Punishment of Lust | Giovanni Segantini

1891 | oil on canvas | 92 ½ x 50 ¾ in / 235 x 129 cm | Walker Art Gallery, Liverpool, UK

Giovanni Segantini (1858–99) was raised by relatives in Milan. He visited the Alps as a child and they remained a significant source of his inspiration. He began his career as a decorative artist. Around 1880, the art critic and art dealer Vittore Grubicy de Dragon discovered and adopted him into the roster of artists whose participation in local and international exhibitions he sponsored. Encouraged by Grubicy to experiment with Divisionism, Segantini expanded beyond painting idyllic pastoral scenes toward using light to convey spirituality. *The Punishment of Lust*, which is also known as *The Punishment of Luxury*, was part of a series infused with Catholic symbolism that Segantini painted between 1891 and 1896 on the theme of "bad mothers" (*cattive madri*).

In Segantini's painting, the souls of the two women are seen floating over the Alps. Their isolation in the mountains, below heaven, is punishment for their having lost unborn children, either through abortion or through neglect. Segantini, whose mother died when he was a young child, passionately believed that motherhood was a woman's sole purpose and that any woman who refused the role of mother was committing a natural sin. Despite having relegated his figures to the Alps as the site of their eternal punishment, Segantini's last recorded words were "I want to see my mountains." After his death, his work developed a wide and diverse range of admirers: Munch, Ensor, and Kandinsky were all awestruck by Segantini's sensual and spiritual paintings. **AH**

The Moret Bridge in the Sun | Alfred Sisley

1892 | oil on canvas | 23 x 28 in / 58.5 x 71 cm | Private collection

Alfred Sisley (1839–99) was born in Paris, the son of English parents. After meeting Monet and Renoir in the 1860s he became associated with the Impressionist group, although he was always a relatively marginal, private personality. Monet had an enduring impact upon Sisley's landscape art, but his work also reflects the influence of Corot, with his gentle feeling for nature. In 1880 Sisley settled in Moret-sur-Loing, a small town of largely medieval buildings on the edge of Fontainebleau forest. During the last two decades of Sisley's life the town and its surroundings became the main subject of his paintings. Sometimes he produced series showing the same view in different atmospheric conditions, but mostly the variation of viewpoints and light in the

different works is less systematic. Sisley painted the bridge at Moret on a number of occasions. This work, painted in 1892, is solidly structured in contrasting areas of water, buildings, and sky, with reflections fastening the town and river together. As in almost all of Sisley's work, human figures are few and small. This is a townscape that aspires to the calm solitude of landscape. With no device to lead the viewer's eye into the picture, the gaze is free to roam over the sundrenched medieval walls, the variegated surface of the water, and the soft luminous sky. Sisley adapts his brushstroke and color with consummate skill to the demands of different areas of the picture. The gentle, charming, seductive quality of Sisley's painting can easily lead to its being underrated. **RG**

Circus
Georges Seurat

1891 | oil on canvas | 73 x 59 ⅞ in / 185.5 x 152 cm
Musée d'Orsay, Paris, France

The last picture Georges Seurat (1859–91) painted was this unfinished, stylized depiction of the Parisian entertainment Cirque Fernando. Seurat considered it good enough to exhibit in 1891 and it was on show when he died suddenly of diphtheria. By the time he painted *Circus*, Seurat had abandoned his early interest in Naturalism. Whereas his adoption of the *pointilliste* style of dot painting had been inspired by the science of optics, here he explores the emotional qualities of color and line. The dashes of primary red, blue, and yellow are not deployed to create an illusion of artificial lighting but with expressive intent. Where Seurat's earlier large-scale works had been static, here all is movement. The arc of the ring and the foreground clown's curving streamer or curtain set up a vertiginous movement continued by the acrobatic bareback rider and the leaping clown. **RG**

Chica in a Bar
Ramón Casas

1892 | oil on canvas | 46 x 35 ½ in / 117 x 90 cm
Museo de la Abadia, Montserrat, Spain

Ramón Casas (1866–1932) was one of the foremost painters of *Modernisme*, a cultural movement striving to bring Catalan art on a par with the rest of Europe. Casas was also well known as a portraitist who sketched and painted the cultural and economic elite of Barcelona, Paris, and the rest of the world. In the first half of the 1890s he exhibited in Paris, Berlin, Madrid, and Chicago. *Chica in a Bar* is typical of his style at the time. The painting seems to lie somewhere between the French Impressionists and an academic style. The red of the girl's hair matches the strong color of her blouse and her drink. This is offset by the white of the skirt and the back wall. The girl's expression gives away little: perhaps she is shy, perhaps miserable, or maybe merely bored although she looks too involved with her surroundings for that to be the case. Either way, this is a fine example of Casas's gift for portraiture. **OR**

Young Girls at the Piano
Pierre-Auguste Renoir

1892 | oil on canvas | 45 ⁵⁄₈ x 35 ³⁄₈ in / 116 x 90 cm
Musée d'Orsay, Paris, France

Woman with a Birdcage
József Rippl-Rónai

1892 | oil on canvas | 73 ¼ x 51 ³⁄₈ in / 186 x 130.5 cm
Hungarian National Gallery, Budapest, Hungary

One of the best loved Impressionist painters, Pierre-Auguste Renoir (1844–1919) depicted Parisian daily life with the feathery touch of his brush and a palette heavy on pastels. His lovely, lush paintings of jolly crowds flirting and drinking, angelic children playing, voluptuous women bathing, and mothers cuddling their infants are still astoundingly popular. *Young Girls at the Piano* is one of Renoir's most enduring images and an excellent example of his frothy technique, known during this time as his "pearly" period, in which he replaced his linear drawing techniques with a more fluid brushstroke. In late 1891 or early 1892, he was invited by the French government to contribute to a new museum in Paris, the Musée du Luxembourg, devoted to the work of living artists. He produced five canvases in an attempt to perfect his vision of the intimacy of bourgeois domestic life. **AH**

József Rippl-Rónai (1861–1927) was a member of the *Nabis*, a group of Symbolist artists active in Paris in the 1890s. *Nabis* is Hebrew for "prophets" and the name refers to the zeal with which they promoted Gauguin's use of color. Rippl-Rónai developed his own style, with a severely limited palette. *Woman with a Birdcage* is typical of the dark interiors he produced at the time. The picture evokes the gloom of the drawing room with its heavy drapes and dark furnishings. The woman is bending slightly backward to balance the cage and its canary, which she is admiring. The curve of her back is in harmony with the curve at the back of the seat of the sofa behind her. She is dressed in a somber brown, yet she is a young attractive woman and her hat sits jauntily on her head—is her garb fashionable or funereal? The only bright patches are her hands and face, the cage, and its contents. **RA**

Ta Matete (We Shall Not Go to the Market Today) | Paul Gauguin

1892 | oil on canvas | 28 ¾ x 36 ¼ in / 73 x 92 cm | Kunstmuseum, Basel, Switzerland

By the time Paul Gauguin (1848–1903) reached his "paradise" in 1891, French colonialists and Christian missionaries had destroyed much of the culture. The Tahiti described in his preparatory reading no longer existed. In some works he attempted to reconstruct Tahiti through invented gods and myths, often drawing on other sources to do so. It was unusual for him to depict contemporary social reality as he does in Ta Matete, which shows a group of prostitutes. The title alludes to a flesh market and the women are shown holding their certificates of health. As if to emphasize the infiltration of Western decadence, he shows one woman with a cigarette in her hand. The women are seated in a row and are not making themselves available; soliciting seems to be the last thing on their minds. In spite of the small procession of fishermen in the background, the painting is as flat as an Egyptian frieze, probably inspired by a photograph of an Egyptian tomb which he took to Tahiti. The most striking feature of this colorful painting is the dancelike hand gestures of the women, and it is likely that Gauguin was drawing on the dance movements of Javanese dancers that he had seen at the Exposition Universelle, Paris, in 1889, which impressed him greatly at the time. Dance was an activity that was strongly discouraged by the colonialists. Gauguin frequently depicted song and dance as the last remnants of authentic culture yet his support for the indigenous people and their culture did not prevent an eclectic attitude to his painting. **WO**

The Bed | Henri de Toulouse-Lautrec

1892 | oil on cardboard | 21 x 27 in / 54 x 70.5 cm | Musée d'Orsay, Paris, France

Although Henri de Toulouse-Lautrec (1864–1901) was raised in the country, by the 1880s he was immersed in the Parisian scene and had become a true city dweller. During this period Lautrec was fascinated by the flamboyance and "life beneath the surface" of Paris after dark. He drew his inspiration from the cafes, circus, brothels, dance halls, and the people— especially the women whose swirling-colored forms were recreated through his paints and pencils. Lautrec sometimes lodged in brothels for weeks at a time and the prostitutes came to regard him as a friend. He concentrated on depicting the everyday aspects of their lives and was particularly sensitive in depicting the lesbian relationships that often developed between them. In the early 1890s Lautrec made a series of drawings and paintings of lesbians in their intimate surroundings and *The Bed* is part of this series. Here he has created an image of infinite ease and tenderness as the two women talk to each other, and he represents their lives with no attempt to moralize or glamorize. He also sets up a divergent dynamic between the voyeur and the sympathizer. Lautrec was primarily a documenter of character and his work is full of human sympathy: he often captured the fatigue masked by powdered faces, or the weariness of the prostitute at the end of the evening. There are few artists who equaled Lautrec in terms of sensitivity to subject combined with a strident, bold use of color, line, and movement, and he was truly one of the masters of nineteenth-century painting. **TP**

The Relic | Joaquín Sorolla y Bastida

c.1893 | oil on canvas | 41 x 49 ³/₈ in / 103.5 x 125.5 cm | Museo de Bellas Artes de Bilbao, Bilbao, Spain

Joaquín Sorolla y Bastida (1863–1923) was an incredibly prolific painter, one who developed his style through many diverse phases. Born in Valencia, his formative period was spent in Madrid, Paris, and Rome. Sorolla then centered his interest on capturing the immediacy of everyday life and the expressivity of popular figures. This period is defined by the term Social Realism due to its detailed style of depicting populist subjects, such as landscapes and portraits. Sorolla was also strongly influenced by classical painters, especially the work of Velázquez and Goya, whose paintings he admired. His early work was greatly accepted across Europe, evidenced by many honors and awards, including the Grand Prix at the Exposition Universelle in Paris. This period lasted until

the turn of the century, when Sorolla began to adopt the Impressionist features that characterized his later works. The Relic shows a line of women and children waiting to kiss a relic held by a priest. This simple scene takes place in a small Baroque chapel of a Valencian church. Sorolla emphasizes the aesthetic value of the daily ritual in the detail of his work. The figures' spontaneous gestures coupled with the close perspective help to convey the sensation of an ephemeral moment caught by the painter's eye. The Relic belongs to a period when Sorolla was focused on achieving a style that satisfied the Salon requirements, a nineteenth-century Realist tenet. Consequently he often chose Baroque backgrounds, as depicted here. **DC**

Storm Clouds | Karl Fredrik Nordström

1893 | oil on canvas | 28 x 31 in / 72 x 80 cm | Nationalmuseum, Stockholm, Sweden

The artist Karl Nordström (1855–1923) played a significant role in the development of Swedish landscape painting at the end of the nineteenth century, and through his active protests helped to break the rigidly conservative attitudes of Konstakademin in Stockholm. He studied at the academy he would later attack and while there met like-minded artists Richard Bergh (1858–1919) and Nils Kreuger (1858–1930), who became allies in their quest to find a new expression for their art. In 1882 Nordström visited Paris where he saw, and was greatly influenced by, the work of the Impressionists. By the time he painted *Storm Clouds* in 1893 he had also become interested in the works of Japanese artists, and the simple, bold composition here owes much to the Japanese woodblock prints that had become so popular at this time. There is an echo of Vincent van Gogh and Paul Gauguin present in this evocative painting that captures the dramatic scenery of Sweden's landscape, particularly evident in his treatment of the swirling sky. It is romantic in feel but expressed with a modern hand, and defines Sweden's scenery with a heroic and nationalist sense of pride. The same year he painted this work, Nordström moved to Varberg on the Swedish coast and established an artists' colony with his friends Bergh and Kreuger. Nordström was a strident voice for the arts during his life and a key contributor toward a new direction in Sweden's landscape painting in the twentieth century. **TP**

Summary
Gunnar Berndtson

1893 | oil on canvas | 24 x 17 ³/₈ in / 61 x 44 cm
Turku Art Museum, Finland

Finnish painter Gunnar Berndtson (1854–95) mainly depicted genre subjects. *Summer* brings together Finnish landscape and nineteenth-century bourgeois life. This romanticized view of a summer day is in direct contrast with the reality of Finnish life at the time, which was mostly agricultural and in places even impoverished. The languid mood of the painting speaks of the leisures of upper-class life; for most of the country, the summer would have been the time for farming and harvesting. The female figure appears to have been startled from her reading by the boy on the boat, or perhaps she is a doting mother or nanny. The landscape is unmistakably Nordic. Berndtson's attention to detail is impeccable: rocks can be seen under the water, the hazy summer sunlight is reflected on the surface of the lake, and the folds in the central figure's clothes are intricate and lifelike. **RK**

Loie Fuller at the Folies-Bergère
Henri de Toulouse-Lautrec

1893 | oil on cardboard | 24 ⁷/₈ x 17 ⁷/₈ in / 63 x 45.5 cm
Musée Toulouse-Lautrec, Albi, France

One of the colorful characters that Henri de Toulouse-Lautrec (1864–1901) was drawn to was the American dance pioneer Loie Fuller (1862–1928). In November 1892 she opened at the Folies-Bergère with four acts that caused a sensation in Paris. She used great swathes of silk that she twirled around her in a sensuous dance, using lighting and mirrors to heighten the effect. Lautrec captured her movement in this oil sketch, which he then used as a base for the design of a series of lithographs. It is this work, more than the lithographs, that retains the immediacy of movement, aided by the strong vertical lines. Although Lautrec had created posters for a number of stars, Fuller chose different artists for her promotional material. In a humorous act of revenge Lautrec included a dish called the *"Foie gras de l'oie Fuller"* on the menu for the opening dinner of the Salon des Indépendants in 1895. **TP**

The Scream
Edvard Munch

1893 | oil, tempera, and pastel on cardboard | 36 x 29 in / 91 x 73.5 cm | National Gallery, Oslo, Norway

This is one of the most familiar images in modern art. It stemmed from a terrifying panic attack suffered by the artist in 1892. Edvard Munch (1863–1944) described how it occurred, as he was strolling along a path outside Kristiania (now Oslo): "The sun was setting and the clouds turned as red as blood. I sensed a scream passing through nature. I felt as though I could actually hear the scream. I painted this picture, painted the clouds like real blood. The colors shrieked." Munch represented the scream through a series of undulating lines that pressed in on the figure like shock waves, reducing its face to a primal image of fear. He accentuated this effect by showing that his two companions were unscathed, thus implying that the trauma came from his own mind, rather than the world outside. On a copy of the picture, Munch wrote: "Could only have been painted by a madman." **IZ**

Oculi
Pál Szinyei Merse

1894 | oil on canvas | 23 5/8 x 18 5/8 in / 60.5 x 47.8 cm | Magyar Nemzeti Galeria, Budapest, Hungary

Pál Szinyei Merse (1845–1920) was a Hungarian artist and politician who produced some of the earliest works of Impressionism in Central Europe. In the late 1860s he began to experiment with color and light, and some critics believe that his *plein-air* technique influenced some of the later French Impressionists. Early in his career, critics harshly denounced his vivid use of color. It was not until the 1890s that Merse began to receive proper recognition for his work. Paintings such as the 1894 *Oculi* demonstrate Merse's interest in the effect of harmonious and contrasting colors and light. Essentially a rural landscape, *Oculi* shows a hunter out with his dog in typical Central European countryside. The colors are autumnal: rustic reds, greens, and browns. The hunter is neatly camouflaged in the underbrush, while the trees form strong verticals, drawing the eye down to him. **AV**

Norwegian Fishing Village | Laurits Bernard Holst

c.1894 | oil on canvas | 15 x 19 in / 38.1 x 48.3 cm | Russell-Cotes Art Gallery, Bournemouth, UK

Self-taught Danish itinerant marine painter Laurits Bernard Holst (1848–1934) traveled to the United States at the age of twenty. There he perfected the art of illustrating the sea, becoming a member of the Academy in Chicago in 1871. After the Great Chicago Fire of October 1871 he returned to Denmark, yet, he still felt the need for varied inspiration and traveled to England in 1873. Holst was fascinated by the sea, and both its roughness and its beauty became his constant inspirational source. *Norwegian Fishing Village* is composed in three sections: the mountains and the sky make up the background, the village is in the center, and the sea is in the foreground. The viewer is left wondering whether Holst used his imagination to conceive this view, or whether he actually sat in a small boat some distance from the shore. The sea is somber, gray, and icily uninviting, a typical depiction of the sea close to the Arctic Circle. With the use of gray color tones, and a slight hint of silver, Holst effectively conveys a sense of extreme cold. The village, which is nestled at the bottom of the fjord, appears tiny and somewhat insignificant compared to its rough surroundings. Rocks and steep mountainsides rise above and around the village, enclosing the inhabitants below. The wide recognition Holst received from the Danish and English royal houses, and the Russian Tsar, absolutely defined him as a well-respected, self-taught marine painter. Fittingly, after his death his ashes were scattered on the sea off the coast at Bournemouth. **SML**

Painting the Birds | Franz Dvorak

1885–95 | oil on canvas | 55 x 36 ¼ in / 140 x 92 cm | Private collection

Symbolism originated in France but spread across Europe in the late nineteenth century. The Symbolist movement was pivotal for the development of later movements such as Expressionism and Surrealism. As an escape from a materialistic world, this artistic genre brought fantasy and imagination to the fore. Influenced by both Romanticism and the Pre-Raphaelites, Symbolist painters opposed the visual realism of the Impressionists and the seriousness of the Industrial Age, wishing to provoke mysterious and ambiguous interpretations of emotions by using symbols. Hungarian artist Franz Dvorak (1862–1927) produced works that encourage flights of the imagination in the viewer. In his *Painting the Birds*, a beautiful young woman is seen holding a large shell palette in the crook of her left arm, a paintbrush in the other. Below her are two *putti* (the plump naked boys often seen in Renaissance, Mannerist, Baroque, and Rococo art) with their angel wings barely discernible amid the flurry of activity. Their presence symbolizes love, whether divine or of a more earthly nature. The group, painted in a dreamlike manner, is caught up in the wonder of representing multicolored birds on canvas—in a sense, capturing them from life. Dvorak's energetic brushstrokes and colorful swirls suggest vital creativity of an indirect and esoteric nature. As an artist he was more interested in the expression of inner life than artistic style or form. *Painting the Birds* is designed to produce a sense of emotional uplift in the viewer that resonates with the innocent joy of the group. **AA**

The Boy in the Red Waistcoat | Paul Cézanne

1894–95 | oil on canvas | 31 x 25 in / 80 x 64 cm | E.G. Bührle Collection, Zürich, Switzerland

The Boy in the Red Waistcoat could only be by Paul Cézanne (1839–1906), with his distinctive style that was so progressive for its time. He mixed Impressionism with classicism and an intense intellectualism. *The Boy in the Red Waistcoat* is a straightforward portrait that, on closer study, dissolves into something very different. Cézanne produced several paintings of this red-vested model. This one is a strikingly modern essay in color and form, with distinctive blocks of red, brown, blue or blue-green, and white with clear-cut, simple shapes. The limited palette creates harmony, borrowing colors from one area to use on another. Blue-green shadows on the skin and shirt unify the picture and place the boy and his surroundings on the same plane. A series of diagonals intersect and echo each other: the curtain on the left, the boy's bent back, his left arm, and the right arm resting on a surface that tips away from the picture plane. Cézanne has dismantled an ordinary scene and rebuilt it from scratch. *The Boy in the Red Waistcoat* shows two of the artist's main preoccupations. Firstly, exploring the underlying structure of the world around him; and secondly, solving the puzzle of representing a three-dimensional world on a flat, painted surface that still says something about the forms being depicted. Cézanne has succeeded here. His painting works as a whole while paving a way to the Cubist work of Braque and Picasso, who famously called Cézanne the "father" of modern painting. **AK**

In the Garden | Édouard Vuillard

1894–95 | oil on canvas | 20 x 32 ½ in / 51 x 83 cm | Pushkin Museum of Fine Arts, Moscow, Russia

Édouard Vuillard's (1868–1940) art is associated with the interplay of family and friends in comfortable, at times claustrophobic, interiors where dappled patterns and dusky colors play against a flattened sense of space. Often the figures seem to disappear into the patterns. Yet the artist, who was influenced by symbolic and spiritual art, was equally at home with his many studies of Parisian public parks and gardens, especially his series of large, wall-panel decorations for private patrons. In such outdoor scenes, the French artist showed an altogether lighter, warmer, fresher touch and, apart from the fin-de-siècle fashions, a thoroughly modern feel. Here two ladies seek shade and company on a wicker chair and stool. They are mothers or nurses perhaps, watching after young children playing out of view. The mottled shadows and light on the gravel are subtly and delightfully exposed and the sunlit patches "feel" warm. Vuillard gives the gardens an Impressionistic character without ever losing his trademark Intimist lyricism. Some years later he was to use his Kodak Brownie camera to snap his family and friends at every opportunity. Although not a man of the world, he was neither entirely isolated. From 1900 to 1940 Vuillard continued both indoor and outdoor studies, as well as more formal portraits and large-scale decorations and murals (including the League of Nations in Geneva in 1939), but his style became somewhat blander and formal and he never quite bettered his supreme Post-Impressionist oeuvre of the 1890s. **JH**

Woman Sewing Before a Garden | Édouard Vuillard

1895 | oil on paper and canvas | 12 x 14 ½ in / 30.5 x 37 cm | Museum of Fine Arts, Boston, MA, USA

"Intimist" is how Édouard Vuillard's (1868–1940) style has been labeled, and from this compact and muted study of his mother one can see why. She is absorbed in her needlework, oblivious to her son's nearby refinements and tiny touches on the canvas. The viewer can imagine perhaps a touching conversation unfolding as Madame Vuillard, not looking up, takes pleasure in her son's company and vice versa. The artist invites one's eyes to wander over his rich mosaiclike detail where discreet areas of neutral color and pale light play on an intimate scene to create a great atmosphere of calm. The patterns given out by the sunlight behind the lattice-work shutters, for example, add to the sense of life being quietly played out by the bent figure sewing by the window. That was Vuillard's mastery: he transformed his home interiors, in themselves nothing special for a bourgeois home in the city of Paris, into magical reflections of sublime beauty. Vuillard never married, sharing his life instead with his widowed mother—his "muse" as he described her—until her death in 1928. They lived together in fin-de-siècle Paris in a host of rooms that became, via his sensitive brushstrokes, the set pieces of their joint lives. Not surprisingly, most of his charming paintings are domestic scenes. Madame Vuillard was a dressmaker, and this inspired Vuillard's interests in textiles and patterns and his almost obsessive attention to these decorative aspects on the canvas. His mother's fine, shimmering blouse is a case in point. **JH**

Interior | Peter Vilhelm Ilsted

1896 | oil on canvas | 27 ⅝ x 27 ½ in / 70.5 x 70 cm | Musée d'Orsay, Paris, France

Peter Vilhelm Ilsted (1861–1933) was one of the foremost late-nineteenth to early-twentieth-century artists in Denmark. His work expresses the essence of contemporary life in Copenhagen and his figures are removed from the political and social turmoil that affected southern Denmark at the time. Tranquillity, neatness, contentment, and peace are the main subjects of his work and his figures merely appear to emphasize this. Heavily influenced by seventeenth-century Dutch genre painting, Ilsted belonged to the Copenhagen Interior School, which concentrated on painting interiors bathed in subtle light. Ilsted's accomplished style and use of color articulate the tonal gradation and shimmering highlights of this quiet interior. The sparsely furnished room is delicately lit by diffused sunlight filtering through the window. The still coolness of the room, the dappling of light over the walls, furniture, and floors, and the tactile appeal of the fabrics and glass, create equanimity and quietude. Sensitively applied paint in muted and understated colors emphasizes the plainness of the interior, while minimal furniture and a few homely objects contribute to the simplistic composition. Nothing dramatic or assertive disrupts the atmosphere of peaceful serenity as the girl quietly replaces a jug in a dresser, going about her daily business. The female figure often plays an important role in Ilsted's work. This intimate and voyeuristic style echoes Degas's works and emerged as photography became more accessible. **SH**

Still Life with Wine and Chestnuts | Albert Anker

1897 | oil on canvas | 15 ³/₈ x 17 ³/₄ in / 39 x 45 cm | Private collection

Despite much vitality in painting between 1750 and 1850, a truly Swiss school of art failed to materialize. French-speaking Swiss artists ventured to Paris, German-speaking to Berlin, Dresden, or Düsseldorf, and Italian Swiss artists settled in Rome or Florence. The Realist painter Albert Anker (1831–1910), who moved to Paris in 1854 to study with Charles Gleyre (1806–74), another Swiss artist, belongs to this group of expatriates. By the 1860s many of Switzerland's artists were working in mainstream Europe, having established careers outside of their country. The majority of Anker's paintings, although essentially "Swiss," would not be out of place alongside those of Barbizon artists in France or Victorian art in England. *Still Life with Wine and Chestnuts* employs an almost analytical rendering of surfaces and objects to convey the expressive power of everyday things. The lugubrious background sets off the luminous wine carafe and glass perfectly. In the foreground a dish of chestnuts rests on a linen tablecloth. Devoid of artifice, the artist masterfully explores the quality of light and volume and betrays both Dutch and Caravaggesque influences. Accuracy of depiction was particularly prized in Swiss art and in still life generally. Other quintessential traits include a lean formality, a sense of craft, and visual ingenuity. As a genre, still lifes can be seen as a starting point for a broad analysis of the relationship between allegory and naturalism. Anker's still lifes foreshadowed the twentieth-century Expressionists. **AA**

Nevermore | Paul Gauguin

1897 | oil on canvas | 23 ⁷⁄₈ x 45 ⁵⁄₈ in / 60.5 x 116 cm | Courtauld Institute of Art Gallery, London, UK

In 1895 Paul Gauguin (1848–1903) returned to Tahiti for the last time after a difficult period in Paris where his work was not successful. He produced a number of large paintings including *Nevermore*, which was prompted by the death of his daughter Aline. It is a long painting with little perspectival depth and includes a familiar motif of two people whispering, and a raven suggesting misfortune. The raven refers to Edgar Allen Poe's poem of the same name, which Mallarmé recited at the Café Voltaire when Gauguin left Paris. In the poem a man imagines that the bird flapping at the window repeating the word "nevermore" is the spirit of his dead lover. The girl faces the viewer but her body is not for erotic consumption as in the tradition of Western painting. The curve of her hip is exaggerated to mimic the furniture or screen behind, both accentuated by strong verticals in the background. She is watchful as she listens to the whisperers, and the raven, in turn, watches her. The melancholia and implied threat in this painting is an indication of Gauguin's unstable state of mind. Later that year he unsuccessfully attempted suicide. In recent years Gauguin has been the subject of much criticism for this painting. Yet it is difficult to view the past and the complex social structure of another culture from a twenty-first-century perspective. It is perhaps too easy to criticize his "primitive" nudes as misogynist. It is the "Eve" of the Western imagination, Gauguin told Strindberg, that makes men misogynists and only the "primitive Eve" is naturally naked. **WO**

The Sleeping Gypsy | Henri Rousseau

1897 | oil on canvas | 51 x 79 in / 129.5 x 201 cm | Museum of Modern Art, New York, NY, USA

Henri Rousseau (1844–1910) was entirely self-taught and did not embark upon an artistic career until relatively late in life. He worked in a number of minor administrative jobs before retiring on a small pension to paint full time, and he exhibited regularly at the Salon des Indépendants. Throughout his life he had a great love of music, and he supplemented his income by teaching music, and later by taking in art students. His work was highly criticized during his life, and mostly regarded as uneducated and immature. Rousseau worked slowly and carefully using many layers of paint and exotic, jewellike colors, and had a fairly small output. *The Sleeping Gypsy* is one of the most famous images of the modern era, and is stunning in the simplicity of its composition combined with the subtlety of its execution. The beautiful and monumental figure of the gypsy sleeps quietly while the lion watches over her, the whole scene bathed in the eerie light of a full moon. The image is both intensely surreal and dreamlike, but also strangely real and the image works on both levels of interpretation. Rousseau offered the painting to the town of Laval, his hometown, for two or three hundred francs, but the town turned it down on account of the painting being "too childish." Yet Rousseau's simplified forms and imaginative use of space and symbol was admired by many artists, especially those who made the transition into Modernist painting, among whom were Picasso, Delaunay, Kandinsky, Brancusi, and Matisse. **TP**

Boulevard Montmartre | Camille Pissarro

1897 | oil on canvas | 21 ¼ x 26 in / 54 x 66 cm | Private collection

High up on the Rue Drouot, from his rented room in the Grand Hôtel de Russie, Camille Pissarro (1830–1903) looked out of the left of his window onto one of Paris's grandest boulevards. He had come here specifically to paint a series of Parisian views, partly because his eyesight was failing, and painting out of doors was increasingly difficult. This is one of fourteen views of Boulevard Montmartre spied from his window between winter and spring of 1897, showing different times of day and different weathers. This particular picture shows the boulevard on a late winter's morning, with fog, sun, and snow. As with the whole series, the strong central shape of the receding boulevard, flanked by rows of trees and impressive buildings, dictates the simple, powerful composition

and perspective, given drama by the high viewpoint. Strong brushstrokes on the sky and road help to draw the eye down this busy thoroughfare. Sketchily painted figures and carriages, like blurred photos, add a bustling movement, although the effect of pearly winter sun diffused through mist makes this view calmer than some of the others. In many places, such a on the road surface, a broad pointillism is used. Pissarro had previously experimented with this technique, and abandoned it, but its influence remains. By the 1890s, Pissarro felt that series paintings such as this gave him the artistic direction he craved. They showed that his heart was in exploring the changing light and weather effects found all around us—a major Impressionist preoccupation. **AK**

Mrs. Walter Rathbone Bacon
Anders Zorn

1897 | oil on canvas | 67 ¼ x 42 ½ in / 171 x 108 cm
Metropolitan Museum of Art, New York, NY, USA

Receiving early acclaim for his watercolors, during the 1880s Anders Zorn (1860–1920) traveled extensively before settling in Paris and taking up oil painting. Over the next few years he produced the work that was to make him one of the most sought-after society portraitists of the age. It was on his second visit to America that Zorn painted this portrait of Mrs. Walter Rathbone Bacon (aka Virginia Purdy Bacon). Virginia's cousin, George Washington Vanderbilt II, had recently had John Singer Sargent—Zorn's great rival—paint her portrait to hang in the halls of Biltmore House, the largest home in the country. It was probably in response to this that Zorn was commissioned by her husband in early 1897. Zorn was linked with Realism and placed his sitters in familiar surroundings. Here, although elegantly dressed and bejeweled, Virginia sits informally at home accompanied by her dog. **RB**

At Breakfast
Laurits Andersen Ring

1898 | oil on canvas | 20 ½ x 15 ¾ in / 52 x 40.5 cm
Nationalmuseum, Stockholm, Sweden

This low-key scene captures the feeling of a leisurely breakfast spent in a room flooded with morning light. It also reflects a major preoccupation of artists around the turn of the century—the balance between depicting something in a naturalistic way and conveying a deeper truth. This picture shows Ring's (1854–1933) Symbolist credentials by using mood and unusual compositional devices to dig beneath the surface of everyday life. It is a convincing portrayal of a woman at breakfast, but painted in a way that fills it with moody immediacy, giving it a more powerful kind of realism. The main subject has her back to us but this emphasizes the fact that she is in a casual, everyday pose, leaning in to read her paper. The table on which she leans is cut off abruptly on the left and forms a strong foreground object, reminiscent of the Japanese prints that influenced so many artists at this time. **AK**

Interior
Vilhelm Hammershøi

1898 | oil on canvas | 20 ¼ x 18 ⅛ in / 51.5 x 46 cm
Nationalmuseum, Stockholm, Sweden

Girls on the Jetty
Edvard Munch

1899 | oil on canvas | 53 ½ x 49 ⅜ in / 136 x 125.5 cm
Munch Museum, Oslo, Norway

Vilhelm Hammershøi (1864–1916), like his better-known contemporary Edvard Munch (1863–1944), had a similar interest in depicting lonely figures in silent interiors. A well-traveled Danish artist, Hammershøi was a great admirer of Whistler and echoed his use of subtle, muted colors. Today Hammershøi is remembered almost exclusively for the hidden drama of his interiors. These interiors exude an air of calm and still. They may be empty, but more often they contain a single, female figure, usually seen from behind. These female figures are enigmatic: their faces are hidden, as is their precise activity. Often the head is bowed slightly, to indicate that the woman is doing something, although this is concealed from the viewer. Hammershøi's chief concern in these scenes was to capture the play of light and create a mysterious atmosphere. **IZ**

Edvard Munch's (1863–1944) art is so associated with themes of anguish and despair that it is easy to forget that he also painted scenes of great lyrical beauty. The scene is set on a bridge leading to the steamship pier at Åsgårdstrand in Norway, where Munch rented a house during the summer. This is an early version of the subject but, as was his custom when he was happy with an image, Munch reworked the theme endlessly, experimenting with different arrangements of the figures. He also tried it out in different media: along with several paintings of this subject, he also produced lithograph and woodcut versions. On one level, Munch's painting is a celebration of the long summer nights in Norway, when it never got completely dark. Indeed, the original title of this picture was *Summer Night*. In addition, though, it is also about the sexual awakening of the girls. **IZ**

Summer Night | Harald Sohlberg

1899 | oil on canvas | 45 x 53 ½ in / 114 x 136 cm | Nasjonalgalleriet, Oslo, Norway

Rather than drawing inspiration from artistic developments in France and Germany, at the end of the nineteenth century, a growing sense of nationalism led Scandinavian painters to place a greater emphasis on the unique qualities of their respective homelands. This trend was particularly evident in the realm of landscape painting. The vogue for capturing minute changes in light and atmospheric conditions took an unusual turn in the far north, where artists became fascinated by the magical half-light of their long summer nights. Harald Sohlberg (1869–1935) was only one of many painters to choose this as a subject. This picture features Sohlberg's apartment, in an eastern suburb of Kristiania (later Oslo). By the end of the century, Nordic artists were increasingly using landscape to create a mood or convey symbolic meanings. The Swedish painter Richard Bergh (1858–1919) summed up a common feeling, when he remarked that "the landscape, that tract in which we live, affects our lives . . . by the purely suggestive influence it has on our soul. . . . Every landscape is a state of mind." In Sohlberg's case, the symbolism of his *Summer Night* relates to his own forthcoming marriage. The table is laid out for two people, and a woman's hat and gloves can be seen. In this context, the beautiful landscape stands as a metaphor for the promise of the couple's future life together. Sohlberg later moved to the bleak, mountainous region of central Norway, where his landscapes acquired more mystical overtones. **IZ**

Woman in a Yellow Dress | Max Kurzweil

1899 | oil on canvas | 67 ½ x 67 ⅜ in / 171.5 x 171 cm | Historisches Museum der Stadt, Vienna, Austria

At the end of the nineteenth century, the arts in Vienna were to undergo a pivotal transformation, signaling the birth of Art Nouveau. The artistic climate immediately preceding this was one of constraint, as most Viennese artists trained at the conservative Academy of Fine Arts and exhibited at the Kunstlerhaus, the only exhibition space in Vienna, which dictated the movements of public taste. A growing dissatisfaction among certain progressive members of the Kunstlerhaus had led to meetings in cafés and clubs until finally, in 1897, Max Kurzweil (1867–1916) and eighteen others broke free of the establishment and founded the "Vienna Secession," headed by Gustav Klimt. This stunning painting of 1899 was displayed in the Secession's new exhibition building. Kurzweil's wife, Martha, gazes out at the viewer in a languid, stylized pose, illustrating Art Nouveau's new code of aesthetics, which borrowed strong curves and flowing lines from the Baroque era. The chair is draped in decorative green fabric, a precursor to the movement's obsession with ornamental design. Rejecting mass-produced art, the Vienna Secessionists sought artistic individualism coupled with decorative unity across architecture, painting, crafts, and the graphic arts. They published their ideas in an art journal entitled *Ver sacrum* ("Sacred Spring"). This iconoclastic period saw the writings of Freud emerge alongside the works of avant-garde artists, without whom Expressionism would never have been possible. **SLF**

The Studio of Bertel Thorvaldsen | Christian Bang

1899 | oil on canvas | 55 ¾ x 65 ⅛ in / 141.5 x 165.5 cm | Private collection

Danish artist Christian Bang's (1868–1950) oeuvre includes alterpieces and landscapes, as well as numerous interiors. Bang taught drawing at the Danish Royal Court and won myriad awards for his paintings. *The Studio of Bertel Thorvaldsen*, pays homage to Danish sculptor and collector Bertel Thorvaldsen, who spent most of his working life in Rome, where he took over from Antonio Canova as the foremost Neoclassical master sculptor. The painting portrays this towering Danish figure—not just as a fellow artist but as one of the leading lights of the Neoclassical movement. Bang's choice of Thorvaldsen's studio in Rome as the focus for his painting is deliberate: the remarkable productivity of the studio was possible both because of its

organization and the unique working methods used. Thorvaldsen's reputation was such that he received a constant stream of important public and private commissions and, to meet supply with demand, he employed several marble sculptors and students. These employees would mold Thorvaldsen's sketches in clay, create plaster models, and finally reproduce as many copies of a piece as needed. As the taste for Neoclassicism waned in succeeding decades, Thorvaldsen's sculpture was momentarily forgotten and it was not until the middle of the twentieth century that his artistic output came to be re-evaluated. Bang's interpretation of Thorvaldsen's studio monumentalizes the great figure, a worthy tribute from a fellow compatriot. **AA**

The Tuileries Gardens, Rainy Weather | Camille Pissarro

1899 | oil on canvas | 25 ⅝ x 36 ¼ in / 65 x 92 cm | Ashmolean Museum, Oxford, UK

Relying on practical experience and not abstract theories, the original aim of the Impressionists was to paint what they saw at one given moment in time. In 1860s France, they moved art quite literally out of the studio, often painting *en plein air*, using rapid brushstrokes and experimenting with color to capture the play of light and shadow and the ever-changing, fleeting mood, not only in landscapes, but also in scenes of modern life. Camille Pissarro (1830–1903) was the only member of the group to exhibit at all eight of their shows, held between 1874 and 1886. Although a central figure to the movement, in his early career he shunned depicting Paris, preferring instead to paint rural landscapes outside the city. However, during the 1890s, forced inside a rented Paris apartment by failing eyesight, he became the preeminent painter of the modern city. *The Tuileries Gardens, Rainy Weather* is one of a series of "weather studies," canvases painted from the window of an apartment looking out over the gardens toward the River Seine. It shows Pissarro's dedication to the Impressionist style: his use of complementary colors, the pale blue sky, and brownish-orange pathways, juxtaposed with flecks of white and silvery gray to capture the unique atmosphere of a rainy day. Pissarro's dedication to his art and his encouragement to artists, such as Cézanne and Gauguin, to use "nature as a guide" meant that he bridged the gap between one generation of artists and the next, from Impressionism to Post-Impressionism. **AIB**

1900s

Magnolia | Wilhelm List

*c.*1900 | oil on canvas | 43 ¼ x 39 ¼ in / 110 x 100 cm | Private collection

There was a great blossoming of art at the turn of the twentieth century when artists such as Wilhelm List (1864–1918), who had been influenced by the Impressionists, discovered, and indeed contributed to, Art Nouveau. List studied at the Academy of Fine Arts in Vienna, and then in Munich and Paris. He has been compared to Gustav Klimt, a fellow student just two years his senior. In 1897 he was one of nineteen Viennese artists—including Klimt, Egon Shiele, and Carl Moll—who formed the Vienna Secession group, and List was the first artist to exhibit at the Secession building. He collaborated on the review "Ver Sacrum" from 1898 to 1903, and he was one of the twelve illustrators of their 1902 catalogue, which was dedicated to Beethoven. He left the Vienna Secession,

together with Klimt, in 1905. In *Magnolia*, the artist has just suggested the finer details in the lake and background trees, and the grass in the foreshore could be by van Gogh. However, the magnolia tree itself is highly detailed. It seems as though one could just reach out and pluck the blooms from the branches. There is also an Impressionist feel: if there were a few waterlilies on the lake, the painting would resemble a work by Monet. The tightly framed composition is almost photographic, reflecting the fascination with early photography at this time. List was also a remarkable portraitist who typically used a technique of divided colors and fine, long brushstrokes, but he is best known for his engravings, where he used wood and lithography in turn. **RA**

Wheat Field | Emil Nolde

*c.*1900 | watercolor on paper | Private collection

Emil Nolde (1867–1956) came to painting at the age of forty after first studying woodcarving and working as a furniture designer and then teaching ornamental drawing. Born on a farm in Schleswig, Germany, his early paintings were fantastical rural landscapes, with mountains humanized as giant trolls, which once published gave him the financial dependence to study painting full-time. Nolde attended art schools from 1898 and 1901 and also spent time with the Dachau "landscapists" so was still studying when he executed *Wheat Field* in 1900. Here, a dark, dense ground of deep blue is shot through with vivid flashes of gold from right and left, which direct the viewer's eye to the earth itself and a vision of a home illuminated in shocking scarlet. Nolde strongly felt that color could evoke emotional responses and he was a great admirer of the work of Manet, Cézanne, Munch, and the French Symbolists. "I had an infinite number of visions at this time, for wherever I turned my eyes nature, the sky, the clouds were alive … and they aroused my enthusiasm as well as tormented me with demands that I paint them". *Wheat Field*, bathed in ethereal light, shows an almost spiritual connection to the landscape. This is a theme to which Nolde was to return many times. It demonstrates his aim to transform nature by infusing it with a sense of emotional expression. In 1906 he asked to become a member of the German Expressionist group, *Die Brücke* (The Bridge), which he joined briefly. He is considered one of the great watercolor painters of the twentieth century. **AIB**

Blue Roofs | Pablo Picasso

1901 | oil on millboard | 15 ³/₈ x 22 ³/₄ in / 39 x 57.7 cm | Ashmolean Museum, Oxford, UK

This painting is of the view from Pablo Ruiz y Picasso's (1881–1973) room on the top floor of an apartment in the Boulevard de Clichy. The penetrating blue of the slate Parisian roofs is briefly mirrored in the sky overhead, where yellow and green flashes are also evident in the thickly rendered clouds. The side of the roofs are washed with a pale sunlight. This is a reflective painting of the scene that Picasso saw from the window of the room where he lived and worked; it is dreamlike and provides clues to the artist's concerns at this embryonic stage of his career. This was a period of discovery and experimentation for Picasso. A critique of his exhibition at the gallery of Ambroise Vollard in June 1901 compared his work to a broad range of contemporary artists, from Toulouse-Lautrec to Matisse. Picasso had a magpie instinct for uncovering the new and vital, and creating coherent images that referenced these evolving styles. In *Blue Roofs* the Impressionist style is strongly evident in the short, energetic brushstrokes. Yet the serenity of this scene belies the turmoil of Picasso's life at the time. His friend Casagemas had committed suicide and a grieving Picasso was only to stay in Paris for a short period, returning to Barcelona in 1902. Before leaving France he embarked upon a series of paintings that later matured into his Blue Period: melancholic evocations of the poor and stricken, death and mortality. *Blue Roofs* is an unknowing precursor to these images, in that it silently evokes a fleeting moment of calm contemplation. **RW/JP**

Autumn, the Five Crosses | Akseli Gallen-Kallela

1902 | tempera and oil on canvas | 29 ¾ x 57 in / 76 x 145 cm | Private collection

Prior to painting *Autumn, the Five Crosses*, Akseli Gallen-Kallela (1865–1931) had triumphed at the Paris World Fair of 1900 with an impressive display of creativity: he produced frescoes, furniture, textiles, paintings, and graphic design work for the Finnish Pavilion, winning medals for his efforts. This painting is a sketch for a fresco at a private mausoleum in Pori, Finland. It combines various elements typical of his work, particularly in this period—Expressionism, the stylized touches of Art Nouveau, and his fascination with the Finnish landscape. Gallen-Kallela was strongly influenced by his country of origin, its scenery, and its people, and often depicted his countrymen or silent, elegant views of nature as seen in this painting. *Autumn, the Five Crosses* is a melancholy ode to nature

in the process of falling asleep for the winter; the dark sky predicts a storm, the water in the lake is black, and the leaves are already golden brown. The mausoleum for which this was designed was built in memory of an eleven-year-old girl: the five crosses stand in mourning, symbolizing the death of summer. The color palette is striking in its simplicity, including only about half a dozen colors. Although the painting does not refer directly to a specific location, it is firmly rooted in his passion for his country, and specifically, its dramatic landscape. Gallen-Kallela was a member of the German Expressionist group *Die Brücke*, and this painting echoes the vivid emotions of the genre. He was a passionate promoter of a distinct, Finnish cultural identity, to which his work contributed. **RK**

Landing of Captain Cook at Botany Bay, 1770
Emmanuel Phillips Fox

1902 | oil on canvas | 75 ½ x 104 ½ in / 192 x 265 cm | National Gallery of Victoria, Melbourne, Australia

In 1770, the explorer and naval captain James Cook stepped onto the beach at Botany Bay—an event that led to the founding of a new colony and, eventually, the birth of a nation. Parts of Australia had been mapped by previous explorers, but Cook discovered an excellent spot for settlement. More than a century later, Emmanuel Phillips Fox (1865–1915) commemorated this moment, creating one of the most enduring images in Australian art. The work was commissioned to mark another great moment in Australian history—the six colonies became a commonwealth and finally had their own parliament on January 1, 1901. Fox was a natural choice for the job. He was probably the most eminent native-born Australian artist at the turn of the twentieth century, recognized in Europe as well as at

home for his vigorous brushwork and subtle use of color. He had already founded an art school in Melbourne and been elected an associate of the Société Nationale des Beaux Arts in Paris, as well as exhibiting regularly at London's Royal Academy. The subject matter of *Landing of Captain Cook at Botany Bay, 1770* is in the heroic mold, recalling French nineteenth-century historical painting. One of Fox's teachers had been Jean-Léon Gerome, who was well known for this style of work. In the painting, Cook directs his men to plant the Union Jack, claiming the territory for Great Britain. A red-coated soldier kneels to do his master's bidding. Fox was perhaps referring to the fact that Australia was still very much under the influence of Great Britain. **CR**

The Knight's Dream
Richard Mauch

1902 | oil on canvas | Private collection

A knight on horseback picks his way through an erotic dreamscape filled with naked nymphs cavorting in a natural setting. In many ways, the Austrian-born portraitist Richard Mauch (1874–1921) has created a classic painting of the turn-of-the-century Art Nouveau period, featuring romantic medieval myth, fantasy, natural motifs, and a certain "decadent" sexuality. By the time Mauch painted this picture, he had been strongly connected to Art Nouveau in both Germany and Austria and in particular to the Munich Secession. This association of Munich artists broke away from the mainstream art world and paved the way for the enormously influential *Jugendstil* movement. Unlike Raphael's *Vision of a Knight* (*c*.1504), in which a sleeping knight dreams of making a choice between

Virtue and Pleasure, Mauch's knight, like the free-thinking artists with whom he associated, appears to break away from this art of the past and its traditional issues and dilemmas. Here the knight makes his way very directly along a flower-strewn path to a naked maiden, whose pose is unambiguously welcoming. The impending liaison is underlined by the red of her cloak—held symbolically opened out—echoing the red of the knight's costume. The artist's soft brushwork convincingly conveys the sense of being in a dream. Mauch's erotic pictures were considered scandalous at the time but placed him in the mood of his era, along with contemporary artists such as fellow Austrian Gustav Klimt, whose love of the female form and nudity caused great sensations. **AK/SaP**

The City
August Strindberg

1903 | oil on canvas | 37 ¼ x 20 ⅞ in / 94.5 x 53 cm
Nationalmuseum, Stockholm, Sweden

The Swedish playwright, poet, and novelist Johan August Strindberg (1849–1912) also had an interest in photography and painting. In his autobiographical novel, *Son of a Servant*, he says how painting made him "indescribably happy—as if he'd just taken hashish." Strindberg suffered from mental illness and his psychotic episodes and introspective personality are revealed in his paintings of stormy landscapes and seascapes. In *The City* his native Stockholm appears a tiny but luminous, welcoming light on the horizon, trapped between a violent, dark sea and sky. It has been said that such paintings of violent weather were a representation of the churning emotions that often gripped Strindberg. The motif of a turbulent sea storm and a distant horizon is one he used again and again. Without explanation, Strindberg stopped painting in 1905, seven years before he died. **TS**

The Old Farmer
Paula Modersohn-Becker

1903 | oil on canvas | 27 ¾ x 23 ⅓ in / 71 x 59 cm
Hamburger Kunsthalle, Hamburg, Germany

Inspired by the primitivism that had Paul Gauguin globetrotting to the Pacific, Paula Modersohn-Becker (1876–1907) found it in her own backyard in the artists' colony of Worpswede, near Bremen, Germany. The artists there shared a romantic, symbolic view, looking to the "lyrical" landscape as a reaction to encroaching urbanization. In this painting, an old farmer woman sits tired and resigned to her labors. It is a sympathetic portrait, subdued and timeless, drawn on a flat plane with strong outlines that distill the "natural" appearance of the figure to her essence—her expressiveness, which is evoked especially in her eyes. The effect can be seen as a precursor for the experiments in form by Pablo Picasso, culminating four years later in *Les Demoiselles d'Avignon*. Sadly, Modersohn-Becker produced only a decade of work; she died of a heart attack after giving birth to her first child. **JH**

Vanity
Otto Friedrich

1904 | oil on canvas | 51 ⅛ x 49 ¼ in / 130 x 125 cm
Private collection

Sir James Matthew Barrie
William Nicholson

1904 | oil on canvas | 22 x 20 ½ in / 56 x 52 cm
Scottish National Portrait Gallery, Edinburgh, UK

Hungarian Otto Friedrich (1862–1937) worked in turn-of-the-century Vienna, home of Sigmund Freud, whose writings on the unconscious and the development of sexuality influenced contemporary art. A series of exhibitions of modernist design by the Vienna Secession, held from 1898 to 1905, engaged Viennese artists in new concepts about the inner self. *Vanity* was painted against this backdrop of intellectual and artistic activity. In *Vanity*, the kneeling young woman, whose naked body reflects the pale, luminescent violet around her, admires herself in a hand mirror that reflects yet another mirror behind her. The plush folds of a white dress suggest she is preparing to dress for a night out and she is checking her painted lips. In a characteristically Viennese style, Friedrich uses evocative lines and bright, unnatural coloring to seduce the viewer into a boudoir of reflections and conceit. **SWW**

Sir William Nicholson (1872–1949) worked in portraiture and theatrical design in the early twentieth century. In 1904 he designed sets and costumes for the first stage production of James Matthew Barrie's *Peter Pan* in London. It was then that Barrie agreed, with some reluctance, to sit for his portrait. It is an extraordinarily downbeat presentation of a writer then at the pinnacle of success. Barrie stands almost in profile, hands in pockets. His features are sallow, although there is a keenness about the eyes. Most of the canvas is filled with emptiness, the figure shrunken and isolated by its surroundings. Not a single detail or splash of brightness relieves what humorist Sir Max Beerbohm described as Nicholson's "passion for low tones." The portrait can be read as an expression of Barrie's inner loneliness, or perhaps it is a reflection of Nicholson's commitment to the avoidance of self-importance. **RG**

Mont Sainte-Victoire | Paul Cézanne

1902–04 | oil on canvas | 27 ½ x 38 in / 70 x 89.5 cm | Philadelphia Museum of Art, Philadelphia, PA, USA

At the heart of Paul Cézanne's (1839–1906) ambitions for painting was the desire to ascertain nature in its most rudimentary and elementary form. Often this meant depicting a landscape, still life, or figure study in an abbreviated manner. *Mont Sainte-Victoire* can be read in this way, as a series of decisions committed to the canvas only when the artist was sure that there was some fidelity between the form seen and its corresponding inscription. Cézanne had known and climbed this mountain in the south of France near his hometown of Aix-en-Provence since he was a child. In adulthood up until his death he retraced his steps, continuing to follow the trails that wended their way across the mountain. He first painted the mountain in 1882, although the mountain in these studies was one of several elements within the overall landscape. From 1886 onward the mountain came to dominate his paintings of this region. With this study, Cézanne's brushstrokes, while remaining discrete, cohere as a whole. Although the mountain only occupies the upper-third band of the composition, it remains set apart from the houses and largely undifferentiated treatment of foliage in the foreground by the artist's use of the same range of blues to depict both mountain and sky. *Mont Sainte-Victoire*'s reduction of nature into essential units not only denotes the degree of visual scrutiny and exactitude Cézanne brought to the subject, but also anticipates the experiments with form, perception, and space carried out under Cubism. **CS**

The Birth of Venus | Odilon Redon

c.1905 | oil on canvas | 21 ¼ x 28 ¾ in / 54 x 73 cm | Private collection

The manifestations of Symbolism were observed all over Europe at the turn of the nineteenth century in both art and literature. In France Odilon Redon (1840–1916) was a visual artist associated with this movement. He settled in Paris after serving in the Franco-Prussian war, during which he produced a large number of astonishing lithographs and charcoal drawings. He remained relatively unknown, however, until his appearance in the celebrated 1884 Symbolist novel *A Rebours* (*Against Nature*) by J.K. Huysmans. The Symbolists were searching for ways to escape their contemporary industrialized world through art. In 1899 Redon exhibited with the *Nabis*—a group of painters with an essentially Symbolist outlook—at Paul Durand-Ruel's gallery in Paris. In 1913 his work appeared at the New York Armory Show. Redon developed an unprecedented style, constantly transforming natural landscapes into somber visions and odd fantasies. In *The Birth of Venus*, he offers his own interpretation of a well-known classical myth. This image is typical of the work Redon started to produce at the beginning of the twentieth century when he abandoned his earlier dark images to create colorful pastel and oil paintings. Here, Venus is painted in a very unusual manner, emphasizing the contours of her silhouette, as if she had been drawn in a cave. The background is surreal—it is not clear where Venus is—she could be in the skies or in a shell under the sea. Redon leaves it to the viewer's imagination. **JJ**

Boats in the Harbor, Collioure | André Derain

1905 | oil on canvas | 15 x 18 in / 38 x 46 cm | Royal Academy of Arts, London, UK

André Derain (1880–1954) was born into a middle-class family in the small town of Chatou, just outside Paris. He refused to follow his father into the family business as a patisserie chef and, instead, attended a fine art course at the Académie Carriere in Paris, where he met the more senior artist, Henri Matisse (1869–1954). It was under Matisse's tutelage that Derain was subsequently introduced to the work of Paul Signac (1863–1935) and Georges Seurat (1859–91). This, together with the developments of the Symbolists and the Neo-Impressionists, informed his own art. *Boats in the Harbor, Collioure* was painted in the summer of 1905, when Derain, together with Matisse, worked in this small Mediterranean fishing port near the Spanish border. Although using a traditional subject matter, the bright colors—applied in fragmented blocks—must have appeared unfinished and almost clumsy to a contemporary audience but, for Derain, it was the most effective means of conveying the effect of bright light where tonal contrast is completely eradicated. In 1906, Derain was commissioned to execute a series of London cityscape paintings, in which scenes of the River Thames—reminiscent of the work of Claude Monet (1840–1926) from two decades earlier—were reinterpreted with dazzling color. Although a surprising traditionalist, Derain was an influential contributor to the Fauves, a group that experimented with non-naturalistic colors and laid the groundwork for Abstract Expressionism. **JG**

Collioure | André Derain

1905 | oil on canvas | 23 ¾ x 29 in / 60 x 73.5 cm | Scottish National Gallery of Modern Art, Edinburgh, UK

André Derain (1880–1954) spent most of his childhood in the small French town of Chatou, close to Paris. Twenty years later he shared a studio there, above a disused restaurant, with his friend and fellow artist, Maurice de Vlaminck (1876–1958). The two painters were highly influential on each other, utilizing a similarly bright palette, applied in rough dabs of color to obtain the effects of light in their depictions of the Mediterranean landscape. Both artists were closely associated with Henri Matisse (1869–1954) and Pablo Picasso (1881–1973), constituting the first generation of Fauves and Cubists. *Collioure* was completed in the summer of 1905, after Derain was released from military service. In this southern French harbor the artist,

working alongside Matisse, primed his canvas with white paint before applying a close mosaic of brilliant color to achieve the effect of bright light that casts no shadow. Derain, already well versed in Neo-Impressionist painting, applied the color theories of artists such as Georges Seurat (1859–91) to combine the effects of artificial composition in intense color with an observed reality. The work was later bought by dealer Ambroise Vollard and exhibited in the Salon d'Automne together with work by Matisse, Vlaminck, and others. Hung as a group, these paintings were promptly dubbed the *Cage aux Fauves* (Cage of Wild Beasts) because of their "wild" use of vibrant color. This marked the birth of Fauvism. **JG**

Landscape from Lejre | Vilhelm Hammershøi

1905 | oil on canvas | 16 x 26 ½ in / 41 x 68 cm | Nationalmuseum, Stockholm, Sweden

This undulating and calm summer landscape was painted in 1905 by Danish artist Vilhelm Hammershøi (1864–1916), at a time when Hammershøi was a widely recognized artist. He studied at the Royal Academy of Arts in Copenhagen, and later at Kunstnernes Studieskole (The Artists' Study School) where he was introduced to the *plein-air* technique. He received acclamation from contemporary cultural figures such as the French artist Pierre-August Renoir (1841–1919) and the German poet Rainer Maria Rilke (1875–1926). *Landscape from Lejre* provides us with a view over the countryside near Roskilde, southwest of Copenhagen. The countryside makes up one-third of the painting; the sky, with its fluffy clouds, occupies the remainder. Hammershøi has repeated the softness of the clouds in the fields, which are equally faint and gentle. The lack of detail and clear focus is evident throughout this landscape, and we are left with an even, almost metaphysical sphere, in which soft tones of shade and light dominate. The yellow field, on the right, is the only real complementary color. Such stillness speaks of aesthetic scrutiny; a visual characteristic that is evident in the artist's other paintings, especially his interiors. Hammershøi traveled throughout Europe—Holland and England were favorite places, and James Abbot McNeill Whistler (1834–1903) was an inspiration to him. The painting opens up a pictorial world that invites us to reflect on an environment that serves to instigate yet more thought and contemplation. **SML**

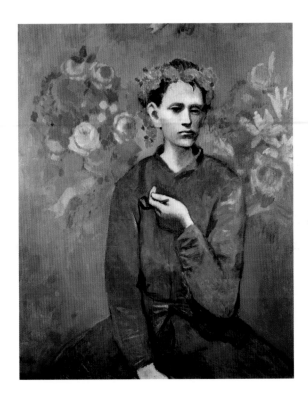

Boy with a Pipe | Pablo Picasso

1905 | oil on canvas | 39 ³/₈ x 32 in / 100 x 81.5 cm | Private collection

In 2004, *Garçon à la Pipe*—or *Boy with a Pipe*, sold for $104m (£58m) to an anonymous bidder at Sotheby's New York, becoming at that time, the world's most expensive painting. Pablo Picasso (1881–1973) was twenty-four when he painted it and it is one of the most poetic of his Rose Period paintings, emerging at the transition from the cool and somber tones of his Blue Period. He had been living in poverty in Montmartre since 1904, and during 1905 he turned away from his stylized, gaunt figures of the previous eighteen months in favor of a more harmonious classicism, inspired by the circus acrobats and clowns who performed nearby. For six months he lightened and brightened both his palette and his subject matter, becoming increasingly fascinated by people who did not fit in with the rest of society. This painting is one of his most celebrated images of adolescent beauty. The model was probably "petit Louis," a boy who regularly visited the artist's studio. According to Picasso, the boy "stayed there, sometimes the whole day. He watched me work. He loved that." A number of preliminary studies for the painting show the boy in a variety of different positions, but the most thoroughly worked study depicts him sitting in a similar pose to that of the final composition. The final painting is nevertheless different from any of the preliminary studies, and the boy's indifferent expression lends an ambiguity to the image. Crowned with roses, holding a pipe, and framed by bouquets on the wall behind him, "petit Louis" becomes a mysterious figure. **SH**

Les Grandes Baigneuses | Paul Cézanne

1900–06 | oil on canvas | 50 ⅛ x 77 ¼ in / 127 x 196 cm | National Gallery, London, UK

During his career Paul Cézanne (1839–1906) repeatedly returned to certain subjects. Mont Sainte-Victoire, the mountain that bordered the artist's hometown of Aix-en-Provence was one such subject, and the sheer volume of canvases based upon this particular mountain are testimony to the lengths the artist was prepared to go to in order to render explicable some aspect of the external, recognizable world. From the early 1870s, the bather became another recurring subject within Cézanne's oeuvre. In 1895, he began work on a series of large canvases based around the theme of bathers that he continued to work on until his death in 1906. Today three large canvases, each depicting a group of female bathers, represent the culmination, if not necessarily the resolution of a theme that, like his studies of Mont Sainte-Victoire, afforded the means by which the underlying structure of the sensate world might be rendered visible. Organized around a grouping of eleven bathers, Cézanne depicts the figures in such a way that they appear to visually interlock and can be read as a visual continuum from left to right across the picture plane. This sense of formal continuity is further conveyed through the artist's brushstrokes carrying equal weight, or "touch," both in their depiction of the figure and its immediate surroundings. Although the subject, on one level, remained indebted to classical precedent, Cézanne applied what were a set of radical techniques to create a thoroughly "modern" conception of the human form. **CS**

Fields, Rueil | Maurice de Vlaminck

c.1906 | oil on canvas | 21 ½ x 25 ½ in / 55 x 65 cm | Museo Thyssen-Bornemisza, Madrid, Spain

Virtually untrained as an artist, Maurice de Vlaminck (1876–1958) earned a living as a racing cyclist, violinist, and soldier before dedicating himself to painting. In 1901 he established a studio in Chatou, outside Paris, with fellow artist André Derain. In the same year he was inspired by an exhibition of paintings by van Gogh, which had a profound influence on his work. By the time this picture was painted, Vlaminck and Derain were recognized as leading members of the Fauvist movement, a group of artists who outraged established taste by the non-naturalistic use of intense, unmixed colors. Vlaminck declared "instinct and talent" the only essentials for painting, scorning learning from the masters of the past. Yet this landscape stands clearly in line of descent from van Gogh and, beyond him, the Impressionists. With these predecessors Vlaminck shared a commitment to painting in the open air and to landscape as a celebration of nature. The broken touch with which paint is dabbed over most of the canvas (the flat color on the roofs is the main exception) also recalls the work of Monet or Sisley. The cursive drawing style is pure van Gogh. Yet Vlaminck's use of color is radically different. Pure colors straight from the tube and heightened tones transform a potentially tame scene of French suburban countryside into a virtuoso firework display. This landscape may now appear exquisite and charming, but we can still imagine how its energy might have struck the public of its day as crude and primitive. **RG**

Fritza von Riedler | Gustav Klimt

1906 | oil on canvas | 60 ¼ x 52 ¼ in / 153 x 133 cm | Österreichische Galerie Belvedere, Vienna, Austria

As the son of an engraver in gold and silver, it is not surprising that the later works of Gustav Klimt (1862–1918) dazzle with the splendor of a Byzantine mosaic. In fact Klimt visited Ravenna, Italy, in 1903 to see the mosaics of San Vitale. He began his career in architectural decoration during the development of the great Ringstrasse in Vienna working on the Burgtheatre and the Museum of Art History. Nothing prepared him, however, for the strong objections to his murals for the University of Vienna where, according to critics, his panels, *Philosophy*, *Medicine*, and *Jurisprudence* were inappropriate and immoral. Recoiling from the controversy he embarked on a series of portraits of women between 1904 and 1906. Fritza von Riedler emerges from a stylized chair in a froth of white lace and heavy satin ribbons. Only her aristocratic bearing, size, and position in the pyramidal composition keep her from being swamped by the decorative elements. Every part of the canvas is adorned with geometrical and organic forms, in gold and silver. Von Riedler's head is framed by an ornate stained glass window; this framing marks her out as a person of importance although Klimt used this device before with *Emilie Flöge* (1902) and *Margaret Stonborough-Wittgenstein* (1905). The flattening out of the chair also acts as a frame in that it allows the sitter to exist as the only three-dimensional object in the interior. Klimt's painting seems the antithesis of that of the younger generation of Expressionists but his influence on them is indisputable. **WO**

Self-examination | Carl Larsson

1906 | oil on canvas | 37 ⅝ x 24 ¼ in / 95.5 x 61.5 cm | Uffizi, Florence, Italy

A national institution in his homeland, Carl Larsson (1853–1919) rose from miserable childhood poverty to become a leading Swedish artist. His great success rested on paintings of an idealized domestic life he shared with his wife, Karin, and their children. The couple designed a home at their farm in the village of Sundborn that combined Swedish folk charm with artistic sophistication. Printed versions of these pictures, and Larsson's cheery accompanying stories, reached a wide public. They loved what they saw as a return to traditional Swedish country life. This picture, however, hints that the idyll was not perfect. Larsson presses up against the front of the picture, in close self-examination, with a quietly grim expression. He grasps a macabre doll with pent-up force. Karin is in the background, closeted away behind a window, her face partly obscured. These two people, apparently the most loving of couples, seem shut off from one another in their own isolated worlds. No one knows whether Karin felt resentful at giving up her earlier career as a painter to become a wife and mother— albeit a highly creative one. Yet it seems fairly certain that Larsson sometimes felt trapped by his wife, by repeatedly painting the interiors she created, and by the public expectation that he would go on doing the same thing. Whatever lies behind this painting, Larsson considered this his most successful self-portrait. It shows his talents as a draftsman and painter, often overlooked by those who see his pictures as just another example of sentimental Victorian art. **AK**

The Harbor at Marseilles | Paul Signac

1907 | oil on canvas | 18 ⅛ x 21 ⅝ in / 46 x 55 cm | State Hermitage Museum, St. Petersburg, Russia

Paul Signac (1863–1935) originally planned to be an architect, but in 1884 he met Claude Monet and Georges Seurat and was struck by the colors of the former and the systematic working methods and color theory of the latter. At twenty-one, he became Seurat's faithful supporter and turned from architecture to painting. Under Seurat's influence, he discarded his Impressionistic sketchy brushstrokes, to experiment with the *pointilliste* style. Each summer, he left Paris and painted vibrantly colored views of the French coasts. He loved sailing and from 1892 he took a small boat to almost all the ports of France, the Netherlands and around the Mediterranean. He returned with bright watercolors, sketched speedily from what he had seen and from which he painted large canvases in his studio. The *pointilliste* technique used in this painting consists of small dotted applications of paint, and is sometimes described as "divisionism." He went even further than Seurat in his methodical divisions of light into its elements of pure color, and he arranged rectangular brushstrokes that seem like little pieces of colored glass. In 1901 he had painted a smaller, less vibrant version of this view of the harbor at Marseilles. The rich luminosity of this painting emerges from his application of pure, unmixed pigments, and the influence of the younger painters, Henri-Edmond Cross, André Derain, and Henri Matisse is apparent. The artists mutually inspired each other, and Signac played a significant role in the development of Fauvism. **SH**

Les Demoiselles d'Avignon | Pablo Picasso

1907 | oil on canvas | 96 x 92 in / 244 x 234 cm | Museum of Modern Art, New York, NY, USA

At twenty-five, with an already serious reputation as an artist, Pablo Ruiz y Picasso (1881–1973) began work on a painting that he referred to as "*mon bordel*." The starting point for a painting that was to become one of the most notorious and celebrated images of the twentieth century was his memory of a brothel that had been located on the Calle Avignon in Barcelona, Spain. This source provided an unconventional subject to inspire a radical step forward as an artist. The painting was viewed, initially, by a collection of friends—including Matisse and Derain—in July 1907. Their reaction was so negative, however, that Picasso did not exhibit it to the public for almost a decade. It is not surprising that this painting caused offense. Five nude women stare provocatively out of the canvas,

locking the viewer in their unsettling gaze. Picasso presents us with a visual challenge—the multiplicity of viewpoints, the provocative poses assumed by the prostitutes, and the masks distorting the faces of the two women on the right all combine to generate the painting's power to disturb (even without knowledge of the subject matter). This memory of a *bordello* has become a vision of sexual power, rendered in a radical geometric style that signaled Picasso's advances toward Cubism. *Les Demoiselles d'Avignon* is acknowledged as an essential reference point for art in the twentieth century. It contains elements that would be taken up by the Modernist movement, and ideas that would repeatedly challenge the art world and the public. **RW**

Three Women and a Young Girl Playing in the Water
Félix Edouard Vallotton

1907 | oil on canvas | 51 ³/₈ x 77 in / 130.5 x 195.5 cm | Kunstmuseum, Basel, Switzerland

Born in Lausanne, Félix Edouard Vallotton (1865–1925) left Switzerland when he was seventeen to become a painter in Paris. He studied at the Académie Julian and became associated with the Post-Impressionist *Les Nabis* ("prophets" in Hebrew) group of artists that included Pierre Bonnard and Édouard Vuillard. They were influenced by the work of Paul Gauguin, Vincent van Gogh, and the Symbolists. In addition to the fine arts, *Les Nabis* worked in a variety of media including printmaking, illustration, textiles, furniture, and theater design. Vallotton's work is also diverse, comprising drawing, painting, sculpture, and writing. He regularly exhibited and the Modernism of his work, particularly his woodcuts, brought him much attention. Toward the turn of the century, he chose to concentrate on painting, especially nudes and landscapes. The stylized, simple lines of *Three Women and a Young Girl Playing in the Water* reveal Vallotton's interest in Symbolism and Art Nouveau, as well as the influence of Japanese woodcuts. Its figures depict several ages of feminity, from childhood to womanhood and middle age. The open pose of innocence of the young girl on the right contrasts with that of the older woman on the left, who with her folded arms and sour expression, reveals her distaste for her own body with its thickening thighs and sagging breasts. She casts an envious glance at the two younger women with their sensual, fecund bodies, and obvious sense of freedom. Whereas the child eagerly anticipates her adulthood. **OR/CK**

In the Washroom
Pierre Bonnard

1907 | oil on canvas | 19 ⅝ x 28 ¾ in / 50 x 73 cm | Galerie Daniel Malingue, Paris, France

When Pierre Bonnard (1867–1947) took art classes at the École des Beaux-Arts and the Académie Julian in Paris in the late 1880s, he was also a law student. It was during this time that he met Édouard Vuillard, Maurice Denis, and Paul Sérusier; they all became members of the group that would become known as Les Nabis (from the Hebrew word for "prophet"). He was called to the Bar in 1889, but gave up law in the 1890s to become a full-time artist. By then he had become strongly influenced by the works of Paul Gauguin (as were all Les Nabis), and an admirer of Japanese art. From 1891 to 1899, Les Nabis held regular exhibitions of their work, which included designs for books, posters, stained glass, and theatrical performances, as well as paintings. By the end of this period, Bonnard was moving away from the group and his first one-man show was held in 1896 at the Durand-Ruel gallery in Paris. In the Washroom is a perfect example of the style of painting that led to Bonnard's works being described as Intimisme, referring to intimate, domestic scenes. Like Degas, Bonnard was inspired by the eroticism of the bathroom, the pleasure the bather takes in drying herself, and the warm hues he could use to depict flushed, damp skin. His favorite model for such paintings was his wife, Marthe. Bonnard was also a keen photographer and his fondness for framing images as if in a photograph can be seen in many of his works, such as The Mirror (1908), in which a provocative scene of a woman bathing can be seen partially reflected in the mirror. **LH**

Pennsylvania Station Excavation | George Bellows

1907–08 | oil on canvas | 31 ⅛ x 38 ¼ in / 79 x 97 cm | Brooklyn Museum of Art, Brooklyn, NY, USA

The American painter and lithographer George Wesley Bellows (1882–1925) was born in Columbus, Ohio. A year younger than Picasso, he attended classes at the New York School of Art under Robert Henri, and he became associated with the Ashcan School, a group of artists that specialized in depicting New York City and its people. Bellows's short career (he died at the age of forty-two) did not prevent him from becoming one of the greatest artists of his time. At the early age of twenty-six, he was elected an associate member of the National Academy of Design in New York, the same year he painted *Pennsylvania Station Excavation*. He also exhibited and helped organize the seminal Armory Show in 1913. Six years later he moved from New York to become a professor at the Art Institute

of Chicago. *Pennsylvania Station Excavation* stands as one of his most memorable works. The building of Pennsylvania Station was considered then to be the height of modernity. In this painting, one can appreciate Bellows's fantastic mastery of light, and the contrast of somber colors with a gorgeous orange and blue sky. Also typical of his early paintings are his vigorous brushstrokes and the thickness of his paint, which provide a great visual texture to this highly detailed image. But Bellows remains best known for his wonderfully crude and chaotic depictions of urban New York City life. His paintings are now part of the greatest American collections such as the National Gallery in Washington and the Whitney and Museum of Modern Art in New York. **JJ**

The Kiss | Gustav Klimt

1907–08 | oil and gold on canvas | 71 x 71 in / 180 x 180 cm | Österreichische Galerie, Vienna, Austria

The Vienna Secession of 1900 included Charles Rennie Mackintosh and the Glasgow Four who were to influence the direction of European art and craft. Although Gustav Klimt (1862–1918) left the Secession in 1905, he was influenced by Margaret Macdonald, Mackintosh's wife, whose linear style included the use of semiprecious gems. Klimt had attempted the subject of fulfillment before, most notably in the final panel of the *Beethoven Frieze* of 1902, which refers to a phrase from Schiller's *Ode to Joy*, "the kiss to the whole world." Klimt turned Schiller's wider political meaning into something much more personal and located the embrace in a womblike space, which remains in *The Kiss*. Here it is decorated with circular biomorphic forms that are echoed in the woman's dress, where they are filled with flowers. By contrast the man's robe is decorated with strong, rectangular shapes. Both patterns have developed from Klimt's own personal symbolism. The image is so seductive that it is easy to miss the other, proto-Expressionist element of Klimt's style, which can be seen in the hideously bent toes and contorted hand of the woman, and in the coloration of her flesh, which suggests putrefaction. This expressive graphic style sits provocatively alongside the voluptuous decorative excess in Klimt's work, and led to many of his works, particularly *Medicine, Jurisprudence,* and *Philosophy*, being received with revulsion. However, it was this aspect of his work that influenced his younger contemporaries. **WO**

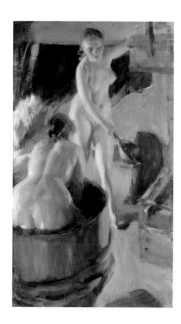

Girls from Dalarna Having a Bath | Anders Zorn

c.1908 | oil on canvas | 33 ⅛ x 19 ⅞ in / 84 x 50 cm
Nationalmuseum, Stockholm, Sweden

This oil painting by Swedish artist Anders Zorn (1860–1920) is a highly atmospheric piece depicting two girls bathing in a tub, the scene lit by the flickering glow of a fire. Zorn was greatly concerned with the effects of light, and especially of light reflecting on water and flesh, and many of his paintings convey a striking clarity of light and atmosphere, and have a photographic quality. *Girls from Dalarna* is an unusual composition and somewhat reminiscent of Degas, whom Zorn had become acquainted with while in Paris. He also socialized with Renoir and particularly Rodin, and there is a sense of each of these within Zorn's work. By the time he painted *Girls from Dalarna* the artist had moved from Paris back to his hometown of Mora, where he stayed until his death. He contributed to the development of the town, and chose the local people and scenery for many of his paintings. **TP**

Mornington Crescent
Walter Richard Sickert

1908 | oil on canvas
Private collection

Walter Richard Sickert (1860–1942) lived at Mornington Crescent, in north London, and used the area in many of his paintings. He created several series, exploring a subject or location repeatedly, and these included music halls, Venice, Dieppe, and the Camden paintings, in particular his notorious *Camden Town Murder* series. His ability to work on several paintings and drawings simultaneously made him a prolific artist. *Mornington Crescent* is one of several paintings of prostitutes. In this picture, the warm light bathing the woman's skin is suggestive of her profession, lighting up only the most provocatively sexual areas of her body and leaving her legs and face in shadow. The light of *Mornington Crescent* is much kinder than the stark light of his famous *La Hollandaise* (1906), in which a naked woman reclines on a bed, her flesh unflatteringly dappled by sunlight from an unseen window. **LH**

Woman in a Black Hat
Kees van Dongen

1908 | oil on canvas | 39 x 32 in / 100 x 81 cm
State Hermitage Museum, St. Petersburg, Russia

Dutch painter Kees van Dongen (1877–1968) moved to Paris in 1897 where he spent much of the rest of his life, and worked at first in a somewhat Impressionist manner. His paintings became increasingly colored and bold, and by 1906 he had joined *Les Fauves*, "the wild beasts." Two years later he briefly joined the German Expressionist group *Die Brücke*, "The Bridge," whose paintings were also brightly colored and often wrought with emotional intensity. *Woman in a Black Hat* was one of several paintings he made of women in headgear that are minimal in composition, but are charged with a sensuous undertone. The restricted palette of green, red, and black and the simple forms with sparing use of line make the image intensely focused. Van Dongen painted a number of society portraits, but the quality of his later works never matched that from his earlier career. **TP**

Brita at the Piano
Carl Larsson

1908 | pencil, charcoal, and watercolor on paper
38 ¼ x 24 ¾ in / 97 x 63 cm | Private collection

This is one of the pictures of Carl Larsson's (1853–1919) rural home life at Sundborn that made the Swedish artist well known. It shows his young daughter Brita, one of seven Larsson children who appeared regularly in their father's paintings. Larsson is especially noted for his watercolors. Like many other European artists at the time, he was a great admirer of Japanese prints, with their flat, decorative qualities. This image has strongly outlined objects and a decoratively shaped piano leg and music stand. The unusual composition features a large, cut-off foreground object (the piano) and a subject (Brita) that is mostly hidden. All these features echo Japanese prints circulating at the time. Typical of his watercolor style—although with perhaps a little more mood, light, and shade—it has the quality of a storybook illustration. Larsson himself had worked as an illustrator. **AK**

Molen Mill: The Winkel Mill in Sunlight, 1908 | Piet Mondrian

1908 | oil on canvas | 44 ⅞ x 34 ¼ in / 114 x 87 cm | Haags Gemeentemuseum, The Hague, Netherlands

Although best known today as an abstract artist, Piet Mondrian (1872–1944) originally adopted a broad range of styles, believing that a painting's subject was just as important as the way in which it was painted. Mondrian maintained that it was the function of art to delineate a clear vision of the world, and it was this notion that finally led him to abolish from his work any illusion of pictorial space in favor of a mode of composition more appropriate to the two-dimensional surface of the canvas. Even in his earliest landscapes—competent imitations of the moody and Impressionistic work of his fellow countrymen—Mondrian expressed a need to create an environment that was pure and complete in its beauty. In his depictions of mills, churches, and dunes, done in a brilliantly colored,

Luminist style, Mondrian devoted close attention to the play of natural light on objects. *The Winkel Mill in Sunlight*, perhaps his finest painting in this style, finds its most immediate source in the highly charged, Fauvist paintings of Matisse and Derain. In it we can already see Mondrian combining abstract geometries with blocks of unadulterated color. No view of Mondrian, however, is more misleading than the one of him as a detached formalist engaged in the search for exclusively decorative harmonies. The heartfelt utopian convictions that led him into abstraction were based on a Platonic vision of reality—on a belief that the reality around us is merely a reflection of a deeper truth—and that vision is already on the way to being realized in paintings like *The Winkel Mill in Sunlight*. **PB**

María y Elena en la playa | Joaquín Sorolla y Bastida

1908 | oil on canvas | 10 ½ x 8 ⅞ in / 26.5 x 22.5 cm | Museo Sorolla, Madrid, Spain

Around 1900, Joaquín Sorolla y Bastida (1863–1923) moved away from Social Realism and entered into a more mature phase. In the following years Sorolla advanced to the forefront of Spanish Impressionism. The greatest change involved a renunciation of the rigidity of classical forms and a new interest in open-air painting. Sorolla gained international recognition as the foremost painter of Mediterranean light and the sensation of movement. He painted portraits and everyday subjects, but his brightest and most luscious pictures were his beach paintings. He was fascinated by the blinding sunlight of his native Valencia, reflected in his spontaneous and daring perspectives. *Maria y Elena en la playa* is a perfect example of Sorolla's strengths. The real protagonist of this painting is the sunlight—its intensity and its shades are reflected in the painting's beach, sand, and sea, and the artist's fluent brushstrokes dominate the carefully arranged composition. The artist uses the children's white clothing and the sail of the boat out at sea to capture the vibrant light of the beach. Black is eliminated from the shadows in the painting, replaced with a range of blue, ocher, and clay. One French critic described Sorolla's painting thus: "Never has a paintbrush contained so much sun. It is not Impressionism, but it is amazingly impressive." Although the luminous treatment of shadows and the painting's fluent style closely follow the ideals of the French School, Sorolla presents a more personal interpretation of color. **DC**

Landscape, Murnau | Alexei von Jawlensky

1908–09 | oil on cardboard | 19 ⅝ x 20 ½ in / 50 x 52 cm | Museum Kunst Palast, Düsseldorf, Germany

This painting, one of a series executed *en plein air* on cardboard, is a fine example of the high Expressionist style of Alexei von Jawlensky (1864–1941), marking an important stage in the emergence of abstract art. Like his close friend Kandinsky, Jawlensky was a Russian who spent most of his life in Germany. The two first met at the Azbé School of Painting in Munich in 1897. Eleven years later, having traveled in France and absorbed the lessons of the Post-Impressionists and Cubists, they, with their companions Marianne von Werefkin and Gabriele Münter, spent the summer in Murnau, below the Bavarian Alps. Kandinsky and Münter bought a house there and the following year Jawlensky and Werefkin joined them again. In this painting we see the white walls and steep red roofs of Murnau in the distance. However, the composition is organized into areas of contrasting color with no real attempt to suggest volume or depth. The dark outlines are derived from the stained glass of Orthodox churches—the influence of religious and Russian folk art was central to the artist's desire to imbue his art with a spiritual intensity he found lacking in the more formal experiments of the avant-garde. Münter later said of this time: "I made a huge leap forward … from an imitation of nature, more or less impressionistic, to a feeling of what lies inside, teasing it out into abstraction." For all four painters it was a period of great creativity but, arguably, it was Jawlensky who was the most advanced, and his influence upon Kandinsky was to be profound. **RB**

Portrait of a Young Woman in Red, 1908–09 | Piet Mondrian

1908–09 | oil on canvas | 19 ¼ x 16 ⅜ in / 49 x 41.5 cm | Haags Gemeentemuseum, The Hague, Netherlands

Pieter Cornelis Mondriaan (1872–1944)—known as Piet Mondrian, he dropped an "*a*" in 1912—is associated more than anything else with the Neoplasticism mode of painting that approximates to the condition of a universal pictorial language, and with the utopian circle of mostly Dutch artists that congregated from 1917 around the periodical *De Stijl (The Style)*. Nonetheless, his involvement with *De Stijl* was always as an independent and the lexicon of painterly components that has become synonymous with Neoplasticism—black grids and red, yellow, blue, and white rectangles—came about only after a long and studious process of artistic and philosophical development. Mondrian's well-documented interest in theosophy, a belief system that insisted it was

possible to attain profound knowledge by other than empirical means, began around 1900. *Portrait of a Young Woman in Red* finds its origins in theosophy. Occupying a frozen world of silence, Mondrian's red-dressed girl is centrally positioned on the canvas and organized in a manner that prefigures the artist's rectilinear canvases of the 1920s and 30s. The painting suggests that even before he embarked on his Cubist-inspired compositions of 1911 to 1912, Mondrian was disposed toward paring down his subject until it contained only the minimum of referential content. A remarkable figurative painter long before he became a great abstract painter, Mondrian was perhaps one of the last artists to believe that his work could alter the forms and conventions of society. **PB**

Mountain Scene | Ferdinand Hodler

1909 | oil on canvas | Private collection

At fourteen the Swiss painter Ferdinand Hodler (1853–1918) was apprenticed to the landscape artist Ferdinand Sommer and was later taught by Barthelemy Menn, a pupil of Ingres. This early training introduced him to some of the great European artists. Later in Paris he was impressed by Gauguin and Seurat. This mixture of influences explains both his interest in the topographical elements of nature, and his aim to reveal more than is normally possible when seeing a landscape as it appears before us. The subject of this painting is pared down to its essentials. Hodler removed detail and largely ignored the tradition of perspective. The mountain becomes a looming flat shape. Framed by a strip of grass and a crescent of cloud, it is both a portrait and an object of meditation.

It fills the frame and its closeness forces us to think about our relationship to it. The curious overlaying of two cloud forms in front of the mountain serves to separate the lighter blue of the bottom half from the inky blue-black of the peak. The use of dots—which is less scientifically rigorous but more expressive than in the work of the *pointilliste* painters—emphasizes the brightness of the lower slopes and forces the eye into movement. At the top of the mountain the eye rests. Hodler's belief that the painter must practice seeing nature as a flat surface has echoes in Maurice Denis's dictum that before a painting is a battle horse, a nude model, or some anecdote, it is essentially a flat surface covered with colors assembled in a certain order. In this Hodler anticipates Abstractionism. **WO**

Toward Evening | Gabriele Münter

1909 | oil on panel | 19 ¼ x 27 ½ in / 49 x 70 cm | Galerie Daniel Malingue, Paris, France

Because most official German art academies did not admit women at the turn of the century, Gabriele Münter (1877–1962) studied at the Phalanx School founded by Kandinsky in Munich. Here she discovered Post-Impressionism and her future partner. At first glance, *Toward Evening* is apparently inspired by Gauguin or perhaps the Fauves with its large, flat areas of intense color. While this may be a contributory factor, the painting owes more to Münter's discovery of Bavarian glass painting in 1908. She learned the technique from one of the craftsmen and transmitted her enthusiasm to Jawlensky and Kandinsky who also experimented with the medium. Although this is an oil painting on panel rather than glass, it has the same simple shapes, often outlined, and the same glowing color. It has also been suggested that Münter was the first of the future *Der Blaue Reiter* group to discover children's drawings. The colors are arbitrary, and although the subject matter of an individual strolling across a red road in the late afternoon is prosaic, the painting has a fairy tale quality. The blue mountains are an oblique reference to her partner Kandinsky who was at this time developing his theories on color and form, as manifested in his *Blue Mountain* (1909). By this time he had ceased to be her teacher. He began to break down his subjects into simplified childlike shapes as a direct response to Münter's initiative. Münter's work has been eclipsed by Kandinsky's success for many years but is now beginning to achieve the recognition it deserves. **WO**

Dance I | Henri Matisse

1909 | oil on canvas | 102 x 153 ½ in / 260 x 390 cm | Museum of Modern Art, New York, NY, USA

This huge painting by Henri Matisse (1869–1954) is the full-size study for a work commissioned by the Russian textile baron Sergei Shchukin. Shchukin was Matisse's greatest patron long before the striking colors and radically simplified forms of Matisse's work were widely appreciated in his native France. Matisse was born in northern France; he worked as a lawyer's clerk before an attack of appendicitis changed his life. While convalescing Matisse began to paint and he moved to Paris in 1891 to become an artist. In 1908 Matisse published the article "Notes of a Painter," which describes the essence of his art. "The whole arrangement of my paintings is expressive. The place occupied by figures or objects, the empty space . . . everything plays its part," he wrote. The motif of a circle of dancers had been used by artists since classical times, and it was a theme to which Matisse returned throughout his career. As in *Dance II* (1910), the dancers are painted in flat color and set against flat areas of blue for the sky and green for the hill. Stretched across the canvas, almost bursting out of it, the dancers form a circular pattern of rhythmic movement. Where two outstretched hands do not quite touch, Matisse creates a sense of dynamic tension. When first seen in 1910, the final version of *Dance I* was criticized for its flatness, lack of perspective, and crudeness of form. However, in its revolutionary use of color, line, and form lay the seeds of two important movements of twentieth-century painting: Expressionism and Abstractionism. **JW**

Two Nudes | Marcel Duchamp

1910 | oil on canvas | 38 ⅞ x 32 ¼ in / 99 x 82 cm | Museum of Modern Art, New York, NY, USA

Marcel Duchamp (1887–1968) was from an artistic family; his brothers, Jacques and Raymond, and his sister, Suzanne, also became artists. Duchamp is best known for his Surrealist paintings and provocative, witty works, such as *Chocolate Grinder No.2* (1914) and *Mona Lisa with a Moustache* (1919). Intrigued by a subject, he would create a whole series around a similar title, reworking themes again and again. *Two Nudes* is an example of Duchamp's Post-Impressionist style and shows the great influence artists such as Renoir and Degas had upon his early works. This painting is a world away from his controversial *Nude Descending a Staircase No.2* and his readymades, the most perplexing of which to contemporary audiences was *Fountain* (1917)—actually a urinal. In 1913, the artist moved to New York where he became a leading figure in the Dada and Surrealist movements. Around this time he decided to move away from art that appealed to the visual senses (which he described as "retinal art") and create an art that appealed to the brain—his works thus became more geometric. By 1920, Duchamp had abandoned the concept of painting altogether and worked only in mixed media, enjoying constantly pushing the boundaries of what was considered "artistic." Duchamp once said about his art: "The creative act is not performed by the artist alone; the spectator brings the work in contact with the external world by deciphering and interpreting its inner qualifications and thus adds his contribution to the creative act." **LH**

Kandinsky
Gabriele Münter

c.1910 | oil on canvas | 35 ¼ x 17 ⅛ in / 90 x 43.5 cm
Private collection

In 1908, Gabriele Münter (1877–1962) and Kandinsky moved to the Bavarian Alps. Their house became an artistic center with constant visitors, including Arnold Schoenberg, Paul Klee, Franz Marc, August Macke, Alexei von Jawlensky, and Marianne von Werefkin. Münter painted portraits of these friends, and several of Kandinsky, which illustrate her relationship with him. Romantic ideas of man as the Godhead in nature were rife in German Expressionism and influenced the way women functioned within the movement, but Kandinsky constantly encouraged Münter, and both exhibited with the Munich New Artists' Association at this time. Unlike other colorful, childlike portraits she did of Kandinsky, this one uses an Impressionistic style with quieter, descriptive colors. The hands placed near the heart, coupled with the romantic image above and the two teacups, betray Münter's feelings. **WO**

A Lady in an Interior
Carl Holsøe

1900–10 | oil on canvas | 15 x 20 in / 38 x 51 cm
Private collection

A Lady in an Interior represents the epitome of peacefulness. We see a lady in dark clothes with her back toward us, appearing to be reading or looking out of the window. Her dark armchair is positioned against a small dresser with a matching mirror and a dark wooden frame. This dark furniture contrasts with the two windows, which welcome the sun and fill the room with light. We suddenly note, however, that we are looking in a mirror, and the room is in fact behind us. The frame of the mirror becomes a frame within a frame. Although Carl Vilhelm Holsøe (1863–1935) also did flower painting and still lifes, he kept returning to the subject of elegant, middle-class interiors, perfecting the representation of architectural details to a greater extent than the portrayal of its residents. This aim for balance within a restricted area was successful in his day; his interior paintings are still widely acclaimed. **SML**

The Artist in Her Room in Paris
Gwen John

c.1910 | oil on canvas
Private collection

Head
Alexei von Jawlensky

c.1910 | oil on canvas over cardboard | 16 x 13 in /
41 x 33 cm | Museum of Modern Art, New York, NY, USA

This intimate scene invites the viewer to look into the artist's room. There are two versions of this painting, one with the window open and the other with the window closed and shielded by thin curtains. The curtains are, in turn, trapped behind the small table, a frustrating obstacle to anyone who would attempt to open the window. These paintings can be read as the two sides of Welsh artist Gwen John's (1876–1939) personality: the open-window scene is one of optimism but the closed curtain scene is claustrophobic and—despite the light colors—depressing. She veered between high and low periods in her life, with her mood echoing the complications she encountered. Her relationship with sculptor Auguste Rodin was often troubled and painful, but it also brought her times of great happiness. She was a very private person, and her reputation is still similarly private today. **LH**

In 1909, a group of like-minded figures founded the Munich New Artists' Association. The group's chairman was Wassily Kandinsky; its deputy, his great friend Alexei von Jawlensky (1864–1941). But while Kandinsky's art became increasingly abstract, Jawlensky stayed rooted to representational idioms—the landscape, the still life and, as we see here, the portrait. While ostensibly a portrait, the subject of this painting is unknown and the baldly descriptive title indicates that his or her identity is irrelevant. Jawlensky applies the same techniques he had used in his landscapes, dividing the planes of the face into broad swaths of bright color contoured by thick black lines. The eyes stare out with a startling hieratic power. For much of his career, Jawlensky concentrated almost exclusively on "head" paintings, gradually simplifying their elements into abstract forms that have been likened to latter-day religious icons. **RB**

Lake Thun and the Stockhorn Mountains | Ferdinand Hodler

1910 | oil on canvas | 33 x 42 in / 83 x 106 cm | Scottish National Gallery of Modern Art, Edinburgh, UK

This painting is one of a series of mountain landscapes near Lake Thun, produced late in the career of Ferdinand Hodler (1853–1918). From the mid-nineteenth century, Switzerland began to experience industrial development and a tourist invasion, but nothing of this is seen in Hodler's Swiss landscapes. As a Symbolist influenced by his reading of the philosopher Schopenhauer, Hodler is more interested in the mood of the scene rather than the superficial world of appearances. To achieve this he deformed the scene through his own subjectivity. In Symbolism, objects are flattened, simplified, and turned into patterns. Horizontality is the key to this particular painting. Apart from its clear, if not realistic, resemblance to grass, water, mountain, sky, and cloud, it can be read as six rhythmic bands of color. The horizontal signified death to Hodler, a common theme in his painting and that of other Symbolists, but in this work death is not an end but simply one part of the endless life cycle expressed through the symmetry of forms in the earth and the clouds. The mountains are encircled in a halo of cloud and in themselves are evocative of Kandinsky's later mystical rendition of mountains. In 1919 Hodler stated that in his contemplation of nature he felt that he was standing on the edge of the earth and communicating with the universe. He cut away the space where the viewer would stand to stress the vastness of the world and to suggest a reality beyond the physical experience of seeing. **WO**

A Fight in the Arcade | Umberto Boccioni

1910 | oil on burlap | 30 x 25 in / 76 x 64 cm | Pinacoteca di Brera, Milan, Italy

Written the same year that he executed this painting, Umberto Boccioni's (1882–1916) *Manifesto of Futurist Painters* is full of active and aggressive words such as "fight," "vicious," and "contempt." This violence is also present in *A Fight in the Arcade*, showing a large group of upper-class people breaking out in hysteria in Milan's most famous shopping arcade. Most of the formally dressed figures are running with their arms above them, all converging on the work's focal point as if it is a vortex sucking them in. In this area are two women, most likely prostitutes, engaged in a fight. Yet Boccioni does not draw us into the scene—in fact, he scares the viewer off through the blinding lights of the café and the man facing toward us in the foreground who gestures for us to leave. By emphasizing the speed and movement of the modern city, the painting can be likened to other Futurist works. Futurism was largely an early twentieth-century Italian and Russian movement. Led by the Italian Filippo Tommaso Marinetti, Futurists rejected traditional notions of art and the past in general. In spite of such claims, one cannot refute that *A Fight in the Arcade* exhibits a debt to art of the recent past. It is known that Boccioni studied Impressionist and Post-Impressionist styles in Paris in 1902, and his use of color here reflects this knowledge. Furthermore, the way in which he often applies the paint in small rather than continuous lines is similar to pointillism (or "dot") technique that was pioneered by the late-nineteenth-century artist, Georges Seurat. **WD**

The Red Studio | Henri Matisse

1911 | oil on canvas | 71 x 72 ¼ in / 181 x 219 cm | Museum of Modern Art, New York, NY, USA

Henri Matisse (1869–1954) is known as the great colorist of the twentieth century and *The Red Studio* is one of the best examples of this talent. An exhibition of Islamic art, which Matisse saw in Munich in 1911, inspired a series of interiors swamped with a single color. The subjects of the art on display in the room are less important than the fact that they operate as patterns on the surface. One or two objects overlap but on the whole they exist as individual artifacts connected by red paint. But it would be a mistake to think of this painting as simply an exploration of the color red, it is principally a painting about the act of painting. The furniture is merely suggested—it barely exists. Because of their color, only the paintings depicted in the image—his own paintings—have a sense of tangibility. The nudes lead the eye around the room from left to right, ending in a deep curl incorporating the chair (a symbolic nude) and the pink nudes leaning against the chest. It is only possible to read this as a room because of the window and the angle of the table and chair, which suggest recession, and the propped-up painting on the left, above which everything flattens out. The only obvious reference to the production of art is an open box of crayons. Instead, it is the idea of painting that is suggested, by allowing an empty frame to capture a portion of the red. Matisse's obvious successor was Mark Rothko (1903–70), who acknowledged his debt after making daily pilgrimages to see *The Red Studio* when it was installed at the Museum of Modern Art in New York in 1949. **WO**

Morning in Paris | Pierre Bonnard

1911 | oil on canvas | 30 x 48 in / 76 x 122 cm | State Hermitage Museum, St. Petersburg, Russia

Despite the subject matter, at around the time he created this painting, Pierre Bonnard (1867–1947) was spending less and less time in Paris. During 1911, he made several prolonged trips to St. Tropez and in 1912 he bought a home at Vernon, near Giverny. In addition to spending much of his time in the south of France, he and fellow painter Édouard Vuillard took regular trips abroad. At around the time *Morning in Paris* was painted, however, Bonnard also took on a new Parisian studio at 22 rue Tourlaque for the weeks he was there. Perhaps it was this move and the studio's new views over the city that prompted him to create such a nostalgic scene. *Morning in Paris* emphasizes the strong influence the Impressionists had on Bonnard's work as he too became fixed on trying to recreate the

effects of light, particularly in his later decades and in landscape scenes. (In the 1920s, Bonnard would become friends with Monet and Renoir.) Bonnard wrote vivid descriptions of scenes or objects he had encountered in his diaries, interpreting the particular composition of their colors and describing what combination of paint colors he would use if he were trying to recreate that particular hue or light effect. His use of so many figures in *Morning in Paris* is interesting —those in the background are less formed than those at the forefront not only because they are in the shadows but because, for his purposes, they are less real, more illusory. Bonnard was always intrigued by the human form and this interest was enhanced by his forays into puppet design and photography. **LH**

Charlotte Corinth at Her Dressing Table | Lovis Corinth

1911 | oil on canvas | 47 x 35 in / 120 x 90 cm | Hamburger Kunsthalle, Hamburg, Germany

In 1903 Lovis Corinth (1858–1925) married Charlotte Berend, a student at the School of Painting for Women that he had opened the previous year. Twenty-two years younger than her husband, Charlotte became his inspiration and his spiritual companion, as well as the mother of his two children. Corinth painted many domestic scenes, in particular delighting in depicting Charlotte in the intimate everyday activities of washing, dressing, and grooming herself. In this picture she is having her hair coiffured by a visiting hairdresser. The room is flooded with sunlight, reflecting off the fabric of her clothing and the hairdresser's white coat. His stiff, pedantic attention to his job contrasts with the loose sensuality of Charlotte's evident pleasure in her own physical existence. There is a joyous sensuality to the image, capturing a moment of unalloyed happiness and well-being. Although Corinth was to speak out against the influence of foreign art on Germany, the picture shows clearly the impression made on him by French artists, especially Édouard Manet. This painting is one of sixty-three produced in 1911, an astonishingly prolific year. In December of the same year he suffered a stroke from which he never fully recovered, though he continued as an artist and took on the prestigious role of president of the Berlin Secession, in succession to Max Liebermann. But he was partially paralyzed on his left side and although Charlotte remained the mainstay of his life, the simple happiness that shines through this painting became more elusive. **RG**

Composition IV | Wassily Kandinsky

1911 | oil on canvas | 63 x 99 in / 160 x 251 cm | Kunstsammlung Nordrhein-Westfalen, Düsseldorf, Germany

In the years before World War I many European artists and intellectuals felt an uneasy sense of impending change. Wassily Kandinsky (1866–1944), one of the main theorists of German Expressionism, rationalized this through his understanding of Nietzsche's ideas of creation through destruction. But this painting is specifically linked to biblical ideas of apocalypse, promulgated by the philosopher Rudolf Steiner and others. The left of the painting is agitated and bristling with dark activity, depicting a world that is out of kilter. The sun is encircled by the rainbow and shrouded in a black ring. The lances of a phalanx of fighters enter the picture from the left, while above them two horses rear up with interlocked legs. A great wave threatens annihilation. A group of three Cossacks appear in the center and above them a walled city perches precariously on a mountain top. The lighter and calmer right side of the painting indicates spiritual regeneration, symbolized by the central blue mountain. The two awakened dead bodies in winding sheets refer to the moment when the dead shall rise again, as described in the Book of Revelation. While it is fascinating to decipher the symbols, Kandinsky intended the colors and lines to work together subliminally to foster a new spiritual understanding. Rather than replicate the world, he abstracted from it to stimulate a vision beyond material existence. After the war, Kandinsky further developed his ideas on empathy which he expressed in *Concerning the Spiritual in Art*, written in 1912. **WO**

Peasants
Natalia Goncharova

1911 | oil on canvas | 51½ x 39½ in / 131 x 100.5 cm
State Russian Museum, St. Petersburg, Russia

The diverse creative output of Russian artist Natalia Goncharova (1881–1962) included illustration, painting, and theater design. With Mikhail Larionov, she initiated Neo-Primitivism, inspired by traditional Russian art and artifacts such as icons, *lubki* (colored popular prints), wooden toys, and textiles. *Peasants* was one of a group of nine paintings known as *Vintage* or *Grape Harvest*. Two peasants move rhythmically across the canvas under the weight of baskets of grapes. The vibrant colors sing out, particularly the orange against the intense blue background; the flat shapes of the figures recall Byzantine art, while the thick outlines clearly reference the woodblock prints in illustrated *lubki*. Two Matisse paintings had recently arrived in Moscow and when the *Vintage* paintings were shown in 1913, Goncharova acknowledged her debt to Fauvism, which led her to discover Russian folk and popular art. **WO**

Blue Horse II
Franz Marc

1911 | oil on canvas | 44 ⅛ x 33 ⅝ in / 112 x 86 cm
Private collection

In 1903, Franz Marc (1880–1916) saw work by Gauguin and van Gogh in Paris; their use of color to describe something other than material reality prompted the development of his own color theories. Believing that animals are purer than humans, Marc thought that the "animalization" of art could evoke the sense of God in everything. By the time he began his animal paintings in 1911, he had befriended August Macke, with whom he discussed color theory, and met Kandinsky, with whom he formed the group *Der Blaue Reiter* (The Blue Rider). *Blue Horse II* shows a blue horse looking across a multicolored landscape (for Marc, the horse was a conduit to spiritual knowledge); viewers are invited to see the landscape through the horse's sensibility. "Blue is the male principle, astringent and spiritual," he wrote. The predominant color, however, is yellow, which for Marc symbolized joy and the female element. **WO**

Portrait of Professor Dr.
Eduard Meyer | Lovis Corinth

1911 | oil on canvas | 24 ¾ x 17 ¾ in / 63 x 45 cm
Hamburger Kunsthalle, Hamburg, Germany

I and the Village
Marc Chagall

1911 | oil on canvas | 75 ⅝ x 59 ½ in / 192 x 151 cm
Museum of Modern Art, New York, NY, USA

In 1910, Alfred Lichtwerk, the director of the Hamburger Kunsthalle, commissioned Lovis Corinth (1858–1925) to paint Eduard Meyer—professor of history at Berlin University. Although a member of the Berlin Secession, Corinth was relatively unknown. Lichtwerk wanted a formal portrait in academic garb, but Corinth and Meyer opted for a more informal pose. This study for the portrait shows the intensity that Corinth brought to the depiction of Meyer's head. There is no attempt to soften the coarseness of the facial features; Meyer's lips are parted and his direct, almost hostile stare implies the energy of his mind. Something of the expressive touch of the study was lost in the finished portrait, but the head remained unsettling. The work did not correspond to Lichtwerk's intended celebration of a pillar of German society, and he commissioned Corinth to paint Meyer again. **RG**

The Jewish identity of Russian-born artist Marc Chagall (1887–1985) is central to his work, with its symbolic, nostalgic, and surreal imagery of *shtetl* scenes and Jewish folktales. *I and the Village* is an early example of his signature style of nostalgic Surrealism. As in a dream, themes, images, references, and impressions overlap in illogical proximity. In the foreground, a man and a goat stare intimately at each other. Superimposed on the animal's cheek is another scene in which a woman is milking another goat. Or perhaps this is a flashback that might explain the relationship between the man and his animal. Interwoven in the painting is an image of a burning bush taken from the Old Testament story in which God appeared to Moses to tell him the prophecy of Israel. There is also an Orthodox church in the background. Nostalgia and ethnic pride connect these seemingly disparate references. **AH**

Ring Gymnast No.2 | Eugène Jansson

1912 | oil on canvas | 75 ¼ x 79 ⅝ in / 190 x 201 cm | Detroit Institute of Arts, Detroit, MI, USA

This work belongs to a period, starting in the early 1900s, when Eugène Jansson (1862–1915) produced several pictures of naked men bathing, lifting weights, and performing gymnastics. These images—influenced partly by a new fashion for healthy living, and partly by the artist's preoccupations with his constant poor health and his sexuality—were shockingly frank for their time and duly outraged many people. This gymnast is painted in such a way that the detail of his body position dissolves on close scrutiny. His body looks as if it is turned inside out, with his upper torso and shoulders resembling a curved but rather two-dimensional piece of carved wood. This adds to the sense that he is doing an almost impossible maneuver. The striated style, especially exaggerated on the limbs, evokes a real feeling of strong muscles being stretched to their limit. At the same time, however, the muted palette, with both human skin and simple background painted in the same tones, and the balletic quality of the man's pose, lend the work a simple harmony. The unusual, stylized approach for which Jansson is known is present, as is the influence of Norwegian artist Edvard Munch (1863–1944), whose work Jansson had seen exhibited in Stockholm in 1894. Underappreciated in his time, Jansson is now recognized as a genuine, highly individual talent. In the stylized, almost Symbolist lingering over the muscular male form seen in pictures such as this one, he added an unusual and progressive note to the history of the male nude. **AK**

Park Restaurant | August Macke

1912 | oil on canvas | 31 ⁷⁄₈ x 41 ³⁄₈ in / 81 x 105 cm | Kunstmuseum, Basel, Switzerland

Although he wrote an essay titled "Masks" for the *Blue Rider Almanac*, August Macke (1887–1914) was a non-theorist whereas Kandinsky and Franz Marc, the founders of *Der Blaue Reiter* (the Blue Rider) formed in Munich, Germany, thrived on theoretical debate. Macke exhibited with the group and shared many of their concerns, particularly the importance of the "primitive" in painting. His paintings are filled with people shopping, sitting in cafes, and strolling through parks. Although he was an Expressionist—the angst of *Die Brücke* (The Bridge) in Berlin and the spiritual strivings of *Der Blaue Reiter* did not form part of his visual vocabulary—he was essentially a colorist. Heat bounces out of the image, while the people in *Park Restaurant* relax with tea and newspapers under the shade of overarching trees. Rather than living beings, however, the figures are mere shapes. The pattern of whites in the composition, the red and orange swirling ground, and the rhythm of hats, show that Macke is very close to pure abstraction, but he never fully engaged with it, preferring the Orphism of Robert Delaunay. Macke clearly absorbed his ideas on color relationships and the breaking down and interpenetration of form. In April 1914 he visited Tunisia with Paul Klee. The color and light revolutionized Klee's work and confirmed Macke's. On his return he was conscripted and died in September 1914 on the front line, aged twenty-seven. In his short life Macke had absorbed many influences and proved himself a supreme colorist. **WO**

Tours de Laon
Robert Delaunay

1912 | oil on canvas | 64 x 51 in / 162 x 130 cm
Musée National d'Art Moderne, Paris, France

Nude Descending a Staircase
No.2 | Marcel Duchamp

1912 | oil on canvas | 57 ½ x 35 in / 146 x 89 cm
Philadelphia Museum of Art, Philadelphia, PA, USA

The gray structures of Braque and Picasso's Cubism had astonished Robert Delaunay (1885–1941) with their cobweblike appearance. His response was to flesh out their silvery skeletons with vivid, delicately applied color, as seen in this painting of the spires of a fourteenth-century Gothic church rising above a town. Shards of pink foliation are indicated by a flurry of brushmarks, reverberating against the greens and violets of the town's walls. Delaunay's rhomboids of shifting light and shade destabilize a fixed viewing position. Within a year of this painting, his color experiments shifted toward an increasingly abstract language in which architectural forms flattened into a kaleidoscope of interlocking shapes. Termed "Orphism," Delaunay believed this non-representational "pure painting" could affect consciousness as deeply as the music of Orpheus had charmed the ancient gods. **ZT**

This was the painting that launched Marcel Duchamp (1887–1968) into the realms of notoriety, although it took months to find its way into the public gaze. Intended for the Paris Salon des Independants show of 1912, it appears to have been too "independent" for the committee to approve and was vetoed. Duchamp looked elsewhere and the painting traveled abroad, where it was seen at an exhibition in Barcelona before being moved on to New York's Armory Show in 1913. At the time, many critics were shocked by their first glimpse of a Cubist-Futurist painting. Cartoonists even ridiculed the piece in which motion is depicted by successive superimposed images. The stark color and harsh angles are suggestive of an aggression that many viewers found unsettling. But despite its Futurist overtones, Duchamp later said that while painting it he was totally unaware of the Futurist style. **LH**

Materia
Umberto Boccioni

1912 | oil on canvas | 89 x 59 in / 35 x 23 cm
Peggy Guggenheim Collection, Venice, Italy

Portrait of Pablo Picasso
Juan Gris

1912 | oil on canvas | 66 ¼ x 29 ⅛ in / 93 x 74 cm
Art Institute of Chicago, Chicago, IL, USA

Umberto Boccioni (1882–1916) created this portrait of his mother shortly before giving up painting to focus on sculpture. The image is one of the most powerful and unsettling of its time, and the culmination of the Italian response to Cubism. The Futurists celebrated technology, the machine, and the industrialized city while advocating the rejection of traditional values. Influenced by the works of Picasso, Braque, and Duchamp, *Materia* embodies an Italian approach that adapted Cubism's static, analytical manner, and infused it with a dynamic, heated activity. In a kaleidoscope of clashing planes and feverish colors, a mother stands on her balcony, halfway between the interior and exterior worlds, fragments of the street beyond and the room behind compete for our attention. The whole is a stunning realization of the Cubist goal of depicting the "simultaneity" of modern experience. **RB**

Juan Gris (1887–1927) left Madrid for Paris in 1906. Six years later, when he was working close to Picasso in a dilapidated studio block, Gris painted one of the great masterpieces of Spanish art. It depicts the artist looking out at the viewer in a relaxed and confident manner. In his left hand, he is shown holding a palette bearing elliptical smears of black and the three primary colors. The painting is made up of a series of facetted planes, the edges of which are delineated with a decisive clarity. The artist constructs these planes out of blocklike touches of warm and cool color, a technique adopted from Picasso and Georges Braque, although Gris places them on the surface of the canvas with a regularity rarely employed by the other artists. The refined, crystalline beauty of his paintings and his unerring sense of composition ensures his reputation as one of the supreme painters of the modern age. **PB**

Dynamism of a Dog on a Leash | Giacomo Balla

1912 | oil on canvas | 35 ³⁄₈ x 43 ¼ in / 90 x 110 cm | Albright-Knox Art Gallery, Buffalo, NY, USA

Born in Turin, Italy, Giacomo Balla (1871–1958) was the son of an industrial chemist. After studying music in his childhood, he switched to art, studying at the Accademia Albertina di Belle Arti and the Liceo Artistico in Turin. He also attended classes at the University of Turin with Cesare Lombroso. Balla moved to Rome in 1895 and worked as illustrator and caricaturist. Influenced by Filippo Tommaso Marinetti, he adopted the Futurism aesthetic, and signed the Futurist Manifesto in 1910, along with Umberto Boccioni, Luigi Russolo, Carlo Carrà, and Gino Severini. These artists fought for the sake of a contemporary art form that would challenge traditions and its conventions. Their art was directed toward an unprecedented expression of speed, technology, and dynamism, in accordance with their contemporary industrial era. Balla's most important Futurist experimentations were developed between 1909 and 1916. He studied the optical possibilities revealed by the photo-scientific research on the representation of time, led by Étienne-Jules Marey and Eadweard Muybridge. Their images led them to invent the first dynamic painted analysis of form in movement. Photographic influence can clearly be seen in *Dynamism of a Dog on a Leash*, one of his most famous works. An incredible number of lines are painted so as to put the emphasis on the action of the dog walking in the street. This painting announced Balla's future work, in which the depiction of movement and speed led to astonishing abstract compositions. **JJ**

Le Nord-Sud | Gino Severini

c.1913 | oil on canvas | 19 ¼ x 25 ¼ in / 49 x 64 cm | Pinacoteca di Brera, Milan, Italy

Italian Gino Severini (1883–1966) moved to Paris from Rome to be at the epicenter of avant-garde activity, where, by 1912, his early Divisionist work exploring the constituents of light was integrated with the fragmented and overlapping forms of Cubism. In contact with his compatriot Marinetti, leader of the Italian Futurists, Severini signed on to the movement in the first Manifesto, embracing the speed and energy of the modern age and setting his subjects in motion. Extended northbound in 1912, the Nord-Sud Line A ran from Notre-Dame-de-Lorette to Jules Joffrin, passing through Pigalle, Severini's local station. The Metro offered the kind of dynamic subject beloved of the Futurist painters, although unusual for Severini, who tended to focus on the modern

movements of dancers in popular nightclubs. His *Le Nord-Sud* hops about with complementary colors mauve and yellow partnering one another, applied densely in a mosaic of patches. Suggesting the glazed tiles under electric light, these dappled surfaces are pierced by chevrons and semi-circles in gray, brown, and black, tunnel openings, staircases and reflections on glass. Truncated advertising and platform announcements add to the impression of noise as well as movement. The effect is analogous to the accumulation of sensations in the mind of a traveling passenger. Exhibited in London in 1913, *Le Nord-Sud* particularly impressed the British painter Christopher Nevinson, who became involved in the Futurist movement. **ZT**

Portrait of Countess Mathieu de Noailles | Ignacio Zuloaga

*c.*1913 | oil on canvas | 59 ⁷/₈ x 77 in / 152 x 195.5 cm | Museo de Bellas Artes, Bilbao, Spain

Born in Eibar, Spain, Ignacio Zuloaga (1870–1945) was principally self-taught, spending his time at museums where he would copy famous paintings. In 1890, he moved to Paris where he fell under the spell of Impressionism. He began using bright palettes, mixing pastels and vivid colors and creating his own style. In 1892 he returned to Spain, where he was inspired by the rich colors of traditional costume and Andalucian life, the results of which can be seen in *Portrait of Countess Mathieu de Noailles*. This wonderfully decadent portrait of French poet and novelist Anna Isabel de Brancovan (1876–1933) is evocative of Spain's rich past, echoing the works of Velázquez in its subject matter and clarity, yet it is also firmly identified with the Spain of the artist's lifetime.

The manner in which the countess looks directly out at the viewer, as if daring one to drop her gaze, is provocative and challenging. Both she and the artist appear to be saying "judge me if you choose." The countess lived in Paris, where she mixed with artists and writers, receiving them at home while reclining on a sofa, as shown here. There is a pleasing symmetry to the picture: the peonies on the curtains alongside those in the vase, the pattern of the vase which emulates the folds of the bedcovers, the dark, patterned stockings to match her dark hair, all in sharp contrast to the demure color of her dress. The dress is so close in tone to her skin color that it takes a while to realize how much of the adventurous countess's bare shoulder is on display. **LH**

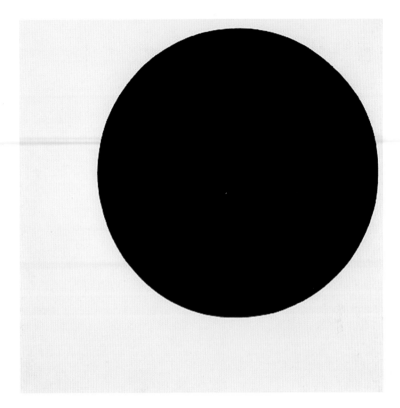

Black Circle | Kasimir Malevich

1913 | oil on canvas | 41½ x 41½ in / 105 x 105 cm | State Russian Museum, St. Petersburg, Russia

Born in Ukraine, Kasimir Malevich (1878–1935) briefly attended art classes at the Drawing School in Kiev, then at the Moscow School of Painting, Sculpture, and Architecture. In 1911, he showed some of his work at the second exhibition of the Union of Youth group ("Soyus Molod'ozhi") in St. Petersburg. Three years later, he was exhibited at the Salon des Indépendants in Paris, along with Sonia Delaunay and Alexander Archipenko. Malevich taught at the Vitebsk Practical Art School (1919–22); then in 1926, he published his seminal book *The World as a Nonobjectivity* while teaching at the Leningrad Academy of Arts. For two years, he gave art classes at the Kiev State Art Institute, and finally in 1930 at the House of Arts in Leningrad (now St. Petersburg). Persecuted by the Stalinist regime, he died in poverty and oblivion. *Black Circle* remains one of the best examples of the work the artist started developing in the mid-1910s. All references to figurative elements are abandoned in favor of a total abstract composition. Here, he chose to depict a perfect circle—a pure geometrical figure— standing on a complete white background. From this period onward, Malevich started to paint new abstract "nonobjective" paintings, an idea he introduced in his famous manifesto, *From Cubism to Suprematism*, published in 1915. Such work would later have a huge impact on art movements to come, such as Op art. His influence would not only be felt in painting, but would also have a great impact on 1920s and 30s European photography. **JJ**

Composition VII | Wassily Kandinsky

1913 | oil on canvas | 78 ¾ x 118 ⅛ in / 200 x 300 cm | State Tretyakov Gallery, Moscow, Russia

In November 1913, Wassily Kandinsky (1866–1944) executed this, the largest and most ambitious painting of his career, over the course of three and a half intense days in his Munich studio. In many ways it marked the summation of everything he had been working toward over the previous five years. Kandinsky described his *Compositions* as "inner visions," analogous in form and construction to a symphony. For *Composition VII*, he carried out more than thirty preliminary studies—more than for any other painting he attempted. He began work in the center left of the frame, flowering out from this nucleus in sweeps of contrasting colors, shapes, and dissecting lines, alternating thickly applied paint with thin washes. Despite the presence of certain motifs from earlier paintings (for example, a boat in the bottom left corner) their purpose here is nonrepresentational. Here at last is a painterly language of complete abstraction—although decidedly not without meaning. Kandinsky stated that his intention was to create art that acted as a spiritual remedy for a sick, materialist world; paintings that allowed "the viewer to stroll around within the picture . . . and so become part of the picture." The theme of *VII* is apocalyptic but unlike the terrifyingly destructive waves of the Flood alluded to in *VI*, here there seems to be an explosive rebirth of joyous, chaotic possibility: an ecstatic cry of hope in the face of the looming violence of World War I and revolution in his Russian homeland. **RB**

Swifts: Paths of Movement + Dynamic Sequences | Giacomo Balla

1913 | oil on canvas | 38 x 47 ¼ in / 96.8 x 120 cm | Museum of Modern Art, New York, NY, USA

Giacomo Balla's (1871–1958) participation at the Venice Biennale in 1899 led him to be exhibited in major venues in Europe during the following years. His work could be seen in Italy (Rome and Venice), Germany (Munich, Berlin, and Düsseldorf), the Netherlands (Rotterdam), and in France (during the 1919 Salon d'Automne held in Paris). In 1912, he traveled to London and to Düsseldorf, where he began painting his most famous abstract light studies. During World War I, Balla's studio became the major meeting place for young Italian artists. Although the Futurist movement started to decline in the mid-1910s, Balla's experimentations continued to represent a major influence on the international art world until the 1940s. In his masterpiece *Swifts: Paths of Movement*

+ Dynamic Sequences Balla offers the viewer a total abstract image, mixing a colorful palette of bright orange, yellow, green, blue, and white touches. This painting is a wonderful example of the work developed by this artist between 1913 and 1914, in which the analysis of movement and dynamism leads to a complete decomposition of forms. Here it can also be noted how Balla wonderfully depicted the extraordinary effects of reflected light. In doing so, he emphasizes the optical vibrations produced by the painting on the viewer's retina. The image is reduced to the representation of essential lines of forces, strengthened by a complementary strong contrast of colors that increases the viewer's feeling of constant rhythm in the image. **JJ**

The Three Judges | Georges Rouault

1913 | gouache, oil on card | 30 x 41 in / 76 x 105 cm | Museum of Modern Art, New York, NY, USA

In the 1890s, French Catholic artist Georges Rouault (1871–1958) belonged to the Symbolist school as a follower of Gustave Moreau (1826–98). In the early twentieth century, he was associated with Henri Matisse (1869–1954) and the Fauves. However, by 1913, he had achieved a totally individual style, employed upon a distinctive subject matter. His trademark is the use of heavy black outlines, giving his paintings something of the appearance of stained-glass windows. His work shows the influence of Paul Cézanne (1839–1906), and his use of color is bold and intense, but without the pagan joyousness of Matisse. Judges figure repeatedly in Rouault's work, as do prostitutes and other social outcasts. The judges are not depicted in the spirit of social realism, or even of hostile political caricature, as they had been by Honoré Daumier (1808–79). This is the work of a deeply religious man whose notion of Christianity focuses on the suffering of Christ and of the oppressed. Dressed in the distinctive robes and hats of the French Republican judiciary, the judges are presented as malevolent priests of a false religion—the worship of the state and its pitiless secular justice. Like all Rouault's subjects, they belong to a fallen humanity, without grace or beauty, but whereas his prostitutes are pitiable, his judges are threatening objects of fear. This is not an image to delight the eye, but an invitation to engage with art on a moral and spiritual plane. **RG**

Udnie, Young American Girl | Francis Picabia

1913 | oil on canvas | 118 x 118 in / 300 x 300 cm | Musée National d'Art Moderne, Paris, France

Francis Picabia (1879–1953) set out on his artistic adventure at the outset of the twentieth century—an exciting time for modern French painting. Not happy to settle with one particular style, from 1902 to 1908 Picabia drew from several influences. Experimenting first with Impressionism then Fauvism, he constantly pushed the boundaries of his art, until he found a brief resting place in 1911 with Section d'Or—a group of painters who, fueled by the questions posed by Cubism, began to move the pictorial plane in new directions. Following a trip to New York, where he worked on what he called "abstractions" or "pure paintings" no longer enslaved by reality—Udnie, Young American Girl seems to take what Cubism offers and toys with it. Dancing curves reminiscent of a female frame mark a softening of Cubist forms, while Picabia's palette—infused with vivid blues and greens, hints of copper, and metallic steel—breaks free from subdued Cubist colors. This playful interpretation of Cubism became known as Orphism. Udnie is thought to have been inspired by a ballerina. Strangely, in Picabia's bid to escape reality, the bounds to this work seem set by its title. But "Udnie," perhaps an anagram of "Nudie," has a distinct erotic overtone which is seen later in more overtly sexual works such as I See Again in Memory My Dear Udnie. From 1913 to 1919, Picabia embraced the Dada movement, traveling again to the United States to disseminate its ideas, which influenced Surrealism, Abstract Expressionism, and Conceptual art. **AIB**

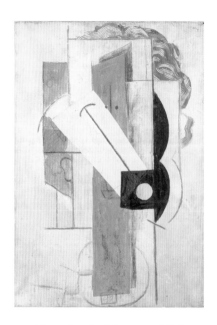

Head of a Young Girl
Pablo Picasso

1913 | oil on canvas | 21 ⁵⁄₈ x 15 in / 55 x 38 cm
Musée National d'Art Moderne, Paris, France

Berlin Street Scene
Ernst Ludwig Kirchner

1913 | oil on canvas | 47 ⁵⁄₈ x 37 ³⁄₈ in / 121 x 95 cm
Private collection

Pablo Picasso (1881–1973) was an artistic prodigy from an early age. However, he became frustrated by traditional methods of representation, and inspired by Cézanne's flattened depiction of space, he worked with Georges Braque to reinvent artistic expression. Their Cubist approach revolutionized the art world. Picasso experimented furiously, stripping down an object to its essentials and constructing something less naturalistic. In 1912, he began creating collage works that featured the recurring use of objects, such as guitar, violin, and the human head. Picasso collated objects in ways that initially elicit feelings of confusion, but with further viewing offer myriad interpretations. Is that a smile? Is the girl hiding something, or is that a door waiting to be opened? However, interpretations may be foolhardy, for as Picasso himself said, "To search means nothing in painting. To find is the thing." **SG**

Ernst Ludwig Kirchner (1880–1938) was a founding member of the *Die Brücke* group in Dresden, Germany. In 1910 the group began to migrate to Berlin, the center of the arts in Germany. Kirchner arrived there in 1911. At that time Berlin was a city of contradictions and in continual political ferment. Kirchner's streets bustle with activity but there is an inescapable mood of degeneracy in the scenes of bars and cabarets, traffic, shop windows, and the faceless masses. Prostitutes strut through the street like brilliant cockatoos, but are hemmed in by the men on the right and the traffic on the left. It is a claustrophobic and alien world; there is no physical or emotional human contact. Compared to Kirchner's work in Dresden, in which artists and models frolicked naked in nature, this work is darker and has jagged and splintered forms that partly show the influence of Futurism. **WO**

Song in the Distance
Ferdinand Hodler

1914 | oil on canvas | 71 x 49 ¼ in / 179 x 125 cm
Hamburger Kunsthalle, Hamburg, Germany

Ferdinand Hodler (1853–1918) formed a theory known as "parallelism"—the symmetrical repetition of elements to reveal harmony and an underlying order in creation. At the same time his friend Emile Jaques-Dalcroze was developing "eurythmics," a system of movement that encourages the body to respond to the rhythms of music. Rather than merely illustrate his subject, Hodler used parallelism and references to eurythmics and dance to create a timeless, universal subject with no content or history. This figure is in blue, the color of the sky, and seems to be momentarily caught between movements. A strong dark outline detaches her from the background. The horizon's arc indicates the edge of the world and, as a portion of a circle, symbolizes the female. Life and death are this painting's themes; life symbolized by the vertical and death by the horizontal. **WO**

The Cyclops
Odilon Redon

c.1914 | oil on canvas | 25 ¼ x 20 ⅛ in / 64 x 51 cm
Museum Kröller-Müller, Otterlo, Netherlands

French Symbolist painter Odilon Redon (1840–1916) had shown great skill at drawing ever since childhood. Between 1879 and 1889 he published lithography albums, most with literary associations. From the 1890s, Redon worked increasingly in color, using a palette of pastel tones to paint flowers, one of his central preoccupations at that time. Above the dreamlike landscape of *The Cyclops*, a huge one-eyed monster looks straight at the viewer, while a naked woman lies in colorful flowers, as if she belongs to another scene. Redon had already explored the theme of the cyclops in the famous chalk and charcoal *Eye-Balloon*. This type of mysterious and disturbing image-making recalls the work of other Symbolist painters, whose aim was to create timeless, imaginary worlds through art, while the Surrealists later came to regard Redon's paintings as a precursor to their own movement. **JJ**

Prismes Électriques | Sonia Delaunay-Terk

1914 | oil on canvas | 98 ³/₈ x 98 ³/₈ in / 250 x 250 cm | Musée National d'Art Moderne, Paris, France

Sonia Delaunay-Terk (née Sarah Stern, 1885–1979) grew up in Gradizhsk, Ukraine, before moving to Paris in 1905, where she met and married Robert Delaunay in 1910. In 1912, they developed Orphism, a style of painting that was closely related to Futurism and Cubism and emerged at the same time, although it was generally more abstract and colorful. Orphism was named after Orpheus, the mythological Greek poet and musician, by the poet Guillaume Apollinaire, who saw links with the harmonious overlapping planes of bright, contrasting colors and harmonies in music. It was also called "Simultanism," as it combined geometric forms, bold patterns and intense color simultaneously. In 1914, Paris was gradually replacing its hazy gas street lamps with bright electric ones. Obsessed with the nature of light, especially the way in which light from these electric lamps distorted into prisms and halos as it fell onto the streets, Delaunay-Terk painted *Prismes Électriques* (Electric Prisms). The work emphasizes luminosity and vibrant color with rhythmic circles of light, evoking movement and depth. By layering color and pattern, she suggests action and excitement, in contrast to the static composition and subdued palette of Cubism. She produced many studies for this piece, using crayons, cut papers, watercolor, and oil paints, which were originally exhibited in the Salon des Indépendants. Also a designer of clothes, furniture, theater sets, and ballet costumes, she was arguably the inventor of the polka dot and used zigzags and other innovative designs in fabric and on canvas. **SH**

Village in the Forest | Fernand Léger

1914 | oil on canvas | 29 ⅛ x 36 ⅝ in / 73 x 93 cm | Albright-Knox Art Gallery, Buffalo, NY, USA

Village in the Forest represents a formative moment in the development of the work of Fernand Léger (1881–1955), one of the first generation of twentieth-century Modernist painters. During the 1910s, Léger increasingly turned away from the Impressionism that influenced his early work, and began to create paintings that allied him stylistically with the French avante-garde. In *Village in the Forest* the influence of Paul Cézanne, a spiritual leader of the Cubists, is clearly evident. This work represents Léger's preoccupation with "contrasts of form," as he also named the series of which this painting is part. We see Léger exploring Cézanne's dictum that "nature should be handled with cylinder, sphere, and cone." The dry, angular surfaces of the houses cut a ladder vertically through the rounded trees and shrubs. The two species of forms, sketched furiously in charcoal black, define and clarify one another. Léger's unhesitating application of primary and secondary color adds another layer of contrasts that animate the traditional landscape scene. The reds of the houses against the greens of the hill seem almost to sizzle, making it easy not to notice the more subtle application of the same complementary colors toward the edges of the painting. The chromatic contrasts not only animate the canvas, but add a bulk and volume to the forms. Though Léger brought his crisp colors and shapes along as his style developed, few of his later, better known works exhibit the same bold experimentation with painting's formal components. **AR**

Landscape with Red Cloud | Konrad Mägi

1913–14 | oil on canvas | 27 ¾ x 30 ¾ in / 70.4 x 78 cm | Art Museum of Estonia, Tallinn, Estonia

Konrad Mägi (1878–1925) was one of the pioneering Estonian artists who eschewed the official painting styles that dominated the country at the time—and that originated outside Estonia—to help create a truly modern art for his homeland. This painting is a strikingly passionate response to light, color, and the beauty of the landscape. The shoreline scene moves from shadowy, richly colored rocks and plants in the foreground to a water's edge sparkling with the intensity of evening light. The water darkens as it gains depth toward a horizon boiling with the flaming shades of sunset. Like other contemporary Estonian artists, Mägi had absorbed a bewildering array of influences. By the time he painted this work, he had lived or worked in Russia, Paris, and Norway. His bright colors echo German-Dutch Impressionism and dabs of varying color in the foreground represent a kind of pointillism. The bold technique, glowing colors, and emotional engagement with the subject recall Vincent van Gogh, and there are also echoes of Fauvism, which embraced intense, non-naturalistic coloring and anticipated German Expressionism. Among all these influences, however, Mägi's very personal response to the landscape sings out. Estonians traditionally have a deep love of their countryside. The painting creates the sense of the artist being alone in a deserted seascape, while experiencing a spiritual connection with it. There is a feeling of living in a land of such long, dark wintry days that, when summer arrives, the desire is to immerse oneself in the sun and light. **AK**

Portrait of the Marchesa Casati | Giovanni Boldini

1914 | oil on canvas | 53 x 73 in / 136 x 186 cm | Galleria Nazionale d'Arte Moderna, Rome, Italy

Giovanni Boldini (1842–1931) was known as the "Master of Swish" because of his exuberantly flattering portraiture, brilliant coloring, and sensuous depiction of the leading socialites in Paris and London. Boldini was born in Ferrara and trained in Florence, where he came into contact with a group of Realist painters—the *Macchiaioli*—whose influence can be seen clearly in his landscapes. However, portraiture was to become the artist's forte, and during a trip to London in 1869 he received a number of portrait commissions. In 1872 he moved to Paris, where his dazzling style captured the imagination of the city's most prestigious women. Boldini became friends with Edward Degas, and painted portraits of his contemporaries John Singer Sargent and James McNeill Whistler, as well as Paul-César Helleu and his wife. *Portrait of the Marchesa Casati* is a work of intense, almost breathless beauty—the quickly painted, Impressionistic brushstrokes evoke the vibrant energy of a flamboyant woman. Marchesa Casati (1881–1957), a wealthy Italian heiress, was brazenly forthright about her bisexuality, held lavish parties, and was often seen in Venice with two cheetahs on leashes. Here she appears to emerge from the swirling lines of her dress and the background, her face, in contrast to the rest of the painting, exquisitely detailed and modeled with utterly convincing rose-flesh tones. Boldini enjoyed huge success throughout his career. He spent his later life in France and died in Paris in 1931. **TP**

Still Life with Dancers | Emil Nolde

1914 | oil on canvas | 28 ¾ x 35 in / 73 x 89 cm | Musée National d'Art Moderne, Paris, France

Although Emil Nolde (1867–1956) was a member of *Die Brücke*, a group that played a pivotal role in German Expressionism, he was a distinctly individual painter who remained an isolated figure for much of his life. In spite of this he traveled widely—to Russia, the Far East, and the South Sea islands—as part of an ethnographic trip that further informed him of primitive art. Nolde's painting *Still Life with Dancers* seems to be an experiment, drawing together the familiar, domestic scene with some of the exotic images he had seen on his travels. In the foreground are two vases of yellow and red tulips and a cow gravy jug reminiscent of home. Upon the warm, earthy backdrop hangs a picture of two bare-chested, skirted female figures dancing with wild abandon—natives

of a faraway place. His simplified depiction of primitive human forms seems to have psychological rather than anthropological aims. Nolde often described his awkwardness in dealing with people, including women. Here we get the sense that he is able to express his emotions unchecked through the sensuous movements of the dancers but kept at a safe distance by their de-individualized blank faces and by the fact that they are within the confines of another picture. A prolific artist and a deeply religious man, Nolde went on to paint visionary figures of the Old and New Testament, but throughout his life he continued to paint simple subjects such as flowers, and with the same intensity. His ability to capture the essence of an object was central to his art. **AIB**

The Song of Love | Giorgio de Chirico

1914 | oil on canvas | 28 ¾ x 23 ⅜ in / 73 x 59.1 cm | Museum of Modern Art, New York, NY, USA

Giorgio de Chirico (1888–1978) was an influential pre-Surrealist Greek-Italian painter and founder of the *scuola metafisica* art movement. After studying in Athens and Florence, De Chirico moved to Munich where he enrolled at the Akademie der Bildenden Künste in 1906. There he became interested in Max Klinger's prints and the Symbolist paintings of Arnold Böcklin. In 1911 De Chirico moved to Paris, where he met Guillaume Apollinaire, who would be the first to qualify his art as "metaphysical." Through him, De Chirico met major artists such as Picasso and Brancusi. Many artists have acknowledged his influence, especially the Surrealists Yves Tanguy, Max Ernst, Salvador Dalí, and René Magritte. De Chirico is best known for the work he produced between 1909 and 1919, his metaphysical period, and *The Song of Love* is one of the most famous paintings. The architectural structure on the right is inspired by the Mediterranean's ancient cityscapes. The one on the left may recall contemporary smoking rooftop chimneys or the wafting steam of a running locomotive. An improbable wall in the center, set arbitrarily behind a huge Greek-style head and a shiny red plastic glove, separates the pictorial space. A big green balloon lies on a darkened floor. By depicting a haunted view of an imaginary, enigmatic scene, De Chirico demonstrates his ability to reveal a parallel reality by means of art—a process inspired in part by De Chirico's reading of Nietzsche—and of crucial importance for the metaphysical movement. **JJ**

The Enigma of a Day | Giorgio de Chirico

1914 | oil on canvas | 73 ¼ x 55 in / 185.5 x 139.7 cm | Museum of Modern Art, New York, NY, USA

Often known as Népo, Giorgio de Chirico (1888–1978) was born in Vólos, Greece, to a Genovese mother and a Sicilian father. After studying art in Athens and Florence, he moved to Germany in 1906 and entered the Academy of Fine Arts in Munich, where he read the writings of the philosophers Friedrich Nietzsche and Arthur Schopenhauer, and studied the works of Arnold Böcklin and Max Klinger. This painting is from the so-called *pittura metafisica*, or metaphysical, period of De Chirico's work that lasted until about 1918. The subject of the painting, as with many of his from the period, is a city square, deserted except for two distant figures and a statue. Dark, impenetrable shadows are cast under the arches of a classical but featureless arcade; a closed railway wagon and two tall chimneys provide an unexpectedly industrial juxtaposition to the architecture. The perspective is equally unsettling—obviously not an observed site, this is a place that is dreamt or imagined. The artist turns the logic of perspective—a system devised to place us securely in the picture—into a disturbing and unsettling device. This period of De Chirico's work was enormously influential on the Surrealists, in particular the illusionist painters such as Dalí and Magritte; his motifs of urban estrangement can also be found in the work of later artists such as George Grosz. The places that De Chirico creates in his paintings are now part of our collective imagination. His work has much to say about dream states and displacement that educates the viewer. **RW**

Self-Portrait in Armor | Lovis Corinth

1914 | oil on canvas | 39 ³/₈ x 33 ½ in / 100 x 85 cm | Hamburger Kunsthalle, Hamburg, Germany

In the spring of 1914, when this portrait was painted, German artist Lovis Corinth (1858–1925) was engaged in a cultural battle that divided the Berlin art world. The Berlin Secession, of which he was president, had split, with Modernist artists such as Max Beckmann rejecting Corinth's conservative leadership. Finding himself left in control of a rump Secession of relatively minor painters, he counterattacked with a public campaign against foreign influence on German art and in favor of traditional artistic values. "We must have the highest esteem for the masters of the past," he said in an address to Berlin art students. "Whoever does not honor the past has no hopeful prospects for the future." With the onset of World War I the following fall, cultural warfare was replaced by the real

thing. He adopted an aggressively nationalist stance in support of the German war effort. Armor had become one of Corinth's favorite studio props—he had donned it to project a heroic self-image in a 1911 portrait. In this work, however, the armor is worn by an embattled artist assailed by self-doubt. The hard gleaming steel surfaces contrast with the vulnerable fleshiness of the face, which carries an expression of baffled puzzlement. A scarf separates the head from the metal carapace of the body. There is a suggestion that he may be struck by the absurdity of dressing up in medieval fancy dress, a heroic posturing at odds with life in twentieth-century Berlin. Yet he seems committed to upholding the banner of his faith, uncomfortably open to ridicule as it may be. **RG**

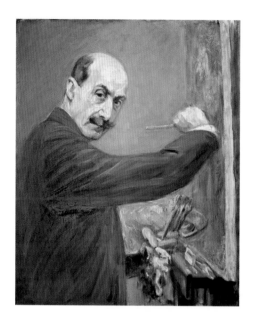

Self-Portrait
Max Liebermann

c.1915 | oil on canvas | 10 x 7 in / 25.7 x 18.4 cm
Uffizi, Florence, Italy

Portrait of Lyonel Feininger
Karl Schmidt-Rottluff

1915 | oil on canvas | 35 ½ x 30 in | Germanisches
Nationalmuseum, Nuremberg, Germany

Max Liebermann (1847–1935) was born into a rich Jewish family at a time when Jews were oppressed. He was a young adult when the laws were changed in 1871 and Jews were granted the same rights as other German citizens. His Realist paintings depicted working people as they actually were—not idealized or denigrated—and were seen as subversive. In the German parliament, Liebermann's *Twelve-Year-Old Jesus in the Temple* (1879) was condemned as blasphemous because his Jesus was said to be "too Jewish looking." In *Self-Portrait*, Liebermann shows himself as a confident, determined man. The background of palette, easel, and cloth is painted impressionistically, but his own image is painted in a more realistic style—he is the main focus, the viewer must not be distracted by anything. After Liebermann's death, the Hitler regime removed his works from German art galleries. **LH**

Karl Schmidt (1884–1976) was born in Saxony and appended the name of his home town to his surname in 1905 while a student in Dresden. This coincided with his formation of the Expressionist group *Die Brücke* (The Bridge), along with four other students. Inspired by summer visits to the Baltic coast, his early landscapes and bathing scenes featured bright, dense color and thick, impulsive brushwork. In this portrait, Feininger's face and body are defined with thick, angular contours (like a woodcut), the paint thinned down and smoothly applied. The color palette is subdued, mirroring Schmidt's concerns about the outbreak of World War I. This would have reflected Feininger's feelings too: as a U.S. citizen, he was to suffer anti-American prejudice during the war. Schmidt remained active until his death, at the age of ninety-one; the youngest member of *Die Brücke*, he was the last to die. **RB**

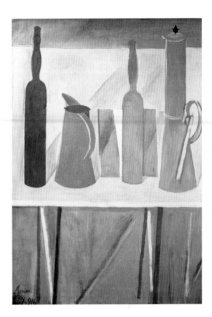

The Sock Knitter
Grace Cossington Smith

1915 | oil on canvas | 24 ¼ x 20 in / 61.5 x 51 cm
Art Gallery of New South Wales, Sydney, Australia

Grace Cossington Smith (1892–1984) became one of Australia's leading artists during the early twentieth century. Credited as the first Post-Impressionist work by an Australian artist, this painting has an oblique link to the horrors of World War I, despite the fact that it portrays a domestic interior thousands of miles from the front. The model was the artist's sister, depicted in the act of knitting socks for soldiers in the European trenches. The painting's structure is based on single brushstrokes of vivid color built up into blocks that lend the composition its form—in this, Smith was following the European Post-Impressionists. But in her bold use of color and the elongation of her lines, she evolved a distinct and individual style that became a rallying cry for Australian Modernists. The bright foreground and prominent shadows are a hallmark of her landscape paintings in particular. **DD**

Still Life
Giorgio Morandi

1916 | oil on canvas | 32 ½ x 22 ⅝ in / 82.5 x 57.5 cm
Museum of Modern Art, New York, NY, USA

Still Life by Giorgio Morandi (1890–1964) anticipates, in its somewhat stylized treatment of the objects, what would subsequently become a lifelong project for the artist. Perhaps partly because of the genre's attempted downgrading, there was a tendency for artists to use still life to signify other potential meanings. However, Morandi's understanding of the genre was one whereby the objects depicted were only ever expected to represent themselves in what could be construed as their essentialized state. Morandi's method usually consisted of arranging around half a dozen bottles, jugs, and other vessels in a configuration whose plainness was reciprocated in the humble nature of the objects themselves. In *Still Life* the economy of form, line, tone, and color represents the artist's attempt to strip away the superfluous and render visible some deeper aspect of the everyday. **CS**

Fruit Dish, Book, and Newspaper | Juan Gris

1916 | oil on canvas | 13 x 18 ⅛ in / 33 x 46 cm | Private collection

José Victoriano González-Pérez (1887–1927), known as Juan Gris, is justly celebrated as a still-life painter of humble objects. Indeed, in the whole of Western art history he is matched only by Chardin, Cézanne, and Morandi in his devotion to the mundane. By 1916 Gris had moved away from an analytic approach to Cubism and begun to embrace synthetic forms. This new approach to picture-making was developed in order to resolve the contradictions inherent in his previous use of collage. Starting in 1912, Gris had introduced paper and cloth into his work as a means of achieving a more intimate relationship with the world beyond the canvas, even as he was breaking down its forms. The use of labels and pieces of newsprint and wallpaper emphatically underscored

that bond, yet these devices remained foreign to the integrity of the picture as a painting. Alongside Picasso and Braque, the inventors of collage, Gris embarked on finding a solution to the integrity problem, and canvases such as *Fruit Dish, Book, and Newspaper* signal a renewed interest in the invention of painterly signs that marks a departure from his earlier work. Arranged on a tabletop that has been fashioned to give an illusion of reality, the dish, book, newspaper, and glass are defined as partially modeled forms on differently tilting axes. Gris wrote about such paintings, "I think I have really made progress . . . and that my pictures begin to have a unity they have lacked until now. They are no longer those inventories of objects which used to depress me so much." **PB**

Bottles and Fruit Bowl | Giorgio Morandi

1916 | oil on canvas | 23 ⅝ x 21¼ in / 60 x 54 cm | Peggy Guggenheim Collection, Venice, Italy

Although Morandi's (1890–1964) name has become virtually synonymous with the genre of still life, his origins as an artist were rooted not in the observable world, but in what might be loosely described as metaphysical art. Like Giorgio de Chirico (1888–1978) and Carlo Carrà (1881–1966), Morandi produced a series of paintings whose precise meanings remained deliberately enigmatic. None of these three artists felt entirely comfortable being associated with this genre, yet Morandi's subsequent still lifes never fully relinquished their connection to these artistic beginnings. *Bottles and Fruit Bowl* is intriguing partly because it encompasses the tendency to imbue a group of ill-defined objects with a certain quality of otherworldliness, coupled with a more direct engagement with the quotidian. The potential is there for us to read three objects in an area of indeterminate space anthropomorphically, as figures that inhabit an ill-defined landscape. Increasingly, Morandi came to use a limited range of modest-sized objects (mostly vessels, bottles, and jars) precisely because they appeared for all intents and purposes as themselves—inert, mundane, and free from association or "meaning." The artist used the convention of still life as a means to distill, harmonize, and calibrate some aspect of the concrete world. *Bottles and Fruit Bowl* affords a degree of insight into the inner workings of the artist's sensibility, both in terms of the original impetus behind what he did, and how this then became refined. **CS**

The Piano Lesson | Henri Matisse

1916 | oil on canvas | 96 x 71 in / 244 x 180 cm | Museum of Modern Art, New York, NY, USA

Henri Matisse (1869–1954) painted pretty pictures during one of history's ugliest eras. Within his lifetime there were two world wars, vicious international ideological rivalries, and relentless urbanization through industry; but Matisse turned a blind eye to these explosive social changes. Unlike his equally influential peer and rival, Picasso, the French Cubist pioneer's impact on art and history was more stylistic than sociological. Yet despite distancing his work from the issues surrounding him, his iconic experiments in drawing, painting, graphic art, book illustration, and sculpture permanently altered the course of modern art and visual culture. Nearing abstraction but marked mainly by an adherence to geometric forms and austere color pairings, the collagelike assembly of color patches in *The Piano Lesson* marked an entirely new direction for Matisse. The image's literal subject matter depicts a young boy struggling to concentrate at a piano as his mother hovers behind. An open window above him seductively reveals a distracting slice of nature green. Open windows were a recurring motif in Matisse's work, yet here the painting's somber hues and sense of introspection undermine the window's soothing symbolism. After a short dalliance with Cubism, exemplified by *The Piano Lesson*, Matisse would return to his original signature love for bright colors, female figures, nudes, and Islamic-inspired decorative composition. His context-free attitude toward genre and technique has inspired subsequent generations of artists. **SE**

Metropolis | George Grosz

1916–17 | oil on canvas | 39 ¼ x 40 ⅛ in / 100 x 102 cm | Museo Thyssen-Bornemisza, Madrid, Spain

Born in Berlin, George Grosz (1893–1959) studied at the Royal Academy in Dresden and later with graphic artist Emile Orlik in Berlin. He developed a taste for the grotesque and the satirical fueled by World War I. After a nervous breakdown in 1917 he was declared unfit for service. His low opinion of his fellow human beings is evident in all his work. He used oil and canvas, the traditional materials of high art, although he despised the tradition of art-making. The subject matter is far from traditional: *Metropolis* is a scene from hell, with blood-red dominating the canvas. The composition is based on vertiginous verticals and depicts hideous wraithlike creatures fleeing from terror. Although he distanced himself from Expressionism, the angular distortions and crazy perspective have grown from the work of artists such as Kirchner. The imagery in *Metropolis* suggests disaster on a huge scale: the city is collapsing on itself and the overall color suggests conflagration. With revolution and World War II around the corner, it is horribly prescient. The work is satirical and openly critical of bourgeois society and particularly of authority. Later, together with Otto Dix, he developed *Die Neue Sachlichkeit* (The New Objectivity)—moving away from Expressionism by calling for the unemotional perception of the object, a focus on the banal, insignificant, and ugly, and painting devoid of context or compositional wholeness. In 1917 Malik Verlag began publishing his graphic works, bringing him to the attention of a wider audience. **WO**

Suprematist Painting
Kasimir Malevich

1916–17 | oil on canvas | 38 ½ x 26 ⅛ in / 98 x 66 cm
Museum of Modern Art, New York, NY, USA

The early work of Russian painter Kasimir Malevich (1878–1935) was influenced by the Cubo-Futurist aesthetic. After publishing his manifesto *From Cubism to Suprematism* in 1915, his aim was to represent pure abstract geometrical compositions. In 1927 Malevich had a retrospective show in Germany that brought him international recognition and permitted him to leave a number of his paintings in safety. Malevich was then persecuted by the Stalinist regime in Russia and many of his works were confiscated or destroyed. While he had previously produced totally abstract pictures, depicting single geometrical shapes on white backgrounds, in this work he proposed a new kind of visual experience. A wide range of different abstract shapes seem to float in an undefined space. As a result, Malevich fulfilled his desire to depict in a two-dimensional image both dynamism and space. **JJ**

Nude Series VII
Georgia O'Keeffe

1917 | watercolor on paper | 18 x 13 ½ in / 45 x 34.5 cm
Georgia O'Keeffe Museum, Santa Fe, NM, USA

The watercolors Georgia O'Keeffe (1887–1986) executed between 1916 and 1918 formed part of a process of renewal that was vital to her emergence as a major artist. In despair at the limitations of her academic training, she worked as an illustrator and only began painting again when teaching art in rural Texas. The breakthrough came in 1915 with a series of charcoal drawings, which led to a remarkable sequence of watercolors. The brushwork is spontaneous yet assured; form is modeled in a few simple strokes; colors are bold and expressive. In this example from her series of self-posed nudes, the warm flesh tones are shaded with blue; her newfound confidence evident in the casual frankness of her pose. O'Keeffe moved on to pastels before finally returning to oils, but her work had already attracted the attention of Alfred Stieglitz, who hosted her first solo exhibition in 1917. **RB**

The Metaphysical Muse
Carlo Carrà

1917 | oil on canvas | 35 x 25 ⅝ in / 89 x 65 cm
Pinacoteca di Brera, Milan, Italy

A mannequin-style female tennis player stands, ball and racket ready, stage left of a visually arresting juxtaposition of geometric objects and images set in a claustrophobic interior. This is a prime example of Carlo Carrà's (1881–1966) *pittura metafisica* (metaphysical painting), a movement influenced by his friend and fellow Italian painter Giorgio de Chirico. The pair set out to convey in their paintings the extraordinary in ordinary, everyday objects. It is surreal in its effect but there is something mathematical as much as metaphysical about the tableaux with the two canvases on which are painted factories and a map of Greece. Carrà dabbled in Futurism, an art movement that espoused dynamism and new technology, which he rejected to pursue his *pittura metafisica*. He eventually abandoned the latter to paint more melancholy, well-constructed works such as *Morning by the Sea* (1928). **JH**

Woman Undressing
Egon Schiele

1917 | oil on paper | 18 ⅛ x 11 ⅝ in / 46 x 29.5 cm
Private collection

Egon Schiele (1890–1918) attracted much criticism in his lifetime for his blatantly erotic images of women and his explicit self-portraits. Recognized as a prodigy, he was eventually taken up by Klimt, whose influence is very evident in his work; however, Schiele is even more of a draftsman and gives the elegant, sensuous *Jugendstil* line directional force. Under his hand it becomes angular and angst-ridden. These characteristics align him with German Expressionism although he was not affiliated to any particular group. The woman in *Woman Undressing* is in an awkward position, reminiscent of Degas, as well as some of Klimt's paintings. The line is taut and edgy, even in the large sweep delineating the buttocks. Color seems almost incidental, but has a purpose. The black of the stockings and the mauve of the dress are used to frame and eroticize the area of focus. **WO**

The Embrace | Egon Schiele

1917 | oil on canvas | 39 ³/₈ x 67 in / 100 x 170 cm | Österreichische Galerie Belvedere, Vienna, Austria

In 1915 Egon Schiele (1890–1918) married Edith Harms. In the following months his paintings and drawings became less tortured. Four days after the wedding he was called up for army service but still managed to paint and exhibit. An enlightened officer in Mühling had a storeroom turned into a studio for him, and when posted to Vienna in 1917 he even had the privilege of being allowed to sleep at home. In this large canvas a couple lie on a rumpled white sheet over a yellow cover with their arms interlocked. The woman's hair tumbles over the pillow, her face is turned away and her hand is placed on the man's shoulder in a manner reminiscent of Klimt's *The Kiss*, which Schiele, as a friend and protégé of Klimt, knew well. The man, who must be Schiele himself, is gaunt

and contorted but less so than in previous self-portraits. Schiele's drawings and paintings have frequently drawn the accusation of pornography but, as others have pointed out, they are imbued with humanity, which sets them apart from such works. His obsession with sexuality, however, is akin to religious fervor, and he is reported as saying that he wanted his works to be experienced in that way. The tender unity of *The Embrace* marks a distinct change from the explicitly sexual paintings and drawings that preceded it and reflects Schiele's growing contentment in married life. However, at six months pregnant, Edith died in the Spanish influenza epidemic that swept through Europe after the war. Schiele died three days later, at the age of twenty-eight. **WO**

Nude, 1917 | Amedeo Modigliani

1917 | oil on canvas | 28 ¾ x 45 ⅞ in / 73 x 116.5 cm | Guggenheim Museum, New York, NY, USA

Jewish Italian painter and sculptor Amedeo Clemente Modigliani (1884–1920) was born in Livorno, Italy. He briefly attended art classes at Scuola Libera di Nudo (the Free School of Nude Studies) in Florence, and then at the Instituto per le Belle Arti in Venice. In 1906, he moved to Paris and worked with the artistic community in Montmartre. There, he discovered works by Gauguin, Cézanne, and Toulouse-Lautrec—all of whom would become major influences on his work. Three years later, Modigliani was introduced to the sculptor Constantin Brancusi who remained a close friend and an important artistic inspiration. From 1909 to 1914, he concentrated on sculpture, an aesthetic interest that can be found in his later paintings. Modigliani exhibited during the Salon d'Automne in 1907 and 1912 and at the Salon des Indépendants in 1908, 1910, and 1911. At the end of 1917, a solo exhibition was organized at the Berthe Weill Gallery in Paris. His luscious nudes provoked a scandal that led to the closure of the show by the Parisian police only a few hours after its opening. The Italian artist asked his close entourage to pose for his portraits, and it is known that he used models for his nude paintings. In *Nude, 1917* the influence of primitive art can be clearly observed, in particular by Modigliani's treatment of the masklike face. But this image also demonstrates how well aware he was of the previous artistic tradition: the pose of this naked, lying model recalls famous paintings by Titian, Goya, and Velázquez. **JJ**

Tiger in the Jungle | Max Slevogt

1917 | oil on canvas | 22 ⅝ x 27 ⅝ in / 57.4 x 70 cm | Hamburger Kunsthalle, Hamburg, Germany

This image erupts with a thrilling but unsettling mix of energy, passion, savagery, and eroticism. Little surprise that its creator, a German artist considered to be one of his country's leading Impressionists, is often credited with helping to lay the foundations of Expressionism. Max Slevogt (1868–1932) is known for his free, broad brushwork and his ability to capture movement—*Tiger in the Jungle* is the perfect example of this. Also a talented and successful printmaker and illustrator, Slevogt made every line count when expressing himself, and that skill is abundantly clear in this picture. It is a recognizable image of a tiger crashing through dense jungle with naked female prey in its jaws, but there is no unnecessary detail and the actual brushstrokes stand out very clearly, with

all their bold vigor, especially on the undergrowth. Here are the bright, fresh colors that helped to make Slevogt a successful Impressionist, but the emphasis is on a strong subjective and emotional response to the subject that was so important in Expressionism; this work was painted at the height of that movement. The naked woman, hair flying out with the tiger's movement, lends a progressive abandonment to the picture—Slevogt had met official disapproval some years before over a painting in which he showed naked male wrestlers in a way that was deemed to be overly erotic. This very modern image shows Slevogt as a true man of his times—its violence a reminder that Slevogt was horrified by the atrocities of World War I, raging as he painted this. **AK**

The New Gogh Gold Mine | Robert Gwelo Goodman

1917 | oil on canvas | 20 ⅛ x 23 ⅞ in / 51 x 60.7 cm | Johannesburg Art Gallery, South Africa

Toward the end of the nineteenth century, painters such as Jan Volschenk and Hugo Naudé, along with the sculptor Anton van Wouw, began to break away from the constraints of Eurocentric art and started to establish an art locally rooted in South Africa. Previously, the art of those who had gone to South Africa was merely a report to their colonial overseers. With the Union in 1910, the stage was set for the development of a more original type of South African art. Robert Gwelo Goodman (1871–1939) was born in England, but went to South Africa with his parents when he was fifteen. South Africa became his home and he died in Cape Town. He studied under J.S. Morland in Cape Town and then at the Académie Julian in Paris. He went to London, where he had three

landscapes accepted at the Royal Academy. He returned to South Africa in 1900; sketching battlefield scenes of the Boer War. While in what was then Rhodesia, he visited a town called Gwelo and adopted the name for himself. Goodman is known as a landscape painter and he considered himself a Realist. In England after the Boer War his reputation was founded on paintings such as *The New Gogh Gold Mine*. Contentiously, and as in the majority of works by white South African painters, his landscapes are often unpopulated, leaving the impression of a land without inhabitants, a land in need of rule. It seems unlikely that this was Goodman's remit and in focusing his attention on the land in front of him he is able to deliver a scene in extraordinary detail. **OR**

Waterlilies: The Clouds | Claude Monet

1914–18 | oil on canvas | 78 ¾ x 167 ⅜ in / 200 x 425 cm | Musée de l'Orangerie, Paris, France

While van Gogh is associated in the public consciousness with sunflowers, Claude Monet's (1840–1926) name is inextricably linked with waterlilies. Almost as passionate a gardener as he was a painter, Monet bought a boggy piece of land next to his house at Giverny in 1892, with the intention of transforming it into an oriental water garden "for the pleasure of the eye, and for motifs to paint." He created a pond surrounded by weeping willows and covered with exotic waterlilies, which became the focus of his art for the rest of his life. He painted the waterlily-covered surface of the pond over and over again, day after day, year after year, and held in his mind the idea of turning his waterlily canvases into a giant decorative scheme that would encircle the viewer. In 1914, his friend, the French prime minister Georges Clemenceau, persuaded him to embark upon the project. For the next decade Monet worked obsessively on his waterlily paintings in a vast studio specially built to house the six-foot-high canvases, which were mounted on mobile easels so that he could experiment with grouping them together. Selected canvases were joined to create eight waterlily panels. These were presented to the State and eventually installed in two oval rooms in the Orangerie the year after Monet's death. After six years' renovations, the rooms were reopened to the public in 2006, allowing once again the experience of being surrounded by the peace and beauty of Monet's "enchanted pond" while the hubbub of Paris continues outside. **JW**

Adam and Eve | Gustav Klimt

1917–18 | oil on canvas | 17 ½ x 23 ⅝ in / 173 x 60 cm | Österreichische Galerie Belvedere, Vienna, Austria

This unfinished painting is one of the last undertaken by Gustav Klimt (1862–1918) before he died. By this time he was the undisputed master of Viennese painting having overcome earlier objections to his work. Beautiful though it is, this work seems to be a relic from the perfumed decadence of Vienna's fin-de-siècle. It is difficult to believe that Futurism, Cubism, and Expressionism had burst into the world, and that the "war to end all wars" was running its course. As the generators of life on Earth, Adam and Eve are curiously lethargic. The abundant flora and fauna of paradise is represented by a few anemones at Eve's feet and the skin of a dead leopard, which also serves to suggest Eve's calculating sensuality. Adam sleeps and is barely distinguishable from the dark background. Eve is awake, pink, and glowing with touches of gold. Her knowingness, as well as her position, makes her the dominant figure. A femme fatale, a desired and dangerous woman, she has reduced Adam to a sleeping shadow, and both are as yet unaware of their fate. The incomplete state of this painting allows us to see Klimt's use of drawing in the creation of his composition. In 1908 Alfred Loos had declared that ornament was no longer an expression of Austrian culture. By 1918 Klimt's paintings seemed to belong to a past world that had been entirely destroyed by the war after which decoration could only be seen as indulgent and irrelevant. However, his extraordinary draftsmanship and use of color have contributed to his lasting popularity. **WO**

Composition VIII (The Cow) | Theo van Doesburg

c.1918 | oil on canvas | 14 ³/₄ x 25 in / 37.5 x 63.5 cm | Museum of Modern Art, New York, NY, USA

Theo van Doesburg (1883–1931) was a Dutch painter, architect, and designer who began his career exploring Impressionism, Expressionism, and Cubism. Only when he met Piet Mondrian in 1915, did he move toward Abstraction. In 1917, he and Mondrian founded the magazine *De Stijl*, which endorsed a new way of working: reducing objects to their simplest forms, while balancing clarity and harmony. From 1921 to 1923, he taught at the Bauhaus and in Berlin, disseminating the influence of the movement across Europe. This painting has two names: *Composition VIII*, which implies an image devoid of any reference to the visual world, and *The Cow*, which links it to the natural world. When compared with a photograph of a grazing cow, which Van Doesburg provided when the painting was shown, the sequence of black, red, yellow, blue, and green rectangles becomes the simplified structure of the animal's body with lowered head and neck to the right. Fourteen rectangles are arranged on the picture plane in flat chunks of smooth color. Van Doesburg was one of the only adherents to *De Stijl* theories who retained the color green and diagonal lines in his work; these were seen as impure by others in the movement. Appearing as it did at the end of World War I, this work heralded the emergence of a new art that would translate into every aspect of art and design—architecture, graphic design, and painting. Van Doesburg, with his tireless energy and inexhaustible intellectual curiosity, produced work in all of these areas. **SH**

A Battery Shelled | Wyndham Lewis

c.1919 | oil on canvas | 72 x 125 ⅛ in / 182.8 x 317.8 cm | Imperial War Museum, London, UK

The Canadian-born British painter Percy Wyndham Lewis (1882–1957) pursued studies in England, first at Rugby School, then at the Slade School of Art in London. During the early 1900s he spent his time traveling in Europe, where he visited many major museums. At the end of 1908, Lewis came back to London, where he settled as a painter and as a satirical short-story writer. In 1911 he played an active role in the Camden Town Group and exhibited some of his paintings at the Second Post-Impressionist exhibition. By 1913, he was popularly regarded as a leader of the British avant-garde. Along with his friend Ezra Pound, he co-founded the short-lived but major Vorticists' revue, *Blast* (1914–15). Vorticism relied on a virulent critique of contemporary society, combining the aesthetic of the two major European art movements at that time, Cubism and Futurism. *A Battery Shelled* is undoubtedly one of the artist's masterpieces and offers an amazing pictorial Modernist interpretation of his experience as an artillery soldier during World War I. Recalling the Vorticist aesthetic, the composition relies on a strong geometrical stylization, with emphasized angles and lines, and a strong schematization of the figures. The three dark-colored soldiers on the left look impassively at the scene of total devastation taking place in front of them. No humanity remains here: the soulless bodies depicted in the battlefield are painted with the same reddish color used by the painter for the fire and for the other objects standing in the background. **JJ**

Abstract Composition
Alexander Rodchenko

c.1919 | oil on canvas | State Russian Museum,
St. Petersburg, Russia

Alexander Rodchenko (1891–1956) was a Russian
artist, sculptor, and photographer who became the
main figure within Constructivism, a movement
based on the idea that art should reflect the forms
and processes of modern technology and machinery.
Trying to make sense of the evolving world
around him, he sought to simplify forms into basic
elements—analytical lines, abstract geometric shapes,
colors, and surfaces. In this painting, dynamic circular
and rectangular shapes seem to float on the canvas.
They do not represent anything in particular from the
"real" world, but do evoke the idea of heavy machinery
at work. At first, the almost toneless and subdued
shades of green, yellow, blue, orange, and black could
be mistaken for a collage. On closer inspection, the
clean lines and solid washes of color form something
almost recognizable and man-made. **SH**

Swan Upping at Cookham
Stanley Spencer

c.1919 | oil on canvas | 58 ¼ x 45 ½ in /
148 x 115.5 cm | Tate Collection, London, UK

In 1915, Stanley Spencer (1891–1959) reported for duty
in the Royal Army Medical Corps at Beaufort Hospital,
Bristol, England. The war years were only his second
time spent away from his home in Cookham, Berkshire.
Swan Upping holds an important place within his
oeuvre, as it was begun shortly before Spencer left for
Bristol and completed only after his return in 1919. The
title refers to an annual event held on the River Thames
when young swans are collected and marked;
Cookham Bridge is seen in the background. The idea
for the work came to Spencer while he was in church.
He could hear the activities of people outside, which
inspired him to transfer the spiritual atmosphere of
the church on to the secular landscape of Cookham.
The unfinished work—the top two-thirds were
completed before he left—haunted Spencer during the
war, but once home he found it hard to complete. **TP**

Woman Seated in an Armchair
Chaim Soutine

c.1919 | oil on canvas | 36 x 25 in / 92.1 x 65.4 cm
Barnes Foundation, Merion, PA, USA

Russian painter Chaim Soutine (1893–1943) was raised in a poor Jewish ghetto. He rapidly developed an interest in drawing and between 1910 and 1913 he attended art classes in Vilnius, where he was exposed for the first time to the major Russian avant-garde movements. In 1913, Soutine went to Paris and studied for two years under the painter Fernand Cormon—who had taught Matisse, van Gogh, and Toulouse-Lautrec. Portraits were a major theme in Soutine's art, and he painted friends, artists, and even strangers. *Woman Seated in an Armchair* is typical of his Expressionist style. The figure is depicted representationally, but many physical characteristics are exaggerated—her hands and fingers in particular seem to have sloughed off their human form. Lost in her thoughts, she sits on a big red armchair in front of an undefined dark background, a *mise en scène* that Soutine often utilized. **JJ**

Portrait of Jeanne Hébuterne
Amedeo Modigliani

1919 | oil on canvas | 39 ³/₈ x 25 ½ in / 100 x 64.7 cm
Guggenheim Museum, New York, NY, USA

In 1917, Amedeo Modigliani (1884–1920) met Jeanne Hébuterne, a student who worked as an artists' model. Their relationship led her to be renounced by her Roman Catholic family—Modigliani was famous for living a debauched life. In 1918 the couple moved from Paris to Nice, where Hébuterne gave birth to a girl. When the artist died in 1920 from tubercular meningitis, Jeanne was heavily pregnant; she committed suicide two days after his death. Here, the influence of primitive art on Modigliani's work is clear. The face—with its almond eyes and its elongated neck and nose—recalls African masks, an aesthetic being explored by avant-garde artists at the time. The emphasis on Jeanne's large hips and thighs alludes to the form of a fertility goddess. There is a somber overtone to the work—the warm colors of the woman and her sweater, deeply contrast with the gray interior in which she is depicted. **JJ**

The Clowns | José Gutiérrez Solana

c.1919 | oil on canvas | 38 x 48 in / 96.5 x 121.9 cm | Museo Centro de Arte Reina Sofia, Madrid, Spain

José Solana (1886–1945) was born in Madrid, where he was to spend much of his life, and his work reflects both the aesthetic qualities of the Spain he experienced from day to day and his concept of the character of the times. He started his artistic training in 1893, taking private lessons before entering the Real Academia de Bellas Artes de San Fernando in Madrid in 1900. In 1904 Solana became involved with the Generation of 1898 movement—a group of writers and philosophers attempting to re-create Spain as an intellectual and literary leader in response to the sociopolitical disaster of its defeat in the 1898 Spanish-American War. Solana's paintings and writing reflect the group's somber, ironic attitude, and throughout his career his work remained largely melancholic. The clown figure was adopted by several artists of the era as the ultimate parody— the tragic hero defined by the comic mask of his existence, and there was an identification between artists and the clown in the struggle for their art in the face of modern criticism. Staring impassively with a disquieting detachment, Solana's clowns evoke neither sympathy nor fear, but a polarity of menace and tragedy. Drawn in a precisely linear manner and colored with the subdued palette that was typical of his work, the two clowns border on the mechanical, which further emphasizes the surreal quality of the painting. Solana was greatly influenced by fellow artists and countrymen Juan de Valdés Leal (1622–90) and Francisco de Goya (1746–1828). **TP**

The India of Tehuantepec | Alfredo Ramos Martínez

1920 | oil on canvas | Private collection

Regarded by many to be the founding father of Mexican art, Alfredo Ramos Martínez (1872–1946) centers his richly evocative portrait on the face of a young *india* (native woman) from Tehuantepec, a region set apart for its matriarchal society within a country dominated by machismo culture. The artist's powers of observation focus on the sensual indigenous features of the subject—the full lips, high cheekbones, coppery skin, lustrous hair, and narrow, slanted eyes. The hairstyle is characteristic of the area and an arresting assertion of ethnic pride. It recalls that of Frida Kahlo in her many self-portraits, where her hair is braided with colored ribbon. Described by fellow painter Covarrubias as a "bottleneck of jungle and brush," the Mexican isthmus of Tehuantepec lies

between the Bay of Campeche on the north of the Mexican coastline and the Gulf of Tehuantepec on the south. It is the natural frontier, both geographically and culturally, between North America and Central America. Despite numerous conquests, colonizations, and invasions from pre-Columbian to modern times, its diverse indigenous inhabitants have maintained a distinct linguistic and cultural heritage. The work elevates Mexico's great indigenous heritage and honors an area proud to preserve its traditions. To this day, Tehuantepec remains largely underdeveloped, despite various Mexican governments' attempts to exploit its natural resources and peoples. This painting celebrates a culture infused with *indian* essence as a source of artistic inspiration. **AA**

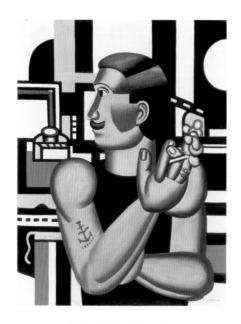

The Mechanic
Fernand Léger

1920 | oil on canvas | 36 ¼ x 27 ½ in / 92 x 70 cm
Art Gallery of Ontario, Toronto, Canada

Believing that mechanized production was giving birth to a new aesthetic that would upturn Europe's artistic conventions, French artist and designer Fernand Léger (1881–1955) endeavored in *The Mechanic* to articulate an emergent standard of beauty as embodied in the industrial worker. While closely associated with Cubism, Léger's work is distinct from that movement. For example, the forms out of which Léger constructed his compositions are tubular and spherical. Here, both the figure and the industrial background typify this distinctive style. Critics have noted that one of the most gripping aspects of the painting is the tension between the impersonal treatment of the shapes of the man's body and the individuality with which Léger endows him—with rings, a mustache, and a tattoo. He envisions an industrialized society that elevates the working man, not one that dehumanizes him. **AR**

Celebes
Max Ernst

1921 | oil on canvas | 55 x 47 ⅝ in / 139 x 121 cm
Tate Collection, London, UK

German-born artist, sculptor, and collagist Max Ernst (1891–1976) formed the German Dada group in Cologne in 1920. He left Germany in 1922 to join the Surrealist group in Paris. There he invented the technique of "frottage." *Celebes* dates from a period in Ernst's career when he combined Dada and Surrealist aesthetics. This, his first large-scale picture in Cologne, evolved out of his use of collage to create bizarre combinations of images. At the center of the painting stands a gigantic figure that seems to resemble both an elephant and a boiler; it appears to have a trunk, tusks, and pipes sprouting from it. This monstrous figure, apparently inspired by a photograph of a communal corn-bin in Sudan, is surrounded by several unrecognizable objects, including a headless female mannequin. As a Dadaist, Ernst often reused found images, which he combined with others to create original, imaginary works. **JJ**

Town of Amecameca
Francisco Díaz de León

1921 | pastel paint on paper | 38 x 30 ¾ in /
96.5 x 78 cm | Private collection

The paintings of Mexican artist Francisco Díaz de León (1897–1975) reveal an interest in Impressionism and, as in *Town of Amecameca with Popocatepetl*, the influence of Cubism and the Open Air School. Popocatepetl, meaning "smoking mountain" in the language of the Aztecs, is the only active volcano in the area of the town of Amecameca in south central Mexico. It was one of the most sacred mountains for the Aztecs and the center of the most fertile and heavily populated area of pre-Columbian Mexico. In vital colors, and loosely structured variations of rectangles, a cloud of foreboding smoke above Popocatepetl descends into rich greens and clear whites. The dark roof on the right, equally foreboding, is contrasted with the lively light of the town. Díaz contrasts the natural history of his area to his local community, using a perspective that is both natural and sophisticated. **SWW**

Fortune's Well, Portland
Edward Wadsworth

1921 | oil on canvas | 29 ½ x 19 ¼ in / 75 x 49 cm
Mayor Gallery, London, UK

Edward Alexander Wadsworth (1889–1949) was raised in industrial northern England—a factor that had a strong effect on his work. In 1914, his friendship with Wyndham Lewis led to their founding of the Vorticist movement. Based on Cubism and Futurism, Vorticism focused on the dynamic impact of industrial and technological advancement on urban environments, of which *Fortune's Well, Portland* is a prime example. The angular, Cubist shapes of the rooftops, forming geometric diagonals that zigzag through the painting, center around a towering industrial smokestack that dominates the town. The palette of beige, gray, white, black, and blue adds to the cold, harsh atmosphere of the townscape. The only circular shapes in the painting are either reminiscent of machine gears or form the dark, blue-black, sooty clouds from the factory chimneys that loom behind the town. **SM**

Black Quarter Circle with Red Stripes | László Moholy-Nagy

1921 | oil on canvas | Private collection

László Moholy-Nagy (1895–1946) was a law student before the traumatic experience of service in the Austro-Hungarian army in World War I changed his life. He emerged from the war convinced that he could "project [his] vitality through light, color, form" and "give life as a painter." He was also caught up in the revolutionary ferment that swept postwar Europe and, under the influence of Russian Constructivists such as El Lissitzky and Naum Gabo, sought to develop art forms that would contribute to building a new society on socialist principles. This suggested both the rejection of "bourgeois" art and erasing the distinction between art and mass-produced industrial design. As part of his effort to build a new art from basic colors and shapes, Moholy-Nagy experimented with gluing colored strips of paper onto various backgrounds. *Black Quarter Circle with Red Stripes* reflects these experiments, appearing to be made out of an assemblage of partially translucent, cut-out shapes. Although the black quarter circle introduces a dynamic instability to the arrangement, the overall impression is of clarity and radical simplification. The clearing away of the superfluous and the rejection of decorative frills were to be the touchstones of European Modernism. Moholy-Nagy went on to become an influential teacher at the Bauhaus college in Weimar, Germany, from 1923. His work ranged from experimental photography to typographic design. After the Nazis came to power in 1933 he went into exile, ending his life in the United States. **SF**

Proun 19D | El Lissitzky

c.1922 | gesso, oil, paper on wood | 38 x 38 in / 97 x 97 cm | Museum of Modern Art, New York, NY, USA

Rejected from art school in his native Russia, Lazar Markovich El Lissitzky (1890–1941), better known as El Lissitzky, trained as an architect in Germany, and later as an illustrator. Perhaps the artist's technical background explains his career-long preoccupation with "goal-oriented construction." El Lissitzky was convinced that the role of the artist was to make practical change, and saw his artistic creation as "a symbol of a new world, which is being built upon and which exists by way of the people." *19D* is part of a series called *Proun* (prounounced with two syllables: "pro-oon"), a term that El Lissitzky coined for a series of abstract works exploring the relationship between the formal concerns of two-dimensional painting and architectural construction. Each piece was conceived

as neither two- nor three-dimensional, but as a self-sufficient aesthetic concept, which could be applied in any medium. El Lissitzky's *Proun* were executed variously as paintings, lithographs, and installations. *19D* was done in oil, but the three-dimensional conception is evident. Not only do the shapes and colors suggest depth, but the shift in axis from the left to the right side of the composition creates an architectural geometry. Despite the massive forms El Lissitzky evokes, *Proun 19D* has a light quality about it; its forms seem to swing gracefully into the air. Something of the heady spirit that El Lissitzky's work shared with the project of the Soviet experiment is a faith in progress toward a world constructed in accordance with visionary ideas. **AR**

Yellow Cross Q.7 | László Moholy-Nagy

1922 | oil on canvas | 37 ¾ x 28 in / 96 x 71 cm | Galleria Nazionale d'Arte Moderna, Rome, Italy

The Hungarian painter and photographer, László Moholy-Nagy (1895–1946) studied law in Budapest before serving in the army during World War I. At the end of the conflict, he went to Vienna, Austria, where he discovered Suprematist and Constructivist works by Naum Gabo, El Lissitzky, and Kazimir Malevich; art that would influence his own artistic development. In 1923 Moholy-Nagy was offered a teaching post at the Bauhaus art school in Weimar, Germany. There, he advocated the integration of technology and industry in the arts. In doing so, he, along with the other members of this institution, broke the long-time frontier between fine and applied arts. To create *Yellow Cross Q.7*, Moholy-Nagy voluntarily worked with a pure and simple geometrical composition. This image is the result of a particular attempt for a visual language that would be able to express his contemporary era, a quest that started within the Russian avant-garde movements such as Suprematism and Constructivism. On a plain cream background, Moholy-Nagy painted a bright translucent yellow cross; its linear perfection is emphasized by a strong black underlining. Behind it are depicted two other geometrical figures. Each of these two rectangles are divided in three different parts, all of them parallel to each other. Moholy-Nagy painted these rectilinear figures on the canvas creating a depth of field, a subtle complexity best observed in the specific passages where the cross lays on top of the two rectangles. **JJ**

The Lady in Mauve | Lyonel Feininger

1922 | oil on canvas | 39 ½ x 31 ¾ in / 100.5 x 80.5 cm | Museo Thyssen-Bornemisza, Madrid, Spain

Born in New York to German parents, Lyonel Feininger's (1871–1956) career was shaped by a conflict of national loyalties, ethnic tension, and political turmoil. Moving to Germany to study, Feininger became a magazine illustrator, caricaturist, and a pioneer of that distinctively American art form, the comic strip. The strips he briefly produced for the *Chicago Tribune* are among the most innovative ever made, but his refusal to move back to America curtailed his contract and he resolved to abandon commercial art. Feininger began to develop his own style of analytical Cubism and, in 1919, became one of the founding members of the Bauhaus. It was while teaching there that he painted *The Lady in Mauve*. Feininger's careful layering of overlapping planes of color and form to create a nocturnal, urban tableau is infused with the city's bustling energy. The central image of a purposefully striding young woman is based on a much earlier drawing of 1906, *The Beautiful Girl*. Thus, the painting functions as both homage to the dynamic Parisian art scene that first inspired him, and as a celebration of the confidence of the early Weimar Republic, when Germany had surpassed France as the locus of the European avant-garde. It was not to last and Feininger and his Jewish wife were compelled to flee Germany in 1936. Settling once more in New York, Feininger found renewed inspiration in the scenes of his childhood and, in the last twenty years of his life, became a key figure in the development of Abstract Expressionism. **RB**

Pimp with Prostitutes
Otto Dix

1922 | oil on canvas | 27 ½ x 21 ⅝ in / 70 x 55 cm
Private collection

Champs de Mars: La Tour Rouge
Robert Delaunay

1911–23 | oil on canvas | 63 ¼ x 50 ⅝ in / 160.7 x 128.6 cm
Art Institute of Chicago, Chicago, IL, USA

German artist Wilhelm Heinrich Otto Dix (1891–1969) served as a volunteer during World War I, an experience that had a huge impact on him. After the war, he played a key role in the creation of the Dresden Secession in 1919, a group of Expressionists and Dada artists. When the Nazis came to power in Germany in the early 1930s, Dix was banished from his teaching position in Dresden. His art was then considered to be morally offensive toward the new regime. In this painting, Dix offers the viewer a dark representation. Three figures stand in front of a red brick wall. The pimp, a man dressed in a suit and a crème cravat, looks down to the right. Is he staring with disdain at his two prostitutes? Has he spotted clients for his expressionless employees? The color used by Dix to paint the coat of the woman on the right echoes the wall behind her. Doing so, Dix creates a somber parallel, which reifies the prostitute. **JJ**

A few years before he created the Cubist piece *Champs de Mars: La Tour Rouge*, Robert Delaunay (1885–1941) was painting in the Impressionist style of the previous century. The artist chose a fitting subject for his new style: the Eiffel Tower. This is one of a series of paintings of what was then the world's tallest man-made structure. In 1911 Delaunay exhibited his work with the Munich-based *Der Blaue Reiter* (The Blue Rider) group. Under the group's Abstractionist influence, Delaunay's work began to evolve. His red tower rises like a phoenix, as if in a flame or a plume of smoke, from among the drab Parisian apartment blocks. The gray cityscape serves to frame Delaunay's subject and objects are broken down on the canvas. The obvious interest of *Champs de Mars* is his treatment of light. Delaunay subjects the air around the tower to similar analysis, deconstructing the atmosphere into an array of vibrant color. **AR**

Landscape with Red Donkey
Chaim Soutine

1922–23 | oil on canvas | 31 ⁷⁄₈ x 24 ³⁄₈ in / 81 x 62 cm
Private collection

Portrait of Mademoiselle Chanel
Marie Laurencin

1923 | oil on canvas | 36 ¼ x 28 ¾ in / 92 x 73 cm
Musée de l'Orangerie, Paris, France

The Russian painter Chaim Soutine (1893–1943) is regarded as one of the most important Expressionist painters of his time. In Paris, where he emigrated in 1913, he lived for a time in La Ruche, a famous residence for artists in Montparnasse. At that time, Soutine claimed Rembrandt, Goya, and Cézanne as his most important influences. In *Landscape with Red Donkey*, the distorted landscape of a peaceful countryside scene is depicted with wonderful mastery, a style that earned him many comparisons with Vincent van Gogh. The strength of the composition relies on the amazing depiction of the abundant, majestic trees. From the 1920s, the tree became an obsessive theme in Soutine's art. His aggressive brushstrokes and his violent use of colors have often been said to prefigure the experiments of the Abstract Expressionist and CoBrA movements. **SP**

In 1923, the French artist Marie Laurencin (1883–1956) was working on the costumes and sets for Serge Diaghilev's *Ballets Russes*. When she met the fashion designer Gabrielle "Coco" Chanel, they were both designing costumes for the same company's *Le Train Bleu*. Laurencin was a well-known set designer when Chanel asked the artist to paint her portrait. The Chanel suit, which would forever alter the way women dress, was introduced to the public in 1923, the year Laurencin painted this portrait. Here, the couturier sits in a sensual, dreamy daze with her Pomeranian puppy in her lap. Chanel is shown in an erotic state of undress, with one shoulder of her draped gown falling off her arm and exposing her chest. The soft, curving, fluid lines, smoky colors, and languid mood are typical of Laurencin's work. However, Chanel decided that the portrait did not look sufficiently like her and rejected it. **AH**

Woman in the Wilderness | Alphonse Mucha

1923 | oil on canvas | 79 ³/₈ x 118 in / 201.5 x 299.5 cm | Mucha Museum, Prague, Czech Republic

At the end of the nineteenth century, Czech Alphonse Mucha (1860–1939) moved to Paris in order to pursue his artistic ambitions. He soon found plenty of work, from paintings, posters, advertisements and book illustrations, to designs for jewelry, carpets, wallpaper and theater sets. In 1894, he had a lucky break when the celebrated actress, Sarah Bernhardt, admired one of his posters and from then on his success was assured. His works feature beautiful young women in flowing clothes, often surrounded by flowers and his style was acclaimed as the zenith of Art Nouveau. His painting, *Woman in the Wilderness*, was the result of at least four preparatory studies. A Russian peasant woman looks up to the sky, desperate as she anticipates her fate. She is alone in a desolate landscape lit by a lone star and a pack of wolves are looming and ready to pounce. Also known as *Star and Siberia*, the painting expresses some of Mucha's sympathies for the Russian people. This was his response to the sufferings they endured after the Bolshevik Revolution, when the subsequent civil war from 1918 to 1920 meant that the largely peasant population starved to death. Mucha had visited Russia in 1913 to make preliminary sketches for his project, *The Slav Epic*—twenty huge paintings chronicling major events in the Slav nation. Although he still earned money from his signature graphic style, this perceptive and atmospheric painting shows his ability to communicate with the world at a more emotive level. **SH**

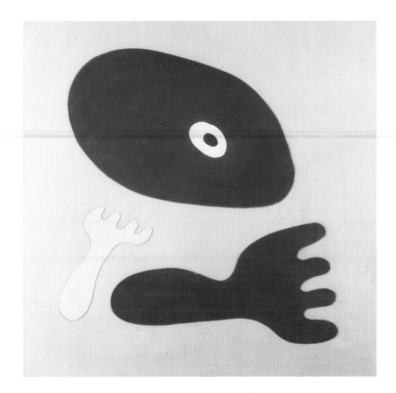

Teller, Gabel und Nabel | Jean Arp

1923 | oil on wood relief | 23 ¼ x 24 in / 59 x 61 cm | Private collection

Jean (Hans) Arp (1887–1966) was born in Strasbourg to a German father and French mother. A poet, sculptor, and abstract artist, he was one of the pivotal figures of Dadaism and allied to the Constructivists and Surrealists; he was also a founder of the Swiss movement *Moderne Bund*. An exponent of so many movements, he exhibited alongside a number of diverse artists. His works are refreshing for their seeming simplicity, beauty of movement, and enduring appeal. Many artists since have followed in his wake, and though his works—to modern viewers—no longer appear avant-garde, in his time he was a forerunner of many of the most controversial art movements. He studied at the Kunstschule in Weimar, Germany, before moving to Paris in 1908 to attend the Académie Julian. He traveled extensively, befriending writers and artists such as Picasso, Kandinsky, Apollinaire, and Modigliani. At the outbreak of World War I, he moved to Switzerland, where he met abstract artist Sophie Taeuber. They married in 1922 and worked on joint projects in a variety of media, including collage and textiles. Arp had favorite motifs that he used repeatedly: specific parts of the human body, such as lips, mustaches, or the navel (as can be seen in *Teller, Gabel und Nabel*); objects, such as cutlery (also included in this painting) and bottles; and stylized motifs from nature. His sensual sculptures, such as *Navel and Two Thoughts* (1932), *Sheaf Torso* (1959), and *Figure from the Woods* (1961) seem to entice the art lover to touch them. **LH**

Pietà or Revolution by Night | Max Ernst

1923 | oil on canvas | 45 ¾ x 35 in / 116.2 x 88.9 cm | Tate Collection, London, UK

In 1911, the German Surrealist painter Max Ernst (1891–1976) met the artist August Macke with whom he became close friends, and joined the *Rheinische Expressionisten* group in Bonn. His first exhibition was held in Cologne in 1912 at the Galerie Feldman. That same year, he discovered works by Paul Cézanne, Edward Munch, Pablo Picasso, and Vincent van Gogh, who made a deep impression on his own artistic development. The following year he traveled to Paris, where he met fellow artists Guillaume Apollinaire and Robert Delaunay. In the early 1920s, he participated in the Surrealist movement in Paris and is regarded as one of its leaders. *Pietà or Revolution by Night* was painted in 1923, a year before André Breton published the first *Manifesto of Surrealism*. The Surrealists sought to find a means to depict not only the outer reality but the working of the human mind, and were influenced by Sigmund Freud's theory of the unconscious. In this painting, Ernst replaced the traditional figures of the the mourning Virgin Mary holding the body of her crucified son Jesus in her arms by a portrait of himself held by his bowler-hatted father. Although no one can give a definitive analysis of the image, it has often been regarded as the expression of the troubled relationship between Ernst and his father, who being a fervent Catholic had previously denounced his son's work. Both appear as statues, perhaps reflecting the frozen nature of their relationship, yet the choice of the pose of the *pietà* suggests Ernst's desire for change and paternal affection. **JJ**

Composition VIII | Wassily Kandinsky

1923 | oil on canvas | 55 x 79 in / 140 x 201 cm | Guggenheim Museum, New York, NY, USA

Credited with being one of the founders of abstract painting, as well as one of the most important art theorists of the twentieth century, Wassily Kandinsky (1866–1944) lived his artistic life pushing the boundaries of Abstractionism. Born in Moscow, Kandinsky spent most of his career in Germany and Paris. *Composition VIII*, one of ten *Composition* paintings created over a thirty-year span, was painted during Kandinsky's tenure as a professor at the Weimar Bauhaus, the innovative art and design school in Germany. In *Composition VIII*, geometrical elements of varying forms and colors are scattered dynamically and interactively over a cool background. The most striking shape is the large black circle on the canvas's upper-left-hand corner, which serves both as a reference point for the smaller circles, and as a powerful contrast to the sharp lines and triangles. Both fiercely vivacious and quiet, *Composition VIII* ranks as one of the artist's most important works in the years after World War I. During his years at the Bauhaus between 1922 and 1926, Kandinsky taught extensively on his theories of form. *Composition VIII* was the artist's first methodical application of his ideas about the relationship between color and form, and his understanding of their spiritual and psychological effects. This painting also marks the beginning of Kandinsky's long association with the circle. In his view, this primary form pointed most clearly to the fourth dimension, and held within it immense and beautiful opposition. **AR**

The Japanese Bridge | Claude Monet

1918–24 | oil on canvas | 35 x 39 ⅜ in / 89 x 100 cm | Musée Marmottan, Paris, France

At the beginning of the twentieth century, landscape painting was the dominant genre of modern art. The Impressionists' bright and spontaneous depictions of nature appealed to the town-dwelling middle classes, for whom the countryside was primarily a place for leisure and enjoyment. In 1890, Claude Monet (1840–1926) bought a house in Giverny, France. He developed its gardens, introducing an ornamental lily pond, a Japanese-style bridge and other stunning features. The garden became his main focus and he spent most of his time painting visions of evanescent light and color from his surroundings. Painting outdoors at first, he would then return to his studio to work and rework his canvases, which became layered and complex. The Japanese bridge was one of his favorite subjects and he painted it over and again, catching it in different moods and lights. From 1908, his eyesight suffered as cataracts formed, distorting his vision. It is interesting to note that the paintings produced while the cataracts affected his vision have a general reddish tone, which is a characteristic symptom of cataracts. He had effective treatment in 1923, but this painting, completed after surgery, remained one of his most abstract works. While the bridge can be delineated at the center, the energetic brushstrokes form a swirl of trees, plants and water. He explored his subject so closely that the whole dissolved into the interplay of color, light, foliage and reflection. The thick, *impasto* brushwork later influenced the Abstract Expressionists. **SH**

Double Portrait | Felice Casorati

1924 | oil on canvas | 47 ¼ x 39 ⅜ in / 120 x 100 cm | Galleria d'Arte Narciso, Turin, Italy

Italian painter Felice Casorati (1886–1963) had his first work shown at 1907's Venice Biennale. He started out painting in a naturalistic way before shifting to a Symbolist style. After serving in the military in World War I he became associated with the Metaphysical movement, and was increasingly interested in the Renaissance. *Double Portrait* was painted during this period. Its title implies Casorati is alluding to Jan van Eyck's *The Arnolfini Portrait*. Like his predecessor, Casorati depicts a man and a woman in a domestic interior, a window lies on the left of the painting, and the woman is wearing a green dress. His painting is also as enigmatic as van Eyck's. Given the evident age difference between the duo, and the placing of the woman's arm protectively around the man, it seems reasonable to assume that they are father and daughter. This is a comment on gender relationships, where the woman is in a caring and dominant role rather than the man: she looks directly at the viewer, while the man looks out of the window to the wider world. But his expression is one of nostalgic yearning for a past connection with that world. He clutches a large book, but significantly it is dull beige, and there is no hint regarding its title. A third shadowy figure lies behind the pair; perhaps a nurse, or even the ghost of a dead wife and mother. And with a touch of humor and play on the title of this work, Casorati shows portraits on the wall of the room, suggesting both the inhabitants' wealth, and indicating that his portrait will survive long after the people it portrays. **CK**

Self-Portrait with Palette | Lovis Corinth

1924 | oil on canvas | 39 ⅜ x 31 ½ in / 100 x 80 cm | Museum of Modern Art, New York, NY, USA

This was among the last of the many self-portraits that German artist Lovis Corinth (1858–1925) painted in his prolific career. It was made for a retrospective exhibition of Corinth's work mounted as part of celebrations for the bicentenary of philosopher Immanuel Kant in Konigsburg, East Prussia. The painting shows the artist at work in his studio in Berlin. In technique it exhibits most of the typical features of Corinth's later style. After suffering a stroke in 1911, he had to cope with a measure of disability, including a trembling right hand. In response, he developed the use of broad, agitated brushstrokes, often angled diagonally from upper right to lower left, which gave his work more expressive intensity than before. Much of his later work shows a bold use of color, but this painting employs a subdued brown tonality. The mood is nervous and intense. Slightly stooped, the artist seems to raise his palette as a shield protecting him from the onlooker. There is a sense of excitement at the total concentration of a painter at work, but also of a man cramped by paintings that hem him in. The key to the strained mood is possibly found in one of Corinth's diary entries around this time, which reads: "A constant ambition to achieve a goal I never reached has made my life bitter." Corinth died the following year. For different reasons, his work was subsequently scorned by Nazis and modernists alike, but since the 1980s it has undergone a major reevaluation. Corinth is now judged one of the finest German artists of the twentieth century. **RG**

Snow on the Hillside | Frederick Nicholas Loveroff

*c.*1925 | oil on canvas | 33 ¼ x 37 ½ in / 84.5 x 95.5 cm | New Walk Museum, Leicester, UK

In this work, Frederick Nicholas Loveroff (1894–1960) presents a charming exploration of a Canadian winter landscape. The high pitch of the color and broad brushwork are elements of Canadian Impressionism, whereas the tendency to flatten and simplify forms points toward the works of the Canadian exhibitors known as the Group of Seven, a group of painters who became famous in the early twentieth century for exploring new ways to represent the Canadian landscape. The composition is, in some ways, unusual and it sets this work apart from the conventions of the European landscape genre. A "rule" of European landscapes was to use cooler tones in the background and warmer tones in the foreground, because warmer tones naturally tend to rise to the foreground

and thus reinforce the illusion of depth. Ignoring this principle, Loveroff presented a scene in which the foreground is covered in a cool-blue shadow, while the hill in the background basks in the warm, yellow light of the sun. The image, nonetheless, works. The cool, shadowed foreground does not "ground" the painting, but rather strengthens the uplifting qualities of the hill, which, despite being in the background, appears to float forward. In this way, Loveroff was moving away from the picturesque and pastoral tradition of European landscapes by choosing to represent scenes that did not "fit into" the traditions of the genre. Although not the most important of Canadian paintings of this era, *Snow on the Hillside* is a distinguished and accomplished work. **SS**

Rhapsody in Blue | Miguel Covarrubias

c.1925 | oil on canvas | 25 ¼ x 31 in / 64 x 78.5 cm | Private collection

Miguel Covarrubias (1904-57) was a prolific painter, caricaturist, illustrator, draftsman, writer, archaeologist, and anthropologist. Known as "El Chamaco" (The Boy), as a teenager he demonstrated a precocious, satirical wit, and was involved in the Mexican mural movement begun in 1922 by Diego Rivera in the wake of the Mexican Revolution. In 1923 Covarrubias went to New York on a government scholarship. His "certain clairvoyance" for penetrating caricatures was soon in demand, and he contributed to magazines such as *Vanity Fair*. The flowering of artistic endeavor in Mexico in the 1920s paralleled the Harlem Renaissance in New York, and Covarrubias had a hand in both. With his penchant for observing and recording, the artist illustrated several publications emerging from

jazz and blues culture, and his depictions of the African-American experience had some influence on mainstream perceptions. Evoking the exuberant mood of the times, this painting shows a performance of George Gershwin's *Rhapsody in Blue* in a Harlem club. The artist's mural painting training and love of caricature are evident in the distorted, colorful, cartoonlike figures, which have the stylized smooth, shiny, and colorful qualities of work by fellow South Americans Rivera, Kahlo, and Botero. The influence of Cubism is also apparent in the geometric shapes and play with perspective—the central figure in the spotlight almost jumps out of the picture. Yet her pose is magnificently rendered, reflecting the artist's fine draftsmanship and bringing some observational truth. **KM**

House by the Railroad | Edward Hopper

1925 | oil on canvas | 24 x 29 in / 61 x 73.7 cm | Museum of Modern Art, New York, NY, USA

The modernization of the transportation system in the 1920s prompted a massive shift in the American populace from small towns to urban centers. No artist has expressed this change in American life—and its resulting sense of isolation and melancholy—as movingly or specifically as Edward Hopper (1882–1967). The artist's unsentimental, realist works—depicting urban and country people and settings alike—capture the felt sense of American life in the early- to mid-twentieth century. In *House by the Railroad*, a huge gray Victorian house stands alone before a cloudless blue-gray sky. A rusty railroad track—a common theme in Hopper's work—slices the bottom of the painting, contributing to the feeling that this house, along with the era to which it belonged, has been left behind by the growth of a bustling, faraway city. The windows reflect the sun's dim yellow light, rendering it impossible to know who lives behind them. *House by the Railroad* was Hopper's first painting in a series that became emblematic of his work—definitively capturing the loneliness of his American subjects. Hopper's most significant artistic impact is in his ability to reveal the timeless and universal meaning in what is seemingly obsolete, outdated, and quintessentially American. His paintings point to the sadness of the human condition, the uncontrollable passage of time, and to the fissures that prohibit his subjects' ability to truly connect to one another or to the changing world they inhabit. **ARA**

Self-Portrait with a Model | Ernst Ludwig Kirchner

1910–26 | oil on canvas | 59 ¼ x 39 ⅜ in / 150.5 x 100 cm | Hamburger Kunsthalle, Hamburg, Germany

The Expressionist group *Die Brücke* drew on "primitive" sources for their imagery. Ernst Ludwig Kirchner (1880–1938) was influenced by artifacts in the Dresden Ethnographical Museum and from them he has produced a reference to Oceanic or African textiles in the background drapes. His ordinary room thus becomes, by implication, a place outside bourgeois constraints, where people can behave naturally. Beneath the striking blue and orange robe he is clearly naked, as the model will also shortly be. The paradox in this painting is the model's awkwardness and inhibition. For all that Kirchner attempts to transpose a primitive Eden into contemporary Dresden, she is the antithesis of a "primitive" Eve capable of lithe, sensual movement. But

perhaps that is the point, in her incomplete state of undress she is less than halfway to Dionysian freedom. There is some indebtedness to Munch's *Puberty* (1895) in the pose and the looming blue phallic shadow behind the girl. Compositionally the shadow connects the gray area to the pink in the flattened out background. Kirchner's position in relation to the viewer is close and almost confrontational. Grasping the paintbrush in his left hand, he projects himself as a dominant, virile creator. His style, consisting of bold, flat areas of color and often heavy outlines, developed through his work with woodcuts. Color had a universal, primordial significance to him in this period and cannot be separated from his passion for Nietzsche and Walt Whitman. **WO**

London, View of the Thames in the Evening | Oskar Kokoschka

1926 | oil on canvas | 24 x 32 in / 61 x 81 cm | Private collection

It is astonishing that the artistic career of Oskar Kokoschka (1886–1980) began in the Vienna of Freud, Klimt, Schiele, Mahler, and Wittgenstein. His early portraits were likened to caricatures, developed from an edgy graphic line. During a period in Berlin, he came into contact with the Expressionists and, as a result, developed his use of color. An admiration for Titian, Tintoretto, and El Greco also fed into his developing mature style. He traveled extensively, but it was London that made the strongest impression. He saw the River Thames as an "artery of life flowing from century to century." To get the broadest view of the Thames he rented a room on the eighth floor of the Savoy Hotel and from here he painted a series of riverscapes. This painting, with its yellow sunset, highlights the buildings on the right with Westminster as the focal point, as in Monet's paintings of 1871, but Kokoschka pulls back, placing Waterloo Bridge in the foreground. He described himself as a "psychological tin opener" when painting portraits. The same could be said of his approach to the river, which he interrogated with the same intensity. This painting is full of the sound of the city's life and history. Kokoschka believed in the experiences of the senses above theory, writing that taste, touch, smell, hearing, and seeing are a means to knowledge. After periods living in Vienna and Prague, he returned to England in 1938, where he lived for many years. It took some time for his style to be accepted; now his work is internationally acclaimed. **WO**

Street, New York I
Georgia O'Keeffe

1926 | oil on canvas | 48 ⅛ x 29 ⅞ in / 122.2 x 75.8 cm
Private collection

In 1916, Georgia O'Keeffe (1887–1986) came to the attention of photographer Alfred Stieglitz, who became a tireless promoter of her work. In the mid 1920s O'Keeffe began to produce the paintings that were to make her famous, among them a series of cityscapes. Influenced by Stieglitz's work and Cubism, they also expressed her abiding interest in landscape and her ambivalent attitude toward New York. Some seem celebratory, conveying the mystery, glamour, and thrilling modernity of the city. Others, like this example, painted from street level with the dark buildings towering up like canyon walls over a solitary, forlorn street lamp, suggest O'Keeffe's urban claustrophobia. In 1929, she visited New Mexico and it was in the very different landscape of the southwestern deserts that she found the motifs that would occupy her for the rest of her career. **RB**

The Pillars of Society
George Grosz

1926 | oil on canvas | 78 ¾ x 42 ½ in / 200 x 108 cm
Nationalgalerie, Berlin, Germany

A member of the Dada movement from 1917 to 1920, George Grosz (1893–1959) satirized corrupt bourgeois society. As the moving force behind the *Neue Sachlichkeit* (New Objectivity) movement, his attacks began to focus on the rising Nazi party. Constantly in trouble with the authorities, he continued to express his revulsion with postwar Germany. The title *The Pillars of Society* refers to a play by Henrik Ibsen. It shows an old aristocrat in the foreground, his head full of the pageant of war, sporting a dueling scar on his cheek. In his hands he holds a beer glass and a foil. His monocle is opaque, he cannot see. On the left is a nationalist with a chamber pot on his head clutching his newspapers. To the right a Social Democrat, his head full of steaming dung, holds a flag and socialist flyer. Behind them is a clergyman, bloated and preaching peace while the city burns and mayhem continues behind him. **WO**

Self-Portrait in a Tuxedo
Max Beckmann

1927 | oil on canvas | 55 x 37 in / 140 x 95 cm
Busch-Reisinger Museum, Cambridge, MA, USA

Early in his career, German artist Max Beckmann (1884–1950) often depicted mythological and religious subjects. By the end of World War I, his work adopted a Cubist character and he turned to a contemporary cultural context. Circus performers and masked revellers emerged as a signature motif. The term coined to describe this style was *Neue Sachlichkeit* (New Objectivity) and it was typified by Beckmann as well as by satirical painters such as Otto Dix and George Grosz. The self-portrait he painted in 1927 depicts him as a dapper, middle-aged man posing with a cigarette dangling between his fingers and an expression of mild impatience on his handsome yet stern features. Though not wholly flattering, the portrait, a model of New Objectivity, presents the artist as an intelligent, self-confident, and idealistic man disappointed by, but still hopeful for, the society around him. **AH**

Landscape with Woodcutters
Max Beckmann

1927 | oil on canvas | 39 ³/₄ x 24 in / 100 x 61 cm
Musée National d'Art Moderne, Paris, France

Max Beckmann (1884–1950) is known more for his works' violent energy than for bucolic forest scenes, so at first glance *Landscape with Woodcutters* seems anomalous. The interior of the canvas, however, evinces Beckmann's singular sense of space. Between the trees, the dwellings, boughs, and foliage are crowded into a vertical composition dominated by dark colors. The deconstructed forms heaped on top of one another create a feeling of closure and disorientation. The figures stand in the open foreground, and by situating the subject outside the confusion of the forest the artist suggests relative, if temporary, security. But the woodcutters are tiny in comparison with the vastness of the trees, suggesting the turmoil of the background is impossible to resist. The oddly situated ladder appears as a symbolic element; the heightened color contrasts imbue a dreamlike light. **AR**

Young Girl in Green | Tamara de Lempicka

c.1927 | oil on canvas | 24 ¼ x 17 ⅝ in / 61.5 x 45.5 cm | Musée National d'Art Moderne, Paris, France

Tamara de Lempicka (1898–1980) was born Maria Gorska to affluent parents in fin-de-siècle Poland. After her parents divorced, her wealthy grandmother adopted her and sent her to a prestigious boarding school in Switzerland. When she was sixteen, and already startlingly beautiful and spoiled, she fell in love with a young lawyer, reputed to be the most handsome bachelor in Warsaw. He had no money of his own, but her uncle provided a dowry and they were married in St. Petersburg, in a high fashion wedding. A year later her husband was arrested by the Bolsheviks. She was said to have charmed the officials into freeing him and the couple fled to Paris, where she changed her name. Paris was where she developed her distinctive Art Deco style of painting.

Her paintings are the pure expression of sex and power. Her male and female figures, whether nude or clad in sensual fabric, are usually set against imposing urban settings, and her paintings and her aesthetic have inspired countless fashion shoots, films, art, and artists. Between the wars, she painted portraits of writers, entertainers, artists, scientists, industrialists, and Eastern Europe's exiled nobility—many of whom were also her lovers. When World War II began, she and her husband moved to Hollywood, where she became a "painter to the stars." She subsequently lived in Manhattan and Houston, Texas, before moving to Mexico. After she died there, she was cremated, so her ashes could be spread on the top of the volcano Popocatepetl according to her wishes. **AH**

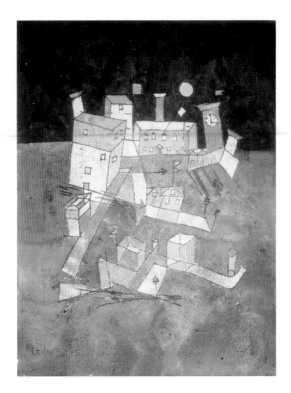

Part of G | Paul Klee

1927 | watercolor and oil transfer on paper | 12 x 9 in / 32.5 x 24 cm | Staatliche Museen, Berlin, Germany

In 1925, the famous art school the Bauhaus moved to Dessau. Paul Klee (1879–1940) joined the staff in 1926. Although he was in charge of the bookbinding workshop (and later the glass painting workshop), it was arguably his lecture series on the theory of form, given from 1921 to 1931, that had the most influence, not only on his students but also on his own work. By 1931 the preparatory notes and drawings ran to thousands of pages. In 1926 he went to Porquerolles Island and Corsica for some inspiration. He said that he wanted something to stimulate the harmonies inside him, "small or big adventures in color." He was probably thinking of the effects of an earlier trip with August Macke to Tunisia. He was not disappointed. Two-thirds of this composition is muddy brown and a third is dark blue. A small town rises from the mud. The title is ambiguous and could refer to a place, a musical key or perhaps the capital letter G with its cross bar that is echoed in the curl of the town. The perspective is askew—the irregular buildings tilt crazily. Roads become ramps and go nowhere. Flags flutter in all directions regardless of the wind. The town clock says four o'clock although this is not corroborated by the light or the position of the sun. It is permanently late afternoon in this deserted toy town of colored bricks despite the night sky above. However, in spite of the jauntiness, there is a mathematical precision. It is Bach and not Offenbach. Klee was in a constant search for harmonies of color and form, which resulted in a great diversity of style. **WO**

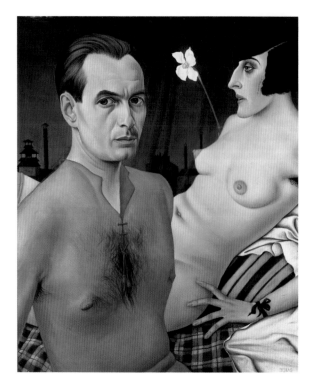

Self-Portrait with Model | Christian Schad

1927 | oil on wood panel | 29 ⅞ x 24 ⅜ in / 76 x 62 cm | Tate Collection, London, UK

German painter Christian Schad (1894–1982) studied briefly in Munich before moving to Switzerland around 1914. There he began to experiment with photography and to participate in the Dada movement. Schad left Switzerland in 1920 for Italy, before returning to Germany in 1928 and settling in Berlin. There, he continued to develop the sober and Realist style for which he is best known. He is traditionally linked with the *Neue Sachlichkeit* (New Objectivity) movement that took place mainly in Germany and Italy in the mid-1920s. Schad's mysterious *Self-Portrait with Model* is considered one of his masterpieces. The relationship between the two figures in the painting is ambiguous. Aside from its title, nothing in the frame indicates that the viewer is looking at a portrait of the artist and his model. There are no obvious features, such as an easel, to suggest that this is an artist's studio. The artist's position in front of the model partly conceals her nakedness. Although not naked himself, the male figure is clothed in a skillfully painted transparent garment that graphically reveals his torso. The image is loaded with symbolism. A narcissus, signifying vanity, leans toward the artist. Both subjects are narcissistically depicted and exude sexual power; they do not look at each other despite the inference that they have recently made love. Disturbingly, the woman's face is marked with a scar, or *freggio*. Such scars were inflicted by males in southern Italy on their lovers as a sign of their passion and possession of their lover's body. **JJ**

Three Generations | Sarkis Katchadourian

*c.*1928 | oil on canvas | 31 ⁷/₈ x 26 ³/₈ in / 81 x 67 cm | Royal Pump Rooms, Royal Leamington Spa, UK

Born in Iran (formerly Persia), of Armenian parents, Sarkis Katchadourian (1886–1947) studied and worked in Rome, Paris, Munich, and India, and settled in New York City. Katchadourian became known for his portraits and genre scenes, as well as for his fascination with life in the east and especially traditional Persian and Indian culture. Here he combines these interests to give us a very simple portrayal of three generations of Muslim womanhood seen in traditional dress—grandmother (in black), mother, and daughter. The bold brushwork, and the interesting mixture of colors on the wall behind the women and on their white garments, would not be out of place in a nineteenth-century French painting. Katchadourian, however, always remained bewitched by the magic and mystery of Eastern art, and this work displays an elegance of line in its clear, simple shapes that is intrinsically Iranian. So, too, is the feeling for decorative color in the splashes of warm red and yellow emerging from beneath the women's white robes. The idealized sweetness of the daughter's face, with her dark, dramatic eyes, is a clear reminder of the style of traditional Persian painting. Katchadourian established an impressive reputation for raising the profile of traditional Eastern art. He is famed in particular for his reconstructions of seventeenth-century frescoes from the palaces of the powerful Persian king, Shah Abbas the Great, and of nearly-lost fifth- and sixth-century Buddhist cave paintings that he studied on visits to India and Ceylon. **AK**

Dama de Blanco | Frida Kahlo

1928 | oil on panel | 31 ¼ x 23 ⅝ in / 79 x 60 cm | Private collection

One of four sisters, Frida Kahlo (1907–54) painted this portrait of her sister Cristina at an early stage in her career. In 1928 she was unknown, although she had already attracted the attention of the celebrated Mexican artist Diego Rivera (1886–1957) whom she married a year later. The image gains a layer of retrospective meaning with the knowledge that Rivera had an extramarital affair with Cristina several years after this was painted, which affected Frida greatly. The family resemblance is clear when compared with Kahlo's many self-portraits. Although Cristina is shown here wearing contemporary dress and a fashionable bob, the rendering of her face is reminiscent of Roman tomb portraits—stylized and remote. She is placed on a diagonal inside a drawn frame, which has the effect of constraining her within the composition. By contrast, the two bushes on the right, one near and one far, gives the impression of a veering perspective. The uncharacteristically restrained range of colors gives this painting a strange ethereal quality. Kahlo was painting in a Surrealist style completely independently from artists in France. Not until André Breton visited Mexico in 1938 was she aware of this, although she strongly disapproved of the Surrealist label. Breton was a great admirer, describing her work as "ribbon around a bomb." In 1938 Kahlo had her first solo exhibition at the Julien Levy Gallery in New York. In 1939 she exhibited in Paris and became an overnight success, earning the admiration of established artists including Picasso. **WO**

Race Track at Deauville, The Start | Raoul Dufy

1929 | oil on canvas | 25 ¾ x 32 ⅛ in / 65.5 x 81.5 cm | Fogg Art Museum, Boston, MA, USA

French artist Raoul Dufy (1877–1953) painted more than 9,000 oils and watercolors during his career, as well as numerous drawings. The essential verve, uplifting character, and aesthetic appeal of his work has contributed to it being widely reproduced. Characteristically his canvases are brilliantly colored and intrinsically patterned, making them instantly appealing. Dufy often painted scenes of people at leisure—enjoying activities such as regattas or horse races—and in a way devoid of social comment. As a result his work was often undeservedly passed over by the critics of his day. However, the decorative quality and cheerful countenance of his paintings made his work popular among the public, a position that it retains today. He was born in Le Havre,

Normandy, where he first started taking evening art lessons at the age of eighteen. While studying in Paris at the Ecole des Beaux-Arts in 1900, he came into contact with Georges Braque (1882–1963) and was also influenced by Édouard Manet (1832–83) and the Impressionists. He later directed his attention toward Fauvism and Cubism, but developed his own highly unique style from this broad base of influences. This painting was one of several of the racecourse. The hive of activity in bright colors and simple forms adds to a sense of pattern, while the short, quick brushstrokes and rapidly applied broad color washes increase the movement and energy of the scene. Even the empty chairs appear to be watching the track with animation. **TP**

Portrait of a Young Woman
Lasar Segall

*c.*1930 | oil on canvas | 23 x 16 in / 58 x 40 cm
Musée d'Art Moderne de la Ville de Paris, France

The sensual, expressionistic style of Lithuanian artist Lasar Segall (1891–1957) was transformed after he moved to São Paulo in Brazil. His unique perspective as an Eastern European immigrant enriched the diversity of modern Brazilian art. Segall joined the Modernist movement as a member of São Paulo's controversial Pro Modern Art Society. *Portrait of a Young Woman* embodies the most compelling and unconventional attributes of the movement. Segall focused on the texture of his medium and his representation of Brazil's magnificent natural light. His rendering of his subject reflects her potentially complex personality: Segall's Cubist influences are visible in his subject's disproportionately large hands and small shoulders. The subject's skeptical expression lends an aspect of reality to the painting that undermines its flatness and the romantic mixture of shadows and pastels. **SWW**

Woman with a Bowl of Fruit
Béla Kádár

*c.*1930 | gouache on paper | 40 ⅛ x 29 ⅛ in / 102 x 74 cm | Private collection

Most of the works of Hungarian artist Béla Kádár (1877–1955) reflect a dreamy quality. His work changed dramatically during the 1920s, as he began to make a living from his art and leave the bitter years of World War I behind him. Despite Kádár's Jewish ancestry, *Woman with a Bowl of Fruit* appears to have Christian overtones. The woman's veil is of the vivid blue usually associated with the Virgin Mary in Renaissance art and on the wall behind her is a rose, seemingly resonant with a halolike glow. In other works, Kádár drew on themes from Hungarian folklore and peasant history. He was influenced by several artistic styles, including Cubism, Expressionism, and Constructivism. He drew on parts of these contemporary movements, but managed to keep his style unique, refusing to conform to any one of them. His own style was one of warmth and harmony, drawing the viewer into his world. **LH**

Rhythmical
Paul Klee

1930 | oil on canvas | 27 ¼ x 19 ⅞ in / 69 x 50.5 cm
Musée National d'Art Moderne, Paris, France

As a violinist married to a pianist, it is not surprising that Paul Klee (1879–1940) became fascinated by the relationship between music and art. After settling in Munich, Klee met Wassily Kandinsky, Franz Marc, and August Macke, who believed that the purpose of art is to unite the inner world of feeling and outer world of color and form, and that music is the key to achieving this. This deceptively simple painting consists of three colors—the equivalent of three beats to the bar—against a rich brown background. Klee stacked up his brushstrokes resulting in a heavy impasto. The "beats" are not evenly spaced; the numbers in each row vary between six and eight. It is tempting to read the painting like a musical score from left to right and top to bottom, but this is not the only way to read this image—the squares of color have relationships vertically and diagonally as well as horizontally. **WO**

Five Girls from Guaratingueta
Emiliano di Cavalcanti

1930 | oil on canvas | 38 x 27 ½ in / 97 x 70 cm
Museu de Arte de São Paulo, Brazil

Emiliano di Cavalcanti (1897–1976) was born in Rio de Janeiro and participated in the organization of the 1922 "Week of Modern Art." He displayed twelve of his own paintings in the influential show, which introduced Brazilian Modernism to the world. In 1923, di Cavalcanti traveled to Paris, where he moved in the circles of Picasso, Braque, and Matisse. *Five Girls from Guaratingueta* is representative of di Cavalcanti's vibrant, cosmopolitan sensibility. In this Cubist canvas, the women's stylish accessories focus the seemingly haphazard arrangement of bold lines on their lush curves. The figures' lips, full breasts, and heavy-lidded, flirtatious eyes, contribute to the canvas's overall sense of seduction and languid eroticism. The girls are sexual and sophisticated and the soft, fleshy, pink setting surrounding them indicates that the world around them is also one steeped in sensuality. **AH/SWW**

American Gothic
Grant Wood

1930 | oil on beaverboard | 29 ¼ x 24 ⅝ in / 74.5 x 62.5 cm | Art Institute of Chicago, Chicago, IL, USA

Iowan artist Grant Wood (1891–1942) was a member of the Regionalist movement in American art, which championed the solid rural values of central America against the complexities of European-influenced East Coast Modernism. Yet Wood's most famous painting is artificially staged, absorbingly complex, and irresolvably ambivalent. Its most obvious inspiration is the work of Flemish artists such as Van Eyck that Wood had seen on visits to Europe, though it may also show an awareness of the contemporary German *Neue Sachlichkeit* (New Objectivity) movement. Wood noticed the white house with its Gothic pinnacle in the small town of Eldon, southern Iowa. He used his sister Nan and his dentist Dr. B.H. McKeeby as models for the couple standing in front of it. The pitchfork suggests the man is a farmer, although whether this is a husband and wife or a father and daughter is unclear. They are a tight-lipped, buttoned-up couple. The farmer's pose is defensive, the pitchfork planted to repel trespassers. The woman's sideways glance is open to any reading. Some have found in it, as in the stray hair curling at her strangely elongated neck and the brooch at her throat, hints of a strictly repressed sensuality. Superficially simple and naive, the image is rich in visual puns and echoes, for example between the pitchfork and the bib of the farmer's overalls. Wood consistently rejected suggestions that the painting was a satire of the Midwest and its conservative values. An icon of American popular culture, it remains as ambiguous as its title. **RG**

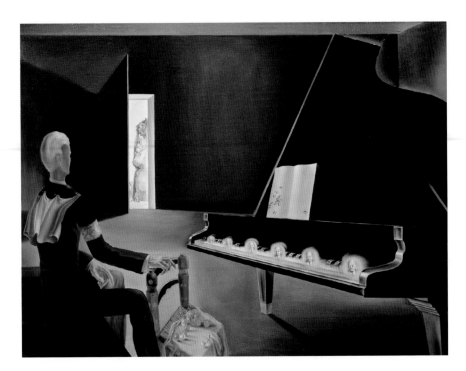

Partial Hallucinations: Six Apparitions of Lenin on a Grand Piano
Salvador Dalí

1931 | oil on canvas | 57 ½ x 44 ⅞ in / 146 x 114 cm | Musée National d'Art Moderne, Paris, France

Throughout his life, Salvador Felip Jacint Dalí Domènech (1904–89) demonstrated a rapacious ability to assimilate an array of different styles and forms, ranging from a refined academic classicism to the most cutting-edge avant-garde. Initial exhibitions of Dalí's drawings in Barcelona attracted significant attention, with a response of both vehement praise and scorn. (He was even excommunicated from his family home owing to the perverse antics of his art.) This divided reaction continues to this day. According to Dalí, *Partial Hallucination: Six Apparitions of Lenin on a Grand Piano* is a "hypnogogic picture" whose genesis he describes as follows: "At sunset, I saw the bluish, shiny keyboard of my piano, where the perspective exposed to my view a series in miniature of little yellow, phosphorescent halos surrounding Lenin's visage." Ironically, Dalí did not identify himself with the revolutionary tendencies of the Paris Surrealist group. Instead he claimed his ambiguous stance as that of an "anarcho-monarchist," refusing to fight in the Spanish Civil War or align himself with any political party. He provoked much controversy when residing in Spain as a supporter of the military dictator Francisco Franco, as most artists had fled the country in renunciation of his fascist leadership. This led to Dalí's expulsion from the Surrealist group in 1937 by its leader André Breton, who renamed the artist with the anagram Avida Dollars, foreseeing the great wealth and fame he would achieve later in life, after moving to the United States in 1940. **JG**

Chicken Boy | Gilbert Spencer

1931 | oil on panel | 17 ⁷/₈ x 12 ³/₄ in / 45.4 x 32.5 cm | Leamington Spa Art Gallery and Museum, UK

Gilbert Spencer (1892–1979) was a distinguished artist and educator. The younger brother of Sir Stanley Spencer, he was born in Cookham, Berkshire, UK. He studied at the Camberwell School of Arts and Crafts, the Royal College of Art (RCA), and the Slade School of Fine Art in London, then in 1919 served one year with the Royal Army Medical Corps in Salonika and the Eastern Mediterranean. During his career as a teacher he was the Professor of Painting at the RCA and Head of Painting at Glasgow School of Art and Camberwell School. In 1960 he was elected a Royal Academician. As an artist Spencer made his name painting landscapes, working mainly in the counties of Berkshire, Oxfordshire, and Dorset, and the Lake District. At first sight *Chicken Boy* may appear to be just another rural scene with not much to do with modern art. In this painting, however, Spencer clearly takes on much bigger issues. The makeshift apron worn by the boy is clearly an acknowledgment of the work Braque and Picasso completed during the previous two decades—introducing flatness, collage, and what became known as Cubism into contemporary painting. Spencer places a flat machine-printed object in the center of an otherwise romantic farmyard scene, then drags the chickens into a space that is midway between two and three dimensions. This painting illustrates quite perfectly the difficulty so many artists experienced during the early twentieth century in making the paradigm shift from a nineteenth-century aesthetic to Modernism. **SF**

The Persistence of Memory | Salvador Dalí

1931 | oil on canvas | 9 ½ x 13 in / 24 x 33 cm | Museum of Modern Art, New York, NY, USA

Salvador Felip Jacint Dalí Domènech (1904–89) was a Catalan Spanish artist who became one of the most important painters of the twentieth century. He was also an accomplished sculptor, draftsman, and designer whose imagery came to influence not only the art world but also fashion, advertising, theater, and film. He is best known for his Surrealist work with its bizarre images. In 1922 he went to study in Madrid at the Residencia de Estudiantes, initiating lifelong artistic partnerships with men such as Luis Buñuel, with whom he made the film *Un Chien Andalou* (1922), as well as Frederico García Lorca. Dalí divided his time between his birthplace in Catalonia and Paris and New York, gaining wealth and fame as the Spanish eccentric who added a Surrealist touch to film and theater sets. *The Persistence of Memory*, also known as *Soft Watches* or *Melting Clocks*, is one of Dalí's most famous pieces. Several of his favorite recurring images are present in this work. The setting is one he often used: the seashore of Catalonia at Cape Creus. His well-known melting-clock imagery mocks the rigidity of chronometric time. The watches themselves look like soft cheese—indeed by Dalí's own admission they were inspired by hallucinations after eating Camembert cheese. In the center of the picture, under one of the watches, is a distorted human face in profile, an image that also appears in his earlier work *The Great Masturbator* (1929). The ants on the plate represent decay. The painting was first exhibited in New York in 1932 and sold for $250. **JG**

In Summer | Pierre Bonnard

1931 | oil on canvas | 79 ½ x 100 in / 202 x 254 cm | Pushkin State Museum of Fine Arts, Moscow, Russia

Pierre Bonnard (1867–1947) gained artistic recognition and wealth during his lifetime, particularly in the 1920s and 30s when his works were selling well at home and abroad. In the 1920s several books about Bonnard were published (one of which was written by his nephew, Charles Terasse). Yet, although he was acclaimed in his public life, Bonnard's private life often proved painful and complicated. In 1925 he married Marthe, one of his favorite models. He had, however, previously been involved with another model, Renée Monchaty. Less than a month after the wedding, Renée committed suicide. By the second half of the 1920s, Bonnard was a regular visitor to the United States and had attracted some prominent, and wealthy, American patrons. In 1928 he held his first one-man show in America at the De Hauke Gallery in New York and then, in 1932, Bonnard and Vuillard held a major joint exhibition at the Zurich Kunsthaus. During the year that *In Summer* was painted, Bonnard spent his time moving around the French countryside, spending his summer painting at Vernonnet and the fall in Le Cannet, a small town not far from Cannes on the French Riviera. From this time onward, Le Cannet became one of Bonnard's favorite places to paint, inspiring many of his landscapes. In 1939 he chose to make his home there and it was in that house that he died in 1947. Bonnard was one of the most distinguished upholders of the Impressionist tradition, adding his own vibrant sense of color to traditional subjects. **LH**

Map Reading | Stanley Spencer

1926–32 | oil on canvas | 85 x 73 in / 208.5 x 185.5 cm | Sandham Memorial Chapel, Burghclere, UK

World War I marked the end of innocence for Stanley Spencer (1891–1959), as it did for many young men of his generation, and it was some time before he could assimilate and find expression for his experiences. The opportunity came when he was commissioned to paint a series of murals for a new chapel in the small Hampshire village of Burghclere. The chapel was to be dedicated to Henry Sandham, a soldier who, like Spencer, had served in the Macedonian campaign. Unconcerned with traditional heroic war narratives, Spencer turned to his own memories and the spiritual significance he attached to ostensibly mundane things. The scenes depicted, therefore, are mainly the routine chores of ordinary soldiers and orderlies. This panel, with its strange flattened, distorted perspective, shows a company of soldiers resting by a roadside, some picking bilberries, others collapsed in exhaustion. Spencer disliked authority, and the mounted officer in the center is the only figure of high military rank among the hundreds of soldiers he painted. The lush countryside is arcadian in contrast to the dark, earth hues of the hospital wards and campsites in the other panels. As such, it seems to prefigure the paradise promised in the monumental *Resurrection of the Soldiers* which, occupying the whole eastern wall of the chapel, is one of the most astonishing achievements in British art. For Spencer, the murals were a six-year process of remembrance and exorcism. Afterward he revealed: "By this means I recover my lost self." **RB**

Palacio Almi | Xul Solar

1932 | watercolor on paper | 15 ½ x 21 ½ in / 40 x 55 cm | Museo Xul Solar, Buenos Aires, Argentina

Xul Solar (Oscar Agustín Alejandro Schulz Solari, 1887–1963) had traveled and exhibited extensively throughout Europe by the time he painted *Palacio Almi*. Solar was greatly influenced by his travels and reflections of the Abstract style of artists such as Paul Klee and Wassily Kandinsky can be seen in the work he produced after returning, twelve years later, to his native Argentina. This is one of many imagined cityscapes that he painted. A futuristic world arranged in space appears to be floating among planets and moons, supported only by the poles and pathways that stretch into the foreground and draw the eye into the bustling array of palace buildings, chimney pots, and arches. Solar's use of bright colors and regular shapes points to his experience of both Expressionism

and Futurism and their integration into his stylistic vocabulary. The snakelike creature in the foreground figures in many of his landscapes in more or less detailed variations. It is almost exactly replicated in his watercolor *Rocas Lagui* created the following year. The otherworldly setting and the symbolism of snakes, moons, and planets reflect the artist's interest in astrology. By the 1930s, Solar had begun to draw astrological tables and as late as the 1950s he painted portraits and other works that directly referenced the signs of the zodiac. Solar also invented two imaginary languages and used symbols from these in his work. Like most of his paintings, *Palacio Almi* was created on a very intimate scale, its limited size reflecting the personal nature of his imagined worlds. **HH**

La Condition Humaine | René Magritte

1933 | oil on canvas | 39 ³⁄₈ x 31 ⁷⁄₈ in / 100 x 81 cm | National Gallery of Art, Washington, DC, USA

René Magritte (1898–1967) was born in Lessines, Belgium. After studying at the Academy of Fine Arts in Brussels, he worked in a wallpaper factory and was a poster and advertisement designer until 1926. Magritte settled in Paris at the end of the 1920s, where he met members of the Surrealist movement, and soon became one of the most significant artists of the group. He returned to Brussels a few years later and opened an advertising agency. Magritte's fame was secured in 1936, after his first exhibition in New York. Since then, New York has been the location of two of his most important retrospective shows— at the Museum of Modern Art in 1965 and at the Metropolitan Museum of Art in 1992. *La Condition Humaine* is one of many versions Magritte painted on the same theme. The picture is emblematic of the work he produced in Paris during the 1930s, when he was still under the spell of the Surrealists. Here, Magritte executes a kind of optical illusion. He depicts an actual painting of a landscape displayed in front of an open window. He makes the image on the painted picture match perfectly with the "true" landscape outdoors. In doing so, Magritte proposed, in one unique image, the association between nature and its representation through the means of art. This work also stands as an assertion of the artist's power to reproduce nature at will and proves how ambiguous and impalpable the border between exterior and interior, objectivity and subjectivity, and reality and imagination can be. **SP**

The Seven Deadly Sins | Otto Dix

1933 | oil on canvas | 70 ½ x 47 ¼ in / 179 x 120 cm | Staatsgalerie, Stuttgart, Germany

Otto Dix's (1891–1969) first solo exhibition took place in 1923, at the Galerie I.B. Neumann in Berlin. In 1925, he participated in the first New Objectivity exhibition at the Mannheim museum, and started to organize collective exhibitions in major German cities. At the end of 1926, Dix was given a teaching position at the Dresden Academy, one he would immediately lose when the Nazis came to power. Dix's work was extremely critical of contemporary German society and, as a consequence, he was forbidden to exhibit his works, many of which were shown at the first Degenerate Art exhibition in 1937. Dix was forced to join the Nazi-controlled Imperial Chamber of Fine Arts in order to be able to work as an artist, promising to produce only landscapes. Still, he continued his allegorical paintings criticizing Nazi ideals. *The Seven Deadly Sins* was painted just after Dix was forced by the Nazis to resign his professorship in Dresden. In this masterpiece, he provides a pictorial interpretation of the political situation in Germany. In the foreground of the image is Avarice, figured as an old person in rags clutching at money on the floor. On its back, Envy, a ridiculously childlike man, wears a mask of Adolf Hitler, whose mustache was only painted by Dix after the war, for obvious reasons. Behind him stands Sloth, a skeleton representing the lack of alarm and concern in the German people—considered by Dix as one of the primary reason for the Nazis' rise. From left to right, behind these central figures, are Anger, Pride, Gluttony, and Lust. **JJ**

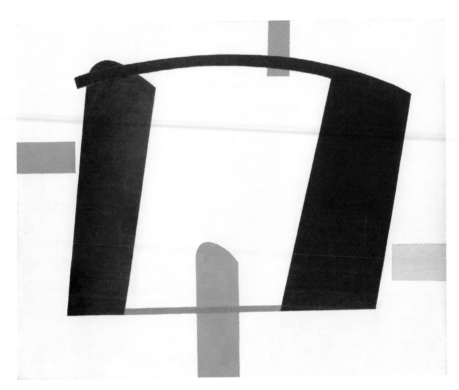

Balance | Jean Hélion

1933 | oil on canvas | 31 ⅞ x 39 ⅜ in / 81 x 100 cm | Hamburger Kunsthalle, Hamburg, Germany

Originally an architectural draftsman, Jean Hélion (1904–87) turned first to traditional representational art, then to abstraction. In about 1933–34, Hélion began to translate the concepts of balance, equilibrium, and tension onto canvas in a group of related paintings. The central black form in *Balance* vaguely suggests one pan on a pair of scales—a traditional image of the concept of balance—but Hélion explores the subject of balance from other angles, literally and figuratively, without recourse to a visual language of symmetry or regularity. Instead the elements of the composition balance one another out through contrast and counterpoint. The main contrast lies in the distinction of color and form between the black box, which appears to swing outward toward the viewer, creating a sense of movement, and the surrounding blue void. The blue area framed by the box is paler than that outside, creating an illusion of receding space. The asymmetrical placement of the colored rectangles gives equal weight to top and bottom, left and right of the composition, while front and back are counterbalanced by the receding black vertical plane to the left and projecting plane to the right. With his architectural background, Hélion would have become accustomed to articulating and enclosing volume, space, and mass—equilibrium and tension must be correctly calculated for any building to remain upright. Here, space has been enclosed in a black shape in order to give a paradoxically concrete form to an abstract idea. **SC**

Winter, Charlevoix County | A.Y. Jackson

1933 | oil on canvas | 25 x 32 in / 63.5 x 81.5 cm | Art Gallery of Ontario, Canada

A.Y. Jackson (1882–1974) is best known for being a member of the exhibitors' group formed in 1920 and known as The Group of Seven, a collection of Canadian painters who sought to eschew the traditions of European landscape painting in an attempt to forge a uniquely Canadian voice. *Winter, Charlevoix County* depicts the artist's native province of Quebec. Jackson's style intensifies colors but remains essentially naturalistic. The way in which he has simplified the rhythmically rolling hills into solid, almost plastic forms, encourages our eyes to trace his brush as it follows the open road, which opens up into the foreground, and then as it moves to the simple cottages in the background. Every curve and irregularity in the telephone wires and fence posts are lovingly remembered, as is each and every track made in the snow. The presence of a horse reminds the viewer that though scarcely populated, this is a landscape in which people live. Jackson's treatment of the landscape was a departure from the more neutral and detached Impressionistic tradition that still lingered in Canada up until that point. The attitude toward the subject that is manifested by this approach sits somewhere between awe at the grandeur of the land and a love for the land that comes from close acquaintanceship. Images such as these were among the first to show Canadians their own landscape free from European generic conventions; today they are regarded as formative works of Canadian heritage. **SS**

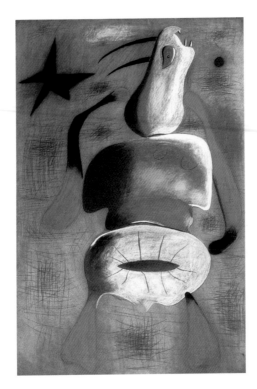

Woman | Joan Miró

1934 | pastel on paper | 13 x 17 in / 41 x 29 cm | Private collection

Refusing his father's wish that he attend business school, Joan Miró (1893–1983) studied at La Lonja school of fine arts in his hometown of Barcelona. He later became one of Spain's most famous Surrealist artists, demonstrating an admirable versatility as a painter, sculptor, and ceramicist. Although he publicly rejected membership of any artistic movement, he played a crucial role in influencing fellow Surrealists Salvador Dalí and Max Ernst. *Woman* is one of five pastels completed in the summer of 1934, in which Miró explores the connection between the living and the dead through his primitive fossilized forms. Works produced in this year were known as the artist's "peintures sauvages," and are typified by grotesquely distorted biomorphic forms that float over a shaded background. Here, the exaggerated genitalia and aggressive glare of the woman, baring her fanglike teeth, imbues the work with a violence uncommon among previous depictions of the female form. The intense feeling of terror evoked in *Woman* has been linked to the mounting political tension of the period, and anticipates the coming turmoil of the Spanish Civil War and World War II. His distorted figures act as a metaphor for human regression into an animalistic condition, as with of Picasso's *Guernica*, which was completed three years later in 1937. In that year, both artists became crucial contributors to the Spanish Pavilion at the Paris World's Fair, producing work that, though not overtly political, became visual symbols of the anti-war protest. **JG**

Fascist Creations | Gerardo Dottori

1925–35 | oil on canvas | Galleria Nazionale d'Arte Moderna, Rome, Italy

Gerardo Dottori (1884–1977) joined the Italian Futurist movement in 1914. The early Futurists actively supported the rise of fascism, as both movements sought a forceful regeneration of Italy, rejected "'backward" tradition, and celebrated modernity, vigor, masculinity, and the glory of war. After Mussolini came to power and aligned himself with Adolf Hitler, he adopted Hitler's taste for Neoclassicism and distanced himself from his Futurist allies. With Mussolini's backing, a group named *Il Novecento* formed in the 1920s that supported a return to a classical, figurative tradition. Meanwhile, Dottori forged ahead with a "Manifesto of Aerial Painting" in 1929, signaling a new branch of Futurism devoted to the sensations of flight, with landscapes distorted by the effects of speed and

height. *Fascist Creations* virtually explodes with symbolism of power and modernity. Scaffolding looms over smoke-filled chimneys, spewing out the mechanical impersonal message of fascism. A threatening warship takes aim at the viewer, while an airplane hurtles through the sky—macho symbols of war and the machine age. Dottori's violently fractured planes are typical of the "Aeropittura" works he was obsessed with at this time. Many of the *Novecento* painters became state propagandists under Mussolini and Dottori and his group contributed to the first *Novecento* exhibition in 1926. Italian Futurism remained active until Mussolini's demise in 1945, influencing many art movements along the way, including Dada, Constructivism, Vorticism, and even Pop art. **SLF**

The Spanish Conquest of Mexico | Diego Rivera

1929–35 | mural (detail) | Palacio Nacional, Mexico City, Mexico

Diego Rivera (1886–1957) is perhaps as famous for his marriage to Mexican artist Frida Kahlo (1907–54) as he is for his own work. Born in Mexico, Rivera studied and traveled widely in Spain, France, Italy, and Russia. His style was influenced by Cubism, but it was his ardent communism that was to influence its content. He believed that art should have a social function, which led him to become involved in the Mexican mural movement, which produced large-scale narrative works for public spaces, in the same vein as Italian fresco artists during the Renaissance. His hope was that they would enable his people in a quest for national and cultural identity and convey a political ideology in a similar fashion to Soviet Social Realists. *The Spanish Conquest of Mexico* stretches around the courtyard of Mexico City's Palacio Nacional and is typical of his colorful tableaux of historical events. It depicts Rivera's view of Mexico's history, from the arrival of Quetzalcoatl—the mythic plumed serpent god who native Indians believed had returned in the form of Spanish conquistador Hernán Cortés in 1519—to the revolution in 1910. The detail shown here depicts the Spanish killing native Indians, exploiting them as slaves, looting their gold, and paving the way for Catholic missionaries. Given his atheism, it is interesting that Rivera shows the Church positively as a protector of the oppressed, in the form of a priest embracing exhausted Indian children and brandishing a crucifix in the face of the greedy conquistadors. **CK**

Le Dimanche | Oscar Domínguez

1935 | oil on canvas | Instituto Oscar Domínguez de Arte y Cultura Contemporanea, Santa Cruz, Tenerife

Born in San Cristóbal de La Laguna on the island of Tenerife, Oscar Domínguez (1906–57) lived with his grandmother during his youth. After suffering a serious illness, which caused the deformation of his face and limbs, the young Domínguez turned to painting as a form of escape and expression. He moved to Paris, working for his family's banana export business before going to various fine-art schools in the city. His early work is heavily indebted to the avant-garde painting of Pablo Picasso and Yves Tanguy. In 1933, Domínguez met, and was influenced by, the Surrealists André Breton and Paul Eluard. A year later, Domínguez's work was featured at the Surrealist exhibition in Copenhagen and, in 1936, it was shown at similar exhibitions in London and

Tenerife. *Le Dimanche* dates from 1935, the year Domínguez was accepted into the Surrealist circle. His early Surrealist work had been rather naive but this piece shows a real growth in style and execution, after Domínguez, inspired by Salvador Dalí (1904–89), had overhauled and improved his painting technique. The figures of the horses hint at his later obsession with the blood of animals (Domínguez and Picasso shared a love of bull fighting) but here the scene is far less brutal. During the 1930s, while obviously influenced by Dalí and Max Ernst, Domínguez invented a new transfer process he called "desire transfers." Ernst, who had influenced Domínguez so profoundly, often made use of this technique. Domínguez committed suicide at the age of fifty-one. **OR**

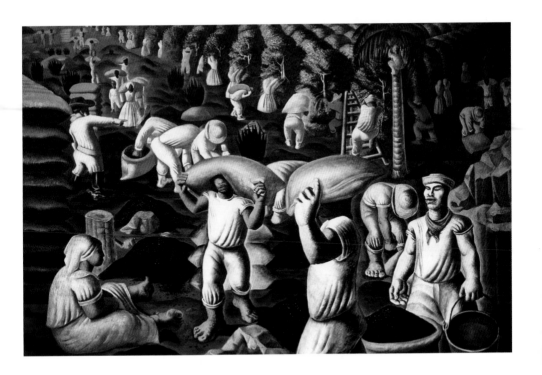

Coffee | Cândido Portinari

1935 | oil on canvas | 51 x 76 ¾ in / 130 x 195 cm | Museo Nacional de Belas Artes, Rio de Janeiro, Brazil

Cândido Portinari (1903–62), the son of Italian immigrants, was born on a coffee plantation near São Paulo and studied art in Rio de Janeiro and Paris. Like many of his peers, he was influenced by French Modernism and painted scenes from Brazilian daily life in a style blending Cubism and politically motivated Brazilian Neo-Realism. In 1922, Portinari participated in São Paulo's "Week of Modern Art," an influential art festival sponsored by wealthy local coffee barons. That year, he also joined the Brazilian Communist Party—of which he remained an active member throughout his life. *Coffee* depicts the arduous life of agricultural workers on coffee plantations. Painted with dramatic movement and great empathy, the work depicts a swarm of men and women lugging bulky bags of coffee beans while a uniformed foreman directs them with his aggressively pointed arm. The geometric repetition of lines of workers and rows of trees heightens the sense of oppressive toil, yet Portinari's use of warm tones neutralizes the composition's rigid angles and humanizes the workers. He depicts their bodies with limbs exaggerated to express exhaustion and animalistic bulk intended to represent the bestial lifestyle they are forced to live. During his life, Portinari enjoyed international success and he was friends with influential circles of poets, writers, journalists, and diplomats. In 1948, however, he was forced to flee Brazil when persecution of the communists began. He returned to Brazil in 1951 but died in 1962 from lead poisoning caused by his use of lead-based paint. **AH/SWW**

Jimson Weed | Georgia O'Keeffe

1936 | oil on linen | 70 x 83 ½ in / 178 x 212 cm | Indianapolis Museum of Art, Indianapolis, IN, USA

Pioneering American painter Georgia O'Keeffe (1887–1986) discovered her distinctive artistic voice after rejecting her traditional training and embracing the theories of her art teacher Arthur Wesley Dow (1857–1922), who advocated the expression of emotions through harmonious compositions of shapes and colors. By 1924, the artist had started work on a series of large-scale flower paintings, that along with her desert and bleached animal bone depictions are among her most recognizable works. *Jimson Weed* is a simple, swirling depiction of a group of trumpet flowers found near the artist's New Mexico home. O'Keeffe found inspiration in the architectural forms and fauna of the New Mexico desert when she began to spend winters there from the late 1920s. The natural subject matter is familiar and comfortable, but the style is distinctly modern. The enormous scale highlights the beauty and importance of the natural world, while the vibrant colors and use of space move away from the natural and evoke a strangeness that forces the viewer to look at the subject afresh. Rejecting Freudian interpretations of the blooming, sensuous petals as sexual symbolism, O'Keeffe claimed she was simply painting a magnification of her own experiences: "I'll paint what I see—what the flower is to me but I'll paint it big and they will be surprised into taking time to look at it—I will make even busy New Yorkers take time to see what I see of flowers." **JB**

Soft Construction with Boiled Beans | Salvador Dalí

1936 | oil on canvas | 39 x 39 in / 99 x 99 cm | Philadelphia Museum of Art, Philadelphia, PA, USA

Salvador Dalí (1904–89) held his first one-man show in Paris in 1929, having just joined the Surrealists who were led by former Dadaist, André Breton. That year, Dalí also met Gala Eluard, the then wife of Paul Eluard, who later became Dalí's lover, muse, business manager, and chief inspiration, encouraging him in the life of excessive wealth and artistic eccentricities for which he is now renowned. As an artist, Dalí was not limited to a particular style or medium. The body of his work, from early Impressionist paintings through his transitional Surrealist works and into his classical period, reveals a constantly growing and evolving artist. *Soft Construction with Boiled Beans (Premonition of Civil War)* depicts a dismembered figure that acts as a visual metaphor for the physical and emotional constraints of the civil war that was taking place in Spain at the time of the painting's execution. The figure grimaces as its own tight fist squeezes its breast with violent aggression, unable to escape its own strangulation as its foot is held down in an equally forceful grasp. Painted in 1936, the year in which war broke out, the work foresees the self-destruction of the Spanish people, while the boiled beans symbolize the decaying corpses of mass destruction. Dalí himself refused to be affiliated to a political party during the war, causing much controversy. Having been a prominent contributor to various international Surrealist exhibitions, he then moved into a new type of painting characterized by a preoccupation with science and religion. **JG**

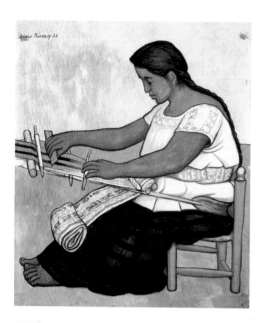

Tejedora
Diego Rivera

1936 | watercolor on rice paper | 22 x 20 in / 57 x 52 cm
Private collection

André Derain
Balthus

1936 | oil on wood | 44 ³⁄₈ x 28 ¹⁄₂ in / 112 x 72.4 cm
Museum of Modern Art, New York, NY, USA

Tejedora (*Weaver*) is one of a series of paintings by Diego Rivera (1886–1957) showing mestiza women spinning or weaving, and he produced another version in oils that shows the entire loom. Painting portraits of indigenous peoples in native dress was Rivera's way of showing his respect for them at a time when portraiture had been the preserve of the wealthy. He shows a young woman working, which indicates that he appreciates the skills of the working class and celebrates the youthful energy that will help shape the future of his country. The artist uses a bold color palette, and the weaver is painted using her backstrap loom to weave a narrow strip of cloth, perhaps for a belt. The choice of loom is significant because backstrap looms were used until the Spanish colonization in the sixteenth century when Dominican missionaries introduced harness looms— and Roman Catholicism. **CK**

Despite knowing some of the period's most avant-garde artists, Balthus (Balthazar Klossowski de Rola, 1908–2001) was opposed to all forms of abstraction. Largely self-taught, he learned his craft by copying the great masters and making observational studies of the real world. The classically styled painting *André Derain* is executed with smooth, incisive brushstrokes in muted colors. In this large portrait, Balthus has tried to capture the monumentality of Renaissance works, with their almost microscopic attention to detail. He admired Derain immensely, yet the painting has disrespectful and ambivalent connotations. Derain is in his studio with a model behind him, but she is sitting in an awkward, almost gauche position and Derain is attired in his dressing gown, leading us to wonder whether this is really just an image of an artist and his model or something less innocent. **SH**

The Strand by Night
Christopher R.W. Nevinson

1937 | oil on panel | 29 x 24 in / 76 x 61 cm
Bradford Art Galleries and Museums, UK

Memory
Frida Kahlo

1937 | oil on canvas | 19 x 15 in / 48.2 x 38 cm
Private collection

Christopher Richard Wynne Nevinson (1889–1946) was influenced by the Futurist style, and worked as an official wartime artist at the Western Front. After the war he returned to a naturalistic style, frequently painting cityscapes in New York, Paris, and London, and his *The Strand by Night* falls into this category. This painting shows the chic London street on a rainy night. Nevinson does not choose to depict the street's glamour, however. Rather this is a dark, wet night, and the street is viewed from a dark, damp alley. The eye is drawn to the bright lights of big city life by his dramatic use of perspective, but as much as the central focus of light and frantic activity celebrates the dynamism of the metropolis, Nevinson also emphasizes the dehumanization of urban life and its grayness by choosing to frame most of his canvas with a painting of a dull back alley. **CK**

Frida Kahlo (1907–54) produced more than fifty-five self-portraits all dealing with issues of identity. In self-portraiture, the artist enters into a conspiracy with the mirror and there is either a conscious construction of a persona or, to varying degrees, an honest investigation. *Memory* contains clues to the artist's state of mind. Here she has shown herself three times, once in a white dress and jacket, with cropped hair, and without arms and hands. She appears twice more represented by contemporary and Mexican clothes, empty except for the missing limbs. An arrow pierces the chest where the heart should be. The enlarged heart lies on the shore, bleeding into the sea. The cropped hair and the displaced heart refer to her husband Diego Rivera's infidelities. The clothing signifies her place in the world as a contemporary artist with a strong link to her Mexican-Indian heritage. **WO**

Guernica | Pablo Picasso

1937 | oil on canvas | 137 x 305 in / 349 x 776 cm | Museo Nacional Centro de Arte Reina Sofia, Madrid, Spain

Pablo Picasso (1881–1973) painted *Guernica* as a vitriolic attack on Spain's fascist government, despite the fact that it had been commissioned by representatives of the Spanish Republic for exhibition in the Paris World's Fair. A portrayal of the Nazi carpet bombing of a Basque city in northern Spain, the painting's importance transcended its historical source, becoming a universal symbol of all atrocities and consequences of war. *Guernica*'s power lies in its mixture of epic and realistic elements. Painted in Picasso's signature Cubist style and replete with characters that recur in his work (such as the Minotaur, Spanish bulls, and women in the throes of pain and suffering), this entirely black-and-white painting has the stark immediacy of a newspaper article. *Guernica* is heavily infused with narrative symbolism. A disembodied eye hovering over the horror is either a bomb or a symbol of hope and freedom, and scholars have read the figure of a horse trampling a wailing woman as representing dictators *in extremis*—Franco, Hitler, and Mussolini. Despite the weighty iconography, the artist's decision to strip his canvas of color provided his abstracted forms and mythic symbolism with the appearance of journalistic credibility. During Picasso's lifetime, *Guernica* toured extensively through America and Europe and, in spite of Franco's repeated requests, he refused to return the painting to Spain until the country was once again a republic. Only in 1981, after both Picasso and Franco had died, was *Guernica* moved from New York to its native Spain. **SE**

Nocturnal Landscape | Paul Nash

1938 | oil on canvas | 30 x 39 ¾ in / 76.5 x 101.5 cm | Manchester Art Gallery, UK

Paul Nash (1889–1946) was the son of a successful London attorney. His brother John became a painter, illustrator, and engraver without formal training, but Paul studied at the Slade Art School and had his first solo show when he was twenty-three. As a lieutenant in World War I, he sketched life in the trenches and produced a series of well-received war paintings after being invalided home due to a nonmilitary-related injury. On the strength of these, he was recruited as a military artist in 1917 to document the fighting on the Western Front. When he returned from the war, Nash championed the aesthetics of Abstraction and Modernism as a founding member of the influential modern-art movement Unit One, along with fellow artists Henry Moore, Barbara Hepworth, and art critic Henry Read. When World War II began, Nash was enlisted by the Ministry of Information and the Air Ministry and created a series of paintings documenting the fighting. Perhaps in contrast to the tension, tedium, and terror of war, Nash painted a series of innovative, geometric, Surrealist English landscapes, inspired by locations that articulated a sense of permanence and long-reaching history, such as burial mounds, Iron Age hill forts, or Bronze Age megalithic sites such as Stonehenge. *Nocturnal Landscape* transforms an actual physical place into dreamlike terrain, distilling reality down to geometry and symbolism. This mystical abstraction of reality reflects the turbulence of his era, as if he longed for the seemingly impossible serenity and permanence of the places he painted. **AH**

Fair in Transylvania | Vilmos Aba-Novák

1938 | oil on canvas | 25 ½ x 31 in / 65 x 79 cm | Nicolas M. Salgo Collection, New York, NY, USA

A number of prominent artistic movements developed at the turn of the century in Hungary, which led to a revival in the tradition of Hungarian painting. The School of Nagybánya was an artists' colony formed by a group of painters from Munich who had settled at Nagybánya and painted under the influence of Simon Hollosy. Working *en plein air* and in a strident Naturalist and Realist manner, they aimed to create a new artistic aesthetic reflective of the Hungarian people. At around the same time another artistic group, the Szolnok Artists' Colony, formed with the artist Adolf Fényes as one of the leading members. Their style was defined by a romantic realism that developed into a strong expressiveness and was often conceived with an attitude of social criticism. The Hungarian artist Vilmos

Aba-Novák (1894–1942) worked within the School of Nagybánya and painted his best works from 1930 to 1938—the year of *Fair in Transylvania*. His paintings reflect a combination of Naturalist detail, semi-Cubist arrangement, and energetic activity. The vibrant *Fair in Transylvania* is typical of this style, with strong, bold lines and forms that create a rich, busy pattern across the painting's surface. The composition is based on strong diagonals that are emphasized by the rounded wagon tops above the people, with the energy focused through this swath of activity. Aba-Novák favored scenes such as this, which depicted fairs, markets, and the hustle-and-bustle of rural peasant life. His Realist approach is representative of this period of Hungarian genre painting. **TP**

Haystack | Thomas Hart Benton

1938 | tempera with oil on linen | 24 x 30 in / 61 x 76 cm | Museum of Fine Arts, Houston, TX, USA

Thomas Hart Benton (1889–1975) was born in Neosho, Missouri, into the miserable marriage of his artist mother, Elizabeth, and Colonel Maecenas Benton, a conservative Congressman who sent his son to military school. As an advocate of populist socialism, Benton believed American artists should address issues of the homeland instead of striving to compete with their European counterparts. He rejected modernism and is widely regarded as the father of the Regionalist artistic movement, in which artists endeavored to paint familiar, everyday scenes in a naturalistic and representational manner. *Haystack* is a quintessential image of idealized manual labor. In this pastoral ideal of farm life, painted shortly after the Great Depression, Benton illustrates the possibility of self-contained, self-generated plenty through his swirling brushstrokes and circular composition. The artist was also a teacher, his most famous student being Jackson Pollock, whose aggressive, masculine form of Abstract Expressionist art distilled Benton's muscular aesthetic down to pure gesture and line. Despite his love of Middle America, Benton lived most of his adult life in New York, yet the force of his conviction meant that, regardless of inconsistencies between his persona and reality, he remained a man who had modeled himself after his concept of an ideal American artist. And, as that artist, he painted an image of America that Americans should always look to in order to remember what truly makes America capable of greatness. **AH**

Composition with Figures on a Terrace | Leonor Fini

1938 | oil on canvas | 39 x 32 in / 99.5 x 81 cm | Edward James Foundation Collection, Chichester, UK

Born in Buenos Aires and raised in Trieste, Italy, Leonor Fini (1908–96) was from an early age attracted to a wide variety of artistic styles, including Renaissance art, Mannerism, and Romanticism. Largely self-taught in her artistic pursuits, Fini moved to Paris in 1936 where she befriended the core progenitors of Surrealism, among them Max Ernst, Salvador Dalí, and René Magritte. While in Paris, Fini was involved in a number of Surrealist exhibitions, but never formally included herself within the group. She worked meticulously on her creations, building up the canvas with paint in tiny brushstrokes of color. In *Composition with Figures on a Terrace,* she explores the notion of a fantastic dreamscape of the unconscious, inspired by the psychoanalytic theories of Sigmund Freud.

Dominating the foreground space is a self-portrait of the artist situated as if on a theatrical stage. By taking control of her own image in the form of a self-portrait, Fini offers herself up as a proto-feminist artistic construction of a sexual and autonomous subject. The figures surrounding Fini are images of her friends, including the male subject, Alexandre Iolas, who is the only figure to engage the viewer's gaze. Random objects—feathers, stockings, a shoe—are scattered about the scene, adding to the dreamlike quality of this imaginary gathering. Throughout her career Fini maintained the primary importance of unconscious thought and the notion of the desiring woman. This focus translated into all aspects of her life, including the three novels that she scripted in the 1970s. **MV**

The Lilienstein on the Elbe | Franz Radziwill

c.1939 | oil on canvas | 33 ½ x 39 ½ in / 85 x 100.5 cm | Hamburger Kunsthalle, Hamburg, Germany

While the early work of German artist Franz Radziwill (1895–1983) had a surreal, Chagall-esque patchwork quality, *The Lilienstein on the Elbe* demonstrates the territory Radziwill made his own. An ostensibly Realist landscape, it subtly combines a Romantic, monolithic quality with restrained, contemporary detail. Initially, Radziwill was a member of the optimistic, Socialist-leaning *Novembergruppe* and painted at a time when economic devastation, following the German defeat in World War I, helped to create a political climate rife with extremism, as charted by the grotesque satire of the era's Expressionist painting. As the Weimar Republic foundered, political extremism gave way to the more Realist, less overt New Objectivity. Radziwill's work became more refined and restrained,

which is perfectly exemplified by this painting. Landscapes and skies figure heavily, monolithic structures are recurrent, and the painting references a sublime, romantic view of nature. The brushstrokes are precise; grays and whites are numerous, adding to the static, frozen atmosphere. The image is Realist, similar to the equally chilling contemporary paintings of Otto Dix. The banal urban foreground is juxtaposed with the terrifyingly wild background, suggesting a looming, implacable yet silent threat. *The Lilienstein on the Elbe* is part of a body of work that developed away from the blatant societal criticism of Expressionism. Through its mix of traditional, accessible technique and subtly jarring images, it provided a more refined critique of current realities. **JCo**

Gas | Edward Hopper

1940 | oil on canvas | 26 ¼ x 40 ¼ in / 66.7 x 102 cm | Museum of Modern Art, New York, NY, USA

This superbly evoked composition feels like a movie-still about to dissolve into a moving image—perhaps a road movie or horror flick? A balding, waistcoated attendant checks his forecourt at a Mobil gas station (actually in Truro, Massachusetts). Bounded by a dense swath of New England locust trees, a long road sweeps away diagonally into an almost tunnellike gloom. It lies in sharp contrast to the reassuring small-town American vernacular of the red-and-white pumps and New England garage building under a protective dusky blue sky—"Welcome Break" meets *Twilight Zone*. The natural light of the sky also contrasts with the artificial light from the gas station. At the time of painting, Edward Hopper (1882–1967) was suffering from tiredness, depression, and had undergone a succession of minor operations. As a direct result he was struggling to paint. He had learned his superb blending of color and light in Paris as a student of Robert Henri from 1901 to 1906. Henri was a member of a group of painters known as the Ashcan school who aimed to depict realistically America's burgeoning metropolitan life—its tenements, docks, sports arenas, factories, and streets. But Hopper pursued his own interpretation of America's homespun architecture and everyday street facades that had been overlooked or ignored by other homegrown artists. Whether it was railroad stations or carriages, bars or diners, front porches or rows of houses, Hopper painted America as he saw it—a documentary artist with a highly poetic visual style. **JH**

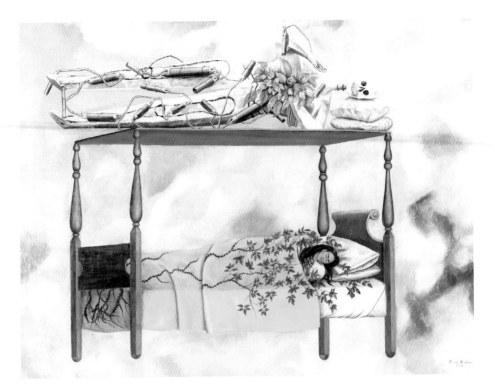

The Dream | Frida Kahlo

1940 | oil on canvas | 29 ⅛ x 38 ¾ in / 74 x 98.5 cm | Private collection

Born in 1907 in Coyoacán, Mexico, Frida Kahlo (1907–54) suffered from polio as a child, and at eighteen survived a bus crash that left her with multiple injuries. She endured over thirty operations, several miscarriages, and constant pain. Death was Frida Kahlo's companion. In this self-portrait, Kahlo dreams in an old, wooden, four-poster bed floating in the clouds. The skeleton that lies on the canopy of her bed was a copy of a papier-mâché skeleton that she had made for the Mexican pre-Easter celebrations. She frequently used images of death in her work as a reference to her culture and to express more personal concerns. This figure of death holding a faded bunch of flowers could refer to her own demise or that of Leon Trotsky, at one time her lover, who was assassinated in 1940. The skirt of one of her most elaborate Mexican costumes had a pattern of vines. Here, vines creep over the bright yellow sheet and encircle her head as a living counterpoint to the tendrils of wire connected to explosives "growing" over the skeleton. There is a play here between the tendrils of life and death, the irony being that Kahlo was incapable of producing life. All the important events take place in bed: conception, birth, and death. Beds are symbolically resonant, measurers of time, and for Kahlo an ever-present reality, as she was confined to hers as a child, teenager, and woman. It was also in bed that she began to paint. Kahlo's self-portraits are inextricable from her much-documented biography; she unashamedly made the personal public. **WO**

Seascape | Cândido Portinari

1940 | oil on canvas | 11 x 18 ½ in / 27.5 x 47 cm | Private collection

Cândido Portinari (1903–62) was a prominent and prolific Brazilian painter. Like the Mexican Communist painter Diego Rivera and the American Socialist artist Thomas Hart Benton, Portinari created elaborate, Expressionistic murals as a method of promoting his ideological principles. His art blatantly expressed his Communist beliefs, but nevertheless he achieved much success in Brazil and in the United States. During his life he exhibited works at the Ministério da Educação e Saúde in Rio de Janeiro, the center church in Pampulha, near Belo Horizonte, the Brazilian pavilion at the 1939 New York World's Fair, the Library of Congress in Washington, DC, and the headquarters of the United Nations in New York. *Seascape*, an image of sailors and fishermen laboring on choppy waters, is a comparatively small painting, but is nevertheless a politically motivated portrait of oppressed workers. With a palette primarily reduced to blue, brown, and cream, the eye is drawn to a pulsed red line on the sail, a symbol of impending violence and rebellion. The Cubist-influenced mural style incorporates naive elements and distorted perspective, which expresses movement and emotion, yet is also distancing, so that the political message is conveyed to both heart and head. Portinari's painting career flourished during the 1940s but his political career suffered. He was awarded several prestigious international awards, including a French legion of honor, but a year after he ran for senator in 1947 he was exiled from Brazil for his affiliation with the Communist party. **AH/SWW**

Head of Woman | Jesús Guerrero Galván

1940 | oil on canvas | 18 x 15 in / 46 x 38 cm | Private collection

Jesús Guerrero Galván (1910–73) was part of the *Banderas de Provincia* (Provincial Flags) group in Jalisco, Mexico, made up of painters, writers, and poets such as Raúl Anguiano, José Guadalupe Zuno, and Agustín Yáñez. A member of the Mexican muralist movement, he joined the ranks of Rivera, Siquieros, and Orozco as one of the most influential twentieth-century painters to contribute to the development of Mexican pictorial art. His signature is a use of oversized body parts, including heads, hands, arms, and legs. *Head of Woman* is representative of this form of stylized representation. The subject displays an inexpressive bearing, as if in a dreamy reflection, close to the models of the Madonnas of Renaissance painters whom Galván admired, and communicates an incipient sensuality and a contained modesty. An Italian influence can be discerned in the face, but the artist's depiction of the enlarged features, especially the nose and mouth, is reminiscent of Picasso. The elements of naive realism, borrowed from Aztec drawing and the *retablo votive* tradition, showcase Galván's appreciation and understanding of local folk traditions. The chosen color palette is used expressively and suffuses the work with a soft, earthy glow. Referred to as an "Italianized" painter by his critics, his compositions are resonant of the study of sketches by great masters such as Leonardo da Vinci. Classical influences also come from his study of and admiration for Pablo Picasso, evident from the monolithic quality of some of his figures. **AA**

Untitled | Victor Vasarely

1941 | oil on cardboard | Israel Museum, Jerusalem

Hungarian-born Victor Vasarely (1908–97) settled in Paris in 1932. He worked as a graphic artist and as a creative consultant in advertising while developing his own style of scientifically based abstract art. Three decades later, he was acclaimed as the father of Op (optical) art. In the process of developing his art, Vasarely experimented with color, textural effects, perspective, geometric patterns, rhythm, and tone. He worked especially on the ways in which static images can create the optical illusion of movement. During the 1930s, he was influenced by Constructivism. His intent was that art should influence our entire environment, from architecture, furniture, and fashion to education and culture. By the 1940s, he had achieved a strong, characteristic style of painting dynamic geometric forms with interacting colors. In this painting, not intended as a final, finished piece, Vasarely links similar tones and colors to create harmony and order, and to create a relationship between his art and the viewer. He believed that "To experience a work of art is more important than to understand it." Here, the red, pink, and brown shapes are not representative of any element or idea in the real world. Instead, the combination of shape and color offers a heightened visual stimulation. The viewer experiences a noticeable sensation and a linked emotional response whether this is calm, excitement, curiosity, or even annoyance. The emphasis is very much on the viewer's reaction to a work of art rather than on searching for the artist's intention. **SH**

Constellation: Awakening in the Early Morning | Joan Miró

1941 | gouache and oil on paper | 18 x 15 in / 46 x 38 cm | Kimbell Art Foundation, Fort Worth, TX, USA

Born in Barcelona, Joan Miró (1893–1983) was one of Spain's leading Surrealist artists, and made his name as a painter, sculptor, and ceramicist. In 1920 he left his home in Catalunya for Paris, where he came under the influence of the Surrealist poets and writers based there. However, throughout his artistic development, in which he incorporated the bright colors of the Fauves and the broken forms of Cubism, his work retains the flat two-dimensionality of Catalan folk art, which continued to inform his work during his career. *Constellation: Awakening in the Early Morning* is the fifteenth in a series of twenty-three small gouache and oil-wash paintings on paper, all known as *Constellations*. This small work displays Miró's playful style in which, under the influence of Surrealism, he explored the creative potential of automatism, allowing a childlike spontaneity to inspire the formation of his doodled creatures, afloat in fluid fields of color. This particular *Constellation* was completed in Mallorca, where the Miró family fled following the beginning of the Nazi occupation of France in May 1940. The entire series of *Constellations* was smuggled to New York during World War II, where part of it was exhibited at the Pierre Matisse Gallery in 1945. Like Picasso's famous painting *Guernica*, Miro's *Constellations* serve as an example of symbolic works of art that have survived the conflict of war. Once in the United States, Miró's paintings subsequently went on to influence the emerging generation of Abstract Expressionists, such as Jackson Pollock. **JG**

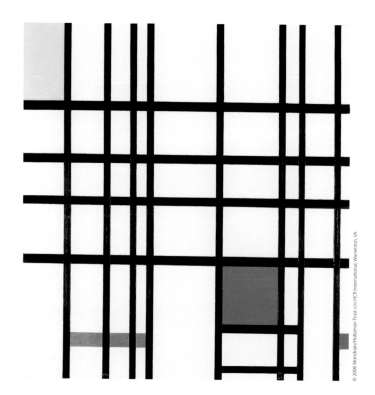

Composition with Yellow, Blue and Red, 1937–42 | Piet Mondrian

1937–42 | oil on canvas | 28 ⅝ x 27 ¼ in / 72.5 x 69 cm | Tate Collection, London, UK

Piet Mondrian (1872–1944) is one of the most important figures in the development of abstract art. Mondrian was keen to develop a purely non-representational mode of painting, based on a set of formal terms. Underlying Mondran's ambitions for painting was the aim to express a "pure" reality. His style, now known as Neoplasticism, did not refer to the external, recognizable world. Having removed all imagery from the canvas, what are conventionally seen as the key elements of painting—line, form, hue—were now mobilized to serve very different ends, namely the embodiment of "plastic expression." To this end, Mondrian was able to restrict himself to straight lines and basic colors. In *Composition with Yellow, Blue and Red*, he organizes the composition around a series of vertical and horizontal lines that overlap to form a grid. Four discrete areas of primary color are "weighted" so that color functions as a form of counterbalance in relation to each line's ascribed role. *Composition with Yellow, Blue and Red* is a mature representation of this approach. Mondrian began the piece while he was living in Paris; in 1938, he went to live in London, then moved to New York two years later, where the painting was completed. In New York, the artist took a further step in his program of formal experimentation, by giving complex color planes precedence over lines. The significance of this work resides in its ability to take what is fundamental to painting and create a reality entirely in accordance with Mondrian's quest for plastic expression. **CS**

The Flower Seller | Diego Rivera

1942 | oil on canvas | 59 x 47 in / 150 x 120 cm | Private collection

When Diego Rivera (1886–1957) painted *The Flower Seller*, he had just finished a series of paintings in San Francisco, and was about to begin a series of frescoes at the National Gallery in Mexico, and to build Anahuacalli, a structure that would house his collection of pre-colonial objects and art. Three years earlier, he had severed his friendship with Leon Trotsky, after hosting him in exile in Mexico, and had broken up with his wife, Mexican painter Frida Kahlo, only to remarry her the following year. By all accounts, Diego Rivera had the makings of a great artist and a great celebrity. Seen in this context, *The Flower Seller* is seemingly insignificant, yet it represents a fusion of the fundamental artistic and political principles that drive Diego Rivera's work. Artistically, Rivera studied Cubist painters such as Picasso, whom he met in his early life in Paris, but was also influenced by Mexican muralists such as revolutionary David Alfaro Siqueiros and Rufino Tamayo, whose robust approach he adopted to generate a specifically Mexican style. Politically, Rivera spent his life as an active member of Mexico's Communist Party and often undertook historical and political subjects for his work. In this painting Diego displays an intimate knowledge of the 1910 Mexican Revolution and promotes the fervent belief of its hero, Emiliano Zapata, who encouraged Mexico's peasants to return to the land that was rightfully theirs. Ironically, it is in the lone figure of a humble Mexican peasant flower seller that these great ideologies and disciplines are delineated. **JSD**

Nighthawks | Edward Hopper

1942 | oil on canvas | 33 ⅛ x 60 in / 84 x 152.5 cm | Art Institute of Chicago, Chicago, IL, USA

Curved geometric forms accentuated by an Art Deco facade and angular light provide an almost theatrical setting for a group of insulated and isolated figures. The Phillies cigars advert on top of the diner shows this is not an upmarket location, since Phillies is a brand of American-made popular, cheap cigars commonly sold at convenience stores and gas stations. These "nighthawks" are bathed in an oasis of fluorescent light in an all-night diner in an otherwise dark urban street: it's a film noir, Chandler-esque setting. There is no doubt that American Edward Hopper's (1882–1967) expressive use of artificial light playing upon the simplified shapes gives the painting its beauty. The Bogart-and-Bacall couple stare at the bar boy bending below the counter while their hands almost touch—a tableaux that makes the solitary diner across the counter, and with his back to the viewer, look even more conspicuous. Hopper claimed that the street itself wasn't particularly lonely, but perhaps unconsciously he was conceptualizing the crushing loneliness of a large city. In any event, there is no visible diner's entrance, the viewer is shut out from the scene, making it more intriguing. The diner itself was inspired by one in Greenwich Village, Manhattan, where Hopper lived for fifty-four years. Hopper's practice was to make sketches while he was out and about in New York and then come back to his studio and sketch a combination of poses together with his wife, Josephine, as he did here for what has become one of the iconic images of the twentieth century. **JH**

The Archer | Paul Nash

1930–42 | oil on canvas | 28 x 36 in / 71 x 91.5 cm | Southampton City Art Gallery, Hampshire, UK

Paul Nash (1889–1946) is one of the most important landscape artists of the first half of the twentieth century, and was central to the development of Modernism within English art. When Nash was twelve his family moved from London to Buckinghamshire, where the beautiful rolling countryside was to instill in him a lifelong appreciation for landscape. He trained at the Slade School of Art in London, where he met Stanley Spencer (1891–1959) and Mark Gertler (1891–1939), and was influenced by the work of William Blake (1757–1827). Although grounded in nature, his work was highly imaginative and cerebral. Nash was a key player in promoting British Surrealism and abstraction. He took everyday inanimate objects and placed them in the landscape, giving them their own identity and symbolism, and referring to them as "objects personages." *The Archer* alludes to a sexual dynamism of unattainable desire, with the "object personage" taken from a toy boat casting a long shadow toward the target. In Nash's words, "The Archer himself . . . is masculine . . . and he is generally after . . . the target . . . But his real headache, as you might say, is a countermenacing shadow in the form of a woman with long, flowing hair." Nash worked in a traditional genre, that of landscape, and sought to propel it into the modern era through his use of abstracted ideas and surreal concepts. The melding of "landscape" and "modern" is not easy, but Nash created a new language for natural imagery that was highly influential in twentieth-century art. **TP**

Portrait of Mr. Dahesh | Marie Hadad

1942 | oil on canvas | 29 ½ x 26 in / 75 x 66 cm | Dahesh Museum of Art, New York, NY, USA

Marie Hadad (1889–1973) was a pioneering figure in the Lebanese arts movement and headed the Association des Artistes du Liban. Born into a prominent Beirut banking family, she was also known as the "Bedouin's artist," as many of her portraits featured the Bedouin. Hadad's career was cut short in 1945 when she stopped painting and withdrew from public life after the death of her daughter, Magda. Among the many paintings that Hadad produced during her career was this portrait of the influential figure Dr. Dahesh, the pen name of writer, philosopher, and intellectual Salim Moussa Achi, who founded the spiritual philosophy "Daheshism" that gave instruction on such matters as God, the cosmic order, and divine justice. Dahesh's philosophy attracted thousands of followers, but also led him to fall foul of the Lebanese authorities, who exiled him in 1944. One of Dahesh's earliest supporters, Hadad wrote about the spiritual leader and painted this portrait in the same year that he founded Daheshism. Here, the subject is shown seated in a low-back chair, dressed formally in a black suit and tie. His pose is quite informal: his head is tilted to one side as he rests his cheek against the knuckles of his right hand. Much more muted in tone than many of Hadad's earlier vibrantly colored paintings, *Portrait of Mr. Dahesh* portrays a handsome and intelligent man, lost in thought. Dahesh's face, through Hadad's use of light and shadow, appears almost luminous, a comment perhaps on his spirituality. **AV**

Sun, Moon, Stars | Meret Oppenheim

1942 | oil on canvas | 18 ⅞ x 20 ⅛ in / 48 x 51 cm | Private collection

Meret Oppenheim (1913–85) was mainly known for the *Fur Teacup* (*Object Le Déjeuner en Fourrure*) of 1936, and for the nude photograph covered in printing ink (*Veiled Erotic*, 1933) taken by Man Ray (1890–1976), both of which earned her some notoriety, but for many years eclipsed her painting. Her uninhibited attitude to sexuality gained her a place in Surrealism, but principally as a woman-child rather than as an artist. *Sun, Moon, Stars* was produced during an extended period of depression, when she keenly felt the inferior position of women artists. The sun god is placed centrally, crowned by stars; the more ambiguous female figure representing the moon drifts away, emitting a faint flowering of light. Oppenheim's use of gender stereotypes makes this an evocative dream-scape rather than a feminist critique. The German-Swiss artist recorded her own dreams long before she encountered the Surrealists and discovered their fascination with the workings of the unconscious. The other most prominent feature in this painting is the sarcophagus with its lid of hollowed-out spheres, like the impression of breasts in plaster. The themes of night, the irrational, creativity, and death reveal the dark side of Surrealism, and for Oppenheim they represented the difficulties faced by women artists. From the 1970s, Oppenheim's work became known to a wider audience. Today she is an artist recognized for her own compelling body of work and not merely as the muse of Surrealism. **WO**

Composition in Magenta: The End of Everything | Matta

1942 | oil on canvas | 36 x 29 in / 92 x 74 cm | University of Essex Collection of Latin American Art, UK

Portrait of Dora Maar
Pablo Picasso

1942 | oil on canvas | 25 ⅝ x 18 ⅛ in / 65 x 46 cm
Private collection

Chilean Roberto Matta Echaurren (1911–2002) originally trained in his native country as an architect and interior designer. He left for Paris in 1932 to work as a draftsman in Le Corbusier's studio before turning to painting and joining the Surrealist movement in 1938. This painting belongs to a series of works that Matta called "inscapes." These landscapes of the mind explore the realms of conscious and unconscious thought, as well as evoking images of the wider cosmos. The painting could be interpreted as the end of the universe or the destruction of humankind during World War II. It uses line, space, motion, and a luminous palette of crimson, black, and white to create a fluid, dreamlike depiction of space. Matta's eerie paintings of inner space influenced pivotal Abstract Expressionist painters. He created new spatial dimensions using a blend of organic and cosmic forms, being one of the first artists to take this abstract leap. **CM**

Pablo Picasso (1881–1973) and Dora Maar were together for a decade through the 1930s and 40s. Raised in Argentina, Maar was the daughter of a Yugoslavian father and a French mother. Though initially trained as a painter, she became one of the foremost Surrealist photographers of the 1930s. Their relationship was tumultuous but yielded more interesting work than the periods Picasso spent with less challenging partners. For the better part of a decade, Maar was Picasso's muse, his model, his companion, and his intellectual sparring partner. Maar is believed to have helped Picasso paint *Guernica*, his anti-war masterpiece, and though she was quoted by her biographer James Lord as saying, "All his portraits of me are lies. They're all Picassos. Not one is Dora Maar," the series of portraits he painted of her are among his most revered. **AH**

Birthday
Dorothea Tanning

1942 | oil on canvas | 40 ¼ x 25 ½ in / 102 x 65 cm
Philadelphia Museum of Art, Philadelphia, PA, USA

The Singing Bird
Rufino Tamayo

1943 | oil on canvas
Private collection

Dorothea Tanning (b.1910) was inspired to become a painter by the *Fantastic Art: Dada and Surrealism* exhibition held at New York's Museum of Modern Art in 1936. At the age of thirty, she painted this self-portrait. According to her memoirs, she often bought secondhand clothes and this ruffled purple jacket was from a Shakespearean costume. Coupled with the brown skirt of twigs, it gives her the appearance of a strange bird. There is a strong latent eroticism in the painting, which is less to do with her bare breasts than with the writhing twigs, which on closer inspection contain figures, and the uncertain invitation of the open doors. At her feet is an extraordinary composite creature, which adds an air of menace. The irrational is constantly present in Tanning's work and this scene is disturbing because—like any dreamscape—it is at once strange and familiar. **WO**

Three of the greatest influences on Rufino Tamayo's (1899–1991) work are evident in this painting: ancient Mexican art and sculpture, Western art, and the opulent color of South American folk art. The angular forms of the figure in *The Singing Bird* reflect Tamayo's interest in pre-Columbian sculpture but also display a simplicity of line and form characteristic of his oeuvre. Tamayo traveled abroad on many occasions, living for a total of twenty years in New York and twelve in Paris, mixing with artists and intellectuals from many countries. The influence of Cubism and artists such as Braque, Miró, and Picasso is evident in his geometrical figures and abstracted forms. The artist's skillful and economical use of color is one of the distinguishing features of his work. Here the rich tones, especially the red that highlights areas of the figure, fill the canvas and bring the almost flat planes of the forms to life. **HH**

Burial at Sea
Thomas Harold Beament

c.1943 | oil on canvas | 23 ¾ x 29 ⅞ in / 60.5 x 76 cm | Canadian War Museum, Ottawa, Canada

Trained as both a lawyer and an artist, Thomas Harold Beament (1898–1985) served as an officer in the Canadian navy from 1939, was an official war artist from 1943 to 1947, and retired with the rank of commander. Created during World War II, *Burial at Sea* offers an intimate glimpse into what one must imagine was one of the most somber events aboard a ship. Beament launches the viewer into the middle of a burial scene, as the flag-cloaked body is about to be cast off to sea. In the background, mourners with bowed heads decorously pay their respects, while in the foreground three men go about the practical business of deposing the body. The color of the flag's stripe is echoed in the skin tones of the sailors' faces. At first glance, the viewer has difficulty orientating the space of the image and its crowded composition; only the title of the work indicates that the large white form dominating the foreground is a body draped in a flag. The face of one of the three men supporting the stretcher seems to strain under the weight of the body; his engagement in his task is in sharp contrast to the calm of the group of mourners behind him, including a saluting officer. The differences between these two groups of people, as well as the unusual spatial composition of the image, cleverly and quietly convey to the viewer the untidy, difficult, and sometimes morbid business of life aboard ship. In this way, Beament was able to capture a unique psychological dimension of life in the navy. **SS**

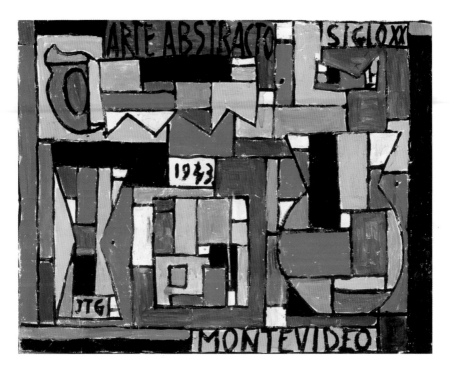

Abstract Art in Five Tones and Complementaries
Joaquín Torres-García

1943 | oil on board | 20 ½ x 26 ½ in / 52 x 67.5 cm | Albright-Knox Art Gallery, Buffalo, NY, USA

Best known for developing the style Constructive Universalism, Joaquín Torres-García's (1874–1949) career began at the age of seventeen, when his family relocated to Barcelona from Montevideo. After completing his studies at the Escuela Oficial de Bellas Artes and the Academia Baixas, he continued to paint, assist Antoni Gaudí with the glass for the Cathedral Sagrada Familia, and enjoy café society with Picasso and Julio Gonzalez. In 1920, he moved to New York, then in 1926 to Paris, where he met Van Doesburg and Mondrian and founded the group *Cercle et Carré*. In 1934 he returned to Montevideo, where he founded his own art school and the Asociación de Arte Constructivo. *Abstract Art in Five Tones and Complementaries* is typical of his mature work: like a compositor's box, each compartment contributes to an overall meaning. At first sight totally formalist, abstract, and geometric, the work is fundamentally biographical. On the top left is a large-toothed carpenter's saw, reflecting the fact that both Torres-García's father and grandfather were carpenters. On the right, a stylized primitive pot; on the lower left, an hourglass. Then there are the words: MONTEVIDEO, Torres-García's birthplace; ARTE ABSTRACTO, his professional preoccupation; SIGLO XX, the twentieth century; and his initials JTG. An exceptionally well-traveled and networked artist, Torres-García's work was a major influence on Latin American art and art education throughout the twentieth century. As a Uruguayan painter his international standing is unique. **SF**

The Palladist | Victor Brauner

1943 | oil on canvas | 51 x 63 ¾ in / 130 x 162 cm | Musée National d'Art Moderne, Paris, France

After a brief stint at the School of Fine Arts in Bucharest, the Romanian artist Victor Brauner (1903–66) initially painted landscapes reflective of Cézanne's influence, but his work became increasingly Expressionist and abstract. He founded the Dadaist magazine *15HP* with the avant-garde poet Ilarie Voronca in 1924, and between 1929 and 1931 contributed articles to *Unu*, a Dadaist and Surrealist paper. By 1930 he had moved to Paris, where he became friendly with Yves Tanguy, who introduced him to other members of the Surrealist movement. *The Palladist* was painted after Brauner had recovered from a serious illness in 1943, and it is a disturbing and unsettling image typical of his work. Created with the smooth glacial tones of classical sculpture, the two abstracted and distorted figures in the foreground represent Adam and Eve, while behind them writhe the snakes of Lucifer. Adam and Eve are posed statuelike within a simple frame, suggestive of a theater stage. The large eyes that dominate the heads of the two figures were a recurring feature in the artist's work. During the 1930s he painted a series of human figures with a distorted eye, and ironically in 1938 the artist himself lost an eye during a fight, which lent his work a strangely prophetic air. In his notebooks Brauner wrote that every image he produced was fundamentally linked to his personal fears and worries, a fact that gives his art a poignant immediacy and helps to unravel the source of his extraordinary works. **TP**

Composition, 1943 | Lee Krasner

1943 | oil on canvas | 30 ⅛ x 24 ¼ in / 76 x 61 cm | Smithsonian Institution, Washington, DC, USA

Before she met Jackson Pollock, Lee Krasner (1908–84) was a better-known artist than the man she would marry and who would later eclipse her. The Brooklyn-born artist collaborated with Pollock from the time they met in 1942. When she met Pollock she became less prolific as a painter but no less experimental, and she pushed the boundaries of Cubism toward Abstract Expressionism. Pollock's influence and interest in myth, ritual, and Jungian theory empowered her to break free of figuration. In turn, Krasner gave Pollock structure and an art history foundation for his feral "action" paintings. She would often incorporate bits of his old canvases in her paintings. More than a muse or wife; Krasner was his peer and, in many ways, his teacher. She painted this floral still life after she had been introduced to the work of Cubists, such as Picasso, Miró, and Matisse. The choppy, dense paint texture Krasner uses to create her bold shapes establishes a compelling tactile component to the heavily abstracted image. The flowers and vase are reduced to circles, trapezoids, triangles, and other geometric shapes delineated by thick, black outlines. Krasner's curling signature (signed with a double "s," which she later dropped) adds a contrasting set of curves to the otherwise ordered forms. Krasner's relationship with Pollock has dominated discussion of her work but, in her role as one of the few female members of the New York School, Krasner made a vital contribution to a movement that would alter painting profoundly. **AH**

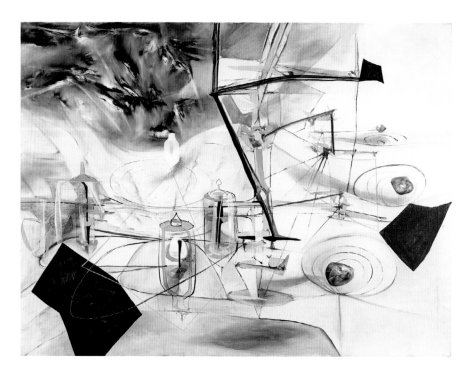

The Bachelors Twenty Years After
Matta

1943 | oil on canvas | 38 x 50 in / 96.5 x 127 cm | Philadelphia Museum of Art, Philadelphia, PA, USA

Chilean-born Surrealist Roberto Matta Echaurren, or simply "Matta" (1911–2002), once said: "Painting has one foot in architecture and one foot in the dream." No words could sum up this painting, and Matta's approach, any better. The picture was painted just six years after he abandoned architecture for painting, at a time when he had settled in New York and was causing a splash in the city's progressive art world. The title refers to a major work by the French avant-garde artist, Marcel Duchamp: *The Bride Stripped Bare by Her Bachelors, Even* (also called *Large Glass*, 1915–23). Like Duchamp's work, which challenged accepted notions of what art was, Matta's painting creates its own reality. With an architect's understanding of spatial construction, Matta builds up a different kind of perpetually shifting, slightly receding space. Planes of transparent color intersect with strange, mechanistic objects that echo those in Duchamp's masterwork. Painted delicately but with a draftsman's precision, these objects seem to be moving. The painting's powerful, dreamlike quality accords with Matta's visionary quest to reveal the "economic, cultural, and emotional forces" and constant transformations that he felt shaped the modern world. As *The Bachelors Twenty Years After* was being painted, artists such as Jackson Pollock and Robert Motherwell were gathering at Matta's studio. In discussions about new ways forward, Matta had a real influence on these leading Abstract Expressionists, and by extension on later developments of twentieth-century art. **AK**

Outcast Coal Production: Dragline Depositing Excavated Earth
Graham Sutherland

1943 | pen, chalk, and watercolor on paper | 27 ½ x 25 in / 69.5 x 66.5 cm | Leeds City Art Gallery, UK

The English artist Graham Sutherland (1903–80) worked as a railroad engineer in Derby before enrolling in 1921 at Goldsmith's College, London, where he studied engraving. In 1930 Sutherland had to withdraw from the print market, which was suffering drastically as a result of the Depression. He then started to produce paintings, mostly landscapes. He was fascinated by the strange forms he saw in the land that surrounded him, which lent a surreal quality to his work, and indeed he participated in the 1936 International Surrealist exhibition in London. During World War II, Sutherland served in the army as an official artist. He made drawings of bomb damage in London and South Wales and also produced depictions of tin mining in Cornwall and of the Liberation of France. After the war, Sutherland took a more traditional approach to nature, painting plants and animals, mostly birds. He spent a lot of time in Pembrokeshire, Wales, where in 1976 he opened a gallery for his work at Picton Castle. *Outcast Coal Production: Dragline Depositing Excavated Earth* was painted in 1943, while he was still a war artist. Here Sutherland uses a childlike style to depict huge pyramidlike mountains of earth excavated by draglines at a mine. The image presents an industrial landscape that has been made and worked by humans, but no humans can be seen—the mechanical engines appear to be their own masters. Sutherland thus succeeds in creating a disturbing and surreal atmosphere in the painting. **JJ**

The Leaf of the Artichoke Is an Owl | Arshile Gorky

1944 | oil on canvas | 28 x 35 ⅞ in / 71.1 x 91.2 cm | Museum of Modern Art, New York, NY, USA

Arshile Gorky (Vosdanik Manook Adoian, 1904–48) was born in Turkish-occupied Armenia. In 1910, fleeing conscription into the Turkish army, Gorky's father left his family for America. Gorky, his mother, and his younger sister, Vartoosh, suffered persecution, including an enforced 120-mile (193-kilometer) march over eight days; Gorky's mother died in his arms. In April 1920, Gorky and Vartoosh escaped to America. Gorky studied in Boston and in New York, where he later became a teacher. Vartoosh was one of Gorky's favorite models and she appears in works such as the poignant *Woman with Necklace*, in which the necklace is much less arresting than the sad look in the model's eyes. Another of Gorky's main influences was the memory of his mother—his portrait *The Artist*

and His Mother illustrates how much he was haunted by her death and his loss. As in this painting, Gorky often mixed together diverse natural elements as a means of suggesting a reconnection with nature. Many of his works reflect a longing to return to Armenia, especially to the garden of his childhood. In a letter to his sister toward the end of his life, Gorky wrote: "I dream of [the garden] always and it is as if some ancient Armenian spirit within me moves my hand to create so far from our homeland the shapes of nature we loved in the gardens, wheat fields, and orchards . . . in Khorkom." For the last few years of his life, Gorky worked on a series titled *The Plough and the Song*, both symbols he considered integral to Armenian culture and history. **LH**

1943–45 (St. Ives, Cornwall) | Ben Nicholson

1943–45 | oil and pencil on canvasboard | 16 x 19 ¾ in / 40.5 x 50 cm | Tate Collection, London, UK

Shortly before the outbreak of World War II, British artist Ben Nicholson (1894–1982) moved to the small Cornish fishing community of St. Ives, England. His Cubist-inspired still lifes and geometrical reliefs had brought him success and, by the late 1930s, he had secured his place as a leading figure in avant-garde European art. The decade had seen his work become increasingly abstract, but his move to the coast sparked another change in direction when he once again turned his attention to the British landscape. It was a more lucrative subject matter, particularly at a time of heightened wartime patriotism and isolation from the forward-looking world of European art. The clear Cornish light, the geometry of the flat-faced fishermen's cottages and the blocky colors of the sea and sand made up his working environment. In this painting, one of a series begun in 1939, a harbor scene of boats and rooftops is viewed through a still life arranged on a windowsill. The geometric shapes embody his fascination with the positioning of objects in space. The flattened forms also demonstrate an interest in naive and primitive art. Completed in 1945, the work includes a Union Jack in the foreground. Primarily a celebration of V-E Day, the flag hints at the new and optimistic era following the end of the war. Although influenced by Picasso, Mondrian, Rousseau, and other giants of European art, Nicholson found a personal, distinctly British take on Modernism. He was also personally committed to encouraging emerging artists of the period. **JB**

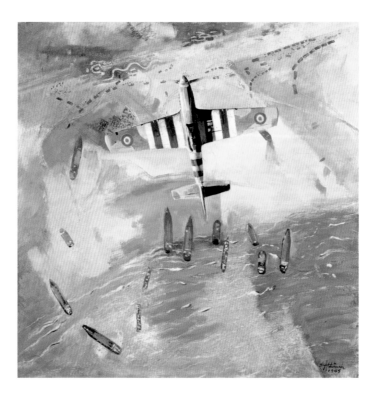

Invasion Pattern, Normandy | Eric Aldwinckle

1945 | oil on canvas | 33 ¾ x 33 ¾ in / 85.6 x 85.6 cm | Canadian War Museum, Ottawa, Canada

Born in England, Eric Aldwinckle (1909–80) relocated to Canada in 1922 and became a graphic designer in Toronto. From 1943 to 1945 he held the rank of flight lieutenant with the Royal Canadian Air Force with whom he served as an official war artist. *Invasion Pattern, Normandy* depicts from above a fighter aircraft of the Allied air forces (which can be identified by the pattern on its wings) flying over the coast of Normandy. The schematic, maplike quality of the painting, and its cool, mostly monochromatic hues, imbue the painting with stillness and calm. Aldwinckle dispassionately observes the scene as though it were simply an abstract arrangement of beige, green, and blue, and not a scene of war. As such, *Invasion Pattern* forces the viewer to adopt an emotionally detached perspective on a view of one of the most decisive battles of World War II. By doing this, Aldwinckle creates a tension between the subject matter and the way in which it is depicted: draining the scene of freneticism and of any of the conventional emotional reactions to war. It is as though he is saying that any attempt to convey the horror of the reality would fall short of its ambition. Instead, he offers us an even more powerful evocation of this horror: an absolute emotional detachment that is emphasized by the physical distance between the viewer's vantage point and the landing beach below. As a war artist, Aldwinckle had free rein to paint whatever he chose, and his cool contemplation of the coast of Normandy is an exercise in restraint and control. **SS**

A Calabrian Worker's Sunday in Rome | Renato Guttuso

1945 | oil on canvas | Pushkin Museum, Moscow, Russia

Born near Palermo, Sicily, Renato Guttuso (1912–87) discovered his artistic talent at a very young age. Not one to be pigeonholed into any one artistic movement, as an adult Guttuso was guided by his strong political beliefs and sense of social responsibility. His direct and arresting style of painting revealed a natural empathy for the common man striving to find a place for himself in the turbulent climate of a world first at, and then recovering from, war. In 1945, Guttuso founded *Fronte Nuovo delle Arti* (New Arts Front), a group of artists united by their commitment to exposing social injustice through unbridled artistic expression, a freedom that had been stifled during fascist rule under Mussolini. The viewer can readily relate to the subject's predicament

in *A Calabrian Worker's Sunday in Rome* (also known as *Rocco with the Gramophone*). Rocco is caught in a snapshot pose, with cigarette smoldering in his fingers, a record spinning, and, importantly, a face that resonates with wearied emotion. As Guttuso himself said, "Face is everything, in faces there is the history we are living, the anguish of our times." The man and his environment are in unison—the checkered rooftops echo the bold red-and-black check of the worker's lumber jacket. He may be trapped by circumstance, but the opened window suggests freedom, and the gramophone an optimistic symbol of personal choice. Guttuso is a fine example of an artist who challenged boundaries to create art that spoke directly to his public—a rebel artist with soul. **JC**

The Rocaille Armchair | Henri Matisse

1946 | oil on canvas | 36 ¼ x 28 ¾ in / 92 x 73 cm | Musée Matisse, Nice, France

After World War II ended, Henri Matisse (1869–1954) returned from Paris where he found himself fêted as a symbol of a free France. The septuagenarian settled in his southern villa for the winter and painted *The Rocaille Armchair*. Matisse uses the bright colors and simplified forms typical of his style to convert a piece of furniture into a vivid two-dimensional image. The rocaille, named for its characteristic forms that imitate the natural curved shapes of rocks and shells, was developed during the eighteenth century. Matisse exaggerates the chair's curvaceous armrests and paints them bright green—they morph into a great serpentine form, which wraps around the back of the chair. At the time, Matisse was also experimenting with collages, and we can almost imagine the artist breaking down the representation of his armchair into a few yellow and green shapes, cutting them out and pasting them onto a red piece of paper. This simplicity of depiction places no barrier of illusion between the viewer and the object: it is at once figurative and abstract. Matisse sees the armchair not as an object to be looked at and evaluated from a detached, clinical distance, but rather as something to be felt, experienced, and viewed creatively. In contrast to the bleak prospects of postwar Europe, the warmth and imaginativeness of Matisse's art spoke a message of hope for those who would listen. Matisse would be delighted to know that people imagine the arms of his rocaille chair as a slithering serpent sixty years after he finished painting it. **DK**

Painting | Francis Bacon

1946 | oil on linen | 78 x 52 in / 198 x 132 cm | Museum of Modern Art, New York, NY, USA

Although long considered a key artist of postwar Europe, Francis Bacon's (1909–92) painting has a timeless quality. His perfectly placed, powerful brushstrokes place him with the greatest artists of Expressionist oil painting from Vincent van Gogh to Wassily Kandinsky. Although Bacon committed his artistic work almost exclusively to painting (very few drawings survive), he has continued to both captivate and unsettle audiences for nearly half a century since he first unveiled his tortured figures in their positions of pain and anguish. The potent homoerotic and sexual impulses of his work juxtaposed against the sickly sweet colors of his raw canvases announced the British artist as a new, forward-thinking, if controversial, painter at a time when the medium was waning in

popularity. In Bacon's world, large-scale picture-making was a way of life. With his 1946 *Painting* —a significant early image and a prescient purchase by Alfred Barr for New York's Museum of Modern Art—Bacon offers a canvas rife with the subjects that would obsess him for the rest of his life: the disembodied head, the gaping mouth, the opened umbrella, the raw meat, the dangling cords, the pastel grounds, the cagelike framing devices. In short, packed into this picture is the very disorder of Bacon's famously chaotic studio at 7 Reece Mews in South Kensington. It is rumored that when Bacon viewed the painting in New York decades after he painted it, the color of the background had changed to a disagreeable pink. He demanded the right to repaint it, but the curators refused. **SP**

Holborn Circus, London, 1947, with Bomb Damage | Carel Weight

c.1947 | oil on canvas | 17 ³/₈ x 24 ³/₄ in / 44 x 63 cm | Brandler Galleries, Brentwood, UK

Carel Weight's (1908–97) canvases are distinctively unassuming—so much so that some may find it remarkable that he has been among the most influential figures in twentieth-century British painting. He began his career in the 1920s as a scene painter and ended it at the Royal Academy of Art in London, having exerted his influence on a generation of new British artists, among them David Hockney, Ron Kitaj, Allen Jones, and Peter Blake. Weight was appointed official war artist in 1945. Though the post took him around Europe, London remained his central preoccupation. This painting depicts central London in the wake of World War II. Weight paints a beautiful day, capturing the English light expertly—diffuse sunlight illuminates the street, and the morning sky is a muted but brilliant combination of pinks and yellows. The bird's-eye perspective, however, reveals the barriers that have been erected between the street's traffic and the hole in the cityscape left by the bombs that devastated the city. Weight reveals Londoners going about their lives, the destruction beside them veiled but not yet repaired. The viewer's position somewhere above the scene creates a sense of distance, both spatial and figurative. The pedestrians are isolated from the viewer, as they are from one another. Weight said of his students that his job was not to "teach them how to paint, but to teach them to paint how they want to paint." His own legacy is an unparalleled clarity of expression, an ability to capture a place and historic moment with brilliant specificity. **AR**

Pad No.4 | Stuart Davis

1947 | oil on canvas | 14 x 18 in / 35.5 x 45.7 cm | Brooklyn Museum of Art, Brooklyn, NY, USA

Stuart Davis's (1894–1964) work sprang from a background of historic upheaval and considerable artistic stimulation. His mother was a sculptor and, as art director at the *Philadelphia Press*, his father worked with prominent figures from a new artistic movement inspired by the realism of modern American life. Davis was one of the youngest artists to exhibit at the controversial Armory Show of 1913, which introduced Americans to modern art. As a new age of hope, jazz, and swing emerged from the ashes of two world wars, Davis sought to capture the spirit of this incredible sea change. As he does in the title of this work, he used words such as "pad" or "swing" as part of his witty take on the new urban life of twentieth-century America. This painting shows him well established in his abstract style, after more figurative earlier works. Strong, contrasting colors and clearly delineated shapes linger on from his artistic past, linked to his great interest in French Cubism and to the commercial art world in which he grew up. Davis is widely regarded as America's greatest Cubist, developing a uniquely American approach to this style. The dynamism of many of his paintings also reflects his love of jazz music, as one critic observed in 1957: "his art relates to jazz, to movie marquees, to the streamlined decor and brutal colors of gasoline stations, to the glare of neon lights … to the big bright words that are shouted at us from billboards." Or as the artist himself put it "I paint the American Scene." Davis is often heralded as a founder of Pop Art. **AK**

Baby Giant
Leonora Carrington

1947 | oil on canvas
Edward James Foundation, Sussex, UK

Betrothal I
Arshile Gorky

1947 | oil on paper | 51 x 40 in / 129.5 x 102 cm
Museum of Contemporary Art, Los Angeles, CA, USA

Although born in England, Leonora Carrington (*b*. 1917) is usually associated with her adopted home of Mexico. She became a pivotal figure in the Surrealist movement, famous for her writing as well as her paintings. In *Baby Giant*, the enormous baby holds an egg in one hand, symbolic of rebirth, spiritual awakening, and mystical powers. Its tiny head atop the huge body and the swirling mass of red-gold hair—so similar in color to the sunset (or sunrise)—are babylike and give the figure a sense of being lost in the middle of a hostile world. The giant birds circling around the infant and swirling out from under her cloak do not seem threatening—instead they seem to be protecting her. Despite the suggestion of insecurity, the baby giant is dominating the landscape, partially blotting out even the powerful sun and looming huge over nature, in the form of tiny trees at her feet. **LH**

Arshile Gorky (1904–48) was influenced by the Surrealism of Miró and abstraction of Kandinsky, but developed his own style in the 1940s, later known as Abstract Expressionism. His techniques included layering paint onto the canvas, then shaving off the excess with a razor blade, leaving an unusually smooth finish. He had a strong regard for drawing, believing that it was the essence of painting. *Betrothal I* was painted at the height of his Abstract Expressionism. The poetic personal vocabulary and sensuous use of color infuse the loosely contoured shapes, which flow into one another in a style that has been described as "lyrical abstraction." These "loose" forms have been said to express his emotional disintegration at the time, when a series of tragedies—his studio burning down, a cancer diagnosis, a car crash, and his wife leaving him—led to him hanging himself the following year. **LH**

Girl with Roses
Lucian Freud

1947–48 | oil on canvas | 42 x 30 in / 106 x 76 cm
British Council Collection, London, UK

Child with a Watermelon
Antoni Clavé

1947–48 | oil on canvas | 21⅝ x 18 in /
54.9 x 45.7 cm | Tate Collection, London, UK

With his signature clots of oil paint and muddy palette, Lucian Freud (b.1922) poignantly portrays the universal battles between external reality and interior urges that his grandfather, Sigmund Freud, deconstructed in his psychoanalytical writings. Freud rose to fame in the 1950s alongside fellow British artists Francis Bacon and Frank Auerbach. He has painted friends, family, and lovers, often undressed and always psychologically naked. Recognized as the masterwork of his early career, Girl with Roses is a portrait of Freud's first wife, Kitty, painted early on in their brief marriage. Freud shows Kitty nervously toying with the thorny stem of a yellow-and-red rose, a hybrid developed shortly after World War II as the "Peace Rose." In Freud's meticulously detailed, flat, and precisely structured composition, each strand of Kitty's hair is carefully delineated and yet her character remains compellingly elusive. **AH**

Barcelona-born Antoni Clavé (1913–2005) fought with the left-wing Republicans in the Spanish Civil War of 1936–39. After their defeat, he fled to France. In 1944 he met Picasso, and Child with a Watermelon suggests that Clavé was strongly influenced by his compatriot. The child here emulates that of Picasso's depiction of his son Paulo as a harlequin in 1924. Harlequins featured in many of Picasso's early works, and the harlequin is a character of the commedia dell'arte, which had been part of Barcelona street theater and carnivals. This is a fitting subject for Clavé, whose oeuvre included stage sets, theatrical costume design, and poster design. Yet Clavé's harlequin is a melancholy figure; the colors of his diamond-patterned costume are dark. He looks like a hungry and grateful beggar, ready to eat the fruit in his hands with its rich red flesh, reflecting the blood spilled in the Spanish Civil War. **LH**

The Abandoned Mine | Sidney Nolan

1947–48 | ripolin enamel on hardboard | 14 ⅛ x 18 ⅞ in / 36 x 48 cm | Private collection

Few artists have portrayed the soul of their homeland with greater skill and devotion than Sir Sidney Nolan (1917–92). His paintings captured the harsh beauty of Australia's landscape as well as the resilient pioneering spirit of its people. In the early 1940s, Nolan belonged to a circle of artists and writers linked with *Angry Penguins*, an avant-garde journal that aimed to promote an Australian art free from European and American influences. Nolan made real progress in this direction after his extensive travels around the country, especially from his journey into the outback in 1948. On this journey he traversed New South Wales and crossed through the "dead heart" of the land to Borroloola and Darwin in the Northern Territory, and explored the coastline of Western Australia. Some of the resulting pictures focused on the vast emptiness of the country, some on the flora and fauna of the desert, and others on the settlers' determination to survive in this tough environment. *The Abandoned Mine* belongs in the latter category and is one of a series of paintings depicting bleak, desert townships, isolated hotels, derelict farm machinery, and forlorn prospectors with their mines. The work proved to be one of the artist's most important paintings. Sir Kenneth Clark, a former director of the National Gallery in London, noticed the painting at an exhibition in Sydney and arranged to meet the artist. Clark was "confident that [he] had stumbled on a genius," and his support helped to establish Nolan's reputation on the international stage. **IZ**

The Reform and the Fall of the Empire | José Clemente Orozco

1948 | fresco (detail) | Museo Nacional de Historia, Castle of Chapultepéc, Mexico City, Mexico

Mexican José Clemente Orozco (1883–1949) was born in Zapotlán el Grande (now Ciudad Guzmán). He studied at Mexico City's San Carlos Academy, and became part of the Mexican mural movement along with other Mexican artists such as Diego Rivera (1886–1957) and David Alfaro Siqueiros (1898–1974). His work is particularly noted for its emotional portrayal of the human condition, and of the suffering of Mexico's Indian population. One of his last works, *The Reform and the Fall of the Empire* (also known as *Juárez Reborn* or *Chapultepéc Reborn*) is a large fresco of Benito Juárez (1806–72), who was Mexican president from 1861 to 1863 and again from 1867 to 1872. Juárez was a Zapotec Indian who became a leading lawyer and liberal politician, and he was held

in high esteem as a defender of human liberty. Here, Juárez's portrait is shown center; to his right are bare-chested figures carrying weapons and torches representing the liberals. Beneath lies the shrouded corpse of the Austrian archduke and former Emperor of Mexico, Maximilian of Hapsburg, who had at one time resided in the Castle of Chapultepéc. His crown has fallen and he is borne by figures representing the beaten conservative aristocracy and clergy. Maximilian was defeated by forces loyal to Juárez at Querétaro in 1867 and was executed shortly after by firing squad. Orozco's red palette reflects the bloody violence of Mexico's struggle against colonization by Napoleon III, who had made Maximilian emperor, as well as paying tribute to Juárez's triumph. **CK**

Christina's World | Andrew Wyeth

1948 | tempera on panel | 32 x 48 in / 82 x 121 cm | Museum of Modern Art, New York, NY, USA

Just as life appeared to be in Cushing, Maine, where most of Andrew Wyeth's (*b.*1917) paintings were set, his style remained steady for more than fifty years. The son of Newell Convers Wyeth, a famous American illustrator and artist, Andrew Wyeth was the youngest of five children who were all home-schooled and taught art by their father. The house in the far distance of *Christina's World* was the location of Wyeth's studio for almost three decades. The austerity of its stark rooms and somber exterior were captured in many of his paintings and lithographs. As Wyeth explained, "I happen to paint things that reflect the basic truths of life: sky, earth, friends." In Wyeth's painting, Christina Olson, a reclusive young friend of Wyeth and his wife, who had been crippled in childhood with polio, feebly raises herself on skeletal arms and gazes at her home in the distance. Her disability is not obvious from the painting, but her body's subtle contortions create a disquieting impression. Initially, the painting may seem to represent a pastoral ideal, but it harbors a pervasive undercurrent of loneliness, longing, and unease. Art historian Sir David Piper said of the painting, "It seems to express both the tragedy and the joy of life with such vivid poignancy that the painting becomes a universal symbol of the human condition." When Olson died in 1969, she had lived her life in the house Wyeth painted in the distance. Neighbors say she never knew Wyeth's image of her had become one of the most well-known and haunting paintings in American art history. **AH**

The Painter's Studio | Raoul Dufy

1949 | oil on canvas | 18 x 21⅝ in / 46 x 55 cm | Musée National d'Art Moderne, Paris, France

In 1905 Raoul Dufy (1877–1953) saw the painting *Luxe, Calme et Volupté* by Henri Matisse at the Salon des Indépendants, and it had a profound effect on the young artist. The brilliantly colored, intense, and emotive work encouraged Dufy toward the style of the Fauves, whose work directly affected him until around 1909, at which time he came under the spell of Cézanne. At this point his approach became softer and more subtle, though he never lost his love of pure color and the technique of short, quick brushstrokes. From around 1920 the artist developed his own unique approach to painting, characterized by bright color, broad washes, and a patterned surface. Dufy's work is universally positive and upbeat, making him one of the most refreshingly untormented artists of

the twentieth century. His studio was a subject that Dufy depicted several times, a habit popular with his contemporaries. Here he shows a view through a window (again characteristic of his interior scenes) and another view through an open door. The view through his window appears to impinge on his studio as the red-roofed house is seen in front of the window frame. This shows the artist manipulating the rules of composition and perspective in a manner that recalls of his Cubist forays, and creating a diverting take on illusion. The bright colors and decorative nature of his linear drawing again contribute to the encompassing aesthetic appeal of his work. Dufy was also an important illustrator, fabric designer, and decorator. **TP**

Study from the Human Body
Francis Bacon

1949 | oil on canvas | 57 ⁷⁄₈ x 52 ⁷⁄₈ in / 147 x 134 cm
National Gallery of Victoria, Melbourne, Australia

Abstract Composition
Nicolas de Staël

1949 | oil on canvas | 64 x 44 ⁷⁄₈ in / 162.5 x 114 cm
Musée National d'Art Moderne, Paris, France

Francis Bacon's (1909–92) raw, unnerving, and arousing images prod his viewers' emotions, forcing them to question how their ideas about life, desire, and death correspond with his. Bacon's life comprised a series of abusive and abused lovers, drug and drinking binges, and professional successes. *Study from the Human Body* exemplifies the aesthetic and psychological concerns that dominate his entire body of work. His paint is as slippery as a secretion and soaks into his canvases like a stain. His composition blends the key figure into his environment and his rendering of the form establishes a foreboding sense of psychological or even physical sadism. Barred from the viewer by a curtain created from the same tones as his flesh, the figure appears decorative and objectified as the object of Bacon's erotic interest. Contemporary English artists such as Damien Hirst cite Bacon as a primary influence. **AH**

Nicolas de Staël (1914–55) began painting still lifes and portraits, but between 1942 and 1952 he adopted a primarily non-figurative style. *Abstract Composition*, a canvas from the latter half of de Staël's abstract period, consists of a series of flat areas of discrete color, applied using a palette knife. The complementary range of gray-browns, browns, and yellow ochres forms a credible, unified whole through the juxtaposition of these colors and the repertoire of angular shapes within which they are contained. The generic title is one the artist employed at this stage of his career to imply the composed nature of the canvases. Although *Abstract Composition* bears the hallmarks of certain precedents within the context of "modern" painting, including Cubism, de Staël managed to actualize a language for painting that, in effect, was nevertheless singular in its contribution to postwar European abstraction. **CS**

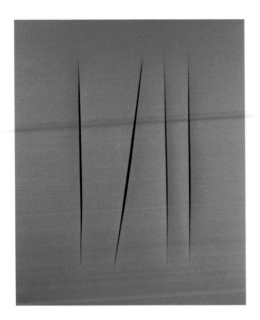

Spatial Concept
Lucio Fontana

c.1949 | oil on canvas
Fondazione Lucio Fontana, Milan, Italy

Perspective II: Manet's Balcony
René Magritte

1950 | oil on canvas | 31 ½ x 23 ½ in / 80 x 60 cm
Museum voor Schone Kunsten, Ghent, Belgium

Having experimented with Abstraction and Futurism in the 1930s, Argentine-born Lucio Fontana (1899–1968) published his *White Manifesto* in 1946, setting out the details of Spatialism, the theoretical basis upon which his so-called *buchi* were created. He began this series of works at the end of the 1940s; they included slashed canvases, punctured metal sheets, and other altered materials that stretched the boundaries between painting and sculpture. *Spatial Concept* signifies the artist's desire to create a "tetradimensional art" that superseded all known artistic and sculptural forms. He once explained how the three dimensions of color, sound, and motion were to be united in the fourth dimension—space—in order for modern art to be truly dynamic. Expressed in the slashes and disruptions of the painted surface, these four dimensions resulted in a free art that broke with the constraints of the past. **HH**

The work of the Italian metaphysical painter Giorgio de Chirico was a major influence on René Magritte (1898–1967). Depressed by the failure of the exhibition of his first Surrealist paintings in 1927 in Brussels, Magritte settled in Paris where he met André Breton and began his involvement with Surrealism. In *Perspective II: Manet's Balcony* the artist has painted a strange replica of Édouard Manet's *Balcony* (1868–69), itself inspired from *Maja and Celestina on a Balcony* by Goya. Here Magritte has created an unusual and striking mode of representation whereby each of the four figures in Manet's painting are replaced by a wooden coffin. The positions of the coffins perfectly mimic those of the original figures, to the extent that one coffin is "posed" as if bent-kneed and seated on a chair. By anthropomorphizing objects usually associated with death, Magritte offers a disturbing *memento mori*. **JJ**

Volcán Iztaccíhuatl | Dr. Atl

1930–50 | resin-based pigment on canvas | 29 ⅛ x 46 ⅛ in / 74 x 117 cm | Private collection

Mexico, a land of the fantastical and supernatural, owes its rich folklore in part to a remarkable landscape. The epic landscape painter Dr. Atl (Gerardo Murillo, 1875–1964) uniquely captured the dramatic beauty of his native country with its changing lights, hues, and contours. Atl created special resin-based pigments for his landscapes, known as "Atl-colors," and painted several panoramic views of immense size. He was a keen vulcanologist and *Volcán Iztaccíhuatl* conveys the deep power exerted by a mystical land on its native sons and daughters. Southeast of Mexico City and the ancient Aztec capital of Tenochtitlán stands the sacred mountain of Iztaccíhuatl (Sleeping Lady). Numerous ruins discovered there confirm that it was an important religious center for the Aztecs and earlier pre-Columbian communities. A pre-conquest legend relates that the great warrior Popocatépetl loved Iztaccíhuatl, daughter of a tribal king, but could only marry her after returning victorious from battle. A rival suitor spread rumors of his death and the maiden died of grief. When Popocatépetl returned, he laid her body atop a mountain range that then assumed the shape of a sleeping woman. (Nearby there is another volcano named after Popocatépetl.) Murillo was given the Aztec name Atl (meaning "water" in the Nahuatl language) and signed his work as Dr. Atl. His interests and unique sense of identity inspired fellow Mexicans Orozco and Rivera to find their own artistic sensibilities in a country of vast cultural and geographical complexity. **AA**

Child with Birds | Karel Appel

1950 | oil on canvas | 16 x 16 in / 40.5 x 40.5 cm | Museum of Modern Art, New York, NY, USA

Christiaan Karel Appel (1921–2006) is considered one of the most significant Dutch artists of the modern era and contributed a new voice of Abstract and Expressionist tone. During his long career—he was also a sculptor and a poet—Appel's style went through several distinct phases in terms of inspiration and technique, although his work remained immediately recognizable through his characteristic use of bold color, line, and form. *Child with Birds* was painted around the time the artist moved to Amsterdam and reflects his interest in children's art. In 1948, he had formed the avant-garde art movement CoBrA, whose members included Corneille (b.1922), Asger Jorn (1914–73), and Constant Nieuwenhuys (1920–2005); they shared an interest in Marxism as well as Modernism. CoBrA advocated the use of primitive forms and symbols and the abstract imagery found in children's art. The style drew heavy criticism in the Netherlands—a mural by Appel, *Inquisitive Children*, painted in the former Amsterdam City Hall in 1949, was covered up for ten years because it provoked such public outrage. The brilliantly colored *Child with Birds* is primitive in concept and abstract in form, but the figures remain identifiable once the pattern of their color has been digested. Appel was greatly taken with the work of Vincent van Gogh (1853–90), especially in his Expressionistic use of color, and the bold use of line seen in Joan Miró's (1893–1983) paintings. Both these influences are evident in *Child with Birds*. **TP**

Biblical Landscape | Reuven Rubin

*c.*1950 | oil on canvas | 23 ½ x 32 in / 60 x 81 cm | Private collection

Reuven Rubin (1893–1974) was the most prominent artist in Eretz Israel's pioneering school of Modernism. He rejected the Western orientation of Jerusalem's Bezalel Academy, embracing the work of local artists who preferred "oriental" motifs and allegorical depictions of local life. Rubin was born in Romania and trained in Paris, where he was drawn to the faux-primitive work of Henri Rousseau (1844–1910). He frequently painted biblical scenes in Fauvist and Expressionist styles, setting them in contemporary Palestinian landscapes. He had his first one-man show, with the help of the photographer Alfred Stieglitz (1864–1946), at the Anderson Gallery in New York in 1920. Rubin contributed to the first official art exhibitions in Israel, and his solo exhibit of 1924 was the first documented one-man show in Jerusalem. He also served as Israel's first ambassador to Romania—from 1948 to 1950—and a show of his work launched the Tel Aviv Museum of Art. Despite his European influences, Rubin's sensitivity to natural light, color, and architecture helped create definitive images for the developing Israeli culture—which strove to distinguish itself from Jewish culture in the Diaspora—and today he is still referred to as the patriarch of Israel's painters. *Biblical Landscape* exemplifies Rubin's romantic vision and love of the Israeli landscape. In this image, a couple embrace under the soft canopy of leaves. The painting's breezy textures and delicate lighting, borrowed from Fauvism, lend it a dreamy, fantastical quality. **AH**

Chief | Franz Kline

1950 | oil on canvas | 58 x 73 in / 148 x 186 cm | Museum of Modern Art, New York, NY, USA

In 1948, William de Kooning (1904–97) introduced Franz Kline (1910–62) to a Bell Opticon projector and encouraged him to look at enlarged images of some of his drawings. Kline first chose a small drawing of his favorite chair, and was astonished at the abstract form the chair's image made when projected onto a canvas and blown up so that the edges of the chair overlapped the picture frame. It was a decisive moment in the artist's life and completely changed the way he perceived his art. Having started his artistic career relatively late, and along conservative lines, he now worked in an almost entirely abstract manner. *Chief* was one of a series of large works in black and white that Kline made shortly after his move from figuration toward abstraction. It is a work of intense, controlled brushstrokes; the application of paint is swift, bold, and as integral to the piece as the composition itself. There is an essentially masculine quality to this painting, as there is in the rest of his images of this ilk: the heavy black linear forms are almost threatening. In 1950, the year that *Chief* was painted, Kline staged his first one-man show at the Egan Gallery, New York—a popular venue for emerging Abstract Expressionist artists. The show was comprised entirely of paintings in his new style, and was an enormous success. After years of financial hardship, the artist finally began to achieve recognition, and a second show in 1951 confirmed Kline as a leading Abstract Expressionist painter. **TP**

Aline and Valcour | Man Ray

1950 | oil on canvas | 30 x 38 in / 76.5 x 96.5 cm | Private collection

Dadaist and Surrealist Man Ray (Emmanuel Radnitzky, 1890–1976) was raised in Brooklyn, New York, although he lived in Paris for twenty years. *Aline and Valcour* was executed during a brief period living in Los Angeles, California. The painting refers to a novel of the same name by the Marquis Sade (1740–1814), a French aristocrat who was imprisoned for his sexual exploits and wrote several novels. The torture of the weak and innocent by cruel tormentors was a common theme in de Sade's often sexually explicit works, hence the use of his name in the word "sadism." The Surrealists saw the Marquis as a free spirit—indeed, Guillaume Apollinaire (1880–1918) deemed him "the freest spirit that has yet existed"—whose work outlined psychological ideas long before Sigmund Freud. In Sade's novel, Aline and Valcour are young lovers, but Aline's father cruelly tries to stop her marrying Valcour. In Man Ray's painting, Aline's blindfolded head is enclosed by a bell jar on a chest of drawers. The blindfold suggests that the head has been severed by a guillotine. Aline's father is represented as a faceless artist's mannequin lying as though relaxing after a recent sexual encounter, his arms enfolding a sphere and a cone, and his head clearly averted from his daughter. His psychological and physical subjugation of Aline is complete, but a question is raised: who is manipulating his puppetlike figure? Sade was preoccupied with the source of cruelty, and Man Ray provides an eloquent visual commentary on the inhumanity of men. **MC**

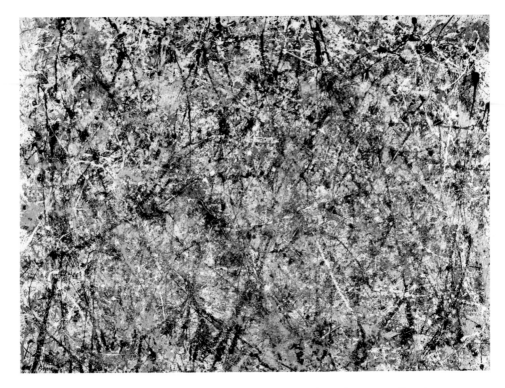

Number 1, 1950 (Lavender Mist) | Jackson Pollock

1950 | oil, enamel, and aluminum on canvas | 87 x 118 in | National Gallery of Art, Washington, DC, USA

The subject of numerous books, documentaries, and a Hollywood movie, celebrated American artist Jackson Pollock (1912–56) is a twentieth-century cultural icon. After studying at the Art Students' League in 1929 under Regionalist painter Thomas Hart Benton, he became influenced by the work of the Mexican Social Realist muralists. He studied at David Alfaro Siqueiros's experimental workshop in New York, where he began painting with enamel. He later used commercial enamel house paint in his work, claiming it allowed him greater fluidity. By the late 1940s Pollock had developed the "drip and splash" method, which some critics claim was influenced by the automatism of the Surrealists. Abandoning a paintbrush and easel, Pollock worked on a canvas laid out on the floor, using sticks, knives, and other implements to fling, dribble, or manipulate the paint from every aspect of the canvas, while building up layer-upon-layer of color. Sometimes he introduced other materials, such as sand and glass, to create different textures. *Number 1, 1950* helped cement Pollock's reputation as a groundbreaking artist. It is a mixture of long black-and-white strokes and arcs, short, sharp drips, spattered lines, and thick blotches of enamel paint and it manages to combine physical action with a soft and airy feel. Pollock's friend, art critic Clement Greenberg, suggested the title *Lavender Mist* to reflect the painting's atmospheric tone, even though no lavender was used in the work: it is composed primarily of white, blue, yellow, gray, umber, rosy pink, and black paint. **AV**

Umbral | Wifredo Lam

1950 | oil on canvas | 72 x 66 in / 185 x 170 cm | Musée National d'Art Moderne, Paris, France

While the majority of artists in Cuba tended to use their work to explore their national identity, Wifredo Lam (1902–82) traveled to Europe, becoming a member of the artistic vanguard, and his primitive Surrealist style was directed through a Western, rather than Cuban perspective. Lam certainly made use of aspects of his own culture and mixed nationality within his work, but his work was not defined by them. The Surrealist qualities of Lam's art display themselves in his use of primitive iconography in works such as *Umbral*. The three dominant objects suspended within this dark canvas appear like horned masks displayed on a wall. Simply constructed of a series of flat shapes and lines, these objects are almost unrecognizable as figures, either human or animal. In a magical way their pose and outstretched limbs give them life. The central positioning of the figures creates space and volume within the canvas, giving the overall composition order and stability. Although each shape at first appears static, the repetition of the main figure creates a distinct sense of motion and energy. The yellow rhombuses between the figures reinforce this as the single dot on the left-hand side becomes two on the right. This implies some kind of evolution or transition—a movement over a threshold. The fourth figure lies prostrate at the foot of the dominant three, almost punctured by their daggerlike bases. This points perhaps, to the significance of multiple thresholds separating the living world from death and the world of the unconscious mind from reality. **HH**

The Empire of Light, II | René Magritte

1950 | oil on canvas | 31 ¼ x 39 ¼ in / 80 x 100 cm | Museum of Modern Art, New York, NY, USA

René Magritte's (1898–1967) Parisian gallery, Le Centaure, closed its doors in 1930. The gallery's stock consisted of approximately two hundred then-recent paintings by the Belgian painter, which were purchased by his friend E.L.T. Mesens, a fellow Belgian artist and the director of his future London gallery. Through him, Magritte's reputation grew considerably in the UK during the late 1930s, at which time he continued to exhibit along with the Surrealist group. Magritte gained international recognition after 1948, when he signed a contract with Alexandre Iolas, a New York art dealer who remained his agent until Magritte's death from cancer in 1967. Regarded as one of the major Surrealists, Magritte's reputation continued to grow in the 1960s. His influence on later art movements, in particular on Pop and conceptual art, is nowadays largely acknowledged. Although many Surrealists experimented with the "automatism" technique—a practice that led to the creation of totally abstract paintings—Magritte always remained attached to a representational style. This approach, which he used in The Empire of Light, II, permitted him to create a more reinforced Surrealist image. The lower part of this picture is a street scene at night, in which there are no people to be seen. Creating a strong psychological contrast, the upper part of the image does not depict a moon or stars in a dark sky but a bright blue afternoon sky full of small, fluffy white clouds. There are more than twenty versions of this painting, the first dating from 1949. **AH**

Harbour Window with Two Figures, St. Ives: July 1950 | Patrick Heron

1950 | oil on board | 48 x 60 in / 122 x 152 cm | Tate Collection, London, UK

There have been a few artists in history who have also been active art critics. Producing art may give a critic a more empathetic and intimate understanding of the art that he or she views. However, evaluating other artists' work can also be a problem for someone who is primarily an artist. British artist Patrick Heron (1920–99) wrote about art for the *New English Weekly*, New York's *Nation and Arts*, and the British political magazine, the *New Statesman*, from 1945 to 1958. In these publications, he questioned the necessity for reducing form to pure abstraction. Instead, during this part of his career, he was trying to synthesize his admiration for painters like Matisse and Braque. Heron's intellectual relationship with art can be seen in this work. Stiffer and less harmonious than his later abstract work, this Cubist painting of a nude model standing by a window nevertheless shows Heron's sensitive understanding of form and graceful handling of difficult color combinations. The key relationship in this composition is between orange or yellow and royal blue, yet Heron tempers this potentially overwhelming contrast with great reserve. The effect successfully recalls Matisse. Heron's early canvases are perhaps too overtly intellectual. In these, one can observe him struggling with abstraction and trying to put his love of Cubism to use. But once he broke from this style and delved fully into abstraction, he was able to balance his appreciation for art with his own ability to produce some of England's most beautiful and direct paintings. **AH**

One: Number 31 | Jackson Pollock

1950 | oil and enamel on canvas | 106 x 209 in / 269 x 530 cm | Museum of Modern Art, New York, NY, USA

By 1950, Jackson Pollock (1912–56) was seen as the figure who perhaps best epitomized the ethos of Abstract Expressionism. While the ascension of Pollock's reputation as an artist of national, if not international, significance was due to a number of factors, it was perhaps the series of photographs Hans Namuth, a German émigré and photography student, took of the artist at work in his studio in East Hampton that elevated his profile to an almost mythological level. The euphoric *Autumn Rhythm* then came at the zenith of Pollock's artistic production when he also produced at least two other canvases of equal stature. Both *One: Number 31* and *Number 1, 1950 (Lavender Mist)* were created using a specific technique that entailed Pollock dribbling lines of enamel house paint onto a length of unstretched and unprimed canvas that he had placed on the studio floor. By approaching the canvas in this way, Pollock was able to be almost "in" the painting itself. Although *One: Number 31* is not the only painting whereby Pollock chose to encourage association with the natural world, any overt reference seems to be at best a pretext when the viewer is confronted with what is a profoundly complex arrangement of line. Here, line is used not to describe form, but rather is form. What Pollock presents is a compelling narrative of separate energies transposed through the act of markmaking, an event or the remnants thereof that articulates in a highly sophisticated and nuanced way the fact that a painting has its own nature. **CS**

Vir Heroicus Sublimis | Barnett Newman

1950–51 | oil on canvas | 95 ⅜ x 213 ¼ in / 242 x 542 cm | Museum of Modern Art, New York, NY, USA

What sets Barnett Newman's (1905–70) oeuvre apart from his Abstract Expressionist peers is the artist's cerebral, measured, and highly calibrated approach to the realization of his vision. The register of Newman's canvases generally entails a single field of color, whose continuity is punctuated only by a subtle series of thin vertical lines, or "zips" as the artist called them. *Vir Heroicus Sublimis*, (the title translates as "Man, Heroic and Sublime"), is a vast canvas that incorporates, at various points across its length, five such "zips." What becomes apparent at a very early point upon viewing this vast unmodulated expanse of cadmium red (its height alone reaches eight feet), is the way it literally fills one's field of vision. Due to the immense scale of the piece, the "zips" play a crucial role in terms of how

one orientates oneself in front of the piece, functioning as visual and physical anchors. When the painting was first exhibited in 1951 at the Betty Parsons Gallery in New York, the artist posted a statement on a wall near the painting which read: "There is a tendency to look at large pictures from a distance. The large pictures in this exhibition are intended to be seen from a short distance." This statement seems to be entirely in accordance with the artist's interest in the "sublime": while we might be able to grasp the idea of the whole, the fragmented nature of lived experience is such that it works against such an idea. *Vir Heroicus Sublimis* becomes analogous to François de La Rochefoucauld's maxim that neither death nor the sun can be looked at directly. **CS**

Atelier VI | Georges Braque

1950–51 | oil on canvas | 51 x 64 in / 130 x 162.5 cm | Fondation Maeght, Saint-Paul de Vence, France

Georges Braque (1882–1963) was born in Argenteuil near Paris to a family of painters and decorators, a profession that would have a significant effect on his painterly techniques in later life. In 1900 he moved to Paris and began his formal artistic training by enrolling in the École des Beaux-Arts before joining the Académie Humbert in 1902. In these early years in Paris he became friends with Raoul Dufy (1877–1953) and Othon Friesz (c.1879–1949), and later came under the influence of the Fauvist movement. By 1907 Braque had met Picasso (1881–1973), and seen the Spanish artist's Les Demoiselles d'Avignon, which would have a significant effect on his style. The two artists began working in a similar style of muted tones and complex spatially organized compositions, and were

given the label Cubists. Toward the end of his career, and seen in the series of Atelier or Studio paintings of which this is one, Braque's style again developed, becoming more personal, decorative, and richly colored. The Studio series consists of nine canvases that incorporate the bird symbol, which appeared in the artist's later work, and often depict a picture within a picture. Here the bird is an inspiring element that is perched on top of an easel and surveys the surrounding pattern of studio equipment with a slightly humorous air. The spatially complex interior achieves an aesthetic harmony that is visually compelling and deeply reflective, and though the artist denied a symbolic content in his art, it is difficult not to view it as having one. **TP**

Portrait Group | Rodrigo Moynihan

1951 | oil on canvas | 84 x 132 in / 213.4 x 334.6 cm | Tate Collection, London, UK

Rodrigo Moynihan's (1910–90) remarkably diverse artistic output includes abstract paintings, portraits, still lifes, landscapes, and figures in oils, gouache, watercolors, pen, and wash. Unlike the tide of Realist painters who gradually morphed into abstract artists, Moynihan was producing experimental works in the 1930s. These paintings, which focused on tone and color, were heavily influenced by Monet, Cézanne, and Turner. Moynihan began making realistic, tonal, and figurative images during the late 1950s, and during the 1970s he focused on portraits and still lifes painted in an anachronistically academic style with muted palette and a sense of pictorial economy. Toward the end of his life, he was simultaneously creating abstract canvases and landscapes influenced by Chinese calligraphic tradition. *Portrait Group* exemplifies the sobriety and physiological sensitivity of Moynihan's Realist period. The painting is alternately titled *The Teaching Staff of the Painting School at the Royal College of Art, 1949–50*, and represents, from left to right: John Minton, Colin Hayes, Carel Weight, Rodney Burn, Robert Buhler, Charles Mahoney, Kenneth Rowntree, Ruskin Spear, and Rodrigo Moynihan himself. The narrative relationships between the figures and their position in the space would be compelling without any knowledge of Moynihan's sitters or their own work, but the fact that this is a painting of painters adds the intriguing question of whether his sitters harbored competitive feelings when they saw the fine result produced by Moynihan's flexible talent. **AH**

Composition with Figures | Corneille

1951 | oil on canvas | Private collection

Cornelis van Beverloo (*b*.1922), better known as Corneille, was an influential figure in the development of Modern art in Scandinavia. After training at the Academy of Art in Amsterdam he went on to form the Nederlandse Experimentele Groep (NEG) in 1948. At around the same time he became involved with the avant-garde movement CoBrA, an abstract Surrealist and Expressionist group that published poetry and painted using vibrant colors and distorted figures based on inspiration from primitive and folk art. *Composition with Figures* shows the influence of Paul Klee and Miró in the bold use of bright color and strident, simple forms that take on a symbollike mantle. It was painted on his return from a trip to North Africa, after Corneille had settled in Paris. He had begun to collect African artifacts and drew on these and his travel experiences for inspiration. In this work the central face echoes the form of African masks while the black lines and dots to the left are reminiscent of tribal paintings. The brilliant colors, contrasted against the dense black traversing the middle of the canvas, evoke the richness of the exotic foreign land. Conversely though the inspiration is primitive and even ancient in tone, the painting itself is an expression of Futurism and abstraction, so that the art of old and new is combined. Corneille's work draws on strong symbolic imagery and is often lyrical in conception. He favors intense colors—as seen in this painting—combined with primitive forms that make his work a vibrant expression of Modern art. **TP**

Two Women on a Veranda | Emiliano di Cavalcanti

1951 | oil on canvas | 45 ¼ x 57 ⅞ in / 115 x 147 cm | Private collection

In *Two Women on a Veranda*, Emiliano di Cavalcanti (1897–1967) created one of the most sensitive and psychologically intimate portraits in Brazilian modern art. Born in 1897 and raised by wet nurses in the old district of São Cristóvão in Rio de Janeiro, Di Cavalcanti worked in an art movement preoccupied by the themes of social awareness and individualistic power which, by the mid-twentieth century, was shifting its focus rapidly to geometric abstraction. His idealistic personality, fraught with contradictions, gave him the ability to paint both abiding sadness and the bright and festive spirit of Brazil. *Two Women on a Veranda* has the vigorous color and bold expression typical of a country known for carnival. The luminous, sensual women in the hot atmosphere—one woman distant, the other confrontational—suggest the inhabitants of a brothel, a common theme of Di Cavalcanti. Yet the pensive faces and defensive stances of the two women, coupled with the moody sky above, locate the painting within the complex social reality of Brazil. The tension between the red blanket on the right, representing passion and sexual power, and the poignant counterpoint of the small white girl facing a far statue, summoning up innocence, privilege, and social power, emphasizes the inability of the two women to truly know and govern themselves. A self-taught artist, Di Cavalcanti was a great individualist and a social progressive, as well as a master of conveying joy combined with the deepest sobriety and conflicted internal depths. **AH/SWW**

The Golden Mannequin Shop | Jean Hélion

1951 | oil on canvas | 31 ⅞ x 39 ⅜ in / 81 x 100 cm | Galerie Daniel Malingue, Paris, France

As an artist, Jean Hélion (1904–87) underwent several changes of direction, leaping from representational art to abstraction, which he helped to popularize in the United States in the 1930s. After World War II (in which he fought in his native France, was captured, and escaped) he returned to live in Paris. Thereafter his art took a completely different turn, returning to a form of representational art, yet with a surreal aspect. All objects in his paintings from the 1940s and 50s are recognizable, but mix the everyday and the normal in odd ways. Outside a plain, slightly shabby shop, an abandoned umbrella, a crack in the pavement, and dirt piling up by the doorstep point the way to an invitingly open door, leading to a mysterious gloom. We cannot see what the shop sells, but, judging from the window display, it is clearly a place where magical things happen. The title gives it away—the golden mannequin shop, a romantic, fairy tale title. On the traditional headless shop dummy to the left, the jacket hangs loose and boxy, whereas the jacket on the right shows how it looks, filled out by a male body, accessorized with white shirt and bow tie. Is it a shop you enter at your peril, turning into a dummy, or is it a place where the dummies come alive, yet are curiously emasculated, lacking trousers? The original ideas of Surrealism were almost thirty years old at the time this was painted, yet were still being developed. The mannequins show a force of magical realism, which emerged as a dominant theme in art, literature, and television in the later twentieth century. **SC**

Interior at Paddington
Lucian Freud

1951 | oil on canvas | 60 x 45 in / 152.4 x 114.3 cm
Walker Art Gallery, Liverpool, UK

Ebony and Blue
Ceri Richards

1951 | oil on canvas
Private collection

Lucian Freud (b.1922) was born in Berlin, the son of the architect Ernst Ludwig Freud and the grandson of Sigmund Freud. He spent most of his time working in Paddington. The gloomy atmosphere of this London neighborhood can be seen in many of his cityscapes and interiors. Here, a young man wearing a dirty raincoat stands still in a room, holding a cigarette in his left hand while clenching his right fist. As suggested in the title, his humanity is denied as his strange stiffness echoes the man-sized withered potted plant in front of him. The picture frame seems to imprison the elements depicted, emphasizing its claustrophobic tone. Freud used a matt paint, making the surface of the image appear more like gouache than oil. The crumpled carpet's bright red color competes with the general gray-bluish overtones of the picture, adding a feeling of uneasiness to the scene. **JJ**

Welsh painter Ceri Richards (1903–71) was indubitably tied to the land where he grew up. The natural forms and energies of his native Wales shine through many of his canvases but his style was shaped by modernity. His career referenced myriad artistic influences and other interests, such as music. In *Ebony and Blue,* the influence of Picasso is unmistakable. Cubist shapes and a tendency toward abstraction figure strongly in this work. Richards's somber blue color palette pays homage to the emotionality of Picasso's blue period. Like the guitars Picasso painted forty years earlier, Richards renders a piano abstractly in this painting in which a woman sits at the keyboard. Her hands are out of proportion; she sits on a chair too small for her hulking body and prepares to play, while the keyboard stretches out vertically. Richards uses the delights of Cubism to break the subject from pure pictorialism. **SE**

The Friend's Room
Dorothea Tanning

1950–52 | oil on canvas | 60 ¼ x 42 ⅛ in / 153 x 107 cm
Private collection

Woman I
Willem de Kooning

1950–52 | oil on canvas | 75 ⅞ x 58 in / 193 x 147.5 cm
Museum of Modern Art, New York, NY, USA

Dorothea Tanning's (*b*.1910) early work centered on adolescent sexuality and dreams. Beds, mirrors, and tables are familiar symbolic objects. Here they form the three points of the composition around which a strange tableau of doubled imagery is constructed. The whole scene is encircled with grays, in the draped fabric and the mirror glass. It is illuminated from the left by an unnatural light. The girl in the bed is doubled by the doll with broken limbs. The girl in the foreground is doubled by her altered reflection. The dwarf in cowboy boots and spurs is mirrored by the ambiguous hooded figure in the background. This pairing is echoed by the two pairs of boiled eggs. This painting is about awakening and seeing—the eggs stand both for eyes, in Surrealist terms, and regeneration or awakening in traditional symbolism. The doubles are blind, but the girls see; they are sexually awakened. **WO**

Along with Jackson Pollock, Willem de Kooning (1904–97) was perhaps the artist whose paintings most closely adhere to the popular understanding of Abstract Expressionism. Both artists, albeit in a very different way, were concerned with what role the figurative might continue to play within a mode of painting that, in the first instance, appeared entirely non-figurative. Nowhere is this felt more keenly than in de Kooning's paintings of women. This painting, which he reworked several times, is comprised of a series of jagged lines of varying thickness, momentum, weight, and direction that attempt to capture the primacy of the figure, before it becomes encoded by the norms of language and society. The work is figured by a specific tension between the two realms of the figurative and the abstract. It is this tension that ensures de Kooning's treatment of the figure remains entirely compelling. **CS**

Blue Poles, Number 11, 1952 | Jackson Pollock

1952 | mixed media on canvas | 83 x 191 in / 212 x 488 cm | National Gallery of Australia, Canberra

Born in Cody, Wyoming, the youngest of five sons, Jackson Pollock's (1912–56) childhood was disrupted by the family's constant moving in search of work. His youth was spent in search of an artistic vocation that he found increasingly illusive and frustrating. Plagued by insecurities, his moods swung between wild, alcohol-fueled, attention-seeking and shy, inarticulate, desperation. His first solo show was in 1943. His marriage to the artist Lee Krasner in 1945, and their move to a house in the countryside, prompted a new type of painting—his so-called "drip paintings." These paintings made Pollock's name, and the commercial value of his paintings rose. However, as the first drip paintings were shown at the Betty Parsons Gallery, postwar euphoria was replaced by the emerging specter of the Cold War. With this new mood came a resistance to what was perceived as European-inflected Modernism, and voices in Congress claimed there was a link between abstraction and communism. Pollock's technique was ridiculed by *Time* magazine, which named him "Jack the Dripper." His desire for a greater financial return on his work led him to change dealers, and in 1952 he moved to the nearby Sidney Janis Gallery. The major new work on exhibition was *Blue Poles, Number 11*. This marked a new intensity in Pollock's painting with its range of marks, drips, pours, and splodges of paint in enamel, aluminum paint, and glass. The colors also broke free from Pollock's previously restrained palette. This is a painting that is celebratory in its excess. **RW**

The Death of Nelson | John Minton

1952 | oil on canvas | 72 x 96 ⅛ in / 183 x 244 cm | Royal College of Art, London, UK

Artist and illustrator John Minton (1917–57) was associated with the British Neoromantic movement in art and poetry, an imaginative reaction against the 1930s preoccupation with gritty social issues and the austerity of Britain in the 1940s. In 1952 Minton decided to depict the death of Admiral Horatio Nelson at the battle of Trafalgar, not an unusual choice of subject given that this was the patriotic period of the Festival of Britain and the Coronation. Minton's painting is a reworking of a famous mural in the House of Lords, made by nineteenth-century history painter Daniel Maclise. This mural had long fascinated Minton because a reproduction of the work had hung in his schoolroom. The key elements of Maclise's painting are present—Nelson dying in the arms of

Hardy, the black sailor pointing to the sniper who has just shot the admiral on the deck of HMS *Victory*—but they have been transformed to reinforce the work's theatrical quality. The most obvious distortion is the near vertical deck; Minton said that he was hoping to reproduce the effect of a newsreel shot through a telephoto lens. He handles the composition coherently, the somber crowd swirling around the spotlit Nelson. It is possible to detect homoerotic undertones in the portrayal of the half-naked men in the foreground. The semi-Cubist elements in the details of masts, sails, and some of the figures may seem a halfhearted nod to Modernism, but the overall effect is dramatic and visually satisfying—perhaps an eccentric project carried off with verve and style. **RG**

HMATISSE 52

Blue Nude III | Henri Matisse

1952–53 | gouache on paper | 44 x 29 in / 112 x 73 cm | Musée National d'Art Moderne, Paris, France

The highly original series of four *Blue Nudes* created by Henri Matisse (1869–1954) during the period 1952–54 was born from a combination of tradition and experiment. *Blue Nude III* represents a definitive stage on Matisse's journey toward abstraction, while remaining recognizably representative of the human form. The color blue signified distance and volume to Matisse. Frustrated in his attempts to successfully marry dominant and contrasting tones, the artist was moved to use solid slabs of single color early in his career, a technique that became known as Fauvism. The painted gouache cut-outs that comprise the *Blue Nudes* were inspired by Matisse's collection of African sculpture and a visit that he made to Tahiti in 1930. It took another twenty years and a period of incapacity

after an operation before Matisse synthesized these influences into this seminal series. The artist found the process of arranging cut-out sections of painted gouache far more manageable than working directly with paint on canvas. He named the process "drawing in paper," and the definition of the figure is found in the spaces between the cut-outs. The effect is almost that of a relief, but in two dimensions. As a culmination of Matisse's long search for a perfect blend of color and form, the *Blue Nudes* represent an ending of sorts. Yet, in their originality they led to new beginnings for Matisse's successors. French artists of the 1960s, such as Viallat, and American abstractionists, like Rothko, built on the foundations laid by Matisse and won great acclaim in their own right. **DD**

Sack 5P | Alberto Burri

1953 | mixed media | 59 x 51 in | Fondazione Palazzo Albizzini Collezione Burri, Città di Castello, Italy

Burri (1915–95) took up painting while a prisoner of war in Texas, having served as a doctor in the Italian army. On his return to Rome, he abandoned medicine as a career and began his first collages with old pieces of sacking, and later charred wood and plastic. Associated with the Art Informel tendency of the postwar period, his work is evocative of bomb-damaged European streets and the bandaged flesh of war casualties. It was intended to offer a critique of the purely decorative aspects of contemporary abstraction. *Sack 5P* is constructed from patched-together layers of jute, a gash of red plastic pulling open below a bluer, bladelike form. Close to the lower edge a row of crude stitches forms a ridge, echoed by a second line halfway up the damaged sacking,

petering out where it meets the vertical lake of red. Running stitches separate rectangular fields of stained cloth, gold turning to brown, a misshapen grid trapping the cutaway figure of an imperfect disk. The whole resembles a failed Modernist abstraction, neoplatonic forms mangled out of all recognition. In the context of Italian painting of the 1950s and 60s, Burri's pock-marked surfaces and peeling skins have been compared with the radicalism of the cleaner, more elegantly sliced canvases of his contemporary Lucio Fontana, and the hygienic "achromes" of Fontana's protégé Piero Manzoni. Nevertheless, Burri's sacks represented an emotionally charged response to the time, his unaesthetic, raw materials taken up by the Italian Arte Povera movement in the 1970s. **ZT**

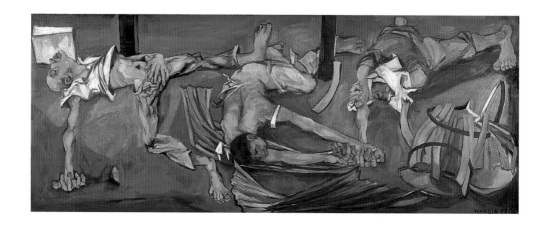

The Execution of Beloyannis | Peter de Francia

1953 | oil on board | 49 x 121 in / 124.5 x 307.3 cm | James Hyman Fine Art Gallery, London, UK

The British artist Peter de Francia (b.1921), previously head of painting at the Royal College of Art, employed his deep understanding of Expressionism to portray nudes and other similar subjects. However, he also used his skill to articulate the horrors of political injustice in a series of three major paintings in the postwar period. This series included *The Bombing of Sakiet* (1958), *African Prison* (1959–60), and the one shown here, *The Execution of Beloyannis*. This painting, one of De Francia's largest, illustrates the execution of the Communist partisan Nikos Beloyannis by the Greek government after the civil war. Beloyannis was executed in the night of March 30, 1952, along with seven other men. Allegedly, he was killed after being charged with high treason, but European intellectuals,

including Jean-Paul Sartre and Picasso, claimed that Beloyannis was killed simply for being a Communist activist. During this period, a portrait of Beloyannis holding a red carnation was circulated and he became known as the "man with the red carnation." In the painting, De Francia depicts the political dissident holding the red carnation in his open hand. Using his art as a form of protest, De Francia manages to lend a tragic beauty to this violent scene with poignant details such as the clasped hands of two of the dead men. The artist kept *The Execution of Beloyannis* and it was not publicly exhibited until 2005, although the Marxist art critic John Berger included a pencil study for the painting in his 1953 traveling exhibition, "Looking Forward." **AH**

Washington Crossing the Delaware | Larry Rivers

1953 | oil, graphite, and charcoal on linen | 83 ½ x 111 ⅜ in / 212 x 283 cm | Museum of Modern Art, New York, NY, USA

After serving in World War II, Bronx native Larry Rivers (Yitzoch Loiza Grossber, 1923–2002) studied at New York's Julliard School of Music. Supporting himself as a jazz saxophonist, Rivers took up painting in 1946 and enrolled in the Hans Hoffman School in 1947. Although grouped with Abstract Expressionist painters of the period, Rivers was highly influenced by the French figurative artists Matisse and Courbet. In the 1950s he became a leading figure in the revival of figurative art and later, in the 1960s, in the development of Pop art. *Washington Crossing the Delaware* is a riff on Emanuel Leutze's 1851 painting of the same title. Leutze's original, which portrays an epic moment in American history, is dominated by Washington's commanding leadership and his crew's navigational skills. In Rivers's version, Washington appears to be standing alone in a stranded rowing boat, which floats uneasily down a freezing river. His soldiers and their horses are scattered randomly about. Painted in ochers and umbers, the image strips Washington of his heroism and allows a human fearfulness to seep through. *Washington Crossing the Delaware* generated substantial controversy when it was first shown in New York in 1953 and some critics interpreted it as a parody of Leutze's work. Rivers's painting encouraged many artists to explore banal subjects as well as American icons, and enabled Rivers to reclaim the course of painting and portraiture. By infusing the field with irony and a deviant wit, Rivers thrust painting into new, uncharted territory. **AR**

Painting, 23 May 1953
Pierre Soulages

1953 | oil on canvas | 7 ⅝ x 5 ¼ in / 19.5 x 13.3 cm
Tate Collection, London, UK

Study of a Baboon
Francis Bacon

1953 | oil on canvas | 78 ⅛ x 54 ⅛ in / 198 x 137 cm
Museum of Modern Art, New York, NY, USA

Pierre Soulages (b.1919) was a member of the group of artists practicing Tachisme. This style concerned mark-making and was influenced by the calligraphy of the East. Their dynamic work expressed the physical procedure of painting as much as the resulting image. Soulages experimented with abstraction, using long brushstrokes of black paint against light backgrounds. The title of this work refers to the date it was completed. Smooth, almost slick slabs and swathes of rich, dark paint overlay each other, creating a latticelike network of flat bands that dominate the image. The sweeping brushstrokes are reminiscent of oriental scripts with their gestural and energetic calligraphic shapes and the strong marks emphasize the process of painting. Despite the small size of the canvas, the shiny black paint commands attention, intensified by the small gleams of light colors glinting through the darkness. **SH**

One of the most complex figures in English art history, Francis Bacon (1909–92) moved to London on his own at age sixteen. There, he survived as a petty thief and rentboy before drifting to Berlin and Paris. Art was never his interest until he saw a Picasso exhibition in Paris. *Study of a Baboon* is a nightmarish, Expressionistic vision of a baboon shrieking upward into a pitch black night and depicts the uncontrollable, unknowable aspects of animals. Although the baboon is perched in what appears to be a caged environment, the animal's physical strength is intensely intimidating as Bacon contrasts the body of the baboon with its background, creating an unnerving relationship between the animal and its artificial surroundings. Bacon painted life at its closest to death. His bruised palette and manic, aggressive strokes created iconic images teeming with rage, brutality, and sadistic, bestial energy. **AH**

Presence of the Past
Günther Gerszo

1953 | oil on masonite | 28 ¾ x 21 ¼ in / 73 x 54 cm
Private collection

Born in Mexico City to a Hungarian father and a German mother, Günther Gerszo's (1915–2000) early work reflects his exposure to Cézanne and Matisse. Gerszo returned to Mexico in 1931. Before turning to art, he worked in the theater designing stage sets, an influence prominent in his compositions. Instead of a realist depiction of nature, Gerszo's landscapes are constructed with geometric shapes and become abstracted in the process. The colors, composition, and shapes simply suggest the type of landscape that is being shown. *Presence of the Past* showcases Gerszo's obsession in planning his paintings according to the Golden Ratio to mathematically guarantee their compositional beauty. Shapes defined by this number have long been seen as aesthetically pleasing in Western culture. The painting's earthy textures and cold color palette clearly distill the essence of Mexico's pre-Columbian history. **AA**

Woman
Willem de Kooning

1953–54 | oil on paper board | 35 ¾ x 24 ½ in /
91 x 62 cm | Brooklyn Museum of Art, Brooklyn, NY, USA

Although Abstract Expressionism became the dominant art movement in postwar America, any affinities each of the respective artists had with each other were potentially sketchy and tenuous. What set Dutch-born painter Willem de Kooning (1904–97) apart from his contemporaries was his insistence upon maintaining an overtly figurative element to what he produced. *Woman*, painted between 1953 and 1954, is wholly affecting as an image. Depicting the figure as assuming a frontal pose, the flurry of brushmarks appear to converge upon the woman's torso, as if this was the perceived center of energy by which her identity, as such, radiated outward. Intriguingly, de Kooning depicts her actual face as almost a cartoonlike, vestigial form of caricature, as if wholly mistrustful of the genre of portraiture's founding precept of "likeness." **CS**

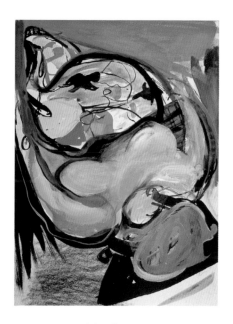

Painting T-54-16
Hans Hartung

1954 | oil on canvas | 512 x 382 in / 1,300 x 970 cm
Centre Pompidou, Paris, France

Nude 54
Peter Lanyon

1954 | watercolor, gouache, and black chalk on paper
42 x 61 in | Whitworth Art Gallery, Manchester, UK

German-born Abstract painter Hans Hartung (1904–89) was one of the prime movers of Art Informel in postwar Paris. Art Informel was a type of abstract art broadly similar to Abstract Expressionism in the United States. In *Painting T-54-16* energetic, black lines swirl and part as if a Zen calligrapher had decided to unleash his emotions via his brushstrokes. Yet there is also something poetic about the lines converging and sweeping out, showing the influence of Chinese brushwork. The fanlike scrawl is ultimately serene and reassuring in effect, while the white slice below appears to anchor these dramatic swirls in some foundation. This work is titled with the medium ("T" standing for toile, implying oil on canvas), the year it was made, 1954, and the order in which it was painted that year. From 1954 Hartung's work changed greatly, becoming even barer in style, with fewer brushstrokes. **JH**

Painter and sculptor Peter Lanyon (1918–64) was born in the small English seaside town of St. Ives, Cornwall, an area that had attracted painters since the late 1800s. Yet when pioneering artists Barbara Hepworth, Ben Nicholson, and Naum Gabo settled there in the late 1930s it was placed firmly on the progressive art map. Lanyon avidly absorbed the creative input of St. Ives's new inhabitants, taking lessons with Nicholson and establishing himself at the heart of the "St. Ives School." The form of Lanyon's nude has been abstracted to some extent but, characteristically for the St. Ives School, he retains a strong naturalistic element. His image exudes a powerfully sculptural curvaceousness, aided by the flowing quality of both the composition and its broad strokes. The fact that he also worked as a sculptor is clear here, as is the influence of sculptor Barbara Hepworth's curving forms. **AK**

Huelga
David Alfaro Siqueiros

1954 | mural in mixed media
Private collection

Annette
Alberto Giacometti

1954 | oil on canvas
Private collection

David Siqueiros (1896–1974) was one of the three great Mexican muralists known as "Tres Grandes," along with Diego Rivera and José Orozco. Siqueiros believed in mural paintings as a public art and as a means to reach the masses, and worked in the style of Social Realism, blending art with political commentary. The Spanish title *Huelga* translates as "strike." The subject matter relates to Siqueiros's passionate involvement in labor politics. The dynamic composition is comprised of varying curvilinear lines, drawing the eye downward to the bottom left corner. Under the bare right foot of the striking worker lies a sickle—a visual reference to Soviet Russia. In the 1930s, Siqueiros ran an experimental workshop in New York City at which he encouraged younger artists to try new techniques and materials. Among them was a young Jackson Pollock, who later used Siqueiros's teachings in his "drip paintings." **MV**

The Swiss painter Alberto Giacometti (1901–66) met Annette Arm in 1943. She began posing for him and they later married. The artist's portrait of her shows intense brushwork; the succession of painterly lines etched onto the canvas are testimony to the artist's acute perceptual awareness. The painting's reduced palette lends a certain sobriety to the work's atmosphere, but also has the effect of placing emphasis on the role played by line. In part what makes *Annette* so compelling is the fact that while Giacometti's use of line is emphatic, searching, almost unrelenting in its pursuit to render empirical data (in this case, a portrait) truthfully, the painting nevertheless appears in a half-formed state. Indeed, the painting is necessarily indeterminate, unfolding as it does across the lived dimensions of both space and time. It is perhaps Giacometti who first reveals this truth to us. **CS**

Still Life with a Green Box | Giorgio Morandi

1954 | oil on canvas | 13 ¾ x 16 ⅛ in / 35 x 41 cm | Haags Gemeentemuseum, The Hague, Netherlands

Giorgio Morandi (1890–1964) was born in Bologna, Italy, and studied at the academy there from 1907 to 1913. He eventually worked at the academy until 1956 as a professor of engraving and etching. Initially Morandi was closely aligned—together with Carlo Carrà (1881–1966) and Giorgio de Chirico (1888–1978)—with the Italian school of Metaphysical painting, but by 1920 he was focusing more intently upon the genre of still life. *Still Life with a Green Box* is, in many respects, the quintessential expression of Morandi's vision. Set against a horizon line—presumably a table top or work surface—are eight rather nondescript objects that effectively occupy a single area of space within the overall composition. Morandi further refines the arrangement by dividing the canvas up into roughly three equal-sized horizontal bands and six vertical bands. He places the objects within this implied latticelike structure so that they occupy the lower two horizontal and middle four vertical bands. The objects themselves are painted with a restricted palette, although Morandi does lend a certain definition to them through a subtle suggestion of shadow. In this quiet, reflective study of eight objects in space, the essence of Morandi's oeuvre is discernible. Free from embellishment or overt detail, such as labels, Morandi tries to get as close as possible to the things themselves, and in doing so, offers us a glimpse of the concrete world in its most elemental state. **CS**

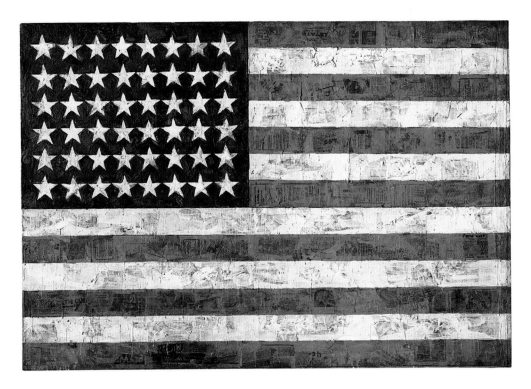

Flag (1954–55) | Jasper Johns

1954–55 | encaustic, oil on panel | 42 x 61 in / 107 x 154 cm | Museum of Modern Art, New York, NY, USA

Along with his friend and fellow artist Robert Rauschenberg, Jasper Johns (b.1930) set about dismantling, if not deflating, the bombastic rhetoric of Abstract Expressionism. While Rauschenberg flooded his canvases with a sprawling heterogeneity of imagery, Johns favored a more cerebral, measured approach and initially focused on a single motif, be it a flag, a target, or a map. Although the generative basis of this painting entailed a direct transcription of the United States flag onto a given support, which in this case was plywood, several subtle but highly important changes were made to what was now a representation of a flag. And at this very moment the paradoxical basis of Johns's undertaking, namely when is a flag merely a representation of a flag,

becomes apparent. Perhaps the most significant change occurred through Johns's employment of encaustic, a fast-drying, wax-based medium capable of creating a thick, *impasto*-like surface that looks quasi-Expressionistic in its appearance. Johns's use of such a medium, in effect, short-circuited the potential for any mark to be read as a signifier of the artist's subjectivity while at the same time it also interrupted the efficacy of the image as such by lending it an obdurate materiality which, ordinarily, it would be entirely lacking, and necessarily so. *Flag* then, as both a riposte to and critique of the legacy of Abstract Expressionism, successfully managed to negotiate a number of artistic precedents without pledging allegiance to any particular sensibility or school. **CS**

Izzy Orts | Edward Burra

1955 | watercolor and pencil on paper | 29 x 41 in / 74 x 105 cm | Gallery of Modern Art, Edinburgh, UK

British painter, printmaker, and theater set designer Edward Burra (1905–76) studied at London's Chelsea School of Art and the Royal College of Art. Although he became a member of Unit One in 1933 and exhibited with the English Surrealists in the late 1930s, his membership of any art group was largely a flirtation, such was his distinctive style. More than anything, Burra was a master at depicting the camp, the Catholic, the dive, and the dance hall. The wit and irony of his work has parallels with contemporary fiction, especially that of writers such as Ronald Firbank and Evelyn Waugh. Burra traveled extensively, to Europe, Mexico, and the USA, and his work reflects this, particularly his depictions of Harlem in the 1930s. He socialized with jazz musicians, and his penchant

for showing the seedier side of nightclubs with a sense of *joie de vivre* is apparent in *Izzy Orts*. This is postwar America, and Burra revels in painting the jazz band, smoky atmosphere, dancing couples, and sailors on leave in Izzy Orts, which was once a bar in Boston. The figure in the foreground on the left is thought to be a self-portrait. In typical Burra fashion, the artist does not merely concentrate on the gaiety of the occasion. The predominant figure is that of the black sailor staring at the viewer with empty eyes and downturned mouth smoking alone at the bar. Perhaps Burra is suggesting that although he wears his country's uniform this sailor feels lonely and out of place, prior to the advances of the American Civil Rights movement in the 1960s. **CK**

Girls on the Couch | Balthus

1955 | oil on canvas | Tazzoli Collection, Turin, Italy

The style employed by Balthus (Balthazar Klossowski de Rola; 1908–2001) varies from classically styled, precise, and meticulous work to techniques and compositions that seem inspired by pre-Renaissance painters who used a flatter, less detailed approach. At times, there are also influences by Surrealists like Giorgio de Chirico. After 1945 Balthus began painting nudes, in particular adolescent girls sleeping, chatting, or in ambiguous private moments. Some of this work is almost dreamlike: figures exist in their own private worlds, indifferent to each other and their surroundings. Despite his traditional approach, an element of menace haunts many of his paintings and his work has always presented something of an enigma. A conventional, middle-class living room,

such as this, was also a frequent theme. The inelegant postures of the two young girls are strangely alarming. They look out of the canvas as if we have disturbed them, confused and not pleased. As always with Balthus's paintings of young women, it could suggest sexual awakening; one girl sits with her legs apart, the other, at her feet, is about to bite an apple. The space is still and calm; yet we, the viewers, seem to have disturbed the rhythm of the scene and interrupted the moment. Reminiscent of a snapshot in time, he had learned methods of framing compositions using cameras from other artists, such as Pierre Bonnard. This painting and others on this theme were admired by other painters, including André Breton and Pablo Picasso. **SH**

Diego
Alberto Giacometti

c.1955 | oil on canvas | 16 ⅛ x 13 in / 41 x 33 cm
Private collection

Color Totem
Lee Krasner

1955 | oil and paper on duck cotton
Betty Parsons Collection, New York, NY, USA

Having initially been aligned with Surrealism, Alberto Giacometti (1901–66) moved away from imagery derived from the "unconscious" toward an engagement with the so-called "furniture" of the sensible world. While the hesitant use of line in *Diego*—the sitter appears to emerge, semi-formed, out of a flurry of brushmarks—would appear to suggest that Giacometti was unwilling to fully relinquish the idea of the inexplicable, the motivating force now for the artist appears to be one of rendering explicable some aspect of lived reality. Although part of the fascination held by *Diego* is that it can be understood as a personalized, idiosyncratic continuation of a long tradition, the painting's significance ultimately resides in the way it manages to reinterpret this tradition. While the success of any portrait hinges upon capturing a "likeness" of the sitter, this painting suggests that can be a philosophical undertaking. **CS**

History has had a hard time knowing how to handle Lee Krasner (1908–84). Feminist scholars have tried to separate her story and her work from the more famous art produced by her husband, Jackson Pollock, and the male members of the New York School, which was responsible for the rise of Abstract Expressionism. The reality is that the development of this new genre is a heavily interwoven history, and the collaboration between Krasner and Pollock enhanced them both. *Color Totem* is one of a series of works that Krasner created by incorporating scraps of drawings by Pollock into her own energetic color compositions. Bits of Pollock's paintings are integrated into Krasner's canvas, in which patches of color swirl like leaves taken up by the wind. The organic and harmonious merger between his work and hers is a beautiful metaphor for collaboration between creative equals. **AH**

Butcher's Shop No. 1
Peter Coker

1955 | oil on board | 72 x 48 in / 182. 8 x 121.9 cm
Graves Art Gallery, Sheffield, UK

Young Woman in White
Celia Calderón

1955 | oil on canvas
Private collection

Peter Coker (1926–2004) was one of British Realism's leading practitioners in the postwar period. His gritty aesthetic themes earned him a place in the movement that critics dubbed "kitchen sink" art. In *Butcher's Shop No. 1*, the hulking back of the butcher at work appears slightly threatening. Just as this butcher cut and carved into animal flesh, Coker used his palette knife to aggressively shape the thick mounds of paint he applied on his canvas. When Coker's work was bought from his first one-man show in 1958 by the Tate Gallery and Contemporary Art Society, it seemed likely that Coker would become a great artistic influence in England. But then Abstract Expressionism arrived from the United States and shifted the art world's focus away from Realism. Ironically, Coker's tactile method of applying paint was akin to abstraction's, but he instead began painting textured landscapes. **AH**

Mexican artist Celia Calderón (1921–69) was chiefly known for her graphic work, although she was also a skillful oil painter and watercolorist. In Mexico, it is economic status that determines the psyche, temperament, and outlook on life of individuals, rather than blood or race. Calderón's *Young Woman in White* is a mestiza; her aquiline nose, coppery skin, braided hairstyle, embroidered white camisole, and bare feet all confirm her indigenous heritage. Her semi-recumbent body and the position of her hands suggest an air of surrender. It is up to onlookers to fill in the gaps: is she rich or poor, liberated or oppressed, a member of the family or a servant? The fact that the subject is portrayed alone and in a corner creates within viewers a dialogue of ambiguity and unease. With little to go on, they are invited to project their prejudices upon an otherwise unknown subject. **AA**

Ned Kelly | Sir Sidney Nolan

1955 | ripolin enamel on hardboard | 24 ½ x 29 ½ in / 62.5 x 75 cm | Private collection

Sir Sidney Nolan (1917–92) is widely acknowledged as Australia's greatest artist. This painting depicts the outlaw Ned Kelly (1854–80), a subject that Nolan returned to again and again throughout his career. The Kelly pictures enabled him to explore the idea of Australia's national identity, as well as a variety of more personal issues. Nolan's early semi-abstract works met with a mixed response in his homeland; it was only after World War II that his art began to find its true direction. Working in a more figurative style, he portrayed Australia's harsh landscape and its rich folklore. Kelly had been a cattle thief and bank robber, although many Australians regarded him as a folk hero for his determined stand against the authorities. Nolan's initial interest in the outlaw stemmed from the tales of his grandfather, who had been one of the police officers involved in the chase for Kelly's gang. In 1946, the artist went to see the bleak landscape of "Kelly Country" in northeast Victoria, before embarking on his first series of pictures about the outlaw, painted in a naive style. The second series, dating from 1955, was far superior. Many of the pictures show Kelly wearing the homemade armor that he and his gang members fashioned out of stolen plow-shares. The square shape of these outfits enabled Nolan to turn the bushranger into a "strong totem figure," which provided a versatile springboard for a wide variety of compositions. The armor, incidentally, did not save Kelly, as the police simply shot him several times in the legs. **IZ**

Creation of the Birds | Remedios Varo

c.1957 | oil on masonite | 20 x 24 in / 52 x 62 cm | Museo de Arte Moderno, Mexico City, Mexico

Surrealist painter Remedios Varo Uranga (1908–63) was born in Anglés, Spain, but spent much of her life in Mexico. She studied at the prestigious Academia de San Fernando in Madrid, and in Barcelona before moving to Paris in 1937 to avoid the Spanish Civil War. There she came into contact with the Surrealists via her husband, the poet Benjamin Péret. She went on to participate in the International Surrealist Exhibition of 1938, but moved to Mexico in 1941, where she spent the rest of her life. Her paintings have variously been described as surreal, mystic, religious, and alchemic in the tradition of Hieronymus Bosch—*Creation of the Birds* is a synthesis of all of these elements. The almond-eyed woman in a feathered owl costume could almost be a self-portrait as the painting symbolically depicts the creative act of painting itself. She sits alone in a studio more akin to a laboratory with its fantasy machines. Varo's interest in the mechanical is often cited as revealing the influence of her father, a hydraulic engineer. The owl represents the wisdom of the artist who harnesses the mechanics of painting by means of the imaginary palette contraption to paint birds. The birds themselves are brought to life by the light from a star, (representing the universe), amplified by a triangular magnifying glass. They fly away through a window, just as Varo's paintings depart to various buyers. The owl artist's paintbrush, attached to the violin placed near the heart, suggests that the artist's creative power comes from harnessing the soul within. **CK**

Russet | Morris Louis

1958 | synthetic polymer paint on canvas | 92 x 173 in / 235.6 x 441 cm | Museum of Modern Art, New York, NY, USA

Morris Louis Bernstein (1912–62) worked briefly at David Siqueiros's art workshop in 1936, where industrial paint and automatist techniques were employed, but it was a visit to Helen Frankenthaler's studio in 1953 that transformed his work from the brooding figurative images that he later destroyed to the light-filled canvases of his last years. Impressed by the staining effect Frankenthaler achieved by thinning oil paint to the consistency of watercolor, Louis resorted exclusively to this method. He rarely allowed anyone in his studio. The room's small scale meant that he could only work on one painting at a time on a bolt of canvas with a standard measurement of 8 feet (2.4 meters), the painting often stretching beyond the confines of the studio. Stapling the canvas loosely to a working stretcher, he poured over the liquid paint, moving the cloth to aid the direction and flow of each color. The darker vertical lines record where pigment collected as the heavy wet canvas lay in contact with the crossmembers, a pattern repeated in the series *Veils* of 1958 and 1959. The appearance of *Russet* candidly reveals the process of its making— the butterfly-thin membranes extending fanlike across the canvas. Color infusing the fiber capillaries causes the difference between figure and ground to dissolve; the forces of nature intuited in the fusion of two bodies. Reducing the significance of the artist's autograph gesture, Louis loosened the ties between Color Field painting and the celebrated action of Abstract Expressionism. **ZT**

Paysage | Syed Haider Raza

1958 | oil on canvas | 18 x 21¾ in / 45.8 x 55.2 cm | Private collection

Syed Haider Raza (b. 1922) is one of the founders of the Progressive Artists' Group (PAG)—which sought to focus on social issues in art rather than nationalistic agendas—created in 1947 in Bombay. Members of this collective sought to embrace Modernism in their art, unlike the work of the more traditional Bengal School, and were praised for using their work to voice demands for social justice, particularly in rural India. Raza became internationally famous after he graduated from the École Nationale des Beaux-Arts in Paris in 1953, and three years later, in the same city, he was awarded the prestigious Prix de la Critique. Raza made regular trips back to India, however, to refamiliarize himself with his roots, and the iconography of his native land. First known as a landscape painter, his style became more abstract in the 1950s. *Paysage* was inspired by the intensity of color in the work of artists such as Cézanne and van Gogh. The artist had changed media from watercolor to oil not long before this work was created, prompted by his studies of Western painting techniques while abroad. His use of color here is symbolic: the dominant red represents the suffering during the famine in rural India; the dark browns strike a somber note. Raza employed abstract geometrical lines for the houses and human forms, and the overall result is an absorbing blend of Rajput miniature and Post-Impressionist styles. His combination of Indian symbolism and European techniques has given Raza's work a multicultural audience. **SZ**

Cadmium
Emil Schumacher

1958 | oil on canvas | 67 x 51 in / 170 x 131 cm
Hamburger Kunsthalle, Hamburg, Germany

Solvejg
Asger Jorn

1959 | oil on canvas
Private collection

The end of World War II saw a change in the arts in Germany, and Emil Schumacher's (1912–99) work can be divided stylistically into prewar and postwar eras. *Cadmium* is typical of the artist's light-filled and color-oriented postwar works. During the 1950s Schumacher was increasingly building on the surface texture of his works, so that the lines between painting and sculpture became blurred. Color was allowed to burst through from the conventional constraints of line, taking on an equal importance to the work's composition. There is a lyrical feel to *Cadmium*, sensed through the luminous quality of the yellow that flows through the gray-blue surrounding, while the delicate tendrils of dark paint weave across the surface. Schumacher's treatment of line and color gave art a new direction, and he is considered one of the most influential of modern German artists. **TP**

Danish artist Asger Jorn (1914–73) was a member of several avant-garde movements that inform his revolutionary artistic gestures. *Solvejg* exemplifies the violent brushwork and vibrant primary colors that Jorn often employed in his fantastical paintings, which embraced folklore and myth. Expressionist in nature, this work conjures action and process because of its lively hand. Although Jorn argued against an abstract style, his work adheres to its principles of unrestrained frenetic movement. However, *Solvejg* retains a loose compositional structure by engaging the diagonal of the picture plane so that the ambiguous object appears to be propelled upward leaving behind bright blue traces in its wake. Jorn's independent style is enlivened by his activism outside the art arena. Constantly stressing the importance of the study of culture, he is known as a painter who wanted to reshape society. **MG**

The Prancing Horse
M.F. Husain

1950–59 | oil on canvas | 29 ¾ x 25 ¾ in /
75.5 x 65.5 cm | Private collection

Abstract Painting Diptych
Ad Reinhardt

1959 | oil on canvas | 15 ¾ x 7 ⅞ in / 40 x 20 cm
Private collection

Born in 1915, Maqbool Fida Husain, known as M.F. Husain, is a controversial Indian painter, sculptor, printmaker, photographer, and filmmaker. He first came to public attention in 1947 when one of his paintings was exhibited by the Bombay Art Society. Husain made a series of paintings of horses, and *The Prancing Horse* reflects his mature work. His paintings are a mixture of Indian and European elements adapted to his distinctive taste. Although Husain's style is unique, the Cubist influence of Pablo Picasso is notable. However, his technique in the outline and use of color is a hallmark of his style. He uses a limited palette: white and brown for the body, black for the mane and tail, and an intriguing yellow for the face. The stark red background contrasts perfectly with the white horse. Husain's confident brushstrokes give an incredible sense of movement to the legs of the animal. **SZ**

Ad Reinhardt's (1913–67) early paintings were inspired by Mondrian: loosely brushed paint applied horizontally and vertically in rhythmic configurations. *Abstract Painting Diptych* is an example of the "black" painting style for which Reinhardt is best known. These canvases appear uniformly black—an art devoid of color and light. Seen up close, however, the carefully painted layers disclose small amounts of blue, yellow, or red, which form the simple shape of a Greek cross. The emphatic, repeated form of this work paradoxically eclipses the painting while insisting on its continued presence in serial and grid extension. Reinhardt's visual code, accompanied by his theoretical texts, was influential for a generation of artists working in three dimensions. Reacting against the emotionalism of Abstract Expressionism, these artists preferred prefabricated materials, geometric forms, and sequential arrangements. **ZT**

Orange and Black Wall | Franz Kline

1959 | oil on canvas | 66 ½ x 144 in / 169 x 366 cm | Museo Thyssen-Bornemisza, Madrid, Spain

Franz Kline (1910–62) described his paintings as "situations," and believed that good art accurately conveyed the emotions of its creator. His best known works are monumentally scaled abstract canvases that retain a visible residue of the highly physical process behind their creation. Though Kline claimed that these works reference specific places, they do not seem guided by any objective logic. Like the works of fellow action painters Jackson Pollock and Willem de Kooning, Kline's paintings appear to be a spontaneous, muscular translation of the artist's will into material form. Kline typically worked in a monochromatic palette of black and white. The addition of bold, thick streaks of color in *Orange and Black Wall* adds yet another dimension of vitality and dynamism to the finished work. The black lines appear to form an Expressionistic grid, out of which the orange, green, and red spill. Despite the lack of a clear division between figure and ground, the painting never becomes static. It resounds with an array of potential emotive origins and so invites constant speculation as to its meanings. Kline's dramatic life has only fueled his iconic status—he struggled for years to find success as a portrait and landscape painter, rose rapidly to international prominence in the 1950s when he began painting in pure abstractions, then died of heart failure in 1962, only fifty-one years old and at the height of his fame. As a public figure, he reflects the "celebrity artist" phenomenon that pervaded the mid-twentieth-century American art world. **NKM**

Second Story Sunlight | Edward Hopper

1960 | oil on canvas | 40 x 50 in / 101.6 x 127 cm | Whitney Museum of American Art, New York, NY, USA

Two women sunbathing on the upper floor of an attractive weather-boarded house might sound like a subject for something stylish, sexy, and fun—a bit of frivolity—but with Edward Hopper (1882–1967) it becomes a stark scene full of frisson. It is a snapshot, a novella, and we want to know what is going on. Why do they appear so disconnected? Is the older woman, draped in a somber black dress, about to make some remark to the younger one, clad in a bikini? Or is the younger woman, confident in her fine figure, simply ignoring the elderly woman? But before such questions take any earnest root we are drawn to the overall composition—the imposing white geometry and sharply peaked roofs punctuated by semi-drawn blinds, and framed by dense green trees and soft sky. As with his other paintings, especially in his later period, Hopper, an American painter and etcher, is fixated by light—in this case sunlight—and the contrasts and shadows it can create. His anonymous characters turn toward it, bask in it, or are simply exposed by it. He had an incredible ability to produce natural-looking sunlight and is quoted to have said that the only thing he wanted to do was "paint sunlight on the side of a house." Often his characters sit, as in this painting as well as in *People in the Sun* (also 1960), isolated from each other, detached, clothed, and motionless. This is Hopper at the peak of his powers, constantly refining his approach to light, shade, and color—a palette that has echoes of Mondrian. **JH**

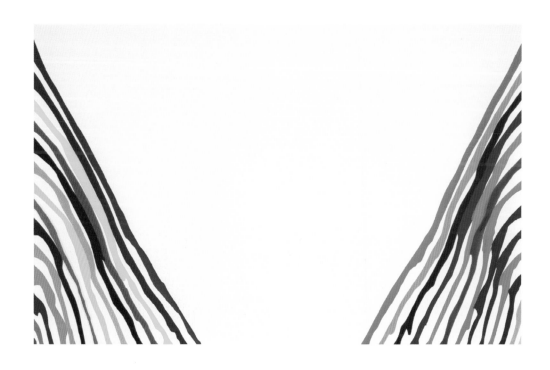

Beta Lambda | Morris Louis

1960 | polymer on canvas | 103 x 160 in / 262 x 407 cm | Museum of Modern Art, New York, NY, USA

In 1953, after a private viewing of New York artist Helen Frankenthaler's stain painting, *Mountains and Sea* (1952), American artist Morris Louis (Morris Louis Bernstein, 1912–62) began exploring groundbreaking methods of paint application. Working with fellow artist Kenneth Noland, and later in virtual isolation in Washington, DC, Louis's experiments transformed the course of painting. *Beta Lambda* is one of approximately 160 paintings in the artist's *Unfurled* series, created in 1960–61. This enormous painting consists of two opposing bands of multicolored paint separated by a gaping white hole. The rivulets of color in each bank undulate simultaneously, meeting occasionally on their way down the canvas. The technique involved leaning unprimed canvases

against the wall and allowing the liquid Magna paint to both flow over, and be absorbed into, its fabric. The paint, and to some extent the artist, were thus subject to the canvases' unstretched condition (hence the asymmetrical relationship of the two banks to one another, and the slight wave in both banks mid-descent). *Beta Lambda* and the *Unfurleds* are considered some of the most radical paintings of the early 1960s. Literally nothing is presented—a massive portion of the canvas is left blank—and Louis also eliminated the brush gesture altogether. In doing so, he downplayed the Abstract Expressionists' emphasis on the individual hand and mind of the painter, placing him as a leader in the movement from Abstract Expressionism to Color Field painting. **AR**

Untitled | Mark Rothko

1960–61 | oil on canvas | 24 x 19 in / 60.8 x 48.2 cm | Private collection

Mark Rothko (1903–70) is considered an abstract artist, though he personally rejected this classification. Born in Latvia (then part of the Russian Empire) into a Jewish family, Rothko emigrated to the United States in 1913. He spent his childhood in Portland, Oregon. Gifted a grant, Rothko attended classes at Yale between 1921 and 1923. Before graduating, he moved to New York where he attended classes at the Art Students' League under the painter Max Weber. Nevertheless, as an artist Rothko was mainly self-taught. His early work consisted of Expressionist landscapes, genre scenes, and still lifes. During World War II, many European artists emigrated to the United States, including those associated with the Surrealist movement. They were a major influence on Rothko who began to attempt to apply Jung's theories on the collective unconscious to his work, and he started to orient his art toward a more abstract style. After the late 1940s, Rothko chose to eliminate representational figures in his paintings completely, creating the abstract, colorful works for which he is today best known. Apparently simple, this painting in fact shows a wonderfully complex process at work. Filled with bright red, the upper part of the painting comes to create a strong opposition with the dark blue area below it, itself encircled by a nimbus of vivid pink. Rothko's saturated colors are emotive and meditative. As one's eyes adjust to the light that the painting emits, the color field envelops the mind, and the palette's warm interplay of tones mesmerizes. **JJ**

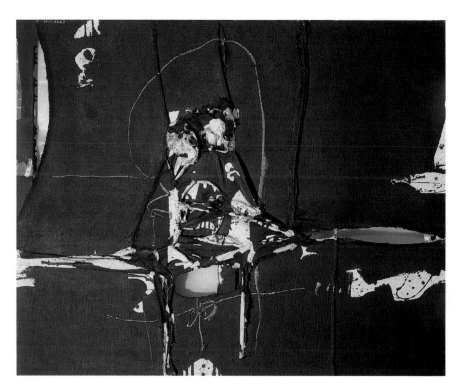

Painting 150 | Manolo Millares

1961 | oil on canvas | 51½ x 63 ⅞ in / 131 x 162 cm | Tate Collection, Liverpool, UK

Born in the Canary Islands, Manolo Millares (1926–72) was self-taught and one of the founding members of the avant-garde group *El Paso* ("The Step"). He is also associated with the Informalists, a group of artists who believed that art should be removed from theory and concept. Millares is perhaps most famous for his collages using materials such as sand, newspaper, ceramics, wood, and fabric, and his particular method of tearing, bunching, tying, and stitching his materials together helped establish him as a leading international artist. Affected by the bloody and bitter period of the Spanish Civil War, the artist became fascinated by the polar opposites of destruction and construction. In the 1940s he was influenced by the work of the Surrealists, notably Paul Klee, and Millares

began producing fantastic pictograms. Until the mid-1960s he employed a particularly austere and limited color palette, creating images that, although abstract, often evoked some kind of human entity. He was fascinated with the idea of the homunculus, the miniature human being that can represent man in a primitive state. This theme appeared in his paintings after 1958, including *Painting 150*. Painted in blacks, beiges, browns, and blues, the painting provides a great contrast to the more colorful work produced by Millares in his later years. The viewer can just about make out a figure, arms stretched out, suspended in the depths of black despair. *Painting 150* embodies Millares's ideas of destruction and construction, and is among the artist's most celebrated works. **AV**

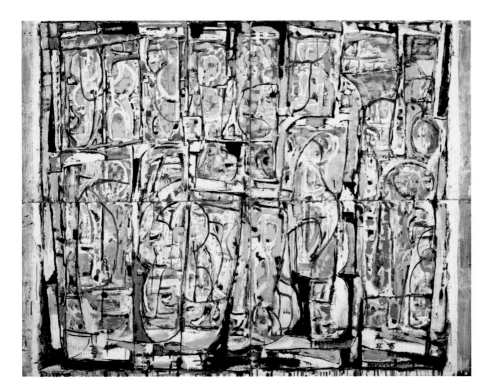

Monastery | Ian Fairweather

1961 | polymer paint and gouache on cardboard | 56 ⅞ x 73 in | National Gallery of Australia, Canberra

Born in Scotland, Ian Fairweather (1891–1974) began to draw in earnest while he was a prisoner of war in World War I. During that time he also taught himself Chinese and became interested in East Asian life. In the 1930s he began working with Australian artists, eventually settling in the country after years of traveling around China, Bali, and other Far Eastern countries. He spent many years living as a recluse on Bribie Island, north of Brisbane. His interest in calligraphy and the Chinese written language informed his art, and he moved from producing tonal figures to a more linear style and restrained use of color. In the 1950s, Fairweather began to produce larger works, and moved from using thick gouache on poor materials to synthetic polymer paint, often mixed with gouache. At the end of the 1950s Fairweather sent thirty-six abstract paintings to the Macquarie Gallery, which were very well received. These pieces led to *Monastery*, which won the John McCaughey Prize; and *Epiphany*, which Fairweather often said was his best work, painted the following year. Many consider *Monastery*, which was bought by the National Gallery of Australia, to be a masterpiece. It shows Cubist influences and portrays Fairweather's interest in calligraphy. At the time, the Australian artist James Gleeson said that *Monastery* was "an extraordinary, fascinating hybrid from the pictorial traditions of Europe and the calligraphy of China." *Monastery* helped cement Fairweather's reputation as one of Australia's greatest artists. **AV**

Map | Jasper Johns

1961 | oil on canvas | 78 x 123 ⅛ in / 198 x 313 cm | Museum of Modern Art, New York, NY, USA

It was in 1435 that the analogy of painting as a window was first introduced. Writing in *De Pictura*, Leon Battista Alberti used the analogy to suggest that painting functioned primarily as an open window affording a view onto the world it framed. At least up until the onset of Modernism during the latter half of the nineteenth century, painting conformed to this model and was considered as something intrinsically illusionistic. But Modernism, with its repertoire of radical painting techniques, challenged this dominant model to the extent that the contiguity between reality and illusion was something that was now no longer automatically given. The significance of *Map* primarily resides in its ability to polarize the distinction between what is real and what is illusory to

the extent that the two appear almost irreconcilable. On the one hand, Jasper Johns (*b.*1930) introduces fragments of stenciled lettering that denote place names. But the two-dimensional, graphic nature of this information is tendentiously set against a range of crudely rendered, Expressionistic brushstrokes and elements of collaged material, both of which work to root the work firmly within the realm of three dimensions. What makes *Map* so compelling is its ability to conflate mutually exclusive realms—in this instance two and three dimensions, but also separate forms of signification. These visual paradoxes are just one aspect of Johns's project as a whole, a project that is both a critique and a meditation upon what constitutes painting as a visual language. **CS**

Le Gros | Franz Kline

1961 | oil on canvas | 41 ³/₈ x 52 ³/₄ in / 105 x 134 cm | Museum of Modern Art, New York, NY, USA

Franz Kline (1910–62) was born in Wilkes Barre, Pennsylvania, and had a traumatic childhood that included the suicide of his father in 1917, his mother's subsequent remarriage, and some years spent in an institution for fatherless boys. In later years the artist later referred to the latter as an "orphanage." It was while Kline was at high school that he developed an interest in the arts, and during recuperation from an accident that left him temporarily immobile, he started to draw. In 1931 his formal artistic training began in Boston, and in 1935 he traveled to England to start studying at the Heatherley's School of Fine Art in London. His early artistic career was defined by his figurative work and on his return to the United States he began producing Realist urban views in a softly

Expressionistic manner. Willem de Kooning was to profoundly influence Kline, who at the end of the 1940s adopted a radically abstract style—a complete departure from his early figurative work. Le Gros is one of a series of large works defined by their strong black and white linear form and strident composition. Kline used large industrial paintbrushes to achieve the wide, swift slashes of black that formed a vibrant cage to the planes and pockets of white space. His abstract works were well received after an exhibition in 1950 at the Egan Gallery, and subsequently his career, which until this point had been dogged by lack of success, took off. His work is particularly unique and distinctive, and places him at the head of the Abstract Expressionist movement. **TP**

Sleeping Child
Will Barnet

1961 | oil on canvas | 62 x 48 in / 157 x 122 cm
Smithsonian American Art Museum, Washington, DC, USA

Untitled Anthropometry
Yves Klein

1961 | acrylic on paper on canvas | 61½ x 42 ½ in /
156 x 108 cm | Musée Cantini, Marseille, France

Will Barnet (b.1911) was influenced by the minimalist qualities of printmaking, evident in the graphic quality in his signature figurative-abstract style. In *Sleeping Child*, he creates a tender graphic image of his young daughter Ona asleep on his wife Elena's lap that is free of perspective, and where austerity of line, flatness of form, minimal use of color, and harmony of design are the driving forces. The result is a visual and intellectual paradox of figuration and abstraction. At first glance, one sees a quiet moment between a mother and child. On closer inspection one realizes that this is not illustrative realism but a pure abstraction of the figures created by the deliberate placement of flat minimalist shapes on the canvas. Nor is the canvas still, but bursting with energy as the juxtaposition of the vertical and horizontal forms creates such strong tension that both mother and child seem to break free of the canvas. **SA**

Yves Klein (1928–62) is best known for painting without a brush. Instead, during performances, he pressed his International Klein Blue paint against paper using naked models. Where Abstract Expressionists were obsessed with exploring the medium of paint, Klein forced viewers to think about the canvas. By burning canvases, he emphasized the vulnerability of fabric, transforming a material used to create the illusion of pictorial immortality into something painfully mortal. In this work Klein reinvents the notion of the nude. Repeated blurred images of a female nude seem to emerge from the canvas, as though walking toward the viewer through some sort of veil. The nudes are not fully formed, or even recognizably naked. The naked body has been the instrument of execution as well as the object of this painting. Hauntingly beautiful and thought-provoking, Klein's painting redefines the concept of "painting." **AH**

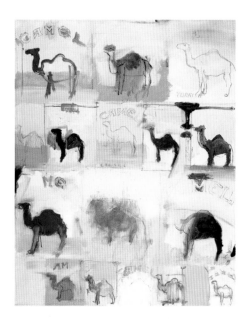

I'm in the Mood for Love
David Hockney

1961 | oil on canvas | 50 ½ x 40 in / 128 x 101 cm
Royal College of Art, London, UK

David Hockney (b.1937) has experimented with a variety of styles and media, working not just as a painter, but as a draftsman, printmaker, and photographer. *I'm in the Mood for Love* incorporates handwritten text and stencilled letters and numerals recalling graffiti. The deliberately naive rendering of the figure and buildings belies the artist's mastery as a draftsman. But despite the presence of these hallmark elements of Pop art, this piece has an emotional depth that distinguishes it from other works linked with the movement. The large brushstrokes in the top left-hand corner, which point downward toward the figure lend a particularly charged and brooding sense to the piece. The indistinct face of the central figure both draws the viewer into a suggested narrative and leads to a search for meaning in symbols like the red heart and white crescent. *I'm in the Mood for Love* evinces Hockney's visual wit. **AR**

Camels
Larry Rivers

c.1962 | oil with collage on canvas | 64 x 51 in / 162.5 x 129.5 cm | Fitzwilliam Museum, Cambridge, UK

New York musician, artist, sculptor, and designer Larry Rivers (1923–2002) was a major figure in the group of New York artists who took contemporary Abstract Expressionism in a more figurative direction. In *Camels*, Rivers plays around with the familiar image and wording from packets of Camel cigarettes—the epitome of "cool" American culture in his era. He loved painting cigarette packets in general, fascinated by what their imagery symbolized and the meeting of art and commercialism. The main camel image is given sixteen different treatments in this painting, including expertly drawn (top right), freely painted (second row, far right), and hardly there at all (bottom row, center). Sometimes the whole word "camel" appears, other times it is just a couple of letters. The repeated image—used to iconic effect by Andy Warhol—was a favorite with Rivers, as was the inclusion of collage. **AK**

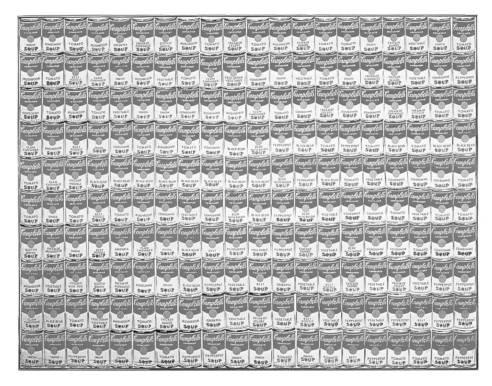

200 Soup Cans | Andy Warhol

1962 | polymer paint on canvas | 72 x 100 in / 183 x 254 cm | Private collection

Born in Pittsburgh, Pennsylvania, Andy Warhol (1928–87) is without a doubt one of the most important artists of the twentieth century. He studied commercial art at Carnegie Mellon University, Pittsburgh before moving to New York in 1949. He worked as a successful magazine and advertising illustrator. Cofounder of Pop art, a movement that emerged in the United States in the 1950s, he progressively became an artistic director and a producer for other artists working in music and film. Many of them worked with him as his assistants in his infamous studio known as The Factory. Pop art stood as an alternative to Abstract Expressionism, which was prevalent in America at that time. Pop artists were interested in the language, the imagery, and the mass media of American postwar culture. In the 1960s, Warhol became interested in the visual power of American objects, such as Coca-Cola and Campbell's soup cans. Painted in 1962, *200 Soup Cans* is emblematic of Warhol's interest in American cultural values. He painted a series of two hundred, identical, red, white, and yellow soup cans based on the famous Campbell's product, arranging them in perfect manufactured order. This particular way of appropriating objects from the American everyday, and reusing them in commercial work became Warhol's own signature. *200 Soup Cans* was an attempt to define a universally recognized American symbol. Warhol claimed to have eaten Campbell's soup for lunch everyday for most of his life. **JJ**

Leda and the Swan | Cy Twombly

1962 | oil, crayon on canvas | 75 x 78 in / 190 x 200 cm | Museum of Modern Art, New York, NY, USA

American abstract artist Cy Twombly (*b*.1928) was born in Lexington, Virginia. He attended art classes in several great institutions, including at the School of the Museum of Fine Arts in Boston (1947–49), at Washington and Lee University in Lexington, and from 1950 to 1951 at the Art Students' League in New York. There, he was introduced to the artist Robert Rauschenberg, who urged him to continue his studies at the Black Mountain College, North Carolina, where he met the musical impresario John Cage. Important artists taught in this school at that time such as Franz Kline, Robert Motherwell, and Ben Shahn. Kline in particular stood out as a major influence. Twombly had his first solo exhibition at the Kootz Gallery in New York in 1951. A grant from the Virginia Museum of Fine Arts provided him with the opportunity to travel to north Africa, France, Spain, and Italy. During the 1950s, the artist enrolled in the army as a cryptologist, an experience that led to an important turning point in his art. In 1959, Twombly emigrated to Rome, Italy, where he based most of his career. In *Leda and the Swan*, he playfully associated painting, writing, and drawing in an unprecedented style. Blurring the frontier between these mediums, Twombly offers the viewer a new visual and artistic experience in his own interpretation of the famous Greek myth. This work is typical of his 1960s style, where he used subjective and erotic signs, and started to paint with intensely bright colors contrasted against white backgrounds. **JJ**

Jackpot Machine | Wayne Thiebaud

1962 | oil on canvas | 38 x 27 in / 97 x 69 cm | Smithsonian American Art Museum, Washington, DC, USA

Born in Mesa, Arizona, to Mormon parents, Wayne Thiebaud's (*b.*1920) diverse career has involved working as an animator for the Walt Disney studios and as an illustrator of a regular comic strip while in the United States Air Force during World War II. Thiebaud was a key figure in defining contemporary American Realism with his deadpan paintings of everyday Americana, such as sandwiches, gumball machines, toys, and cafeteria foods. He composes these still life paintings with simple geometric shapes and a solid use of light that often suggests photorealism. With an unmistakable undertone of nostalgia, Thiebaud's semi-abstract style paints a regressive advertisement for the forgotten pleasures of American middle-class life. The colors and shapes

in *Jackpot Machine*—bold reds, honest blues, and even stars—manufacture the American flag into a novelty product. The sleek design and metal colors solidly convey an example of the many factory-produced pleasures of American consumer culture. With variations of rectangles and ovals structured by emphatic pigments and well-defined shadows, *Jackpot Machine* portrays the American dream of get-rich opportunity in a sweet and digestible portrait of a toy. Such themes of consumer excess link much of Thiebaud's work to Pop art, but he generally lacks the moral judgment of that movement. Instead, Thiebaud recalls the innocence and novelty of childhood, where commercial consumption formulates the memories and desires of an American dream. **SWW**

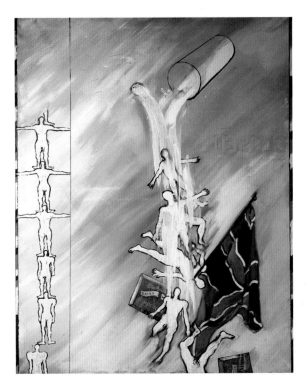

Drinka Pinta Milka | Derek Boshier

1962 | oil on canvas | 58 ¾ x 47 ½ in / 152 x 121 cm | Royal College of Art Collection, London, UK

During his Pop period, Derek Boshier (b.1937) made a number of figural paintings exploring the effects of consumerism and mass media on British society at the time. These were exhibited in "Image In Revolt" at Grabowski Gallery, London, in 1962, along with work by Frank Bowling. *Drinka Pinta Milka* refers to a long-running Cadbury's ad campaign for their Dairy Milk chocolate bar that featured the much-remembered but meaningless slogan "a glass and a half of full cream milk per half pound." Boshier paints their trademark glass of milk being poured over and into people falling through space along with the chocolate bars. The title refers to a public information campaign in which citizens were advised to "Drinka Pinta Milka Day" to stay healthy. To Boshier, such information represented the sinister side of the postwar British welfare state—a nannying social control over many by an elite few. His uniform, faceless humans, shaped and displaced by the milk, are part of an "identi-kit" set that forms a larger, rigid structure—it is not only the milk that is being homogenized. Pop art concerned itself with "smashing" previously sacred images and while Jasper Johns recontextualized the stars and stripes, Boshier used the Union Jack, drooping and falling down with the figures, to suggest the downfall of the old imperial nation in the wake of global consumerism. Starting as a Pop motif, the Union Jack then became a fashionable commodity itself when it was placed on many mass-produced items, undermining its representational authority, yet celebrating British national identity. **KM**

First Toothpaste | Derek Boshier

1962 | oil on canvas | 30 x 54 in / 76 x 137 cm | Sheffield Galleries and Museums Trust, Sheffield, UK

Derek Boshier (b.1937) trained at the Royal College of Art, London, and came to prominence in the early 1960s as part of the British Pop art movement. His paintings frequently confront the world of consumer goods: there is often a comic-ironic play with popular imagery and everyday graphics. Boshier painted a series of works inspired by a toothpaste commercial, including this one, and the paintings are usually read as a criticism of how easy it is for the media to manipulate the viewer. In *First Toothpaste*, a man is represented as trapped inside a toothpaste tube—a typical mass consumer product—struggling to escape. The man is tiny in comparison to the huge, overwhelming, garish red and white squirt of the toothpaste. The figure with his outstretched arms echoes the symmetry and form of Da Vinci's *Vitruvian Man*, the famous Renaisssance image of human beauty. It could be argued that Boshier inverts this figure to create a vivid impression of man's entrapment. Pop artists also set about breaking down hierarchies between "high" and "low" art in technique as well as subject matter. What Warhol achieved with flat silkscreen color, Boshier creates with paint. The flat colors look almost printed rather than painted. They help to depersonalize the figure in the image and represent him as a participant, a cog-in-the-wheel of a mass-produced world. Boshier has had an eclectic career, not only working as a painter, but also as a conceptual artist, filmmaker, photographer, and graphic artist for David Bowie and The Clash. **CM**

Delaware Crossing | Frank Stella

1962 | alkyd on raw canvas | 12 x 12 in / 30.5 x 30.5 cm | Brooklyn Museum of Art, Brooklyn, NY, USA

Delaware Crossing is one of a series of six minimalist works that the young Frank Stella (*b*.1936) called his "Benjamin Moore paintings"—Benjamin Moore being the brand name of the alkyd house paint he used to cover the canvases. Each work in the series consists of a pattern made of regular lines separated by pinstripes on a square canvas. Each is painted using a different color from the Benjamin Moore range. Stella underlined his taste for mathematical combinations of form and color by making thirty-six smaller versions of these paintings, presenting each of the six patterns in each of the six colors. In revolt against the Abstract Expressionists then dominant on the American art scene, Stella sought to make paintings that would rigorously exclude not only representation but also the Romantic individualist goals of self-expression and spontaneity. The use of color is neither emotive nor decorative. The viewer is confronted with a painted surface that is neither more nor less than exactly that. As Stella quipped: "What you see is what you see". In a less pithy mood, the artist described his objective as forcing "illusionistic space out of the paintings at a constant rate by using a regulated pattern." Stella was criticized for making painting mechanical and impersonal—a view that the artist himself encouraged with his talk of "systemic" painting generated by following a set of rules. Yet *Delaware Crossing* is as individual and distinctive as any twentieth-century work of art. In its purity and power, the painting could be by no one but Stella. **RG**

Forget It! Forget Me! | Roy Lichtenstein

1962 | oil and magna on canvas | 80 x 68 in / 203.2 x 172.7 cm | Rose Art Museum, Waltham, MA, USA

In 1964, a now infamous article in *Life* magazine asked "Is Roy Lichtenstein the worst artist in the US?" The article testified to Lichtenstein's (1923–97) unique ability to provoke controversy with his deadpan imitations of comic book illustrations on a blown-up scale. Like his contemporaries Andy Warhol and Claes Oldenburg, he rejected the notion of the artist as spontaneous creative genius. Instead, he embraced a style of art that came to be known as Pop, characterized by explicit references to mass culture and attempting to undermine the gravity of traditional "high" art. *Forget It! Forget Me!* has the distinctly playful, ironic feel that pervades much of Lichtenstein's output. The colors are bold—almost garish; the Benday Dots that give the painting its texture make it seem mass produced, even though each dot was tediously drawn by hand; and the characters are not plausible depictions of actual people but idealized versions of women and men. The text bubble and its equally ambiguous, stereotyped content makes the painting vacant of any attempt to convey genuine emotion or profound meaning. The entire scene is so formulaic that it appears deceptively familiar. But the precision of its execution and its enormous scale belie the apparent lightness of its content. Lichtenstein's idea of critiquing culture by reproducing its most familiar icons in a new context would go on to become a major trend in late twentieth-century art. He is now widely regarded as one of the pre-eminent American painters of his time. **NKM**

Passing | Alex Katz

1962–63 | oil on canvas | 71 ¾ x 79 ⅝ in / 182 x 202 cm | Museum of Modern Art, New York, NY, USA

Alex Katz's (b.1927) flat, hard-edged, and boldly colored portraits of elegant, affluent urbanites and country-home dwellers have become part of America's visual lexicon, earning him a secure place in American painting's pantheon. New York–born and bred, Katz creates a series of colorful, reduced paintings that illustrate the people and places most important to him. His subjects live graceful lives filled with cocktail parties and summerhouses in Maine. Their portraits exemplify the modern realism where abstraction and figuration meet to create images of often recognizable faces—less portraits of people than of the lifestyle they have. Although the chic images have become synonymous with Manhattan's intellectual and wealthy elite, they have wide-ranging appeal.

Passing is one of Katz's most physiologically unnerving images. The painting appears to be of a stranger, in a porkpie hat and sharp suit, whose somewhat hostile expression might be directed at us, or might be the result of his internal thoughts. Its mystery adds depth to its flat surface. Katz's signature cool style keeps the subject at a distance, yet the enigmatic man is not a stranger who Katz has passed on the street—it is the artist himself. As a self-portrait, Passing is intriguingly unconventional since it portrays the artist as unknowable to us, and possibly even to himself. Its mood strongly evokes Felix Nussbaum's Self-Portrait with Jewish Passport, adding another meaning to the title since "passing" is a term used to describe the experience of assimilation for minorities. **AH**

Christ at Emmaus | Patrick Caulfield

1963 | house paint on board | 40 x 50 in / 102 x 127 cm | Royal College of Art Collection, London, UK

In 1963, students at the Royal College of Art in London were set an Easter project. They were given the choice of two themes: "Figures in a High Wind" and "Christ at Emmaus." One of these students was a young painter called Patrick Caulfield (1936–2005). Taking on both themes, he portrayed a windblown Christ at Emmaus. *Christ at Emmaus* is a fascinating painting when considered in the context of its time and in relation to Caulfield's maturing style. Along with many of his peers, Caulfield was drawn toward Pop art, and this work has Pop's characteristic impersonal flatness and graphic aesthetic. Another aspect of the Pop approach is shown here in the artist's appropriation of existing visual imagery: the pattern around the border of the image was derived from the design of packets of dates. Caulfield did not generally refer to religious subjects in his later work but he was inspired by ancient art, in particular decorative Minoan artifacts and frescoes. This influence can be seen in his depiction of the large vase next to the figure under the tree; pottery of this kind is a recurring image in later works. Other indications of Caulfield's stylistic direction are evident in this painting—the clear black outline, use of alkyd house paint on board, and flat, linear composition are all present. His paintings over the next ten years were concerned with the subtlety of still lifes and interiors, his subject matter refined with a brilliant use of color and pattern. *Christ at Emmaus* is an extraordinary early work by one of the most important British artists of recent times. **RW/JP**

The Bay | Helen Frankenthaler

1963 | acrylic on canvas | 80 ³⁄₈ x 81 ¹⁄₈ in / 204 x 206 cm | Detroit Institute of Arts, Detroit, MI, USA

Helen Frankenthaler (b.1928) was the inventor of Color Field painting, and her creations are among the most beautiful and poetic examples of abstraction in the genre's history. Frankenthaler, who was the youngest daughter of a justice on the New York State Supreme Court, attended New York City's leading private high school, Dalton, where she studied under the Mexican painter, Rufino Tamayo, before earning her BA from Bennington College, Vermont. She was introduced to the New York art scene through pioneering critic Clement Greenberg and her artistic mentor Hans Hoffman, and later married the Abstract painter Robert Motherwell. In 1952, Frankenthaler became known in the New York art community through *Sea and Mountains*, an enormous, luminous canvas. The ethereal beauty of Frankenthaler's abstraction derives from her signature "staining" technique, in which she paints with oil paint heavily diluted with turpentine or kerosene onto an unprepared canvas, so that the fabric soaks up colors. She termed this technique "soak stain," and it was later adopted by painters such as Morris Louis and Kenneth Noland. *The Bay* is an impressive, poetic example of her graceful compositions and elegant, impassioned, use of color. In a 1975 interview, Frankenthaler described her act of creation: "I think very often it takes ten of those over-labored efforts to produce one really beautiful wrist motion that is synchronized with your head and heart, and you have it, and therefore it looks as if it were born in a minute." **AH**

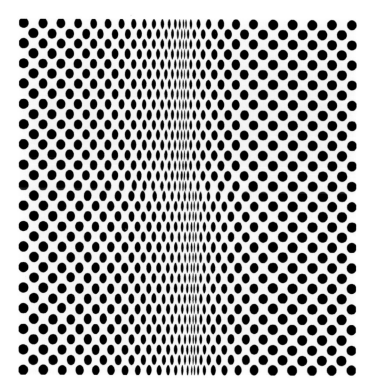

Fission | Bridget Riley

1963 | tempera on board | 35 x 33 ⅞ in / 89 x 86 cm | Museum of Modern Art, New York, NY, USA

Bridget Riley (b.1931) burst onto the London cultural scene in the early 1960s with illusionistic abstract paintings that earned her celebrity status well beyond the confines of the art world. Her monochromatic works used simple shapes such as circles, squares, or stripes, arranged in subtle, complex, repetitive patterns to create unstable optical effects. In *Fission*, a classic example of Riley's work in this period, a square covered in black dots is rendered vertiginous by progressive warping of the circles and compression of their spacing. The mind of the viewer cannot fix a stable version of the image, which constantly alters as the eyes scan the picture. The image appears to hover queasily between the painting and the viewer. Included in the 1965 New York show The Responsive

Eye, Riley's black-and-white paintings were celebrated as Op art, the next big thing after Pop art. Against the artist's wishes, her work was appropriated by the fashion industry to pattern trendy clothing. It is now clear that this initial response to Riley's painting misunderstood the seriousness and privacy of her intentions. Riley later explained her work as devoted to "the pleasures of sight." Her inspiration stemmed from a childhood in Cornwall, where the "changing seas and skies" excited her vision. The optical illusions were an attempt to create afresh the wonder of seeing, which could not be captured by a representational image. Riley has continued to pursue her artistic course without regard for the fashions of the day through more than four decades. **RG**

Standard Station, Amarillo, Texas | Ed Ruscha

1963 | oil on canvas | 65 x 121 in / 165.1 x 307.3 cm | Hood Museum of Art, Hanover, NH, USA

Born in 1937, Ed Ruscha was raised in Oklahoma City, and in 1956 moved to Los Angeles, California. There, he enrolled at the Chouinard Art Institute, a school that provided training in both commercial and fine arts. Ruscha started gaining recognition in the late 1960s, particularly with his famous "liquid words" pictures. He was then associated with the Ferus Gallery group, along with Robert Irwin, Edward Moses, and Ken Price. Ruscha also worked with photography and produced a great number of photographic art books, most made in Southern California between 1963 and 1978. His oeuvre is regarded as one of the most significant artistic precedents of Conceptualism. Influenced by Pop art, he experimented with the new language and iconography of popular culture, and *Standard Station* is emblematic of the style he developed during the 1960s. It depicts a typical American gasoline station, and uses only a few colors applied flatly to the canvas. In painting such a structured composition, with its striking architectural delineation, Ruscha enlivens what might otherwise be a banal scene. The painting is typically Pop in its melding of fine and graphic arts. "Standard" is the brand name, but here it is also a play on the standardization of modern culture and society. It also comments on the standardization of the image itself, which is streamlined and reproduced— Ruscha made a series of screen prints of this painting, now in the collections of several museums including the Museum of Modern Art in New York. **JJ**

Man Woman
Allen Jones

1963 | oil on canvas | 84 ½ x 74 ¼ in / 215 x 187 cm
Tate Collection, London, UK

In the Sixties Allen Jones (b.1937) explicitly drew from culturally unacceptable sources—John Willie's *Bizarre* magazine, Eric Stanton's bondage cartoons, brown-paper-bag-wrapped porn—all of which led to his controversial apotheosis, the 1969 life-size statues of women-as-furniture (*Chair, Hat Stand, Table*). *Man Woman* is one of a series of paintings exploring notions of transgenderism and the breaking down of sexual stereotypes. Here, Jones fuses the male and female archetypes, both headless but, in his powerful green-against-red polarizing color scheme, he subverts cliché in dressing the man in a red shirt (red being redolent of erotica: lipstick, rouge, red-light areas) against the green tones of the woman. Jones's brushwork is unmannered, loose, and free; the colors vivid and bold. He is an unapologetic sensualist, up there with Matisse and Dufy. **PH**

Celia and Her Heroes
Pauline Boty

1963 | oil on canvas | 48 x 60 in / 122 x 152 cm
Private collection

Pauline Boty (1938–66) was at the heart of London's Swinging Sixties set: an actress, she appeared as one of Sir Michael Caine's girlfriends in *Alfie* and was one of the artists featured in Ken Russell's documentary *Monitor: Pop Goes the Easel*. Boty studied stained glass at London's Royal College of Art. Her portrait of textile designer Celia Birtwell, *Celia and Her Heroes* is typical of the fashion for painting celebrities—Birtwell was at the heart of London's avant garde. Boty surrounds her subject with a painting by Blake, a portrait of Hockney, and an image of Elvis Presley, emphasizing the designer's own celebrity status, and putting a woman on a par with successful men. In a defiant gesture, Birtwell's blouse is unbuttoned to reveal her bra, but at the same time Birtwell's breasts are not revealed: she is an independent modern woman rather than the mere subject for the male gaze. **CK**

Gray and Red Composition
Serge Poliakoff

1964 | oil on canvas | 62 ¾ x 51 in / 160 x 130 cm
Musée National d'Art Moderne, Paris, France

Lock
Robert Rauschenberg

1964 | mixed media on canvas | 40 x 30 in /
101 x 76 cm | Private collection

Serge Poliakoff (1906–69) fled Moscow during the 1917 Russian Revolution and eventually settled in Paris in 1923. He was fascinated with the technical aspects of painting, especially the unique methods of color-layering showcased on the surfaces of the Egyptian sarcophagi in the British Museum, London. Poliakoff experimented with the thickness of the painted surface and engaged viscerally with the material properties of color. He prepared his own paints, almost as a homage to the Old Masters. Seemingly inspired by the Egyptian sarcophagi, in *Gray and Red Composition* he superimposes layers of contrasting blocks of color in order to obtain a heightened sense of inner luminescence and intensity. He worked to break new ground in the formal systems of color composition, and his work today holds an important place in postwar abstract painting. **AT**

From the early 1950s, Robert Rauschenberg (*b.*1925) began to create experimental works, such as the well-known work *Erased de Kooning Drawing* (1953), in which he actually erased a drawing by the Abstract Expressionist artist Willem de Kooning. In doing so, he challenged the accepted definition of art. Many other works by Rauschenberg can be associated with this aesthetic, such as the work *Lock*, made with various media including paint and magazine clippings. *Lock* is emblematic of a new style that would become one of the characteristic features of the artist's oeuvre. It was also a way to move away from Abstract Expressionism. In doing so, Rauschenberg succeeded in bridging the gap between art and life, a credo already defended by his fellow artists Andy Warhol and Jasper Johns. *Lock* reflects Rauschenberg's involvement in Pop art, which posited an alternative to Abstract Expressionism. **JJ**

Flowers | Andy Warhol

c.1964 | acrylic and silkscreen ink on canvas | 85 x 84 in | Andy Warhol Museum, Pittsburgh, PA, USA

Andy Warhol (1928–87) was a cofounder of the Pop art movement, which was in part a reaction to the hegemony of Abstract Expressionism. In his works, Warhol appropriated and explored the visual language of mass American culture. Among his most well-known works are his manufactured portraits of famous personalities, such as Marilyn Monroe, and his paintings of disasters. His New York studio, The Factory, became the birthplace for many art projects including music productions. In 1965 Warhol became the manager of the American rock band The Velvet Underground. They became the house band at The Factory and Warhol's banana design appeared on the album cover of *The Velvet Underground & Nico* in 1967. In the 1950s, Warhol turned to flowers for inspiration, doing book illustrations and early commissioned art works. *Flowers* is part of a series based on blossoming hibiscus. Through the ages, the flower has always been an iconic and powerful symbol in the history of art. With his flower series, Warhol offered his own interpretation—flat, stylized, and luridly colored. The flowers in this painting owe more to commercial advertising than to actual hibiscus. By the 1970s painting was no longer Warhol's preferred medium—most of his new flower works were screenprints. By then Warhol had become more and more concerned with the suppression of all handmade processes in favor of a "manufactured" style for which he is best known. **JJ**

Red and White Still Life | Patrick Caulfield

1964 | oil on board | 63 x 83 ⅞ in / 160 x 213 cm | Birmingham Museum and Art Gallery, Birmingham, UK

A red, white, and black patterned vase sits on a round sky-blue table. Next to it stands a blue bowl, intricately patterned with red diamonds, swirls, and dots. A tendril of green leaf motif curls around the inner rim. The three objects—table, vase, and bowl—are posed against a dramatically layered background; a shard of white pressing onto a larger, angular red shape, leaning against a densely black background littered with small ovals of red. This is a daring still life where color offsets shape, reestablishes form, and unifies the final composition in a balancing act that is as sophisticated as it is subtle. *Red and White Still Life* is a particularly striking and successful example of Patrick Caulfield's (1936–2005) art, connecting the traditional genre of still life to contemporary representation. The artist painted the work a year after graduating from the Royal College of Art in London. The Pop art movement was then well established in the United States, and Caulfield's flat aesthetic bore comparison to the stylistic explorations of the period. His choice of subject matter was never as starkly commercial as his Pop contemporaries, however, and the influence of Cubist artists such as Fernand Léger (1881–1955) and Juan Gris (1887–1927) are evident in his work. Caulfield's great economy of means and aesthetic refinement transform seemingly simple scenes, through close observation, into images of great poignancy. The glass of wine, an abandoned ashtray, the occasional figure—all are rendered in the same flat, linear style. **RW/JP**

The King of the Heart | Jean Dubuffet

1964 | oil on canvas | 38 ¼ x 51 ⅛ in / 97 x 130 cm | Private collection

Jean Dubuffet's (1901–85) tumultuous relationship with painting reflected his critical attitude toward Western art-making techniques. He found the principles of the formal academy oppressive and took two hiatuses from painting to join his family wine business. The Frenchman's triumphant return to paint was marked by the concurrent postwar devastation that drove him toward a primitive vision that manifested itself in his paintings. From the *Hourloupe* cycle that occupied him through the 1960s, *The King of the Heart* is characterized by jigsaw pieces that seem to simultaneously advance and recede. The series was inspired by doodles that Dubuffet made with a ballpoint pen while talking on the telephone. The arbitrary and restrictive palette of red, blue, and

black complicates the process of discerning the individual elements within the larger framework. Each figure and action is perceived as existing in both a real and imagined visual plane, ultimately suggesting that the real world may in fact be illusionary. In the aftermath of the war, Dubuffet relied on the primitive values of instinct, madness, and passion to counteract the trauma created in the modern world. He felt that the raw energy he derived from earlier historical periods was a necessary articulation in his contemporary moment. An emphasis on primal culture inspired the subversive artist to reject the trends of his contemporaries and project the universal truths that he considered best expressed through both insanity and imagination. **MG**

The Schmidt Family | Gerhard Richter

1964 | oil on canvas | 49 x 51 in / 125 x 130 cm | Hamburger Kunsthalle, Hamburg, Germany

Gerhard Richter (*b.*1932), was born in Dresden, Germany, and joined the Hitler Youth as a child. His experiences made him wary of political fanaticism, and he has remained detached from contemporary artistic movements, although some of his work can sometimes be linked to Abstract Expressionism, Pop art, monochrome painting, and Photorealism. As a student he started painting from photographic sources, but whereas the Photorealists depict reality with the precision and sharp focus of a camera, Richter blurs the images, transforming them into paintings that make a personal statement. *The Schmidt Family* is based on a typical 1960s family photo, but the blurring of outlines and forms renders the image slightly disturbing. The father and son merge into a two-headed body, while the cushion behind them becomes a grotesque animal, its claw suggested by the son's fuzzy hand. Stripped of sharp definition, the family members' poses attract attention—the father's legs are crossed away from his wife, and as she looks toward the family, he looks forward, caught in the moment of saying something to make the boys laugh. But why must laughter be provoked, and why does the wife sit tentatively on the sofa? Richter heightens light and shade, intensifying the feeling of unease. This image was created in 1960s postwar Germany—a time of prosperity and ongoing reconstruction, when a collective silence fell over the past. Richter's reinvention of a family snapshot discusses the past's relevance to the present. **SH/MC**

Homage to the Square: Joy | Josef Albers

1964 | oil on wood fiberboard | 30 x 30 in / 76 x 76 cm | Private collection

The many hundreds of works in the *Homage to the Square* series by Josef Albers (1888–1976) conform to a similar pattern—all are based around either three or four squares of solid color. These works were produced in conditions that have been described as similar to those of a scientific laboratory. Albers set up a specific arrangement of florescent lights in his studio, always ensuring that the alternation of warm and cool lights was kept in the same order, so he could vary the lighting he worked by. Albers began his work by priming the rough side of a panel of wood fiberboard known as masonite. The priming would be done with several coats of white liquitex or chalk. On top of this he would add paint straight from the tube, choosing not to mix his colors. The paint was applied with a palette knife and the white background caused the colors to glow. Albers varied his technique by occasionally changing his pattern as to which area he would begin working on first (though he would usually begin in the middle and work outward). Despite this obsessive routine, the paintings in the *Homage to the Square* series are not homogeneous—not only are the colors varied, but the style of the paintings differs from one to another. Albers's intention was to discover how many times the same technique could be used to create a range of individual paintings. He also experimented with reworking *Homage to the Square* in other media, including tapestry and printmaking. Albers wrote a much-praised book, *Interaction of Color* in 1963. **LH**

The End of Madame Gardenia | Jacques Monory

1964 | oil on canvas, wood, plexiglass | 110 x 126 in / 280 x 320 cm | Musée des Beaux-Arts, Pau, France

Jacques Monory (*b*.1944) worked for ten years as an art director in Paris, which helped to form his highly charged, graphic style of painting. He experimented with color photography collages, lithographs, and 16mm films before creating a series of paintings in the early 1960s that defined his cold, figurative narratives. Despite his cruel, modern themes—often featuring guns and other symbols of power—his images, rendered with a disturbingly commercial cleanliness, are pleasing overall. His figures are juxtaposed against a playful color scheme that verges on technicolor, recalling the vivid scale of early polaroids or film chemicals. *The End of Madame Gardenia* is dominated by the eponymous flower, known for its sweet, heady perfume. Its errant, pink petals resemble drops of blood or falling tears. A woman's black-and-white image, charged with perfection as if taken from a contemporary fashion magazine, is cracked in pieces like shrapnel, suggesting a breach of sanity. With the city architecture behind her, she symbolizes the European lady—refined, beautiful, but often fractured by loneliness. A gun on the table suggests suicide and the black dots scattered across the painting look like bullet holes. The well-kept, ideal French wife, as presented in Gustave Flaubert's *Madame Bovary*, has her neurosis deconstructed into a basic, bold palette of white, pink, and black. With the visual vocabulary of his American Pop art contemporaries, Monory creates a mythology of the everyday, evoking characters that are both everyone and no one. **SWW**

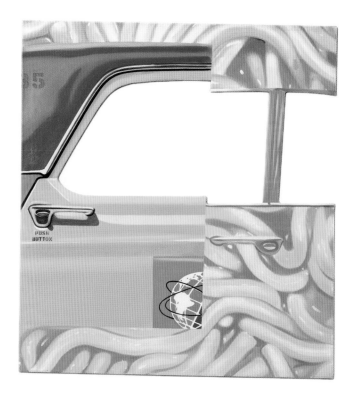

The Friction Disappears | James Rosenquist

1965 | oil on canvas | 48 x 44 in / 122 x 112 cm | Smithsonian American Art Museum, Washington, DC, USA

American consumer culture in the 1950s inspired Pop artists to represent commercial products and advertising images of everyday life in a bright, energetic style. Early in his career, James Rosenquist (b.1933) painted commercial billboards in Times Square, New York, but began creating large-scale studio paintings in 1960. With clever, subversive comments on affluence, mass production, and the sexualization of selling, the artist represents the modern divorce from nature as a rather upbeat affair. More intimate than political, *The Friction Disappears* overlaps product fragments of a typical, everyday, safe, and clean suburban life. Rosenquist juxtaposes two products that represent the ease of modernity and are a trademark of consumer societies: prepared, refined food and the automobile.

The thick, smooth noodles on the upper left effortlessly lend themselves to the bright red, canned spaghetti sauce applied to the right fragment. The ultimate leisure product, the automobile, adds structure to the looping noodles. Friction equals atomic energy—in the painting an atomic globe seems to be disappearing amid the excess of cultural production. A commercially refined life of gloss and ease provides, above all, a life without friction. Rosenquist is known for his skillful manipulation of scale, color, and repetition of shapes to recreate the impulse and fascination of buying new things. With extreme realism and vast size, Rosenquist turns consumer products into abstraction, entering and expanding the popular mindset that equally turns modern economies. **SWW**

Two Boys in the Pool, Hollywood | David Hockney

1965 | acrylic on canvas | Private collection

In the 1960s, David Hockney (*b.*1937) moved to Los Angeles, and began painting the pleasures of a carefree southern California existence: sun-drenched gardens, swimming pools, and boys. Hockney switched from oil to acrylic paint to create these images, and like *Two Boys in the Pool, Hollywood*, they tend to have a graphical quality. The painting's stylized perspective and strong parallel lines recall Japanese prints, as does the handling of the surfaces as areas of pure color and pattern. The abstraction of the swimming pool into a psychedelic design, contained squarely within the austere composition, illustrates Hockney's competence as a graphic artist—not to mention the artist's sense of humor. A longer look at the painting, however, shows that the treatment of

the forms is not uniform; Hockney has painted the skin of the pair emerging from the pool with a level of detail and sensitivity absent from the rest of the image—and the men are without a doubt the focus of attention. The perspective seems to suggest an observer who has caught the moment from an upper-story window; the framing of the scene reinforces the sense of voyeurism. Hockney has been criticized for the unabashedly erotic choice and treatment of his subject. The artist responds by highlighting the intrinsic role that pleasure plays in our appreciation of painting. On his subject matter, Hockney states, "Cézanne's apples are lovely and very special, but what finally can compare to the image of another human being?" **AR**

Red Nude | Karel Appel

1965 | oil on canvas | 76 x 51 in / 195 x 130 cm | Museum voor Schone Kunsten, Ghent, Belgium

The influential Dutch abstract painter Karel Appel (1921–2006) was an energetic innovator, ceaselessly seeking a new expression for his bold artistic ideals and working with a wide range of media and techniques. Though his style changed during his long career he remained true to the essential Expressionist and abstract concept behind his work, which can be broadly characterized by his use of vigorous brushwork and expressionistic color. He trained at the Academy in Amsterdam from 1940 to 1943 during which time he met and befriended Corneille, another leading Dutch artist of the modern age. He drew on primitive symbols, folk art, and children's painting for inspiration and was influenced by Matisse, Klee, Miró, and Picasso. By the time he painted *Red Nude*, Appel's

childlike forms with simple, structured composition had evolved into a more frenetic and passionate expression. This painting has a vibrant buzz created through the explosion of line and color that at first appears random, but on examination reveals the abstracted form of a female nude. Appel was also inspired by jazz music, and there is a resonance of the vibrancy and soul of this music apparent in this image. During the period that Appel painted *Red Nude* he was also working on three-dimensional paintings and sculptures and used mediums as diverse as wood, ceramic, plastic, and polyester. It was a time of enormous artistic diversity and energy for the artist, and this quality of unbridled creativity remains most apparent in his work. **TP**

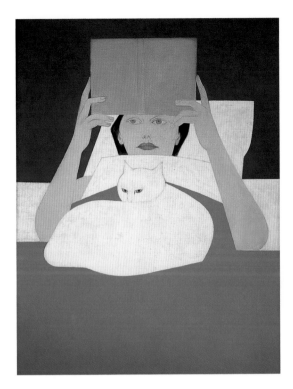

Woman Reading | Will Barnet

1965 | oil on canvas | 45 x 35 in / 114.3 x 88.9 cm | Private collection

In 1919 at age eight, Will Barnet (*b*.1911) decided he wanted to be an artist and soon after set up a studio in the basement of his childhood home in Beverly, Massachusetts. There he spent hours drawing and painting portraits of his family and pets, placing the light source at the left to emulate his favorite painter Rembrandt van Rijn. By the age of twenty-one, Barnet had completed several years of strict academic training in Boston and had moved to Manhattan. There he studied lithography with Charles Locke and painting with Stuart Davis at the Art Students' League and soon emerged as their youngest master printer and instructor of graphic arts, then of painting. Considered one of Barnet's master works, *Woman Reading*, a study of his wife Elena with the family cat, exemplifies his inimitable style of combining poetic figuration with graphic abstraction in order to create a modern humanistic portrait. Barnet explores, deconstructs, and then reinvents artistic traditions, ultimately producing an image so refined it is reduced to the very essence of emotional and visual intensity. Barnet achieves this powerful effect by constructing a complex composition of monumental shapes of bold, flat color juxtaposed vertically and horizontally on the canvas—while maintaining the spiritual grace and structural integrity of the subjects. For many decades, Will Barnet has influenced American art as a painter, printmaker, and teacher with arguably his greatest contribution being his redefinition of the principles of abstract composition and the image. **SA**

War | Marc Chagall

1964–66 | oil on canvas | 64 x 91 in / 163 x 231 cm | Kunsthaus, Zürich, Switzerland

Marc Chagall (1887–1985) was born in Belarus, the eldest of nine children in a close-knit Jewish family. This was a happy though impoverished period in his life. He moved to Paris when he was twenty-three, where he was enthused by what he saw at the Louvre. Mixing those ideas with inspiration from his early life, he began painting biblical themes using thick, colorful paint. He became involved with avant-garde currents in Paris, including Cubism and Fauvism, but never wholly surrendered his style. During World War I, he was called to military service, but to avoid serving at the Front, he worked in an office in St. Petersburg. In 1922, he returned to Paris and by World War II he had become a French citizen, although he spent most of the war in America. Themes of flight and exile appear in this painting, which Chagall began almost twenty years after World War II. It took him two years to complete. A rickety and overloaded cart is slowly leaving the burning city. A man is plodding along behind the cart, a sack over his shoulder, saving his worldly goods from the flames. Most of the people cling to each other in despair, while the people and animals that have remained in the city are helplessly at the mercy of the intense blaze. Jesus is on the Cross to the right of the painting and a huge white lamb emerges from the ground, representing the sacrifice of both Jesus and the innocent people. Chagall, who often used animals as symbols in his work, is portraying blameless people's dreadful plight during the war, bestowing on them the status of martyrs. **SH**

Peinture aux Formes Indéfinies | Daniel Buren

1966 | painted fabric | Private collection

Contemporary French artist Daniel Buren (*b.*1938) is famous for his signature stripes that he has incorporated in his work since the early 1960s. Buren's legacy is his site-specific works created *in situ*. His interest in integrating art within the praxis of life is exaggerated by his strategic placement of the stripe pattern within the city landscape. He has adorned public spaces ranging from stairwells to street billboards and buses. One of his most controversial projects was his transformation of the Palais Royale in 1986 in which he created *Les Deux Plateaux* showcasing 260 short, striped columns in the courtyard of the palace. In the mid sixties, Buren began making striped paintings that were formed by an alternating pattern of white stripes juxtaposed with one additional color, such as the red in this painting. Buren used ready-made linen canvases from Marche Saint-Pierre, a Parisian textiles market, that were pre-printed and resembled mass produced awnings. His artistic choices are governed by a strong contrasting palette and sharp geometric lines with stripe widths measuring a uniform 3 ⅛ inches, a scale that he patented. Buren's conceptual goal was to eliminate all illusionary and expressive pictorial elements. He achieved this minimalist canon through his regulated and precise style. Buren defied the conventional notions of painting. His trademark stripes, although seemingly anonymous because of their striking simplicity, register as a bold statement associated directly with his artistic persona. **MG**

SS Amsterdam in Front of Rotterdam | Malcolm Morley

1966 | liquitex on canvas | 64 x 84 in / 163 x 213 cm | Private collection

Malcolm Morley (b.1931), the inaugural winner of the Turner Prize in 1984, discovered art while serving a three-year stint in Wormwood Scrubs prison for petty theft. After his release he studied art in London, but a 1956 exhibition of Abstract Expressionism at the Tate led him to become obsessed with that style and he moved to Manhattan to be closer to the New York school of painters. He began to delve into his turbulent childhood and produced images inspired by his childhood memories of the Blitz. Over time, his interest in Abstraction waned and he returned to the representational images that had shaped his consciousness. His early exposure to war was the foundation for a subsequent series of paintings with military motifs. Bombed-out cities,

the Royal Navy, and model airplanes were the themes of his bright, colorful, photorealist work, which he termed "Superrealism." Morley borrowed these images from travel brochures, calendars, and old paintings. In the 1960s, he developed a method of transferring photographs to canvas, using a grid system. SS Amsterdam in Front of Rotterdam is an early example. This picture was taken from a brochure and painted square by square while the rest of the painting was covered up. The canvas was often flipped as he painted each section—in effect, he painted each square in an abstract way to produce a representational image. The resulting painting is a hyperrealistic, meticulously executed, large, vibrant canvas full of light and movement. **AH**

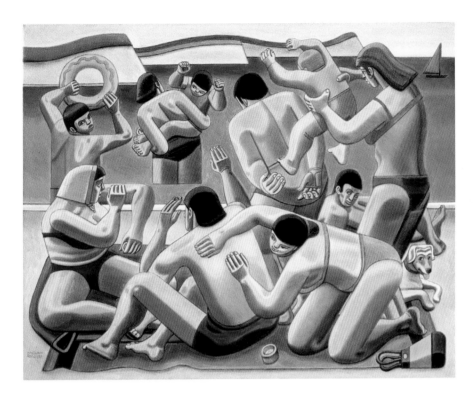

The Seaside | William Patrick Roberts

*c.*1966 | oil on canvas | 24 x 30 in / 61 x 76.2 cm | Arts Council Collection, Hayward Gallery, London, UK

English painter William Patrick Roberts (1895–1980) was born a working-class Londoner, and started out as an apprentice draughtsman in an advertising firm with the aim of becoming a poster designer. He then attended evening classes at London's St. Martin's School of Art, and won a scholarship to the Slade School of Art at the age of fifteen. When he left three years later he traveled to France and Italy, and became interested in Cubism. He went on to become a founding member of the British Vorticist movement. During World War I he served in the military before being commissioned as an official war artist. After the war he concentrated on painting portraits and scenes of urban life, often with a satirical edge, and became known as an English Cubist. *The Seaside* is typical of his works depicting the lives of the working class. With the white cliffs of Dover in the background, this can only be England. It is a masterpiece of social observation of a 1960s English family holidaying at the seaside. The flat, bulky shapes of his Cubist style give his figures a sculptural quality in this portrait of several generations of one family. He places the family within their social context: the older woman on the left is wearing a scarf, typical attire for a working-class mother at that time, and he wittily crams the family together on one beach towel. His early training as a draughtsman is evident in the posterlike vivid colors, and the dynamic cohesion of the figures that tumble across the canvas like a group sculpture depicts the nobility of the apparently ordinary. **CK**

Elegy to the Spanish Republic, 108 | Robert Motherwell

1965–67 | oil on canvas | 81 ⁷⁄₈ x 138 ¼ in / 208 x 351 cm | Museum of Modern Art, New York, NY, USA

Robert Motherwell (1915–91) was in his early twenties when the Spanish Civil War began in 1936. The three-year conflict, which witnessed more than half a million casualties and the first air-bombings of civilians, had a profound effect on the intellectuals of his generation. Intended as a lamentation for the victims of that war, Motherwell's series of *Elegies* confront human suffering through a highly formal, abstract, visual language. Picasso famously made his own response to the same war with *Guernica*. *Elegy to the Spanish Republic, 108*, one of the largest paintings in the series that consists of more than one hundred works, is composed from the recurring motif of black, irregular, ovoid shapes against vertical bands or rectangles on a white field. Standing in the pictorial field rather than appearing as an absence—and marked by rhythm and a subtle interaction of color—the black forms are set against suggested earth tones. Motherwell's use of black as a color stems from a long tradition that includes Velázquez and Manet. Motherwell's painting lends a richness of suggestion to purely abstract forms. It has been proposed, for example, that the large, black shapes in the series make reference to the Spanish custom of displaying the dead bull's testicles after a bullfight. In bringing such a literary weight to what is a disciplined meditation on a troubling event, Motherwell suggested that artists could use the terse visual language of abstraction to make work of remarkable depth and humanity, acting as keen witnesses to the conflicting forces in it. **JR**

A Bigger Splash | David Hockney

1967 | acrylic on canvas | 95 ½ x 96 in / 242.5 x 243.5 cm | Private collection

David Hockney's (*b.*1937) colleague and critic R.B. Kitaj commented, "It is a rare event in our modern art when a sense of place is achieved at the level of very fine painting." Kitaj noted Hockney's work of the 1960s as an outstanding contemporary example, alongside Edward Hopper's images of 1940s America. *A Bigger Splash* captures the desolation of a southwestern American midday outside a Modernist California home. The sense of stillness is reinforced by the strong horizontals and verticals of the composition. Hockney created the flat, rectilinear shapes by masking the canvas and applying the acrylic paint with rollers. Human presence is almost entirely absent both from the canvas and from the scene itself. The only element interrupting the painting's discipline is the diving board jutting diagonally into the frame and, of course, the splash. The subject of the painting announces himself with a chaotic explosion of white but remains, nevertheless, submerged by the calm blue surface. However, the painting's central themes tend to obscure its often surprising details. The two palm trees in the background, which appear either strangely proportioned or exceedingly far away, are a humorous addition. The splash itself was added on top of the flat blue surface of the pool, using small brushes. Hockney evidently enjoyed himself, saying "I loved the idea of painting this thing that lasts for two seconds. It takes me two weeks to paint this event." The immediacy of its appeal has made this vibrant and pleasing painting an icon of Pop art as well as of southern California. **AR**

The Presidential Family | Fernando Botero

1967 | oil on canvas | 80 ⅛ x 77 ¼ in / 203.5 x 196 cm | Museum of Modern Art, New York, NY, USA

Influenced by Mexican muralist Diego Rivera's volumetric forms, Colombian artist Fernando Botero (b.1932) produced exaggerated, inflated human figures and still lifes. Botero experimented with distorted proportion and oversized shapes to enhance the sensuality of his forms or to emphasize the comic nature of his characters. *The Presidential Family* confirms Botero's satirical attitude toward the stereotypical Latin-American, upper-class families in which sons are destined to become politicians, members of the military, or of the Church. Standing in the foreground is the mother wearing a fox stole as an indicator of her wealth; sitting to the left is the grandmother with the youngest member of the family sitting on her lap. Both mother and grandmother stare impassively at the child who will soon be at the age to marry, while the grandmother watches over the virtue of the young girl. As with many of Botero's works, *The Presidential Family* is a parody of well-known works of art. It has the formal composition of Goya's *Family of Carlos IV* (1800) and parodies the artist's self-portrait in Velázquez's *Las Meninas* (1656), replacing the family dog in the latter with a cat. Botero's use of the crawling snake at the bottom of the painting is a brash reference to medieval iconography, and is an omen of trouble to come. The use of bright, flat colors in Botero's work is a partial homage to Latin-American popular folk art but also serves to lighten his political and social subject matter that condemns greed and corruption. **RJ**

Untitled | Mark Rothko

1967 | oil on canvas | 68 ⅛ x 60 ¼ in / 173 x 153 cm | Private collection

Mark Rothko (1903–70) is undoubtedly one of the most important American painters of the twentieth century. From 1947 to 1949, he taught at the California School of Fine Arts, along with Clyfford Still. Since then, he moved progressively toward a total Abstract style, eliminating any kind of representational figures in his work. In 1948, he founded The Subjects of the Artists, an independent art school, with fellow artists Robert Motherwell, William Baziotes, and Barnett Newman. In 1959, Rothko was commissioned to paint a series of works for the Four Seasons Restaurant in New York's Seagram Building, designed by Mies van der Rohe and Philip Johnson. But he later withdrew from the project, considering the location inappropriate. The paintings are now part of London's Tate Collection. *Untitled* dates from Rothko's mature period, in which he used darker tones than he had earlier in his career. Critics and historians have seen this choice as a reflection of his fragile mental health—he committed suicide three years after painting this work. Looking at the picture, the viewer can easily be overwhelmed by a sense of melancholy suggested by the large blocks of somber colors. The predominant pink and red colors, usually associated with brightness, do not alleviate the general impression of darkness, which is reinforced by the deep black paint in the bottom part of the image. Rothko stressed that even though this kind of work looked "abstract," he never stopped depicting the human figure—not in terms of figurative language, but by the means of shapes and symbols. **JJ**

The Lord Mayor's Reception | Michael Andrews

1965–68 | oil, screened photograph on canvas | 84 x 84 in | Norwich Castle Museum, Norwich, UK

Michael Andrews (1928–98) began his studies at the Slade School of Fine Art, London, under William Coldstream (known for imparting to his life class students a rigorous system of measuring). Andrews followed his time at the Slade with a brief spell in Italy. From 1959 he taught at Slade and at the Chelsea School of Art. In the 1960s, Andrews began a series of works depicting parties, among which is *The Lord Mayor's Reception in Norwich Castle Keep*, which he began in 1965 and completed in 1968. As the title suggests, the scene features a reception for the Lord Mayor in the Great Hall of Norwich Castle. Andrews chose to look down on the party from the upstairs gallery. Faces of local dignitaries slip in and out of focus, some engaged in conversation, others caught

in a moment of reflection, gazing up and out toward the viewer. A group of five waitresses hangs back to the left of the painting's mid-ground, waiting to weave their way among the crowd serving drinks and refilling glasses. The high viewpoint lends a sense of antlike activity to the gathering beneath, and the mixed media of oil and screened photograph enables Andrews to freeze the moment in time while losing nothing of the excitement of the scene—delivered by swift strokes of his brush and pen. Andrews's *Party* series was to give way to aerial scenes in the 1970s *Lights* series. A visit to Ayers Rock in 1983 was to make a great impression on his painting, but in later years, the last of his works were inspired by scenes from London and Scotland. **JN**

Agbatana II | Frank Stella

1968 | polymer on canvas | 120 x 180 ¼ in | Musée d'Art Moderne de Saint-Etienne-Métropole, France

Agbatana II is one of a series of wall-size paintings by American Frank Stella (*b*.1936). It is known as the *Protractor* series because the shapes of the paintings are based on the instrument used to measure and draw angles. The titles of the paintings refer to cities of the ancient Middle East and to Islamic architectural features—a less abstract source of inspiration. Agbatana (better known as Ecbatana) was the capital of the ancient Persian empire and was reputedly built to a circular plan. This was the first time Stella, by then a leading Minimalist abstract artist, had used curves in his work and he went about it in a typically systematic fashion. The artist planned the series as thirty-one different protractor-based shapes, each painted in three versions using different decorative surface patterns—the interlace, the rainbow, and the fan. *Agbatana II* is the "rainbow" version of the Agbatana shape. It is in four framed sections with three sets of eight concentric semicircles—the rainbows. Stella insisted on flat canvases, with no illusion of receding space, yet the eye inevitably sees the semicircles as running behind the frames and, in places, behind one another. Applied in a single coat, the paint creates a delicate insubstantial impression despite the psychedelic brilliance of the fluorescent paint. The overall effect is architectural, with the vaulting circles anchored to the horizontal and vertical straight lines. It is an overwhelmingly joyous, materialistic painting, its lucid physical presence unsullied by turbid emotions. **RG**

Portrait of George Dyer in a Mirror | Francis Bacon

1968 | oil on canvas | 78 x 58 in / 198 x 147.5 cm | Museo Thyssen-Bornemisza, Madrid, Spain

Francis Bacon (1909–92) spent his early years moving between England and Ireland, and had a troubled family life, which instilled in him a strong sense of displacement. He lived for a short time in Berlin and Paris, where he decided to become a painter, but was mainly based in London. The self-educated artist increasingly turned to painting dark, emotional, and unsettling subject matter with existential themes, and he gained recognition in the postwar years. Recurrent preoccupations in his work include war, raw meat, political and sexual power, and decapitation. Bacon also revived and subverted the use of the triptych, which, in the history of Christian iconography, emphasized the omnipresence of the Holy Trinity. This is an image of Bacon's lover and muse, George

Dyer, who Bacon claimed to have met when Dyer was robbing his house. The figure of Dyer, dressed in a gangster's lounge suit, is deformed and severed, the reflection of his face fractured in the mirror. The portrait confronts the viewer with the sexual nature of the painter's relation to the subject—it has been suggested that the splashes of white paint represent semen. An additional series of naked portraits of Dyer reveals the intimacy of their union. Here, Dyer looks askance at his own image, reflecting his narcissistic behavior, and the sense of isolation and detachment Bacon felt in their often stormy relationship. Dyer committed suicide in Paris on the eve of the artist's major retrospective at the Grand Palais. His broken face here foreshadows his early demise. **SP/KM**

Mornington Crescent, Winter | Frank Auerbach

1967–69 | oil on board | 45 x 55 in / 114.5 x 140.5 cm | Private collection

Frank Auerbach's (b.1931) first major retrospective took place in 1978 at the Hayward Gallery, London. Since then, Auerbach's works have been exhibited in many major international art venues. He represented Great Britain at the Venice Biennale in 1986, where he shared the Golden Lion prize with Sigmar Polke. His most recent exhibitions were held at London's Royal Academy (2001), the Scottish National Gallery of Modern Art (2002), and Marlborough Fine Art, London (2004). Auerbach is represented in many museum collections such as the Art Institute of Chicago, the Metropolitan Museum of Art and the Museum of Modern Art in New York, and the National Portrait Gallery and Tate Gallery in London. Indisputably one of the most established painters of our time, Auerbach

is associated with the British artists Lucian Freud and Francis Bacon. Mornington Crescent, Winter intimidates the viewer with its pulsating architecture. This urban street scene is one of numerous works on the same theme painted by Auerbach. The composition of this chaotic cityscape relies on heavy lines, as well as a fascinating struggle between dark and bright colors. One cannot be certain of the origin of the brilliant light that streams through the windows of the prominent building in the background. In painting this, Auerbach succeeds in producing a disturbing scene that gives the impression of fire and chaos. Typical of Auerbach's style from that period, this painting wears an extremely thick impasto that makes it look almost like a sculptural relief. **JJ**

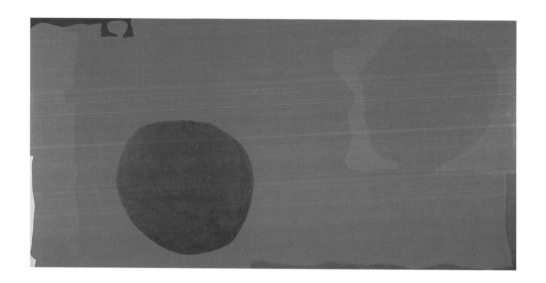

Cadmium with Violet, Scarlet, Emerald, Lemon and Venetian: 1969
Patrick Heron

1969 | oil on canvas | 77 x 149 in / 198 x 379 cm | Tate Collection, London, UK

Patrick Heron (1920–99) resisted the drive toward abstraction in the 1950s until the end of the decade, when he started producing canvases composed of horizontal blocks of color. Before then, he had been making muddled and often muddy Cubist images. But once he cleared his palette, he began incorporating other shapes and more complex compositions, and produced some of the genre's most moving and magnificent canvases. Circles and circular forms became his signature, but color was his obvious area of interest. His balletic balancing of contrasting colors far surpassed other Abstract painters and his technique created the illusion of soft textures and pliant surfaces. As a young man, Heron worked as a textile designer for his father's firm. His understanding of design and fabric is evident in his method of composing the beautiful, rich patches of pure color saturating his canvases. *Cadmium with Violet, Scarlet, Emerald, Lemon and Venetian: 1969* is a perfect example of how Heron's early intimacy with textiles informed his mature work. The painting gives the impression of being a silkscreen, as the color is absorbed into the canvas, allowing the reds, greens, and purples to meld together, yet still arrest the eye. Heron published extensively as a critic, but temporarily stopped writing criticism once he began painting Abstraction. Writing arguably hobbled Heron's creativity and his ability to emote on canvas. His painting blossomed after he broke from criticism, as this extraordinary work testifies. **AH**

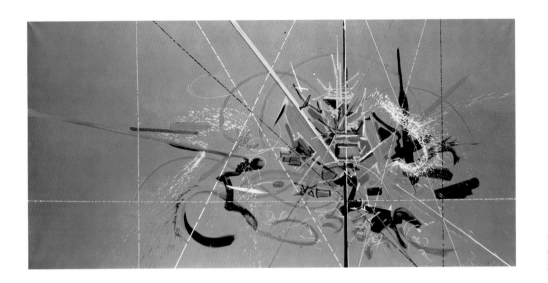

Homage to Monsieur de Vauban
Georges Mathieu

1969 | oil on canvas | 116 x 236 ¼ in / 295 x 600 cm | Musée d'Unterlinden, Colmar, France

Georges Mathieu, born in 1921 in Boulogne-sur-Mer near Calais, France, was a precursor and pioneer of the kind of performance or body art that would become prevalent in the 1960s, although his preferred medium was the more traditional paint on canvas. Unlike most of his contemporary American "Action Painters", such as Jackson Pollock, Mathieu relished the public demonstration of his art, defining the process of painting itself as so "interesting and exciting" as to be worthy of exhibition itself. He could frequently be found flinging paint in front of an audience while sporting a ridiculous mustache or dressed in outlandish, futuristic costumes. The intuitive gestures and free-form production of his pictures were often contradicted by their very specific, historical titles, as in *Homage to Monsieur de Vauban*, which refers to the French seventeenth century architect Sébastien Le Prestre de Vauban. In fact, for many of his public performances he would re-enact famous historical scenes, even incorporating carefully researched details by initiating the painting at the same time of day as the battle was waged. A self-taught artist, he drew his calligraphic style from the random results of the kind of automatic writing advocated by the Surrealists and from the 1950s' abstract painting of Hans Hartung and Franz Kline. He became a leading exponent of a loose, expressive style of painting dubbed *Tachisme* or "Art Informel" that had a wide-ranging influence on the Japanese Gutai Group, the Vienna Actionists, and Yves Klein. **OW**

Our Grandparents | Jorge González Camarena

1960–70 | oil on canvas | Private collection

Our Grandparents addresses the ongoing and complex issue of Mexican identity through a visual exploration of the region's clashing Latin American ancestry. Mexicans are born into a culture that was shaped by the forces of colonial oppression. Jorge González Camarena's (1908–80) startling composition *Our Grandparents* addresses the dual— and, in many ways, contradictory—nature of Mexican consciousness: half-Spanish conquistador, half-Aztec Indian; oppressor and oppressed. Abandoning the traditional Realist roots characteristic of much Mexican art, Jalisco-born Camarena has opted for deeply symbolic magic-realism to deal with such a personal subject matter; his sympathies are thinly disguised. The decrepit state of the Spanish soldier's decaying face—little more than a skull—and his rusty, bullet-riddled helmet point at a diminishing European influence struggling for relevance in the modern Mexican mind. By way of contrast, the powerful and forceful lateral projection of the chiseled Aztec profile seems to highlight the ascendant, defiant, mystical power of Mexico's indigenous legacy. The feathered headdress and animist details point to the ceremonial and ritualistic aspects of a unique culture—at once poignant and terrible—lost in the mists of time. The painting's composition is reminiscent of Janus, the two-headed Roman god, who symbolized transitions. Camerana uses strong fiery and earthy tones to convey the ongoing struggle faced by Mexicans in laying their country's turbulent past to rest. **AA**

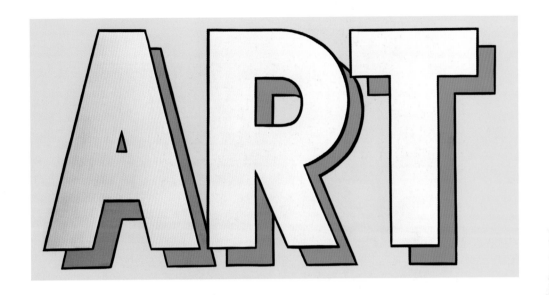

Art | Edward Ruscha

*c.*1970 | acrylic on canvas | Private collection

The American painter Edward (Ed) Ruscha (*b.*1937) is aligned with Pop artists such as Andy Warhol and Roy Lichtenstein. Reacting against the heavy textured surfaces and the intense brushstrokes of the Abstract Expressionist works, the Pop artists advocated a new art style that was inspired by commercial mechanical reproduction. Along with his fellow artists, Ruscha took inspiration from popular culture such as magazines and comic books. In *Art* Ruscha employs his particular idiom, practiced by him since the 1960s, of painting a large, isolated word with a bright monochrome background. This painting is a bold appropriation of the word—and, therefore, the concept of—"art." Retreating from a traditional conception of art and its quasi-divine *chef d'oeuvres,*

the composition of this image is purposefully simple and looks like an industrial product. The provocative use of words to make us question the meaning of art has its precedents—Marcel Duchamp's readymades is one significant example. Ruscha's image stands as a complex conceptual assessment on the identity of "art" while blurring the distinctions between an object and its sign. As well as questioning the nature of art, *Art* strongly reaffirms art's commercial value. Indeed, Ruscha seems to have only needed to put his "label" on the canvas to turn his painting into a valuable commodity, the buyer becoming part of the game. Ruscha's work remains popular, and in 2002 the Museo Nacional Centro de Arte in Madrid, Spain, organized an important exhibition of his works. **JJ**

Las Meninas, 1970 | Equipo Crónica

1970 | acrylic on canvas | 78 ¾ x 78 ¾ in / 200 x 200 cm | Fundación Juan March, Madrid, Spain

Born in Valencia, Spain, Manuel (Manolo) Valdés (*b*.1942) began training as a painter at the age of fifteen when he spent two years at the Fine Arts Academy of San Carlos in Valencia. In 1964 Valdés, along with Rafael Solbes (1940–81) and Joan Toledo, formed an artistic team called *Equipo Crónica*. Valdés has now emerged as a unique artist in his own right, who fuses and reinvents traditional techniques, styles, and even specific works of art. He does this through a wide variety of media such as drawing, painting, sculpture, collage, and printmaking. His encyclopedic knowledge of art history enables him to draw on numerous influences and reconfigure them for a modern audience. He is often startling in his bold use of familiar imagery to make a new point. *Las Meninas*

(*The Maids of Honor*) is a reworking of the famous painting by Velázquez, which has influenced many artists with its play on the nature of an artist's work. Valdés has since made *Las Meninas* into a modern icon, painting, drawing, and sculpting details of it over and over again. In this version, the princess and her imploring maids are removed from their seventeenth-century palace and placed in a 1960s-style living room with a collection of plastic toys. Valdés and Solbes are perhaps inviting us to assign significance to the ball and the toy duck as critics have been assigning significance to every element of Velázquez's painting over the centuries. The point is that the original enigma created by Velázquez cannot be solved by analysis, only by intuition. **TS**

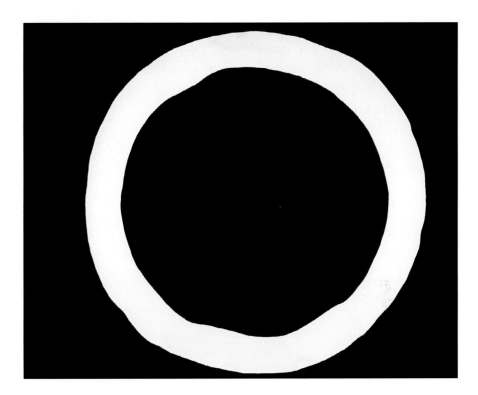

To Martha's Memory | Jiro Yoshihara

1970 | oil on canvas | 28 ¾ x 36 ¼ in / 73 x 92 cm | Albright-Knox Art Gallery, Buffalo, NY, USA

After earning his fortune as an industrialist, Jiro Yoshihara (1905–72) taught himself to paint and became one of Japan's first abstract painters. His work hangs in many international collections all over the world. In 1954 he founded and funded the Gutai Group, a circle of avant-garde performance artists and painters based in Osaka. Some of the "happenings" the Gutai Group staged would involve dancers carrying paper screens into public areas and shredding and jumping through them impromptu. In the 1950s Yoshihara began to exhibit with midtown Manhattan's Martha Jackson Gallery. Jackson had been born into the prominent Kellogg family, but was hardly a pampered socialite. Instead she attended the intellectually rigorous all-women's Smith College and worked at what is now known as the Albright-Knox Art Gallery (that owns most of her private collection). After she married her second husband, she began avidly collecting art, met and befriended artists such as John Marin, Reginald Marsh, Hans Hoffman, Franz Kline, and Jackson Pollock, and established her iconoclastic art gallery in New York in 1953. Part of Martha Jackson's mission was to exhibit works by emerging Abstract Expressionist and Pop artists, especially those still unknown in the United States. Yoshihara was one of her proudest discoveries. After her death in 1969, several artists in her gallery's roster created memorial art, but Yoshihara's jagged white circle on a black background was perhaps the purest representation of her minimalist aesthetic. **AH**

Travels of an Old Tingari Man | Ronnie Tjampitjinpa

1970 | acrylic on linen | 60 ¼ x 48 in / 153 x 122 cm | Private collection

Australian Aborigines have produced many of the country's most respected artists. The power of their work lies in the narrative and in the way in which it reflects some of their ancient traditions. Aboriginal belief focuses on immortal ancestor spirits; the Tingari are one of these groups of ancestral beings, who brought law and culture to the people of the western desert. For thousands of years, the Aborigines have communicated with their ancestors through art and ritual to invoke their protection and blessings. Ronnie Tjampitjinpa was born around 1943 in Western Australia. He started painting in about 1970, following the Pintupi style, which involves strong circles joined together by connecting lines that relate to the people, the country, and Dreamtime. This latter is a mystical part of Aboriginal culture, which is unlike anything in western beliefs as it includes the story of many things that have happened, how the universe came to be, how human beings were created, and how the Creator intended humans to function within the cosmos. Tjampitjinpa's depiction of Tingari cycles contains information that is forbidden to the general public but integral to the continuity of physical, cultural, and spiritual life in the western desert. He was among the first group of artists who effectively linked ancient stories with modern materials. This painting tells the story of an old man who, in mythical times, traveled through Western Australia. The lines and circles represent his journey, and the angular circles represent the sites he visited. **SH**

Chance and Order 5 (Red) | Kenneth Martin

1970 | oil on canvas | 48 x 48 in / 122 x 122 cm | Arts Council Collection, Hayward Gallery, London, UK

British artist Kenneth Martin (1905–84) worked as a designer and created naturalistic paintings for two decades. He came to abstract painting in the late 1940s and became a leading and influential member of the British postwar group of Constructivists. Martin explored the method and process of creating art and described his interest "in the form-making power of sequence, of monotony, and of changing rhythm." In the late 1960s Martin started a set of works on both paper and canvas that he termed the *Chance and Order* series, and this painting is fifth in the sequence. To create the paintings, Martin set up a grid on the canvas and numbered its points of intersection. He then drew corresponding numbers "out of a hat"—by chance. Each pair of numbers then became a line on

the grid. Although the underlying grid structure remained the same for each painting in the series, the resulting correspondences produced a seemingly endless succession of combinations. With this painting there is, therefore, a dual invitation to explore it as a statement about an inventive process, and also to look at the painting that has been generated by this process—a combination of ordered structure and randomness. A similar series followed, entitled *Chance, Order, Change*. The painting *Chance and Order 5 (Red)* consists of bold red lines carefully painted on a white background. For Martin, the color and line sequence of the series becomes part of the constructing rhythm of the whole, and can be in harmony or in opposition, rather like a piece of music. **CM**

Ocean Park No. 27 | Richard Diebenkorn

1970 | oil on canvas | 80 x 100 in / 203 x 254 cm | Brooklyn Museum of Art, Brooklyn, NY, USA

The *Ocean Park* series takes its name from the Californian beachfront community where Richard Diebenkorn (1922–93) painted from 1966 to 1988. These large, abstract canvases represent the culmination of his career as one of the most noted American artists of the twentieth century. Diebenkorn's return to abstraction from the figurative paintings he produced in the early 1960s was born out of a desire to be unconstrained in the formal development of his canvases. "The abstract paintings," Diebenkorn explained, "permit an all-over light which wasn't possible for me in the representational works, which seem somehow dingy by comparison." *Ocean Park No. 27* exemplifies the artist's attitude toward painting as a forum for the exploration of the purity of color and shape. The bold swathes of primary color are matched in force by the triangular nexus at the center of the canvas. Their white borders serve to reinforce the formal geometry of the composition, recalling Mondrian's treatment of similar themes. Yet the geometric design of this work is counterbalanced by an atmospheric quality, achieved by the thin application of paint to the canvas, the evidence of brushwork in the bottom left-hand corner, and the presence of *pentimenti*—marks of earlier layers of painting that show through at the surface. Despite the painting's abstract nature, continuities with figurative work are evident; the sense of light and sea air is less typical of Abstract Expressionism than of the work of Turner and Whistler. **AR**

Mr. and Mrs. Clark and Percy | David Hockney

1970–71 | acrylic on canvas | 120 x 84 in / 304 x 213 cm | Tate Collection, London, UK

Mr. and Mrs. Clark and Percy by David Hockney (*b*.1937) is one of a series of double portraits of the artist's famous friends made during the 1970s. Critics have remarked on Hockney's ability to appeal to viewers' escapist instincts; the Los Angeles swimming pools series and the celebrity portraits share this characteristic. Along with *The Room, Manchester Street 1967*, this is the only explicit picture of London that Hockney painted before he moved to California. In this work, the furnishings, the view through the balcony, and the muted light in the picture establish the sense of place. Hockney's own comments on the painting suggest that achieving the quality of light was his main concern; he worked both from life and from a series of photographs to achieve the desired

effect. Leaving behind the stylistic devices of his previous works, which draw attention to the status of his subjects as pictures, the artist here returns to a more traditional style. The couple's formal poses and their relationship to one another in the room reinforce the reference to eighteenth- and ninteenth-century portraiture. However, on close examination of Hockney's treatment of large areas of the canvas, the viewer finds that the artist has abstracted the room's background surfaces, while paying significant attention to detail in his subjects' faces, the telephone, and the vase of flowers. It would be a mistake to take this work as an example of simple, realistic naturalism; here, Hockney is experimenting with new ways of constructing and painting the portrait. **AR**

White over Red on Blue | Tony Tuckson

1971 | polymer paint on board | 84 x 96 in / 213 x 244 cm | National Gallery of Australia, Canberra, Australia

As well as being a curator and deputy director of the Art Gallery of New South Wales for sixteen years, Australian Abstract Expressionist Tony Tuckson (1921–73) was a prolific artist, producing more than four hundred canvases and more than ten thousand drawings. Despite this, he only held his first exhibition in 1970, just three years before his death. Over the course of his artistic career, Tuckson became increasingly interested in, and influenced by, Abstract Expressionism. *White over Red on Blue* is one of the artist's later paintings, and this large canvas seems a roughly produced work. Tuckson applies layers of synthetic polymer paint on composition board, building up layer upon layer of blue and reddish-brown pigment (reminiscent of the Australian earth), before slapping broad strokes of white paint across and down his canvas. The dripping of the white paint down the canvas is in keeping with Abstract Expressionistic style, but overall Tuckson's work is more controlled and contained in this painting than in some earlier works. The viewer is confronted with the rough texture of the paint in *White over Red on Blue*, the immediate contrast between dark and light on the canvas, and also the sheer impressive size of the painting. Tuckson helped to bring Aboriginal and Melanesian art into major art collections in Australia. He also collected Aboriginal grave posts, which were often painted in clay and ocher. Some critics claim that *White over Red on Blue* is reminiscent of these posts and draws on Aboriginal culture. **AV**

The Window | Francisco Zúñiga

1971 | oil on canvas | Private collection

The Costa Rican painter and sculptor Francisco Zúñiga (1912–98) belonged to a generation of artists who perfected the xylograph technique. His paintings undeniably betray the influence of older European artists, such as Paul Cézanne, Paul Gaugin, and Henri Matisse, but Zúñiga broke away from academic art and began exploring more radical terrain and incorporating Primitivist and Surrealist elements into his work. He traveled to Mexico in 1936, where he painted and made public monuments for the Mexican state. His main artistic interest was in articulating the sensuality of the human figure, especially the essence of the feminine, through a visual celebration of the vigor of life. Mexico proved to be a rich source of inspiration for these inclinations. Zúñiga's earthy, poignant drawings and paintings depict Mexico's indigenous people in naturalistic settings. The native woman shown here appears strong and impassive, her dark face cradled by a powerful hand, her gaze deliberately turned away. Her seeming reticence and lack of interaction with the artist make the painting especially compelling. It clearly reflects the deep understanding and respect that Zúñiga had for his adopted country and its people. Having obtained Mexican citizenship, he worked and lived there until his death. His body of work is not underpinned by moralistic or sociological tendencies but is influential because of its ability to produce an intense, almost palpable sensation of the power and mystery of life that pulsates behind even the most insignificant face. **AA**

Cluster of Grapes | Markus Lüpertz

1971 | oil on canvas | 86 ⅝ x 86 ⅝ in / 220 x 220 cm | Hamburger Kunsthalle, Hamburg, Germany

Markus Lüpertz (*b*.1941) was among several German Neo-Expressionists whose work was widely shown in the United States and Western Europe during the 1980s. He always appeared to be a more formidable force than his fellow Neo-Expressionists, and his "traditional" panel painting bears witness to his vitality and power. The beginning of his career in the 1960s saw him confront the dominant art trends of the time: figurative Pop art and Abstract Expressionism. Expertly blending the classical and the abstract, Lüpertz sees himself as an "abstract painter," without having to be bound to the strict, technical guidelines of non-representational painting. In the 1970s Lüpertz's compositions began to take on the character of still lifes, being based on objects such as snail shells, coats,

and painters' palettes. These motifs called up manifold associations from the history of art, as well as containing direct political references. *Cluster of Grapes* shows the artist's eye for detail and his unique use of shading and color. The jagged lines and sharp edges of the gold leaves at the top of the work and the shading are offset by the round abundance of the grapes, which resemble soldiers' helmets. A German artist living in the shadow of Theodor Adorno's famous proclamation that after the Holocaust no poetry could be written, Lüpertz has nevertheless managed to create intelligent art that celebrates the simple and traditional, (as seen in *Cluster of Grapes*, for example) as well as paintings and sculpture that throw up abstract, more complicated scenes. **OR**

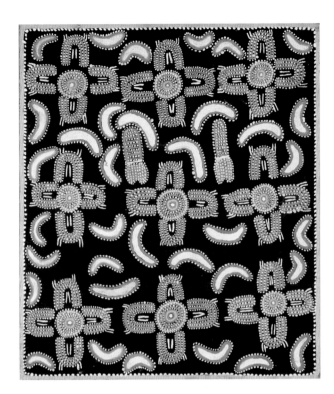

Boy's Story | Don Ellis Tjapanangka

1971 | polymer paint on panel | 20 ⅜ x 17 ⅝ in / 52 x 44.5 cm | Corbally Stourton Contemporary Art, London, UK

The vast Australian outback where most Aborigines have lived has long been regarded by the rest of the world as inhospitable and uninhabitable, but the Native Aborigines have always seen it differently. They not only inhabit the land, they feel part of it, and their surroundings are the physical manifestations of the spirits of their ancestors. They believe that Aboriginal society, the spirits of their ancestors, and the ancestors' powers are all parts of a complete world. Some Aborigines call this world *Jukurrpa*, which translates as "dreaming" or "dreamtime." This dreaming does not refer to dreaming in your sleep but signifies the world created by ancestors. Yet the artists do not create the art themselves. In this cosmology art is created by the ancestors and given to the artists, who reproduce it for others to see. Thus the artists' challenge is to find ways to revive, copy, and stimulate the images of dreaming using worldly materials. The materials traditionally came from their surroundings, but in the early 1970s Aboriginal artists, such as Don Ellis Tjapanangka (c.1925–76), began using acrylic paints on canvas, board, paper, and bark. Here, a boy, represented by some of the smaller, shallow U-shapes, journeys through life. As he grows, he mixes with different people: friends and family. The most dominant forces in his life are women, represented by the four U-shapes around the circles, which traditionally symbolize four women sitting. The painting represents a traditional Aboriginal view of life, untainted by Western thinking, but with a universal appeal. **SH**

E VIII (Towards Disappearance) SFP71-14 | Sam Francis

1971| oil on canvas | Private collection

Sam Francis (1923–94) attended the University of California at Berkeley, to study botany, medicine and psychology, but was soon involved in World War II, serving in the United States Air Force. Francis took up painting after surviving a horrific plane crash during the war, eventually returning to Berkeley where he rejected his previous studies in the sciences in favor of art. Francis spent the 1950s living and working in Paris, absorbing the influence of earlier French artists, including Monet and Matisse. His return to the United States in the 1960s brought about new explorations in design and color patterning, as well as a turn toward Jungian psychoanalytic thought. *E VIII (Towards Disappearance)* demonstrates Francis's mature style where swatches of vibrant colors are pressed to the edges of the canvas. The resulting sea of white in the center of the painting appears as an absence of color, or void, relating to the production of Minimalist art in the United States during the 1960s. The distinctness of the brushstroke on the canvas emphasizes the inherent two-dimensional flatness of painting, a notion propagated by the theorist Clement Greenberg. The dynamic interplay of intense, pure color draws the eye in a continuous movement across the canvas adding to the emotional engagement of the viewer. Francis was associated with such movements as Tachisme, Art Informel, and Post-Painterly Abstraction during his career, but personally resisted being grouped with other artists in what he viewed as a limiting manner. **MV**

The Beach of Rome Ostia I | Werner Tübke

1973 | oil on panel | 31½ x 67 in / 80 x 170 cm | Hamburger Kunsthalle, Hamburg, Germany

This allusive painting is a fine example of the controversial style and subject matter for which Werner Tübke (1929–2004) became famous. Together with Bernhard Heisig and Wolfgang Mattheuer, Tübke formed part of the Leipzig School: East German painters adhering to Socialist Realism, supposedly exalting Marxist theories of social emancipation and collective living. In line with these theories, this painting's elongated shape allows for a mass of extended, reclining human forms. The figures are not shackled and are ostensibly at leisure; the variety of uninhibited poses highlights their freedom. Though the influence of Titian is discernible, the center-heavy framing, modern detail, and muted colors clash with the Classical allusions. Tübke was also significantly influenced by the pre-Surrealist painter Giorgio de Chirico, and the notion of some sort of psychodrama being played out in this scene is enhanced by the almost Surrealist composition, in which the sea is bordered by dark shapes. The actions and emotions of those in the picture's foreground seem indeterminate; their faces hidden from view, their stances neither leisured nor panicked but suspended between the two states. In the 1980s Tübke and his assistants painted the *Peasant's War Panorama*, which at 1,722m² is the largest oil painting in the world. A tribute to the suffering of the masses, it raises a similar issue to this work: that the aims of Socialist Realism, while necessarily executed on a large scale, might also be undermined by Tübke's own unique vision. **JCo**

Paintings in the Studio: "Figure Supporting Back Legs" and "Interior with Black Rabbit" | Arthur Boyd

1973–74 | oil on canvas | 123 ¾ x 170 ¾ in / 313.5 x 433.2 cm | National Gallery of Australia, Canberra

Arthur Boyd (1920–99) was one of Australia's best-loved artists but hated to be described as such, preferring instead "painter" or "tradesman." Born in Murrumbeena, Victoria, Boyd grew up in an artistic family. However, his parents' marriage was troubled and his father faced financial ruin after his studio burned down. Boyd lived and traveled with his grandfather, the artist Arthur Merric Boyd (1862–1940), who nurtured his grandson's talent. Confronted by brutality and racism in World War II, Boyd produced a series of Expressionist works featuring maimed soldiers and the dispossessed. Back in his homeland, Boyd was distressed to discover how badly Aborigines were treated; he highlighted their experiences in several paintings known as the Bride series. In the late 1950s,

Boyd moved to London, England, where he created his celebrated Nebuchadnezzar series as a response to the Vietnam War. In the last twenty-five years of his life, Boyd and his wife divided their time between Italy, England, and Australia. In the early 1970s, Boyd created a series of paintings featuring figures languishing in the Australian landscape. This painting shows a naked artist being held up by his back legs, clutching paintbrushes in one hand and a pile of gold in the other. The artist later explained, "You really don't want to hang on to possessions. You want to hang on to concepts. Concepts involve the future whereas possessions don't." Boyd donated more than three thousand of his paintings, drawings, and other work to the National Gallery of Australia. **AV**

Small Naked Portrait
Lucian Freud

1973–74 | oil on canvas | 8 ½ x 10 ½ in / 22 x 27 cm | Ashmolean Museum, Oxford, UK

Born in Berlin, Lucian Freud (*b*.1922) became a British national in 1939. He studied at the Central School of Art, London, and then at Cedric Morris's East Anglian School of Painting and Drawing. After having briefly served in the British army as a merchant seaman during World War II, he had his first solo exhibition in 1944 at Lefevre Gallery, London. His first paintings were associated with Surrealism, but from the 1950s onward he began to paint Realist portraits. From the mid-1960s he usually painted nudes, using a thick *impasto* technique. Preferring an autobiographical quality to his subjects, for models he took friends, lovers, family members, and fellow artists such as Frank Auerbach, Francis Bacon, and Leigh Bowery. In *Small Naked Portrait* Freud depicts a young woman with short black hair, lying naked, exposed, and vulnerable on a white mattress. Apart from the plain mattress and dark wall, there are no background or external elements. Consequently, the viewer's eye is forced to confront the unprotected body, lit up brightly with an artificial studio light, a process typically used by the artist. Freud concentrated his study on the painting of the model's flesh; its volume is created by a palette of pink, gray, and white. The composition of the painting, the unusual and graphic pose of the figure, and the fact that the model has her eyes shut, all draw the viewer's eye to her left nipple at the center of the image, which appears like an extra eye, almost forming a surreal other face in the flesh surrounding it. **JJ**

The Chrysanthemum | Claudio Bravo

1974 | oil on canvas | Private collection

Born in Valparaiso, Chile, Claudio Bravo (b.1936) first established himself as a professional artist in Madrid in the 1960s, where he became a highly successful society portraitist. Since 1972 he has lived in Tangier, Morocco, where he continues to paint figuratively but perhaps more conceptually. His recent work demonstrates an extraordinary attention to detail and a highly developed craft skill. *The Chrysanthemum* was painted at a time when figurative painting and Realism was far from fashionable. Today, however, in the light of the ironies of postmodernism, Bravo's eerily academic style tends to steer us toward understanding the image as a quite formal event and as such sits somewhere between Realism and total Abstraction. The flower and the girl's tied-back hair act as formal devices, designed to keep the rhythm of the image moving, not tell some deeper story. The pleasure of studying Bravo's superb draftsmanship and exquisite eye for textural details—recalling Spanish masters such as Velázquez and Zurbarán—is an end in itself. As the artist himself has observed, "I have always been an aesthetic painter. If I am called a *preciosista* I consider it a compliment." If one wants meaning over and above the pleasure of looking at paint, then *The Chrysanthemum* probably places the viewer in the life room or artist's studio, sitting at an easel behind the model. Bravo's works feature in the collections of the Baltimore Museum of Art, The Metropolitan Museum of Art, New York, Museo Nacional de Bellas Artes, Santiago, and Museo Rufino Tamayo, Mexico City. **SF**

Flat Pack Rothmans | Stephen Farthing

1975 | oil and mixed media on canvas | 84 ¼ x 43 ¼ in / 214 x 110 cm | Royal College of Art, London, UK

British artist Stephen Farthing (*b*.1950) was educated in London—at St. Martin's School of Art and the Royal College of Art—but moved to New York in 2000. He works in a variety of media, is an accomplished portrait painter, landscape artist, draftsman, and designer. He held his first solo exhibition in 1977, his work was featured in the São Paulo Biennale of 1989, and he was elected to the Royal Academy in 1998. Farthing's commissions have been numerous and varied, for example, the carpet design that was commissioned by the Grosvenor Estate and the architectural drawings of the Oxford University Press buildings in England. In 1999, he was commissioned by the National Portrait Gallery in London to paint six eminent historians, in a work titled *Past and Present*. To prepare for the work, Farthing took more than one hundred photos of the sitters and asked the historians to fill in a questionnaire, so that he could build up a mental picture of their personalities, as well as a visual image of their faces. A number of components went into the creation of *Flat Pack Rothmans*, including acrylic, gloss paint, gesso, paper, resin, spray paint, and screenprinting. The work owes a great debt to Pop art and is one of a number of Farthing's images that make use of everyday objects. The objects used here are layered one upon the other, as if in a collage. The several pairs of scissors, cigarette packets, and miscellaneous scraps of paper intertwine to make a hypnotic image, which suggests hidden layers beneath the superficial. **LH**

Ocean Park No. 79 | Richard Diebenkorn

1975 | oil on canvas | 93 x 81 in / 236 x 206 cm | Philadelphia Museum of Art, Philadelphia, PA, USA

No. 79 was among the later works in the *Ocean Park* series which established Richard Diebenkorn (1922–93) as an artist of international stature. Based for most of his career in the San Francisco Bay area of California, Diebenkorn evokes a sense of sun, sky, and sea in his *Ocean Park* paintings. Painted five years after *Ocean Park No. 27*, *No. 79* illustrates the artist taking a more deliberate approach to his canvas than in earlier examples of the series. In marked contrast to the thin washes used in earlier work, the colors here are bold and opaque. A drip of paint is allowed to remain in the bottom right-hand area of the canvas, evidence of Diebenkorn's over-painting and corrections. In this work we see the artist engaged with, and laboring over, the canvas in a heightened self-consciousness of the painting process. Not lost, however, is the allusion to physical space and place, which Diebenkorn's abstract work evokes. The thin horizontals of warm color at the top of the frame recall landscape—their proportions making the large indigo areas below appear vast—recalling an expanse of sea or sky. The thin wash of paint at the left of the canvas and to the center foster a sense of depth, creating a relief from the weightiness of the paint's application on the rest of the canvas. Meanwhile, the strong diagonals in the upper left-hand corner create a dynamism on the canvas, animating *Ocean Park No. 79* despite its austere composition. In this painting, Diebenkorn's second round of explorations with abstraction truly come into maturity. **AR**

Cross + R | Antoni Tàpies

1975 | mixed media on wood | 64 x 64 in / 162.5 x 162.5 cm | Museu d'Art Contemporani de Barcelona, Spain

The son of a Catalan Nationalist lawyer, Antoni Tàpies (*b*.1923) was born in Barcelona not long before the start of the Spanish Civil War. He first read for a law degree, then, probably as a result of a long illness, gave up the law to devote himself entirely to painting. As a largely self-taught artist he was at first influenced by Eastern philosophy and then by the Surrealist artists Max Ernst, Joan Miro, and Paul Klee. By 1952, however, in common with many of the more fashionable painters of his day, Tàpies turned away from his figurative starting point to concentrate more on contemporary and abstract concerns. *Cross + R* is typical of these later paintings. Influenced by his Buddhist beliefs, the painting starts with a heavy impasto of paint polluted with earth, stone, and sand,

and ends in contrast with a much lighter, poetically driven calligraphy. Tàpies was acclaimed by Robert Motherwell as the greatest living European artist. In 1958 he was awarded First Prize for Painting at the Pittsburgh International, and the UNESCO and David E. Bright Prizes at the Venice Biennale. In 1992 he was elected an honorary member of the Royal Academy of Arts in London. It seems quite probable that Tàpies's obsession with earth, dust, and detritus came from his experiences growing up during the Spanish Civil War as well as World War I and World War II. Clearly, whether this is true or not, his physical handling of paint and matter has influenced a whole generation of younger artists, and probably no one more than German artist Anselm Kiefer. **SF**

American Girl and Doll | Carel Weight

1975 | oil on board | 29 ½ x 29 ½ in / 75 x 75 cm | Private collection

Carel Weight's (1908–97) portraits have long been acclaimed for capturing their subject remarkably well—most famously his portrait of Orovida Pissarro, granddaughter of the French Impressionist. The artist did not confine himself to famous sitters, however; fascinated with faces, Weight painted portraits that bring out the odd in the ordinary. *American Girl and Doll* was painted in the artist's London studio; the model was a young woman traveling through Europe, who became captivated by the carved Spanish doll pictured at the bottom right. The warm colors and printed textiles evoke a rather domestic, familiar setting, yet Weight chooses an angle on the otherwise banal scene that speaks volumes. Here the viewer is nearly on top of the subject, looking down on her.

Though seated, the girl cuts a vertical column through the square composition, creating a sense of tension. The girl's face is upturned, but she looks off into the distance, her gaze strangely vacant. The labored brushstrokes on her neck and head contrast with the looser handling of the paint on the rest of the canvas, as though the artist is working hard to decipher her expression. Meanwhile the scalp of the wooden doll signals a strange semi-human presence in the room, but the face is hidden, and the body cut off by the bottom of the composition. Much as in Goya's eerie formal portraits and Munch's interior scenes, the details in Weight's *American Girl and Doll* are unsettling, suggesting that below banal respectability, madness is never submerged too deeply. **AR**

The Ballroom | Marion Pinto

1976 | oil and acrylic on canvas | 96 x 168 in / 244 x 426.5 cm | Museum of the City of New York, NY, USA

In 1976 Gregory Dawson, one of three owners of The Ballroom, the popular cabaret restaurant in Manhattan (which at the time was at 458 West Broadway), commissioned Soho artist Marion Pinto (*b*.1935) to paint a picture for and of the restaurant. Dawson wanted the painting to honor the regular diners at his restaurant responsible for pioneering Soho's conversion from a run-down commercial area to a fashionable arts community who enjoyed late-night dining and entertainment. Inspired by Degas's *The Cotton Exchange*, Pinto's *The Ballroom* started life as a set of *in situ* photographs of the nineteen prime movers in the Soho art world who regularly ate at the restaurant. Pinto invited each of them to The Ballroom to pose for a photo portrait. The photographs were then grouped and organized into a composition. The resulting photomontage was then photographically transferred onto the canvas and painstakingly translated into paint. Pinto composed and executed the painting over a period of about six months. Among those present are art dealers Paula Cooper and Max Hutchinson, and artists Alex Katz, Larry Rivers, Deborah Remington, and Robert Indiana. The painting was removed from its original setting when the restaurant closed due to a dramatic rent increase. It was then installed some two and a half years later at the New Ballroom restaurant club in Chelsea, which closed in 1994. At that point the owners of the first Ballroom on West Broadway donated the painting to the Museum of the City of New York. **SF**

Stilleben | Georg Baselitz

1976–77 | oil on canvas | 98 ½ x 78 ⅞ in / 250.1 x 200.4 cm | Museum of Modern Art, New York, NY, USA

Georg Baselitz (Hans-Georg Kern, b.1938) is one of the world's biggest-selling living artists. This postmodern painter specializes in painting his subjects upside down. In *Stilleben*, the still life performs the function (as any other standard subject matter might) of a stage on which painting can perform. The components of the still life are only relevant in that they lend themselves to the painterly needs of the artist. That painterly performance has been labeled "wild, incompetent, and brutal" and while there is an energy and attack in these paintings, it is as much strategic as it is expressive. As with his other paintings of the period, Baselitz inverts the image—a device intended to detach the viewer from the task of recognition that relegates other forms of observation

and appreciation. Baselitz wants us to see the painting rather than the subject. This device also liberates the painter and it is quite apparent, in the period following the first inverted images, just how far Baselitz has been able to develop the structure, color, and handling of the image. While many assumed the upside-down pictures were an attention-grabbing tactic in an ever more competitive art market, Baselitz showed us how this simple physical change could release new levels of visual invention for the artist and of experience for the viewer. In this and other works of the period we find a mixture of sensuality and vulgarity of illusion and abstraction and, above all, paintings that are recognizable and distinctive while avoiding the entrapment of style. **RW**

Dry Creek Bed, Werribee Gorge I | Fred Williams

1977 | oil on canvas | 71 ¾ x 59 ⅞ in / 182 x 152 cm | Tate Collection, London, UK

Fred Williams (1927–82) was undoubtedly one of the most significant and influential Australian artists of the twentieth century. Born in Melbourne, he studied for a while at the National Gallery of Victoria Art School before traveling to London in 1951. There he worked as a picture framer and studied at the Chelsea School of Art, and Central School of Arts and Crafts. While in London, Williams produced a series of scenes of music halls. On his return to Australia he developed his skills as a printmaker and turned his attention to depicting the landscape of his native country in new and extraordinary ways. It was not long before his unique vision began to emerge, and he tried to convey through his paintings the enormity and timelessness of the outback. Viewing his subjects from a great height we see, as if from a glider or through the eye of an eagle, the features of this wild and rugged place in the form of abstract patterns and marks. The use of color and subtle markings give an eerie sense of soaring to a great height. Werribee Gorge is located in Victoria, Australia, and is a spectacular natural phenomenon. Such a significant feature takes pride of place in this picture, and is illuminated by the parched colors and mysterious markings. *Werribee* is an Aboriginal word meaning "backbone" and the curving line suggests, perhaps, the outline of a snake. Williams's paintings became sparer as he progressed. These later landscapes are excellent examples of an artist who has, after a long journey, found his authentic voice. **SF**

Black Sea | Philip Guston

1977 | oil on canvas | 68 x 117 in / 173 x 297 cm | Tate Collection, London, UK

Philip Guston (1913–80) can best be understood as two painters: before and after. The "before" Guston was a comfortably successful Abstract Expressionist. His canvases from the 1950s usually consisted of swatches of solid red, black, or white concentrated in the picture's center. By contrast, a repeated cast of pink cartoon figures and objects dominated his "after" work. In tone, the particular pink that became his signature was reminiscent of old chewing gum, but despite the sugariness of this association, little was sweet in Guston's later canvases. These paintings are populated by stained coffee cups, cigarette butts, dirty boots, messy beds, and lonely men whose puffy pink faces are reduced to big, frightened eyes and mouths plugged up by cigarettes. Guston's embrace of one of these diametrically oppositional styles of painting and his rejection of the other was a defining break from the cultish reverence for abstraction that ruled the art world of the 1950s. Though painted with a darker, more somber palette than was typical of this time in his career, *Black Sea* is otherwise emblematic of Guston's mature, iconoclastic work. Over the sea is a blue sky streaked with light, like the sky at dawn, but instead of the sun, the heel of a shoe rises ominously above the horizon line. The influence of Guston's later paintings can be seen everywhere today—from graphic novels to the paintings of a new generation of artists more interested in emotional impact, psychological complexity, and satire than pure forms and patches of pigment floating above reality. **AH**

Hope and Despair of Ángel Ganivet | Eduardo Arroyo

1977 | oil on canvas | 57 ½ x 44 ⅞ in / 146 x 114 cm | Musée d'Art Moderne de la Ville de Paris, France

Born in Madrid in 1937, Spanish artist Eduardo Arroyo initially studied journalism, and in 1958 he went to live in Paris with the aim of becoming a writer, but instead took to caricature and painting. His early work was figurative but soon he was to be influenced by Pop art and his painting began to adopt a flat, graphic, cinematic style, while its content revealed his opposition to General Francisco Franco's regime in his homeland. In 1963, this lead to his exhibition at the Biosca Gallery in Madrid being shut down by the Spanish government. On a return visit to Spain in 1974 he was arrested and expelled. He lived in France as a political refugee until 1976, when he was able to go back to his native country following Franco's death. His *Hope and Despair of Ángel Ganivet* takes the suicide of Spanish novelist and essayist Ángel Ganivet y Garcia (1865–98) as its theme. Ganivet was director of Spanish consul in Riga, Latvia, when, depressed and disillusioned, he drowned himself in the Dvina River, having been diagnosed with a progressive disease. Like Arroyo, Ganivet had been concerned about the fate of his country, was far from home, and parodied its politics and temperament. Arroyo too parodies his culture with the jaunty hat on the top of the sherry bottle on the table. His faceless Ganivet has three legs and sits on a floating chair; the open window reveals a fractured icy view outside. This is a world in which nothing is as it should be and nothing is as it originally seems, just as Arroyo, with the longing of an exile, sees his own country under a dictatorship. **CK**

Gears | James Rosenquist

1977 | oil on canvas | Private collection

Created between the sexual revolution of the early 1970s and the conspicuous consumption of the 1980s, *Gears* confirms James Rosenquist's (*b*.1933) ability to represent the modern consumer mind in its vividly stimulated fragments. Since his early comparison to Lichtenstein and Warhol, Rosenquist appropriates the visual language of advertising and pop culture in his collage-based paintings. A commercial billboard artist by training, Rosenquist is intrigued by large-scale fragments of everyday objects, using them to comment on material plentitude, cultural narcissism, and sexually charged commercial media. Rosenquist's use of size and color conveys, above all, intelligence and humor. If there were ever an atomic war, Rosenquist once said, he would really have a great view being blasted off a signboard in Times Square, New York. *Gears* is sexually charged, with stereotypically masculine machinery on the left, feminine pearls on the right, with the central, governing gear controlled by one of the penetrating red lipsticks. These lipsticks, open and ready for application, come out of an icy background—a color scheme of commercial product lighting in industrial blues, cool metals, and severe reds. Rosenquist is a dynamic conversationalist using color, shape, and popular culture. He abstracts common consumer culture to uncommonly large sizes, articulating the modern visual reality of disparate images in constant flux, and the modern creative impulse to consume in order to understand. **SWW**

The Paris Commune | Bernhard Heisig

1979 | oil on canvas | 63 x 29 ¾ in / 160 x 75.5 cm | Hamburger Kunsthalle, Hamburg, Germany

Bernhard Heisig's (b.1925) work is a battleground of political conflict, public controversy, and private trauma. Born in Breslau, Heisig fought for Hitler in Normandy at the age of sixteen and joined the Waffen-SS at eighteen. One of the greatest East German representational artists, Heisig painted in the Leipzig School alongside Wolfgang Mattheuer and Werner Tübke, and challenged the aesthetic doctrine of Socialist Realism in the GDR in the 1960s with graphic depictions of fascism and the Nazi regime. A painter of explosive emotion, Heisig never surrenders his vision, once declaring, "I'm no loner. I want my pictures to be seen. I want them to provoke." *The Paris Commune* is a triptych depicting the fighters of the Paris Commune of 1871. The figures are not portrayed as dutiful and heroic; instead they are wild and misplaced, emerging in thrashing layers and screaming variations. In the left panel the gentlemen below look up to a woman in an exalted, defiant position. At center, men burn red flags alongside leaders with twisted heads. Alongside Prussian helmets in the right panel, European dignitaries cower under the dress of an ironic can-can dancer or revolutionary female. Here Heisig uses the safer distance of nineteenth-century France to express his political views about Germany. His art was criticized by Walter Ulbricht, the East German leader, but he was also awarded prizes by the state, which he later returned. Heisig may have sometimes acquiesced to power, but he always talked back. **SWW**

West Interior | Alex Katz

1979 | oil on canvas | 96 x 72 in / 243.8 x 182.9 cm | Philadelphia Museum of Art, Philadelphia, PA, USA

Alex Katz's (b.1927) most tenderly felt portraits are those of his wife Ada, who has been the subject of his paintings for almost fifty years. Few artists in history have paid such prolonged, prolific attention to one subject. Katz's spare visual vocabulary has become associated with portraits of Manhattan's affluent, intellectual cocktail party and country-house crowd, but his body of work concerning Ada adds profound depth, intimacy, and personality to his oeuvre of flat, cool, representational paintings. Like Ingres, Katz is sensitive to clothing and style. Through his images of his effortlessly well-dressed wife, one can chart changing fashions and observe defining differences in mood and style through the last five decades. In *West Interior*, Ada rests her head on her fist and looks at Katz with an expression of calm contentment. She wears a casual sweater but the red, patterned shirt underneath reflects the style of the era. Her relaxed posture and loving look give this painting its pervasive sense of pleasure, warmth, and tenderness. Thanks to Katz, Ada's elegant and intelligent face, classically chic style, and wave of black hair have become iconic images. But despite this focus, Katz offers little discernable insight into his wife's personality. Instead, his signature hyper-reduced style articulates their mutual affection and intimacy while still retaining a distanced sense of privacy. In his images of Ada, she comes to represent universal yet singular aspects of every woman in love who is being viewed by the person who loves her. **AH**

Portrait of a Youth | Mohammad Reza Irani

1979 | oil on canvas | 19 ½ x 15 ¾ in / 50 x 40 cm | Private collection

Mohammad Reza Irani (1954–94) was born in Tabriz, in the Azerbaijan province of Iran. He studied art at the Mirak Art College in Tabriz, then received a degree in painting from Tehran University's School of Fine Arts in 1974. Afterward, he returned to Tabriz to teach. In 1985 his paintings were exhibited in Münich, Germany, and in 1988 he exhibited in Istanbul and in his native Iran. His influences came from a wide range of sources, and there are clear signs in some of his studies of his admiration for van Gogh and the Impressionists. His still-life studies and flower pictures are exquisitely observed, but there is no stylistic consistency that can be identified. Irani also produced many affectionate depictions of daily life in the villages of Southern Azerbaijan. His portraits, too, including his famous self-portrait, are widely admired for their honesty and simplicity. This study of an unnamed youth is typical in its unfussy directness. But at the same time, the lack of detail leaves many questions unanswered. Who is this boy? Where is he? There are no artifacts to give the viewer clues, no landscape to give context, no costume to tell of class or origin. There is nothing to distract from the face, but also nothing about why the youth wears such a serious, even melancholic, expression. This all adds to the sense of anonymity, but it also points to the subject's androgynous features—the long eyelashes, generous lips, and large eyes. Sadly, at the height of his creativity, Irani was killed in a road accident in Tehran on September 3, 1994. **TS**

Red Bermudas | Howard Hodgkin

1978–80 | oil on wood | 27 ¾ x 27 ¾ in / 70.5 x 70.5 cm | Museum of Modern Art, New York, NY, USA

A British artist who studied at Camberwell School of Art in London, Sir Howard Hodgkin (*b*.1932) can create art around the most everyday objects. Often described as an "Intimist," in his works the most ordinary items—bedsheets, clothing, or a dirty mirror—become objects for study. His style is typified by brilliant colors, erratic shapes, and witty use of perspective. At first glance, *Red Bermudas* looks like a fruit and vegetable display on a market stall or perhaps a tessellation of Italian roof tiles; it is only as the viewer explores the title that the columnlike legs poking out of the bermuda shorts become perceptible. Hodgkin grew up in an artistic environment, through family connections to the Bloomsbury Group. His father was a garden designer

and this perhaps explains Hodgkin's depictions of trees and flowers in a simplistic but reverential style. The people in his paintings appear rather like a child would draw them, yet they also seem real, as though one would recognize them if they walked into the room. Many of his works are inspired by travel, such as *In the Bay of Naples* (1980–82) and *Bombay Sunset* (1972–73), while others spring from simple, everyday affairs, such as the strangely compelling *Dinner at Smith's Square* (1975–79) in which neither people nor food are discernible. The latter seems to bear out Hodgkin's comment, "The picture is instead of what happened. We don't need to know the story, generally the story's trivial anyway. The more people want to know the story, the less they'll look at the picture." **LH**

Ferocious Painting | Enzo Cucchi

1980 | oil on canvas | 79 x 144 ½ in / 200.7 x 367 cm | Detroit Institute of Arts, Detroit, MI, USA

Enzo Cucchi (*b.*1949) began drawing in the 1970s and held his first one-man show in 1977. A member of the Transavanguardia movement, Cucchi has always lived in Italy and uses the Italian landscape, people, and experiences as inspiration for his work. His oeuvre encompasses many different styles and media. He produces ceramics, sculptures, drawings, and paintings. Much of his work is inspired by early Etruscan art or biblical stories. *Ferocious Painting* is one of his earlier works and representative of one of his most well-known styles—visionary figure painting employing bold primary and secondary colors. The imagery employed here—of the venerable bearded religious icon-style figure about to be obliterated by a very commonplace ballpoint pen—shows a clever melding of old and new styles and a comment on the old being written off by modernity. The bright yellow human figure is burdened with what appears to be a sacrificial lamb, a symbol for Jesus Christ. The man's frightened face appears in a square-cut tunnel in the velvety green hillside. From the same tunnel issues forth a train, but is the train coming out of the hillside or out of the man? It is a steam train in smart red and black design, harking back to a golden age, or perhaps to a less enlightened age than our age of modernity and gleaming bullet trains; the steam train could symbolize both. Is this a comment on Christianity versus older religions or is it about modern society versus history? Questions are raised but it is left to the viewer to find the answers within themselves. **LH**

Large Shower | Rainer Fetting

1980 | acrylic on canvas | 105 x 120 in / 269 x 305 cm | Private collection

In the early 1980s, a group of young German artists wowed the art world with their bold painterly work—a direct challenge to the minimalism and conceptualism so ubiquitous at the time. They were the *Neuen Wilden* (Young Wild Ones) and their work was soon commanding top prices. Rainer Fetting's (*b.*1949) big paintings especially impressed the critics. He used old-fashioned oil on canvas and his work was figurative, a breath of fresh air at the time. His vivid colors and depictions of Berlin nightlife harked back to the great German painters of the first half of the century, such as Max Beckmann. The art world began to talk about the return of painting and, even more thrilling, the return of the figure. This particular work shows several athletically built young men taking a communal shower—a homoerotic scene. Yet the dark background and hidden faces create an air of uncertainty, menace, and mystery. One figure, his face half hidden, stares boldly out of the canvas. The figure on the left could be stretching or he could almost be hanging by the arms, suggesting a kind of torture. In the background, a grid pattern recalls the bars of a jail. Bondage has been a recurring theme in Fetting's work. Are these men in prison, have they been working in a coalmine, or are they in a gay bathhouse? The menace so palpable in *Large Shower* is more sinister with hindsight. This painting was made just before AIDS devastated the gay community. In fact, by 1980, the virus was already doing its deadly work although it had not yet been identified. **CR**

Euston Steps | Frank Auerbach

1980–81 | oil on hardboard | 48 ½ x 60 in / 123 x 153 cm | Hayward Gallery, London, UK

The art of Frank Auerbach (*b.*1931) occupies a significant place in both the development of English art and the European tradition. Born in Germany, Auerbach was sent to school in England in 1939 to escape the Nazis—he never saw his parents again. As a figurative painter, Auerbach's individualism rests in his staunch adherence to the figurative style in the face of its rejection by much of contemporary art. As a result his art is often associated with the School of London, which included Lucian Freud, Francis Bacon, and Leon Kossuff. *Euston Steps* represents a slice of London, just near Auerbach's home, reverberating with the life of individuals mounting the steps and tracing a line in English art history from Hogarth and Constable through to Sickert, while still retaining links

to Expressionism. Auerbach's entire oeuvre portrays the people and places both physically and emotionally closest to him—the places exhibiting as much personality as the portraits. Auerbach's thickly applied paint and broad brushstrokes accentuate the already rampant diagonals of the composition, thus enhancing their ability to convey energy and movement. Even the figures themselves receive equal treatment and barely emerge from the muted, earth tones of their urban surroundings. An exhibition at the Royal Academy in London marking Auerbach's seventy-first year highlighted the almost obsessive quality of his focus on specific landscapes and specific individuals—the repetition of representing the same scene to capture its mutable nature. **AEH**

Drifting Smoke | Fred Williams

1981 | oil on canvas | 59 ⁷/₈ x 71 ⁷/₈ in / 152 x 183 cm | National Gallery of Victoria, Melbourne, Australia

Fred Williams (1927–82) started his art education in 1943 at the National Gallery School in Melbourne, Australia. During the 1950s he traveled to England where he stayed for five years to study at both Chelsea and the Central Schools of Art. After his clearly academic start in Australia his English experience opened his eyes to modern art, particularly Impressionism and Post-Impressionism. From the time he was in London, Williams's practice as an etcher influenced his development as a painter and resulted in a cross-fertilization of ideas between the two techniques. With hindsight it seems highly probable that this interplay between painting and printmaking is at least partly responsible for the shift he finally made from his early rather European-looking work to the groundbreaking approach we see in *Drifting Smoke*. Back in Australia during the late 1950s and early 1960s his work continued to show a strong European influence, his paintings being usually of the figure and clearly influenced by Modigliani. During the 1960s, however, Williams managed to shake off the weight of history and found a way of describing the Australian landscape that was both original and persuasive. In *Drifting Smoke*, a field of hot, dusty earth pictured after a bush fire is first dotted with small sharply focused objects, then introduced to the sky by wisps of drifting smoke. Made at a time when cutting-edge artists were weighing abstraction against figuration, this painting sits neatly between what at that time seemed to be the two poles of painting. **SF**

Head of J.Y.M. No.1 | Frank Auerbach

1981 | oil on board | 22 x 20 in / 56 x 51 cm | Southampton City Art Gallery, Hampshire, UK

British painter and printmaker Frank Auerbach (*b*.1931) was born in Berlin but his Jewish family sent him to England in 1939 to escape the Nazis. After both his parents died in concentration camps, he stayed on, acquiring British citizenship in 1947. Between 1947 and 1952 he attended art classes under David Bomberg at the Borough Polytechnic, and at St. Martin's School of Art. Bomberg encouraged him to take inspiration from the French painter Paul Cézanne, and helped him develop an unconventional and Expressionist approach in his figurative painting. From 1952 to 1955, Auerbach studied at London's Royal College of Art. His first solo exhibition was held in 1956, at the Beaux Arts Gallery in London, at which he was criticized for his thick application of paint. Auerbach

has always preferred to keep an intimate approach to his work—his landscapes tend to be building sites close to London and his figurative works often have his friends and family as subjects. His recurrent models were his wife Julia, his close acquaintance Stella West (usually referred to as E.O.W.), and Juliet Yardley Mills (J.Y.M.), subject of this painting. She was a professional model who posed regularly for the artist since 1963. Looking straight forward, she is seen slightly from a low-angled vantage point. In his early works, Auerbach insisted on texture and asserted the importance of the paint's materiality. In contrast, this portrait is a wonderful example of his later style, where a particular freedom and fluid movement of paint can be clearly noted. **JJ**

Innenraum | Anselm Kiefer

1981 | mixed media | 112 x 122 in / 287 x 310 cm | Stedelijk Museum, Amsterdam, Netherlands

The noisy arrival of Neoexpressionism in the early 1980s signaled a confident break with the Pop art of the 1960s, while challenging the ideals of Modernism that had dominated both popular taste and the art market for a generation or more. Neoexpressionism differed from the earliest form of Expressionism produced by pre-World War I European painters and showed little interest in Abstract Expressionism, which by the 1980s had already been consigned to the museum. Neoexpressionism restored a fresh level of confidence and ambition in painting, as well as infusing a sense of personal vision and immediacy in philosophical, poetic, and political subjects. Anselm Kiefer, born at the end of World War II in 1945, in Donaueschingen, Germany, produced some of the most challenging paintings of the 1980s. After initially studying law and French, he went on to study art from 1966 to 1972, the last two years at Düsseldorf with Joseph Beuys. Kiefer's *Innenraum* (meaning "Interior Space") shows a vast interior resembling a stateroom—an image that is at once monumental and distressed. Like much of his work, it confronts images of national identity and institutions of power, and the paint is coarsely applied and mixed with industrial materials on a vast canvas. The cold, fragile edifice speaks of a nation's history entirely without sentiment but with the memory of a painful past. Kiefer's forceful depictions of the ruins of German Third Reich culture establish him as a rare and powerful contemporary painter of modern history. **RW**

View of Madrid from Torres Blancas | Antonio López García

1976–82 | oil on board | 57 ⅛ x 96 ⅛ in / 145 x 244 cm | Private collection

Spanish painter and sculptor Antonio López García (also known as Antonio López, b.1936) is a master at painting the mundane. He paints still lifes of clothes racks, bathrooms, and fridges. But each painting is arresting in its realism as he sees the beautiful in the ordinary, taking years to complete a canvas. In this way he continues in the tradition of Spanish painters such as Juan Sánchez Cotán (1561–1627) and Francisco de Zurburán (1598–1664). López's prodigious talent was spotted and encouraged by his artist uncle when he was young, which led to him studying at Madrid's School of Fine Arts. After graduating, López initially adopted Surrealist and Magical Realist styles, but by the late 1950s his work became more realistic as he adopted a hyperrealist approach. He said of this shift: "The physical world gained more prestige in my eyes." *View of Madrid from Torres Blancas* is typical of the cityscapes of Madrid he started to paint in the 1970s in its incredible attention to detail and use of light. Dawn rises over the city, and López's delicate color palette gives the sky a Baroque feel; its strained early morning light would not be out of place in a sunrise by Claude Lorraine (1600–82). His dramatic use of perspective over the skyline and the sweeping road trailing off into the city gives the unsightly 1960s tower blocks a majestic grandeur. This is not a painting of an architectural gem such as the Palacio Real or the Plaza Mayor, but a depiction of the ordinary, ugly, and urban, yet his loving portrayal reveals a Madrid of hope and significance. **CK**

Donut Revenge | Jean-Michel Basquiat

1982 | acrylic, oilstick, and paper collage on canvas | 95 ¼ x 72 in / 241.9 x 182.8 cm | Private collection

Jean-Michel Basquiat (1960–88) first made his name as the graffiti artist-poet "SAMO" (Same Old Shit), whose satirical haikus in black capital letters became a ubiquitous part of downtown Manhattan. He often scrawled his SAMO sentences outside art galleries and created a SAMO character, who served as an alternative to the established art world. By the time Basquiat was twenty-two, however, he was no longer an antidote to art's establishment system, he was an art star. He was born in Brooklyn, the son of a black Puerto Rican mother and Haitian father. His friendship with Andy Warhol resulted in a number of collaborative paintings and performances in the mid-eighties. Basquiat's drug use was known and often exploited by art-world figures who wanted to promote his bad-boy status. There are rumors that his first art dealer moonlighted as his drug dealer, supplying him with heroin and speed so he would not leave his studio. Basquiat died of a heroin overdose in his studio in 1988. His Neoexpressionist paintings combined graffiti, hieroglyphic signs, and symbols with text and manic, kinetic, strokes of color. His work has topped sales records at auctions in modern times, defining the aesthetic of the 1980s. Bungled attempts by forgers to pass off faux-Basquiats has proven that even in his most seemingly sloppy images the artist's hand was always unique, and that its essence was the best evidence for his defensive assertion that, "Believe it or not, I can actually draw." **AH**

The Citizen | Richard Hamilton

1981–83 | oil on canvas | 81 ¼ x 82 ½ in / 206.5 x 210 cm | Tate Collection, London, UK

British collage artist and painter Richard Hamilton (*b.*1922) is considered by many to be the first Pop artist. Born into a working-class London family, he dropped out of high school and worked as an apprentice electrician while taking evening art classes at Central Saint Martins. He then entered the Royal Academy, but was expelled for failing courses. After enlisting in the military, Hamilton joined the Slade School of Art for two years before exhibiting independently in London. Greatly inspired by Marcel Duchamp, he eventually befriended him and in 1966 curated the first retrospective of Duchamp's work to be shown in the UK. Like Duchamp, Hamilton borrowed images and references directly from mass culture and recontextualized them to highlight their political, literary, or social meaning. Inspired by a 1980 TV documentary on the "dirty protest" by republican prisoners at the Maze prison in Northern Ireland, *The Citizen* depicts a messianic-looking protester standing in a prison cell smeared with feces. During the Maze protest, inmates who demanded to be classified as political prisoners refused to wash or wear regulation clothing and smeared their cells with excrement. Hamilton represents feces as soft, brown washes of color surrounding the bedraggled yet heroic central figure. The image is "shocking less for its scatological content," Hamilton asserted, "than for its potency… the materialization of Christian martyrdom." The painting's title is borrowed from the nickname given to a character from James Joyce's *Ulysses*. **AH**

Cabalistic Painting | Julian Schnabel

1983 | oil on velvet | 108 x 84 in / 274.3 x 213.3 cm | Detroit Institute of Arts, Detroit, MI, USA

Born in Brooklyn, Julian Schnabel (*b*.1951) moved with his family at the age of fourteen to Texas, and subsequently studied at the University of Texas. In 1973, he returned to New York to follow the independent study program at the Whitney Museum, his successful application apparently comprising of a set of his color slides sandwiched between two slices of bread. Schnabel's first solo exhibition was in 1975 at the Contemporary Arts Museum in Houston. Four years later, he had his first New York show with Mary Boone, in Soho, who during the 1980s was also exhibiting the likes of Georg Baselitz, Francesco Clemente, Enzo Cucchi, Anselm Kiefer, Jannis Kounellis, and Sigmar Polke. *Cabalistic Painting* has all the qualities of a classic Expressionist painting. There

is, however, a twist—it is painted onto intentionally bad-taste velvet. Schnabel transforms a surface more frequently associated with sleazy boudoirs into a dark mysterious space. Schnabel said of his 1980s Neoexpressionist paintings that he was "aiming at an emotional state, a state that people can literally walk into and be engulfed by." During the mid-1990s, as the rebirth of painting became gradually less radical, Schnabel reinvented himself as a screenwriter and director. In 1996, his excellent biopic of his friend the artist Jean-Michel Basquiat (1960–88)—featuring David Bowie as Andy Warhol—was released, to mixed reviews. In 2000, his second film, which tells the story of the life of the Cuban poet and novelist, Reinaldo Arenas (1943–90), was screened. **SF**

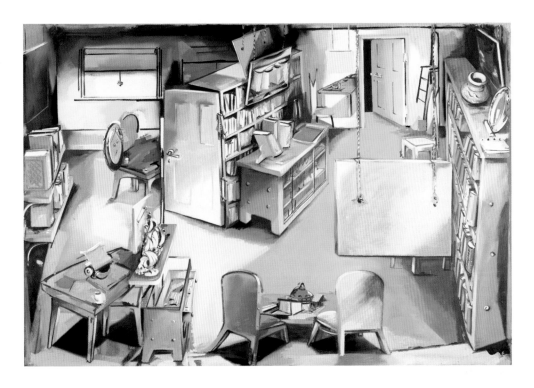

The School at Rome | Stephen Farthing

1983 | oil, beeswax, and damar varnish on cotton duck | 63 x 86 in / 160 x 220 cm | Private collection

Stephen Farthing (*b*.1950) was only twenty-six, just graduated from the Royal College of Art in London, when he was awarded a scholarship to the British School at Rome in 1976. Having already demonstrated an ability to reinterpret art historical conventions and imagery from Rococo portraiture through to Cubism as devices for wholly contemporary paintings, he took full advantage during his year in Rome of the rich possibilities he found embedded in the city's ancient monuments and in its evolving languages of painting. In the early 1980s he embarked on a series of paintings of architectural interiors depicted nearly life size, some of them prompted by descriptions in the naturalistic novels of Balzac. *The School at Rome*, based on his vivid recollections of the grand library

of the institution where he had spent such a happy year, is one of the most haunting of these works. It depicts a stagelike and essentially invented room crowded with books, furniture, decorative and functional objects, and pictures suspended from chains, viewed simultaneously from a multiplicity of contradictory angles. The surface area of the canvas is almost as large as the notional wall through which we view the library and animates its interior with our own presence. Presenting the furnishings of the room as if viewed through transparent walls, the painting invites us to enter into the space of memory and the imagination, the space of art, telescoping time in a post-Cubistic journey through three dimensions on the flat surface of the canvas. **ML**

Paul | Sean Scully

1984 | oil on canvas | 102 x 127 in / 259 x 320 cm | Tate Collection, London, UK

Sean Scully (b.1945) is one of the finest abstract painters of the age. For the past thirty years he has made use of his signature motif, the stripe and all its variants, to create an extraordinarily rich body of work, a testament to the artist's unstinting belief in the transcendent power of repetition. Ever since his student days at the University of Newcastle upon Tyne, Scully has been following a consistently individual path in an effort to reinstate the primacy of abstraction over figuration. The artist has repeatedly argued that abstraction has become divorced from the real world and a desire to imbue it with profound human feelings lies at the core of his ambition. Scully takes inspiration for his work from his own experiences and from his wide knowledge of the history of art. Painted in memory of the artist's son following his untimely death, Paul declares its expressive intentions in the most immediate terms. Its sheer scale evokes a scene of great physical activity in the studio, where the painting's variously colored horizontal and vertical components have been built up on the surface of the canvas. Like so many of the artist's works from the mid-1980s, Paul includes a section of panel that stands proud of its neighbors. This device brings the painting away from the wall and invests it with dramatic sculptural and architectural properties. Although the figure plays no part in Scully's resonant paintings, the forms and colors are charged with an especially earthy and emotional presence. **PB**

Idea of a Passion | Guillermo Kuitca

1984 | acrylic on canvas | 57 ⅛ x 76 ¾ in | University of Essex Collection of Latin American Art, UK

After meeting choreographer Pina Bausch during a trip to Europe in 1981, Argentinian artist Guillermo Kuitca (*b*.1961) started directing experimental theater and this, in turn, led him to paint his series *The Sweet Sea*, from which this painting is taken. The recurrent themes in this series are stagelike interiors, mysterious figures, and an implied narrative as if taken from a scene in a movie. *Idea of a Passion* introduces us to the drama of seven characters positioned around a column contemplating the dead body of an eighth, who lies nude on a blood stain. The unusual angle implies that a third party is watching over, while the physical distance that the picture displays serves to deepen the sense of isolation portrayed through the expansive areas of cobalt blue. The title of this

painting, together with the ambiguity of the imagery, makes strong reference to biblical passages and the death of Christ, as well as to the extreme violence that occurred during the Dirty War (1976–83), a state-sponsored war on dissident citizens in Argentina. Like a movie still, Kuitca has frozen a moment in time after a crucial event. The impassivity of the characters and the uncertain setting of a stage or studio give this work the ability to fluctuate between the spheres of public and private, dream and reality, and art and life. In *The Sweet Sea*, Kuitca not only explores space as an architectural form but also as a psychological setting where emotions live and memories revisit. His later paintings are stripped of characters, leaving the setting of the space to take precedence. **RJ**

Francis Bacon | Ruskin Spear

1984 | oil on board | 30 x 24 ⅞ in / 76.2 x 63.2 cm | National Portrait Gallery, London, UK

Ruskin Spear's (1911–90) portrait of the painter Francis Bacon is a compelling example of one of art's most challenging subgenres: painters painting painters. Spear was a British figurative painter whose main artistic influence was the Victorian artist, Walter Sickert. Spear employed his conservative, illustrative style to capture idiosyncratic moments and intrigue. He often framed his sitters in swirls of dark color, creating a sense of detailed description but also of mystery. In his portrait of the former British Prime Minister, *(James) Harold Wilson, Baron Wilson of Rievaulx* (1974), he shows the politician puffing on a pipe surrounded by big blooms of smoke. With his fat face and cocked pipe, the image could be comical, but Spear's use of shadowing makes the painting seem unnerving—like a still from a Hitchcock film. The notorious painter Bacon was the sitter for more than twenty-five portraits, sitting for Spear when he was seventy-five years old. In the image, Bacon stares intensely at Spear, and at the viewer, from a blood-red background. Unlike other artists who painted Bacon, Spear does not try to replicate his signature style or even hint at his qualities as an artist. Instead, his choice of background color playfully references Bacon's reputation as a painter renowned for frenzied, smeared scenes packed with allusions to violence. Spear surprisingly pictures him as an avuncular character in a frumpy cardigan, yet his choice of colors and passionate use of paint make this a cryptic but telling portrait. **AH**

Table Manners | Graham Crowley

1984 | oil on canvas | 60 x 76 ¾ in / 152.5 x 195 cm | Private collection

Graham Crowley's (b.1950) diverse career has produced a range of painting styles, from bold abstractions to dark figures, as well as exceptional mastery of the rural landscape in his later pieces. His paintings exhibit a subtle social consciousness of his personal and political surroundings. His 1980s works, of which *Table Manners* is a key example, portray common domestic objects of Surrealist size yet with realistic coherency. The unsettling social change of the Thatcher era was a theme for Crowley during this period—from urban landscape paintings of decaying housing estates to scenes conveying the suffocation of domestic intimacy. In England, where manners are the only currency for social mobility, the nationalist title *Table Manners* suggests nothing of the painting's dark and nightmarish tone. With shadows and figurative distortions Crowley paints a feast, seen from the perspective of the one about to eat. The artist admits to using anthropomorphism, in which the pieces of tableware and food are given a human expression of character, leaving space for moral inflection, much like the Dutch still-life paintings of the seventeenth century. *Table Manners* portrays no humans, and so poses the question: If there is no one else at the table, does one still hold one's manners? Crowley positions himself in the contemporary art scene as flexible in style and subtly powerful in social commentary. He explores personal and political landscapes, weaving one into the other with a versatile technique and an intelligent social presence. **SWW**

World of Work | Jörg Immendorff

1984 | oil on canvas | 111 ¾ x 129 ⅞ in / 284 x 330 cm | Hamburger Kunsthalle, Hamburg, Germany

A leading figure of the new German Expressionism, Jörg Immendorff (1945–2007) was raised in postwar Germany, and came to prominence as an artist in the 1970s for his role as translator of the complex German modern identity. Immendorff's paintings are highly charged with allegory and are rendered in a conceptualist, frenetic style. The artist was diagnosed with Lou Gehrig's disease in 1998; when he could no longer paint with his left hand, he switched to the right and, directed others to paint following his instructions. World of Work (Welt der Arbeit) uses heavy symbolism to convey political ideas and dominating cultural values. The atmosphere is dark and ghoulish, with aggressively clawed ravens scowling the scene of a bruised, purple coloring.

The human figures, a disparate mix of working-class men and enthusiastic gallery visitors, are shadows defined by bright outlines. The crack in the ceiling is a reworked swastika, a symbol that appears again in the surrealistic renditions of the raven's claws. An artist with a strong belief in his social and political responsibility, Immendorff believed that evil takes root and flourishes in societies where art and freedom of expression are censored. World of Work presents the struggles of the artist's own work within the art world, as portrayed in the endless gallery hall, and within the complex of work values rooted in Protestantism, the Nazi regime, and German Marxist ideals. Immendorff presents puzzling questions and provides few resolutions. **SWW**

Sapling Forest, Cherry Plum Blossom | Clifton Pugh

1984 | oil on canvas | 36 x 44 in / 91.4 x 111.7 cm | Private collection

Born in Victoria, Australia, Clifton Pugh (1924–90) had his first taste of an artistic career during World War II, when he was sent to Papua New Guinea as a draftsman for Military Intelligence. In 1947, he enrolled at the National Gallery of Victoria Art School, where he became renowned for the quality of his work and his empathy with the natural world. The simple beauty of *Sapling Forest, Cherry Plum Blossom* has overtones of Japanese art. It celebrates the natural world in all its forms with the spiky, dead branch of the tree in the foreground emulating the shape of a bird's head. The slender new growth of the paler wooded trees contrast perfectly with the older, knotty wood, suggestive of the circle of life and the enduring beauty of nature. Pugh was also known for his portraiture. His first solo exhibition in 1957 won him critical acclaim. From then on, Pugh's success within Australia was assured and he went on to become one of the country's most popular artists. He took advantage of this to play a prominent role in the political world. A staunch supporter of the Australian Labour Party, he painted flattering portraits of the party's leading lights, such as his acclaimed 1972 portrait of Gough Whitlam. Pugh was a founding member of the Dunmoochin Artists' Society in 1953, a collection of fellow artists who appreciated the beauty of the Victoria landscape in which they lived. Shortly before his death, Pugh helped to ensure the future of the area, by setting up the Dunmoochin Foundation, a preservation charity. **LH**

Nigredo | Anselm Kiefer

1984 | mixed media on canvas | 130 x 218 ½ in | Philadelphia Museum of Art, Philadelphia, PA, USA

The title of this painting is an alchemical term meaning "decomposition" and is a stage in the process by which the alchemist attempts to turn "base material" into gold. To achieve a state of perfection, it was believed that the mixture of ingredients had to be heated and reduced down to black matter. Here the German artist Anselm Kiefer (b.1945) explores the physical, psychological, philosophical, and spiritual character of such a transformation. The base materials are either represented or physically present in this painting, which incorporates oil, acrylic, and emulsion paints, shellac, straw, a photograph, and a woodcut print. Many thinkers, including Carl Jung, saw nigredo as representing part of a spiritual or psychological process in which chaos and despair are necessary precursors to enlightenment. Kiefer uses this idea to refer to contemporary German society and culture, most notably the legacy of the Third Reich—the "place" represented here is historical rather than geographical. This is an image of a scorched and rutted earth rather than a beautiful landscape, but suggests stubble burning in a field, anticipating new crops, and therefore new life, in the future. Kiefer's landscapes are expressive but not Expressionist; they are used as a stage upon which the artist presents his numerous themes. The combination of paint with other materials highlights the physicality of making and reflecting; Kiefer is thus suggesting that a reflection on the purpose of painting itself is an integral part of the enlightenment process. **RW**

The Vivian Girls with China | Paula Rego

1984 | acrylic on paper | 4 ¾ x 6 in / 12 x 15 cm | Bristol City Museum & Art Gallery, UK

With typically unsettling energy, Paula Rego's (b.1935) mix of childhood fantasy and somewhat fetishistic sex explode onto the paper. The artist had a privileged if rather isolated upbringing in a Lisbon stifled by the dictatorship of António de Oliveira Salazar. Childhood influences included the oral storytelling tradition practiced by the women around her, Roman Catholic culture, the expected female roles of wife and mother, and the prevailing political oppression. Fairy tales, cartoons, childhood fantasy, animals acting as people, overturning accepted norms, and personal and sexual repression—these are Rego's trademarks, and this work is almost a checklist of them. The story of the Vivian Girls, who feature in several of her works, comes from the epic novel by Henry Darger about an imaginary planet where seven Christian princesses—the Vivian sisters—fight an often vicious and bloody campaign against the childhood slavery meted out by their evil overlords. In this picture, the willful girls engage in a variety of tasks, from the innocently childish one of playing a whistle to sexual games akin to bondage and domination—in Rego's world, this is the flip side of sexual and personal repression. The girls, animals, and coloration in this work all have the Pop-arty feel of cartoons. The artist has devised a personal, dreamlike story and the whole forms a kind of chaotic pattern. Rego has transformed the expressive female storytelling of her youth in ways that tell us about female power and make us question accepted values and beliefs. **AK**

The Abgar Head | Georg Baselitz

1984 | oil, acrylic on canvas | 98 ³/₈ x 78 ³/₄ in / 250 x 200 cm | Louisiana Museum, Humlebæk, Denmark

Georg Baselitz (Hans-Georg Kern; *b*.1938) grew up in the schoolhouse where his father taught in the village of Deutschbaselitz, outside Dresden. At eighteen, he went to East Berlin to study art and was expelled after two terms for "socio-political immaturity." Before he left for the West, he took the name of his birthplace as a "reminder of his Saxon roots." Famous for painting upside-down, Baselitz became a leading exponent of Neoexpressionism, which made an impact in the 1980s by reinfusing painting with all that had been edited out through Modernist refinement. Typically containing a surfeit of references ranging from the personally poetic to the erotic and political, the manner in which the Neoexpressionists' liberated content was painted was also unrestrained. The self-

consciousness of the traditionalist and the restraint and denial of the minimalist were overcome by a carefree exuberance that attached the bravura of Abstract Expressionism to a new content. Baselitz's portrait, *The Abgar Head*, owes much to his long-standing interest in African art. The color, ranging from the Fauves to psychedelia, is anchored by vigorous brushwork that weaves the image together. As an abstract image, it rewards our attention through its richness of gesture and color. When we add further layers of meaning, as the masklike black face emerges, prompting an exchange between a sophisticated Western aesthetic and a "primitive" representation, the painting brushes aside any politeness and mounts a frontal attack on our sensibilities. **RW**

Crucifixion 3.85 | Antonio Saura

1985 | oil on canvas | 96 ½ x 76 ¾ in / 245 x 195 cm | Private collection

Antonio Saura (1930–98) was born in Huesca and lived with his family in Madrid, Valencia, and Barcelona. From an early age his father took him to the Prado Museum in Madrid, where works by Velázquez and Goya captured his imagination. Velázquez' *Crucifixion* of 1631 became one of his greatest sources of inspiration. In 1947, while convalescing from a long illness, Saura taught himself to paint. His early works show the influence of Surrealism, and when Saura moved to Paris in 1954 he made contact with leading members of the Surrealist movement. After two years he returned to Spain, and began working in a much more expressionist style. In 1957, in Madrid, he founded the El Paso group, which popularized Art Informel in Spain. Saura won the Guggenheim Prize in

1960 and the Carnegie Prize in 1964. His work became increasingly violent and his stormy monochromatic paintings and later expressive, dark, thick, layered oils are reminiscent of Goya's brooding works. Saura never lost his early fascination with Velázquez' *Crucifixion*, and returned to the theme over and again in later life. His first *Crucifixion* was painted in 1957 and his last in 1996. Each is different, yet similarities are evident. He never includes figures of Christ, but features ordinary people, to illustrate the tragedy of mankind. His figures are dynamic and distorted, helpless in an intimidating world. *Crucifixion 3.85* is an impressive flat black cross on a white background, with touches of heavy yellow and gray paint delineating the figure. It cannot fail to grab your attention. **SH**

Entry into Port of a Ship with a Red Rose Aboard | Enzo Cucchi

1985–86 | fresco | Philadelphia Museum of Art, Philadelphia, PA, USA

This is expressive of Enzo Cucchi's (*b*.1949) more subdued works—somber colors and stark themes, redolent of death and sadness. In this work, the crosses ostensibly mark the moorings of other boats in the port, which the ship must navigate its way beyond. Yet they are sinister, suggestive of cemeteries, or perhaps slave ships. The deliberately smeared black leeching from some of the crosses evokes not only water in the port, but also tears and misery. The ship is heading directly into the most impassable area of the port, into a crevice through which it cannot possibly pass. Cucchi's fondness for mixing media means that his works often include reclaimed objects, such as neon lighting tubes or pieces of wood. He experiments with the use of natural and artificial lights, exploring the painterly properties of both. After the mid-1990s, Cucchi's works began to get smaller in size, but as a result they are often much richer in detail. In recent years, Cucchi has become most renowned for his sculpture, which has been in high demand in Europe and the United States. Just as many of his paintings feature elongated figures, Cucchi's sculptures, like *Fontana d'Italia* (1993), often feature elongated columns or shapes. When asked about his work in 2001, Cucchi said: "I strive to give to others a sense of sacredness, because an art event is not just a formal fact, but also a moment where you put a mark on your dedication. You must have a feeling of joining a tribe where there is the chain of command, because you are in a sacred place with its rules." **LH**

Knights Not Nights | Ross Bleckner

1986–87 | oil and wax on canvas | 108 x 72 in / 274.3 x 182.8 cm | SFMoMA, San Fransisco, CA, USA

Ross Bleckner (*b*.1949) was born in New York where he still lifes and works. As a student at NYU he was encouraged by Chuck Close to enroll at the California Institute for the Arts. Despite the predominance of conceptual and photographic work at that time, he maintained a commitment to painting. Returning to New York in 1974, Bleckner settled in SoHo and was among the first artists to join the then fledgling Mary Boone Gallery along with David Salle and Julian Schnabel. At the time Bleckner's style had little in common with the muscular neo-Expressionism of most of the gallery's artists. His early paintings were formal compositions containing striped and spiraling forms—reworkings of the visual devices of Op Art. The art world's preference was still for expressive figuration and Bleckner was disappointed by the response to his work of this period. The excesses of the art of the 80s, however, gradually appeared overblown and played out, which coincided with the emergence of Bleckner's subtle and symbolic imagery. Despite appearing abstract, the paintings depict real-world things, sometimes at a microscopic level and it is hard to tell whether we are very close or far away from the painting's subject. In this painting we could be gazing at a starry constellation or cell mutation. Bleckner was the first artist to address AIDS in his work and the death of his father through cancer influenced work based on electron-microscopy. His comment that it is a cell wall that separates us from disaster adds melancholy to this sublimely seductive painting. **RW**

The Neo Cubist
R.B. Kitaj

1986–87 | oil on canvas | 70 x 52 in / 178 x 133 cm | Saatchi Collection, London, UK

First sent to Europe with the U.S. army, R.B. Kitaj (1932–2007) remained in England to study—first at the Ruskin School of Drawing, Oxford, and later at the Royal College of Art (1959–61) where he befriended David Hockney. Kitaj was to make a profound impression on his fellow students at the RCA and was credited as "sparking the birth of British Pop art" because of his decision to graft ordinary objects on to his early paintings. Despite the initial label of "Pop artist," Kitaj also looked to history, literature, and politics for inspiration. In the 1970s, Kitaj began *The Neo Cubist*, a portrait of Hockney, his long-time close friend. He left it unfinished until the late 1980s when Hockney's description of the death of his friend, Isherwood, in California, prompted Kitaj to take up the work again and to draw a kind of "alter figure" over the original full-frontal Hockney. The result is that Hockney seems paradoxically contained by, and emerging from, a giant ovoid situated in a vivid sun-baked landscape, ripe with references to Matisse. The work also pays homage to Hockney's experiments with photomontage and prints—heralded by some as the natural successors to the great Cubist masterpieces. In Kitaj's portrait, Hockney has been deconstructed in a Cubist manner to reveal movements not normally possible on a two-dimensional surface. But the painting is not contained by the rules of Cubism and deals as much with the frustration of being trapped by a particular style, as it acknowledges Hockney's then current preoccupation with Neo-Cubist theory. **JN**

If You're Born to Be Hanged Then You Will Never Be Drowned
Sandro Chia

1986–87 | oil on paper on canvas | 7 x 7 ¾ in / 18.1 x 20 cm | Private collection

Sandro Chia (*b.*1946) studied fresco painting and sculpture in Florence in the 1960s before traveling extensively in India, Turkey, and Europe. He settled in Rome in 1970 and experimented with conceptual and performance art, but returned to painting in 1975 and formed part of the Italian movement Transavanguardia ("beyond avant-garde"). It developed as a reaction against the conceptual and minimalist art of the 1970s and celebrated a return to the simple enjoyment of painting, drawing on various artistic influences, and producing large-scale figurative paintings. In 1981–82, he moved to New York and was grouped with the Neoexpressionists who, like the Transavanguardes, returned to portraying recognizable objects, such as the human body (although sometimes in a virtually

abstract manner), in a rough and violently emotional way, using vivid colors and color harmonies. Chia's *If You're Born to Be Hanged Then You Will Never Be Drowned* displays a decorative use of color and pattern. His swirling brushstrokes show his proficiency in fresco and are reminiscent of the dynamic work of the Italian Futurists. Resembling a pile of twisted fabrics entwined in a heap, the distorted textures, undulating shapes, and vibrant colors seem incongruous with the title. Chia said that the art world "is the weirdest scene in the world," alluding to the way in which artists are defined through others' opinions of them and the notion of success and power. Chia believes that modern art has suffered a moral lapse and this painting expresses what little sense it all makes. **SH**

St. John | Gerhard Richter

1988 | oil on canvas | 79 x 102 in / 200 x 260 cm | Tate Collection, London, UK

Born in Dresden, East Germany, where he trained as a painter, Gerhard Richter (*b*.1932) moved to the West just before the Berlin Wall was erected in 1961 and studied at the Düsseldorf Academy. Perhaps due to this early experience of moving from the traditions and certainties of East Germany to the permissive and sceptical West, Richter constructed a practice that stood apart from both the established conventions of painting and the popular voices of the time that predicted painting's ultimate demise. Characterized by breaks in style that do not follow the usual linear chronology from figuration to abstraction, his bodies of works—designated by the artist as "figurative," "constructive," and "abstract"—overlap, and paintings produced in the same period often differ dramatically in their appearance and method. These aesthetic contradictions are central to Richter's approach, as he rejects any singular idea of style as an unnecessary limitation on his practice as an artist. *St. John* is one of a series of abstract paintings known as the "London Paintings", named after chapels in Westminster Abbey. Like all of his paintings of the last two decades or so, it is generated from an initial painting to which a further layer of paint is applied. He then scrapes and drags the surface with spatulas to reveal previous layers. The mixed layers produce a painting that can be neither predicted nor completely controlled and that bears no resemblance to the original image. Richter has spoken of an affinity to music in these paintings, underlining their illusiveness and resistance to description. **RW**

Greenfield | Susan Rothenberg

c.1990 | oil on canvas | 78 x 111 in / 198 x 282 cm | Private collection

Susan Rothenberg (*b*.1945) has been called the Stubbs of contemporary painting. Like the iconic Victorian English painter, Rothenberg is best known for her paintings of horses. Though unlike Stubbs's representational animal portraits, Rothenberg, who was born in Buffalo, New York, tends to straddle the line between abstraction and figuration. Though her work was influenced by her era's experimentation with form, she is known for treading her own path. Though also influenced by Abstract Expressionism, in that her process cries out for as much attention as the finished products, she nevertheless repeatedly refuses to go completely abstract. Like Jasper Johns's flags, Rothenberg employs repetition to deconstruct objects. In *Greenfield*, two eerily slim figures occupy the center of the painting. One is black and the other is Rothenberg's signature red. This opposition creates tension: Why is each figure divided by a heavy line? Perhaps this is emblematic of Rothenberg's oft-stated aim to flatten out and remove the object-ness of what she paints. The faces of the figures have both feline and ursine qualities yet their vertical posture is more human than animal. The dark background behind them lends a stormy, ominous feeling to the whole work. Rothenberg's consistent themes have earned her long-standing institutional and critical respect. The questions she challenges herself with during her process remain intriguingly unanswered in her work—lending a captivating set of cyclical concerns always in evidence in her oeuvre. **SE**

Untitled | Jenny Saville

1990 | oil on canvas | 80 ½ x 72 in / 204.5 x 183 cm | Private collection

The classic tradition of nude portraiture was turned on its head with the arrival of Jenny Saville (b.1970). In Saville's massive canvases, fleshy female bodies and overt physicality dominate. Using oil paint, she maximizes her medium's sculptural and architectural properties by building thick layers of paint. Born in Cambridge, England, Saville's rise to stardom has been swift. England's foremost contemporary art patron, Charles Saatchi, has supported her throughout her career in her preoccupation with radically updating one of art's classic subjects. The entire canvas of Untitled is filled with the hulking neck and chubby cheeks of a young bride. Mottled red dominates the neck area, creating a queasy juxtaposition to her gauzy white veil, under which her small eyes nonchalantly confront the viewer. With no body to match her face, the viewer is not distracted from witnessing what appears to be a personal moment in the subject's life. Untitled provokes questions about the context of the moment Saville depicts: Is the bride alone? Has the ceremony been performed? Is the veil a prop in a lonely woman's fantasy? Saville has been compared to Peter Paul Rubens (1577–1640) and Lucian Freud (1922–2011). However, they do not match her feminist concern with the female form, which confronts the viewer and their prejudices head on. The flesh of Saville's sitters is not being offered for passive viewing. By depicting obese female bodies as simultaneously glorious and grotesque, Saville undermines notions of idealized feminine beauty. **SE**

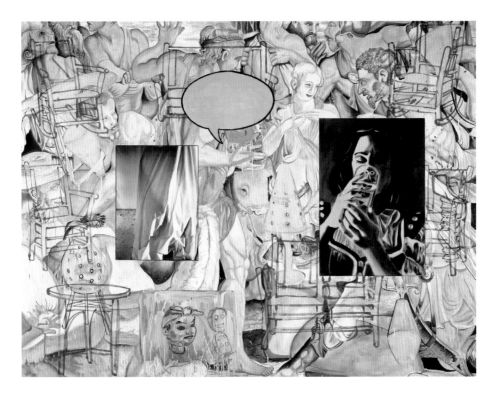

Mingus in Mexico | David Salle

1990 | acrylic and oil on canvas | 96 x 123 in / 244 x 312 cm | Saatchi Gallery, London, UK

David Salle (b.1952) gathers random images from all areas of history and culture, throws them onto his canvases, and paints whatever sticks. His postmodern pastiche paintings have been called "ham-fisted" and "cynical, calculating, and cold" by detractors—to which Salle responds, "Literal-mindedness doesn't get you anywhere very interesting. I want to take bigger leaps." He plunges into art history, popular culture, pornography, and anthropology, and piles images and styles on top of each other in oil paintings. There is no discernible method, meaning, or logic to the juxtapositions on Salle's canvases, where a photorealist representation of a snapshot sits next to a graffitilike scrawl or is forced under a block of solid color. His images are layered the way

posters and advertisements are pasted over each other on city billboards. This scattershot aesthetic is exemplified in *Mingus in Mexico*. Figures extracted from Roman myths are interwoven with an empty cartoon speech bubble, racist memorabilia, ghosts of chairs hovering in outline forms, and a carefully constructed copy of a girl drinking from a cup—an image he repeats in a number of other paintings. The Oklahoma-born Salle studied under conceptual art legend John Baldessari (b.1931). While Baldessari's impatience with the pretensions of art theory and art itself provides the conceptual foundation for Salle's snappy, collagelike paintings, they surely recall Salvador Dalí (1904–89) and his investigations into psychological, not physical, realities. **AH**

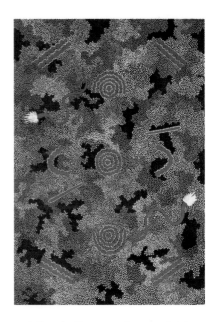

Northwest Territory
Gerrit Greve

c.1990 | acrylic and sand on canvas | 36 x 30 in /
91.4 x 76.2 cm | Private collection

Men's Dreaming, 1990
Clifford Tjapaltjarri

1990 | acrylic on canvas | 52 ¾ in x 36 ⅝ in / 134 x 93 cm
Aranda Art Gallery, Melbourne, Australia

Gerrit Greve has explored a variety of styles, subjects, and materials as a way of maintaining a fresh approach. He works in an analytical way, embracing shape and structure using thick brushstrokes and intense color. His paintings of the American northwest are inspired by Native American blankets and emphasize the rich hues and textures of landscapes lit by the shimmering sun. Pattern is accentuated through strongly contrasting colors. In this painting, Greve shows his love for his adopted America, and although he rejects art movements, both Pop art and Abstract Expressionism appear to have had some bearing on the final result. The vast tundra is represented by the vertical stripes of earthy colors and modern highways by the black and purple horizontal stripes. Fine black stripes border the verticals, and orange stripes outline the horizontals, unifying and empowering the work. **SH**

Clifford Tjapaltjarri (1932–2002) grew up around Jay Creek in the Northern Territory, Australia. He was influenced by the art teacher Geoffrey Bardon, who came to Papunya in the early 1970s to encourage Aboriginal artists. Until then, the Aboriginal people had only drawn their "dreamtime stories" in the sand, and Bardon wanted them to commit them to canvas. Bardon provided the acrylic paint and canvases and left his students to express their cultural and personal visions. As a result, a new movement emerged known as Western Desert Art, and Tjapaltjarri became one of its leading exponents. His paintings fetch large sums at auction and are now held in almost every major collection in the world. Typical of Tjapaltjarri's style, *Men's Dreaming, 1990* is composed of a series of precise dots of paint; the figures of the Dreaming are arranged symmetrically over a maplike design. **TS**

On the Edge of Night
David Austen

1991 | oil on linen | 14 x 12 in / 35.5 x 30.5 cm
Hayward Gallery, London, UK

British artist David Austen (*b.*1960) lives and works in London, and his paintings and sculptures are represented in many major collections. His works are universally bold and moving and rank among the best of British abstract art. *On the Edge of Night* is an intensely evocative image, with the deep velvet darkness of the "night" almost tangible, while the electric blue of "morning" seems to vibrate with an energy of its own. The small blue form is such that it has the illusion of growing, mimicking the slow swell of light as dawn breaks, and shimmers with the concentrated color contrasted against the deep background. His minimal line and form compact the essence of the painting, focusing attention on the two colors and creating a forum for reflection. The artist has created great effect through the application of blue and black, a technique used in many of his paintings of this period. **TP**

Sailing Against the Current
Miquel Barceló

1991 | mixed media on canvas | 118 x 79 in / 300 x 200 cm | Private collection

Spanish artist Miquel Barceló Artigues (*b.*1957) is best known for his paintings that incorporate earth, sand, and organic materials. *Sailing Against the Current* reveals the influence of Jackson Pollock. Like Pollock, Barceló created this painting partly by dripping paint onto a large canvas on the ground. *Sailing Against the Current* also shows the artist's interest in African culture. Since 1988 he has spent time in Mali, and this painting was completed the same year he traveled the six hundred miles separating Ségou from Gao in a canoe, along the River Niger. The small craft inhabited by tiny men struggling against the current could be of almost any part of the world at any time. Yet despite the superhuman effort of these fishermen, Barceló's lovingly painted, thick blue, green, and white paint shows that the environment they are in is a thing of beauty as well as the provider of a livelihood. **CK**

Myth of the Western Man (White Man's Burden) | Gordon Bennett

1992 | polymer paint on canvas | 68 ⁷/₈ x 119 ⁷/₈ in | Art Gallery of New South Wales, Sydney, Australia

Gordon Bennett was born in Monto, Queensland, Australia in 1955. He left school at fifteen, taking on a variety of jobs until, in 1998, he graduated in Fine Arts at the Queensland College of Art. He quickly established himself as an artist addressing the themes of identity and alternative histories. His interest in this area was sparked by the discovery, at the age of eleven, that he had Aboriginal ancestry. He says his work is an expression of the eighteen years it took to come to terms with his own "socialization." Much of Bennett's work is concerned with casual racism in white-dominated Australia, asserting a personal liberation from racial labels and stereotypes. Since 1989, he has held more than fifty solo exhibitions and been in major exhibitions of contemporary art. *Myth*

of the Western Man (White Man's Burden) uses a figure of an Australian pioneer clinging to a collapsing pole or mast. The figure's left leg disappears into a flurry of white dots, possibly indicating how cutural identity can become blurred over the passage of time. There are patches of blue among the white dots, with stenciled dates important in Aboriginal history. The influence of other artists, most notably Jackson Pollock and Aboriginal artists of the desert region, is evident. The use of small dots evokes pointillism, but also reflects the technique used in desert painting for disguising secret knowledge. His melding of styles and referencing of iconic Western imagery challenges the viewer to assess his or her view of both colonial and Aboriginal history. **TS**

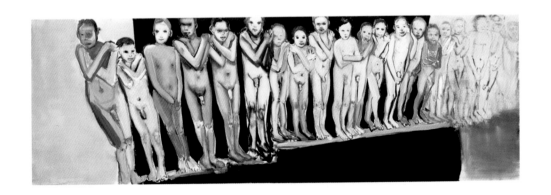

Young Boys | Marlene Dumas

1993 | oil on canvas | 39 ⅜ x 118 ⅛ in / 100 x 300 cm | Saatchi Gallery, London, UK

Born in 1953 in South Africa, Marlene Dumas has been an active painter in the Netherlands since 1976. She began her artistic education during the apartheid era at the University of Cape Town (1972 to 1975). Thanks to a major grant she then continued her studies at the Atelier '63 in Haarlem, Netherlands (now De Ateliers, Amsterdam), where she teaches today. She also attended courses in psychology at the Psychological Institute of the University of Amsterdam between 1979 and 1980. Dumas became famous for her portraits of children and erotic scenes. She has exhibited her work extensively in European venues and has been part of major international expositions such as the Venice Biennale (Italy) and Documenta VII, Kassel (Germany). Combining elements of Expressionism and conceptual art, she paints ink and watercolor pieces, as well as oil on canvas. Her work is often disturbing; she insists on confronting difficult subjects such as childhood abuse and the sexual exploitation of women. Painted in 1993, *Young Boys* is one of Dumas's most impressive paintings. A long line of naked boys fills up the picture's ambiguous space. Toward the right the figures trail off into the distance, becoming mere outlines. Dumas's rapidity of execution provides a real lightness of touch, which deeply contrasts with the gravity and disturbing power of the work upon the viewer. Her palette of colors, ranging from a grayish pink to a pale bluish gray, reinforces the general feeling of strangeness provided by the image. **JJ**

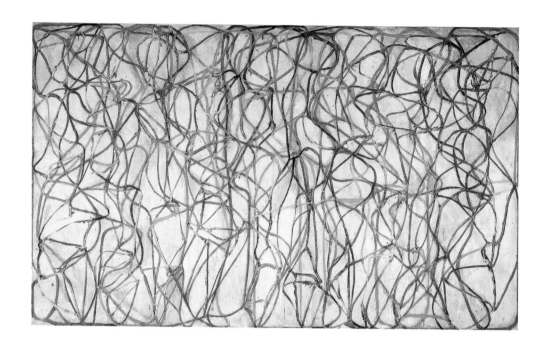

The Muses | Brice Marden

1993 | oil on linen | 108 x 180 in / 274.5 x 458 cm | Daros Collection, Zürich, Switzerland

After decades of painting strict minimalist canvases, New York-based artist Brice Marden (b.1938) turned in the 1980s to Western formalism to express the essence of Eastern spirituality. His monumental series of large-scale calligraphic oil paintings, *Cold Mountain*, was inspired by Han Shan (whose name translates to Cold Mountain), a seventh-century Chinese poet and hermit who wrote of transcendence from the physical "world of dust." Marden's paintings, created by trailing long ailanthus twigs dipped in paint across linen canvases, strive to achieve a sense of the streamlined spirituality he learned from his study of Far-Eastern artistic methods and philosophy. Marden was born in Bronxville, New York, and received his MFA from Yale University. His initial monochromatic beeswax and pigment canvases presented references to his personal history and experiences through abstract forms. Although his great admiration of scholarly work is evident in the titles of his works, and many of Manhattan's most revered intellectuals became his friends, ultimately impressions and instinct guide the work of this erudite artist. Marden's kinetic markings impart an enveloping sense of calm and unity to his canvases. Works in his 1991–97 series *Study for the Muses (Hydra Version)* are categorized by an increased complexity in the interrelationship between lines and background. In this series, the lines interlock and are swallowed in portions by the base color paint, in the same way that inspiration, life, and creativity bleed and blend together. **AH**

The Four Seasons: Spring | Cy Twombly

1993–94 | acrylic, oil, crayon, pencil on canvas | 123 x 74 in / 313 x 189 cm | Tate Collection, London, UK

When the American Abstract artist Cy Twombly (b.1928) settled permanently in Rome in 1959, he moved away from his close association with the New York art scene. In doing so, he succeeded in creating his own personal art, which has earned him a reputation as one of the greatest artists of the second half of the twentieth century. Twombly exhibited his works at the Venice Biennale in 1964, and four years later the Milwaukee Art Center hosted his first retrospective—the first in a long series organized by the greatest museums around the world. In 1995 the architect Renzo Piano designed the Cy Twombly Gallery of The Menil Collection in Houston, Texas. This collection holds more than thirty of Twombly's art works, not only paintings, but also sculptures, drawings, and other works on paper dating from 1953 to 1994. Twombly executed this painting at a point when he was already an internationally celebrated artist. Spring is a work from a famous series entitled The Four Seasons, painted between 1993 and 1994. Being obsessed with the history of art, it is not surprising that Twombly chose such a topic for his masterpiece series. But here, instead of providing the viewer with a traditional representation of the season of rebirth, he has created an ambiguous image, in which the sensuous colors are as peaceful as they are violent. Twombly's early graphic style can be observed here in the numerous inscriptions of random words all over the painting, and the act of painting itself is a theme that he has revisited throughout his career. **JJ**

Road to Zenica | Peter Howson

1994 | oil on canvas | 80 x 125 ½ in / 203 x 319 cm | Flowers East Gallery, London, UK

"Stark" and "uncompromising" are words that have followed Peter Howson (b.1958) throughout his prolific career. Focusing on heroics, conflict, and religion, Howson's works are an apocalyptic, tortured and vivid parody of real life. He studied at Glasgow School of Art and caught the public's attention in the late 1980s with a series of figurative sketches satirizing individual and institutional violence. More recently he has increasingly turned to religious subjects but has also dabbled in caricatures of more contemporary figures from pop star Madonna to the British Queen. In the Spring of 1993, sponsored by London's Imperial War Museum and the *Times* newspaper, Howson traveled with the British forces to Bosnia as an official war artist. He was so horrified by what he saw that he

quickly became ill, and was forced to return home. As Howson said, "I was so moved by what I saw in Bosnia that I didn't think painting had any importance any more." With his family's encouragement he returned in December 1993, and went on to produce thirty-five works including *Road to Zenica*. This painting depicts displaced refugees fleeing the conflict, their faces gaunt and haggard with anxiety and exhaustion. The guns bring home the reality of their plight—this is a life or death situation. It is a shock when the viewer realizes that the children also have the same haunted, despairing expression. Howson's honest portrayal is chilling, but the viewer should not look away. While it's difficult to take in, it's unlikely the viewer will regret having seen the world through Howson's eyes. **JM**

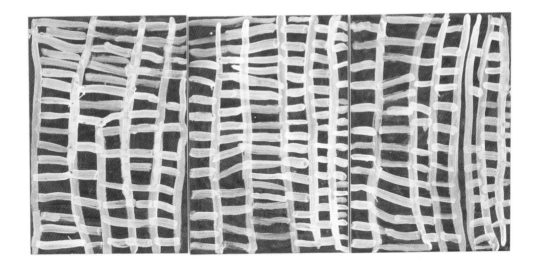

Untitled (Awelye) | Emily Kngwarreye

1994 | acrylic on paper transferred to canvas | 40 x 84 in | Art Gallery of New South Wales, Sydney, Australia

Aboriginal artist Emily Kame Kngwarreye (c.1910–96) painted her first acrylic on canvas in her seventies and soon became one of Australia's great modern painters. She is thought to have been born in 1910 and had already spent a lifetime making art and batik cloth for ceremonial and everyday purposes, especially for *"awelye"*—female-only Aboriginal rituals—to which the subtitle of this triptych also refers. The striped designs traditionally painted on the breasts and necklines of women during ritual ceremonies inspired many of Kngwarreye's paintings, which also respond to the land and spiritual forces through the interplay of lines, dots, and colors. The earthy hues of this austere, late, monochrome work recall the rock formations and red earth of her ancestral home in Alhalkere on a stretch of Aboriginal desert land known as Utopia, northeast of Alice Springs. The white lines may also represent tracks in the physical sense as well as in the metaphorical sense of being tracks through time and history. Before her artistic career, Kngwarreye formed the Utopia Women's Batik Group in 1978 and exhibited her silk designs across the country. She began painting prolifically in 1988, producing around three thousand works on silk, cotton, and canvas in just eight years, the proceeds of which went back into her community. Surprisingly for an indigenous artist, she quickly gained mainstream acceptance in Australia, even representing the nation at the Venice Biennale, albeit a year after her death, in 1997. **OW**

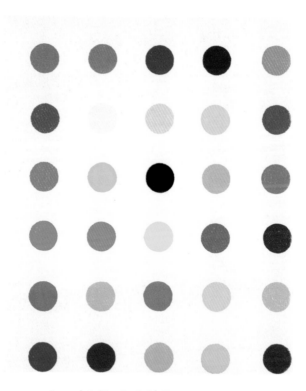

Arachidic Acid | Damien Hirst

1994 | gloss household paint on canvas | 12 x 10 in / 30.5 x 25.4 cm | White Cube, London, UK

The longtime leader of the Young British Artists, a movement that began in earnest in the late 1980s, Damien Hirst (*b.*1965) is a sculptor, installation artist, printmaker, and painter. His declared interest in the darkness of death, the fragility of life, the specter of violence, lust and its aftermath, and the chemical nature of existence has captivated the art world. Among his most famous works are those using the carcasses of dead animals preserved in massive tanks and cabinets filled with odd collections from pharmaceuticals to seashells. *The Physical Impossibility of Death in the Mind of Someone Living*, a villainous shark pickled in formaldehyde, catapulted the artist into international limelight. *Arachidic Acid*, a smallish early spot painting, takes its sinister name from an innocuous saturated fatty acid found in peanut oil. Hirst is fascinated with the difference between drugs and the everyday substances that we ingest, which are often full of insalubrious compounds. Although these inconclusive spots are befuddling at first, they are deeply entrenched in the history of color theory beginning with the French in the nineteenth century. Hirst claims to never repeat the same color twice on the canvas, thereby juxtaposing several different and sometimes similar tones, which recalls the optical process of sight. Several painters before him, from Seurat to Richter, touched upon this same central concept. The irony of what we perceive and how we perceive is evident in Hirst's spots, an elegant examination of color in its most elemental form. **SP**

Lending an Ear to the Past | Ofelia Rodríguez

1994 | mixed media on canvas | 66 x 82 in | University of Essex Collection of Latin American Art, UK

Ofelia Rodríguez was born in Barranquilla, Colombia, in 1946. She studied Fine Arts in Bogotá and later in the United States, where she received a Masters in Fine Arts from Yale University in 1972. She now lives and works in London. *Lending an Ear to the Past (Prestándole un Oido al Pasado)* is an arresting piece that opens up to the eye like a window to a fantastic tropical landscape. Its large scale and the expansive areas of contrasting bold, flat color envelop the viewer. Rodríguez's paintings often include a sculptural element, in this case a small wooden box positioned on the lower edge of the canvas. Rodríguez's boxes are often filled with kitsch objects bought from markets, in the manner of a Dadaist readymade or *objet trouvé*. The doors of this box open

to a mysterious world within which a fetus rests on a bed of plastic grass. Rodríguez has created an object that invites the viewer to look at what is contained within its intimate, small space. What is within may relate to her personal history as she makes the private public. However, the painting's title probably suggests a broader past. Rodríguez's work addresses the scars inflicted on Colombia and Latin America. References to popular culture combine with Western aesthetics in her art, mirroring the melting pot of peoples and cultures existing from the arrival of the conquistadors onward in a search for national or indigenous identity. In Rodríguez's oeuvre, this identity is reflected in bright and surprising creations that heal the wounds of the past with humor and spirit. **HH**

Half-Brothers (Exit to Nowhere–Machiavellian) | Mark Wallinger

1994–95 | oil on canvas | 90 ½ x 118 ½ in / 230 x 300 cm | Tate Collection, London, UK

Art and horseracing have long been interests for British artist Mark Wallinger (*b*.1959). Like art, horseracing subscribes to its own set of invented rules, and so it seemed natural to him that he should work with an activity whose artificiality mirrors the fabrications of his chosen profession. He received a Turner nomination in 1995 following his unorthodox *A Real Work of Art*, where he bought a racehorse and called it an artwork, in the tradition of a Marcel Duchamp "readymade". In addition to acknowledging that the recognition of any object as an artwork involves a leap of faith on the part of the viewer, *A Real Work of Art* touched on the unsettling consequences aroused by the prospect of eugenics. This theme found another outlet in a related group of four naturalistic paintings entitled *Half-Brothers*, in which the front half of one famous British racehorse is paired with the rear end of its maternal and equally famous blood-brother: Diesis with Keen, Unfawain with Nashwan, Jupiter Island with Precocious, and Exit to Nowhere with Machiavellian. Taken together these life-size paintings of racehorses reflect on the complexity of the relationship between a parent and its offspring, and the crucial role played by stud farms in determining the outcome of any thoroughbred breeding program. In his exploration of the issues of cultural and personal identity, and in his works that relate to the turf, Wallinger has created one of the most important bodies of work to come out of the UK on the subject of self and belonging. **PB**

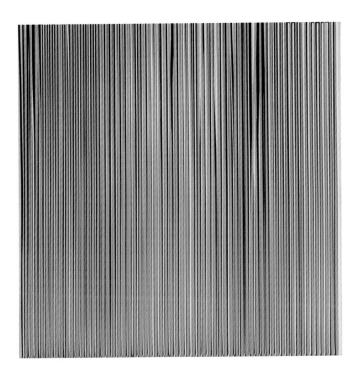

Poured Lines: Light Orange, Blue, Yellow, Dark Green and Orange
Ian Davenport

1995 | household paint on canvas | 84 x 84 in | Arts Council Collection, Hayward Gallery, London, UK

At first glance, *Poured Lines: Light Orange, Blue, Yellow, Dark Green and Orange* is reminiscent of works such as *Winter Palace* (1981) by British Op artist Bridget Riley. The use of flat color and line by abstract artists such as Riley has no doubt exerted its influence on Ian Davenport (*b*.1966), but this painting has a distinctly end-of-the-twentieth-century feel. It is the work of one of the Young British Artists (YBA) and shares the concerns of the group. Davenport studied at Northwich College of Art and Design, Cheshire, and at Goldsmiths College, London. He exhibited in the influential Freeze exhibition, curated by Damien Hirst, in London in 1988. In 1991 he was nominated for the Turner Prize. Like fellow YBA Hirst with his spot and spin paintings, Davenport is interested in color, the

process of painting, and the element of chance in the process of creation. Like YBA Gary Hume he uses an everyday material in the form of household paint, and like YBA Michael Landy he is interested in exploring the concepts of consumerism and mass reproduction. Davenport is as fascinated by how he creates a painting as in the eventual result. *Poured Lines* is one of a series of works created by pouring layers of household paints on to tilted canvases and boards; gravity and the viscosity of the paint determine the final outcome. The large-scale density of the lines, and color combinations—especially the blurring of colors when lines of paint mix—create beautiful objects that require an act of meditation from the viewer, almost like that of Davenport when doing his paintings. **CK**

The Holy Virgin Mary
Chris Ofili

1996 | mixed media on linen | 95 ½ x 71 ½ in / 243 x 182 cm | Private collection

An English painter of Nigerian descent, Chris Ofili (*b*.1968) was born in Manchester. From 1988 to 1991, he studied at London's Chelsea School of Art before going on to the Royal College of Art from 1991 to 1993. Ofili's reputation grew after a series of exhibitions at the Saatchi Gallery in London, in particular the Sensation exhibition, which traveled to several venues in 1997. The following year, Ofili was awarded the Turner Prize. *The Holy Virgin Mary* is a work that shows how the painter draws inspiration from his African origins. He was awarded a grant in 1992 and traveled to Zimbabwe, where he spent his time studying cave paintings—an experience that was a turning point in his art. This painted collage consists of multiple layers of oil paint, resin, glitter, and elephant dung. It depicts the Virgin Mary in an unconventional manner. The African Madonna emerges from a surreal background, made of close-ups of female genitalia cut from pornographic magazines. They were incorporated to reference the cherubs that traditionally accompany the Virgin Mary, and it is these elements that provoke accusations that the painting is blasphemous. In 1999, during its only display in the United States as part of the Sensation exhibition, the painting was one of several works that sparked a legal battle between the mayor of New York City and the host venue, Brooklyn Museum of Art as to whether the exhibition could go ahead—it did. Ofili's works are now in several collections, including the Tate Collection, London, and the Museum of Modern Art, New York. **JJ**

Air Superiority | Vitaly Komar and Alex Melamid

1997 | tempera oil on canvas | 66 x 66 in / 168 x 168 cm | Ronald Feldman Fine Arts, New York, NY, USA

Vitaly Komar (b.1943) and Alex Melamid (b.1945) are highly intelligent and engaging individuals—both were born in Moscow, and both were students there from 1958 to 1967. Their collaboration as artists started in 1965 and formally ended in 2005. Retrospectivism, their first joint show, was held at the Blue Bird Café in Moscow in 1967. An artist statement at the time made the nature of their collaboration clear: "Even if only one of us creates some of the projects and works, we usually sign them together. We are not just an artist, we are a movement." Komar and Melamid's collaboration started at a time when it was unusual for artists to share authorship, but by the end of the twentieth century, collaborations of this type had become positively fashionable. In 1967, they initiated SOTS, the Soviet version of the Western Pop art movement. However, they were expelled from the Youth section of the Soviet Artist Union in 1973, and in 1978 they became residents of the United States. Just three years later they became the first Russians to receive a National Endowment for the Arts grant. In *Air Superiority*, the U.S.'s most famous soldier and president, George Washington, is shown shouldering a grenade launcher. He sits astride the two images of patriotism held most dear to the natives of the artists' adoptive home, the Bald Eagle and the Stars and Stripes. This heraldic image leaves little to the imagination but is designed, just like the paintings they made before relocating to the United States, to challenge the capitalist dream. **SF**

Self-Portrait | Chuck Close

1997 | oil on canvas | 102 x 84 in / 259 x 213.3 cm | Private collection

After studying at the University of Washington and Yale, Chuck Close (*b.*1940) was awarded a Fulbright grant for the Akademie der Bildenen Kunste, Vienna, where he commenced his now trademark process of working from photographs. In 1967, he moved to New York City and began his black-and-white portrait paintings. In 1969, the Annual Exhibition of Contemporary American Painting provided him with his first showing in a museum exhibition. The following year, he held his first solo show and became quickly identified as the central figure in what has become known as Photorealism or Superrealism. For more than thirty years, Close has worked with a single subject—the human figure. The massive heads he creates are often intensely personal images of fellow artists, friends, and family. Using photographs as reference and an underlying grid structure, Close works systematically, beginning in one corner of a picture and working toward its opposite. Each separate element of a painting works like a tessera—an individualized contribution to the whole. In *Self-Portrait*, through the rich patination of a painted mosaic, a head turns toward us with an uncertain gaze and slightly parted lips. The image is cropped, bringing the head closer to the front of the canvas, and therefore to the viewer. As the viewer backs away to allow the image to form, so the face presses forward. The size of the head and scale of the painting transform what might have been a fascinating visual experience into a psychological challenge. **RW**

Honeymoon Nude | John Currin

1998 | oil on canvas | 46 x 36 in / 116.8 x 91.5 cm | Tate Collection, London, UK

New York Times critic Michael Kimmelman described John Currin (*b*.1962) as "a latter-day Jeff Koons" trafficking in postmodern irony, although critic David Cohen views him as a "disingenuous and meretricious hack." Currin is above all a craftsman and a very skillful painter who has opted to work in the spaces left between Botticelli, the great American illustrator Norman Rockwell, and that master of life Austin Powers. Currin is an alumnus of Yale University where he received his MFA in 1986. Just one solo exhibition at the Institute of Contemporary Arts in London in 1995 followed by his inclusions in a number of major international shows secured his status as one of the most successful painters of his generation. His fame has catapulted his artwork into shows in major museums and galleries across the world. With a set of highly seductive craft skills Currin draws his audience into a place they would not normally dare go. His models are professional blonds, constructs who share a spooky and more than passing resemblance with their creator. *Honeymoon Nude* is a contemporary celebration of two old favorites in the story of painting: skill and heterosexual male desire. During the late nineties many critics were angered by his portrayal of his female subjects, particularly by a series of paintings he made featuring women with large, anatomically inflated chests. Too clever and calculating to be unaware of the reaction his paintings have on the public, Currin clearly fools with his audience while enjoying his craft. **SF**

Pasiphaë and the Bull | Ansel Krut

1998 | oil on copper | 9 x 11 in / 23 x 28 cm | Private collection

Born in South Africa in 1959, Ansel Krut studied art in Johannesberg and London. He has also lived and worked in France, Italy, and the United States. Influenced by artists such as Édouard Manet and Goya, Krut's work of the 1990s acknowledges their ghosts by using disguised autobiographical references coupled with subjects that enjoy wider allegorical significance. In Greek mythology Pasiphaë, Queen of Minoan Crete, is enchanted by the god Poseidon whose spell causes her to fall madly in love with a bull. Masquerading in animal form she encourages the beast to inseminate her, and their union leads to the birth of the Minotaur. *Pasiphaë and the Bull* stages the unlikely pair against a twilit backdrop, actors in a fantastical drama, but the anticipated absurdity of the scene is offset by Krut's tender representation, rendering the image one of private eroticism. The small scale of the painting allows the artist's brush to register visibly in an intimate caress of the queen's arched back and legs. Delicate touches of red ocher detailing the bull's decorative harness are a flashing foil to the olive shadows around his neck, a ruddiness picked out again near his horns, nose, and eyes, while the copper support confers a seductive luminosity to the skin of the expectant lover. Pasiphaë's manipulation of the bull might be read as analogous to the artist's performance, provoking responses through alchemical studio constructs, pushing his paint to suggest apparent states of primitive energy and control. **ZT**

Break Domination | Sigmar Polke

1998 | mixed media on polyester fabric | 51 x 59 in | Albright-Knox Art Gallery, Buffalo, NY, USA

Sigmar Polke (1941–2010) grew up in former East Germany before his family moved to Wittich, West Germany, in 1953. Along with Gerhard Richter, a fellow art student at the Kunstakademie in Düsseldorf, Polke established a form of Pop art appropriating ad imagery termed Capitalistic Realism, which has been described as an "anti-style of art." Part of Polke's mission as a German artist was to address Germany's "difficulty purging the demons of Nazism." He weaves swastikas into narrative scenes as if calling forth the assumption that the viewer will always question any German artist's relationship with the Holocaust when looking at their work. This element of playful self-defensiveness can be found in *Break Domination*. The figure of a prankster, half-man and half-animal, is lifted from the margins of illuminated manuscripts. The light, glittering wash of paint on the linen canvas and slashes of dark color lend the image the illusion of antiquity. A hybrid creature, the figure appears to embody the process of evolution. It starts as a plant, its tail sprouting leaves. Further up its body, it resembles a reptile. However, its legs are furry and could be the limbs of a mammal. Once we reach its torso, it has become a man, and by the time we get to its head, it has achieved the intelligence to mock us. It taunts us with its fingers in its mouth, as if we were idiots for wondering what it is and how it came to be that way. In this painting Polke appears to be making a cynical statement about the inanity of questioning creation, either artistic or divine. **AH**

"Is It a Tart, or Is It Ayers Rock?" | Euan Uglow

1998 | oil on canvas laid on panel | 5 x 7 in / 12.7 x 17.8 cm | Private collection

Born in London, the English figurative painter Euan Uglow (1932–2000) studied at Camberwell College of Arts from 1948 to 1950 under William Coldstream. Coldstream was a significant influence on the young Uglow. When Coldstream left Camberwell to begin teaching at the Slade, Uglow followed. He embraced Coldstream's method of measuring, which dictates that the artist stand before the subject to be painted holding a brush, upright and at arm's length, and then, with one eye closed, slide a thumb up or down the brush, taking the measure of an object or interval. Evidence of Uglow's adherence to this method of measuring can be found throughout his works, which feature numerous little horizontal and vertical markings—recording carefully plotted coordinates.

Although Uglow is known primarily as a figure painter, he also painted portraits, landscapes, and still lifes. One such example is *Is It a Tart or Is It Ayers Rock?* which depicts a solitary, pink, Bakewell-style tart against a light, gray-green background. As with so many of Uglow's compositions, it is stark in its simplicity, and stripped of extraneous details. The tart is situated squarely in the center of the rectangular canvas, its shadow falling slightly to the left, and just above a brown strip that marks the edge of a table. The ambiguity of the painting's title lends a degree of mystery, but otherwise the painting is a fine example of how Uglow could take the most banal of subjects, and, through his meticulous method, suffuse it with an air of quiet and studied grandeur. **JN**

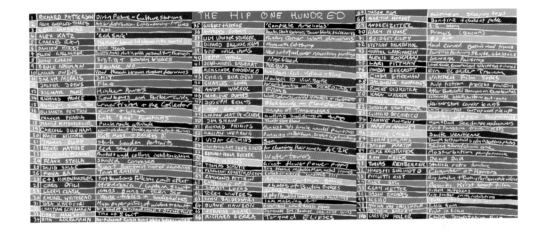

The Hip One Hundred | Peter Davies

1998 | acrylic on canvas | 100 x 240 in / 254 x 609.6 cm | Saatchi Gallery, London, UK

Peter Davies's (b.1970) paintings will be an invaluable primary source for future students' dissertations on the incestuous links within the international art world at the end of the twentieth century. Inspired by late-night Top 100 TV shows and best-seller lists, Davies paints spreadsheet-like lists and Venn diagrams in faux-amateur style. His idiosyncratic charts rank the recognizable names of his friends, peers, and art heroes according to indeterminable attributes such as being "hip" or "fun." Next to each name he appends titles of the artist's works or scathingly funny descriptive sentences. With his squiggly scrawl and use of cheerful basic colors, these works visually resemble props for a grade-school kid's classroom presentation. But their benign appearance does not undermine the intelligent nastiness in his satire of the art-world's cliquey market-driven mentality. The Hip One Hundred rates Richard Patterson, who paints oil paintings of plastic figurines, as number one, five slots above Damien Hirst. When Davies painted The Hip One Hundred, he was twenty-seven years old and his chutzpah in stating "who is who" is part of the piece's charm. Some of the pleasures of viewing Davies's paintings lie in contemplating the rises, falls, and come-backs they relate, as his canvases make contemporary art history out of contemporary art's fickle fashion. Another treat that his paintings provide is the pleasure of arguing with his idiosyncratic ranking system as it pits critically validated, established art stars against emerging downtown starlets. **AH**

2000S

Flower Chucker | Banksy

2000 | stenciled paint on brick

Street artist Banksy (Robert Banks, *b*.1974) has, arguably, done more to further the appreciation of graffiti in Britain than anyone else. His risqué, often illegal antics have gained him both urban legend status and copious newspaper column inches denouncing his work as vandalism. Banksy describes himself as an "art terrorist" and his mainstay is the stencil, usually spray-painted onto a wall without permission. This kind of activity has its origins in "tagging" or signing one's name on trains, subway walls, and public property. However, Banksy's work invites comparison with high art, most obviously in the case of his "vandalized oil paintings" that he smuggled into Tate Britain, the Louvre, and other venerable art galleries before surreptitiously hanging them next to the museums' own collection. Some of these pieces included pastoral nineteenth-century landscapes rudely interrupted by helicopters and CCTV towers, or stiff-looking portraits given an incongruous spray can or gas mask. Much of Banksy's artistic output has role reversal at its heart, whether he is equating traditional art with graffiti, depicting anarchy overturning authority or, as in the case of *Flower Chucker*, replacing a symbol of violence—a Molotov cocktail—with a symbol of peace—a bouquet of flowers. He took this motif to its extreme in 2005 when he painted sections of the two-hundred-mile-long security barrier separating Israel from the Palestinian West Bank with windows showing oases beyond or comical ladders offering a means of

Within | Luc Tuymans

2001 | oil on canvas | 87 ³⁄₄ x 95 ⁵⁄₈ in / 223 x 243 cm | Saatchi Gallery, London, UK

Belgian-born, British-based Luc Tuymans (b.1958) is partially responsible for returning painting, a medium heralded as "dead" during the last half of the twentieth century when installation and conceptual art ruled, back to the forefront of contemporary art. The artist is part of megacollector Charles Saatchi's "chosen few," and in 2003 was one of the youngest artists ever to have a solo show at Tate Modern, London. In the 1980s Tuymans worked primarily as a filmmaker—cinematic influences show in his paintings, which are marked by allusions to cinematic techniques such as closeups, cropped frames, and sequencing. Yet despite these modern touches, Tuymans's return to painting demonstrates his belief that the classic genre remains capable of reflecting the heterogeneity of modern existence. In *Within*, we witness one of Tuymans's signature subjects—the Holocaust. Often dubbed a "poetic painter," instead of illustrating the historical event Tuyman creates a pale, washed-out painting depicting an empty birdcage in which melancholy pervades. The absence of the cage's inhabitants symbolizes death. Feelings of guilt, loss, and a sense of collective consciousness haunt the viewer's experience of this seemingly banal image. The work's large size also contributes to its emotional gravitas—we are sucked in and overwhelmed by the void Tuymans paints in cool blues and grays. This image poses the question: what position do we take when looking? Are we victims trapped behind bars, or are we responsible for the suffering being evoked? **SE**

100 Years Ago | Peter Doig

2001 | oil on canvas | 90 x 141 in / 229 x 358.5 cm | Victoria Miro Gallery, London, UK

Peter Doig was born in Edinburgh in 1959 and brought up in Trinidad and then in Canada. He settled in Britain in 1979, studying painting at St. Martin's School of Art and Chelsea School of Art. Doig came to prominence in 1993 when *Blotter*, his haunting picture of a teenage boy standing on a frozen pond gazing down at his own reflection, won first prize in the prestigious John Moores Liverpool Exhibition. However, it was while he was at Chelsea that Doig began to produce the kinds of poetic paintings for which he is best known, mixing manipulated imagery from existing pictorial sources with invented motifs and scenes from his adopted homes. Anticipating his move to the Caribbean, *100 Years Ago (Carrera)* depicts a long-haired, bearded figure adrift in a

canoe on a turquoise sea. The verdant prison island of Carrera dominates the horizon. Canoes appear in a number of Doig's paintings, sometimes as a linking device between two sections of a composition. The painting's tripartite arrangement further recalls the tiered structure of some of the artist's work from the early 1990s, while the figure in the canoe, adapted from the album cover of a record by the Allman Brothers Band, generates an eerie, almost atavistic resonance. Numerous writers have commented on the fact that Doig's paintings resemble half-remembered dreams. The images we generate in our dreams are among the most vivid that any of us will ever experience, and it is a tribute to the artist's achievement that his pictures fit comfortably

Three Oncologists | Ken Currie

2002 | oil on canvas | 77 x 96 in / 195.6 x 243.8 cm | Scottish National Portrait Gallery, Edinburgh, UK

English artist Ken Currie (*b.*1960) paints an indelible image that articulates the fear people feel when contemplating the reality and myths of cancer, a disease highly stigmatized in Western society. As well as pain, cancer patients often suffer shame, thinking they might have contributed to their disease. In *Three Oncologists*, Currie—an artist who brilliantly explores the emotional ramifications of sickness and the notion of diseases as metaphors for social, political, and personal states—represents the almost spiritual pressure placed on oncologists as putative dispensers of healing in the face of the disease. The three men depicted in this unnerving painting are professors in the Department of Surgery and Molecular Oncology at Ninewells Hospital and Medical School in Dundee, Scotland. Sir Alfred Cuschieri, the Head of Department and Professor of Surgery, is situated in the center with Sir David Lane, Professor of Molecular Oncology, on his right and surgeon Professor R.J. Steele at his left. Through his luminous use of paint—the men surrounded by ominous darkness and posed as if interrupted in mid-operation—Currie casts the figures as spectral figures hovering over the division between life and death. All three wear intelligent, sensitive expressions, yet Professor Steele holds his bloodstained hands away from his body and Sir Alfred Cuschieri holds a mysterious medical implement, summoning up the confusion, fear, and concern felt by the subjects of their struggles when confronted with the perils and

Wake | Mark Tansey

2003 | oil on canvas | 85 ½ x 96 in / 217.2 x 243.8 cm | Broad Art Foundation, Santa Monica, CA, USA

The large-scale, monochromatic canvases of American painter Mark Tansey (*b*.1949), the son of two art historians, are packed with playful, ironic, in-jokes about art, as well as hidden images and portraits that reflect the influence of French Surrealist René Magritte. *Wake* is one of a series painted in ultramarine blue, an apt choice for the shimmering sea that fills most of the canvas, although its acidic vibrancy emphasizes the painting's artifice. The work's title and the depiction of people eating alfresco as in an Impressionist painting implies that it shows an actual event, but Tansey sources his imagery from his own photographs and press clippings. He then rotates, crops, and skews his source material, combining it to produce a cohesive image of an imagined event

that never occurred. He thus carefully structures a reality of his own making from juxtaposed images. The work's title prompts the viewer to question if it refers to the wake of a storm, or even a funeral. On close inspection, it contains an anamorphic portrait of Irish writer James Joyce that is visible in the sea in the wake of the departing boat. This visual pun refers to Joyce's novel, *Finnegans Wake* (1939), which was regarded as highly innovative when it was published because of its use of stream of consciousness, literary allusions, and linguistic puns. Here, like Joyce, Tansey abandons the idea of the conventional narrative to create a witty work that blends images with a dreamlike quality, as he challenges ideas about perception and the artist's ability to innovate given the

Ice Cream Cavern | Will Cotton

2003 | oil on linen | 70 x 80 in / 178 x 203 cm | Mary Boone Gallery, New York, NY, USA

Will Cotton's (b.1965) lavish oil paintings are in the soft-focus, soft-core tradition of eighteenth-century masters Broc, Gerard, Franque, and Fragonard. Like his predecessors, the Massachusetts-born artist paints beautiful, creamy-skinned nudes amid luscious surroundings, but while Cotton's paintings recall their sensuality and delight, he is far from a mere copyist. Instead of painting high on the sugar of that decadent lost age in art, Cotton replaces pastoral love scenes with mountains of sweets and erotic treats. Candy is for Cotton what dark lush forests were for his forefathers: an ideal of plenty and a site for temptation. There are no consequences depicted in these hedonistic scenes but we know that outside the fantasy, indulgence always has its price. Like other girls' late-night indulgences, the lithe but tense model's enclosed ice-cream castle seems a curse as well as a comfort. Cotton paints for an era where delights come in endless quantities but whose sweetness is poisoned by gluttony and guilt. Instead of painting lovers trysting, he paints solitary fashion models, whose aloneness reflects an age of self-obsession, porn fixation, and masturbation. Whether his models are the protagonists of his scenes or just eye candy, they never seem satiated. Candy satisfies emotional needs and frivolous fancies, but it only distracts the body from its genuine hunger, leading to fat not fulfillment. Like the fatty foods he paints, Cotton's paintings might appear light, but they are full of conceptual calories. **AH**

Cockaigne | Vincent Desiderio

2003 | oil on canvas | 111 ⁷⁄₈ x 153 ³⁄₈ in / 284.2 x 389.6 cm | Hirshhorn Museum, Washington, DC, USA

Vincent Desiderio (b.1955) is one of those rare artists for whom the intellectual aspect of art-making is as arduous, uncompromising, and mentally demanding as the formal act of painting itself. In common with other exceptionally literate and gifted American conceptualists active during the last twenty years, Desiderio has engaged with a wide range of subject matter, from the deeply personal to the poetic and narrative. Among his most admired skills is his ability and willingness to debate—with colleagues, critics, and students—the illusive role of history and ideas as they apply to the challenges of making art. With that in mind, it comes as no surprise that *Cockaigne* has attracted such interest and commentary. In this painting, Desiderio has carved out a place for himself at the intersection of the Abstract and Conceptual traditions as they are practiced currently. By the explicit titular reference to Pieter Bruegel's *Land of Cockaigne*, Desiderio acknowledges a portion of his own artistic inheritance. What's more, he references Bruegel's perspective of viewing a scene at some distance above and behind its subject. *Cockaigne* amounts to a visual, pedagogic, and historical mosaic of books, color shapes, and sustenance, all frozen randomly in time. Indeed, with this work Desiderio effectively offers up a snapshot of iconic time travel—through a history of reference material for the Western visual arts—that is so monumental and overwhelming as to beg the painful question of whether painting is meant to have any memory at all. **RL**

Keith (From Gimme Shelter) | Elizabeth Peyton

2004 | oil on board | 10 x 12 in / 25.5 x 30.5 cm | Solomon R. Guggenheim Museum, New York, NY, USA

Elizabeth Peyton (*b*.1965) is one of a group of emerging artists who share the desire to revive figure painting of a seemingly traditional kind. Peyton's gentle portraits indulge in sentiment and nostalgia, but reconcile an ostensibly outmoded genre with a contemporary obsession with celebrity and the media. She matches her small paintings to a suggested intimacy, faces in close up, backgrounds cropped. Based on photographs culled from music and fashion magazines, this closeness is placed at one remove, emphasizing Peyton's interest in the image of the individual rather than in the individual himself. Seen in close up, her "sitter" here is Keith Richards, painted in lush, fluid strokes, hair flowing blue-black against pale skin, ruby red repeated in lips and jewels.

The shadowed eyes and luminous color intensify the expressive flamboyancy of the pose, presenting him as romantic poet and androgynous hero. The original source is an image from the film *Gimme Shelter*, documenting the Rolling Stones's 1969 tour. Peyton's careful transmutation of this arrested moment into oil has poignancy given the notoriously violent end to the Rolling Stones's free concert at Altamont Speedway in the California hills, seen as death knell to sixties rock-and-roll utopianism. Peyton's work offers a fresh approach to traditional portraiture, and her commitment to a medium of poetic affect, demanding of time in execution and viewing, has a critical relationship to an image-loaded world created and dominated by new technologies. **ZT**

1000 Thread Count
Cecily Brown

2004 | oil on canvas | 90 x 78 in / 228.6 x 198.1 cm
Gagosian Gallery, New York, NY, USA

Head in the Clouds
Carlo Maria Mariani

2004 | oil on canvas | 20 ¼ x 14 ¾ in / 51.5 x 37.5 cm
Hackett-Freedman Gallery, San Francisco, CA, USA

Cecily Brown (b.1969), daughter of the art critic David Sylvester, studied painting at the Slade School of Art, London. She relocated to New York, where she attracted attention with what she called the "bunny gang rape" paintings. *1000 Thread Count* grows out of a tradition of painting that started in the hands of Titian and Rembrandt and was further modernized by Francis Bacon and Willem de Kooning. This highly fluid painting goes beyond being a simple celebration of the joys of the human figure and of paint itself to become, what in the mind of most critics is a slipping, sliding, dripping metaphor for sex. The title may relate to the rather expensive Egyptian cotton sheets that pull and twist under the writhing couple. At the start of the twenty-first century, Brown has made a reputation for herself as a real painter's painter, not simply a fabricator of fashionable images.

Influenced by both hyperrealism and conceptualism, Rome-born avant-garde painter Carlo Maria Mariani (b.1931) displays a dazzling craftsmanship that borrows heavily from classical and mythological motifs to conceptualize timeless anxieties such as the reconciliation of past and present, memory and loss, life and death. This enigmatic painting exudes the hushed atmosphere of classic Surrealism yet is whimsical and strangely moving. The youth is cast from the mold of classical perfection, an idea reinforced by the marble head turned on its side floating in the clouds above. The marmoreal flesh of this delicately poised central figure is depicted with exquisite ambiguity; the facial expression suggesting curiosity as well as serenity. Mariani's painterly expertise is visible in his treatment of the skin's luminosity, with the torso laid bare through folds of

Antäus
Anselm Kiefer

2005 | oil, paint, emulsion, shellac, soil on paper
39 ³⁄₈ x 29 ½ in / 100 x 75 cm | Private collection

German artist Anselm Kiefer (*b.*1945) explores history, myth, and literature in his work in an attempt to understand how the past informs the present. He is known in particular for his examinations of Germany under Nazi rule, which represent the struggle for identity of a postwar artist. *Antäus* references the giant of Greek mythology, Antaeus, who killed people for their skulls to build a temple to his father, the god Poseidon. But, Antaeus' strength relied on him staying in contact with the ground and he was killed by Hercules, who discovered the giant's secret. Kiefer shows two towers crumbling against a foreground of crusted mud that represents the primal creation of earth. The artist implies that if the human race refuses to stay in touch with mother earth, civilization will fall. His choice of two towers resonates with imagery of New York's World Trade Center destroyed in 2001. **CK**

A Sleep Alone with Legs Open
Tracey Emin

2005 | gouache, watercolor, and pencil on canvas
24 x 21 ½ in / 62.8 x 54.5 cm | Private collection

Tracey Emin (*b.*1963) became linked with the Young British Artists in the 1990s and came to public attention with her appliquéd tent artwork *Everyone I Have Ever Slept With 1963–1995* (1995). It established Emin as an artist who creates explicit works of a confessional nature. By the turn of the century, she renewed her interest in painting, often creating delicate, nude self-portraits, including *A Sleep Alone with Legs Open*. She admits that her exploration of painting partly comes from a desire to throw off the image of Britain's bête noire artist and to show she has the skill to paint. Yet, the pose, where her face is hidden and her vagina exposed, is in keeping with the transgressive, diarist nature of her earlier work. While in the tradition of sexualized nudes portrayed by Egon Schiele, Emin is a female artist exploring her own body rather than a male artist painting a female nude aimed to pleasure a male

The Blacker Gachet I | Mark Alexander

2005 | oil on canvas | 34 ⅝ x 30 ⅛ in / 88 x 76.5 cm | Haunch of Venison, London, UK

In the last decade, Mark Alexander (b.1966) has developed an original body of figurative work that has entered several important private collections in America and Europe. The artist himself remains something of an enigma. His works are far from numerous—some estimates put his total career output at around two dozen pieces. However, his shows quickly sell out, with the works purchased at prices of $375,000 a piece. Alexander uses known or familiar images and adds his own touches to create original art. He often makes the images monochrome, adds slight distortions, or repeats the image to make it more striking. In doing so, he makes the normal or everyday seem strange and perturbing. The Blacker Gachet I is based on Doctor Gachet, by Vincent van Gogh. This portrait of a melancholy-looking physician was painted by van Gogh in the last months of his life. It became notorious when it vanished from the public eye, after becoming the most expensive painting ever sold, in 1990. Its buyer jokingly stated that he wanted it cremated with him, though after his death in 1996 it was probably sold secretly to a private collector. The Blacker Gachet I is one of three near-identical black-on-near-black paintings in the Doctor Gachet series. The paintings ask us to look again at the original work and reconsider the value, both monetary and artistic, ascribed to it. Alexander's work has been described as "macabre," but his reinterpretation of the familiar should give us pause for thought: it allows us to appreciate how close to each other the known and the

727-727 | Takashi Murakami

2006 | acrylic on canvas | 118 ⅛ x 177 ⅛ in / 300 x 450 cm (three panels) | Private collection

Takashi Murakami (b.1963) has been stirring the art world since the early 1990s with his unconventional approach to both subject matter and artistic production. Born in Tokyo, he works as a curator and designer as well as a painter and sculptor. Murakami was first noticed when he designed backpacks using skins of endangered or exotic animals. Since then he has kept his name in the headlines by turning popular themes from mass media and pop culture into huge sculptures or commercial goods such as figurines or phone caddies. Murakami also creates "Superflat" paintings, which encompass his own postmodern art movement, influenced by manga and anime. *727-727* is a response to the mass popularity of Japanese styles of animation and comics, in particular *otaku*

culture, which refers to young people who take an obsessive interest in manga and anime. For Murakami, this emphasis on otaku culture represents modern day Japanese life. By blending cultures and styles in this way, he is obscuring the boundaries between E a s t and West, past and present and high and low culture, while remaining amusing and accessible. It is Murakami's way of integrating both popular contemporary Japanese cartoons and historic Japanese painting. Dominating the composition is the artist's signature character, Mr. DOB, a cartoon-like creature with sharp teeth, only instead of his usual straightforward self, in this painting Mr. DOB has become almost psychedelic, assimilating with the

Samurai Tree 2U | Gabriel Orozco

2006 | egg tempera on red cedar panels with gold leaf | 21 ⅝ x 21 ⅝ in / 55 x 55 cm | Private collection

Mexican artist Gabriel Orozco (*b*.1962) has traveled extensively throughout the world and his sculptures, photographs, installations, and videos reflect the random encounters he had on his travels, as well as his fascination with chance and spontaneity. *Samurai Tree 2U* is one of a series of paintings under the title *Samurai Tree* that explore spatial representation. They employ circular and elliptical shapes and reflect his interest in mapping and geometry. His choice of materials—gold leaf, egg tempera, and red cedarwood—reference those used in Mexican religious icons and reredos. Although it appears to be an abstract piece, like other paintings in the series, this work's composition reflects the movements within a game of chance—chess. The color sequence of red,

white, and blue imitates the movements of the chess knight piece, which moves in an L-shape, either two squares horizontally and one square vertically, or two squares vertically and one square horizontally. Uniquely, a knight can jump over all the other pieces to its destination square, and Orozco has tried to represent this three-dimensional movement in a two-dimensional plane, inviting comparison with his earlier sculptural work. He started by constructing a circle in the center of the painting, and went on to create a series of increased or decreased circles that reach the edges of the square, illustrating the various permutations of chess moves. The result is an organic shape like the tree referred to in the painting's title and, like a knight in chess, a samurai is a warrior. **CK**

Untitled | Yue Minjun

2006 | oil on canvas | 32 x 32 in / 82 x 82 cm | Private collection

Chinese painter, sculptor, and printmaker Yue Minjun (b.1962) was born in Daqing, Heilongjiang Province, but moved to Beijing as a child, where he continues to live and work. He has become known for his works depicting smiling faces, such as *Untitled*, which reference iconic images of the Laughing Buddha. Minjun was inspired to create his signature pieces when he saw a self-portrait of the smiling face of Chinese artist Geng Jianyi at a show in China in 1989. The same year, Beijing witnessed the Tiananmen Square uprising and the Cynical Realist movement was born when native artists such as Minjun became disillusioned with the collective mindset spawned by the Cultural Revolution and its Communist ethic. Young Chinese artists began to paint in a realistic fashion with a Pop art twist, and examine Chinese society from an individualist perspective in their work. *Untitled* is typical of the witty but biting works of Cynical Realism that use an acidic color palette and graphic lines to give them a raw edge. Looking at this man clad only in his underwear in a fetal position the viewer wonders if the subject is happy or driven mad with hysteria. Is the contorted figure with his cartoonlike grin in the midst of a physical exercise he cannot complete, or is he in pain? Minjun forces the viewer to question whether the figure is symbolic of contemporary China undergoing a painful rebirth and, as the grotesque figure's open mouth gapes to reveal a black hole, he suggests there is a spiritual vacuum at its center. **CK**

The Illusionist | Sigmar Polke

2007 | mixed media on fabric | 86 x 118 in / 219 x 299 cm | The Rachofsky Collection, Dallas, TX, USA

During his lifetime Sigmar Polke (1941–2010) forged a unique and unrelentingly original path as an artist. His experiences as an apprentice at a stained glass factory in Düsseldorf influenced his later works, in particular the Lens Paintings, of which *The Illusionist* is one. Later, in the 1960s, he studied at the Düsseldorf State Art Academy, where he was inspired by Joseph Beuys to experiment with unconventional mediums. The Lens Paintings, which were exhibited at the Michael Werner Gallery, New York, in 2009 are mixed media and strongly three-dimensional. They explore optical illusions and the manipulation of visual and conceptual planes by presenting several different moments in time layered one on top of the other. Polke spent five years creating a polymer gel

sufficiently slow drying to allow him to manipulate its surface into ridges. This gel was applied over the surface of a work, being transparent enough to allow the image beneath to show through. In *The Illusionist* the bottom image is a reproduced engraving of three men sword fighting. Polke painted a further scene on top of the polymer showing two Victorian magicians conducting a séance with a seated woman. The effect is striking and ghostly as the two scenes unfold separately but also relate to one another. The hypnotized woman has been pierced by the sword of the swashbuckler behind her, which could account for the release of the angel and devilish creatures that surround her. Polke's use of color, line, and pattern is exquisite and is complemented by his dry humor. **TP**

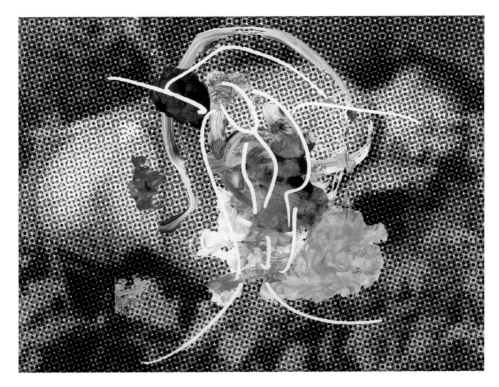

Girl Woods (Dots) | Jeff Koons

2008 | oil on canvas | 108 x 146 ⅛ in / 174.3 x 371.2 cm | Private collection

Jeff Koons (*b*.1955) became known for his controversial conceptual sculptures of banal objects, such as vacuum cleaners and children's toys, that some label as kitsch and others as Neo-Pop art. In later years Koons has turned to painting, and his *Girl Woods (Dots)* is one of a series constructed with dots, referencing the benday dot technique of American Pop artist Roy Lichtenstein and the German painter Sigmar Polke. Like his predecessors, Koons's use of dots recalls Impressionist brushstrokes, printmaking, photography, color television, and comic books. When seen from a distance the dots appear to coalesce so that the viewer is faced with a photorealistic image of a nude woman sleeping in a natural landscape. The fluorescent greens of the

grass and her bright red lips resemble a soft-focus photograph similar to those used in advertising or adult magazines. At first glance the overlaying smears of pastel-colored paint appear abstract in nature, but closer examination reveals they represent a woman's labia. An artist working within historical tradition, Koons deliberately suggests a comparison with French Realist Gustave Courbet's erotic painting *L'Origine du monde* (*The Origin of the World*) that was regarded as shocking in 1866 because of its graphic depiction of a woman's genitals. Here, Koons makes the woman's sexual organs explicit to highlight that, as in nineteenth-century paintings, contemporary imagery of women in the media is still passive and intended for male arousal however much it may be

Pink Vendetta | Charline von Heyl

2009 | acrylic and oil on linen | 82 x 72 in / 208.5 x 183 cm | Private collection

Pink Vendetta is one of New York–based, German painter Charline von Heyl's (*b*.1960) large-scale abstract works known for their highly stylized sense of energy. Its pale pink acrylics form a wash bordered by a white jagged edge that was painted last to create an image that seems to want to burst from its confines. The soft pinks are punctuated by stabbing, bright red brushstrokes that appear like harsh, bloody scratches on the surface. Curved, thick red lines flow around the edges of the image accentuating a central area of swirling, geometric shapes that float harmoniously like those on a Wassily Kandinsky canvas. The visual rhythm of the image is reminiscent of a rose in bloom. The viewer wonders whether the artist is wryly commenting on the fact that in the

seventeenth century, flowers were deemed the only subject suitable for female painters. Following in the footsteps of American painter Georgia O'Keeffe, who brought floral subjects to prominence by exploiting their sensual potential and treating them as almost pure, geometric form, von Heyl suggests her subject by its form and her painting's witty title. *Pink Vendetta* alludes to color, feminism, and the power of the contemporary female artist. The zigzag shapes could be petals, but their pointed, sharp edges explode from the surface like razor-sharp fangs. This is a ferocious painting that has bite and power; it is not a still life that exists to adorn the house of a rich patron. Rather, its sense of menace commands attention and respect and has the capacity to both entertain and

©Rudolf Stingel. Courtesy Paula Cooper Gallery, New York.

Untitled | Rudolf Stingel

2010 | oil on linen | 72 x 60 in / 182.9 x 152.4 cm | Paula Cooper Gallery, New York, NY, USA

The Conceptual works of Italian artist Rudolf Stingel (*b.*1957) attempt to engage the viewer in a dialogue about what makes a work of art. *Untitled* (2010) is one of a series of gold, silver, and black large-format paintings based on the colors and patterns of historical wallpapers. Stingel applies the pattern to the surface of his canvases in a single color through a tulle screen, and then paints subtle highlights over the top to create a shimmering illusion of light and shadow. The work's abstract nature is circumvented by the memories it evokes of the ornate heavy wallpaper that can be seen in opulent settings, such as the Palace of Versailles. The artist has exhibited his brocade paintings alongside portraits, carpeted walls, mirror-tiled floors, and chandeliers to accentuate their artifice and play with the viewer's sense of what an artwork is. Stingel prompts his audience to challenge the notion of what makes a contemporary painting because *Untitled* places painting in the context of architectural space and furnishings, and its shapely brocade forms suggest a particular decorative style associated with the grand homes of nobility and royalty. Stingel's provocative work pushes the viewer to question whether its painterly surface is abstract or decorative. Do paintings merely exist to fill the walls of rich patrons—past and present—to project an image of luxury, wealth, culture, and, sometimes, kitsch, or do they serve a greater purpose and have meaning? So Stingel challenges notions of context and hierarchy: What is decorative and what is High Art? **CK**

10pm Saturday | Lynette Yiadom-Boakye

2012 | Oil on canvas | 79 x 51 in / 200 x 130 cm | Tate Collection

Lynette Yiadom-Boakye was born in London in 1977 to Ghanaian parents. Twenty years later, she left the capital to study at Falmouth College of Art, before returning in 2000 to spend three postgraduate years painting at the Royal Academy Schools. After completing her art school training, Yiadom-Boakye had to fund her painting by taking on a range of menial jobs, including working as a phone tester at a cell phone recycling plant. In 2006, she won an award from a British charity, The Arts Foundation, that enabled her to paint full time. She was shortlisted for the 2013 Turner Prize on the strength of her solo exhibition of traditional portraits, *Extracts and Verses*, at Chisenhale Gallery. Although *10pm Saturday* seems to emerge from ground first laid by Manet, then Degas and Sickert, her paintings are neither painted from life nor from a photograph. *10pm Saturday* gives the impression that it is based on an image that originated in street photography—a photo taken quickly on an iPhone one night while walking down a dimly lit street in search of the next bar. The young man in the red stripped shirt is, however, like all Yiadom-Boakye's figures, an invention. At a technical level, her portraits are each, like the portraits of Alex Katz and Chantal Joffe, the product of a single day's work. When asked why, she will tell you that coming back to a work never improves it. Her portraits were the subject of a solo show at London's Serpentine Gallery in 2015; she has works in the London collections of the Tate Gallery and the Victoria and Albert Museum. **SF**

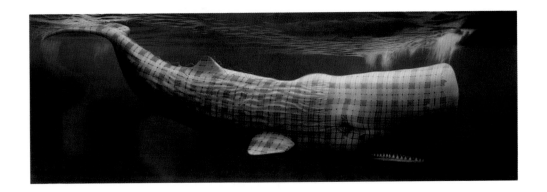

Moby Dick (Merrilees) | Sean Landers

2013 | Oil on linen | 112 x 336 in / 284.5 x 853.4 cm | Petzel Gallery, New York

Sean Landers is an astute commentator on both contemporary life and the contemporary art world. Born in Springfield, Massachusetts in 1962, he was immersed in art from the earliest age: both his mother and grandmother were artists. He first attended the Philadelphia College of Art, then went on to Yale University to take a Master of Fine Arts in sculpture. Today Landers is just as likely to be found working as a painter, performance artist, sculptor, photographer, draftsman, writer, video or audio artist. Through his brilliant understanding of media and contemporary culture, he sets out to reveal the ironies, sadness and humor that lie behind so many of the stories that we see on our TV and computer screens. In his 2014 exhibition at Petzel Gallery in New York, *North*

American Mammals, Landers presented a group of paintings in which different animals have been transformed in a variety of Scottish tartan outfits in a nod to René Magritte's 1947–48 "Période Vache", during which tartan was a recurring motif. *Moby Dick (Merrilees)* references Herman Melville's famous novel, published in 1851, which recounts the tale of Captain Ahab's search for an elusive sperm whale. Landers sees the pursuit of the whale as a metaphor for the artist's pursuit of greatness and immortality; the harpoons that scar the animal's body are symbols of his attempt to make a lasting work of art. Landers spent four months working on the giant linen canvas, which is almost 30 feet (9 meters) in length, toiling to depict the whale exactly as it would look in the wild. **SF**

Vita in the Borgese | Chantal Joffe

2013 | Oil on board | 96 x 72 in / 244 x 183 cm | Galerie Forsblom, Helsinki and Victoria Miro Gallery, London

Chantal Joffe (*b*.1969) has lived and worked in London for most of her professional life. After completing a master's degree in painting at the Royal College of Art in 1994, she was appointed an Abbey Major Scholar at the British School in Rome. Having developed what might be seen as a "late style" while she was still relatively young, Joffe was elected a member of the Royal Academy of Arts in London in 2015. Her meteoric rise to fame saw her being named by the British magazine *Latest Art* as the most important female artist of all time. Joffe's confident, large-scale, photographically informed portraits of women and children sit at the end of a lineage that starts with Edouard Manet, then is carried into the twentieth century by artists such as Alice Neel and David Hockney. Her sources range from family photos and advertising to pornography. Using her photographic source material as a basis, Joffe introduces distortions to her paintings. *Vita in the Borgese* is based on a photograph of Joffe's niece Vita that she took in the gardens of the Villa Borghese, which separate her old studio from the center of Rome. It is the classic snap from the family holiday album, albeit rendered here in oil on board and on a giant scale. Perched on the edge of a fountain, Joffe's subject takes a sideways look at her audience, in a pose that is halfway between innocent child and knowing adult. Although, at first glance, the painting gives an impression of simplicity and childishness, there is an unsettling quality that leaves the audience wanting to know more. **SF**

Flashlight and Sofa | Zhang Xiaogang

2014 | oil on paper | 11 ½ x 15 ⅜ in / 29.5 x 39 cm | Beijing Zhang Xiaogang Art Studio

Zhang Xiaogang, China's most expensive living artist, was born in 1958 in Kunming, the capital of Yunnan Province. When he was eight years old, his parents were forced to leave him and his three brothers to live in a "study camp" in the countryside. This early experience marked the young Zhang profoundly and his preoccupation with the Cultural Revolution can be seen in many of his artworks. He initially came to fame for his large, haunting depictions of families dressed in Mao jackets and comrade's caps. In 1995, he exhibited in an international exhibition called *Identità e Alterità*, installed in the Italian Pavilion during the 46th Venice Biennale; with this, he began to develop an international reputation. Over the years, Zhang's paintings have gradually broken from their compulsion to look back to the Cultural Revolution, and they appear today to be more about art and a broader range of emotions than anger and politics. Although small in size, *Flashlight and Sofa* is big in conception. Painted in oil on paper, with a dreamlike quality to its colors, it shows a shabby couch covered by an array of rectangular fabric pieces. The fabric acts as a screen for a beam of light projected from an old flashlight. An electrical cable, with a plug dangling from one end, draws a line across the composition, producing an image that demands reflection. It is not an image that is designed to reference the Kitchen Sink painters or Tracey Emin's bed; it is a conceptual work that asks the question: can a circular flashlight project a diamond-shaped image? **SF**

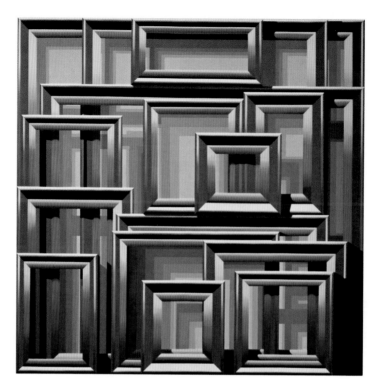

Untitled | Rui Macedo

2014 | Oil on canvas | 78 ¾ x 78 ¾ in / 200 x 200 cm | Amarelonegro Gallery, Rio de Janeiro

Rui Macedo (*b*.1975) began working as a painter at the end of the 1990s, after graduating from the Faculdade de Belas Artes in Lisbon. He collaborated socially and intellectually with classmates José Batista Marques, Jorge Lancinha, José Lourenço, and Manuel Caeiro, thus becoming part of a group of young artists with a shared interest in reimagining the Portuguese tradition of painting. He recently said of his work, "The work of a painter is a challenge that deals directly with a cultural heritage; it is bound to architecture—the space and place where it is seen." This painting, given the enigmatic title *Untitled*, was originally made as a part of an exhibition/installation called *Memorabilia*, which was presented by the artist at the Convento dos Capuchos, Caparica, during the summer of 2014.

Macedo used the painting in that exhibition to remind his audience of art's artifice and to challenge the overly codified context of the exhibition space. Today, the painting is free of the installation; it is a painting that now hangs alone. As such, it is more open to interpretation, but it still presents the viewer with a group of meticulously imagined *trompe-l'oeil* frames that demonstrate the artist's technical virtuosity. Now appearing as the whole story, not a fragment of another bigger story, the painting turns our understanding of authenticity upside down. In doing so, it takes us from the shadows of Renaissance painting through the geometry of modernism to a point where the frame is the subject and no longer simply a protective device and decorative border. **SF**

Sneakers, Computers, Capri Sun | Katherine Bernhardt

2014 | Acrylic and spray paint on canvas | 96 x 120 in / 243.8 x 304.8 cm | CANADA Gallery, New York

Brooklyn-based artist Katherine Bernhardt (b.1975) received her Bachelor of Fine Arts from the School of the Art Institute of Chicago and her Master of Fine Arts from the School of Visual Arts, New York. After a visit to Morocco in 2007, Bernhardt began working on paintings that were abstractions of Moroccan carpets; after these came a less confined, more pragmatic approach to subject matter. Cell phones, fast food, fruit, and cigarettes all became fair game—the most mundane of articles are considered by Bernhardt to be worthy subjects for her work. Her only requirement is that the items that she features must be interesting in shape and color. Bernhardt says that her inspiration for her "pattern paintings"—large-scale works that present these items in jazzy, semi-abstract

combinations—comes from Dutch wax printing on African batik fabrics. They continue the theme of repetition and juxtaposition that began with the Moroccan carpets. It is from this context that Sneakers, Computers, Capri Sun arises. Seemingly random objects—sneakers, computers, and cartons of Capri Sun—are landed in a field of brilliant yellow. Bernhardt has used watered-down spray paint to create a more fluid and watery effect. Although critics have tried to read her paintings as talking about consumerism and environmentalism, the artist resolutely refuses to intellectualize her own work. She has said that color choices and combinations are what matters to her. In terms of art history, her work sits neatly between Wayne Thiebaud, Lisa Milroy, graffiti and hip-hop. **SF**

Dialogue | Lee Ufan

2014 | Oil on canvas | 63 ¾ x 51 in / 162cm x 130cm | Private collection

The minimalist painter and theorist Lee Ufan was born in 1936 in Haman County in the South Kyongsang province of Korea. Having interrupted his studies at Seoul National University to study philosophy at Tokyo's Nihon University, he stayed on in Japan during the 1950s to work as an art critic, philosopher, and artist. He was first acknowledged in the late 1960s as a founder of Japan's first international avant-garde movement, Mono-ha or the "School of Thing," a movement that resembles in many ways the Italian Arte Povera movement. In 1973, Ufan was appointed professor at Tama Art University in Tokyo, a post he held until 2007. *Dialogue* is from a series of medium-size monochrome tonal oil paintings on canvas. The artist has moved away from his traditional grey palette to incorporate stronger colors, such as the intense terracotta red seen here, into his paintings. Each work is a secular icon that has been slowly, ritualistically and systematically built from small meditative brush strokes controlled by the artist's held breath. The paintings were made to be reflected upon, not simply looked at. Ufan intended them to function in a way similar to the icons of the Orthodox Church, but in this case evoking a response to a material presence rather than to a god. The relationship between painted/unpainted and occupied/empty space are at the heart of his work. In his collected writings, *The Art of the Encounter* (2008), the artist expressed the hope that his work might "lead people's eyes to emptiness and turn their eyes to silence." **SF**

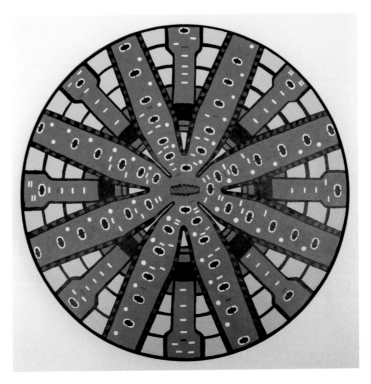

Beat the Drum | Jack Daws

2015 | Deer hide, maple, acrylic, leather | 18 in / 45.7 cm (diameter) | Greg Kucera Gallery, Seattle

Jack Daws (b.1970) is a Seattle-based artist who works with a wide range of different media, including painting, mixed media sculpture, and photography. Recent political events and current public works, among other things, provide rich material for this politically engaged artist. He produces work that comments both on the reinvention and appropriation of racial and cultural identity. Some of his most difficult and controversial works play on stereotypes of African American, Native American, and Mexican American culture. Art critic Regina Hackett said of him, "In Seattle, no white artist has pushed the edge of racial outrage as clearly as Jack Daws." Beat the Drum is, in every sense of the word, Postmodern. It sits midway between being simply a circular painting (a tondo) and a painted object (a tribal drum). The design on the deer hide, inspired by the bold symmetry of Native American imagery, is based on the shape of the tunnel-boring machine, Bertha, used by the Washington State Department of Transportation to dig the Alaskan Way Viaduct tunnel—a project that has encountered many difficulties along the way. For Daws, the bungled infrastructure project raises questions about the use and abuse of landscapes inscribed with the ancient memories of the Native Americans. Beat the Drum can be seen as emerging from either today's hip–hop culture or from a Native American visual tradition that takes us back to Mesoamerica and the Aztecs. It is at once timeless and rooted firmly in the present day. **SF**

Fingering Vanitas | Mequitta Ahuja

2015 | Oil on canvas | 84 x 80 in / 213 x 203 cm | Saatchi Gallery, London

Mequitta Ahuja (b.1976) is renowned for her self-portraits, a form that she describes as "automythography," as she considers her paintings to combine "history, myth, and personal narrative." She describes her choice to use her own image as being related to her "unusual ethnic heritage"—she has both African-American and Indian origins—and her need to "have imagery in the world that reflected [her] identity." Using remote shutter technology, she photographs herself, carefully stage managing her own gaze, posture, and dress, and uses the resulting image as source material for her painting. *Fingering Vanitas* was first exhibited as a part of a series of allegorical paintings that were conceived to go beyond the self-portrait, to reflect on the act of painting itself. Ahuja took as her starting point Giotto's biblical frescoes, with their use of inside-outside perspective. The artist is pictured sitting at a low table in a small, sparsely furnished room, but glimpses of the surrounding landscape can be seen through an open door and window. The colors are vivid and warm. Ahuja's nude figure evokes Paul Gauguin's Tahitian women; however, while Gauguin's paintings objectify the female body and fetishize the women's exoticism, Ahuja's image is in no way sexualized. It represents the artist as a creator, not an exotic muse. While the image contains myriad references to both Western and Eastern art traditions, Ahuja has appropriated and modified these traditions, weaving a complex cultural experience for the viewer. **SF**

Forbidden Fruit Picker | Wangechi Mutu

2015 | Collage painting | Gladstone Gallery, New York

New York-based Kenyan artist Wangechi Mutu (*b.*1972) works as a video artist and sculptor, but is perhaps best known for her collage art. Her large-scale collages often show a female protagonist who is the monstrous product of a grafting process that brings plants, humans and machines together. Her work nods to Surrealist Max Ernst, who scoured scientific manuals for illustrations of unusual plants and strange implements to juxtapose in his collages. Like Ernst, she is careful to hide the joins between morsels of cut paper. Mutu placed the collage painting *Forbidden Fruit Picker* at the entry point to the installation she created for the main exhibition of the 2015 Venice Biennale, *All the World's Futures*, offering a historical backdrop to the sculpture, *She's Got the*

Whole World in Her, and animated video, *The End of Carrying All*, that formed the rest of the installation. The image draws on the biblical story of the fall of man, but also on the traditional story of creation from Mutu's homeland, Kenya. The first woman, Eve, reaches for the forbidden fruit of the title, which hangs from the tree of life. She is a hybrid of human and machine—part-metal, part-flesh—symbolizing the objectification of women. The serpent, a familiar figure in Mutu's work, appears here as a two-headed beast, leering at Eve from the side of the picture, goading her into action. Seductive yet grotesque, the collage draws the audience's attention not only to Eve's appetite for the apple, but the voracious appetite of the human race for material things. **SF**

Glossary

Abstract Art
Style that does not imitate real life but consists of forms, shape, and color, independent of subject matter.

Abstract Expressionism
Post–World War II American art movement characterized by a desire for freedom of expression and the communication of strong emotions through the sensual quality of paint. Chief artists include Jackson Pollock, Willem de Kooning, and Franz Kline.

Action Painting
Technique in which paint is applied with gestural movements, often by pouring or splashing. Its chief exponent was American painter Jackson Pollock.

Art Informel
Term coined by French art critic Michel Tapié to describe abstract painting that was created during the 1940s and 1950s, in an improvised style, by artists such as Dubuffet and Michaux.

Art Nouveau
Decorative style in the art, design, and architecture of Europe and the USA popular from 1890 through World War I. Often consisting of organic, asymmetrical, and stylized flora and foliage forms.

Arte Povera
Italian for "Poor Art." Term coined by critic Germano Celant to describe art made using everyday materials such as newspapers, rather than traditional materials such as oil paint. Predominantly created in the 1960s and 1970s by Italian artists including Fabro and Paolini.

Ashcan School
Group of American artists active from 1908 to 1914 who focused on realistic images of urban city life, with particular emphasis on the poor. Led by Robert Henri, in 1913 they organized an influential exhibition of modern European art in America: the Armory Show.

Atelier
French for "studio." An *atelier libre* was a studio where there was usually no formal tuition. A nude model was provided for fixed sessions and any artist could drop in and work there.

Automatism
A method whereby the act of painting, writing, or drawing is based on chance, free association, suppressed consciousness, dreams, and states of trance. As a means of supposedly tapping into the subconscious mind, it was adopted with particular enthusiasm by the Surrealists.

Avant-garde
Term used to describe any new, innovative, and radically different artistic approach.

Bacchus
In Greek and Roman mythology, the god of fertility and wine, also called Dionysus. His festivals, or "bacchanalia," were celebrated with dancing, revelry, and orgy.

Baroque
Style of European architecture, painting, and sculpture, from 1600 to 1750, that peaked around 1630 to 1680 in Rome, Italy, and is typically dynamic and theatrical. Its chief exponents were Caravaggio and Rubens.

Bauhaus
German school of art, design, and architecture founded in 1919 by Walter Gropius and closed by the Nazis in 1933. Artists such as Russian Wassily Kandinsky and Swiss-German Paul Klee worked there, and its trademark streamlined designs became influential worldwide.

Blaue Reiter, Der
German for "The Blue Rider." A group formed in Munich, in 1911, by artists who epitomized German Expressionism, with a particular focus on abstraction and the spirituality of nature. The name comes from a drawing by Wassily Kandinsky, the leader of the group.

Book of Hours
A prayer book, often in the form of an illuminated manuscript, containing prayers, psalms, biblical text, and illustrations for particular hours of the day, days of the week, months, or seasons. Particularly popular during the fifteenth century.

Brücke, Die
German for "The Bridge." A group founded in Dresden in 1905 by German Expressionist artists, which had disbanded by 1913. The group espoused radical political views and sought to create a new style of painting to reflect modern life. Noted for their landscapes, nudes, vivid color, and use of simple forms. Members included Kirchner and Nolde.

Byzantine
Term for orthodox religious art created during—or influenced by—the Byzantine (Eastern Roman) Empire, from 330 BCE to 1453 CE. Icons are a common feature in the art of this era, which is also typified by exquisite mosaic church interiors.

Camden Town Group
British Post-Impressionist group founded by Walter Richard Sickert in London in 1911, which predominantly painted realistic scenes of city life in a broadly Impressionistic style.

Camera Obscura
Latin for "dark chamber." An optical device used to project an image via a hole or lens onto material such as canvas so that the artist can trace its outline. It was popular from the fifteenth century onward and was famously used by Vermeer in the seventeenth century.

Chiaroscuro
Italian for "light-dark." The dramatic effect created by balancing or strongly contrasting light and shade in a painting.

Cinquecento
Italian for "five hundred." Used to describe sixteenth-century Italian art.

Cercle et Carré
French for "Circle and Square." French abstract group founded in Paris in 1929 by critic and artist Michel Seuphor and artist Joaquín Torres-García. They published a journal of the same name and held a group exhibition in 1930.

Classicism
Term describing the use of the rules or styles of classical antiquity. Renaissance art incorporated many classical elements, and other eras, such as the eighteenth century, have used ancient Greece and Rome as inspiration. The term can also be used to mean formal and restrained.

CoBrA
Group formed in Paris in 1948, and lasting until 1951, by artists from Copenhagen, Brussels, and Amsterdam, the name taken from the first letters of these cities. Leading members included Dutch artist Karel Appel and Danish artist Asger Jorn. Their work was characterized by its fantastical imagery and often naive style.

Collage
Style of picture-making in which materials (typically newspapers, magazines, photographs, etc.) are pasted together on a flat surface. The technique first gained prominence with the rise of Cubism in the early twentieth century, particularly in the work of Picasso and Braque.

Color Field Painting
Term originally used to describe the work of Abstract Expressionist painters Rothko, Newman, and Still in the 1950s and that of Frankenthaler, Louis, and Noland in the 1960s. Works characteristic of this style are notable for large areas of flat, single color.

Commedia dell'Arte
Italian for "comedy of professional artists." Term used to describe comic plays performed in masks popular in sixteenth- to eighteenth-century Italy and France.

Conceptualism
Artistic style in which the ideas or concepts behind an artwork are prioritized over the piece itself, which is sometimes regarded simply as a document of the idea-making process that preceded it. Its heyday was in the 1960s and 1970s, though the same principles were being employed by Duchamp decades beforehand.

Constructivism
Art movement founded by Vladimir Tatlin and Alexander Rodchenko in Russia around 1914, spreading to the rest of Europe by the 1920s. Notable for its abstraction and use of industrial materials such as glass, metal, and plastic.

Cubism
Highly influential and revolutionary European art style invented by Spanish artist Pablo Picasso and French artist Georges Braque and developed between 1907 and 1914. Cubists abandoned the idea of a fixed viewpoint, resulting in the object portrayed appearing fragmented. Cubism gave rise to a succession of other movements, including Constructivism, Futurism, and Vorticism.

Cubo-Futurism
School of Russian Futurism, developed in 1913 by artists such as Malevich, that combined the fragmentary and multiple viewpoints of Cubism with the dynamism and attempt to convey movement that typified Futurism.

Dada
Art movement started in 1916 in Switzerland by writer Hugo Ball as a reaction to the horror of World War I. It aimed to overturn past traditional values in art, and was notable for its introduction of "readymade" objects as art, and its rejection of the notion of craftsmanship. Core artists included Duchamp, Hans Richter, Picabia, Arp, and Schwitters.

De Stijl
Dutch magazine (1917–32) edited by Theo van Doesberg and used to champion the work of cofounder Piet Mondrian and the ideas of Neoplasticism. The term is also applied to the ideas it promoted, which had a significant influence on the Bauhaus movement and on commercial art in general.

Divisionism
Painting theory and technique involving the application of small areas or dots of paint to the canvas in order to obtain color effects optically rather than by mixing colors on a palette. Its most famous practitioners were Seurat and Signac. The technique is also sometimes referred to as "pointillism" or "pointillisme."

Expressionism
Term used to describe a twentieth-century style that distorts color, space, scale, and form for emotional effect and is notable for its intense subject matter. Adopted particularly in Germany by artists such as Kandinsky, Nolde, Beckmann, and Macke.

Fauvism
Derived from the French "fauve," meaning " wild beast." Art movement from about 1905 to 1910 characterized by its wild brushwork, use of bright color, and flat patterns. It was associated with artists such as Matisse and Derain.

Folk Art
Term used to describe art that falls outside the category of fine art and that has been created by a non-formally-trained individual. Its subject matter often involves family or community life and includes crafts, naive art, and quilts.

Fresco
A painting that is applied to wet plaster—as distinct from a mural, which is painted onto a dry surface.

Futurism
Art movement launched by the Italian poet Filippo Tommaso Marinetti in 1909. Characterized by works that expressed the dynamism, energy, and movement of modern life. Integral artists include Severini and Balla.

Golden Ratio
Also known as "Golden Mean," "Golden Section," or "the divine proportion." A mathematical ratio, roughly 8:13, thought to have great aesthetic value in art, architecture, and music, and particularly used during the Renaissance. In art, it is seen where a straight line or rectangle is divided into two unequal parts so that the ratio of the smaller to the greater is the same as that of the greater to the whole. It was adopted by artists as diverse as Leonardo and Mondrian.

Gothic
European style of art and architecture from the 1300s to the 1600s. Work produced during this period is characterized by an elegant, dark, somber style, and by a greater naturalism than the earlier Romanesque period.

Gouache
An opaque watercolor paint, also known as poster paint. It can be used to obtain similar effects to oil paints with more speed and ease. It is often used for making studies for larger paintings in oils.

Graffiti Art
Style inspired by spray-painted graffiti—particularly that which became prevalent in the 1980s in New York. Its most famous practitioner was Basquiat, though Banksy may well be the best-known contemporary graffiti artist.

Grand Tour
A journey around Europe generally taken by wealthy and aristocratic young men as part of their education during the seventeenth to early-nineteenth centuries. The itinerary was designed to educate travelers in the art and architecture of classical antiquity.

Group of Seven
Name for Canadian painters who created the first significant Canadian art movement, typified by Expressionistic, dynamic brushwork and the use of bright, dramatic colors. The artists took their primary inspiration from the landscape of northern Ontario.

Gutai Group
In English, "gutai" means "embodiment." A Japanese avant-garde group formed in 1954 in Osaka by Jiro Yoshihara, Akira Kanayma, Saburo Murakami, Kazuo Shiraga, and Shozo Shimamoto and famed for their theatrical events.

Harlem Renaissance
A flowering of African-American art, literature, music, and social commentary that primarily took place in Harlem, New York, in the 1920s. It aimed to challenge prejudice, promote racial pride and social integration, and break down white European distinctions between "high" and "low" culture.

Hatsuboku
Japanese for "splashed ink." Japanese landscape painting that was imported from China and became popular in the thirteenth century. Artists splashed the ink in an act of meditation to form elements such as mountains before adding more detailed elements.

Hudson River School
Term applied to mid-nineteenth-century American group of landscape painters noted for their Romantic approach and who took inspiration from their native land. Included artists such as Cole and Church.

Hyperrealism
Used to describe a resurgence of high-fidelity realism in painting and sculpture that began in the late 1960s. Proponents include Spaniard Antonio López García and American Chuck Close. Also known as "Superrealism" or "Photorealism."

Iconography
Derived from "ikon" in Greek, meaning "image." Term used to describe imagery in a painting. Originally a picture of a holy person on a panel used as an object of devotion. In art, the word has come to be used to describe any object or image with a special meaning attached to it.

Il Novecento
Italian art movement founded in Milan in 1922 by gallery owner Lino Pesaro and art critic Margherita Sarfatti with the aim of reviving large-scale naturalistic art based on the Italian classical tradition. Artists included Carrà, Morandi, and Sironi.

Impasto
A technique whereby paint is thickly applied using a brush or palette knife, so that the strokes or marks remain visible and in some cases raised from the surface to provide texture.

Impressionism
Revolutionary approach to painting landscape and scenes of everyday life pioneered in France by Monet and others from the early 1860s, and which was later adopted internationally. Often created outdoors (en plein air) and notable for the use of light and color as well as loose brushwork. The first group exhibition held in 1874 was dismissed by critics, particularly Monet's painting Impression, Sunrise, which gave the movement its name. Chief artists include Pissarro, Renoir, Degas, and Manet.

International Gothic
A type of Gothic art developed in Burgundy, Bohemia, and northern Italy in the late-fourteenth and early-fifteenth centuries, characterized by rich, decorative patterns, colorful settings, classical modeling, flowing lines, and use of linear perspective. Notable artists include Italian painters Gentile da Fabriano and Jacopo Bellini.

Isfahan School
Sixteenth- to seventeenth-century Iranian school of miniature painting.

Japanimation
Japanese animation, particularly that of the 1970s and 1980s. Also referred to as "anime."

Jugendstil
German name for Art Nouveau, inspired by the title of the Munich journal Die Jugend, meaning "the youth."

Kanō
School of Japanese painting founded in the fifteenth century. The Kanō style of painting is noted for its large-scale works on sliding doors or screens, depicting nature scenes of birds, plants, water, or other animals.

Lithography
Technique in which a design is drawn onto a surface using a medium such as greasy ink or a crayon and then treated so that it is fixed. Water is applied to the design; this will not adhere to the greasy areas. A greasy ink is then rolled over the surface; this will adhere to the greasy areas of the design, but not to the wet areas. Paper is applied to the surface and the work is passed through a press, creating a reverse image of the design on the paper.

Luminism
1. Term devised c.1950 by John Baur, then director of New York's Whitney Museum, for an aspect of American landscape painting of the 1850s to 1870s. Describes the use of light effects by artists such as Frederic Edwin Church.

2. Alternative name for Light Art from the 1960s onward using electric and neon lighting, lasers, and holography.

3. Belgian name for Neo-Impressionism.

Magic Realism
Term invented by German photographer, art historian, and art critic Franz Roh in 1925. It is used in a broad sense to describe paintings that feature fantastical and dreamlike subject matter that are presented in a realistic, true-to-life style. The paintings of Magritte and Kahlo typify this approach.

Mandorla
Italian for "almond." An ancient symbol of two overlapping circles to form an almond shape. Often found in Christian iconography surrounding the figure of Christ to depict the unification of the divine and human.

Mannerism
Derived from "maniera," meaning "manner," in Italian. A loose term to describe Late Renaissance art from around 1530 to 1580 in which altered perspective, vibrant color, unrealistic lighting, and exaggerated or distorted figures in complex, elongated poses resulted in theatrical and sometimes disturbing images. It was based on the ideals of Raphael and Michelangelo and expanded on by artists such as Parmigianino.

Mazzocchio
Male headdress made of wood or wicker, common in mid-fifteenth-century Florence. Seen in paintings by artists such as Uccello.

Memento Mori
Latin term that loosely translates as "Remember you will die." It was a popular theme in Medieval and Renaissance art and describes paintings or sculptures that were intended to move viewers to contemplate their mortality.

Minimalism
Style of abstract art—characterized by a spare, uncluttered approach and deliberate lack of emotive expression or conventional composition—that arose in the mid-twentieth century and flourished mainly until the 1970s. Practitioners range from Yves Klein and Lucio Fontana to Ellsworth Kelly and Kenneth Noland.

Moderne Bund
German for "Modern League." Exhibition held in Lucerne, Switzerland, in 1911 at which work by artists such as Gauguin, Matisse, Picasso, and Arp—who organized the show—were featured.

Modernism
A broad term used to describe Western artistic, literary, architectural, musical, and political movements in the late-nineteenth and early-twentieth centuries. Applied to that which is typified by constant innovation, formal experimentation, and rejection of the old, and works in which the adoption of the new is seen as being more appropriate to the modern age.

Nabis
Derived from word for "prophets" in Hebrew. Term used to describe a group of Post-Impressionist avant-garde Parisian artists of the 1890s, who were Symbolist in approach and admired the work of Paul Gauguin. Prominent members included Bonnard and Vuillard.

Naturalism
In its broadest sense, a term used to describe art in which the artist attempts to portray objects and people as observed rather than in a conceptual or contrived manner. More generally, it can also be used to suggest that a work is representational rather than abstract.

Neo-Classicism
Prominent late-eighteenth- and early-nineteenth-century movement in European art and architecture, motivated by the impulse to revive the style of ancient Greek and Roman art and architecture. In modern art, the term has also been applied to a similar revival of interest in classical style during the 1920s and 1930s.

Neo-Dadaism
Term used to describe the revival of the spirit of Dada by artists such as Sigmar Polke in their work. The term is frequently associated with Pop artists such as Johns and Oldenburg.

Neo-Expressionism
International movement in painting that started in the 1970s, influenced by the raw personal emotion and bold mark-making characteristic of Expressionism. Often figurative and typified by their large scale and use of mixed media on their surface. Artists include Chia, Clemente, Schnabel, Salle, Baselitz, and Kiefer.

Neo-Impressionism
A French movement in painting, started by Seurat and Signac, that aimed to take a scientific approach to creating light and color using "divisionism" or "pointillism."

Neoplasticism
Term invented by Dutch painter Piet Mondrian in 1914 to describe his theory that art should be non-representational in order to find and express a "universal harmony." Mondrian's paintings are characterized by their restricted palettes and use of horizontal and vertical lines.

Netherlandish
Term used to describe art produced in Flanders—now Belgium—and the Netherlands, and developed by artists such as van Eyck, Memling and Bosch. The style, also known as "Flemish," arose in the fifteenth century, and evolved separately from the art of the Italian Renaissance, especially in the use of oil paint instead of tempera. The early Netherlandish period ended around 1600; the late period lasted until 1830.

Neue Sachlichkeit, Die
German for "The New Objectivity." German art movement of the 1920s that lasted until 1933. It opposed Expressionism and is noted for its unsentimental style and use of satire. Included artists such as Nagel, Dix, and Grosz.

Northern Renaissance
The influence of the Italian Renaissance in northern European painting from around 1500, incorporating the use of human proportion, perspective, and landscape. Albrecht Dürer was an early exponent, having studied in Italy. It was influenced by Protestantism as opposed to the Roman Catholic themes of Italian painting.

Objet Trouvé
French for "found object," signifying a pre-created item that is subsequently chosen to be used unaltered in a work of art.

Op Art
Abbreviation of "Optical Art." Style of abstract art of the 1960s that used optical illusion, employing a range of optical phenomena to make artworks appear to vibrate or flicker. Primary exponents included Riley and Vasarely.

Orphism
French abstract-art movement originated by Jacques Villon and characterized by its use of bright color. The term was first used in 1912 by the poet Guillaume Apollinaire to describe the paintings of Robert Delaunay, which he related to Orpheus, the poet and singer in Greek mythology. Its practitioners introduced a more lyrical element to Cubism. Klee, Marc, and Macke were all influenced by this short-lived movement.

Paleo-Christian
Early Christian art used in Roman catacombs from the first-century CE, incorporating elements of late classical Roman art and using both classical and Christian themes.

Parthian Frontality
Artistic style developed in the second century CE, during the time of the Parthian Empire, in which figures portrayed in frescoes face forward instead of sideways.

Persian Safavid
Art produced during the Safavid dynasty that ruled in what is now Iran from 1501 to 1736. Arts such as miniature painting, bookbinding, decoration, and calligraphy were promoted, as they were believed to encourage foreign trade.

Plein Air
See Impressionism.

Pointillism, Pointillisme
See Divisionism.

Political Pop
Chinese artistic movement, developed in the 1990s by artists such as Wang Guangyi, that takes iconic imagery from Cultural Revolution propaganda and reworks it in a Pop art style.

Pop Art
Term coined by British critic Lawrence Alloway for an Anglo-American art movement that lasted from the 1950s to the 1970s. It is notable for its use of imagery taken from popular cultural forms such as advertising, comics, and mass-produced packaging. Practitioners included American artists Warhol, Lichtenstein, and Johns, and British artists Hockney and Blake.

Post-Impressionism
Term used to describe various works of art and artistic movements influenced by, or reacting against, Impressionism. The phrase was invented by British art critic and painter Roger Fry, who organized a Post-Impressionists show in London in 1910. Painters include Cézanne, Gauguin, and van Gogh.

Pre-Raphaelite Brotherhood
British society of artists founded in London in 1848 that championed the work of artists active prior to Renaissance master Raphael. Members included William Holman Hunt, John Everett Millais, and Dante Gabriel Rossetti. Their work is characterized by its realistic style, attention to detail, and engagement with social problems and religious and literary themes.

Putto (plural, putti)
Italian for "cherub." Winged, naked infant figure, usually male. Commonly found in Italian Renaissance works by artists such as Veronese.

Quattrocento
Italian for "four hundred." Used to describe fifteenth-century Italian art.

Realism
1. Mid-nineteenth-century art movement characterized by subject matter depicting peasant and working-class life, as exemplified by the work of French artist Courbet.

2. Term for a style of painting that appears photographic in its representational accuracy, irrespective of subject matter.

Regionalism
American art movement of the 1930s to 1940s that sought to establish an independent American art and typically depicted scenes from the American Midwest. Core artists include Hart Benton, Curry, and Wood.

Renaissance
French for "rebirth." Used to describe the revival of art in Italy from 1300 under the influence of the rediscovery of classical art and culture. The Renaissance reached its peak—the High Renaissance—from 1500 to 1530 with the work of Michelangelo, Leonardo, and Raphael.

Rococo
From the French "rocaille," meaning "rock-work," referring to carvings in grottoes and on fountains. The term is used to describe the eighteenth-century French style of visual arts that was decorative in nature and often used shell-like curves and shapes.

Romanesque
Initially a term to describe the architecture of eleventh- and twelfth-century Europe—influenced by that of the Roman Empire—but extended to cover painting and sculpture of the era. Typified by stylized devotional works, such as illustrated manuscripts.

Romanticism
Artistic movement of the late-eighteenth and early-nineteenth centuries. Broadly characterized by an emphasis on the experience of the individual; instinct over rationality; and the concept of the "sublime," as seen in the landscapes of Friedrich.

Salon
Refers to exhibitions held by the French Royal Academy of Painting and Sculpture—and later the Academy of Fine Arts—in Paris from 1667 to 1881. Known as the "Salon de Paris" in French. Named for the Salon Carré in the Louvre, where the exhibition was staged from 1737 onward.

Secession
Name used by groups of artists in Germany and Austria in the 1890s who "seceded" from art institutions that they deemed excessively conservative. Led by Klimt in Vienna, von Stuck in Münich, and Liebermann in Berlin.

Section d'Or
French for "Golden Section." Group of French artists who worked from 1912 to 1914 in a loose association. Their predominant style was Cubist, and they were particularly concerned with mathematical proportion (see Golden Ratio). Members included Gris and Picabia.

Sgraffito
Italian term for "scratched." A reference to the practice of scratching through one layer in an artwork to reveal a second layer beneath.

Sfumato
Italian for "faded away," derived from "fumo" meaning "smoke." Painting technique in which colors or tones are blended together so that the transition lines between them vanish. Practiced by artists such as Leonardo.

Shiraz School
A style of Persian miniature painting developed in modern-day Iran, beginning in the thirteenth century and reaching its highest expression in the 1400s. Typical works were highly colored, stylized, and detailed—often with "fairy-tale" or mystical qualities—and often used to illustrate epic poems.

Situationism
Political and artistic ideas advocated by a radical group formed in 1957 and influenced by Marxism and the early European artistic avant-garde. The process of creation was prioritized with an emphasis on the here and now. Relevant members included Debord and Jorn.

Social Realism
Term used to describe art of the nineteenth and twentieth centuries that protested against adverse social conditions and the hardships of everyday life, and employed a broadly representational technique. It is used to describe muralists active in North America during the Great Depression such as Rivera and Orozco.

Socialist Realism
A style that evolved after the Russian Revolution of 1917 and which was intended to further the goals of socialism and communism and was officially sanctioned by the state. It rejected "modern" art such as Impressionism in favor of highly realistic painting that extolled the virtues of the proletariat or communist leaders. Popular in South America in the 1950s to 1970s, it is the prevailing style in modern-day North Korea.

Spatialism
Italian movement launched by Lucio Fontana in 1947. It embraced technology and placed emphasis on gesture or performance in art.

Suprematism
Russian abstract-art movement. Its chief proponent was the Russian artist Kasimir Malevich, who invented the phrase in 1913. Paintings are characterized by a limited color palette and the use of simple geometric forms such as the square, circle, and cross. Other artists associated with the style include El Lissitzky and Moholy-Nagy.

Surrealism
Movement in art and literature launched in Paris in 1924 by French poet André Breton with the publication of his "Manifesto of Surrealism." The movement was characterized by a fascination with the bizarre, the illogical, and the dreamlike and, like Dada—an obvious precursor—sought to shock the viewer. Integral artists include Dalí, Ernst, Magritte, and Miró. Its trademark emphasis on chance, and gestures informed by impulse rather than conscious thought (see Automatism), was highly influential for subsequent artistic movements, such as Abstract Expressionism.

Symbolism
Term invented in 1886 by French critic Jean Moréas to describe the poetry of Stéphane Mallarmé and Paul Verlaine. Applied to art, it describes the use of mythological, religious, and literary subject matter, and art that features emotional and psychological content, with a particular interest in the erotic, perverse, and mystical. Predominant artists include Redon and Gauguin.

Tachisme
Derived from "tache," meaning "stain," or "blot," in French. Term used to describe technique adopted in the 1940s and 1950s by abstract artists, such as Dubuffet and Mathieu, who often painted using spots of paint straight from the tube. It is closely related to Art Informel.

Tempera
Derived from "temperare," meaning "to mix" in Latin. Paint made of powdered pigments, egg yolk, and water. Primarily associated with European art produced from the thirteenth century to the end of the fifteenth century.

Third Style
Roman style of painting from c.20 BCE to 45 CE, notable for figures shown in a three-quarter pose, and trompe l'oeil effects such as the imitation of framed pictures on walls.

Transavanguardia
Italian Neo-Expressionist movement that sought to establish "traditional" artistic priorities such as expressive painting, individuality, and figurative work. Leading artists include Chia, Clemente, Cucchi, de Maria, and Paladino.

Trompe l'Oeil
French for "deceives the eye." Painted features designed to fool the viewer into thinking what is seen is real.

Ukiyo-e
Japanese for "floating world." Style of mass-produced Japanese paintings created from the seventeenth century to the present, noted for bright color and decorativeness, including animals, landscapes, courtesans, and wrestlers.

Vanitas
Latin for "vanity." A still-life containing objects such as a skull, candle, or flowers, as symbolic reminders of the brevity of life. A popular theme in seventeenth-century Dutch and Flemish work.

Vasari, Giorgio
Sixteenth-century Italian architect, painter, and writer. Most famous for his *Lives of the Artists*, which describes the biographies and major works of Italian artists from the fourteenth century onward. First published in 1550, the book remains a cornerstone of art history.

Veduta (plural, vedute)
Italian for "view." A painting depicting a view of a townscape or landscape that is so accurate that the location is identifiable. Particularly associated with eighteenth-century Italian artists Canaletto and Guardi.

Venus Pudica
Term meaning "modest Venus," describing a classical pose, either sitting or standing, of a nude female covering her genitalia.

Vorticism
British art movement founded in 1914, which promoted a Cubist style combined with a Futuristic emphasis on the mechanistic dynamism of the modern world, as a reaction against perceived complacency in British culture. Painters included Lewis, Roberts, and Wadsworth.

Wagnerism
Philosophical ideals based on the writings of nineteenth-century German composer and conductor Richard Wagner, and advocating the perceived attributes of a "true" German.

YBA
Abbreviation of Young British Artists. Used to describe a group of avant-garde British artists, including Davenport, Whiteread, Lucas, and Hirst, prominent from the 1990s.

Artist Index

Contributors

(AA) Anna Amari-Parker has traveled through Europe, Asia, and Latin America as a writer and editor. She has written on Dante Alighieri's *Divine Comedy* and contributed to the *Encyclopedia of Decorative Arts*. She lives and works in London.

(AB) Aliki Braine is an artist who studied at the Ruskin School, Oxford, and the Slade School, London. She is a freelance lecturer for the National Gallery, London, and regularly exhibits her work.

(AlB) Alice Bell studied History of Art and Architecture at the University of Newcastle upon Tyne. She has worked on children's books, adult nonfiction, and magazines and is now a senior editor.

(AEH) Amy Elin Haavik is a graduate student in History of Art at Bryn Mawr College. She received a BA in Art History from Vassar College and an MA in History of Art from the University of Manchester.

(AH) Ana Finel Honigman is a New York- and London-based critic, curator, and arts editor. A Sarah Lawrence graduate, she has completed an MA and is currently reading for a DPhil in History of Art at Oxford.

(AHi) Anne Hildyard is a writer and editor who has worked on numerous publications, including books, encyclopedias, and magazines. Her specialties are book reviewing, wildlife, art, and health issues.

(AK) Ann Kay is a writer and editor with a degree in History of Art and Literature at Kent University and a postgraduate qualification in graphic design from London University. She has also studied book design and jewelry-making.

(AR) Alix Rule grew up in New York and studied in Chicago and then in Oxford. She has worked on *Dissent* and *In These Times* and currently writes freelance. She is also a community organizer, living in London but bound for Berlin.

(ARa) Abigail Rasminsky is a former modern dancer who spent many years performing all over the world. Her work has been published in the *New York Times*, *FitYoga*, and *Elephant Magazine*. She lives and writes in Brooklyn, New York.

(AS) Andrew Smith is a New Zealander who studied English at the University of Cambridge. He graduated in 2006 with an MPhil in Eighteenth-century and Romantic Literature, and currently works in London.

(AT) Abraham Thomas works as assistant curator in the Prints, Drawings and Paintings collection of the Victoria & Albert Museum.

(AV) Aruna Vasudevan is a London-based writer and editor who specializes in popular culture and travel. Her work is featured in *Passion* (about painter Fletcher Sidthorp) and *Twentieth-Century Masterworks*.

(CK) Carol King is a London-based freelance writer with a love of art who studied English Literature at the University of Sussex. She has a degree in Fine Art from London's Central Saint Martins art school.

(CM) Cathy Marriott is a London-based writer and editor specializing in art, food and drink, and entertainment. She has contributed to books such as *The Encyclopedia of Decorative Arts* and *Collector's Guide: Arts and Crafts*.

(CR) Christina Rodenbeck studied History of Art at London University, where she specialized in nineteenth- and twentieth-century culture. She also writes on the subject of religion and spirituality.

(CS) Craig Staff is an artist, writer and lecturer based in Northamptonshire. He has written extensively on the philosophical discourses of painting and has also exhibited in numerous art galleries and museums across the United Kingdom.

(DC) Diana Cermeño graduated in History of Art from Universidad Autónoma de Madrid, Spain, and Essex University. She specialized in Spanish art, with particular emphasis on the collections of the Prado and Thyssen-Bornemisza museums.

(DD) Dan Dunlavey is an editor and writer on various subjects, including art, antiques, and collectables.

(DK) Daniel Robert Koch specializes in nineteenth-century history and art. He received a Master's degree from Oxford University, has written on the Hudson River school, and is currently completing a PhD dissertation on Ralph Waldo Emerson.

(EB) Emma Bryant studied Fine Art and worked as a painter and community artist before becoming a museum educator. She currently works at the Wallace Collection in London.

(EG) Emilie E.S. Gordenker is senior curator of early Netherlandish, Dutch, and Flemish art at the National Gallery of Scotland. She received her doctorate from the Institute of Fine Arts, New York University, and has lectured and published extensively on her specialty—seventeenth-century dress and Anthony van Dyck.

(FN) Fuyubi Nakamura is an anthropologist specializing in the visual and material cultures of Japan, with particular emphasis on contemporary calligraphy. She has a doctorate in Social and Cultural Anthropology from Oxford.

(GD) Geoff Dyer's many books include *But Beautiful*, *Paris Trance*, *Out of Sheer Rage*, *Yoga For People Who Can't Be Bothered to Do It* and, most recently, *The Ongoing Moment*. He has received the E.M. Forster Award from the American Academy of Arts and Letters.

(HC) Lam Wei Ching trained and worked as a fashion designer. She changed career to work in investment property management but has returned to the art field.

(HH) Hannah Hudson studied for a BA in Latin American Studies and an MA in Latin American Art and Architecture at the University of Essex, England. She lived and studied in Mexico for two years.

(IZ) Iain Zaczek is a writer who lives in London. He studied at Wadham College, Oxford, and the Courtauld Institute of Art. His previous books include *The Collins Big Book of Art* and *Masterworks*.

(JB) Jessica Bishop is an editor and writer on art, design, homes, and antiques. Born in Nottingham, she studied in Leeds and now lives in south London.

(JC) Jane Crosland studied History of Art at Newcastle University, England, specializing in the Italian Renaissance. She has worked in magazine publishing and is currently a designer, based in London.

(JCo) Joanna Coates is a filmmaker and writer. She works as a graphic artist, while making music videos, illustrations, and writing a feature film.

(JG) Jessica Gromley graduated from Leeds University with a degree in History and Spanish. She spent a year working in Barcelona as a curator before returning to London to complete a Master's degree in History of Art at the Courtauld Institute.

(JH) James Harrison is a writer on art, culture, and sport. His favorite painting is *A Bigger Splash* by David Hockney and he feels aggrieved he wasn't slated to write about this paean to pools, especially as he coauthored *Learn to Swim in a Weekend* with British Olympic swimmer Sharron Davies.

(JJ) Julie Jones attended the University of Paris I—Sorbonne, France. She is writing a book on the relationship between Abstract Expressionism and experimental photography in the late twentieth century. She lives in Paris and Oxford.

(JM) Jamie Middleton is a freelance writer and editor for numerous lifestyle magazines and books. Based in Bath, he has an extensive classical-art background and has worked on a range of diverse subjects, ranging from the Milau Bridge and Jaguar cars to laptops and fine wines.

(JN) Jane Neal is an Oxford-based freelance journalist and critic. Her particular focus has been the developing art scene in Central and Eastern Europe. She contributes to a wide variety of international art publications.

(JP) Jane Peacock is the assistant to the Head of College at Chelsea College of Art and Design. Her studio work involves the integration of paintings with short stories and other texts. She lives in London.

(JR) João Ribas is a writer, critic, and curator based in New York. His writing appears in several international publications, and he is the author of numerous essays and exhibition catalogues. He is a former editor at *ArtReview* and *LTB Media*.

(JSD) Jenny Doubt has an MA in Postcolonial Literature from the University of Sussex. She has worked as a project editor and online editorial consultant and is one of the founding editors of *Transgressions*.

(JT) Julian Treuherz is Keeper of Art Galleries at National Museums Liverpool. He has curated many exhibitions, including *Rossetti* and *Sir Lawrence Alma-Tadema*, and is an expert in Victorian art.

(JW) Jude Welton studied English and History of Art at Nottingham University. Her numerous books on art include *Monet*, *Impressionism*, *Looking at Paintings*, *Chagall*, and *Matisse*.

(KM) Karen Morden is an editor and writer on art and popular culture. She completed a PhD in Media and Cultural Studies at the University of Sussex and has written for *The Idler* and *Kettering* magazines.

(LH) Lucinda Hawksley is the author of *Katey: The Life and Loves of Dickens's Artist Daughter*, *Lizzie Siddal: The Tragedy of a Pre-Raphaelite Supermodel*, and *Essential Pre-Raphaelites*. She is also an award-winning travel writer.

(MC) Mary Cooch is a freelance magazine and book journalist with a BA (Hons) degree in History from London University. One of her special interests is pre-Renaissance art.

(MF) Michael Farthing is principal and professor of Medicine at St. George's, University of London. He was formerly professor of Gastroenterology at St. Bartholomew's Hospital, London, where he had the privilege to pass and enjoy *The Pool of Bethesda* in the North Wing's Great Hall.

(MG) Megan Green studied History of Art at Stanford University and completed a tutorial at Oxford University focusing on the Young British Artists. She interned at the Museum of Contemporary Art in Chicago and collects contemporary art.

(ML) Marco Livingstone is an art historian and independent curator who has published widely on painting, sculpture, drawing, photography, and video. His books include *Pop Art: A Continuing History* and monographs on David Hockney, R.B. Kitaj, Patrick Caulfield, Allen Jones, and Jim Dine.

(MV) Marissa Vigneault is a PhD candidate in History of Art at Bryn Mawr College, and is currently working on the artistic production of *Mary Kelly*. She was awarded an MA in History of Art by the American University in Washington, DC.

(NKM) Nicholas Kenji Machida is a BA candidate in History of Art at Stanford University. He is writing a senior thesis on contemporary museum design as it relates to the museum's role in the public sphere.

(NMa) Nora Mahony is a graduate of Trinity College, Dublin. She has worked in graphic design and art publishing, and is a freelance critic for *The Times Literary Supplement* and the *Irish Times*.

(NSF) Nathalie Sroka-Fillion recently completed her MA in Medieval Art and Architecture at the Courtauld Institute of Art. She is currently a researcher for English Heritage, living in London and Montreal.

(OR) Oscar Rickett was born in London and completed an MA at the University of Leeds. A semi-professional clarinettist and freelance writer, he spent a year living in Buenos Aires, where he worked with, and wrote about, painters, sculptors, and musicians he befriended there.

(OW) Ossian Ward writes on contemporary art and is a contributor to several newspapers and magazines. Formerly the editor of *ArtReview*, he has also been an editor at the *V&A Magazine* and *The Art Newspaper* and currently edits *The Artist's Yearbook*.

(PB) Paul Bonaventura is senior research Fellow in Fine Art Studies at the University of Oxford.

(PH) Paul Hamilton studied at Portsmouth School of Art. He is the coeditor of *How Very Interesting: Peter Cook's Universe and All That Surrounds It* and writes the film pages of *The Idler* magazine.

(PS) Paige Sweet is a PhD candidate in Comparative Literature at the University of Minnesota. Her research includes figures and processes of forgetting in the contexts of literature and philosophy, ranging from ancient history to the modern day.

(RA) Rex Anderson is a writer, editor, and graphic designer. He has been admiring the work of other artists for more than fifty years but has never completed any of his own paintings.

(RB) Richard Bell studied Visual Cultures at the University of Derby and subsequently completed a postgraduate diploma in Publishing at the London College of Printing. He currently works for an educational publisher in London.

(RG) Reg Grant is a freelance writer who has published more than twenty books on cultural and historical subjects. His special interests include French nineteenth-century painting, Renaissance iconography, and certain aspects of Modernism.

(RJ) Rosalva Johnston was born in Peru and was awarded a BA (Hons) in History of Art from the University of Essex. She was involved in the Latin American Link Project organized by *Firstsite @ The Minories Art Gallery* in Colchester.

(RK) Riikka Kuittinen is assistant curator at the Victoria & Albert Museum in London. She graduated with a BA in Visual Culture from Middlesex University and an MA in History of Art from Goldsmiths College. In 2005, she curated *Street Art* at the V&A.

(RL) Randy Lerner was born in Ohio in 1962. He graduated from Columbia College in 1984 and currently lives in New York. He has known and owned artist Vincent Desiderio's work for more than ten years.

(RM) Rebecca Man graduated from Sussex University with a degree in History of Art. She worked at the National Art Collections Fund and the Arts Council of England before moving to Chelsea College of Art and Design, where she currently works as a researcher for Stephen Farthing.

(RW) Roger Wilson is a painter and academic, currently Head of Chelsea College of Art and Design. Over the last thirty-five years he has worked in colleges and universities in the United Kingdom, the United States, and Europe.

(SA) Sandra April is an arts consultant who lives and works in Manhattan. She is also originating editor of *Will Barnet: In His Own Words*. She has worked at the Museum of Modern Art, Solomon R. Guggenheim Museum, and New York Academy of Art.

(SC) Serena Cant studied Anglo-Saxon art at the University of Exeter. She is an art history lecturer specializing in sign-language talks to deaf audiences on the subject of Western art and architecture.

(SE) Samantha Earl is a freelance arts documentary researcher and producer in London. Since studying Art and Urban History at Columbia University in New York, she has been involved in filmmaking at various levels.

(SF) Stephen Farthing is a painter and the Rootstein Hopkins Research Professor in Drawing at the University of the Arts, London. In 1990, he was elected Master of Ruskin School of Drawing, University of Oxford, and a professional Fellow at St. Edmund Hall, Oxford.

(SG) Simon Gray studied Media at Sheffield Hallam and worked as editor for *Itchy City Guides* for four years before starting up a telecommunications company. He divides his time between his business and writing.

(SH) Susie Hodge is an illustrator, teacher, and author of over fifty books and articles. She also writes web resources and booklets for galleries and museums. She has an MA in History of Art and is a Fellow of the RSA.

(SLF) Susan Flockhart studied History of Art at the University of Newcastle upon Tyne. A painter living in London, she has a particular interest in rediscovering the practical techniques of the Old Masters.

(SM) Sally Young McFall was a Theater and Literature major at Bard College. After graduation, she helped found a band called Ut that used Abstract Expressionism as an approach to making music. She is now an editor and a jazz/blues singer.

(SML) Signe Mellergaard Larsen was born in Aarhus, Denmark. She has an MA from the Courtauld Institute of Art, London, and a BA (Hons) in History of Art from the University of Plymouth, Exeter. Her research includes North European painting from the nineteenth to the twenty-first century.

(SP) Steven Pulimood attended Columbia University and has a Master's degree from Oxford University. Currently, he is a doctoral candidate at Oxford writing a book on Leonardo da Vinci and the development of human anatomy in sixteenth-century Italy.

(SaP) Saskia Pütz teaches History of Art at the Freie Universität of Berlin. Her main areas are German nineteenth-century painting and concepts of artistic identity. She is completing a PhD on artists' autobiographies and has published works on nineteenth- and twentieth-century art.

(SS) Steven Stowell is a DPhil candidate in History of Art at the University of Oxford, researching the concept of allegory written about by Italian Renaissance art theorists.

(SW) Sonia Werner is a graduate student at New York University. Her research includes theories of mimesis in ancient and modern contexts as well as comparative nineteenth-century Realist literature and historiography.

(SWW) Sara White Wilson is an American photographer and journalist working in Paris. She has a degree in the History of Philosophy and Mathematics and was short-listed for the Vogue UK Writing Contest in 2004. She works for European graffiti magazines and in fashion advertising.

(SZ) Sandrine Josefsada was born in Belgium and has a BA in History of Art and Archaeology from the School of Oriental and African Studies, London. She specialized in the Arts of India and has written *Reactions and Functionalities of Eroticism in Indian Art, from Khajuraho to Bollywood*.

(TP) Tamsin Pickeral studied History of Art before furthering her education in Italy. She divides her time between writing about art and horses, her most recent publications being *Turner, Whistler, Monet, Charles Rennie Mackintosh* and *30,000 Years of the Horse in Art*.

(TS) Terry Sanderson is a London-based freelance journalist and commentator. He has written for all of the major newspapers and magazines in Britain and has published a total of nine books.

(WD) William Davies is a London-based writer and researcher. Currently studying at the Courtauld Institute of Art, he was also a press coordinator for the opening of White Cube's Mason's Yard space.

(WM) Wilson McClelland Dunlavey has lived in Berlin, Germany, for the past three years. He is a graduate student of Philosophy and History at Humboldt University.

(WO) Wendy Osgerby is a senior lecturer in History of Art at the University of Northampton, England. Apart from writing on art, she writes fiction and enjoys being involved in curating.

(ZT) Zoë Telford studied Painting at Edinburgh College of Art in Scotland before studying for an MA in Art and Ideology at the University of Southampton, England. She works as a freelance lecturer for a number of galleries and colleges in London.

Picture Credits

of Art, Washington DC, USA/Bridgeman Art Library **338 L:** Scottish National Portrait Gallery, Edinburgh, Scotland/Bridgeman Art Library **338 R:** Arte & Immagini srl/Corbis **339 L:** Fine Art Photographic Library/Corbis **339 R:** ©Dulwich Picture Gallery, London/Bridgeman Art Library **340** Mozart Museum, Salzburg, Austria, Alinari/Bridgeman Art Library **341** Burstein Collection/Corbis **342** Art Archive/Museo del Prado, Madrid **343** Huntington Library & Art Gallery, San Marino, CA, USA/Bridgeman Art Library **344** Kunsthaus, Zurich, Switzerland/Bridgeman Art Library **345** ©Dixson Galleries, State Library of New South Wales/Bridgeman Art Library **346** ©National Gallery of Scotland, Edinburgh, Scotland/Bridgeman Art Library **347** Brooklyn Museum of Art/Corbis **348** ©1990 Photo Scala, Florence **349** akg-images/Sotheby's **350–351** Tate Collection, London UK **352** Art Archive/V&A Museum London/Sally Chappell **353** ©National Trust Picture Library/Mount Stewart House, County Down, UK **354** Priv. coll./Bridgeman Art Library **355** Louvre, Paris, France/Francis G Mayer/Corbis **356** Art Archive/Museo del Prado, Madrid, Spain/Dagli Orti **357** Photo Scala, Florence/Museo del Prado, Madrid, Spain **358** Metropolitan Museum of Art, NY, USA/Francis G Meyer/Corbis **359** Louvre, Paris, France/Peter Willi/Bridgeman Art Library **360** Musée de Picaride, Amiens, France/Giraudon/Bridgeman Art Library **361** Muzeum Narodowe, Warsaw, Poland/Bridgeman Art Library **362** Art Archive, Victoria &Albert Museum, London/Eileen Tweedy **363** National Gallery of Scotland, Edinburgh, UK **364** Art Archive/Museo del Prado, Madrid, Spain/Dagli Orti **365** Tate Collection, UK, London **366** Hamburger Kunsthalle, Hamburg, Germany/Bridgeman Art Library **367** National Gallery, London UK **368** Louvre, Paris, France **369** Priv. coll., Christies Images/Corbis **370** Hamburger Kunsthalle, Hamburg, Germany/Bridgeman Art Library **371** Museo del Prado, Madrid, Spain/Photo Scale, Florence **372** Staatliche museen, Berlin, Germany/Ann Ronan/HIP/Scala, Florence **373** Hamburger Kunsthalle, Hamburg, Germany/AKG Images **374** Musée Conde, Chantilly, France/Bridgeman Art Library **375** akg-images/Erich Lessing **376** Nationalmuseum, Stockholm, Sweden/Bridgeman Art Library **377** Musée des Beaux-Arts, Rouen, France, Lauros/Giraudon/Bridgeman Art Library **378** Museu de Arte da bahia, Salvador, Brazil **379** Art Archive/National Gallery, London/Eileen Tweedy **380** Museum voor Schone Kunsten, Ghent, Belgium/Bridgeman Art Library **381** Museo del Prado, Madrid, Spain/Archivo Iconografico, SA/Corbis **382** Scottish National Portrait Gallery, Edinburgh, UK/Bridgeman Art Library **383** Victoria & Albert Museum, London/Bridgeman Art Library **384** Victoria & Albert Museum, London/Bridgeman Art Library **385** Walker Art Gallery, National Museums Liverpool/Bridgeman Art Library **386** Seattle Art Museum/Corbis **387** Ashmolean Museum, University of Oxford, UK/Bridgeman Art Library **388** Tate Collection, London 2006 **389** ©University of Liverpool Art Gallery & Collections, UK/Bridgeman Art Library **390** Priv. coll., ©Bonhams, London/Bridgeman Art Library **391** Philadelphia Museum of Art/Corbis **392** ©Louvre, Paris, France/Lauros /Giraudon/Bridgeman Art Library **393** Georgian State Picture Gallery, Tbilisi, Georgia/Bridgeman Art Library **394** Christie's Images/Christies Images/Corbis **395** akg-images/Erich Lessing **396** Hamburger Kunsthalle, Hamburg, Germany/Bridgeman Art Library **397** Hamburger Kunsthalle, Hamburg, Germany/Bridgeman Art Library **398** Museum der Bildenden Kunste, Leipzig, Germany/akg-images **399** Hamburger Kunsthalle, Hamburg, Germany/Bridgeman Art Library **400** Elder Bequest Fund 1899, Art Gallery of South Australia, Adelaide **401** Philadelphia Museum of Art, Pennsylvania, PA, USA/Bridgeman Art Library **402** Nationalmuseum, Stockholm, Sweden/Bridgeman Art Library **403** Collection of the New-York Historical Society, USA/Bridgeman Art Library **404** Thorvaldsens Museum, Copenhagen, Denmark/Bridgeman Art Library **405** National Gallery, London/Bridgeman Art Library **406** Louvre, Paris, France, Giraudon/Bridgeman Art Library **407** Tate Collection, London UK **408** Walters Art Gallery, Baltimore, USA/Scala, Florence **409** Detroit Institute of Arts, USA, Gift of Douglas F Roby/Bridgeman Art Library **410** bpk/Gemäldegalerie, SMB/Photo Jörg P Anders **411** Metropolitan Museum of Art, NY, USA/Bridgeman Art Library **412** Geoffrey Clements/Corbis **413** Birmingham Museums & Art Gallery/Bridgeman Art Library **414** Priv. coll., Christie's Images/Bridgeman Art Library **415** Walker Art Gallery, National Museums Liverpool/Bridgeman Art Library **416** Galleria degli Uffizi, Florence, Italy/Bridgeman Art Library **417** Francis G Mayer/Corbis **418 L:** Museum Georg Schafer, Schweinfurt, Germany/Bridgeman Art Library **418 R:** Priv. coll., Index/Bridgeman Art Library **419 L:** Gift of Quincy Adams Shaw through Quincy Adams Shaw, Jr & Mrs Marian Shaw Haughton 17.1485. 2006 Museum of Fine Arts, Boston/Bridgeman Art Library **419 R:** Hamburger Kunsthalle, Hamburg, Germany/Bridgeman Art Library **420** Ashmolean Museum, University of Oxford, UK/Bridgeman Art Library **421** Metropolitan Museum of Art, NY, USA/Bridgeman Art Library **422** United Distillers & Vintners/Bridgeman Art Library **423** Art Archive/Tate Gallery London/Eileen Tweedy **424** Tate Collection, London UK **425** Seattle Art Museum, Gift of Mrs Paul C Carmichael/Corbis **426** Musée Fabre, Montpelier, France/akg-images **427** National Gallery Collection; By kind permission of the Trustees of the National Gallery, London/Corbis **428** Manchester Art Gallery, UK/Bridgeman Art Library **429** Birmingham Museums & Art Gallery/Bridgeman Art Library **430** Art Gallery of Ontario, Toronto, Canada/Bridgeman Art Library **431** Archivo Iconografico, SA/Corbis **432** Musée d'Orsay, Paris, France, Giraudon/Bridgeman Art Library **433** Manchester Art Gallery, UK/Bridgeman Art Library **434** National Gallery Collection; By kind permission of the Trustees of the National Gallery, London/Corbis **435** Birmingham Museums & Art Gallery/Bridgeman Art Library **436** Karnter Landesgalerie, Vienna, Austria/Bridgeman Art Library **437** Schack Galerie, Munich, Germany/Bridgeman Art Library **438** Musée d'orsay, Paris, France/akg-images **439** Statens Museum for Kunst, Copenhagen, Denmark/Bridgeman Art Library **440** ©1990 Photo Scala, Florence Courtesy of Minstero Beni e Att. Culturali **441** State Hermitage, St Petersburg, Russia/Bridgeman Art Library **442** Sangram Singh Collection, City Palace, Jaipur, India/akg-images/Jean-Louis Nou **443** Museu Nacional Belas Artes, Rio de Janeiro, Brazil, Paul Maeyaert/Bridgeman Art Library **444** Priv. coll., Fine Art Photographic Library/Corbis **445** Ayuntamiento de Coruna, Spain /Bridgeman Art Library **446** Royal Holloway & Bedford New College, Surrey, UK/Bridgeman Art Library **447** National Gallery of Australia, Canberra, Australia **448** Musée d'Orsay, Paris/Dagli Orti/Art Archive **449** Musée d'Orsay, Paris/Dagli Orti/Art Archive **450** Muzeum Narodowe, Warsaw, Poland/Bridgeman Art Library **451** Louvre, Paris, France/Scala, Florence **452** Museo Civico Rivoltello, Trieste, Italy, Alinari/Bridgeman Art Library **453**Musée d'Orsay, Paris, France, Lauros/Giraudon/Bridgeman Art Library **454** Museo Historico Nacional, Buenos Aires, Argentina, Index/Bridgeman Art Library **455** Birmingham Museums & Art Gallery/Bridgeman Art Library **456** Musée d'Orsay, Paris, France, Giraudon/Bridgeman Art Library **457** Musée d'Orsay, Paris, France/Scala, Florence **458** Palazzo Pitti Florence/Dagli Orti/Art Archive **459** ©National Gallery of Scotland, Edinburgh, Scotland/Bridgeman Art Library **460** Stadtische Kunsthalle, Mannheim, Germany/Bridgeman Art Library **461** Musée d'Orsay, Paris, France/Scala **462** Hamburger Kunsthalle, Hamburg, Germany/Christie's Images/Corbis **463** Musée d'Orsay, Paris/Dagli Orti/Art Archive **464** Museo de Arte Moderno, Madrid, Spain, Index/Bridgeman Art Library **465** Metropolitan Museum of Art, NY, USA/Bridgeman Art Library **466** Tate Collection/akg-images/Erich Lessing **467** Musée d'Orsay, Paris, France, Giraudon/Bridgeman Art Library **468** Butler Institute of American Art, Youngstown, OH, USA, Museum Purchase 1918/Bridgeman Art Library **469** Staatliche Muséen, Alte Nationalgalerie, Berlin, Germany/akg-images **470** Priv. coll., ©Christie's Images/Bridgeman Art Library **471** Muzeum Narodowe, Warsaw, Poland/Bridgeman Art Library **472** Musée Marmottan, Paris, France, Giraudon/Bridgeman Art Library **473** National Gallery, Budapest, Hungary **474** Musée d'Orsay, Paris, France/Scala, France **475** Museo Perez Chiriboya del Banco Central, Ecuador, Index/Bridgeman Art Library **476** Musée des Beaux-Arts et d'Archaeologie, Bescancon, France/Archivo Iconografico, SA/Corbis **477** Museo del Prado, Madrid, Spain/Bridgeman Art Library **478** Christie's Images/Corbis **479** Scala, France **480** Detroit Institute of Arts, USA, Gift of Dexter M Ferry Jr/Bridgeman Art Library **481** Francis G Mayer/Corbis **482** Musée d'Orsay, Paris, France/akg-images/Laurent Lecat **483** Walters Art Museum, Baltimore, USA/Bridgeman Art Library **484** Musée d'Orsay, Paris, France, Lauros/Giraudon/Bridgeman Art Library **485** Guildhall Art Gallery, City of London/Bridgeman Art Library **486** Nationalmuseum, Stockholm, Sweden/Bridgeman Art Library **487** Priv. coll., Bourne Gallery, Surrey/Bridgeman Art Library **488** Osterreichische Galerie Belvedere, Vienna, Austria/Ali Meyer/Corbis **489** Museo Nacional de Artes Visuales, Montevideo, Uruguay/Archivo Iconografico SA/Corbis **490** Phillips Collection, Washington DC, USA/Bridgeman Art Library **491** Nasjonalgalleriet, Oslo, Norway/Bridgeman Art Library **492** Lady Lever Art Gallery, Wirral, UK/akg-images **493** Magyar Nemzeti Galeria, Budapest, Hungary/Bridgeman Art Library **494 L:** ©De Morgan Centre, London/Bridgeman Art Library **494 R:** Nationalmuseum, Stockholm, Sweden/Bridgeman Art Library **495 L:** Birmingham Museums & Art Gallery/Bridgeman Art Library **495 R:** Musée d'Orsay, Paris, France, Lauros/Giraudon/Bridgeman Art Library **496** ©Musee d'Orsay, Paris, France/Giraudon/Bridgeman Art Library **497** Barnes Foundation, Merion, PA/Corbis **498** Samuel Courtauld Trust, Courtauld Institute of Art Gallery/Bridgeman Art Library **499** Sobieski Room, Vatican City, Italy/Scala, Florence **500** National Gallery, London/Bridgeman Art Library **501** Metropolitan Museum of Art, NY, USA/Geoffrey Clements/Corbis **502** Malmo Museum, Sweden/Bridgeman Art Library **503** Nationalmuseum, Stockholm, Sweden/Bridgeman Art Library **504** Museo de Nittis Barletta Bari/Dagli Orti/Art Archive **505** Albright-Knox Art Gallery/Corbis **506 L:** Fine Art Photographic Library/Corbis **506 R:** Musée d'Orsay, Paris, France, Giraudon/Bridgeman Art Library **507 L:** Metropolitan Museum of Art, NY, USA/Bridgeman Art Library **507 R:** National Gallery London/Eileen Tweedy/Art Archive **508** Art Institute of Chicago/Art Archive **509** Nasjonalgalleriet, Oslo, Norway/Bridgeman Art Library **510** Museum der Bildenden Kunste, Leipzig, Germany/Bridgeman Art Library **511** Priv. coll./Bridgeman Art Library **512** Musée d'Orsay, Paris, France **513** National Gallery of Victoria, Melbourne, Australia, Felton Bequest/Bridgeman Art Library **514** Joseph Winterbottom Collection, Art Institute of Chicago, IL, USA/Bridgeman Art Library **515** National Gallery of Scotland, Edinburgh/Bridgeman Art Library **516** J Paul Getty Museum, Los Angeles, USA, Lauros/Giraudon/Bridgeman Art Library **517** Goteborgs Konstmuseum, Sweden/Bridgeman Art Library **518** Musée d'Orsay, Paris, France, Giraudon/Bridgeman Art Library **519** Nationalmuseum, Stockholm, Sweden/Bridgeman Art Library **520 L:** Burstein Collection, Isabella Stewart Gardner Museum, Boston, USA/Corbis **520 R:** National Gallery, London/Bridgeman Art Library **521 L:** Samuel Courtauld Trust, Courtauld Institute of Art Gallery/Bridgeman Art Library **521 R:** Detroit Institute of Arts, USA, Founders Society Purchase, RH Tannahill Foundation fund/Bridgeman Art Library **522** University of Pennsylvania, Philadelphia, USA,/Geoffrey Clements/Corbis **523** Priv. coll./Peter Willi Bridgeman Art Library **524** Worcester Art Museum, MA, USA/Bridgeman Art Library **525** Van Gogh Museum, Amsterdam, the Netherlands/Francis G Mayer/Corbis **526** ©Leeds Museums & Galleries (City Art Gallery) UK/Bridgeman Art Library **527** Priv. coll., ©Fine Art Society, London/Bridgeman Art Library **528** Ramus Meyers Samlinger, Bergen, Norway/Bridgeman Art Library **529** Pushkin Museum, Moscow, Russia/Bridgeman Art Library **530** ©Nationalmuseum, Stockholm, Sweden/Bridgeman Art Library ©DACS, London 2006 **531** Tate Gallery London/Eileen Tweedy/Art Archive **532** Berko Fine Paintings, Knokke-Zoute, Belgium/Bridgeman Art Library **533** Morgan Thomas Bequest Fund 1951, Art Gallery of South Australia, Adelaide **534** Priv. coll./Bridgeman Art Library **535** Museum of Fine Arts, Boston, Gift of Miss Aimée & Miss Rosamond Lamb in memory of Mr & Mrs Horatio Appleton Lamb/Bridgeman Art Library **536** Museu de Arte de Sao Paulo, Brazil/Francis G Mayer/Corbis **537** National Gallery Collection; By kind permission of the Trustees of the National Gallery, London/Corbis **538** Walker Art Gallery, National Museums Liverpool/Bridgeman Art Library **539** Christie's Images/Corbis **540 L:** Musée d'Orsay, Paris/Dagli Orti/Art Archive **540 R:** Museo de la Abadia, Montserrat, Catalonia, Spain, Index/Bridgeman Art Library **541 L:** Musée d'Orsay, Paris, France/Bridgeman Art Library **541 R:** Magyar Nemzeti Galeria, Budapest, Hungary/Bridgeman Art Library **542** Kunstmuseum, Basel, Switzerland/Bridgeman Art Library **543** Musée d'Orsay, Paris, France/Bridgeman Art Library **544** Fine Art Museum, Bilbao/Dagli Orti/Art Archive **545** Nationalmuseum, Stockholm, Sweden/Bridgeman Art Library **546 L:** Turku Art Museum, Finland/Bridgeman Art Library **546 R:** Musée Toulouse-Lautrec, Albi, France, Giraudon/Bridgeman Art Library **547 L:** Munch Museum/Munch—Ellingsen Group, BONO, Burstein Collection/Corbis **547 R:** Magyar Nemzeti Galeria, Budapest, Hungary/Bridgeman Art Library **548** Russell-Cotes Art Gallery & Museum, Bournemouth, UK/Bridgeman Art Library **549** Priv. coll., Bonhams, London/Bridgeman Art Library **550** EG Buhrle Collection, Zurich, Switzerland/Francis G Mayer/Corbis **551** Archivo Iconografico, SA/Corbis **552** Burstein Collection, Museum of Fine Arts, Boston, MA, USA/Corbis **553** Musée d'Orsay, Paris, France, Lauros/Giraudon/Bridgeman Art Library **554** Priv. coll., Held Collection/Bridgeman Art Library **555** Samuel Courtauld Trust, Courtauld Institute of Art Gallery/Bridgeman Art Library **556** MoMA, NY/Scala, Florence **557** Priv. coll./Edimédia/Corbis **558 L:** Metropolitan Museum of Art, NY, USA/Francis G Mayer/Corbis **558 R:** Nationalmuseum, Stockholm, Sweden/Bridgeman Art Library **559 L:** Nationalmuseum, Stockholm, Sweden/Bridgeman Art Library **559 R:** Burstein Collection/Corbis Munch Museum/Munch—Ellingsen Group, BONO **560** Nasjonalgalleriet, Oslo, Norway/Bridgeman Art Library **561** Historisches Museum der Stadt, Vienna, Austria/Corbis **562** Priv. coll./Bridgeman Art Library **563** Ashmolean Museum, University of Oxford, UK/Bridgeman Art Library **564–565** (detail) Priv. coll./Bridgeman Art Library. ©ADAGP, Paris & DACS, London 2006 **566** Priv. coll./Bridgeman Art Library **567** Burstein Collection/Corbis **568** ©Ashmolean Museum, University of Oxford, UK/Bridgeman Art Library. ©Succession Picasso/DACS, London 2006. **569** Priv. coll. ©Christie's Images/Bridgeman Art Library **570** ©National Gallery of Victoria, Melbourne, Australia, Gilbee Bequest/Bridgeman Art Library **571** Priv. coll., ©Gavin Graham Gallery, London, UK/Bridgeman Art Library **572 L:** ©Nationalmuseum, Stockholm, Sweden/Bridgeman Art Library **572 R:** Hamburger Kunsthalle, Hamburg, Germany/Bridgeman Art Library **573 L:** Priv. coll. ©Whitford Fine Art, London,/Bridgeman Art Library **573 R:** Scottish National Portrait Gallery, Edinburgh/Bridgeman Art Library ©Elizabeth Banks **574** ©Philadelphia Museum of Art/CORBIS **575** Christie's Images/Corbis **576** Christie's Images/Corbis ©ADAGP, Paris & DACS, London 2006 **577** Burstein Collection/Corbis ©ADAGP, Paris & DACS, London 2006 **578** ©Nationalmuseum, Stockholm, Sweden/Bridgeman Art Library **579** Collection of Mr & Mrs John Hay Whitney, New York, USA,/Bridgeman Art Library **580** ©National Gallery Collection; By kind permission of the Trustees of the National Gallery, London/CORBIS **581** Christie's Images/Corbis ©ADAGP, Paris & DACS, London 2006 **582** Österreichische Galerie Belvedere, Vienna, Austria,/Bridgeman Art Library **583** ©1990 Scala—Minstero Beni e Att. Culturali **584** Hermitage, St. Petersburg, Russia/Bridgeman Art Library **585** ©2006. Dig. Image, MOMA, NY/Scala, Florence. ©Succession Picasso/DACS, London 2006 **586** Kunstmuseum, Basel, Switzerland, Giraudon/Bridgeman Art Library **587** Galerie Daniel Malingue, Paris, France/Bridgeman Art Library. ©ADAGP, Paris & DACS, London 2006 **588** ©Brooklyn Museum of Art, NY, Augustus Healy Fund B/Bridgeman Art Library **589** ©Austrian Archives; Österreichische Galerie, Vienna/CORBIS **590 L:** ©Nationalmuseum, Stockholm, Sweden/Bridgeman Art Library **590 R:** Priv. coll./Bridgeman Art Library. ©Estate of Walter R Sickert/DACS, London 2006 **591 L:** ©1990 Photo Scala, Florence ©ADAGP, Paris & DACS, London 2006 **591 R:** Christie's Images/Corbis **592** Haags Gemeentemuseum, The Hague, Netherlands/Bridgeman Art Library ©2006 Mondrian/Holtzman Trust c/o HCR International, Warrenton, VA **593** ©1990 Photo Scala, Florence **594** Kunstmuseum, Dusseldorf, Germany/Bridgeman Art Library. ©DACS, London 2006 **595** Haags Gemeentemuseum, The Hague, Netherlands/Bridgeman Art Library ©2006 Mondrian/Holtzman Trust c/o HCR International, Warrenton, VA **596** Christie's Images/Corbis **597** Galerie Daniel Malingue, Paris, France/Bridgeman Art Library **598** ©2005. Dig. image, MOMA, NY/Scala, Florence ©Succession H Matisse/DACS **599** Musée National d'Art Moderne, Centre Pompidou, Paris, France, J.P. Zenobel/Bridgeman Art Library. ©Succession Marcel Duchamp/ADAGP, Paris & DACS, London 2006 **600 L:** Priv. coll./Bridgeman Art Library. ©DACS, London 2006 **600 R:** ©Christie's Images/Bridgeman Art Library **601 L:** Priv. coll./Bridgeman Art Library ©Estate of Gwen John/DACS, London 2006 **601 R:** ©2006 Dig. image MoMA, NY/Scala, Florence ©DACS, London 2006 **602** Scottish National Gallery of Modern Art, Edinburgh, UK/Bridgeman Art Library **603** Pinacoteca di Brera, Milan, Italy, Alinari/Bridgeman Art Library **604** ©2006 Dig. Image, MOMA, NY/Scala, Florence ©Succession H Matisse/DACS **605** Hermitage, St Petersburg, Russia/Bridgeman Art Library. ©ADAGP, Paris & DACS, London 2006 **606** Hamburger Kunsthalle, Hamburg, Germany/Bridgeman Art Library **607** Kunstsammlung Nordrhein-Westfalen, Dusseldorf, Germany, Peter Willi/Bridgeman Art Library. ©ADAGP, Paris & DACS, London 2006 **608 L:** ©State Russian Museum/Corbis ©ADAGP, Paris & DACS, London 2006 **608 R:** Priv. coll. ©Held Collection/Bridgeman Art Library **609 L:** Hamburger Kunsthalle, Hamburg, Germany/Bridgeman Art Library **609 R:** ©2006. Dig. image, MOMA, NY/Scala, Florence. ©ADAGP, Paris & DACS, London 2006 **610** ©Detroit Institute of Arts, USA, Founders Society Purchase, R.H.

Tannahill Foundation fund/Bridgeman Art Library **611** Bettmann/Corbis **612 L:** Art Archive/Musée National d'art moderne Paris/Dagli Orti ©L&M Services B.V.Amsterdam 20060811 **612 R:** Francis G. Mayer/Corbis. ©Succession Marcel Duchamp/ADAGP, Paris & DACS, London 2006 **613 L:** Priv. coll., Lauros/Giraudon/Bridgeman Art Library **613 R:** Francis G. Mayer/Corbis **614** Albright-Knox Art Gallery/Corbis ©DACS, London 2006 **615** Galleria d'Arte Moderna, Turin, Italy, Alinari/Bridgeman Art Library. ©ADAGP, Paris & DACS, London 2006 **616** Art Archive/Fine Art Museum, Bilbao/Dagli Orti. ©DACS, London 2006 **617** State Russian Museum/Corbis **618** Tretyakov Gallery, Moscow/Bridgeman Art Library ©ADAGP, Paris & DACS, London 2006 **619** ©2006. Dig. Image, MOMA, NY/Scala, Florence ©DACS, London 2006 **620** 2004 ©Dig. Image MoMA, NY/Scala **621** Priv. coll. ©Bonhams, London/Bridgeman Art Library ©ADAGP, Paris & DACS, London 2006 **622 L:** Musée National d'Art Moderne, Centre Pompidou, Paris, France, Peter Willi/Bridgeman Art Library ©Succession Picasso/DACS, London 2006 **622 R:** Brucke Museum, Berlin, Germany/Bridgeman Art Library. ©by Ingeborg & Dr Wolfgang Henze-Ketterer, Wichtrach/Bern **623 L:** Hamburger Kunsthalle, Hamburg, Germany/Bridgeman Art Library **623 R:** Rijksmuseum Kroller-Muller, Otterlo, Netherlands/Bridgeman Art Library **624** ©1990 Photo Scala, Florence ©L&M Services B.V. Amsterdam 20060811 **625** Albright-Knox Art Gallery/Corbis ©ADAGP, Paris & DACS, London 2006 **626** ©Art Museum of Estonia, Tallinn/Bridgeman Art Library **627** Art Archive/Galleria d'Arte Moderna Rome/Dagli Orti **628** ©1990 Photo Scala, Florence **629** ©2004 Dig. Image MoMA, NY/Scala **630** ©2006 Dig. Image, MoMA, NY/Scala, Florence. ©DACS, London 2006 **631** Hamburger Kunsthalle, Hamburg, Germany/Bridgeman Art Library **632 L:** ©1990. Scala—Minstero Beni e Att. Culturali **632 R:** ©2001. Photo Scala, Florence. ©DACS, London 2006 **633 L:** ©Art Gallery of New South Wales, Sydney, Australia/Bridgeman Art Library **633 R:** Bettmann/Corbis. ©DACS, London 2006 **634** Francis G. Mayer/Corbis **635** ©DACS, London 2006 **636** ©2005 Dig. image, MoMA, NY/Scala, Florence. ©Succession H Matisse/DACS **637** Thyssen-Bornemisza Collection, Madrid, Spain/Bridgeman Art Library. ©DACS, London 2006 **638 L:** ©2005 Dig. Image MoMA, NY/Scala **638 R:** ©2006 Georgia O'Keeffe Museum, Santa Fe/Art Resource/Scala, Florence ©ARS, NY & DACS, London 2006 **639 L:** Pinacoteca di Brera, Milan, Italy/Bridgeman Art Library. ©DACS, London 2006 **639 R:** Priv. coll./Bridgeman Art Library **640** Österreichisches Galerie, Vienna, Austria/Bridgeman Art Library **641** Solomon R. Guggenheim Museum, NY/Bridgeman Art Library **642** Hamburger Kunsthalle, Hamburg, Germany/Bridgeman Art Library **643** ©Johannesburg Art Gallery, South Africa/Bridgeman Art Library **644** Musée de l'Orangerie, Paris, France, Lauros/Giraudon/Bridgeman Art Library **645** Österreichische Galerie Belvedere, Vienna, Austria/Bridgeman Art Library **646** ©2004 Dig. Image MoMA, NY/Scala **647** Art Archive/Imperial War Museum, London **648 L:** ©1992. Photo Scala, Florence ©DACS, London 2006 **648 R:** Art Archive/Tate Gallery London/Eileen Tweedy ©Estate of Stanley Spencer/DACS, London 2006 **649 L:** ©Barnes Foundation, Merion, PA/Bridgeman Art Library ©ADAGP, Paris & DACS, London 2006 **649 R:** akg-images/Erich Lessing **650** Museo Nacional Centro de Arte Reina Sofia, Madrid, Spain, Giraudon/Bridgeman Art Library ©DACS, London 2006 **651** Christie's Images/Corbis **652 L:** National Gallery of Canada, Ottawa/Bridgeman Art Library ©ADAGP, Paris & DACS, London 2006 **652 R:** ©Tate, London 2006. ©ADAGP, Paris & DACS, London 2006 **653 L:** Christie's Images/Corbis **653 R:** Mayor Gallery, London, UK/Bridgeman Art Library ©Estate of Edward Wadsworth/DACS, London 2006 **654** Priv. coll./BAL ©Hattula Moholy-Nagy/DACS, London 2006 **655** ©2006. Dig. image, MoMA, NY/Scala, Florence. ©DACS, London 2006 **656** Galleria Nazionale d'Arte Moderna, Rome, Italy, Alinari/Bridgeman Art Library ©Hattula Moholy-Nagy/DACS, London 2006 **657** Thyssen-Bornemisza Collection, Madrid, Spain, Giraudon/Bridgeman Art Library ©DACS, London 2006 **658 L:** Alinari Archives/Corbis. ©DACS, London 2006 **658 R:** Art Institute of Chicago, IL. ©1990 Photo Scala, Florence ©L&M Services B.V. Amsterdam 20060811 **659 L:** Priv. coll./Bridgeman Art Library ©ADAGP, Paris & DACS, London 2006 **659 R:** Musée de l'Orangerie, Paris, France, Peter Willi/Bridgeman Art Library. ©ADAGP, Paris & DACS, London 2006 **660** Mucha Trust/Bridgeman Art Library **661** Priv. coll./Bridgeman Art Library ©DACS, London 2006 **662** ©1990 Photo Scala, Florence. ©ADAGP, Paris & DACS, London 2006 **663** Art Archive/Penny Guggenheim Collection, Venice/HarperCollins Publishers **664** Musée Marmottan, Paris, France, Giraudon/Bridgeman Art Library **665** ©Galleria Narciso, Turin, Italy/Lauros/Giraudon/Bridgeman Art Library **666** ©2006. Dig. image, MoMA, NY/Scala, Florence **667** ©New Walk Museum, Leicester City Museum Service, UK/Bridgeman Art Library **668** Priv. coll. ©Christie's Images/Bridgeman Art Library **669** ©2006. Dig. image, MoMA, NY/Scala, Florence **670** ©Archivo Iconografico, SA/Corbis ©by Ingeborg & Dr Wolfgang Henze-Ketterer, Wichtrach/Bern **671** Priv. coll./Bridgeman Art Library. ©DACS, London 2006 **672 L:** akg-images. ©ARS, NY & DACS, London 2006 **672 R:** Nationalgalerie, Berlin, Germany/Bridgeman Art Library. ©DACS, London 2006 **673 L:** Burstein Collection/CORBIS **673 R:** Musée National d'Art Moderne, Centre Pompidou, Paris, France, Peter Willi/Bridgeman Art Library. ©DACS, London 2006 **674** Musée National d'Art Moderne, Centre Pompidou, Paris, France/Bridgeman Art Library **675** Priv. coll. ©Christie's Images/Bridgeman Art Library. ©DACS, London 2006 **676** Priv. coll. Lauros/Giraudon/Bridgeman Art Library ©Christian Schad Stiftung Aschaffenburg/VG Bild-Kunst, Bonn & DACS, London 2006 **677** ©Leamington Spa Museum & Art Gallery, Warwickshire, UK/Bridgeman Art Library **678** Priv. coll., ©Christie's Images/Bridgeman Art Library **679** Burstein Collection/Corbis. ©ADAGP, Paris & DACS, London 2006 **680 L:** Musée d'Art Moderne de la Ville de Paris, France, Giraudon/Bridgeman Art Library **680 R:** Priv. coll./Bridgeman Art Library. ©DACS, London 2006 **681 L:** Christie's Images/Corbis. ©DACS, London 2006 **681 R:** Archivo Iconografico, S.A./Corbis **682** Bettmann/Corbis. All rights reserved by the Estate of Nan Wood Graham/Licensed by VAGA, NY **683** Musée National d'Art Moderne, Centre Pompidou, Paris, France, Peter Willi/Bridgeman Art Library. ©Salvador Dali, Gala-Salvador Dali Foundation, DACS, London 2006 **684** Leamington Spa Museum & Art Gallery, Warwickshire, UK/Bridgeman Art Library **685** ©2005. Dig. image, MoMA, NY/Scala, Florence. ©Salvador Dali, Gala-Salvador Dali Foundation, DACS, London 2006 **686** Pushkin Museum, Moscow/Bridgeman Art Library. ©ADAGP, Paris & DACS, London 2006 **687** ©National Trust Picture Library. ©Estate of Stanley Spencer/DACS, London 2006 **688** Rights reserved by Pan Klub Foundation Xul Solar Museum **689** Art Archive/Priv. coll./Dagli Orti. ©ADAGP, Paris & Dacs, London 2006 **690** Alinari Archives/Corbis. ©DACS, London 2006 **691** Hamburger Kunsthalle, Hamburg, Germany/Bridgeman Art Library ©ADAGP, Paris & DACS, London 2006 **692** ©Art Gallery of Ontario, Toronto, Canada/Bridgeman Art Library **693** Burstein Collection/Corbis. ©Succession Miro/ADAGP, Paris & DACS, London 2006 **694** Alinari Archives/Corbis **695** ©2006 Photo Schalkwijk/Art Resource/Scala, Florence **696** Galerie Daniel Malingue, Paris, France/Bridgeman Art Library. ©ADAGP, Paris & DACS, London 2006 **697** Archivo Iconografico, S.A./Corbis **698** ©Indianapolis Museum of Art, USA, Gift of Eli Lilly & Company/Bridgeman Art Library. ©ARS, NY & DACS, London 2006 **699** Louise & Walter Arensberg Collection, 1950 ©2004 Photo Philadelphia Museum of Art/Art Resource/Scala, Florence ©Salvador Dali, Gala-Salvador Dali Foundation, DACS, London 2006 **700 L:** © 2010 Banco de México Diego Rivera Frida Kahlo Museums Trust, Mexico, D.F. / DACS **700 R:** ©2006. Dig. image, MoMA, NY/Scala, Florence. ©ADAGP, Paris & DACS, London 2006 **701 L:** © Whitworth Art Gallery, The University of Manchester, UK/Bridgeman Art Library **701 R:** Christie's Images/Corbis **702** Museo Nacional Centro de Arte Reina Sofia, Madrid, Spain/Bridgeman Art Library. ©Succession Picasso/DACS, London 2006 **703** ©Manchester Art Gallery, UK/Bridgeman Art Library **704** Nicolas M. Salgo Collection, USA/Bridgeman Art Library **705** ©Museum of Fine Arts, Houston, Texas, Gift of Mr. Frank J. Hevrdejs/Bridgeman Art Library. ©T.H. Benton & R.P. Benton Testamentary Trusts/DACS, London/VAGA, NY 2006 **706** Ex-Edward James Foundation, Sussex, UK/Bridgeman Art Library. ©ADAGP, Paris & DACS, London 2006 **707** Hamburger Kunsthalle, Germany/Bridgeman Art Library. ©DACS, London 2006 **708** ©2006. Dig. image, MoMA, NY/Scala, Florence **709** Priv. coll., Photo: Jorge Contreras Chacel/Bridgeman Art Library **710** ©Burstein Collection/Corbis **711** Christie's Images/Corbis **712** Israel Museum, Jerusalem. Arthur & Madeleine Chalette Lejwa Collection/Bridgeman Art Library **713** ©Kimbell Art Museum/Corbis ©Succession Miro/ADAGP, Paris & DACS, London 2006 **714** Art Archive/Tate Gallery, London/Eileen Tweedy ©2006 Mondrian/Holtzman Trust c/o HCR International, Warrenton, VA **715** Priv. coll., ©Christie's Images/Bridgeman Art Library **716** Friends of American Art Collection, 1942.51, Art Institute of Chicago Photo ©Art Institute of Chicago. **717** ©Southampton City Art Gallery, Hampshire/Bridgeman Art Library **718** ©Dahesh Museum of Art, NY/Bridgeman Art Library **719** Priv. coll., ©Held Collection/Bridgeman Art Library ©DACS, London 2006 **720 L:** University of Essex Collection of Latin American Art ©ADAGP, Paris & DACS, London 2006 **720 R:** Priv. coll. ©Christie's Images/Bridgeman Art Library ©Succession Picasso/DACS, London 2006 **721 L:** Philadelphia Museum of Art, PA, USA, Lauros/Giraudon/Bridgeman Art Library ©ADAGP, Paris & DACS, London 2006 **721 R:** Priv. coll., Alinari/Bridgeman Art Library ©D.R. Rufino Tamayo/Herederos/México/2006 Fundación Olga y Rufino Tamayo, A.C. **722** ©Canadian War Museum, Ottawa, Canada/Bridgeman Art Library **723** ©Albright-Knox Art Gallery/Corbis ©DACS, London 2006 **724** Musée National d'Art Moderne, Paris, France, Lauros/Giraudon/Bridgeman Art Library ©ADAGP, Paris & DACS, London 2006 **725** ©2000 Photo Smithsonian American Art Museum/Art Resource/Scala, Florence ©ARS, NY & DACS, London 2006 **726** Priv. coll., Lauros/Giraudon/Bridgeman Art Library ©ADAGP, Paris & DACS, London 2006 **727** ©Leeds Museums & Galleries (City Art Gallery) UK/Bridgeman Art Library **728** ©2006 Dig. image, MoMA, NY/Scala, Florence ©ARS, NY & ADAGP, Paris & DACS, London 2006 **729** ©Tate, London 2006 **730** ©Canadian War Museum, Ottawa, Canada/Bridgeman Art Library **731** ©1998 Photo Scala, Florence ©DACS, London 2006 **732** Musée Matisse, Nice-Cimiez, France, Peter Willi/Bridgeman Art Library ©Succession H Matisse/DACS **733** ©2006 Dig. image, MoMA, NY/Scala, Florence ©Estate of Francis Bacon/DACS, London 2006 **734** Art Archive/Brandler Galleries Essex/Eileen Tweedy **735** ©Estate of Stuart Davis/DACS, London/VAGA, New York 2007 **736 L:** Ex-Edward James Foundation, Sussex, UK/Bridgeman Art Library ©ARS, NY & DACS, London 2006 **736 R:** Geoffrey Clements/Corbis ©ARS, NY & ADAGP, Paris & DACS, London 2006. **737 L:** British Council, London/Bridgeman Art Library **737 R:** ©Tate, London 2006 ©ADAGP, Paris & DACS, London 2006 **738** Priv. coll. ©Agnew's, London/Bridgeman Art Library **739** Museo Nacional de Historia, Mexico City, Mexico, Photo: Michel Zabe/AZA/Bridgeman Art Library. ©DACS, London 2006 **740** ©2006 Dig. image, MoMA, NY/Scala, Florence. **741** Francis G Mayer/Corbis ©ADAGP, Paris & DACS, London 2006 **742 L:** ©National Gallery of Victoria, Melbourne, Australia/Bridgeman Art Library ©Estate of Francis Bacon/DACS, London 2006 **742 R:** Musée National d'Art Moderne, Paris, France, Lauros/Giraudon/Bridgeman Art Library ©ADAGP, Paris & DACS, London 2006. **743 L:** Christie's Images/Corbis **743 R:** ©1990 Photo Scala, Florence ©ADAGP, Paris & DACS, London 2006 **744** Priv. coll. Photo: Michel Zabe/AZA/Bridgeman Art Library **745** ©2006 Dig. image MoMA, NY/Scala, Florence ©DACS, London 2006 **746** Priv. coll./Bridgeman Art Library **747** ©2006 Dig. image, MoMA, NY/Scala, Florence ©ARS, NY & DACS, London 2006 **748** Priv. Coll., Peter Willi/Bridgeman Art Library. ©Man Ray Trust/ADAGP, Paris & DACS, London 2006 **749** National Gallery of Art, Washington, DC/Bridgeman Art Library ©ARS, NY & DACS, London 2006 **750** Musée National d'Art Moderne, Paris, France, Peter Willi/Bridgeman Art Library ©ADAGP, Paris & DACS, London 2006 **751** ©2006. Dig. image MoMA, NY/Scala, Florence ©ADAGP, Paris & DACS, London 2006 **752** Tate Collection, London ©Estate of Patrick Heron/DACS, London 2006 **753** ©2005. Dig. image MoMA, NY/Scala, Florence © ARS, NY & DACS, London 2006 **754** MoMA, NY, USA/Scala ©ARS, NY & DACS, London 2006 **755** ©Photo Fondation Maeght, Saint Paul, France ©ADAGP, Paris & DACS, London 2006 **756** Tate Collection, London **757** Kroller-Muller Museum, Otterlo, Netherlands/Bridgeman Art Library **758** Christie's Images/Corbis **759** Galerie Daniel Malingue, Paris, France/ADAGP Paris & DACS, London 2006 **760 L:** ©Walker Art Gallery, National Museums Liverpool/Bridgeman Art Library **760 R:** Priv. coll./DACS, London 2006 ©Estate of Ceri Richards **761 L:** Priv. coll./ADAGP Paris & DACS, London 2006 **761 R:** ©2005. Dig. image MoMA, NY/Scala, Florence ©Willem de Kooning Foundation, NY/ARS, NY & DACS, London 2006 **762** National Gallery of Australia, Canberra/ARS Paris & DACS London 2006 **763** Royal College of Art, London **764** Musée National d'Art Moderne, Paris, France/Bridgeman Art Library ©Succession H Matisse/DACS **765** 2003 Photo Scala, Florence **766** ©Peter de Francia Courtesy James Hyman Fine Art Ltd., London **767** ©2006 Dig. image, MoMA, NY/Scala, Florence ©DACS, London/VAGA, NY 2006 **768 L:** ©Tate, London 2006 ©ADAGP, Paris & DACS, London 2006 **768 R:** ©2006 Dig. image, MoMA, NY/Scala, Florence ©Estate of Francis Bacon/DACS, London 2006 **769 L:** Christie's Images/Corbis **769 R:** ©2005 Dig. image, MoMA, NY/Scala, Florence ©Willem de Kooning Foundation, NY/ARS, NY & DACS, London 2006 **770 L:** Musée National d'Art Moderne, Paris, France, Lauros/Giraudon/Bridgeman Art Library ©ADAGP, Paris & DACS, London 2006 **770 R:** ©Whitworth Art Gallery, University of Manchester, UK/Bridgeman Art Library **771 L:** Christie's Images/Corbis ©DACS, London 2006 **771 R:** Galerie Maeght, Paris, France/Bridgeman Art Library ©ADAGP, Paris & DACS, London 2006. **772** Haags Gemeentemuseum, The Hague, Netherlands/Bridgeman Art Library ©DACS, London 2006 **773** 2005 Dig. image, MoMA, NY/Scala, Florence ©Jasper Johns/VAGA, NY/DACS, London 2006 **774** Scottish National Gallery of Modern Art, Edinburgh, UK/Bridgeman Art Library Courtesy of Lefevre, on behalf of the Edward Burra Estate **775** ©1990 Photo Scala, Florence ©ADAGP, Paris & DACS, London 2006 **776 L:** Priv. coll./Bridgeman Art Library ©ADAGP, Paris & DACS, London 2006 **776 R:** ©Christie's Images/Corbis ©ARS, NY & DACS, London 2006. **777 L:** ©Sheffield Galleries & Museums Trust, UK/Bridgeman Art Library **777 R:** Archivo Iconografico, S.A./Corbis **778** Priv. coll./Bridgeman Art Library **779** Art Archive/Museum of Modern Art Mexico/Dagli Orti ©DACS, London 2006 **780** ©2006 Dig. image, MoMA, NY/Scala, Florence. **781** Priv. coll./Bridgeman Art Library **782 L:** Hamburger Kunsthalle, Hamburg, Germany/Bridgeman Art Library ©DACS, London 2006 **782 R:** Christie's Images/Corbis ©DACS, London 2006 **783 L:** Phillips, International Fine Art Auctioneers, UK/©Bonhams, London/Bridgeman Art Library **783 R:** ©Christie's Images/Corbis ©ARS, NY & DACS, London 2006. **784** ©1990 Photo Scala, Florence ©ARS, NY & DACS, London 2006 **785** Geoffrey Clements/Corbis **786** ©2006 Dig. image, MoMA, NY/Scala, Florence **787** ©Christie's Images/Corbis ©Kate Rothko Prizel & Christopher Rothko ARS, NY & DACS, London 2006 **788** ©Tate, London 2006 ©DACS, London 2006 **789** National Gallery of Australia, Canberra ©Estate of Ian Fairweather/DACS, London 2006. **790** ©David Lees/Corbis ©Jasper Johns/VAGA, NY/DACS, London 2006. **791** ©2006 Dig. Image, MoMA, NY/Scala, Florence ©ARS, NY & DACS, London 2006 **792 L:** ©DACS, London/VAGA, NY 2006 **792 R:** Musée Cantini, Marseille, France, Giraudon/Bridgeman Art Library. ©ADAGP, Paris & DACS, London 2006 **793 L:** Royal College of Art Collection, London ©David Hockney **793 R:** ©Fitzwilliam Museum, University of Cambridge, UK/Bridgeman Art Library ©DACS, London/VAGA, NY 2006. **794** ©2004. Photo the Andy Warhol Foundation/Art Resource/Scala, Florence ©Andy Warhol Foundation for the Visual Arts, Inc./DACS, London, 2006. Trademarks Licensed by Campbell Soup Company. All Rights Reserved **795** ©2006 Dig. image MoMA, NY/Scala, Florence Courtesy Gagosian Gallery **796** ©2006 Photo Smithsonian American Art Museum/Art Resource/Scala, Florence ©DACS, London/VAGA, NY 2006. **797** Royal College of Art Collection, London **798** ©Sheffield Galleries & Museums Trust, UK/Bridgeman Art Library **799** Christie's Images/Corbis ©ARS, NY & DACS, London 2006. **800** Burstein Collection/Corbis ©Estate of Roy Lichtenstein/DACS, London 2006 **801** ©2006 Dig. image, MoMA, NY/Scala, Florence ©DACS, London/VAGA, NY 2006 **802** Royal College of Art Collection, London ©Estate of Patrick Caulfield/DACS, London 2006 **803** ©Detroit Institute of Arts, USA, Founders Society Purchase, Dr & Mrs Hilbert H DeLawter Fund/Bridgeman Art Library **804** ©2006 Dig. image, MoMA, NY/Scala, Florence **805** © Whitford & Hughes, London, UK/Bridgeman Art Library. **806 L:** ©Tate, London 2006 **806 R:** Christie's Images/Corbis ©SODRAC, Montreal & DACS, London 2006 **807 L:** Musée National d'Art Moderne, Paris, France, Lauros/Giraudon/Bridgeman Art Library ©ADAGP, Paris & DACS, London 2006 **807 R:** Christie's Images/Corbis ©DACS, London/VAGA, NY 2006 **808** ©2004. Photo the Andy Warhol Foundation/Art Resource/Scala, Florence ©Licensed by the Andy Warhol Foundation for the Visual Arts, Inc/ARS, NY & DACS London 2006 **809** ©Birmingham Museums & Art Gallery/Bridgeman Art Library ©Estate of Patrick Caulfield/DACS, London 2006 **810** Priv. coll./Bridgeman Art Library ©ADAGP, Paris & DACS, London 2006 **811** On Loan to Hamburg Kunsthalle, Germany/Bridgeman Art Library **812** Priv. coll./Bridgeman Art Library ©Joseph & Anni Albers Foundation/VG Bild-Kunst, Bonn/ARS, NY & DACS, London 2006 **813** Musée des Beaux-Arts, Pau, France, Giraudon/Bridgeman Art Library ©ADAGP, Paris & DACS, London 2006 **814** ©2000 Photo SAAM/Art Resource/Scala,Florence ©DACS, London/VAGA, NY 2006 **815** Priv. coll./Bridgeman Art Library ©David Hockney **816** ©1990 Photo Scala, Florence ©DACS, London 2006 **817** ©DACS, London/VAGA, NY 2006 **818** Kunsthaus, Zurich, Switzerland/Bridgeman Art Library ©ADAGP, Paris & DACS, London 2006 **819** ©Photo CNAC/MNAM, RMN, Paris ©Philippe Migeat ©ADAGP, Paris & DACS, London 2006

Acknowledgments

820 Priv. coll./Bridgeman Art Library **821** ©Arts Council Collection, Hayward Gallery, London, UK/ Bridgeman Art Library. **822** ©2005 Dig. image,MoMA, NY/Scala, Florence ©Dedalus Foundation, Inc/DACS, London/VAGA, NY 2006 **823** ©Tate, London 2006 ©David Hockney **824** ©2006 Dig. image, MoMA, NY/Scala, Florence. **825** Christie's Images/Corbis ©Kate Rothko Prizel & Chritopher Rothko ARS, NY & DACS, London 2006 **826** ©Norwich Castle Museum & Art Gallery/Bridgeman Art Library **827** Musée d'Art et d'Industrie, St. Etienne, France, Lauros/Giraudon/Bridgeman Art Library ©ARS, NY & DACS, London 2006. **828** ©1990 Photo Scala, Florence ©Estate of Francis Bacon/DACS, London 2006 **829** Priv. coll/Bridgeman Art Library ©the artist, Marlborough Fine Art, London Ltd **830** ©Tate, London 2006 ©Estate of Patrick Heron/DACS, London 2006 **831** ©Musee d'Unterlinden, Colmar, France, Lauros/Giraudon/Bridgeman Art Library **832** Priv. coll./Archivo Iconografico SA/ Corbis **833** Priv. coll./MoMA, NY, USA/Scala, Florence ©Ed Ruscha **834** Fundacion Juan March, Madrid, Spain/DACS London 2006 **835** Albright-Knox Art Gallery, Buffalo, NY, USA/Corbis **836** Priv. coll./Dreamtime Gallery, London/Bridgeman Art Library ©The artist licensed by Aboriginal Artists Agency 2006 **837** Arts Council Collection, Hayward Gallery, London/Bridgeman Art Library **838** Brooklyn Museum of Art, NY, USA. Gift of Roebling Society & Mr & Mrs Charles H. Blatt/ Bridgeman Art Library **839** Tate Collection, London/Art Archive/Eileen Tweedy ©David Hockney **840** National Gallery of Australia, Canberra/DACS London 2006 **841** Priv. coll./Christies Images/ Corbis **842** Hamburger Kunsthalle, Germany/Bridgeman Art Library **843** Corbally Stourton Contemporary Art, London/The estate of the artist licensed by Aboriginal Artists Agency/ Bridgeman Art Library **844** Priv. coll./Sam L Francis Foundation/Geoffrey Clements/Corbis/DACS London 2006 **845** Hamburger Kunsthalle, Germany/Bridgeman Art Library/DACS London 2006 **846** National Gallery of Australia, Canberra. Arthur Boyd's work reproduced with the permission of Bundanon **847** Ashmolean Museum, Oxford, UK/Bridgeman Art Library **848** Priv. coll./Christie's Images/Corbis **849** Royal College of Art Collection, London **850** ©2005 Photo Philadelphia Museum of Art/Art Resource/Scala, Florence **851** ©Fondation Antoni Tapies, Barcelona/VEGAP, Madrid and DACS, London 2007 **852** Priv. coll./Royal Pavilion, Libraries & Museums, Brighton, UK/ Bridgeman Art Library **853** Museum of the City of NY, NY, USA/Geoffrey Clements/Corbis **854** ©2006. Dig. image MoMA, NY/Scala, Florence **855** National Gallery of Australia, Canberra, courtesy Lyn Williams **856** Tate Collection, London **857** Musée d'Art Moderne de la Ville de Paris, France/Giraudon/Bridgeman Art Library/ADAGP, Paris & DACS London 2006 **858** Priv. coll./Art Archive/Dagli Orti ©DACS London 2006 & VAGA NY 2006 **859** Hamburger Kunsthalle, Germany/ Bridgeman Art Library ©DACS London 2006 **860** Philadelphia Museum of Art, PA, USA/Gift of Friends of the Philadelphia Museum/Art Resource/Scala, Florence ©DACS London/VAGA NY 2006 **861** Priv. coll./Georgan State Picture Gallery, Tiblisi, Georgia/Bridgeman Art Library **862** ©2006 Dig. image MoMA, NY/Scala, Florence Courtesy Gagosian Gallery **863** Detroit Institute of Arts, Detroit, USA/Founders Society, gift of Mrs George Kamperman/Bridgeman Art Library **864** Priv. coll./ Bridgeman Art Library/DACS London 2006 **865** Arts Council Collection, Hayward Gallery, London/ Bridgeman Art Library/Courtesy of Marlborough Fine Art Gallery, London **866** ©National Gallery of Victoria, Melbourne, Australia, Presented through the NGV Foundation by Rio Tinto Limited/ Bridgeman Art Library Courtesy Lyn Williams **867** ©Southampton City Art Gallery, Hampshire, UK/ Bridgeman Art Library ©The Artist, Marlborough Fine Art, London **868** Collection Stedelijk Museum Amsterdam, Netherlands **869** Priv. coll./Bridgeman 2006 Priv. coll./Bridgeman ©ADAGP, Paris & DACS, London 2006 **871** ©Tate, London 2006 ©Richard Hamilton. All Rights Reserved, DACS, London 2006 **872** ©Detroit Institute of Arts, USA, Founders Society purchase, W. Hawkins Ferry fund/Bridgeman Art Library **873** Priv. coll. ©Bonhams, London/Bridgeman Art Library **874** ©Tate, London 2006 **875** University of Essex Collection of Latin American Art, UK **876** National Portrait Gallery, London, UK **877** Priv. coll. ©Bonhams, London/Bridgeman **878** Hamburger Kunsthalle, Germany/Bridgeman Art Library ©The Artist, Marlborough Fine Art, London **879** Priv. coll., ©Crane Kalman, London/Bridgeman **880** ©2004 Photo: Philadelphia Museum of Art/Art Resource/Scala, Florence **881** ©Bristol City Museum & Art Gallery, UK/Bridgeman Art Library. ©The Artist, Marlborough Fine Art, London **882** Louisiana Museum of Modern Art, Humlebaek, Denmark **883** ©Succession Antonio Saura/DACS, London 2007 **884** Gift of Mr & Mrs David N Pincus, 1991 ©2005 Photo: Philadelphia Museum of Art/Art Resource/Scala, Florence **885** Courtesy Mary Boone Gallery, NY **886** ©The Artist, Marlborough Fine Art, London ©DACS, London/VAGA, NY 2006 **887** ©The Artist, Marlborough Fine Art, London ©DACS, London/VAGA, NY 2006 **888** ©Tate, London 2006 **889** Christie's Images/Corbis ©ARS, NY & DACS, London 2006 **890** Lefeuvre Fine Art Ltd, London, UK/Bridgeman Art Library/VAGA New York & DACS, London 2006 **891** Courtesy Mary Boone Gallery ©DACS, London 2006 **892 L:** Artist's collection/Gerrit Greve/Corbis **892 R:** ©2 Estate of the artist 2010, licensed by Aboriginal Artists Agency **893 L:** Arts Council Collection/Bridgeman Art Library. Copyright of the artist. Courtesy Anthony Reynolds Gallery, London **893 R:** Priv. coll., Index/Bridgeman Art Library. ©ADAGP, Paris & DACS, London 2006 **894** ©Art Gallery of New South Wales, Sydney/Bridgeman Art Library. ©DACS, London 2006 **895** Zeno X Gallery, Antwerp, Belgium **896** Daros Collection, Zürich, Switzerland/ARS NY & DACS, London 2006 **897** ©2006. Dig. image, MoMA, NY/Scala, Florence **898** Flowers East Gallery, London **899** ©Art Gallery of New South Wales, Sydney/Bridgeman Art Library **900** Priv. coll., courtesy of Jay Jopling/White Cube, London **901** University of Essex Collection of Latin American Art, UK **902** ©The artist, courtesy Tate Collection, London **903** ©Arts Council Collection, Hayward Gallery, London/Bridgeman Art Library/Afroco **904** ©The artist, courtesy Ronald Feldman Fine Arts, NY **906** ©Dig. image, MoMA, NY/ Scala, Florence **907** ©Tate Gallery, London/Art Resource, NY ©The artist/Gillian Jason Modera & Contemporary Art/Bridgeman Art Library, courtesy of Ansel Krut & Domo Baal **909** Albright-Knox Art Gallery, Buffalo/Corbis. Courtesy Michael Werner Gallery, New York & Cologne. ©Sigmar Polke **910** Priv. coll./Marlborough Fine Art Gallery, London **911** Saatchi Gallery, London **912-913** Courtesy Mary Boone Gallery, NY **914** Courtesy of the artist **915** Courtesy of the artist, Saatchi Gallery, London **916** Victoria Miro Gallery, London **917** Scottish National Portrait Gallery. Courtesy of Flowers, London **918** ©Mark Tansey, Courtesy Gagosian Gallery, NY **919** Courtesy Mary Boone Gallery, NY **920** Hirshhorn Museum, Washington, DC **921** Courtesy Gavin Brown's enterprise **922 L:** Courtesy Gagosian Gallery, NY **922 R:** Hackett-Freedman Gallery, San Francisco, courtesy of the artist & Photocaso/JW White /VAGA NY & DACS, London 2006 **923 L:** ©The artist, Photo: Stephen White, Courtesy White Cube **923 R:** ©Tracey Emin. All rights reserved, DACS 2010 **924** Hackett-Freedman Gallery, San Francisco, courtesy of the artist & Photocaso/JW White/VAGA NY & DACS, London 2006 **925** Courtesy Blum & Poe, Los Angeles, CA ©2006 Takashi Murakami/Kaikai Kiki Co., Ltd. All Rights Reserved **926** ©The artist, Photo: Stephen White, Courtesy White Cube **927** ©The artist **928** ©The Estate of Sigmar Polke, Courtesy Jennifer & John Eagle & the Rachofsky Collection **929** ©The artist **930** Courtesy of the artist and Friedrich Petzel Gallery, NY **931** ©The artist, Courtesy Paula Cooper Gallery, NY **932** ©The artist; Courtesy of the artist, Jack Shainman Gallery, New York, and Corvi-Mora, London **934** Courtesy of the artist, Galerie Forsblom, Helsinki and Victoria Miro, London **935** Courtesy of the artist and Amaralonegro Arte **937** Courtesy of the artist & CANADA **938** © Lee Ufan; Courtesy Lisson Gallery. Photography: Jack Hems **939** ©The artist; Courtesy of Greg Kucera Gallery, Inc. **940** ©The artist **941** ©The artist; Courtesy of Gladstone Gallery, New York/Brussels, Susanne Vielmetter Los Angeles Projects and Victoria Miro, London

Our sincere thanks to the following:

Editors
Antonia Cunningham; Robert Dimery; Ana Finel Honigman; Cathy Marriott; Sally McFall; Fiona Plowman; Francis Ritter

Scatterproofing
Rod Teasdale

Picture Research Assistance
Joanne Forrest-Smith

Fact Checking & Editorial Assistance
Melissa Riggall; Andrew Smith; Olivia Young

Picture Agencies
Scala: Valentina Bandelloni; Veneta Bullen; Andrea Franceschi; Emmanuelle Peri; Vera Silvani

Corbis: Duncan Crawley; Simon Pearson

Bridgeman: Alex Edouard; Jenny Page; Tamzin Phoenix

AKG: David Price-Hughes; Kate Tasker

Art Archive: Anna Barrett

Christie's: Angela Minshull

V&A Images: Stephanie Fawcett

Museums & Galleries
Afroco Ltd.
Archive & Museum at St Bartholomew's Hospital, London; especially Samantha Farhall
The Art Institute of Chicago; especially Aimee Marshall
British Library
British Museum
Chinese Contemporary, London; especially Julia Colman
Daros Collection, Zürich
Flowers East Gallery; especially Siobhan Andrews
The Frick Collection, NY; especially Zoe Browder
Friedrich Petzel Gallery, NY
Gagosian Gallery, NY
Gemäldegalerie, Berlin
Grimm Rosenfeld, NY
Hackett-Freedman Gallery, San Francisco
Haunch of Venison; especially Matt Watkins
Henze & Ketterer Galerie für moderne Kunst, Bern, Switzerland
James Cohan Gallery, NY
Lisson Gallery, London
Louisiana Museum for Moderne Kunst, Denmark
Marlborough Gallery, London
Marlborough Gallery, New York; especially Eric Gleason
Mary Boone Gallery, NY
Museum Rietberg, Zürich
National Gallery of Australia
National Gallery, London
October Gallery, London
Paula Cooper Gallery, NY
Saatchi Gallery, London
Scottish National Portrait Gallery
Shoshana Wayne Gallery, Santa Monica
Sikkema Jenkins & Co., NY
Stedelijk Museum, Amsterdam; especially Hefty Wessels
Tate; especially Lucy Scrivener
Saatchi Gallery, London; especially Philippa Adams
The University of Essex Collection of Latin American Art; especially Valerie Fraser
Victoria & Albert Museum
Victoria Miro Gallery, London
White Cube, London

Thank you also to the following for their assistance:
Sandra April; Mattias Dammgård; Rebecca Man; Wendy Osgerby; Jane Peacock; Jude Welton; Lyn Williams